The Planning of Change

FOURTH EDITION

Warren G. Bennis
University of Southern California

Kenneth D. Benne
Emeritus, Boston University

Robert Chin
Boston University

Holt, Rinehart and Winston
New York   Chicago   San Francisco   Philadelphia
Montreal   Toronto   London   Sydney
Tokyo   Mexico City   Rio de Janeiro   Madrid

Library of Congress Cataloging in Publication Data
Main entry under title:

The Planning of change.

   Includes bibliographies and index.
   1. Social change—Addresses, essays, lectures.
I. Bennis, Warren G.   II. Benne, Kenneth Dean, 1908–
III. Chin, Robert, 1918–
HM101.P558 1984   303.4'84   84–19227

ISBN 0-03-063682-5

Address correspondence to:
383 Madison Avenue
New York, N.Y. 10017
All rights reserved
Printed in the United States of America
Published simultaneously in Canada
5 6 7 8   038   9 8 7 6 5 4 3 2

CBS College Publishing
Holt, Rinehart and Winston
The Dryden Press
Saunders College Publishing

Preface

The first edition of *The Planning of Change* was published in 1961, the second in 1969 and the third in 1976. This fourth edition shows both continuities with the previous editions and departures from them.

All have sought to contribute to the unfinished task of merging and reconciling the arts of social practice and action and the sciences of human behavior. This task, as we see it, presents both an intellectual and a practical, moral challenge to those who would improve the quality of life in American society. Living in an age whose single constant is change, all men and women are in urgent need of whatever resources can be made available as they seek to understand and manage themselves and their environments, to understand and solve the unprecedented personal and social problems that confront them.

The intellectual challenge comes from the necessity to develop an adequate theory of the processes through which knowledge of human behavior and of human systems is applied and utilized. More particularly, a theory of applying and adapting theories of social, interpersonal, and personal dynamics to the special case of deliberate changing is required. All editions have sought to bring together some of the best current conceptualizations of various aspects of utilization and change processes.

The practical, moral challenge lies in inventing and developing social technologies, consistent with our best social and behavioral knowledge and adequate to the practical and moral requirements of contemporary change situations. All editions have sought to present discussions and evaluations of a rapidly growing body of change technologies, viewed not as isolated methods for achieving and guiding change, but rather in their intellectual, practical, and moral bearings and implications.

Another part of the practical challenge is the development of persons who can function effectively and responsibly as agents of planned change. This edition, as well as its predecessors, has been designed to provide material aid in the education of such agents. Change agents are now being educated in various departments of social and behavioral science as well as in various professional schools. We have tried to keep the needs of this scattered academic audience in mind. As in the case of its predecessors, this edition should prove useful in departments of psychology, sociology, and anthropology and in schools of public and business administration, social work, education, theology, nursing and other health professions, and public health as well.

How does this fourth edition differ from the third? About two-fifths of the readings in this edition are new. This change reflects the current rapid expansion and development of theory-building, research, and practical experimentation in applied social and behavioral science in this country and abroad. We have tried to reflect the contours of this developing field of study in this edition.

Changes of emphasis in applied behavioral science have also occurred in response to the turbulent social environment of the 1960s and later and the various liberation movements which that decade released. These changes have been reflected throughout the present edition.

It is hard to know where to begin and where to end in acknowledging the contributions of the many people who have helped us, directly and indirectly, in preparing this book. Our most direct debt is to those contributors whose work we have reprinted. Specific acknowledgement of our obligation to each of them and to their publishers is made at the beginning of each selection.

The index shows many names in addition to those of our contributors. In a number of cases, these writers have published work that we wished to include. Space limitations made inclusion impossible. We are nevertheless grateful for their very real help in maturing our own thinking.

W. G. B.
K. D. B.
R. C.

Contents

v

Introduction

In an important sense this world of ours is a new world, in which the unity of knowledge, the nature of human communities, the order of society, the order of ideas, the very notions of society and culture have changed and will not return to what they have been in the past. What is new is new not because it has never been there before, but because it has changed in quality. One thing that is new is the prevalence of newness, the changing scale and scope of change itself, so that the world alters as we walk in it, so that the years of man's life measure not some small growth or rearrangement or moderation of what he learned in childhood, but a great upheaval. What is new is that in one generation our knowledge of the natural world engulfs, upsets, and complements all knowledge of the natural world before. The techniques, among and by which we live, multiply and ramify, so that the whole world is bound together by communication, blocked here and there by the immense synapses of political tyranny. The global quality of the world is new: our knowledge of and sympathy with remote and diverse peoples, our involvement with them in practical terms, and our commitment to them in terms of brotherhood. What is new in the world is the massive character of the dissolution and corruption of authority, in belief, in ritual, and in temporal order. Yet this is the world that we have to live in. The very difficulties which it presents derive from growth in understanding, in skill, in power. To assail the changes that have unmoored us from the past is futile, and in a deep sense, I think, it is wicked. We need to recognize the change and learn what resources we have.

Robert Oppenheimer[1]

The Problem

Richard Weaver once remarked that the ultimate term in contemporary rhetoric, the "god term," is "progress" or "change":[2] the world, as Oppenheimer remarks, alters as we walk in it. It would appear, then, that we are beyond debating the inevitability of change; most students of our society agree that the one major invariant is the tendency toward movement, growth, development, process: change. The contemporary debate has swung from change versus no change to the methods employed in controlling and directing forces in change. Dewey has remarked that ". . . history in being a process of change generates change not only in details but also in the *method of directing social change*."[3] The predicament we confront, then, concerns method; methods that maximize freedom and limit as little as possible the potentialities of growth; methods that will realize man's dignity as well as bring into fruition desirable social goals.

Concerning the methods of change, we can observe two idea systems in the contemporary scene that are directly counterposed: the law of nonintervention and the law of radical intervention. The former stems from the natural-law and "invisible-hand" ideology of the laissez-faire doctrine—part economic analysis and part ideology. Tampering and social tinkering with man's natural and social universe interferes with the homeostatic forces, which, if left unfettered, will bring about the perfectly optimized good life. Keynesian and welfare economics, as well as the monopolistic structure of contemporary society, have all exposed the weaknesses in the natural-equilibrium position. (Keynes once remarked that classical economic doctrines may well work in the long run; but, he poignantly added, in the long run we'll all be dead.)

Marxian analysis, with its emphasis on conflict, inevitable class struggle, and radical intervention—occasionally at the price of human freedom—represents the other extreme. Although Marxian theory was developed as an indispensable antidote to the elegant rationalizations of

---

[1] Robert Oppenheimer, "Prospects in the Arts and Sciences," *Perspectives USA*, II (Spring 1955), 10–11.

[2] Richard Weaver, "Ultimate Terms in Contemporary Rhetoric," *Perspectives USA*, II (Spring 1955), 123.

[3] John Dewey, *Liberalism and Social Action* (New York: G. P. Putnam's Sons, 1935), p. 83 (our italics).

the laissez-faire doctrine, it now also suffers from an obsolescence wrought by the accelerating changes of the world, including the Marxian world, which its basic theory could not predict or encompass.

Planned change, as we view it, emerges as the only feasible alternative to the methods; that is, a method which self-consciously and experimentally employs social knowledge to help solve the problems of men and societies. One may approve or deplore the concept of planned change—or look on it with scientific detachment. But no one will deny its importance. And this book was designed to bring about greater understanding of its developing methods, the social processes bearing on its use, its potentialities, its consequences, both ethical and pragmatic, as well as its limitations.

Nature of This Book

There is an old parable that has made the rounds about the grasshopper who decided to consult the hoary consultant of the animal kingdom, the owl, about a personal problem. The problem concerned the fact that the grasshopper suffered each winter from severe pains due to the savage temperature. After a number of these painful winters, in which all of the grasshopper's known remedies were of no avail, he presented his case to the venerable and wise owl. The owl, after patiently listening to the grasshopper's misery, so the story goes, prescribed a simple solution. "Simply turn yourself into a cricket, and hibernate during the winter." The grasshopper jumped joyously away, profusely thanking the owl for his wise advice. Later, however, after discovering that this important knowledge could not be transformed into action, the grasshopper returned to the owl and asked him how he could perform this metamorphosis. The owl replied rather curtly, "Look, I gave you the principle. It's up to you to work out the details!"

All parables, supposedly, contain a moral, and the moral here provides one of the main cornerstones of this volume: How can the man of knowledge utilize his hard-won knowledge to help clients and lay personnel? And conversely, how can the lay public provide information and insight that will aid the man of knowledge, the expert, in his role as helper as well as theory builder?

These are not simple questions, and unfortunately ways of answering them are not easily arrived at or even certainly known. And the conditions of the world today—with the often noted communication gap between actionists, practitioners and scientists, clients and professional helpers—and the ever increasing specialization and technocracy of the sciences, tend to exacerbate the problem. In another part of the essay quoted above,

Oppenheimer states eloquently what can be taken as a central leitmotiv of this book of readings and text:

> The specialization of science is an inevitable accompaniment of progress; yet it is full of dangers, and it is cruelly wasteful, since so much that is beautiful and enlightening is cut off from most of the world. Thus it is proper to the role of the scientist that he not merely find new truth and communicate it to his fellows, but that he teach, that he try to bring the most honest and intelligible account of new knowledge to all who will try to learn. This is one reason—it is the decisive organic reason—why scientists belong in universities. It is one reason why the patronage of science by and through universities is its most proper form; for it is here, in teaching, in the association of scholars, and in the friendships of teachers and taught, of men who by profession must themselves be both teachers and taught, that the narrowness of scientific life can best be moderated, and that the analogies, insights, and harmonies of scientific discovery can find their way into the wider life of man.[4]

Putting the problem a little differently, we can say that the major foundation of this book is the *planful application of valid and appropriate knowledge in human* affairs for the purpose of creating intelligent action and change. Thus, this is a book that focuses on *planned change*; conscious, deliberate, and collaborative effort to improve the operations of a human system, whether it be a self-system, social system, or cultural system, through the utilization of valid knowledge.[5]

Let us review briefly some of the organizing features of this volume. First, what is meant by valid and appropriate knowledge? The parable, of course, burlesques just this point. Yet we find that a substantial body of social science literature suffers an owlish deficiency. Whitehead, commenting pungently on this matter, said: "In this modern world the celibacy of the medieval learned class has been replaced by a celibacy of the intellect which is divorced from the concrete contemplation of complete facts."[6]

The relationship between theory and practice must constantly be kept within the same field of vision in order for both to cope with the exigencies of reality. We have developed a substantial body of theory and

---

[4] Oppenheimer, p. 9.

[5] Ronald Lippitt et al., *Dynamics of Planned Change* (New York: Harcourt, Brace & World, Inc., 1958). This book would undoubtedly serve as an excellent companion text to this volume. Any book of readings, by definition, suffers from a lack of systematic integration of its content; Lippitt's book may provide a welcome format for readers of this text. On the other hand, *Dynamics* represents a more constricted view of change than the present volume.

A recent publication, K. Benne, L. Bradford, J. Gibb, and R. Lippitt (Eds.), *The Laboratory Method of Changing and Learning: Theory and Application* (Palo Alto, Calif.: Science and Behavior Books, 1975), significantly overlaps the content of this volume, particularly in the emphasis on the place of re-education in personal and social change. Readers of this volume who wish to explore some of the methodologies and technologies dealt with in this volume in summary fashion, may wish to consult this source.

[6] Alfred North Whitehead, *Science and the Modern World* (New York: Mentor Books).

certainly a rich body of practice, but somehow our failure has been to provide the necessary transformations and bridgings between the two. Kurt Lewin, one of the intellectual forebears of this volume, was preoccupied with this issue of the relationship between the abstract and concrete. He once compared this task to the building of a bridge across the gorge separating theory from full reality. "The research worker can achieve this only if, as a result of a constant intense tension, he can keep both theory and reality fully within his field of vision."[7] We seem, quite often, to become lost at the crossroads of a false dichotomy; the purity and virginity of theory on the one hand and the anti-intellectualism of some knowledge-for-what adherents on the other. This division oversimplifies the issue. The issue is far more complicated; it concerns the transformations and developmental conceptualizing that have to be undertaken before theory can become practical.[8]

Once these intellectual linkages between theory and practice are effectively established, we have to be concerned further with the social processes that bear on the infusion of knowledge into action and policy decisions. These two foci—practical theory and the social dynamics of utilizing knowledge in effecting change—make up two of the dominant themes in this volume.

One other meaning that has implications for the organization of this book can be drawn from our parable. The grasshopper, supplicant, comes to the expert owl for help. The owl listens to the problem, prescribes a remedy, and terminates the relationship. The owl did not discuss implementation or consequences of his therapy, nor did he seem to understand the *dependence* of the client, nor did he recognize the *transference* in the relationship. The owl simply proffered a rational *"solution."* The meaning, then, that now emerges from our parable has to do with the nature of the relationship between the man of knowledge, the expert, and his client. Our conviction, which is reflected in a number of articles in this volume, is that the extent to which knowledge can be effectively utilized by practitioners and clients—especially knowledge provided for social change—depends to a great extent on the nature of the relationship between the client and change agent.[9] In other words, we do not view science in and

[7] Remark attributed to Lewin by his wife, Getrud Weiss Lewin, in her introduction to *Resolving Social Conflicts* (New York: Harper & Row, Publishers, 1948).

[8] Harold Guetzkow writes about the conversion barriers in using the social sciences. "Little attention has been given," he says, "to the way the very structure of knowledge affects its conversion for application. In the social sciences the role of scientist, engineer, technician, practitioner, and policy-maker has not been well differentiated. It may be useful to sketch how the knowledge that the scientist develops may be converted by others for use and then to examine the impact of certain characteristics of basic knowledge upon the application process." This conversion process is one of the main concerns of this volume. See "Conversion Barriers in Using the Social Sciences," *Administrative Science Quarterly*, IV (1959), 68–81.

[9] These terms have been developed in conjunction with the National Training Laboratories and used by Lippitt et al. in *Dynamics of Planned Change* (New York: Harcourt, Brace & World,

of itself as the panacea. This naïve technocratic viewpoint does not take into account the importance of the existential relationship between the man of knowledge (change agent) and the client system. Dewey once said that "Mankind now has in its possession a new method, that of cooperative and experimental science which expresses the method of intelligence."[10] In this book on the theory and practice of planned change we aim to stress the cooperative and collaborative aspects of the various relationships implicated in change—change agent to client, among clients, and among change agents—as well as the scientific findings related to change. (Too often social scientists neglect as legitimate inquiry the collaborative process and the interpersonal and methodological norms and rules distinctively required in the practices of an action science.)

We are now in a better position to express succinctly the nature of this book. Perhaps our greatest emphasis is on the processes of planned changing, on how change is created, implemented, evaluated, maintained, and resisted. The processes of change take us, given its enormous scope, into many fields. The exploration fans out into the various dimensions of change processes (from brainwashing to introducing change in a classroom or a factory), into the social and psychological consequences of change, into the antecedent conditions for effectively planning change, into strategic leverage points for effecting change. Included, also, are some of the major instruments which have been developed for creating and maintaining change: training, consulting, and applied research.

Focusing on the processes and instruments of change, however, does not provide an adequate picture of the complications of change and changing. We have to illuminate the targets or systems to which the change is directed. In this book we make a strong effort to keep in mind four types (or levels) of systems: self, role, interpersonal or group, and larger systems such as formal organizations, communities, and in some cases, cultural systems. "The educational task," Dewey once said, "cannot be accomplished merely by working on men's minds without action that effects actual changes in institutions."[11] We cannot overemphasize the importance of keeping the fact in mind that human behavior is like a centipede, standing on many legs. Nothing that we do has a single determinant. We emphasize this now because we believe there is a danger in focusing too

---

Inc., 1958). Client refers to the person or group being helped, thus client system whether it be person, group, organization, community, culture, family, club, or whatever. Change agent refers to the helper, the person or group who is attempting to effect change. These are fairly clumsy terms but we cannot think of ready substitutes, and they are coming into wider usage.

We might point out now that Lippitt et al. restrict the role of the change agent by defining him as exogenous to the client system, a person from the outside who attempts to effect change. We believe this is too narrow a view, and we have encompassed in our definition the idea that the change agent may be either in or outside the client system.

[10] Dewey, op. cit., p. 83.
[11] Dewey, op. cit., p. 4.

narrowly on personality factors; elements in addition to the *personal* equipment of the client and the change agent must be considered.

In addition to the change processes and the various client systems, we will present material, touched on earlier, relevant to the nature of the collaborative processes in planned-change programs. Moreover, some attention will be given to the strategy and methodology of planned change, its complexities, vicissitudes, and outcomes.

George Santayana once observed that in our changing world we no longer salute our ancestors but bid them good-bye. The temptations to ungrateful impiety are great for all men but perhaps particularly great for practitioners and theorists of planned change with their typical present and future orientation to human affairs. We have tried to resist this temptation to impiety in ourselves by giving attention to the historical roots of contemporary ideas about deliberate changing of men and societies. We have sought to salute our ancestors in this field of intellectual and moral endeavor, both ancestors who have fed our own chosen orientation and those who have nourished variant contemporary orientations. Statements about change become shrill and hollow, when they do not include attention to the conditions of stability and continuity in human life.

No discussion of planned change would be complete without some attention to the perplexing philosophical issues, axiological and ethical, which this subject generates. In these times of "hidden persuaders," brainwashing, "payola," conformity, and manipulation, lay and intellectual publics alike are exceedingly wary, lest social and psychological knowledge bring into actuality the specter of predictable—and thereby helpless—man. We share this concern, as a number of articles in this volume attest; but we also join Spinoza in saying that our job as men of knowledge is not to weep or laugh, but to understand.

One of our problems here is that our ethical-value positions are intimately related to our pragmatic positions. For example when we postulate that collaboration is a *sine qua non* of effective planned change, we are insisting on an ethical imperative as well as on a scientific objective. Value orientations color almost every statement in the book. The best we can hope to do is make our own values as explicit as we can. Throughout the course of the book we have attempted to do this.

A brief word about the outline of this volume is now in order. What is the outline of this fourth edition of the book, and how does it compare and contrast with the third edition? The present edition contains four parts. In Part One, we try to provide perspective on "planned change," as we define it, by discussing its underlying ideas and variant methodologies in two sorts of contexts. The first context is historical. How has thinking about "planned change" and its uses been influenced by the tortuous career of social science and social practice and action in American society? Our second edition was published in 1969 during the cresting of the civil rights and other liberation movements in America and in the midst of American involvement in the Vietnam War. We made no attempt to discuss the effects of the turbulent 1960s on the practice and prospects of planned change. In the third edition, we assessed these effects. The second context we chose for placing planned change in perspective was a mapping of the internal differentiations in its methodologies and technologies which have emerged in its evolution, as a social movement and as a practice profession, in the two and a half decades since our first edition was published in 1961.

In the third as well as in this fourth edition, we devoted Parts Two and Three to the "diagnostic" and "intervention" aspects of planned change, respectively. The meaning and use of four families of concepts in diagnosing change situations are explored in Part Two—"social system," "knowledge utilization," "conflict, power and authority," and "the internal and external environments of organizations." Three intervention modes—"planning structures and processes," "re-education," and "politics"—are dealt with in Part Three. The readings in Parts Two and Three of the present volume differ from the corresponding parts of the previous editions in two ways. (1) We have dealt directly with the structures and processes of "open systems" and "transactive" planning where these were touched only tangentially in the preceding edition. (2) We have, in this edition, honored one legacy from the 1960s in dealing with the difficult problems of mobilizing the efforts and energies of "the poor" and "the oppressed" in pursuing changes which serve their interests as they articulate these for themselves and which augment their continuing exercise of power in community life.

Part Four of this volume, like Part Four of the second and third editions, explores the dilemmas confronted by agents of planned change with respect to the directions and goals to which change programs should be oriented and with respect to the ethical and moral principles which should guide their decisions and actions. The readings in this volume deal more adequately than we were able to do in previous editions with (1) difficulties of imaging the future both of persons and institutions and (2) the ethical problems encountered at the level of public policy-making.

This, in a very general way, indicates the content and emphasis of the present volume. We hope that readers will recognize the editors' difficulties in constructing a book of readings that draw upon so wide a range of sources—from the major disciplines of the behavioral sciences, from the history and philosophy of these sciences, from social and personal ethics, and from theories of application and practice. However, that is, as we see it, the requisite scope of our topic, and hence this book of readings.

I
Planned Change in Perspective

1
Planned Change in Historical Perspective

One way in which people gain perspective on current events which are moving around them, indeed events which are moving in and through them since their choices and actions contribute to shaping the events, is to think of those events historically. How did the events come to be? What human needs, aspirations, and conflicts lent motivation to the events? What changes in life conditions gave them impetus and focus? And what ideas and ideals provided direction and justification for them? In this chapter, we attempt to place that evolving complex of events, which we have called "planned change," in historical perspective.

Another way to get perspective on a field of study and practice is to map the different varieties of thought and practice which have developed internally to the field. "Planned change" has undergone a rapid internal differentiation since the first edition of this book was published in 1961. In Chapter Two we try to make sense of current bewildering differentiations within the advocacy and practice of "planned change."

Our treatment of the history of planned change in this chapter must, of necessity, be impressionistic. No thorough historical study of it has yet been made. One strand in its history is the changing relationships between persons of knowledge and persons of action, between persons who are expert because of their special studies and persons who are in political and managerial control of institutions or who aspire to such control. For,

11

as we have noted, planned change involves a new relationship between social scientists, students of human affairs on the one hand, and practitioners and action planners and leaders, on the other. Planned change requires collaboration between social scientists and action planners. This is in contrast to the segregation and conflict which have marked the relations between "theory" and "practice" traditionally and which persist in contemporary social organization, despite the widespread breaching of the walls of segregation in recent years.

Of course, the use of experts as advisers and consultants to rulers is much older than the relatively recent emergence of the social sciences or the helping professions as research and teaching disciplines in modern universities. In the past the experts may have been sages, priests, shamans, astrologers, or philosophers rather than scientists in the modern sense. George A. Kelly has outlined the changing history of these uneasy relationships in an illuminating essay, "The Expert as Historical Actor."[1]

Kelly makes clear the basis of many of the dilemmas of experts who are drawn into the service of action programs and projects. They must mediate between a system shaped to the production and refinement of knowledge and a system concerned centrally with the exercise and channeling of power in the service of practicable ends. Where the persons of knowledge may espouse a utopian "sociological vision," they must deal with non-utopian action leaders who are committed to the achievement of the possible and practicable within an existing system of power relationships.

As protagonists of planned change, we do not see a utopian end to the contrasting and conflicting mentalities and characters selected and nurtured by systems of knowledge and by systems of power which Kelly's essay illuminates or an end to the tensions in relationship which result when persons from both systems attempt to collaborate in planning for the resolution and melioration of human issues and ills. But we do believe that such unwonted collaborations are increasingly required by an irreversible shift in our society from tradition-directed policies and practices to knowledge-based policies and practices and from unconscious historical selection of viable patterns and forms of living to deliberate human choice, invention, and evaluation of such patterns and forms. Part of the task of planned change is the linkage and re-education of hitherto segregated and conflicting groups toward the practice of creative collaboration. Another strand in the history of planned change would, therefore, be a documentation of this irreversible shift from a nonplanned to a planned way of life in postindustrial societies.

In the first selection in this chapter, "Planned Change in America," the editors sketch shifting and conflicting attitudes and practices among social scientists, social practitioners, policy-makers, and oppressed minorities in America with respect to several distinguishable aspects of planned

[1] *Daedalus*, Volume 92, No. 3.

change since the late nineteenth century. These aspects include consciousness of the need for planning changes in human life; the relations of social scientists to social practice and planning; the professionalization of change agents; and the place of popular participation in the direction and evaluation of programs of changing.

In "General Strategies for Effecting Changes in Human Systems," Chin and Benne attempt two tasks. They propose a three-way classification of the strategies of changing in current use. The authors of this volume are committed to one of these families of strategies, the "normative re-educative," as most appropriate to the conditions of contemporary life and to the advancement of scientific and democratic values in human society. But this commitment does not mean that the authors reject any place for the other two families of strategies—the "rational-empirical" and the "power-coercive," as Chin and Benne name them—in the armamentarium of change agents and change strategists in our time. It is probably safe to predict that all three kinds of strategies will continue to be used in action programs. However, we believe that continuing research, development, and training in the applied behavioral sciences will extend the use of normative re-educative strategies in local, national, and world society.

Chin and Benne also attempt to place the three classes of general strategies within recent historical streams of thought about man and society, which have fed these strategies and their sustaining and supporting rationales. This tracing of the intellectual roots of contemporary ways of thinking about planned change is designed to establish continuities with our past as well as to place alternative contemporary approaches to changing into clearer relief. Although this final piece was prepared primarily for an audience of leaders in public education, it should have meaning for change strategists in other institutional settings as well.

1.1 Planned Change in America

Kenneth D. Benne   Warren G. Bennis
Robert Chin

The idea of social scientists participating in and actively influencing the planning

This piece incorporates material from the first edition of *The Planning of Change: Readings in the Applied Behavioral Sciences*, edited by Warren G. Bennis, Kenneth D. Benne, and Robert Chin. Copyright © 1961 by Holt, Rinehart and Winston, Inc.

and implementation of social change has been a center of controversy in America since the emergence of the idea in the late nineteenth century. The idea of social planning and governmental employment of experts is, of course, much older. But the differentiation of the more behaviorally oriented social sciences—psychology, sociology, and anthropology—as distinct research disciplines, along with tentative acceptance of and support for them within the university structure in the late nineteenth and early twentieth centuries, gave new impetus to the Baconian dream of a New Atlantis governed by scientific thinkers and doers. Controversy over the idea has divided in varying degree action leaders, policy-makers, social scientists, professional practitioners, and the "general public" from 1900 to the present.

The focus of the controversy has shifted during this time, along with the terms in which the issue is discussed. In fact, we see two major shifts in this continuing debate. One shift occurred between 1900 and the 1950s. The shift accompanied the co-optation of liberal progressivism by the New Deal and its domestication of a "brain trust" of professors into the service of government change programs. A new characteristic quality of the controversy is most apparent in the affluent 1950s.

The second shift in the controversy occurred during the 1960s. This period was marked by the emergence and cresting of the civil rights and other liberation movements, by the pressure of various "grass roots" protest movements against the established techno-structure,[1] by the emergence and spread of a survivors' mentality among various segments of American society, and by the Vietnam War and its aftermath. We are too close to these events of the 1960s to see clearly or fully either their motivations or their consequences. But it is clear that they did refocus attitudes toward planned change

and affected its rationale, its opportunities and responsibilities, and its practices. Events, new thoughts, and occurrences in countries abroad have contributed direct and indirect waves of influence on American thinking about the need for and processes of planned change.

Let us return now to the history of planned change in America. In 1900, controversy over planned change was typically stated in sweeping ideological terms. Should or should not men seek, through deliberate and collaborative forethought in the present, to mold the shape of their collective future? Or should confidence rather be placed in a principle of automatic adjustment, operating within the processes of history to reequilibrate, without human forethought yet in the interest of progress and human welfare, the inescapable human upsets and dislocations of a changing society?

This issue raised a corollary issue concerning the proper relations of the emerging social sciences of the time, and of social scientists, to the guidance and management of practical affairs. In general, the "planners" saw an important place for social science in informing policies and in rendering social practice more intelligent and reality-oriented. Proponents of "automatic adjustment" tended to relegate social scientists to an observer role and to deny them participation or leadership in influencing the direction or the form of practical affairs. This conception of "nonintervening" social science fitted the mainline traditions of the natural sciences and of the older social studies—history, economics, and political theory. This view of the proper relationships between social science and social action was further reinforced by aspirations of the younger and more behavior-oriented sciences—psychology and sociology—to achieve and maintain their autonomy and "purity" within the academic world in which they were parvenus. The issue concerning "science" and "practice" has been raised

---

[1] "Techno-structure" is Galbraith's term for the coalition between interests and their spokesmen within both the private and the public (governmental) structures of our political economy. The "military-industrial complex" is one often-mentioned aspect of this coalition. It is this coalition which makes decisions concerning the policies which control our economic and related social and political life. See J. K. Galbraith, *The New Industrial State* (Boston: Houghton Mifflin, 1967; 2d Revised Edition, 1971).

anew as "applied social science" has been encouraged and supported by many policy-makers and social practitioners, and actively promoted by some social scientists.

Lester F. Ward was one of the earliest social scientists in America to proclaim that modern men must extend scientific approaches into the planning of changes in the patterns of their behaviors and relationships. He was well aware that men were already utilizing their accumulating collective and scientific intelligence deliberately to induce changes in their non-human environment. And he saw a major role for the emerging sciences of man in extending a similar planning approach into the management of human affairs.

> Man's destiny is in his own hands. Any law that he can comprehend he can control. He cannot increase or diminish the powers of nature, but he can direct them. . . . His power over nature is unlimited. He can make it his servant and appropriate to his own use all the mighty forces of the universe. . . . Human institutions are not exempt from this all-pervading spirit of improvement. They, too, are artificial, conceived in the ingenious brain and wrought with mental skill born of inventive genius. The passion for their improvement is of a piece with the impulse to improve the plow or the steam engine. . . . Intelligence, heretofore a growth, is destined to become a manufacture. . . . The origination and distribution of knowledge can no longer be left to chance or to nature. They are to be systematized and erected into true arts.[2]

Ward's proclamation seemed foolish boasting, if not downright sacrilege, to many among his contemporaries. William Graham Sumner was one of the leaders in sociology who emphasized both the folly and sacrilege of prophecies like Ward's.

> If we can acquire a science of society based on observation of phenomena and

study of forces, we may hope to gain some ground slowly toward the elimination of old errors and the reestablishment of a sound and natural social order. Whatever we gain that way will be by growth, never in the world by any reconstruction of society on the plan of some enthusiastic social architect. The latter is only repeating the old error over again, and postponing all our chances of real improvement. Society needs first of all to be free from these meddlers—that is, to be let alone. Here we are, then, once more back at the old doctrine *laissez faire*. Let us translate it into blunt English, and it will read—Mind your own business. It is nothing but the doctrine of liberty. Let every man be happy in his own way.[3]

It may be fortunate or unfortunate that American controversies a half century later over the direction and management of social change seldom took the form of sweeping societal prescriptions and counterprescriptions or ideological debates—a form which Ward and Sumner, along with their contemporaries, gave to them. In any event, the form of the controversies shifted. In large measure subsequent events have foreclosed the factual basis for Sumner's argument. *Laissez faire* has been widely abandoned in practice as a principle of social management, whatever ghostly existence it yet enjoys in conservative political platforms and pronunciamentos. Human interventions designed to shape and modify the institutionalized behaviors of men are now familiar features of our social landscape. "Helping professions" have proliferated since Ward's and Sumner's day. Professions of industrial and public management have taken shape. The reason for being of all of these is deliberately to introduce and coach changes in the future behaviors and relationships of their various "client" populations. This is most apparent in "new" professions such as psychiatry, social work, nursing, counseling, management, and consultation in its manifold

[2] Quoted in Henry Commager, *The American Mind* (New Haven, Conn.: Yale University Press, 1950), pp. 208, 210, 213–214.

[3] Quoted in Commager, op cit., pp. 201–202.

forms. But older professions too, such as medicine, law, teaching, and the clergy, have been pressed increasingly to become agencies of social change rather than of social conservation. Resistances to assuming the new role have, of course, developed along with the situational pressures to enact it.

Behavioral scientists, neo-Sumnerians among others, in the first part of the twentieth century, were drawn, with varying degrees of eagerness and resistance, into activities of "changing," such as consultation and applied research. "Helping professionals," "managers," and "policy-makers" in various fields of practice increasingly sought and employed the services of behavioral scientists to anticipate more accurately the consequences of prospective social changes and to inform more validly the processes of planning designed to control these consequences.

We were widely seeking to plan social changes in the fifties. And both the products and the methods of social research were being more and more widely utilized in the processes of such planning. Sumner's ideological advice had been widely rejected in practice.

But it is equally true that Ward's millennial hope seemed far—indeed very far—from realization. Attempts to apply social knowledge in planning and controlling changes tended to be fragmented by the division of contemporary agents of change into specialized and largely noncommunicating professions and disciplines. These attempts were thwarted too by noncommunication and noncollaboration among policy-makers and action planners in the various institutional settings where planning has become familiar practice—industry, government, welfare, health, and education. Advocates and students of planned change became more cautious in their claims, less millennial in their hopes than Ward tended to be. The modal question shifted from "Should we seek to plan change?" to "How to plan

particular changes in particular settings and situations?" Where the wider societal view had not been entirely lost the question "How to interrelate and link the various forms which the planning of change has taken in conventionally isolated but actually interdependent settings of social action and practice?" was raised.

Men in the fifties had thus widely come to believe that they had no actual choice as to whether somebody will seek to plan continuing changes in the patterns of their lives. Men must try to plan their changing futures, and this necessity is seen to be determined by cultural conditions, not primarily by the ideology men happen to hold. "Democratic," "communistic," and "fascist" peoples must alike try to plan social changes. This helped to account for the shift of many questions about planned change from an "ideological" to a "technical" form. This did not mean, as some who would reduce all questions of planning to technical form might believe, that questions about the values which should guide planners can or should disappear from discussions about planning or from the processes of planning. It meant rather that these questions too had taken new forms.

Both Ward and Sumner worked within a framework of common assumptions about the actuality and desirability, if not the inevitability, of Progress. Their ideological differences centered on varying ways of achieving the Progress which both generally assumed to be, in some way, America's destiny, and by patriotic extension, human destiny as well. (The pessimism of Sumner grown old came more from despair over the course of events about him than from relinquishment of this ideal.) Differing means of achieving Progress, of course, if carefully analyzed, meant different meanings of Progress as well. But the values of "rationality," "freedom," "universal education," and the "extension through science of human control over the natural environment" were, in general, values acceptable to "planners" and "antiplanners" as well. Both sought to settle value issues by an appeal to living traditions of "liberalism" and "democracy," traditions not usually clearly distinguished one from the other.

It was a living tradition of "liberal democracy" that could no longer be assumed or taken for granted in discussions of issues of planned change in the period after World War II. Intellectually and practically, consensus in the core values of "liberalism" and "democracy" had been eroded in America. And these values had never been a part of the living tradition of many national cultures outside America in both technologically developed and undeveloped nations. The possibility, desirability, and meaning of Progress, and most emphatically its inevitability, as defined and revered within the liberal tradition, had been challenged fundamentally.

Neoconservative critiques of "liberalism" had been familiar features of the American intellectual scene for a generation before the 1950s. "Liberal" theology had been attacked by religious neoorthodoxies of various types. "Liberal" politics had been denounced as unrealistic and "soft" by political conservatives who sought to meet their security needs through maintaining a militarily strong capitalist state within a hostile world. "Progressive" education had been inveighed against by various conservative critics as negligent of "fundamentals" in knowledge and in morality.

As already noted, the focus of attention of most people interested in planning in the 1950s was on the technical questions of how to plan in particular isolated social settings, rather than on the more fundamental questions of who should be involved in processes of planning and of what overarching values and purposes processes of planning should serve. The prevailing model of planning was an *engineering* model of applied science rather than a clinical model, in terms of Alvin Gouldner's distinction.[4] In the *engineering* model, plans are made by experts to meet the needs of the people affected by the plan as the experts interpret these needs, as well as relevant objective technical and economic conditions and requirements. After the plan is made, the consent of those affected to the plan is engineered by effective means of monologic persuasion. In the *clinical* model, the experts work collaboratively and dialogically with those affected by the policy to be made in order to inform them and to empower them toward participation in making, evaluating, and remaking operating plans. (It is, of course, apparent that the authors of this book are committed to the clinical rather than the engineering model.)

The New Deal, World War II, and the scientific management movement had familiarized our society in the uses of the expertise of economists and other students of people and of society according to the engineering model of planning. Only a minority of critics, for example, in the human relations movement in industry, in mental health, and in community work, advocated an alternative model of participatory planning and of the deployment and use of social science resources. We believe that this preference for "technological" solutions to human problems in the 1950s was by no means accidental.

For the liberal faith in progress in America had become intertwined, in both learned and popular minds, with a faith in technology as the guarantor of progress. Many people believed that the only realistic and dependable index of progress was the development and utilization of an ever more refined and powerful technology. A changing technology, so Veblen and others argued, was the principal motor of social change. Each technological advance in-

4 Alvin W. Gouldner, "Explorations in Applied Social Science," *Social Problems*, Vol. 3, No. 3 (January 1956), pp. 173–181

volved us in new social and human problems. But the devotees of technology, and these included most Americans, believed that a new technology would be invented to solve these problems with a minimum of effort, travail, or responsibility on the part of most people. The technological experts would eventually save us.

It was the evidence of cataclysmic historic events, rather than the criticisms already noted, that cast convincing doubt upon the inherent beneficence of the technological god. After the day in August 1945 when a U.S. bomber dropped a nuclear bomb—a stupendous technological achievement—upon Hiroshima, many sensed that mankind had moved, in Karl Jaspers' term, into a new Axial period of human history. Man's ingenious and inventive cultivation of technology had given him the power to pollute his planet irreparably and to destroy all terrestrial life.

Actually, the germ of the mentality of the lucky and guilty survivors of holocaust was planted during World War II by Nazi genocide and the real possibilities of irreparable nuclear pollution. This mentality did not flower until the 1960s. Most of us persisted through the 1950s in role-playing a dying faith in technological solutions to human problems and watched the increasing gross national product and the proliferation of ingenious gadgets to add to human comfort as evidences of a societal health and growth in which we no longer deeply believed.

This is no place to write the history of the turbulent 1960s in America. But several of its developments have thrown the discussions and practices of planned change into new relief. It is these developments which we will note and attempt to interpret in their influence on the practice of planned change.

The 1960s were marked by a wave of liberation movements which stemmed from persons and groups of persons who felt alienated from the mainstream of American life, alienated from themselves and their "real" nature and potentialities, oppressed by the forms and conventions of established society. Protests against oppressive conditions of life and against those who defended and maintained these conditions began with racial groups, particularly Blacks in America, and spread to students and younger people, to poor people, to women, to homosexuals, to American Indians, and to environmental conservationists.[5]

Almost invariably the language and rhetoric of protest was a language and rhetoric of "power"; the goal of protest, in addition to local and occasional goals, was a redistribution of maldistributed power. Protests were "mass" movements but most often the professed aim was to encourage oppressed persons to lift themselves out of the reactive mass, to encourage individuals to become proactive, to accept and affirm themselves as persons, to reject the attributions of inferiority, powerlessness, and helplessness which those in charge of established society place upon them. The "new" consciousness-raising aimed toward politicizing traditional relationships by exposing and emphasizing their "power" dimension. But the consciousness-raising and self-affirm-

[5] It is interesting to note that the U.S. Supreme Court in its decision in *Brown* v. *Kansas* in 1954 gave unprecedentedly strong weight to the evidence and recommendations of social scientists concerning the educational effects of racial segregation. Thus, this landmark decision, which gave impetus to the civil rights movement, created conflicting public images of "social science" and its relation to the making of public policy. Within the minds of those who opposed the decision, suspicion of "social scientists" as "radicals" was created or reinforced. Within the leadership of the Black community and of other militant supporters of the civil rights movement, this significant contribution by social scientists may have created unrealistic expectations of their continuing support which were partly destroyed and replaced by disillusionment in the light of the neutrality shown by many social scientists when, during the height of the civil rights movement, polarization and conflict deepened and violence flared.

ing actions advocated and practiced were "therapeutic" in intention as they sought self-acceptance and self-assertion for those whom the "establishment" had put down and kept down. And the protest movements also often embodied qualities of religious commitment, putting faith above conventional and "worldly" knowledge and wisdom. Institutionalized compartmentalizations of "politics," "therapy," and "religion" were broken down. Were new mergers of purpose and method and alternative institutions implicit in the razing of old boundaries and walls?

Some of the protest movements, especially those defined along generational lines, young *versus* old, cut across national boundaries and emerged in capitalist, communist, and socialist countries, in developed and developing countries.[6] Were there intimations of a nascent world culture in the youth movements, a nascent consciousness and culture, pressing against the confines of repressive and outmoded social organization and controls?[7]

How have these liberation movements and new experiences in grass-roots participation in community planning affected the status of planned change? What problems and opportunities have they precipitated for students and practitioners of planned change?

They exposed and in a measure cleared away some of the conventional debris that has clouded the realities of existing relationships in our society—the distorting effects of power differentials, the dysfunctional inhibitions of expression of affect, positive and negative, in many human relationships; the gap between professed values and values in use; and the dehumanizing effects of depersonalized relations in many of our bureaucratized

institutions, political, industrial, and educational. These effects are clearly in line with the values of planned change of the sort we are advocating and are supportive of its continuing thrust.

They have unmasked the assimilationist myth of the American melting pot and revealed the pluralism inherent in American life, the variety of groups and group interests that are seeking their place in the sun, and they have thus placed the clarification and negotiation of differing values and value orientations as an inescapable priority upon the agenda of agents of change and their clients. Technical problems remain but they can no longer crowd out the clarification and negotiation of value stances. The stance of value neutrality on the part of applied social scientists and social practitioners has been effectively debunked.

In their emphases on redistribution of power, they have revealed inadequacies in their own conceptions of power and in the conceptions of power held by many of their adversaries as well. The assumption that power exists in a fixed amount and that one must take power away from those who wield it in order to gain power for one's self and one's group vitiated many of their well-intentioned programs of change. Power can be generated by peer support, by a more adequate self-concept, by shared values and goals, by access to more valid knowledge and information. Win-win strategies of changing can be built upon this latter conception of power. Win-lose strategies of changing which lead to destructive polarization are bolstered by the assumption that power exists in a limited and fixed amount. Agents of planned change have an important re-educative task in the conceptual clarification of power and in finding strategies for its generation and use.

This is illustrative of the fact that protestors often were clearer about their values and goals than they were creative in inventing methods and strategies of

---

[6] See, for example, Margaret Mead, *Culture and Commitment* (New York: Natural History Press, 1970).

[7] Charles A. Reich's *The Greening of America* (New York: Random House, 1970), emphatically overstated this view.

changing that were coherent with their values and goals and which led to effects consistent with their intentions. This clearly presents a re-educative task for the agent of change. But, we believe, liberation movements, in general, created a readiness for such re-education that was not there before.

We have stated that one of the values of planned change, as we see it, is the use of valid knowledge and information as a basis for plans and programs of change. And, we believe, much relevant valid knowledge lies in the tested concepts and methods of social scientists. It is at this point that some of our gravest misgivings about the effects of protest movements in America center. For many, protest movements have led to estrangement between the resources of the social sciences and the action strategists and planners of protest movements. They may, in some instances, have strengthened the anti-intellectualism which is always endemic in American life and which has always accompanied the growth of populist movements. This effect, if it in fact is an effect, is, of course, not entirely the "fault" of those in liberation movements. For liberationists are partly right in seeing the resources of the applied social sciences as more oriented and available to the needs of guardians of the status quo than to those who are challenging that guardianship and in interpreting the claim of value neutrality which many in the social sciences still make for themselves as a mask for passive endorsement of the powers that be. But the liberationists are wrong in depriving themselves of resources that could make their projects of changing more coherent and more effective. This widened gap, insofar as it exists, between social scientists and those from the oppressed who take leadership in humanizing our institutions and relationships defines an important task for practitioners of planned change in America.

In characterizing the effects of American experience in the 1960s on the prospects of and challenges to planned change, we cannot fail to mention and assess the effects of that period's most cataclysmic event—American involvement in the Vietnam War. And, because we are still suffering deeply its painful effects, an adequate assessment is currently impossible. We could have no clearer demonstration of the failure of power-coercive strategies of change in the relations between nations and the need to invent and test more collaborative strategies at that level. Our attempt to coerce both North and South Vietnam and the Viet Cong into conformity to what our leaders defined as our national interest failed. In the case of North Vietnam and the Viet Cong, we showed the impotence of technological might against the human power generated by belief in a cause. Our show of force only solidified resistance to the imposition of our alien purpose. In the case of South Vietnam, we showed our inability, though our material investment was stupendous, to engineer popular acceptance of a regime in which people did not believe and to induce high popular morale under the leadership of that regime.

It remains to be seen whether we as a people and a government will be able to face and acknowledge our failures, to learn from them, and to take the lead in instituting more collaborative, more creative, less fundamentally destructive ways of resolving conflicts among nations. Actualizing this desirable outcome should have a high priority on the agenda of agents of planned change in America.

The effects of our involvement in the Vietnam War upon the internal society of our nation were no less drastic than on our international relations. Our potential learning through our mistakes about processes of changing are equally great. The power that stems from the hoarding of relevant information by any elite was vividly illustrated. In the name of national security, access to relevant information was stringently limited to a few in the central government. This limited access left most people and their representatives in Congress relatively helpless in effectively criticizing, redirecting, and altering public policy with respect to the war. And it made possible the dissemination of highly selected and false information in an attempt to engineer acquiescence in the Executive's war policy. That this manipulation of information failed to engineer acquiescence or to still criticism and protest, that it eventually destroyed the credibility of two Presidents, may be a tribute to our system of civil liberties and to the commitment in our people to openness and authenticity in the relationship between leaders and followers. That the policy worked for so long, that it paralyzed public discussion and debate for so long, that it led to governmental invasion of the privacy of so many honest dissenters are facts that are sobering in their implications. More adequate management of the flow of information on which public policy is based and more effective protection of the rights of privacy and of dissent should be high priorities on the agenda of agents of planned change. And this applies to local as well as to national and international change programs.

We have spoken of the survivors' mentality which emerged in America after the Nazi holocaust and the nuclear bombing of Hiroshima and which spread widely during the 1960s. This is a mentality that accepts the premise that the survival of *mankind, not just you or me*, has become problematic in our time and place. It is conjoined with the premise that the extinction of mankind, if it comes, will be through the agency of human beings themselves. Where acceptance of these premises does not lead to a paralyzing and guilty despair, it may engender a new sense of moral responsibility in persons. And this sense of responsibility may lead to a reassessment of even our most hallowed traditional moralities and policies against the criterion of their implications and consequences in terms of human survival.

Richard Means has expressed the contemporary ethical meaning of problematic human survival in this way:

> If the survival of life is a basic good and can be accepted by people throughout the world, then this good is universal. On the practical level, the terror of atomic holocaust maximizes into reality the greatest good for the greatest number, that is, survival and life, as the basic ethical rule. It is the interconnection of terror, the intricate web of world destruction, that now ties us together and lends objectivity to the consequences of our values. Thus the values of industrial civilization, of the warring powers of the East and West, are universalized in their implication and consequences and must be judged in relation to a universal good—the fact of human survival.[8]

Agents of planned change must resist in themselves the despair and accept the deepened ethical responsibility both of which are implicit in acknowledgment of the problematic character of human survival today. And they must invite their clients to open their values, personal, local, political, religious, to a test against this new universal criterion of good—human survival.

[8] Richard L. Means, *The Ethical Imperative: The Crisis in American Values* (Garden City, N.Y.: Doubleday, 1969), p. 56.

1.2 General Strategies for Effecting Changes in Human Systems

Robert Chin   Kenneth D. Benne

Discussing general strategies and procedures for effecting change requires that we set limits to the discussion. For, under a liberal interpretation of the title, we would need to deal with much of the literature of contemporary social and behavioral science, basic and applied.

Therefore, we shall limit our discussion to those changes which are planned changes—in which attempts to bring about change are conscious, deliberate, and intended, at least on the part of one or more agents related to the change attempt. We shall also attempt to categorize strategies and procedures which have a few important elements in common but which, in fact, differ widely in other respects. And we shall neglect many of these differences. In addition, we shall look beyond the description of procedures in common-sense terms and seek some genotypic characteristics of change strategies. We shall seek the roots of the main strategies discussed, including their variants, in ideas and idea systems prominent in contemporary and recent social and psychological thought.

One element in all approaches to planned change is the conscious utilization and application of knowledge as an instrument or tool for modifying patterns and institutions of practice. The knowledge or related technology to be applied may be knowledge of the nonhuman environment in which practice goes on or of some knowledge-based "thing technology" for controlling one or another feature of the practice environment. In educational practice, for example, technologies of communication and calculation, based upon new knowledge of electronics—audiovisual devices, television, computers, teaching machines—loom large among the knowledges and technologies that promise greater efficiency and economy in handling various practices in formal education. As attempts are made to introduce these new thing technologies into school situations the change problem shifts to the human problems of dealing with the resistances, anxieties, threats to morale, conflicts, disrupted interpersonal communications, and so on, which prospective changes in patterns of practice evoke in the people affected by the change. So the change agent, even though focally and initially concerned with modifications in the thing technology of education, finds himself in need of more adequate knowledge of human behavior, individual and social, and in need of developed "people technologies," based on behavioral knowledge, for dealing effectively with the human aspects of deliberate change.

This essay was prepared especially for the second edition of *The Planning of Change*. It was adapted from a paper by Robert Chin prepared for "Designing Education for the Future—An Eight State Project" (Denver, Colo., 1967). Kenneth D. Benne joined in revising and expanding sections of the original paper for inclusion in the second edition. In the process of revision, what was in several respects a new paper emerged. The original focus on changing in education was maintained. Historial roots of ideas and strategies were explored. The first-person style of the original paper was also maintained. Citations have been modified to include articles contained in the present volume, along with other references.

The knowledge which suggests improvements in educational practice may, on the other hand, be behavioral knowledge in the first instance—knowledge about participative learning, about attitude change, about family disruption in inner-city communities, about the cognitive and skill requirements of new careers, and so forth. Such knowledge may suggest changes in school grouping, in the relations between teachers and students, in the relations of teachers and principals to parents, and in counseling practices. Here change agents, initially focused on application of behavioral knowledge and the improvement of people technologies in school settings, must face the problems of using people technologies in planning, installing, and evaluating such changes in educational practice. The new people technologies must be experienced, understood, and accepted by teachers and administrators before they can be used effectively with students.

This line of reasoning suggests that, whether the focus of planned change is in the introduction of more effective thing technologies or people technologies into institutionalized practice, processes of introducing such changes must be based on behavioral knowledge of change and must utilize people technologies based on such knowledge.

A. Types of Strategies for Changing

Our further analysis is based on three types or groups of strategies. The first of these, and probably the most frequently employed by men of knowledge in America and Western Europe, are those we call empirical-rational strategies. One fundamental assumption underlying these strategies is that men are rational. Another assumption is that men will follow their rational self-interest once this is revealed to them. A change is proposed by some person or group which knows of a situation that is desirable, effective, and in line with the self-interest of the person, group, organization, or community which will be affected by the change. Because the person (or group) is assumed to be rational and moved by self-interest, it is assumed that he (or they) will adopt the proposed change if it can be rationally justified and if it can be shown by the proposer(s) that he (or they) will gain by the change.

A second group of strategies we call normative-re-educative. These strategies build upon assumptions about human motivation different from those underlying the first. The rationality and intelligence of men are not denied. Patterns of action and practice are supported by sociocultural norms and by commitments on the part of individuals to these norms. Sociocultural norms are supported by the attitude and value systems of individuals—normative outlooks which undergird their commitments. Change in a pattern of practice or action, according to this view, will occur only as the persons involved are brought to change their normative orientations to old patterns and develop commitments to new ones. And changes in normative orientations involve changes in attitudes, values, skills, and significant relationships, not just changes in knowledge, information, or intellectual rationales for action and practice.

The third group of strategies is based on the application of power in some form, political or otherwise. The influence process involved is basically that of compliance of those with less power to the plans, directions, and leadership of those with greater power. Often the power to be applied is legitimate power or authority. Thus the strategy may involve getting the authority of law or administrative policy behind the change to be effected. Some power strategies may appeal less to the use of authoritative power to effect change than to the massing of coercive power, legitimate or not, in support of the change sought.[1]

1. Empirical-Rational Strategies

A variety of specific strategies are included in what we are calling the empirical-rational approach to effecting change. As we have already pointed out, the rationale underlying most of these is an assumption that men are guided by reason and that they will utilize some rational calculus of self-interest in determining needed changes in behavior.

It is difficult to point to any one person whose ideas express or articulate the orientation underlying commitment to empirical-rational strategies of changing. In Western Europe and America, this orientation might be better identified with the general social orientation of the Enlightenment and of classical liberalism than with the ideas of any one man. On this view, the chief foes to human rationality and to change or progress based on rationality were ignorance and super-

stition. Scientific investigation and research represented the chief ways of extending knowledge and reducing the limitations of ignorance. A corollary of this optimistic view of man and his future was an advocacy of education as a way of disseminating scientific knowledge and of freeing men and women from the shackles of superstition. Although elitist notions played a part in the thinking of many classic liberals, the increasing trend during the nineteenth century was toward the universalization of educational opportunity. The common and universal school, open to all men and women, was the principal instrument by which knowledge would replace ignorance and superstition in the minds of people and become a principal agent in the spread of reason, knowledge, and knowledge-based action and practice (progress) in human society. In American experience, Jefferson may be taken as a principal, early advocate of research and of education as agencies of human progress. And Horace Mann may be taken as the prophet of progress through the institutionalization of universal educational opportunity through the common school.[2]

a. Basic Research and Dissemination of Knowledge through General Education

The strategy of encouraging basic knowledge building and of depending on general education to diffuse the results of

---

[1] Throughout our discussion of strategies and procedures, we will not differentiate these according to the size of the target of change. We assume that there are similarities in processes of changing, whether the change affects an individual, a small group, an organization, a community, or a culture. In addition, we are not attending to differences among the aspects of a system, let us say an educational system, which is being changed—curriculum, audio-visual methods, team teaching, pupil grouping, and so on. Furthermore, because many changes in communities or organizations start with an individual or some small membership group, our general focus will be upon those strategies which lead to and involve individual changes.

We will sidestep the issue of defining change in this paper. As further conceptual work progresses in the study of planned change, we shall eventually have to examine how different definitions of change relate to strategies and procedures for effecting change. But we are not dealing with these issues here.

[2] We have indicated the main roots of ideas and idea systems underlying the principal strategies of changing and their subvariants on a chart which appears as Figure 1 at the end of this essay. It may be useful in seeing both the distinctions and the relationships between various strategies of changing in time perspective. We have emphasized developments of the past twenty-five years more than earlier developments. This makes for historical foreshortening. We hope this is a pardonable distortion, considering our present limited purpose.

research into the minds and thinking of men and women is still by far the most appealing strategy of change to most academic men of knowledge and to large segments of the American population as well. Basic researchers are quite likely to appeal for time for further research when confronted by some unmet need. And many people find this appeal convincing. Both of these facts are well illustrated by difficulties with diseases for which no adequate control measures or cures are available—poliomyelitis, for example. Medical researchers asked for more time and funds for research and people responded with funds for research, both through voluntary channels and through legislative appropriations. And the control measures were forthcoming. The educational problem then shifted to inducing people to comply with immunization procedures based on research findings.

This appeal to a combination of research and education of the public has worked in many areas of new knowledge-based thing technologies where almost universal readiness for accepting the new technology was already present in the population. Where such readiness is not available, as in the case of fluoridation technologies in the management of dental caries, general strategy of basic research plus educational (informational) campaigns to spread knowledge of the findings do not work well. The cases of its inadequacy as a single strategy of change have multiplied, especially where "engineering" problems, which involve a divided and conflicting public or deep resistances due to the threat by the new technology to traditional attitudes and values, have thwarted its effectiveness. But these cases, while they demand attention to other strategies of changing, do not disprove the importance of basic research and of general educational opportunity as elements in a progressive and self-renewing society.

We have noted that the strategy under discussion has worked best in grounding and diffusing generally acceptable thing technologies in society. Some have argued that the main reason the strategy has not worked in the area of people technologies is a relative lack of basic research on people and their behavior, relationships, and institutions and a corresponding lack of emphasis upon social and psychological knowledges in school and college curricula. It would follow in this view that increased basic research on human affairs and relationships and increased efforts to diffuse the results of such research through public education are the ways of making the general strategy work better. Auguste Comte with his emphasis on positivistic sociology in the reorganization of society and Lester F. Ward in America may be taken as late-nineteenth-century representatives of this view. And the spirit of Comte and Ward is by no means dead in American academia or in influential segments of the American public.

b. Personnel Selection and Replacement

Difficulties in getting knowledge effectively into practice may be seen as lying primarily in the lack of fitness of persons occupying positions with job responsibilities for improving practice. The argument goes that we need the right person in the right position, if knowledge is to be optimally applied and if rationally based changes are to become the expectation in organizational and societal affairs. This fits with the liberal reformers' frequently voiced and enacted plea to drive the unfit from office and to replace them with those more fit as a condition of social progress.

That reformers' programs have so often failed has sobered but by no means destroyed the zeal of those who regard personnel selection, assessment, and replacement as a major key to program improvement in education or in other enterprises as well. This strategy was given a scientific boost by the development of scientific testing of potentialities and aptitudes. We will use Binet as a prototype of psychological testing and Moreno as a prototype in sociometric testing, while recognizing the extensive differentiation and elaboration which have occurred in psychometrics and sociometrics since their original work. We recognize too the elaborated modes of practice in personnel work which have been built around psychometric and sociometric tools and techniques. We do not discount their limited value as actual and potential tools for change, while making two observations on the way they have often been used. First, they have been used more often in the interest of system maintenance rather than of system change, since the job descriptions personnel workers seek to fill are defined in terms of system requirements as established. Second, by focusing on the role occupant as the principal barrier to improvement, personnel selection and replacement strategies have tended not to reveal the social and cultural system difficulties which may be in need of change if improvement is to take place.

c. Systems Analysts as Staff and Consultants

Personnel workers in government, industry, and education have typically worked in staff relations to line management, reflecting the bureaucratic, line-staff form of organization which has flourished in the large-scale organization of effort and enterprise in the twentieth century. And other expert workers—systems analysts— more attuned to system difficulties than to the adequacies or inadequacies of persons as role occupants within the system, have found their way into the staff resources of line management in contemporary organizations.

There is no reason why the expert resources of personnel workers and systems analysts might not be used in nonbureaucratic organizations or in proc-

esses of moving bureaucratic organizations toward nonbureaucratic forms. But the fact remains that their use has been shaped, for the most part, in the image of the scientific management of bureaucratically organized enterprises. So we have placed the systems analysts in our chart under Frederick Taylor, the father of scientific management in America.

The line management of an enterprise seeks to organize human and technical effort toward the most efficient service of organizational goals. And these goals are defined in terms of the production of some mandated product, whether a tangible product or a less tangible good or service. In pursuing this quest for efficiency, line management employs experts in the analysis of sociotechnical systems and in the laying out of more efficient systems. The experts employed may work as external consultants or as an internal staff unit. Behavioral scientists have recently found their way, along with mathematicians and engineers, into systems analysis work.

It is interesting to note that the role of these experts is becoming embroiled in discussions of whether or not behavioral science research should be used to sensitize administrators to new organizational possibilities, to new goals, or primarily to implement efficient operation within perspectives and goals as currently defined. Jean Hills has raised the question of whether behavioral science when applied to organizational problems tends to perpetuate established ideology and system relations because of blinders imposed by their being "problem-centered" and by their limited definition of what is "a problem."[3]

We see an emerging strategy, in the use of behavioral scientists as systems

[3] Jean Hills, "Social Science, Ideology and the Purposes of Educational Administration," *Education Administration Quarterly* I (Autumn 1965), 23–40.

analysts and engineers, toward viewing the problem of organizational change and changing as a wide-angled problem, one in which all the input and output features and components of a large-scale system are considered. It is foreseeable that with the use of high-speed and high-capacity computers, and with the growth of substantial theories and hypotheses about how parts of an educational system operate, we shall find more and more applications for systems analysis and operations research in programs of educational change. In fact, it is precisely the quasi-mathematical character of these modes of research that will make possible the rational analysis of qualitatively different aspects of educational work and will bring them into the range of rational planning—masses of students, massive problems of poverty and educational and cultural deprivation, and so on. We see no necessary incompatibility between an ideology which emphasizes the individuality of the student and the use of systems analysis and computers in strategizing the problems of the total system. The actual incompatibilities may lie in the limited uses to which existing organizers and administrators of educational efforts put these technical resources.

d. Applied Research and Linkage Systems for Diffusion of Research Results

The American development of applied research and of a planned system for linking applied researchers with professional practitioners and both of these with centers for basic research and with organized consumers of applied research has been strongly influenced by two distinctive American inventions—the land-grant university and the agricultural extension system. We, therefore, have put the name of Justin Morrill, author of the land-grant college act and of the act which established the cooperative agricultural extension sys-

tem, on our chart. The land-grant colleges or universities were dedicated to doing applied research in the service of agriculture and the mechanic arts. These colleges and universities developed research programs in basic sciences as well and experimental stations for the development and refinement of knowledge-based technologies for use in engineering and agriculture. As the extension services developed, county agents—practitioners—were attached to the state land-grant college or university that received financial support from both state and federal governments. The county agent and his staff developed local organizations of adult farm men and women and of farm youth to provide both a channel toward informing consumers concerning new and better agricultural practices and toward getting awareness of unmet consumer needs and unsolved problems back to centers of knowledge and research. Garth Jones has made one of the more comprehensive studies of the strategies of changing involved in large-scale demonstration.[4]

All applied research has not occurred within a planned system for knowledge discovery, development, and utilization like the one briefly described above. The system has worked better in developing and diffusing thing technologies than in developing and diffusing people technologies, though the development of rural sociology and of agricultural economics shows that extension workers were by no means unaware of the behavioral dimensions of change problems. But the large-scale demonstration, through the land-grant university cooperative extension service, of the stupendous changes which can result from a planned approach to knowledge discovery, development, diffusion, and utilization is a part of the

[4] Garth Jones, "Planned Organizational Change, a Set of Working Documents," Center for Research in Public Organization, School of Public Administration (Los Angeles: University of Southern California, 1964).

consciousness of all Americans concerned with planned change.

1) Applied research and development is an honored part of the tradition of engineering approaches to problem identification and solution. The pioneering work of E. L. Thorndike in applied research in education should be noted on our chart. The processes and slow tempo of diffusion and utilization of research findings and inventions in public education are well illustrated in studies by Paul Mort and his students.[5] More recently, applied research, in its product development aspect, has been utilized in a massive way to contribute curriculum materials and designs for science instruction (as well as in other subjects). When we assess this situation to find reasons why such researches have not been more effective in producing changes in instruction, the answers seem to lie both in the plans of the studies which produced the materials and designs and in the potential users of the findings. Adequate linkage between consumers and researchers was frequently not established. Planned and evaluated demonstrations and experimentations connected with the use of materials were frequently slighted. And training of consumer teachers to use the new materials adaptively and creatively was frequently missing.

Such observations have led to a fresh spurt of interest in evaluation research addressed to educational programs. The fear persists that this too may lead to disappointment if it is not focused for two-way communication between researchers and teachers and if it does not involve collaboratively the ultimate consumers of the results of such research—the students. Evaluation researches conducted in the spirit of justifying a program developed by expert applied researchers will not help to guide teachers and students in their quest for improved practices of teaching and learning, if the concerns of the latter have not been taken centrally into account in the evaluation process.[6]

2) Recently, attempts have been made to link applied research activities in education with basic researchers on the one hand and with persons in action and practice settings on the other through some system of interlocking roles similar to those suggested in the description of the land grant-extension systems in agriculture or in other fields where applied and development researches have flourished.

The linking of research-development efforts with diffusion-innovation efforts has been gaining headway in the field of education with the emergence of federally supported Research and Development Centers based in universities, Regional Laboratories connected with state departments of education, colleges and universities in a geographic area, and with various consortia and institutes confronting problems of educational change and changing. The strategy of change here usually includes a well-researched innovation which seems feasible to install in practice settings. Attention is directed to the question of whether or not the innovation will bring about a desired result, and with what it can accomplish, if given a trial in one or more practice settings. The questions of *how* to get a fair trial and *how* to install an innovation in an already going and crowded school system are ordinarily not built centrally into the strategy. The rationalistic assumption usually precludes research attention to these questions. For, if the invention can be

[5] Paul R. Mort and Donald R. Ross, *Principles of School Administration* (New York: McGraw-Hill, Inc., 1957). Paul R. Mort and Francis G. Cornell, *American Schools in Transition: How our Schools Adapt their Practices to Changing Needs* (New York: Bureau of Publications, Teachers College, Columbia University Press, 1941).

[6] Robert Chin, "Research Approaches to the Problem of Civic Training," in F. Paterson (ed.), *The Adolescent Citizen* (New York: The Free Press, 1960).

rationally shown to have achieved desirable results in some situations, it is assumed that people in other situations will adopt it once they know these results and the rationale behind them. The neglect of the above questions has led to a wastage of much applied research effort in the past.

Attention has been given recently to the roles, communication mechanisms, and processes necessary for innovation and diffusion of improved educational practices.[7] Clark and Guba have formulated very specific processes related to and necessary for change in educational practice following upon research. For them, the necessary processes are: *development*, including invention and design; *diffusion*, including dissemination and demonstration; *adoption*, including trial, installation, and institutionalization. Clark's earnest conviction is summed up in this statement: "In a sense, the educational research community will be the educational community, and the route to educational progress will self-evidently be research and development."[8]

The approach of Havelock and Benne is concerned with the intersystem relationships between basic researchers, applied researchers, practitioners, and consumers in an evolved and evolving organization for knowledge utilization. They are concerned especially with the communication difficulties and role conflicts that occur at points of intersystem exchange. These conflicts are important because they illuminate the normative issues at stake between basic researchers and applied researchers, between applied researchers and practitioners (teachers and administrators), between practitioners and consumers (students). The lines of strategy suggested by their analysis for solving role conflicts and communication difficulties call for transactional and collaborative exchanges across the lines of varied organized interests and orientations within the process of utilization. This brings their analysis into the range of normative-reeducative strategies to be discussed later.

The concepts from the behavioral sciences upon which these strategies of diffusion rest come mainly from two traditions. The first is from studies of the diffusion of traits of culture from one cultural system to another, initiated by the American anthropologist Franz Boas. This type of study has been carried on by Rogers in his work on innovation and diffusion of innovations in contemporary culture and is reflected in a number of recent writers such as Katz and Carlson.[9] The second scientific tradition is in studies of influence in mass communication asso-

[7] Matthew B. Miles, *Some Propositions in Research Utilization in Education* (March 1965). Kenneth Wiles, unpublished paper for seminar on Strategies for Curriculum Change (Columbus, Ohio, Ohio State University). Charles Jung and Ronald Lippitt, "Utilization of Scientific Knowledge for Change in Education," in *Concepts for Social Change* (Washington, D.C.: National Educational Association, National Training Laboratories, 1967). Ronald G. Havelock and Kenneth D. Benne, "An Exploratory Study of Knowledge Utilization," David Clark and Egon Guba, "An Examination of Potential Change Roles in Education," seminar on Innovation in Planning School Curricula (Columbus, Ohio: Ohio State University, 1965).

[8] David Clark, "Educational Research and Development: The Next Decade," in *Implications for Education of Prospective Changes in Society*, a publication of "Designing Education for the Future—An Eight State Project" (Denver, Colo., 1967).

[9] Elihu Katz, "The Social Itinerary of Technical Change: Two Studies on the Diffusion of Innovation," in W. Bennis, K. Benne, and R. Chin, *The Planning of Change*, 2d Edition (New York: Holt, Rinehart and Winston, 1969), Chap. 5, p. 230. Richard Carlson, "Some Needed Research on the Diffusion of Innovations," paper at the Washington Conference on Educational Change (Columbus, Ohio: Ohio State University). Everett Rogers, "What are Innovators Like?" in *Change Processes in the Public Schools*, Center for the Advanced Study of Educational Administration (Eugene, Oregon: University of Oregon, 1965). Everett Rogers, *Diffusion of Innovations* (New York: The Free Press, 1962).

ciated with Carl Hovland and his students.[10] Both traditions have assumed a *relatively passive recipient of input* in diffusion situations. And actions within the process of diffusion are interpreted from the standpoint of an observer of the process. Bauer has pointed out that scientific studies have exaggerated the effectiveness of mass persuasion since they have compared the total number in the audience to the communications with the much smaller proportion of the audience persuaded by the communication.[11] A clearer view of processes of diffusion must include the actions of the receiver as well as those of the transmitter in the transactional events which are the units of diffusion process. And strategies for making diffusion processes more effective must be transactional and collaborative by design.

e. Utopian Thinking as a Strategy of Changing

It may seem strange to include the projection of utopias as a rational-empirical strategy of changing. Yet inventing and designing the shape of the future by extrapolating what we know of in the present is to envision a direction for planning and action in the present. If the image of a potential future is convincing and rationally persuasive to men in the present, the image may become part of the dynamics and motivation of present action. The liberal tradition is not devoid of its utopias. When we think of utopias quickened by an effort to extrapolate from the sciences of man to a future vision of society, the utopia of B. F. Skinner comes to mind.[12] The title of the Eight State Project, "Designing Education for the Future" for which this paper was prepared, reveals a utopian intent and aspiration and illustrates an attempt to employ utopian thinking for practical purposes.[13]

Yet it may be somewhat disheartening to others as it is to us to note the absence of rousing and beckoning normative statements of what both can and ought to be in man's future in most current liberal-democratic utopias, whether these be based on psychological, sociological, political, or philosophical findings and assumptions. The absence of utopias in current society, in this sense, and in the sense that Mannheim studied them in his now classical study,[14] tends to make the forecasting of future directions a problem of technical prediction, rather than equally a process of projecting value orientations and preferences into the shaping of a better future.

f. Perceptual and Conceptual Reorganization through the Clarification of Language

In classical liberalism, one perceived foe of rational change and progress was superstition. And superstitions are carried from man to man and from generation to generation through the agency of unclear and mythical language. British utilitarianism was one important strand of classical liberalism, and one of utilitarianism's important figures, Jeremy Bentham, sought to purify language of its dangerous mystique through his study of fictions.

More recently, Alfred Korzybski and S. I. Hayakawa, in the general semantics movement, have sought a way of clarifying and rectifying the names of things and processes.[15] While their main applied

[10] Carl Hovland, Irving Janis, and Harold Kelley, *Communication and Persuasion* (New Haven: Yale University Press, 1953).

[11] Raymond Bauer, "The Obstinate Audience: The Influence Process from the Point of View of Social Communication," in *The Planning of Change*, 2d Edition, Chap. 9, p. 507.

[12] B. F. Skinner, *Walden Two* (New York: Crowell-Collier and Macmillan, Inc., 1948).

[13] "Designing Education for the Future—An Eight State Project" (Denver, Colo., 1967).

[14] Karl Mannheim, *Ideology and Utopia* (New York: Harcourt, Brace & World, Inc., 1946).

[15] Alfred Korzybski, *Science and Sanity*, 3d Edition (International Non-Aristotelian Library Publishing Company, 1948). S. I. Hayakawa, *Language*

concern was with personal therapy, both, and especially Hayakawa, were also concerned to bring about changes in social systems as well. People disciplined in general semantics, it was hoped, would see more correctly, communicate more adequately, and reason more effectively and thus lay a realistic common basis for action and changing. The strategies of changing associated with general semantics overlap with our next family of strategies, the normative-re-educative, because of their emphasis upon the importance of interpersonal relationships and social contexts within the communication process.

2. Normative—Re-educative Strategies of Changing

We have already suggested that this family of strategies rests on assumptions and hypotheses about man and his motivation which contrast significantly at points with the assumptions and hypotheses of those committed to what we have called rational-empirical strategies. Men are seen as inherently active, in quest of impulse and need satisfaction. The relation between man and his environment is essentially transactional, as Dewey[16] made clear in his famous article on "The Reflex-Arc Concept." Man, the organism, does not passively await given stimuli from his environment in order to respond. He takes stimuli as furthering or thwarting the goals of his ongoing action. Intelligence arises in the process of shaping organism-environmental relations toward more adequate fitting and joining of organismic demands and environmental resources.

Intelligence is social, rather than narrowly individual. Men are guided in their

actions by socially funded and communicated meanings, norms, and institutions, in brief by a normative culture. At the personal level, men are guided by internalized meanings, habits, and values. Changes in patterns of action or practice are, therefore, changes, not alone in the rational informational equipment of men, but at the personal level, in habits and values as well and, at the sociocultural level, changes are alterations in normative structures and in institutionalized roles and relationships, as well as cognitive and perceptual orientations.

For Dewey, the prototype of intelligence in action is the scientific method. And he saw a broadened and humanized scientific method as man's best hope for progress if men could learn to utilize such a method in facing all of the problematic situations of their lives. *Intelligence*, so conceived, rather than *Reason* as defined in classical liberalism, was the key to Dewey's hope for the invention, development, and testing of adequate strategies of changing in human affairs.

Lewin's contribution to normative-re-educative strategies of changing stemmed from his vision of required interrelations between research, training, and action (and, for him, this meant collaborative relationships, often now lacking, between researchers, educators, and activists) in the solution of human problems, in the identification of needs for change, and in the working out of improved knowledge, technology, and patterns of action in meeting these needs. Man must participate in his own re-education if he is to be re-educated at all. And re-education is a normative change as well as a cognitive and perceptual change. These convictions led Lewin[17] to emphasize action research

---

in Thought and Action (New York: Harcourt, Brace & World, Inc., 1941).

[16] John Dewey, *Philosophy, Psychology and Social Practice*, ed. Joseph Ratner (Capricorn Books, 1967).

[17] Kurt Lewin, *Resolving Social Conflicts* (New York: Harper & Row, Publishers, 1948). Kurt Lewin, *Field Theory in Social Science* (New York: Harper & Row, Publishers, 1951).

as a strategy of changing, and participation in groups as a medium of re-education.

Freud's main contributions to normative-re-educative strategies of changing are two. First, he sought to demonstrate the unconscious and preconscious bases of man's actions. Only as a man finds ways of becoming aware of these nonconscious wellsprings of his attitudes and actions will he be able to bring them into conscious self-control. And Freud devoted much of his magnificent genius to developing ways of helping men to become conscious of the mainsprings of their actions and so capable of freedom. Second, in developing therapeutic methods, he discovered and developed ways of utilizing the relationship between change agent (therapist) and client (patient) as a major tool in re-educating the client toward expanded self-awareness, self-understanding, and self-control. Emphasis upon the collaborative relationship in therapeutic change was a major contribution by Freud and his students and colleagues to normative-re-educative strategies of changing in human affairs.[18]

Normative-re-educative approaches to effecting change bring direct interventions by change agents, interventions based on a consciously worked out theory of change and of changing, into the life of a client system, be that system a person, a small group, an organization, or a community. The theory of changing is still crude but it is probably as explicitly stated as possible, granted our present state of knowledge about planned change.[19]

Some of the common elements among variants within this family of change strategies are the following. First, all emphasize the client system and his (or its) involvement in working out programs of change and improvement for himself (or itself). The way the client sees himself and his problem must be brought into dialogic relationship with the way in which he and his problem are seen by the change agent, whether the latter is functioning as researcher, consultant, trainer, therapist, or friend in relation to the client. Second, the problem confronting the client is not assumed *a priori* to be one which can be met by more adequate technical information, though this possibility is not ruled out. The problem may lie rather in the attitudes, values, norms, and the external and internal relationships of the client system and may require alteration or re-education of these as a condition of its solution. Third, the change agent must learn to intervene mutually and collaboratively along with the client into efforts to define and solve the client's problem(s). The here and now experience of the two provide an important basis for diagnosing the problem and for locating needs for re-education in the interest of solving it. Fourth, nonconscious elements which impede problem solution must be brought into consciousness and publicly examined and reconstructed. Fifth, the methods and concepts of the behavioral sciences are resources which change agent and client learn to use selectively, relevantly, and appropriately in learning to deal with the confronting problem and with problems of a similar kind in the future.

These approaches center in the notion that people technology is just as necessary as thing technology in working out desirable changes in human affairs. Put in this bold fashion, it is obvious that for the normative-re-educative change agent, clarification and reconstruction of values is of pivotal importance in changing. By getting the values of various parts of the client

[18] For Freud, an interesting summary is contained in Otto Fenichel, *Problems of Psychoanalytic Technique* (Albany: NT Psychoanalytic Quarterly Inc., 1941).

[19] W. Bennis, K. Benne, and R. Chin, *The Planning of Change* (1st ed.: New York: Holt, Rinehart and Winston, 1961). R. Lippitt, J. Watson and B. Westley, *The Dynamics of Planned Change* (New York: Harcourt, Brace & World, Inc., 1958). W. Bennis, *Changing Organizations* (New York: McGraw-Hill, Inc., 1966).

system along with his own, openly into the arena of change and by working through value conflicts responsibly, the change agent seeks to avoid manipulation and indoctrination of the client, in the morally reprehensible meanings of these terms.

We may use the organization of the National Training Laboratories in 1947 as a milestone in the development of normative-re-educative approaches to changing in America. The first summer laboratory program grew out of earlier collaborations among Kurt Lewin, Ronald Lippitt, Leland Bradford, and Kenneth Benne. The idea behind the laboratory was that participants, staff, and students would learn about themselves and their back-home problems by collaboratively building a laboratory in which participants would become both experimenters and subjects in the study of their own developing interpersonal and group behavior within the laboratory setting. It seems evident that the five conditions of a normative-re-educative approach to changing were met in the conception of the training laboratory. Kurt Lewin died before the 1947 session of the training laboratory opened. Ronald Lippitt was a student of Lewin's and carried many of Lewin's orientations with him into the laboratory staff. Leland Bradford and Kenneth Benne were both students of John Dewey's philosophy of education. Bradford had invented several technologies for participative learning and self-study in his work in WPA adult education programs and as training officer in several agencies of the federal government. Benne came out of a background in educational philosophy and had collaborated with colleagues prior to 1943 in developing a methodology for policy and decision making and for the reconstruction of normative orientations, a methodology which sought to fuse democratic and scientific values and to translate these into principles for resolving conflicting and problematic situations at personal and community levels of human organization.[20] Benne and his colleagues had been much influenced by the work of Mary Follett,[21] her studies of integrative solutions to conflicts in settings of public and business administration, and by the work of Karl Mannheim[22] on the ideology and methodology of planning changes in human affairs, as well as by the work of John Dewey and his colleagues.

The work of the National Training Laboratories has encompassed development and testing of various approaches to changing in institutional settings, in America and abroad, since its beginning. One parallel development in England which grew out of Freud's thinking should be noted. This work developed in efforts at Tavistock Clinic to apply therapeutic approaches to problems of change in industrial organizations and in communities. This work is reported in statements by Elliot Jaques[23] and in this volume by Eric Trist. Another parallel development is represented by the efforts of Roethlisberger and Dickson to use personal counseling in industry as a strategy of organizational change.[24] Roethlisberger and Dickson had been strongly influenced by the pioneer work of Elton Mayo in industrial sociology[25]

[20] Raup, Benne, Smith, and Axtelle, *The Discipline of Practical Judgment in a Democratic Society*, Yearbook No. 28 of the National Society of College Teachers of Education (Chicago: University of Chicago Press, 1943).

[21] Mary Follett, *Creative Experience and Dynamic Administration* (New York: David McKay Company, Inc., 1924).

[22] Karl Mannheim, *Man and Society in an Age of Reconstruction* (New York: Harcourt, Brace & World, Inc., 1940).

[23] Elliot Jaques, *The Changing Culture of a Factory* (New York: Holt, Rinehart and Winston, 1952).

[24] William J. Dickson and F. J. Roethlisberger, *Personal Counseling in an Organization. A Sequel to the Hawthorne Researches* (Boston: Harvard Business School, 1966).

[25] Elton Mayo, *The Social Problems of an Industrial Civilization* (Cambridge, Mass.: Harvard University Press, 1945).

as well as by the counseling theories and methodologies of Carl Rogers.

Various refinements of methodologies for changing have been developed and tested since the establishment of the National Training Laboratories in 1947, both under its auspices and under other auspices as well. For us, the modal developments are worthy of further discussion here. One set of approaches is oriented focally to the improvement of the problem-solving processes utilized by a client system. The other set focuses on helping members of client systems to become aware of their attitude and value orientations and relationship difficulties through a probing of feelings, manifest and latent, involved in the functioning and operation of the client system.[26] Both approaches use the development of "temporary systems" as a medium of re-education of persons and of role occupants in various ongoing social systems.[27]

a. Improving the Problem-Solving Capabilities of a System

This family of approaches to changing rests on several assumptions about change in human systems. Changes in a system, when they are reality-oriented, take the form of problem solving. A system to achieve optimum reality orientation in its adaptations to its changing internal and external environments must develop and institutionalize its own problem-solving structures and processes. These structures and processes must be tuned both to human problems of relationship and morale and to technical problems of

meeting the system's task requirements, set by its goals of production, distribution, and so on.[28] System problems are typically not social *or* technical but actually sociotechnical[29]. The problem-solving structures and processes of a human system must be developed to deal with a range of sociotechnical difficulties, converting them into problems and organizing the relevant processes of data collection, planning, invention, and tryout of solutions, evaluation and feedback of results, replanning, and so forth, which are required for the solution of the problems.

The human parts of the system must learn to function collaboratively in these processes of problem identification and solution and the system must develop institutionalized support and mechanisms for maintaining and improving these processes. Actually, the model of changing in these approaches is a cooperative, action-research model. This model was suggested by Lewin and developed most elaborately for use in educational settings by Stephen M. Corey.[30]

The range of interventions by outside change agents in implementing this approach to changing is rather wide. It has been most fully elaborated in relation to organizational development programs. Within such programs, intervention methods have been most comprehensively tested in industrial settings. Some of these more or less tested intervention methods are listed below. A design for any organizational development program, of course, normally uses a number of these in succession or combination.

---

[26] Leland Bradford, Jack R. Gibb, and Kenneth D. Benne, *T-Group Theory and Laboratory Method* (New York: John Wiley & Sons, Inc., 1964).

[27] Matthew B. Miles, "On Temporary Systems," in M. B. Miles (ed.), *Innovation in Education* (New York: Bureau of Publications, Teachers College, Columbia University Press, 1964), pp. 437–492.

[28] Robert R. Blake and Jane S. Mouton, *The Managerial Grid* (Houston: The Gulf Publishing Company, 1961).

[29] Jay W. Lorsch and Paul Lawrence, "The Diagnosis of Organizational Problems," in *The Planning of Change*, 2d Edition, Chap. 8, p. 468.

[30] Stephen M. Corey, *Action Research to Improve School Practices* (New York: Bureau of Publications, Teachers College, Columbia University Press, 1953).

1. Collection of data about organizational functioning and feedback of data into processes of data interpretation and of planning ways of correcting revealed dysfunctions by system managers and data collectors in collaboration.[31]
2. Training of managers and working organizational units in methods of problem solving through self-examination of present ways of dealing with difficulties and through development and tryout of better ways with consultation by outside and/or inside change agents. Usually, the working unit leaves its working place for parts of its training. These laboratory sessions are ordinarily interspersed with on-the-job consultations.
3. Developing acceptance of feedback (research and development) roles and functions within the organization, training persons to fill these roles, and relating such roles strategically to the ongoing management of the organization.
4. Training internal change agents to function within the organization in carrying on needed applied research, consultation, and training.[32]

Whatever specific strategies of intervention may be employed in developing the system's capabilities for problem solving, change efforts are designed to help the system in developing ways of scanning its operations to detect problems, of diagnosing these problems to determine relevant changeable factors in them, and of moving toward collaboratively determined solutions to the problems.

b. Releasing and Fostering Growth in the Persons Who Make Up the System to Be Changed

Those committed to this family of approaches to changing tend to see the person as the basic unit of social organization. Persons, it is believed, are capable of creative, life-affirming, self- and other-regarding and respecting responses, choices, and actions, if conditions which thwart these kinds of responses are removed and other supporting conditions developed. Rogers has formulated these latter conditions in his analysis of the therapist-client relationship—trustworthiness, empathy, caring, and others.[33] Maslow has worked out a similar idea in his analysis of the hierarchy of needs in persons.[34] If lower needs are met, higher need-meeting actions will take place. McGregor has formulated the ways in which existing organizations operate to fixate persons in lower levels of motivation and has sought to envision an organization designed to release and support the growth of persons in fulfilling their higher motivations as they function within the organization.[35]

Various intervention methods have been designed to help people discover themselves as persons and commit themselves to continuing personal growth in the various relationships of their lives.

1. One early effort to install personal counseling widely and strategically in

---

[31] See contributions by Miles *et al.*, "Data Feedback and Organizational Change in a School System," in *The Planning of Change*, 2d Edition, Chap. 8, p. 457, and Jay W. Lorsch, and Paul Lawrence, "The Diagnosis of Organizational Problems," in *The Planning of Change*, 2d Edition, Chap. 8, p. 468.

[32] C. Argyris, "Explorations in Consulting-Client Relationships," in *The Planning of Change*, 3d Edition (New York: Holt, Rinehart and Winston, 1976), Chap. 8, p. 331. See also Richard Beckhard, "The Confrontation Meeting," in *The Planning of Change*, 2d Edition, Chap. 8, p. 478.

[33] Carl Rogers, "The Characteristics of a Helping Relationship," in *The Planning of Change*, 2d Edition, Chap. 4, p. 153.

[34] Abraham Maslow, *Motivation and Personality* (New York: Harper & Row, Publishers, 1954).

[35] Douglas M. McGregor, "The Human Side of Enterprise," in W. Bennis, K. Benne, and R. Chin, *The Planning of Change* (1st ed.), pp. 422–431.

an organization has been reported by Roethlisberger and Dickson.[36]

2. Training groups designed to facilitate personal confrontation and growth of members in an open, trusting, and accepting atmosphere have been conducted for individuals from various back-home situations and for persons from the same back-home setting. The processes of these groups have sometimes been described as "therapy for normals."[37]

3. Groups and laboratories designed to stimulate and support personal growth have been designed to utilize the resources of nonverbal exchange and communication among members along with verbal dialogue in inducing personal confrontation, discovery, and commitment to continuing growth.

4. Many psychotherapists, building on the work of Freud and Adler, have come to use groups, as well as two-person situations, as media of personal re-education and growth. Such efforts are prominent in mental health approaches to changing and have been conducted in educational, religious, community, industrial, and hospital settings. While these efforts focus primarily upon helping individuals to change themselves toward greater self-clarity and fuller self-actualization, they are frequently designed and conducted in the hope that personal changes will lead to changes in organizations, institutions, and communities as well.

We have presented the two variants of normative-re-educative approaches to

[36] Dickson and Roethlisberger, cited above.
[37] James V. Clark, "A Healthy Organization," in *The Planning of Change*, 2d Edition, Chap. 6, p. 282. Irving Weschler, Fred Massarick, and Robert Tannenbaum, "The Self in Process: A Sensitivity Training Emphasis," in I. R. Weschler and E. Schein (eds.), *Issues in Training*, Selected Reading Series No. 5 (Washington, D.C., National Training Laboratories).

changing in a way to emphasize their differences. Actually, there are many similarities between them as well, which justify placing both under the same general heading. We have already mentioned one of these similarities. Both frequently use temporary systems—a residential laboratory or workshop, a temporary group with special resources built in, an ongoing system which incorporates a change agent (trainer, consultant, counselor, or therapist) temporarily—as an aid to growth in the system and/or in its members.

More fundamentally, both approaches emphasize experience-based learning as an ingredient of all enduring changes in human systems. Yet both accept the principle that people must learn to learn from their experiences if self-directed change is to be maintained and continued. Frequently, people have learned to defend against the potential lessons of experience when these threaten existing equilibria, whether in the person or in the social system. How can these defenses be lowered to let the data of experience get into processes of perceiving the situation, of constructing new and better ways to define it, of inventing new and more appropriate ways of responding to the situation as redefined, of becoming more fully aware of the consequences of actions, of rearticulating value orientations which sanction more responsible ways of managing the consequences of actions, and so forth? Learning to learn from ongoing experience is a major objective in both approaches to changing. Neither denies the relevance or importance of the noncognitive determinants of behavior—feelings, attitudes, norms, and relationships—along with cognitive-perceptual determinants, in effecting behavioral change. The problem-solving approaches emphasize the cognitive determinants more than personal growth approaches do. But exponents of the former do not accept the rationalistic biases of the rational-empirical family of change strategies, already discussed. Since exponents of both problem-solving and personal growth approaches are committed to re-education of persons as integral to effective change in human systems, both emphasize norms of openness of communication, trust between persons, lowering of status barriers between parts of the system, and mutuality between parts as necessary conditions of the re-educative process.

Great emphasis has been placed recently upon the releasing of creativity in persons, groups, and organizations as requisite to coping adaptively with accelerated changes in the conditions of modern living. We have already stressed the emphasis which personal growth approaches put upon the release of creative responses in persons being re-educated. Problem-solving approaches also value creativity, though they focus more upon the group and organizational conditions which increase the probability of creative responses by persons functioning within those conditions than upon persons directly. The approaches do differ in their strategies for releasing creative responses within human systems. But both believe that creative adaptations to changing conditions may arise *within* human systems and do not have to be imported from *outside* them as in innovation-diffusion approaches already discussed and the power-compliance models still to be dealt with.

One developing variant of normative-re-educative approaches to changing, not already noted, focuses upon effective conflict management. It is, of course, a common knowledge that differences within a society which demand interaccommodation often manifest themselves as conflicts. In the process of managing such conflicts, changes in the norms, policies, and relationships of the society occur. Can conflict management be brought into the ambit of planned change as defined in this volume? Stemming from the work of the Sherifs in creating intergroup conflict and seeking to resolve it in a field-laboratory

situation,[38] training in intergroup conflict and conflict resolution found its way into training laboratories through the efforts of Blake and others. Since that time, laboratories for conflict management have been developed under NTL and other auspices and methodologies for conflict resolution and management, in keeping with the values of planned change, have been devised. Blake's and Walton's work represent some of the findings from these pioneering efforts.[39]

Thus, without denying their differences in assumption and strategy, we believe that the differing approaches discussed in this section can be seen together within the framework of normative-re-educative approaches to changing. Two efforts to conceptualize planned change in a way to reveal the similarities in assumptions about changing and in value orientations toward change underlying these variant approaches are those by Lippitt, Watson, and Westley and by Bennis, Benne, and Chin.[40]

Another aspect of changing in human organizations is represented by efforts to conceive human organization in forms that go beyond the bureaucratic form which captured the imagination and fixed the contours of thinking and practice of organizational theorists and practitioners from the latter part of the nineteenth century through the early part of the twentieth century. The bureaucratic form of organization was conceptualized by Max Weber and carried into American thinking by such students of administration as Ur-

[38] Muzafer and Carolyn Sherif, *Groups in Harmony and Tension* (New York: Harper & Row, Publishers, 1953).

[39] Robert Blake *et al.*, "The Union Management Inter-Group Laboratory," in *The Planning of Change*, 2d Edition, Chap. 4, p. 176. Richard Walton, "Two Strategies of Social Change and Their Dilemmas," in *The Planning of Change*, 2d Edition, Chap. 4, p. 167.

[40] R. Lippitt, J. Watson, and B. Westley, *Dynamics of Planned Change* (New York: Harcourt, Brace & World, Inc., 1958). W. Bennis, K. Benne, R. Chin, *The Planning of Change* (1st ed.).

wick.[41] On this view, effective organization of human effort followed the lines of effective division of labor and effective establishment of lines of reporting, control, and supervision from the mass base of the organization up through various levels of control to the top of the pyramidal organization from which legitimate authority and responsibility stemmed.

The work of industrial sociologists like Mayo threw doubt upon the adequacy of such a model of formal organization to deal with the realities of organizational life by revealing the informal organization which grows up within the formal structure to satisfy personal and interpersonal needs not encompassed by or integrated into the goals of the formal organization. Chester Barnard may be seen as a transitional figure who, in discussing the functions of the organizational executive, gave equal emphasis to his responsibilities for task effectiveness and organizational efficiency (optimally meeting the human needs of persons in the organization).[42] Much of the development of subsequent organizational theory and practice has centered on problems of integrating the actualities, criteria, and concepts of organizational effectiveness and of organizational efficiency.

A growing group of thinkers and researchers has sought to move beyond the bureaucratic model toward some new model of organization which might set directions and limits for change efforts in organizational life. Out of many thinkers, we choose four who have theorized out of an orientation consistent with what we have called a normative-re-educative approach to changing.

Rensis Likert has presented an intergroup model of organization. Each working unit strives to develop and function as a group. The group's efforts are linked to other units of the organization by the overlapping membership of supervisors or managers in vertically or horizontally adjacent groups. This view of organization throws problems of delegation, supervision, and internal communication into a new light and emphasizes the importance of linking persons as targets of change and re-education in processes of organizational development.[43]

We have already stressed McGregor's efforts to conceive a form of organization more in keeping with new and more valid views of human nature and motivation (Theory Y) than the limited and false views of human nature and motivation (Theory X) upon which traditional bureaucratic organization has rested. In his work he sought to move thinking and practice relevant to organization and organizational change beyond limits of traditional forms. "The essential task of management is to arrange organizational conditions and methods of operation so that people can achieve their own goals best by directing their own efforts toward organizational objectives."[44]

Bennis has consciously sought to move beyond bureaucracy in tracing the contours of the organization of the future.[45] And Shephard has described an organizational form consistent with support for continual changing and self-renewal, rather than with a primary mission of maintenance and control.[46]

3. Power-Coercive Approaches to Effecting Change

It is not the use of power, in the sense of influence by one person upon another or by one group upon another, which

[41] Lyndall Urwick, *The Pattern of Management* (Minneapolis: University of Minnesota Press, 1956).

[42] Chester I. Barnard, *The Functions of the Executive* (Cambridge: Harvard University Press, 1938).

[43] Rensis Likert, *New Patterns of Management* (New York: McGraw-Hill, Inc., 1961).

[44] McGregor, pp. 422–431.

distinguishes this family of strategies from those already discussed. Power is an ingredient of all human action. The differences lie rather in the ingredients of power upon which the strategies of changing depend and the ways in which power is generated and applied in processes of effecting change. Thus, what we have called rational-empirical approaches depend on knowledge as a major ingredient of power. In this view, men of knowledge are legitimate sources of power and the desirable flow of influence or power is from men who know to men who don't know through processes of education and of dissemination of valid information.

Normative-re-educative strategies of changing do not deny the importance of knowledge as a source of power, especially in the form of knowledge-based technology. Exponents of this approach to changing are committed to redressing the imbalance between the limited use of behavioral knowledge and people technologies and the widespread use of physical-biological knowledge and related thing technologies in effecting changes in human affairs. In addition, exponents of normative-re-educative approaches recognize the importance of noncognitive determinants of behavior as resistances or supports to changing—values, attitudes, and feelings at the personal level and norms and relationships at the social level. Influence must extend to these noncognitive determinants of behavior if voluntary commitments and reliance upon social intelligence are to be maintained and extended in our changing society. Influence of noncognitive determinants of behavior must be exercised in mutual processes of persuasion within collaborative relationships.

[45] W. G. Bennis, "Changing Organizations," in *The Planning of Change*, 2d Ed., Chap. 10, p. 568.
[46] H. A. Shephard, "Innovation-Resisting and Innovation-Producing Organizations," in *The Planning of Change*, 2d Edition, Chap. 9, p. 519.

These strategies are oriented against coercive and nonreciprocal influence, both on moral and on pragmatic grounds.

What ingredients of power do power-coercive strategies emphasize? In general, emphasis is upon political and economic sanctions in the exercise of power. But other coercive strategies emphasize the utilization of moral power, playing upon sentiments of guilt and shame. Political power carries with it legitimacy and the sanctions which accrue to those who break the law. Thus getting a law passed against racial imbalance in the schools brings legitimate coercive power behind efforts to desegregate the schools, threatening those who resist with sanctions under the law and reducing the resistance of others who are morally oriented against breaking the law. Economic power exerts coercive influence over the decisions of those to whom it is applied. Thus federal appropriations granting funds to local schools for increased emphasis upon science instruction tends to exercise coercive influence over the decisions of local school officials concerning the emphasis of the school curriculum. In general, power-coercive strategies of changing seek to mass political and economic power behind the change goals which the strategists of change have decided are desirable. Those who oppose these goals, if they adopt the same strategy, seek to mass political and economic power in opposition. The strategy thus tends to divide the society when there is anything like a division of opinion and of power in that society.

When a person or group is entrenched in power in a social system, in command of political legitimacy and of political and economic sanctions, that person or group can use power-coercive strategies in effecting changes, which they consider desirable, without much awareness on the part of those out of power in the system that such strategies are being employed. A power-coercive way of making decisions is accepted as in the nature of things. The use of such strategies by those in legitimate control of various social systems in our society is much more widespread than most of us might at first be willing or able to admit. This is true in educational systems as well as in other social systems.

When any part of a social system becomes aware that its interests are not being served by those in control of the system, the coercive power of those in control can be challenged. If the minority is committed to power-coercive strategies, or is aware of no alternatives to such strategies, how can they make headway against existing power relations within the system? They may organize discontent against the present controls of the system and achieve power outside the legitimate channels of authority in the system. Thus teachers' unions may develop power against coercive controls by the central administrative group and the school board in a school system. They may threaten concerted resistance to or disregard of administrative rulings and board policies or they may threaten work stoppage or a strike. Those in control may get legislation against teachers' strikes. If the political power of organized teachers grows, they may get legislation requiring collective bargaining between organized teachers and the school board on some range of educational issues. The power struggle then shifts to the negotiation table and compromise between competing interests may become the expected goal of the intergroup exchange. Whether the augmented power of new, relevant knowledge or the generation of common power through joint collaboration and deliberation are lost in the process will depend on the degree of commitment by all parties to the conflict to a continuation and maintenance of power-coercive strategies for effecting change.

What general varieties of power-coercive strategies to be exercised either by those in control as they seek to maintain their power or to be used by those now outside a position of control and seeking to enlarge their power can be identified?

a. Strategies of Nonviolence

Mahatma Gandhi may be seen as the most prominent recent theorist and practitioner of nonviolent strategies for effecting change, although the strategies did not originate with him in the history of mankind, either in idea or in practice. Gandhi spoke of Thoreau's *Essay on Civil Disobedience* as one important influence in his own approach to nonviolent coercive action. Martin Luther King was perhaps America's most distinguished exponent of nonviolent coercion in effecting social change. A minority (or majority) confronted with what they see as an unfair, unjust, or cruel system of coercive social control may dramatize their rejection of the system by publicly and nonviolently witnessing and demonstrating against it. Part of the ingredients of the power of the civilly disobedient is in the guilt which their demonstration of injustice, unfairness, or cruelty of the existing system of control arouses in those exercising control or in others previously committed to the present system of control. The opposition to the disobedient group may be demoralized and may waver in their exercise of control, if they profess the moral values to which the dissidents are appealing.

Weakening or dividing the opposition through moral coercion may be combined with economic sanctions—like Gandhi's refusal to buy salt and other British manufactured commodities in India or like the desegregationists' economic boycott of the products of racially discriminating factories and businesses.

The use of nonviolent strategies for opening up conflicts in values and demonstrating against injustices or inequities in existing patterns of social control has become familiar to educational leaders in the demonstrations and sit-ins of college students in various universities and in the demonstrations of desegregationists against *de facto* segregation of schools. And the widened use of such strategies may be confidently predicted. Whether such strategies will be used to extend collaborative ways of developing policies and normative-re-educative strategies of changing or whether they will be used to augment power struggles as the only practical way of settling conflicts, will depend in some large part upon the strategy commitments of those now in positions of power in educational systems.

b.   Use of Political Institutions to Achieve Change

Political power has traditionally played an important part in achieving changes in our institutional life. And political power will continue to play an important part in shaping and reshaping our institutions of education as well as other institutions. Changes enforced by political coercion need not be oppressive if the quality of our democratic processes can be maintained and improved.

Changes in policies with respect to education have come from various departments of government. By far the most of these have come through legislation on the state level. Under legislation, school administrators have various degrees of discretionary powers, and policy and program changes are frequently put into effect by administrative rulings. Judicial decisions have played an important part in shaping educational policies, none more dramatically than the Supreme Court decision declaring laws and policies supporting school segregation illegal. And the federal courts have played a central part in seeking to implement and enforce this decision.

Some of the difficulty with the use of political institutions to effect changes arises from an overestimation by change agents of the capability of political action to effect changes in practice. When the law is passed, the administrative ruling announced, or the judicial decision handed down legitimizing some new policy or program or illegitimizing some traditional practice, change agents who have worked hard for the law, ruling, or decision frequently assume that the desired change has been made.

Actually, all that has been done is to bring the force of legitimacy behind some envisioned change. The processes of re-education of persons who are to conduct themselves in new ways still have to be carried out. And the new conduct often requires new knowledge, new skills, new attitudes, and new value orientations. And, on the social level, new conduct may require changes in the norms, the roles, and the relationship structures of the institutions involved. This is not to discount the importance of political actions in legitimizing changed policies and practices in educational institutions and in other institutions as well. It is rather to emphasize that normative-re-educative strategies must be combined with political coercion, both before and after the political action, if the public is to be adequately informed and desirable and commonly acceptable changes in practice are to be achieved.

c. Changing through the Recomposition and Manipulation of Power Elites

The idea or practice of a ruling class or of a power elite in social control was by no means original with Karl Marx. What was original with him was his way of relating these concepts to a process and strategy of fundamental social change. The composition of the ruling class was, of course, for Marx those who owned and controlled the means and processes of production of goods and services in a society. Since, for Marx, the ideology of the ruling class set limits to the thinking of most intellectuals and of those in charge of educational processes and of communicating, rationales for the existing state of affairs, including its concentration of political and economic power, are provided and disseminated by intellectuals and educators and communicators within the system.

Since Marx was morally committed to a classless society in which political coercion could disappear because there would be no vested private interests to rationalize and defend, he looked for a counterforce in society to challenge and eventually to overcome the power of the ruling class. And this he found in the economically dispossessed and alienated workers of hand and brain. As this new class gained consciousness of its historic mission and its power increased, the class struggle could be effectively joined. The outcome of this struggle was victory for those best able to organize and maximize the productive power of the instruments of production—for Marx this victory belonged to the now dispossessed workers.

Many of Marx's values would have put him behind what we have called normative-re-educative strategies of changing. And he recognized that such strategies would have to be used after the accession of the workers to state power in order to usher in the classless society. He doubted if the ruling class could be re-educated, since re-education would mean loss of their privileges and coercive power in society. He recognized that the power elite could, within limits, accommodate new interests as these gained articulation and power. But these accommodations must fall short of a radical transfer of power to a class more capable of wielding it. Meanwhile, he remained committed to a power-coercive strategy of changing until the revolutionary transfer of power had been effected.

Marxian concepts have affected the thinking of contemporary men about social change both inside and outside nations in which Marxism has become the official orientation. His concepts have tended to bolster assumptions of the necessity of power-coercive strategies in achieving fundamental redistributions of socioeconomic power or in recomposing or manipulating power elites in a society. Democratic, re-educative methods of changing have a place only after such changes in power allocation have been achieved by power-coercive methods. Non-Marxians as well as Marxians are often committed to this Marxian dictum.

In contemporary America, C. Wright Mills has identified a power elite, essentially composed of industrial, military, and governmental leaders, who direct and limit processes of social change and accommodation in our society. And President Eisenhower warned of the dangerous concentration of power in substantially the same groups in his farewell message to the American people. Educators committed to democratic values should not be blinded to the limitations to advancement of those values, which are set by the less than democratic ideology of our power elites. And normative-re-educative strategists of changing must include power elites among their targets of changing as they seek to diffuse their ways of progress within contemporary society. And they must take seriously Marx's questions about the re-educability of members of the power elites, as they deal with problems and projects of social change.

The operation of a power elite in social units smaller than a nation was revealed in Floyd Hunter's study of decision-making in an American city. Hunter's small group of deciders, with their satellite groups of intellectuals, front men, and implementers, is in a real sense a power elite. The most common reaction of educational leaders to Hunter's "discovery" has been to seek ways in which to persuade and manipulate the deciders toward support of educational ends which educational leaders consider desirable—whether bond issues, building programs, or anything else. This is non-

Marxian in its acceptance of power relations in a city or community as fixed. It would be Marxian if it sought to build counter power to offset and reduce the power of the presently deciding group where this power interfered with the achievement of desirable educational goals. This latter strategy, though not usually Marxian inspired in the propaganda sense of that term, has been more characteristic of organized teacher effort in pressing for collective bargaining or of some student demonstrations and sit-ins. In the poverty program, the federal government in its insistence on participation of the poor in making policies for the program has at least played with a strategy of building countervailing power to offset the existing concentration of power in people not identified with the interests of the poor in reducing their poverty.

Those committed to the advancement of normative-re-educative strategies of changing must take account of present actual concentrations of power wherever they work. This does *not* mean that they must develop a commitment to power-coercive strategies to change the distribution of power except when these may be necessary to effect the spread of their own democratically and scientifically oriented methods of changing within society.

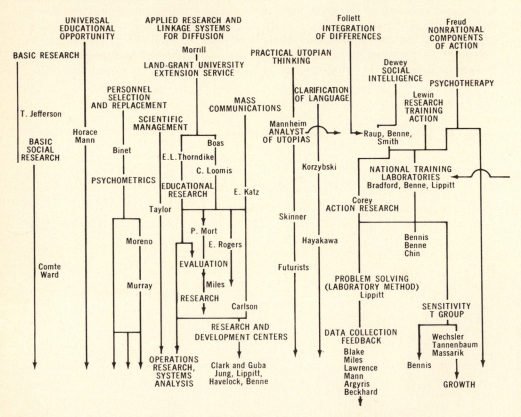

FIGURE 1   Strategies of Deliberate Changing

RE-EDUCATIVE

TRAINERS, AND SITUATION CHANGERS

C. POWER—COERCIVE

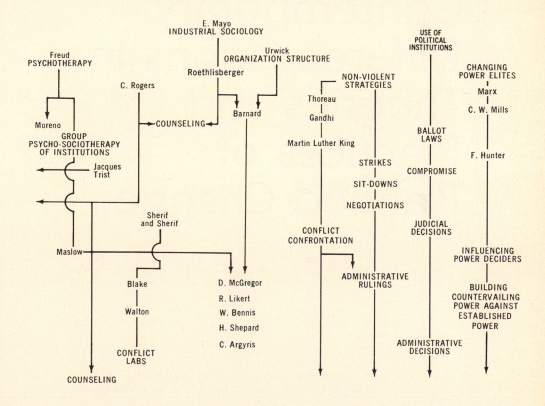

2

Contemporary Differentiations in Theories and Practices of Planned Change

As awareness and acceptance of the need for continuing changes in interpersonal and intergroup relations, institutions, social structures, and ways of life have widened and deepened in the consciousness of contemporary men and women, the volume and variety of efforts to introduce planfulness and deliberateness into processes of social and personal change have expanded correspondingly. The bewildering multiplicity of "therapies," "consciousness-raising methodologies," "development technologies," and "planning-action models" which today confront the student and practitioner of planned change evokes a search for meaningful patterns within this multiplicity.

The functions of a cognitive map of the current profusion of innovations and experimentations in the diagnosis and development of human systems are, at one and the same time, intellectual and practical. Intellectually, it is clarifying to get a meaningful view of the entire scope of the field of planned change. This means a way of identifying the differentiations among prevailing practices and rationales—a categorization that both accounts for the descriptively discernible differences in practice and makes it possible to compare and contrast these differences in their interrelations. Practically, it is useful for a change agent to see the range of approaches available for possible use as that agent confronts situations calling for his or her responsible intervention and shapes an intervention appropriate to himself or herself and to the requirements of the context of decision and action.

In the preceding chapter, Chin and Benne presented a mapping of the field of planned change in terms of "families" of intervention strategies. The bases of differentiation among these generalized strategies were varying images of man and of ways in which changes in human behavior and relationships are best effected, images with historically traceable roots in Western culture and history.

In this chapter, we are seeking to map contemporary differences in the practices and rationales of planned change without reference to their historical origins. Probably the most apparent basis for differentiating practices of planned change is the unit of human organization which is seen and taken as the target of change. The unit may be an individual person. It may be a group or an interpersonal relationship. Or perhaps the target of change is an intergroup complex or interface. An entire organization may be the focus of a change effort. Other change agents may take a society or some societal pattern or practice as their chosen target of changing. The relevant point here is that methods of diagnosis and intervention do vary as the unit-target of change varies.

Blake and Mouton have identified five types or kinds of interventions which applied social scientists are currently making into organizations in the interest of organizational change. These they name acceptant interventions, catalytic interventions, confrontation, prescriptive interventions, and the application and utilization of principles, models, and theories concerning the determination of human change. When Blake and Mouton combine their five types of intervention with the five target-units of change previously identified, a diagnosis/development matrix with twenty-five cells is generated. They provide examples of change efforts, along with bibliographical references, to illustrate the meaning of each cell in their matrix.

While Blake and Mouton recognize variations in the practice of changing as different human units are focused upon, their entire map is designed to clarify the current field of *organizational* diagnosis and development. Thus their concern with personal change, whether through acceptant, catalytic, confrontation, or prescriptive, is limited to changes of persons within an organization, undertaken in the interest of organizational development. And, similarly, their treatments of group, intergroup, and societal change are subsumed under their central concern with the changing of organizations.

There is a general point concerning the changing of human systems which the work of Blake and Mouton makes clear. The various levels and units of human organization as targets of change cannot be dealt with adequately in arbitrary isolation one from the other. For persons, groups, intergroup complexes, organizations, and societies are in actuality overlapping open systems. But a change agent can and does focus attention and effort on one level of human organization or another.

While Blake and Mouton's matrix illuminates admirably differentiations in the current practices and practice-rationales in organizational development, it leaves other areas of change practice and rationales unmapped. In essay 2.2 in this chapter, Benne attempts to map other areas of current practice in deliberate changing, where the focal purpose is not organizational development. His essay has been written to supplement the work of Blake and Mouton and thus deals only tangentially with processes and programs of organizational change.

2.1 Strategies of Consultation

Robert R. Blake   Jane Srygley Mouton

In the process of our studies we have come to recognize that five different kinds of interventions characterize what applied behavioral scientists do as they work with people in organizations. They intervene, in any of these five ways, in five different settings or units of change. So a matrix of twenty-five cells is necessary to describe the significant change efforts that are going on. We would like to explain what these cells are, provide a brief bibliography to pinpoint work going on in each, and provide a few examples that describe the respective intervention/development assumptions that each contains.

"Strategies of Consultation" by Robert R. Blake and Jane Srygley Mouton, Austin: Scientific Methods, Inc., Copyright © 1972. Reproduced with permission.

You will notice that Figure 1 is called the D/D (Diagnosis/Development) Matrix. This is because diagnosis and development are two aspects that are more or less interdependent in planned change efforts, although occasionally they need to be separated for purposes of analysis.

The *rows* of the matrix represent types of interventions. One is acceptant. The next is catalytic. A third is confrontation. The fourth is prescriptive. The fifth and last includes use of principles, theories and models as the determinants of change. Selection of any particular intervention, of course, is a judgmental decision taken on the basis of prior diagnosis.

The *columns* of the matrix refer to settings within which change occurs. The first column identifies the individual *per se*

FIGURE 1   The D/D Matrix[1]

	Unit of Change				
Types of Intervention	Individual	Team (group, project, department)	Intergroup (interdivisional, headquarters-field, union-management, etc.)	Organization	Society
Acceptant	A	B	C	D	E
Catalytic	F	G	H	I	J
Confrontation	K	L	M	N	O
Prescriptive	P	Q	R	S	T
Principles, Models, Theories	U	V	W	X	Y

[1] This way of organizing intervention strategies led us to introduce a third dimension called *focal issues*. There are four: power/authority, morale/cohesion, norms/standards, and goals/objectives. See R. R. Blake, and Jane Srygley Mouton, *Consultation* (Reading, Mass.: Addison-Wesley, 1976).

as a unit of change. The second, or team, column refers mainly to small groups, projects, departments, and managerial "family" groups, but it also includes interpersonal relations on a one-to-one basis. The third column is for intergroup relationships. Examples of intergroup diagnosis/development units are interdivisional, headquarters-field, union-management, and other relationships between any organized groupings within or semi-external to the organization. The fourth column refers to the organization considered as a whole or as a system. The fifth we have labeled "society" because of the broader implications of training and development for planned change of society at large.

Acceptant Intervention

Now let's go along the top. What an "acceptant" intervention does is to enter into contact with the feelings, tensions, and subjective attitudes that often block a person and make it difficult for him to function as effectively as he otherwise might. The developmental objective is to enable him to express, work through and resolve these feelings so that he can then return to a more objective and work-related orientation. This is not the whole area of counseling as it relates to therapy. It is that aspect of counseling which takes place within the framework of organizations and which is intended to help a person perform better. Certainly it is a very important application of counseling.

Here is an example of counseling with individuals from Cell A in the matrix. During the 1930s, at the Hawthorne plant of the Western Electric Company, it was discovered that many employees were blocked, taut, seething with tensions of one kind or another. Generally these tensions were either work-focused or home-focused, or an intricate combination of both. For some years Hawthorne management provided a counseling service that enabled people to be aided through counseling to discharge the emotion laden tensions. We say "to discharge" tensions, as distinct from resolving them more or less permanently. The procedure was, in effect, "Any time you feel overcome by tension, get a slip from your supervisor and go see a counselor." This is comparable—if we adopt an oil-industry analogy—to "flaring off" subterranean natural gas rather than piping it to wherever it can be productively used.

In the peak year of the program, 1948, Hawthorne's department of counseling was manned by fifty-five people. That's a large complement of counselors. This very interesting experiment has been documented by its originators, who were able to return to the scene of their effort and to study the consequences thirty years after the program began.

An example I would like to paraphrase for you is from their book (Dickson & Roethlisberger, 1966, 225–226). The situation takes place in the counselor's office. Charlie enters. He is a semi-skilled worker who has been with the company for some time but has recently been transferred to a new inspection job from another one he had formerly mastered and enjoyed. He is unhappy with his new job.

Counselor: Hi ya Charlie, how are you?
Charlie: Glad to see you. We all set to go?
Counselor: Sure, any time you're ready.
Charlie: Well, I'm ready any time to get out of this g.d. place. *You know, you get shoved around from one place to another.*
Counselor: You mean you don't have one steady job?
Charlie: Steady, hell. When I came from the first floor I was supposed to do this particular bank job. I stayed on that for two or three weeks, not even long enough to learn it, then I got transferred up here. . . . Of course you know what I got. It got me nothing, just this job here which was a cut.*

* (in his hourly rate of pay)

Counselor: Then all that work didn't pay off?
Charlie: Pay off? There's no payoff at all.

As you can see in this brief example, Charlie is ventilating his feelings and frustrations and the counselor is "reflecting"; trying to aid Charlie to clarify them by feeding him back a summary of those tensions so that Charlie might get an understanding of what they are, rather than just feeling the hurt and distress of them. You will notice that the counselor is not attempting to help Charlie solve his "transfer with pay cut" problem. That's one point of application that involves counseling with an individual to promote catharsis.

In recent years—and "way out" from Hawthorne—the continuum of learning through experience has been extended and enriched through experimentation with action-oriented, nonverbal approaches. An advantage here is that the modalities through which an individual is able to experience himself in situations are increased. Results and experiences can be more directly *felt*, in the sense that words are unnecessary to convey whatever emotions are involved. The way in which any particular approach is used, of course, determines its location in the matrix. One of the most common uses of "encountering" is in the effort to promote personal growth through individual cathartic experiences (Watson, 1972, 155–172).

Now let's look to Cell B. This involves acceptant interventions at the team or group level. Here the idea is that before a team can do an effective job of dealing with its work problems, it may have to deal with emotional tensions and feelings that exist within and between its members.

Gibb has for a considerable time been aiding teams to discharge tension in a cathartic way. This example is from his account of his methods (Gibb, 1972). He describes how, in the process of team building, he may begin with what he calls a "preparation meeting." He brings together the people who are going to be leaders of different teams in order to prepare them for their experience. Why does he start this way? "The primary constraint," he says, ". . . is, of course, fear. Participants are given . . . perhaps the first half-day to share and fully explore as many of their fears as they are able to verbalize." What help is this? "Fears dissipate as they are brought into awareness, shared with others, lived with, listed on the board, made public, and made acceptable. The public expression of the fear may take many forms" (Gibb, 1972, 38). So the effort begins with group exploration which aims to remove these constraints so that constructive sessions can take place.

Cell C identifies approaches to planned change utilizing catharsis at the intergroup level. For example, I am sure that many readers have experienced the tensions and emotions that underlie many union-management relationships. Bickering at the bargaining table is a constant feature and, many times, the topics discussed are not the relevant ones that need to be resolved. Sometimes the relevant ones can't even be expressed! Rather, the issues that people concentrate on seemingly are brought to the table in order to provoke a fight. Often such intergroup dynamics emerge from emotions and frustrations which never get uncovered but stay beneath the surface. Catharsis at the intergroup level has as its purpose to uncover feelings that are barriers to problem-solving interaction; to provide the opportunity for them to be made public; and, in this way, to escape from their hidden effects.

Here is an example from a union-management situation we happen to be familiar with. Contract bargaining was underway. It was hopeless. It was going nowhere. We heard management voicing its frustrations and bitching about the union, and we suggested that perhaps the needed activity was to get *away* from the union-management bargaining table and to sit down together in a special conference for the sole purpose of exploring the feelings these groups held toward one another. This was done. The tensions discharged in those three days were destructive, deep-rooted, intense. The grudges and fantasies from the past that were blocking present effectiveness finally got unloaded, and this freeing-up permitted bargainers to get back to their deliberations.

Here is just one example of the many fantasies unveiled during these days. At one time, actual events which were the source of the fantasy had occurred, but now the "truth" of these events was a matter of history. At the present time the varied feelings about these events were in the realm of fantasy.

"In 1933," (this cathartic session took place in *1963*) the union told the management, "you s.o.b.'s had us down and out because of the depression. And what did you do? You cut everybody's pay in half and, having done so, then you turned us out into the yard to dig up all the pipe and repack it. How do you expect us to bargain with a bunch of cutthroats that would do that to human beings who are down?"

The managers, hearing this, did a retake and said, "Oh, but golly, that was not *us*; that was five dynasties of management ago!" But this disclaimer didn't mollify the union. Eventually, 1963 management walked the 1963 union back through the time tunnel in an attempt to reconstitute the thinking that 1933 management had undertaken. This was "We shouldn't let people go home with no job. We should keep them 'whole.' We can't employ them full time because we don't have that much production scheduled—market demand is way down. Rather than laying off people *en masse*, the humane thing to do is to keep everyone on the payroll, but to make the cost burden bearable by reducing wages. Also, we have to keep them occupied somehow. With operational activities currently at such low levels, the only thing we can do that has long-term utility to it is to dig up the yard pipe and repack it.''

So the 1933 management's intentions were probably well-meant, but the union's legend regarding those intentions portrayed them as very maliicious. Yet eventually the 1963 union, after reconsidering that management's dilemma, agreed that it had taken the most humane alternative open to it. So the old legend dissolved away. Only by getting this kind of emotional muck out in the open and discharged was it possible for these union and management representatives to get back to a businesslike basis of working toward a contract. That's an example of acceptant at the intergroup level.

There are many examples of acceptant interventions at the organization level, Cell D.

In another company the entire management engaged in an ''acceptant'' experience prior to bargaining. The reason was that even though management, at an intellectual level, desired to interact on a problem-solving basis with the plant's independent-union representatives, there were many deeply rooted antagonistic attitudes which continually surfaced and stifled the effort. Why? The ostensibly humane attitudes of people who have received formal education sometimes only serve as a mask for deeper feelings of resentment and antipathy. Often there is a lot of hate among managerial people toward the work force. Such feelings are particularly prevalent among engineers, supervisors and foremen who have, in their own careers, only recently risen above the level of the ''blue-collar stiff.''

The consultant determined that to work solely with the bargaining committee would be insufficient as they could only move in a problem-solving direction if they had the support of the rest of management. Thus a series of conferences were held. Participants were the top 100 members of management, who represented all levels of supervision except first and second line foremen. The stated purpose of these meetings was to develop shared convictions in regard to answering the key question, ''How can we create better relations between union and management?''

Participants were put into three ''cross-section'' groups during each conference. Quinn, the plant manager, sat in one group. Van, the operations superintendent, sat in another group and Wes, the personnel chief, in a third. The groups struggled with the problem of how to improve union-management relations. It was fascinating to watch because a fairly substantial cross-section of the managerial group considered the key question a hopeless one to answer. ''There is no way to bring about any improvement vis-à-vis the thugs, thieves and crooks who presently are running the union. How can you cooperate and collaborate with such a rat pack?''

Then as the question got debated, their deep-lying attitudes and feelings were expressed in detail and were looked at from many points of view. A new concept began to appear. Consciousness dawned that one can never look forward to an improvement in union-management relations unless this governing attitude—namely that the union is composed of thugs, thieves and crooks—is erased or at least given an experimental adjournment in the minds of management. After the discharge of emotions was completed, it was concluded in group after group, ''Regardless of what the union officers are personality-wise and what their history has been, the only conceivable way of bringing about a resolution of conflict is through treating the union officers as officers and according them the dignity and respect due to people who are duly elected. It is not our place to judge the people who have been chosen by their membership as lawful representatives. This is not our role. Our role is to meet with these people and to search for whatever conditions of cooperation and collaboration are possible."

As a result of this cathartic experience, it was possible thereafter for management's bargaining team to take a more collaborative stance (Blake & Mouton, 1973).

At the level of society shown in Cell E, there also are mechanisms that provide for catharsis. Religious institutions are one example. More so in American history than now, but still persisting, is the role of the clergyman as one of the persons to whom people turn when in deep emotional trouble, with the expectation of his providing the disturbed person an opportunity to talk through his feelings. In addition, the doctor, teacher, and school or private counselor are often turned to for help during periods of emotional turmoil, as indeed may be true for parents as well. Beyond these, whenever there is a trauma in society it frequently happens that *ad hoc* mechanisms are created which help people work through their distressed emotional feelings. Well remembered American examples include the two Kennedy funeral processions that were carried by television to many parts of the world. These occasions aided people to mourn. Mourning, in this sense, means working through and discharging tensions of a painful emotional character which currently are preventing people from going on living in their customary ways. As is true in the individual case, societal catharsis mechanisms may not have any direct and systematic connection to potential problem-solving steps, although they sometimes stimulate remedial action of one kind or another.

Catalytic Interventions

Let's move to the next row down: catalytic interventions. "Catalytic" intervention means entering a situation and adding something that has the effect of transforming the situation in some degree from what it was at an earlier time. That's quite different from catharsis. When a training manager or consultant is acting to induce catharsis, he is reflecting or restating the problem—or perhaps simply listening in a fashion that gives empathic support. But when a person makes a catalytic intervention, he might provide a suggestion that causes the problem to be seen in a different and more relevant perspective. Or he might suggest a procedure that will lead to a different line of action being adopted.

Here is a catalytic intervention at the individual level, Cell F in the D/D Matrix. In one particular company they have a career-planning project. A young man who had been employed for some time came in to talk about his career hopes. The interviewer said, "What are your aspirations? Where would you like to end up in the company?"

The young man replied, "Well, I think I would like to be president or chairman."

Now then, the interviewer might have said something in a cathartic or reflective way. But he didn't. He said, "Well, that's an interesting aspiration. I would like to think it through with you. How many years of education do you have?"

"Six."

"How many promotions have you had in the last two years?"

"One small wage increase."

"Have you taken any courses on your own initiative?"

"No."

And as the discussion continued, the young man began to see the unrealism in his aspiration to be president. Currently there was *no* realistic possibility either in terms of some evidence of upward progression, or of autonomously achieved preparation, or in terms of anything else he was doing. The consultant thereby brought him to the choice point of whether he was prepared to make the additional sacrifices necessary for him to generate upward movement, or whether he was simply content to go on projecting an unrealistic career fantasy (Gould, 1970, 227–228). That's a catalytic intervention at the *individual* level.

Another example, which uses a laboratory setting for life/career planning, is premised on catalytic intervention at the individual level (Fordyce & Weil, 1971, 131–132).

Catalytic intervening at the *team* level, Cell G, is one of the most popular applied behavioral science developments of the past twenty-five years, and has become a central intervention in industrial life. There are a whole host of names that come to mind at this point. There are people who engage in team-building sessions where the purpose of their interventions is not to direct the team or merely to reflect back members' feelings, but to facilitate the interaction process so that the team comes to have a better understanding of the problems and pitfalls it's gotten into, and so on.

The following is an example of Schein, a consultant, facilitating group action by focusing attention on how the agenda for meetings was determined.

> In the Apex company I sat in for several months on the weekly executive-committee meeting, which included the president and his key subordinates. I quickly became aware that the group was very loose in its manner of operation: people spoke when they felt like it, issues were explored fully, conflict was fairly openly confronted, and members felt free to contribute.

What did this mean to Schein?

> This kind of climate seemed constructive, but it created a major difficulty for the group. No matter how few items were put on the agenda, the group was never able to finish its work. The list of backlog items grew longer and the frustration of group members intensified in proportion to this backlog.

How did members themselves diagnose the situation?

> The group responded by trying to work

harder. They scheduled more meetings and attempted to get more done at each meeting, but with little success. Remarks about the ineffectiveness of groups, too many meetings, and so on, became more and more frequent.

But what did it look like to Schein?

> My diagnosis was that the group was overloaded. Their agenda was too large, they tried to process too many items at any given meeting, and the agenda was a mixture of operational and policy issues without recognition by the group that such items required different allocations of time.

So what did Schein propose?

> I suggested to the group that they seemed overloaded and should discuss how to develop their agenda for their meetings. The suggestion was adopted after a half-hour or so of sharing feelings.

Was Schein passive and reflecting or active in a facilitative way?

> It was then decided, with my help, to sort the agenda items into several categories, and to devote some meetings entirely to operational issues while others would be exclusively policy meetings. The operations meetings would be run more tightly in order to process these items efficiently. The policy questions would be dealt with in depth. (Schein, 1969, 106)

Another example of facilitative or catalytic interaction occurs between boss and subordinate as they engage in "management by objectives." Quite frequently, however, in the introduction of MbO in an organization, people other than just the boss and subordinate are used to develop and facilitate the program. Here is a description of what such facilitators do. It is taken from Humble's work with management by objectives (Humble, 1967, 60). He calls these internal people "company advisers."

> Company Advisers must be selected and trained to a highly professional standard in the various techniques. . . . An Adviser is a source of professional advice on the whole programme. He develops suitable techniques and methods with managers; counsels each individual manager in

the Key Results Analysis preparation; is present at first Reviews; helps to analyse training plans. He is an "educator" and "catalyst," *not* a man who states what the standards should be, nor what the priorities are and how the problems should be solved. That is management's task.

In this description we see a clear distinction between what we later on call prescriptive interventions—where the intervention is for the purpose of telling people what to do—and the facilitative or catalytic type of intervention where the goal is to aid a process of change or development to occur.

Data-gathering procedures frequently are used in a catalytic way. This is where data are intended to add something to the situation in order to change it (Likert, 1961). When these data are returned to their users, the expert's own personal participation is best described as catalytic. Usually he doesn't tell people what the data mean, but he does ask them questions that aid them to probe meanings more directly.

Next to Cell H, intergroup. Catalysis here denotes adding something *between* two groups, in order to enable existing difficulties to rise to the surface or be placed squarely on the examining table so that they can be dealt with.

An intergroup intervention example is described by Beckhard. What he describes is a situation where people from a higher level meet with people from a lower level. The goal is to aid the lower-level people to communicate with the higher-level managers, or discuss specific problems with them, or to bring forth their feelings, attitudes, opinions and ideas regarding what actually is happening in some existing situation. Usually they have been unable, on any prior occasion, to communicate their ideas directly through organizational channels.

The person who organizes and leads the meeting is acting in a catalytic way. He is inserting a procedure into the situation that is facilitating in the sense that it helps the situation to develop toward resolution. In the following description, the meeting leader gives an assignment to each of the groups—say, to a top level group and a middle management group. He does not give directions as to what specifically should be discussed, but he indicates a way to get started on a facilitative discussion.

> Think of yourself as an individual with needs and goals. Also think as a person concerned about the total organization. What are the obstacles, "demotivators," poor procedures or policies, unclear goals, or poor attitudes that exist today? What different conditions, if any, would make the organization more effective and make life in the organization better? (Beckhard, 1967, 154)

Then each unit goes off and discusses this separately. Beckhard's instructions are sufficiently general to permit people to put into their discussion whatever it is that is specifically troubling them in their particular jobs and situations. Then the meeting leader, from there on, continues in his procedurally facilitative role by helping the two units collect their data, analyze their feelings and facts, evaluate and compare them, and generally make progress. A similar example of catalytic intervention with multiple membership groups is provided by Bennis (Bennis, 1970, 158–160). Sometimes this approach is called a confrontation meeting, but this is a misnomer, because it entails no confrontation of the sort correctly described by Argyris (Argyris, 1971) which will be discussed later. Rather, the proceedings have a "group suggestion box" quality.

At the organization level (Cell I), intervention by an "ombudsman," who is empowered to bypass ordinary channels when he problem-solves on behalf of people who are burdened with difficulties because of some mistake or lack of response on the part of his particular company or government department, is catalytic in character, particularly in its facilitative aspects (*Commerce Today*, 1972, 29; Foegen, 1972, 289–294).

At the level of society there are many endeavors that are essentially catalytic, as specified in Cell J. We wish it were possible to say they were being systematically implemented within comprehensive and coherent frameworks of development. But there are some that, considered individually, have become quite systematic by now. Taking a census every five or ten years, one which describes the state of the nation "as of" a given point in time and permits comparisons to be made across several decades, is one way of aiding citizens to review their situation, of aiding national leadership to formulate policy, and of aiding industries to see the contemporary shape of markets, population trends, and many other things. The census is a powerful force in society. So are opinion polls. These are becoming ever more significant in the eyes of the public. Unfortunately their uses are somewhat limited to political affairs, but there are many other points of application that are possible for polling mechanisms, ones that can have a catalytic effect in terms of how society sees itself conducting its affairs.

Confrontation

Let us now look along the next row, which deals with *confrontation* strategies. These represent quite different intervention styles from catalysis and very different from carthartic interventions. Confrontation has much more challenge in it. It's a much more active intrusion into the life experience of other people than could possibly be implied by a catalytic approach, and certainly much more than would be implied by a cathartic one.

There's another distinction here. As you move from catharsis and catalytic approaches into the next three, what you find is that, under the first two, there is

no challenge of the *status quo* by the intervener. In other words, he accepts the definition of the problem, and the associated values and attitudes usually as these are given by the client, and then helps the client to adjust better to the *status quo*. Under a confrontation mode you frequently find a shifting across some kind of "gap"—the existence of this gap having been identified in the locus of the challenge that the intervener implies.

In different ways, each of the next three approaches is much more likely to cause people to challenge the *status quo* and to reject the existing situation as being less preferable than a stronger situation that could be designed to replace it. That's a very important shift in thinking—from simply aiding people to conform or adjust, to assisting people to redesign the situations in which they live and work.

First, we'll describe a confrontation type of intervention at the individual level (Cell K). This occurred in a multinational company where the New York president visited the subsidiary president and said to him, in effect—though it was a whole day in the doing—"Look, Henry, I want you to know that we're very unhappy with how your company is operating. As we look at it, in comparison with other companies in our worldwide group, your profit performance is far below the best, and we just don't see you taking the vigorous action necessary to solve your problems."

Henry *said*—that is, he didn't reply to the specifics of that statement: he couldn't hear them—"If you'll look at our 1949 figures and then look at our latest performance records relative to 1949 when I took over, you'll see that over the years we have made a dramatic shift for the better.

And so they went at it, this way and that, all day, and neither heard the other. From the New York Headquarters president's point of view, this was a company they would willingly sell, because they couldn't exert influence upon it. From the subsidiary president's point of view, a valiant effort over many years that had produced betterment was being disregarded. Now the confrontation was this.

The next day, one of us said to Henry, "My hearing is that two quite different *perspectives* are being employed to evaluate this company's performance. The perspective of the New York president is a here-and-now perspective. He doesn't care what you did for him yesterday, he is asking, 'What are you doing for me today?' By comparison, your perspective is historical. You're saying, 'How much better we're doing now than yesterday and last year and five years ago.' So unless you two can get onto a common perspective and reason from there, I see very little possibility of any collaborative effort occurring." Well, they did eventually get onto that common perspective basis. Once both of them understood what the central issue was, and that they weren't just totally unresponsive to each other, then some very significant changes took place in the subsidiary company, ones which are continuing to have enlivening effects. That's a confrontation that has caused development to get underway. And the *status quo* has been radically changed from what it previously had been.

Gestalt approaches, several of which are engineered to dramatize an encounter between the participant and an absent person, between two or more imaginary people, or even to dramatize ambivalent feelings within the person's own personality, are confrontational in character, even though cathartic elements are present. Conflicts, contradictions, incongruencies, and so on, are focused by the situation as the intervener structures it—or directly through the intervener's own words—in such a way as to permit more insightful resolutions through the elimination of contradictions, rationalizations, etc. (Herman, 1972).

Now let's examine confrontation at the team level (Cell L). An example of this comes during a team-building session conducted by Argyris. During this team-building session, and for the last several hours, members had been insisting that the company has a soft, manipulative, ineffective philosophy. Yet they had not really pinned down examples but were just talking in terms of generalities. So he said, "It is difficult to deal with such an answer, namely that the whole company is at fault. Could you give a specific example?" Nobody could. He continued very directly, saying, "OK fellows, are you going to be soft on these issues? You speak of integrity and courage. Where is it? I cannot be of help, nor you for that matter, if all you do is accuse the company of being ineffective. You said you were ready to talk—OK, I'm taking you at your word" (Argyris, 1971, 84). He is confronting them with the discrepancies between what they can be specific about and the abstractions.

Confrontation at the intergroup level (Cell M) usually involves each in coming to terms with the other. This interaction is not in terms of discharge of emotional tensions—as in the example of union and management given earlier—but in terms of gaining a shared and realistic sense of what their relationship is.

Here is an example. This one involves the headquarters' Division of Manufacturing in a large company and its major plant, which is located thirty miles away. The Division is headed by a vice president. A general manager runs the plant. These two had gotten more and more out of phase with each other over the years until they had nearly reached total impasse. It was very difficult for anyone to see how their misunderstandings had originated and grown into crisis proportions.

Eventually it was arranged for the vice president of manufacturing, and eight or ten people who reported to him, and the plant's general manager and the twelve people who reported to him to get together to study their relationship. The task was for each group to describe what the relationship between headquarters and the plant would be like if it were really a good one. Thereafter, they were to describe what the relationship actually was, here and now. The vice president of manufacturing's group worked in one room and put on newsprint a description of what, from their viewpoint, an ideal relationship would be like. The plant manager's group did the same thing, but in another room. Then they came back together and put their newsprints on the wall so that it could be seen by all what both sides thought a sound relationship would be like. The descriptions were similar and this similarity gave a lot of encouragement. Differences were discussed and resolved.

The next step, working separately, was for each group to describe the relationship as it actually existed here and now. They did this, and brought back their newsprints. Now it seemed like the relationship being described, as viewed from the headquarters point of view, was "totally" different from the relationship being pictured from the plant point of view. These dramatic divergences stimulated confrontation between the two groups on the issue of what, in fact, did characterize their mutual relationship. For several days, with close management of this situation and the interaction maintained by the interventionist to avoid an uncontrolled explosion, they thrashed through many aspects until a more accurate picture of the present relationship emerged. Now it became possible for both groups to see the many deep problems that in fact existed. They then designed some strategies for improvement steps that could lead toward resolution.

There is a comprehensive description of confrontation at the organization (Cell N) level (Jaques, 1951). The project was one of the innovative applied behavioral science interventions of the early post-war period and took place within the Glacier Metal Company in England. Jaques describes how he and others on his research team continually confronted the organization with the character of its internal relationships and objective performance.

At the societal level are found a good many institutionalized as well as informal mechanisms through which problems are confronted. What these are is a function of the kind of society you are looking at. The two-party system provides ways of confronting issues by challenging what's going on. When one party publicizes its point of view, the other side is confronted with the necessity of either accepting the point of view as expressed, or identifying flaws in it. This is not to imply that in *any* political system this is done particularly well. We are only suggesting that two-party mechanisms, as these link into and work through a nation's executive branch, legislatures and public media, constitute one important way of confronting the problems of society and getting them into definition so that actions can be taken in behalf of solving them. Furthermore, the spread of the union-management confrontation mechanism into government, school, university and professional settings has resulted in this mechanism of intervention taking on social dimensions. Beyond that the entire legal system provides mechanisms by which confrontation with redress of injustice is provided for.

Prescriptive

Now let's consider the *prescriptive* row. These are the most forceful types of intervention, ones which I rather doubt are widely practiced by training and development people. But they are widely applied by outside consultants in conjunction with managers in industry, commerce, and government. Higdon describes the prescriptive approach as used in various consulting firms such as McKinsey and Company; Arthur D. Little; Booz, Allen and Hamilton, and many others (Higdon, 1969). The basic procedure is that management asks an expert in, and he and his associates study the situation and provide a recommended solution. The "mainstream" consultant is not working with emotions in a cathartic sense. He is not working catalytically. He is not confronting. He is telling. His recommendations would be directions, if he had the authority of rank. But he is certainly prescribing, and these prescriptions sometimes are very complete and fundamental. Often they involve changing an organization's structure, or getting out of one product line and into another, or applying a more efficient theory of business. Many times they involve firing or laying off people, and so they can have impactful consequences on the development of an organization. Sometimes the prescription is rejected out of hand. Sometimes, when taken, it results in a healthful bracing up of part or all of the organization. There have been numerous instances, however, of consultant prescriptions becoming very frustrating to the organization in terms of the difficulties and side effects left in their wake. These include lowered morale, people leaving because they no longer can give their commitment, and so on.

Here's a description of prescriptive strategy at the individual level (Cell P). It is where a consultant is trying to hold up a mirror in front of a manager to help him see what he is like, and then to prescribe, in concrete and operational terms, what he'd better do. The client is a plant manager who has trouble with his chief accountant, who is a rather "cold and formal" individual. To obtain better results than he was presently getting from this man, the plant manager—a genial fatherly person who likes to develop warm personal relations with his subordinates—was advised to take a forceful, direct, impersonal approach with him. This, the consultant predicted, would resonate much better with the accountant's psyche than the manager's more typical approach had been doing. On the matter of delayed reports the manager was to say the following: "I want your report on my desk at nine o'clock Friday morning, complete in every detail, and no ifs, ands, or buts about it." Having delivered that ultimatum, he was to turn around and leave. The plant manager did just that, although, being the kind of person he was, it was hard for him to do. The new approach brought striking results. The report came in on schedule and it was one of the finest the plant manager had ever received (Flory, 1965, 158–159). The client had been told specifically how he should act and he followed it through in strict accordance with the consultant's plan. In this case it produced effective results. Incidentally, the developing area of "behavior modification" (Krumboltz, 1965) is a training strategy that has prescriptive qualities.

An example of a prescriptive intervention at the group level (Cell Q) is offered by Cohen and Smith. They think this kind of intervention is most suitable toward the end of a group experience. At that time the total group is divided into subgroups of four or five members who are given the following instructions.

> . . . In each subgroup one person will leave the room for ten minutes. During that time the remaining members will first diagnose this person's typical style of interacting with others, and secondly try to pinpoint definite, specific, helpful suggestions as to how he might be helped to engage in atypical but productive behavior both for himself and the group. I must stress the terms "definite" and "specific." Don't make abstract generalizations like "you're too much of an introvert, so try being an extrovert for a while." Instead, give him definite and specific prescriptions to carry out that are generally atypical but productive. Thus, one person might be told to express anger toward the group more directly and verbally instead of remaining quiet. The process continues until everyone has been given a "behavioral prescription."

We will all meet back here in 'X' minutes to see what sort of changes have occurred. (Cohen & Smith, 1972, 103)

Robert's Rules of Order are prescriptive rules for conduct at the group or team level [Robert (1876), 1970]. They tell the leader how to operate meeting procedures. This rather mechanical set of criteria, if followed, prescribes the process parameters of the meeting, provides for expressions of differences, and offers a voting mechanism for resolution.

The third party arbiter is used at the intergroup level to provide for the resolution of differences, and to speed thinking toward further progress (Cell R). Typically, it operates in the following way. Two groups—say, management and a union—reach an impasse. Both agree to submit the disagreement to binding arbitration. The arbitrator, characteristically a distinterested outsider, hears evidence or otherwise studies the case and renders his decision. This usually takes the form of a prescription which both sides in the dispute are obligated to take (Linke, 1968, 158–560, Lazarus *et al.*, 1965).

Prescriptive approaches at the organization level are shown in Cell S. One is vividly described in a case study from *Fortune*. Top management of Philco had engaged an outside firm to study the organization and to propose needed changes. Here's how a crucial meeting was described.

> James M. Skinner, Jr., president of Philco Corp., (arrived) . . . for a momentous meeting that had been six months in the making. Waiting for Skinner in suite 1808 were nine somewhat apprehensive men from Arthur D. Little, Inc., the technical consulting firm of Cambridge, Massachusetts.
> . . . Donham spoke first, outlining in general terms what A.D.L. hoped to accomplish with its reorganization plan. What he was proposing, in brief, was a massive reorganization of Philco's marketing setup, which would: make the job of marketing all

of Philco's consumer products the responsibility of one division; fix profit responsibilities at precise points in the company; get day-to-day pressures off the backs of men who should be doing long-range planning; and provide much closer support for Philco's independent distributors and dealers. (Thompson, 1959, 113–114)

Levinson, operating out of a psychoanalytic tradition, has described his model of organization diagnosis in step-by-step terms. The approach he depicts is prescriptive in character, as demonstrated in the following excerpt which gives a few of the diagnostician's recommendations regarding the improvement of personnel practices at "Claypool Furniture and Appliances."

> The recommendations to be made, following the logic expressed in the last discussion, are as follows:
> *Personnel Practices* The company should establish descriptions and standards and objectives for all positions. It should develop orientation and training programs to properly prepare people for their jobs and provide appraisal devices by which personnel and their superiors can assess progress and training needs. Positions and training in supervision and management are to be included in this process. A procedure for identifying prospective managerial talent should be evolved. The representative council should be abolished, and it should be replaced by employee task forces appointed to solve specific intraorganizational problems. Such groups, to include stock personnel, would end the isolation of the stock people and contribute to organizational identification and group cohesion.
> A continuous and open evaluation of the wage and salary structure below the managerial levels should be undertaken, with the intention of creating and maintaining an equitable and competitive salary structure. . . . (Levinson, 1972, 491)

The Hoover Commission was an effort to use prescriptive techniques of diagnosis and development at the societal level. Ex-President Herbert Hoover and other members of the commission comprised a prestigious group. The presumption was that the voice of their authority behind recommendations would be sufficient, along with a responsive incumbent President, to bring about the recommended reformations in terms of restructuring the design and operations of the executive branch of the government.

> The usual procedure, applied on all levels of government in the United States, is to set up a formal inquiry into existing conditions, in the hope of bringing forth concrete recommendations with a fair chance of adoption. Inquiries of this type on the federal level include the President's Committee on Administrative Management with Louis Brownlow as chairman (reporting in 1937) and the (first) Commission on Organization of the Executive Branch headed by former president Herbert Hoover (reporting in 1949). (Willson, 1968, 632)

Principles, Theories, and Models

The first [fifth] row of the matrix identifies diagnostic and developmental efforts which focus upon aiding people to acquire insights derived from principles, theories, or models. The assumption is that deficiencies of behavior or performance can be resolved best when people responsible for results use relevant principles, theories, or models in terms of which they themselves can test alternatives, decide upon and take action, and predict consequences. It is an approach which emphasizes intervention by concepts and ideas rather than by people.

With regard to Cell U, the particular significance to an individual of theory, principles, and models is that they are capable of providing a map of valid performance against which actual behavior and actual performance can be contrasted. When gaps exist between theory specifications for sound conduct and actual behavior, then change can be introduced

which reduces the gap by increasing the congruence between the two. In this sense—and also, importantly, in the sense of removing self-deception—systematic concepts involving theories, principles, or models constitute a "theory mirror" which has the unique power of enabling people to see themselves, their present situations or future potential more clearly than if reliance is on subjective notions that something feels "right," "natural," or "okay," or simply that others "approve" it. Here are some examples:

Transactional Analysis is a conceptual formulation which provides a mirror into which people can look as a way of seeing themselves. Training designs have been created which enable participants to identify "Parent," "Child," and "Adult" oriented behavior both directly and with the benefit of colleague feedback and to study and practice ways of shifting toward more adultlike behavior (Blansfield, 1972, 149–154).

Also at the individual level, there is the Kepner-Tregoe system which provides managers with a model through which to design an analysis of any given problem and evaluate the quality of decisions they make. The objective is to reduce impulse, spontaneity and reliance on past practice and to shift to a rationality basis for problem analysis and decision making (Kepner & Tregoe, 1965).

There are a variety of theories, principles or models regarding individual behavior, some of which are accompanied by intervention strategies calculated to make the models functionally useful in concrete situations. Some of the more widely known include Theories X and Y (McGregor, 1960), Grid® formulations (Blake & Mouton, 1964, 1968, 1970; Mouton & Blake, 1971), and Systems 1 through 4 (Likert, 1967). However, the approach described by Likert does not involve man-to-man feedback on actual performance. Thus provisions are unavailable for penetrating and correcting self-deception.

FIGURE 2   Actual vs. Ideal Top Culture in a Chemical Plant

Actual	Ideal
Persons only do what is expected of them. Each man runs his own shop. The boss calls the shots.	Synergism is exploited, issues are talked through, and solutions and decisions based on facts are fully thrashed through to understanding and agreement.
Plans come down from the boss without opportunity to review, evaluate, or recommend changes by those who implement them.	Plans based on analysis of facts permit real issues to be treated soundly; plans are produced jointly by those who should be involved; individual responsibilities are clear.
Traditional ways of doing things are rarely questioned; they represent the tried and true operating standards.	Elements of culture are continually evaluated in the light of requirements for peak performance and, if necessary, they are modified or replaced through thoughtful discussions and agreement among team members.
Results are what count, no matter how achieved.	Team members are fully committed to excellence, results are achieved because members are motivated to exceed.

Examples of theory orientation at the individual level include four Grids: Managerial, Sales, Customer, and Marriage; each of which describes several alternative models—9-9, 9-1, 1-9, 5-5, and 1-1—as well as mixed, dominant and backup theories. Once a person has learned the various theories, they can be used to diagnose his own behavior. In addition, he can select any theory as a model to change toward, but the most likely endorsed one is 9-9. He can then study and practice ways of increasing the congruence between his actual behavior and the model (Blake & Mouton, 1968, 34–66).

Some approaches to team building (Cell V) use principles, theories and models as the basis for diagnosing and feedback and for implementing development activities. Central issues, which, for the top team of a large chemical plant, demonstrated the gap between a diagnosis of their present ways of functioning and a model of what they considered ideal, are shown in Figure 2. This actual/ideal comparative diagnosis was used for designing strategies of change to be implemented within the next four months (Blake & Mouton, 1968, 120–157).

Theory, principle and models also have proved useful in strengthening intergroup relations (Cell W). Phase 3 of Grid Organization Development, for example, begins with two groups convening for the purpose of describing what would be an ideal model for their particular relationship. This ideal model is itself based on theories of intergroup conflict and cooperation (Blake & Mouton, 1964; Blake, Shepard & Mouton, 1964). It culminates with an *in situ* design which spells out the properties of a sound and effective relationship in a particular, concrete setting. The modeling stage is followed by implementation strategies for converting "what is" to "what should be." An example of the properties of an ideal management-union relationship as described by one company is shown in Figures 3 and 4 (see pp. 64 and 65).

The development of an Ideal Strategic Corporate Model in Phase 4 of Grid Organization Development is an example of the use of models at the organization level (Cell X). Phase 4 enables a top group, particularly, to isolate itself from the *status quo* long enough to design what would be an "ideal" company, given its realistic access to financial resources. Issues considered include, "What should be the key financial objectives that the company should strive after?" "What should be the nature of the company's business, and the nature of its markets?" "What should its structure be?" "What policies should it operate under?" Finally, "What are development requirements for getting from where it is to where it would go if it were to approach the ideal model?" An example of the change in thinking about financial objectives at the corporate level during Phase 4 is shown in Figure 5 (see p. 65).

The use of principles, models and theories also can be seen at the level of society (Cell Y). The Magna Charta is a well-known historical example. The U.S. Constitution describes the kind of behavior, freedom and control which American society was expected to be modeled after. Over nearly two centuries, several constitutional amendments have updated the model in the light of contemporary perspectives. Legislative and executive actions are always being tested against the Constitution.

Lilienthal's work in Iran can be viewed as intervention at the societal level to bring about change through assisting the eventual users to design models of "what should be" as the basis of specific implementation plans. Lilienthal is a notable industrial statesman who led first the Tennessee Valley Authority and then the U.S. Atomic Energy Commission in their beginning years. He has described his later consulting work (Lilienthal, 1969) when, with his own and his colleagues'

vast knowledge of hydro-electric engineering, community rehabilitation, and agri-business, they helped the Iranian government design a model for water and electric-power resources for the future of its then undeveloped Khuzestan province. That model is being systematically implemented through the building of dams, power irrigation systems, and so on, as well as infrastructure developments such as agricultural advisory programs, health and educational facilities, etc. This is an example of how a consultant can work, not in a prescriptive mode, but as a skillful teacher in aiding people to learn to design and implement complex models. Lilienthal thus has enabled a vast development to occur, one that otherwise would have been piecemeal, suboptimizing, and possibly impractical.

Skinner's recent writings about society are derived from theory and principles and also rest on a model concept (Skinner, 1971).

Summary and Conclusions

The D/D Matrix provides a way of encompassing a wide range of activities now underway for strengthening human performance through diagnosis and development. Illustrations of each approach have been provided without trying to be inclusive.

Using this matrix, anyone who wishes to do so can identify the assumptions underlying his own work, and evaluate their probable consequences for increasing the effectiveness of individuals, groups, groups in relationships with one another, organizations, and society. The acceptant approach of emotional barrier-reduction and the catalytic approach of helping people to make progress in dealing with given situations are most likely to aid

---

FIGURE 3   What a Sound Union-Management Relationship Would Be as Described by Management

---

The Management Would:

Maintain open communications with the union in the following areas:
Economics of industry and company
Goals and objectives of company
Long range company plans
How company profits handled and distributed
Problems facing company
Growth opportunities—company and individual
Security and development of employees
Employee induction and orientation—where person fits in total scheme of things
Participate in prebargaining discussions to:
Identify and clarify current economic climate
Identify and understand company's competitive position
Assess and evaluate indexes for productivity
Identify and agree upon appropriate and objective cost of living standards
Identify and understand employee attitudes and concerns
Assess strengths and weaknesses of present contract
Identify possible obstacles and barriers that could arise during negotiations
Adopt bargaining strategy to:
Develop frame of reference for agenda
Explore problem areas jointly
Explore opportunity areas
Have more joint problem solving—e.g., on:
Evaluating impact on employees from operational changes
Work simplification
Benefits and pension programs
Techniques of training
Job safety
Handle complaints and grievances as follows:
First line supervisors would discharge responsibility for resolving complaints and grievances and act with dispatch
Participate in continuing joint efforts leading to clear interpretation and uniform application of contract clauses at working level
Maintain open door policy—union executives have free access to management executives and vice versa
Establish and maintain open, upper level labor-management dialogue—ongoing critique
Endeavor to understand problem confronting union officers within their frame of reference in their relationship with membership.

The Union Would:

Develop comprehensive understanding of specific nature of the business and concern for it
Understand and consider nature of competition as it relates to company performance and needs for change
Develop understanding of relationships of productivity to wages and benefits
Because of peculiar nature of industry, understand long range impact on both company and employees from work stoppages
Recognize implications of taking fixed positions in approaching problems—win-lose trap
Recognize harm in intragroup (within union) conflict resulting in company and employee backlash
Subdue personal interests in favor of overall company and union objectives
Accept responsibility to communicate facts to employees without prejudice.

Source: Blake, R. R. & Mouton, J. S. Corporate excellence through grid organization development: A systems approach. Houston: Gulf Publishing, 1968, 181–182. Not to be reproduced without permission.

FIGURE 4   What a Sound Union-Management Relationship Would Be as Described by the Union

---
The Management Would:

Exercise authority on complaints, grievances, questions, decisions needed, etc., without needless delay, particularly first level managers

Adopt uniform education program for all supervisors, vertical and horizontal, on understanding, interpreting, and applying the contract

Interpret the contract in an honest and aboveboard way

Consult employees on changes in working schedules, shifts, transfers, location, etc.

Apply a system of seniority and rotation without favoritism, e.g., assigned overtime, easy jobs, time off, vacations, best working schedules, etc.

Rate employees' performance on a uniform, systematic, and fair basis and with employees told where they stand

Coordinate and communicate effectively between department supervisors to prevent needless work by employees and cut down costs and wasted effort.

The Union Would:

Represent all employees fairly

Communicate problems, complaints, contract infractions to management

Have access to top management without runaround at lower levels

Be concerned with costs and amount of production

Insure employee has correct rating for skills he has and that he is paid for job he does, not the classification he has.

(Union had insufficient time remaining to complete this activity.)

Source: Blake, R. R. & Mouton, J. S. Corporate excellence through grid organization development: A systems approach. Houston: Gulf Publishing, 1968, 183. Not to be reproduced without permission.

FIGURE 5   Genuine Concern with the Organization's Earning Capacity Results from Designing an Ideal Strategic Model

---

From	To
Maintain or increase market share while living within a budget.	Optimal 30, minimum 20 percent pretax return on assets employed with an unlimited time horizon.
Dollar profit should improve and not fall behind last year. Return on investment computed and discussed on an after-the-fact calculation which exerted little or no influence on operational decision making.	Each business should have a specified profit improvement factor to be calculated on a business-by-business basis. The objective should be an earnings per share level which would within five years justify a price-earnings ratio of 20 to one or better.
	Share of market objectives should be established within the framework of return on assets and cash generation objectives.

Source: Blake, R. R. & Mouton, J. S. Corporate excellence through grid organization development: A systems approach. Houston: Gulf Publishing 1968, 233. Not to be reproduced without permission.

individuals and groups to do a better job within the existing *status quo*.

Confrontation and prescription are useful in a "fixed" or "frozen" situation. They provide alternatives to those currently present in the *status quo*. Both rely heavily on outside expertise.

The history of society and its capacity to identify and grapple with complex and interrelated problems of the physical environment, new technologies, and community development is significantly linked with the production and use of principles, theories and models for understanding, predicting—and, therefore, managing—natural and human environments. Approaches to diagnosis and development which rely on the use of principles, theories, and models for understanding emotional, intellectual and operational events provide the most powerful and impactful approach to the implementation of planned change.

It is highly unlikely that any single approach will be based solely on one intervention mode. Rather, the likelihood is that several intervention modes will be included, with one of them being central or dominant. For example, the Dickson-Roethlisberger counseling program appears to have been a very "pure" individual-cathartic approach, with minor reliance on counseling as catalytic intervention. Process consultation, as depicted by Schein, relies heavily upon catalytic intervention, with some use of acceptant interventions and very infrequent use of the confrontation mode. Schein makes practically no use of the prescriptive mode, and makes theory interventions only after the fact.

The intervening in T Groups is mainly catalytic, with secondary reliance on the cathartic mode. "Encounter" relies very heavily on catharsis. Grid OD concentrates on theory, principles and models; but it also provides at key points for confrontation, catalytic intervention, and cathartic release. Other approaches can be analyzed in a similar manner.

No one can say, in an abstract sense and without regard to a particular situation, that there is "one best way." While principles, theories, and models constitute the strongest approach, they may lack feasibility until emotional blockages have been reduced through cathartic intervention. Or, perhaps, opening up the possibilities of systematic OD may take little more than a timely catalytic intervention which enables managers to see possibilities not previously envisaged. Statements of a similar character can be made with regard to confrontation and prescription.

In the final analysis, however, acceptant, catalysis, confrontation or prescription constitute means to an end, rather than ends in themselves. The ultimate goal is that people become capable of effective living through utilizing principles, theories and models as the basis of human enrichment.

References

Matrix Cell

L   Argyris, C. *Organization and innovation*. Homewood, Ill.: R. D. Irwin, 1965.

L   Argyris, C. *Intervention theory and method*. Reading, Mass.: Addison-Wesley, 1970.

L   Argyris, C. *Management and organization development*. New York: McGraw-Hill, 1971.

H   Beckhard, R. The confrontation meeting. *Harvard Business Review*, March-April, 1967, 149–155.

H   Bennis, W. G. Organization development: What it is and what it isn't. In D. R. Hampton (Comp.) *Behavioral concepts in management* (second edition) Encino, Calif.: Dickinson, 1972. Pp. 154–163.

U   Blake, R. R. & Mouton, J. S. *The managerial grid: Key orientations for achieving production through people.* Houston: Gulf Publishing, 1964.

W   Blake, R. R., Shepard, H. A. & Mouton, J. S. *Managing intergroup conflict in industry.* Houston: Gulf Publishing, 1964.

C   Blake, R. R., Sloma, R. L. & Mouton, J. S. The union-management intergroup laboratory: Strategy for resolving intergroup conflict. *Journal of Applied Behavioral Science,* 1965, *1,* 1, 25–57.

U,V, W,X   Blake, R. R. & Mouton, J. S. *Corporate excellence through grid organization development: A systems approach.* Houston: Gulf Publishing, 1968.

U   Blake, R. R. & Mouton, J. S. *The grid for sales excellence: Benchmarks for effective salesmanship.* New York: McGraw-Hill, 1970.

X   Blake, R. R. & Mouton, J. S. *How to assess the strengths and weaknesses of a business enterprise.* Austin, Tex.: Scientific Methods, Inc., 1972, 6 vols.

D,I   Blake, R. R. & Mouton, J. S. *Diary of an OD man.* Houston: Gulf Publishing, 1976.

U,V   Blansfield, M. G. Transactional analysis as a training intervention. In W. G. Dyer (Ed.), *Modern theory and method in group training.* New York: Van Nostrand Reinhold, 1972. Pp. 149–154.

Q   Cohen, A. M. & Smith, R. D. The critical-incident approach to leadership in training groups. In W. G. Dyer (Ed.), *Modern theory and method in group training.* New York: Van Nostrand Reinhold, 1972. Pp. 84–196.

I   *Commerce Today,* 2, April 3, 1972, 29.

A   Dickson, W. J. & Roethlisberger, F. J. *Counseling in an organization: A sequel to the Hawthorne researches.* Boston: Division of Research, Graduate School of Business Administration, Harvard University, 1966.

P   Flory, C. D. (Ed.) *Managers for tomorrow.* New York: The New American Library of World Literature, 1965.

I   Foegen, J. H. Ombudsman as complement to the grievance procedure. *Labor Law Journal,* May 1972, 23, 289–294.

F   Fordyce, J. J. & Weil, R. *Managing with people: A manager's handbook of organization development methods.* Reading, Mass.: Addison-Wesley, 1971.

B   Gibb, J. R. TORI theory: Consultantless team building. *Journal of Contemporary Business,* 1972, *1,* 3, 33–41.

F   Gould, M. I. Counseling for self-development. *Personnel Journal,* 1970, *49,* 3, 226–234.

K   Herman, S. M. A Gestalt orientation to organization development. In W. Burke (Ed.), *Contemporary organization development: Approaches and interventions.* Washington, D. C.: NTL Institute for Applied Behavioral Science, 1972.

S   Higdon, H. *The business healers.* New York: Random House, 1969.

G   Humble, J. W. *Improving business results.* Maidenhead, Berks.: McGraw-Hill, 1967.

N   Jaques, E. *The changing culture of a factory.* London: Tavistock, 1951.

U   Kepner, C. H. & Tregoe, B. B. *The rational manager.* New York: McGraw-Hill, 1965.

P   Krumboltz, J. D. (Ed.) *Revolution in counseling: Implications of behavioral science.* Boston: Houghton Mifflin, 1965.

R   Lazarus, S. *et al. Resolving business disputes: The potential of commercial arbitration.* New York: American Management Association, 1965.

S   Levinson, H., with Molinari, J. & Spohn, A. G. *Organizational diagnosis*. Cambridge, Mass.: Harvard University Press, 1972.

G   Likert, R. *New patterns of management*. New York: McGraw-Hill, 1961.

U   Likert, R. *The human organization, its management and value*. New York: McGraw-Hill, 1967.

Y   Lilienthal, D. E. *The journals of David E. Lilienthal*. Vol. IV. *The road to change, 1955–1959*. New York: Harper & Row, 1969.

R   Linke, W. R. The complexities of labor relations law. In R. F. Moore (Ed.), *Law for executives*. New York: American Management Association, 1968.

U   McGregor, D. *The human side of enterprise*. New York: McGraw-Hill, 1960.

U   Mouton, J. S. & Blake, R. R. *The marriage grid*. New York: McGraw-Hill, 1971.

Q   Robert, H. M. *Robert's rules of order* (newly revised). Glenview, Ill.: Scott, Foresman, 1970. First published, 1876.

G   Schein, E. H. *Process consultation: Its role in organization development*. Reading, Mass.: Addison-Wesley, 1969.

Y   Skinner, B. F. *Beyond freedom and dignity*. New York: Knopf, 1971.

S   Thompson, E. T. The upheaval at Philco. *Fortune*, February 1959, 113-116.

A   Watson, G. Nonverbal activities— why? when? how? In W. G. Dyer (Ed.), *Modern theory and method in group training*. New York: Van Nostrand Reinhold, 1972, Pp. 155–172.

T   Willson, F. M. G. Government departments. *Encyclopaedia Britannica*. Vol. 10. Chicago: Encyclopaedia Britannica, Inc., 1968.

2.2 The Current State of Planned Changing in Persons, Groups, Communities, and Societies

Kenneth D. Benne

Without discounting in any way the admirable clarity with which Blake and Mouton have mapped current practices in

This essay was written especially as a supplement to Selection 2.1 by Blake and Mouton. The "matrix" was designed to map and clarify various current practices and rationales in organizational development. This essay seeks to characterize and clarify the present state of planned change efforts in which the focus of the effort is upon some human system other than the organization, more particularly the bureaucratic organization.

the complex field of organizational diagnosis and development, I recognize at the outset that my task of mapping the terrain of planned changing outside the organizational setting is a more difficult one. I recognize further that my mapping will not achieve the elegance or completeness which Blake and Mouton have achieved.

The kinds of practices I am trying to categorize cover a wider spectrum of change targets, stretching from the human individual, through the small group and interpersonal relations, through intergroup relations, to which I have annexed the "community" as a local intersystem of group and organizational systems to the macrosystems of societies and cultures. The ideological element is probably stronger between identifiable streams of practice focused on individual changing than among various practitioners of organizational development. Certainly, the ideological element is much more visible in practices designed to stimulate and guide processes of community and societal changing. And there is probably more collegiality, more sharing of experimental results, more reading of each other's papers and journals, among practitioners of organizational development than among practitioners in any other part of the spectrum of planned changing.

Yet, though we can rightly be more dubious about the clarity of the results, the effort may be worth a try.

I. The Human Individual as the Target of Changing

A generation ago, most informed people would have identified two main forms of social practice, whose aim was deliberately to effect changes in human individuals. One form of practice was psychotherapy, the other education. At that time the two forms of practice seemed relatively easy to distinguish. In general, psychotherapy dealt with the treatment of pathologies and deviations from the norm. It was, therefore, reasonable to assume that the practice of psychotherapy should be carried on or at any rate supervised by specialists from the medical profession—psychiatrists. A division of labor was beginning to occur with nurses, social workers, occupational and physical therapists, and clinical psychologists getting into the therapeutic act. But the "therapeutic" or medical model was for the most part intact.

Education, on the other hand, was identified with the transmission of selected cognitive and skill elements, drawn from the cultural conserve, to "normal" human individuals, more particularly to those who were chronologically immature. This transmission process was designed to equip the individual with the knowledge and skills thought to be required in coping with his or her adult responsibilities as person, as citizen, and as a member of one vocational group or another. The site of education was the school and the classroom, though supervised experiences in field settings were included as part of vocational and professional education.

It is the breakdown of these relatively neat categories and institutions of education and psychotherapy that has led to the differentiation and proliferation of methodologies and technologies designed to facilitate individual changing which now confront the student and practitioner of planned changing. A brief examination of the critiques that have led to the breakdown of the walls between education and therapy may help us to understand the spate of "new" methodologies for individual changing which have followed and suggest a more apt basis for their classification.

There has been a revolt within the medical profession itself against the pathological or medical model of changing.[1] One set of objections to the pathological model is that it draws attention away from the life conditions and environmental stresses which have induced the individual difficulty or trauma. Resources, including the resources of health professionals, should be focused on changing the life

[1] Thomas Szasz, "The myth of mental illness," *American Psychologist*, 1960, *15*, 113, and R. D. Laing and A. Esterson, *Sanity, Madness and the Family* (New York: Basic Books, 1964), represent two quite different forms that revolt, from within the medical profession, against the domination of the pathological model in therapy has taken.

conditions and environmental stresses which induce individual difficulties in functioning. This critique often is phrased as a plea for a *preventive* rather than a therapeutic approach to health problems, for *positive* conceptions of health, particularly of mental health, rather than a negative conception of health as the absence of pathology. This approach, it should be noted, would draw a significant part of the energies of health professionals away from treatment and into processes of prevention. And the core of preventive interventions is a process of *education* and *re-education*. It is consistent with this approach to take treatment, rehabilitation, and re-education processes away from segregated hospital institutions and back into the families, neighborhoods, and work settings of the clients. This requires, of course, a redeployment and reorganization of professional persons and resources.

Another objection to the pathological model in therapy has been that it brings the stereotype of a disease entity between the professional helper and his or her client, be it a stereotype of "schizophrenic," "manic-depressive," or "character disorder." The helper is tempted to treat a disease entity, rather than to deal with a unique, holistic client as a person in all the complexities of his or her strengths, limitations, difficulties, and aspirations. This objection is often combined with a purpose of rehumanizing "treatment" relationships. Here, as elsewhere, stereotypy may obstruct the mutually growthful meeting of persons.

Related to these revolts within "therapy" are claims, supported by some evidence, that responsibility for therapy should be diffused from the psychiatrist and shared with all who have contact with the patient or client—nurses, social workers, psychologists, paraprofessionals, and, indeed, his or her peers—other patients and clients. This would redefine the role of the psychiatrist as counselor, educator, and re-educator to a diversified staff group. This idea is behind movements toward group psychotherapy and reaches its culmination in the idea of therapeutic community.[2]

Comparable revolts have been taking place, or at least are being advocated, on the educational side of the divide. A central object of criticism has been the transmissive model of education. This model, it is argued, diverts the attention of the educator from his or her client in his or her wholeness and uniqueness and introduces a standardization and rigidity into the curriculum which reduce the responsiveness of the school to the service of variegated learning needs and to the utilization of unanticipated learning opportunities. A model, alternative to a transmissive model, is often termed a model of personal growth or of personal and cultural renewal.

Here, as in therapy, the concept of the learning client as a whole person challenges the almost exclusive preoccupation of the traditional school with cognitive development and encourages the assumption of responsibility by the school for the affective and conative development of students as well. In other words, the subject matter of the school should include feelings, values, and interpersonal relations as well as facts, concepts, and intellectual skills. This kind of alternative school is sometimes named humanistic education. It is interesting to note a convergence at this point between the programs of such alternative schooling and preventive-oriented programs in mental health.

Again, as in the case of psychotherapy and the psychiatrist, the traditional centrality and essentiality of the teacher-pupil relationship have been questioned and diffusion and sharing of responsibility for

[2] See Maxwell Jones, *The Therapeutic Community* (New York: Basic Books, 1953), for a description of a pioneer attempt to create and utilize a therapeutic community.

help in learning called for. Not only the teacher but teacher aides and other paraprofessionals, other students—age peers, younger and older students—and community persons, and most of all the student himself or herself—come to share responsibility for the purposing, planning, and evaluation of learning projects. Here, as in the case of the psychiatrist in therapy, the teacher must change to include functions as consultant, team builder, and trainer to other human parts of learning teams within the scope of his or her responsibilities.

A criticism of the segregation of schools from the ongoing life around the schools is also implicit in the revolt against the transmissive model of schooling. On this view, field experiences for students of any and all ages become an expected part of the learning program. Extensions of educational opportunities to individuals at any age or juncture of living are also an implication of this alternative model of education. Finally, this view of education counters the preoccupation, which has characterized many recent "innovators" in schooling, with the elaboration and refinement of thing technologies—audiovisual and multimedia equipment, teaching machines and other "teacher-proof" electronic devices. The view does not oppose the use of such technological aids to learning. It does reassert the view of the educative process as centrally an interpersonal—a social—process.

It should now be clear that the traditional categories of "therapy" and "education" as ways of differentiating processes of individual changing have been breached and broken—deeply, in thought and aspiration, and significantly, though with great resistance, in patterns of practice. Significant "new" methodologies for aiding, stimulating, and supporting individual changing have emerged that are difficult or impossible to classify in traditional terms. Such methodologies are being utilized at present both in health centers and clinics and in "alternative schools." They are probably still practiced most frequently and fully in the "temporary systems" of "growth centers," human relations training laboratories and workshops, and programs of informal continuing education.

How can we classify these methodologies? They vary significantly in their conceptions of the human individual or of the aspect of the human individual that is seen as most strategic in processes of individual changing in our own period of human history. *I felt it convenient to note the aspect of the individual which each methodology seeks to support clients in rediscovering and reevaluating.* I realize I will do an injustice to the complexities of each methodology thus classified. In partial expiation for this injustice, I have noted a reference which includes a more adequate description of the methodology and its rationale.

I have selected representative instances to illustrate my subcategories rather than attempting a complete coverage. My selection has not been grounded in a value judgment that the ones chosen are "better" than those omitted. My basis of selection has been rather to identify the methodologies which are now "better known" both to me and to the general public.

a. Rediscovery and Reevaluation of the Self

Müller-Freienfels, in his history of early-twentieth-century psychology, noted that much "modern" psychology is a study of man without a psyche or self. This is a pardonable exaggeration which emphasizes the behavioristic cast of the main line of "academic psychology" in the first half of this century. There have been strong reactions against the "neglect" of the self by various clinical and humanistic psychologists in recent years. And some of the newer methodologies of individual changing seek to involve individuals in clarifying their self-concepts and self-images and in more fully understanding and affirming themselves as selves.

1) Rogerian counseling and its extension from a two-person setting into the encounter group clearly belongs in this classification. The effort is to create the conditions which allow free persons to learn about themselves, to perceive and affirm the clarified and undistorted image of self that emerges within the interchanges between the learner and the therapist and/or the members of the encounter group. The focus is on the client and his or her needs to learn and grow, not upon the propagation of the values and preferences of the therapist or facilitator.[3]

2) In Gestalt Therapy attention is focused, usually in the presence of other clients, if not in a developed group, upon the client's discovery and acceptance of his or her boundaries as a self as over against the boundaries of other selves. Great emphasis is placed upon each client discovering and owning, in the sense of assuming responsibility for, his or her own feelings and actions and disowning responsibility for the feelings and actions of others. Various ingenious exercises, including spontaneous drama and fantasy, are utilized in the achievement of the change objective.[4]

3) Transactional analysis is an outgrowth and simplification of Freudian analysis. Its practitioners regard the individual as a "family" of introjected selves, including an internalized father, mother, infantile child, growing-learning adult, and so on. When the internalized father, for example, is ascendant in an individual, the other in an interpersonal relationship becomes a child to that individual. Interpersonal relations are confused and strained by this kind of distortion of the other to fit the unconscious role-playing needs of the individual. The goal of changing is to lift the interpersonal games he or she plays into consciousness through interaction with others and interpretation of the interactions. Presumably, such consciousness reduces the compulsion of the individual to play interpersonal games and enables the individual to build and enact more authentic and reality-oriented relationships with others.[5]

4) The T-group, or Training group, was developed on the basis of ideas of self as a social emergent which characterize such social psychologies as those of Kurt Lewin, John Dewey, and George Herbert Mead. Selves emerge within social processes as biologic individuals incorporate significant memberships symbolically into their ways of functioning as differentiated members of a society. The first T-groups focused on helping persons to rediscover and reevaluate themselves as members of groups and of other interpersonal relationships as they helped to build an assemblage of strangers into a functioning group and reflected on their experiences in doing so. The original T-groups also were designed to help members learn experientially about small group development and processes, as we will note later. As clinical psychologists and psychiatrists came to work with T-groups, the emphasis on learning about group processes and membership was relaxed and a variant of T-groups, often called sensitivity groups, sought to focus the learning of members upon expanding awareness of their idiosyncratic selves.[6]

5) A variant learning group has been developed by Max Birnbaum under the name of "clarification group." The process of the clarification group is designed and

---

[3] See Carl R. Rogers, *Client-Centered Therapy* (Boston: Houghton Mifflin, 1951), and Carl R. Rogers, *Carl Rogers on Encounter Groups* (New York: Harper & Row, 1970).

[4] See Fritz Perls, *Gestalt Therapy Verbatim* (Lafayette, Calif.: Real People Press, 1969).

[5] Eric Berne, *Games People Play* (New York: Grove Press, 1964).

[6] See L. P. Bradford, J. Gibb, and K. D. Benne (Eds.), *T-Group Theory and Laboratory Method* (New York: Wiley, 1964).

directed to stimulate and support members in rediscovering and reevaluating their "social selves." This involves a reassessment by members of the influences of racial, ethnic, religious, age, and sex groups to which they belong or have belonged upon their ways of seeing, valuing, and thinking about their social worlds with emphasis upon the influence of these memberships upon their relations with members of other social and cultural groups. This method of self-study was designed originally to augment the self-objectivity of persons who work and live in multiracial, multiethnic, and multireligious community settings. It belongs also, therefore, in the later section of this essay which deals with training and consultation in intergroup and community relations.[7]

6) The last methodology to be noted in this subsection actually unites an emphasis upon the rediscovery and reevaluation of the self with an emphasis upon the rediscovery and reevaluation of the body. This is the "personal growth laboratory" originated and developed by John and Joyce Weir. The laboratory is designed to support participants in achieving self-differentiation and in developing guidelines for their continuing *psychic, somatic,* and *spiritual* development. Methods include bodily movement, fantasies, and spontaneous dramatization and ritualization of significant life events. It seems clear that the Weirs work with a biosocial concept of the individual and of individual growth.[8]

b. Rediscovery and Reevaluation of the Body[9]

In another connection, I wrote as follows:

My social self, as I along with others construct and imagine it, may or may not include my body. But, in a healthy person, the body is lifted up into membership within the inner society of selves and speaks openly and unashamedly, though in its own language in the dialogues through which decisions are made and personal integrity is sought and achieved. This is to accomplish that naturalistic resurrection of the body for which Norman Brown pleads in his *Life Against Death!*[10]

It is the "naturalistic resurrection of the body" to which another set of methodologies concerned with changing human individuals is devoted. Many persons, it is believed, lose touch with their bodies, lose awareness of their bodies in the mazes of their shame and guilt-ridden, value-laden social-symbolic worlds which they must negotiate in living. In the interest of personal wholeness and integrity, the body must be rediscovered and affirmed.

1) I have already mentioned the emphasis in the Weirs' Personal Growth Laboratory on expanding and deepening awareness of bodily processes, both autonomic processes and cerebrally controlled

---

[7] See Max Birnbaum, "The Clarification Group," chapter 15 in Benne, Bradford, Gibb, and Lippitt (Eds.), *The Laboratory Method of Changing and Learning* (Palo Alto, Calif.: Science and Behavior Books, 1975).

[8] John Weir, "The Personal Growth Laboratory," chapter 13 in Benne, Bradford, Gibb, and Lippitt (ibid.)

[9] I have found difficulty in fitting the methodology of individual changing through behavior modification into my classification. It is an application of behaviorist learning theory to processes of unlearning dysfunctional behaviors and of learning more functional behaviors in a wide range of practical settings. It is built primarily upon the theory of learning as operant conditioning originated by B. F. Skinner. It clearly rejects a "pathological" model for explaining dysfunctional behavior and eschews "consciousness" and "inner processes and structures" like self as significant factors in processes of learning and relearning. It seeks to extinguish dysfunctional responses and to instate functional responses to environmental stimuli by programming the rewards which are presented along with the stimuli. See B. F. Skinner, *Beyond Freedom and Dignity* (New York: Knopf, 1971), for an explication of the rationale of behavior modification as a methodology of individual changing.

[10] Kenneth D. Benne, "Something There Is That Doesn't Love a Wall," *Journal of Applied Behavioral Science*, Vol. I., No. 4 (1965), 334.

processes, through methods which involve both relaxation and concentration upon feeling and listening to the body.

2) A methodology known as bioenergetics, strongly influenced by the organismic psychology of Wilhelm Reich, has been developed to help persons expand awareness of their own bodies. It also coaches persons in becoming aware of the bodily correlates of their psychic functions and dysfunctions and, through such awareness, toward altering dysfunctional aspects of their behavior.[11]

3) A most powerful tool for facilitating awareness of bodily proceses is biofeedback. Information about their own bodily functioning is fed back to individuals by converting the electromagnetic waves which accompany organ functioning into forms which they can receive through their own senses. Although biofeedback is in an experimental stage as a method for the treatment of bodily disorders, one observed result is of particular behavioral significance. Individuals can come, through biofeedback, to control consciously processes which are ordinarily experienced as involuntary, as under control of the autonomic nervous system—blood pressure, heart beat, and so forth.

This ability to control involuntary bodily processes achieves the same ends which Yogins, Zen Buddhists, and others had sought to achieve and had in some measure achieved through the "nontechnological" means of meditation, relaxation, and "mental" concentration. The frontiers of "biofeedback" research and practice have recently been intertwined with methodologies for rediscovering and reevaluating the transpersonal or spiritual dimension of human functioning.[12]

[11] See Alexander Lowen, *The Betrayal of the Body* (New York: Macmillan, 1967).

[12] See, for example, G. S. Schwartz, "Biofeedback, Self-Regulation and the Patterning of Physiological Processes," *American Scientist*, Vol. 63, No. 3 (June 1975), 314–324; and J. Kamiya, L. V. DiCara, T. X. Barber, N. E. Miller, D.

c. Rediscovery and Reevaluation of the Transpersonal

Along with the penchant for naturalistic, biosocial explanations of individual development and dynamics, which has flourished in secularized academic and "enlightened" circles in modern Western and Westernized civilizations, belief in a transpersonal, spiritual reality in which human individuals do and/or should participate has coexisted in Western civilization and more emphatically in parts of Eastern cultures as well. And "methodologies" for individual changing—prayer, meditation, mystical experience, religious conversion—have developed concurrently with this belief.

With loss of confidence in established ways of education and therapy in America and other parts of "the West," already noted and described, it is not surprising that methodologies for guiding persons into rediscovery and reevaluation of the transpersonal and spiritual dimensions of their lives have emerged, along with others which have emphasized rediscovery and reevaluation of self and body. Jungian therapy and analysis and some forms of pastoral counseling were precursors of these developments in Europe and America.

In general, two main kinds of methodological developments concerned with planfully guiding individuals into rediscovery and reevaluation of the transpersonal are now apparent in America. The first is an outgrowth from indigenous "Western" ways of thinking about the spiritual dimension of life. The second is a more or less conscious acculturation and adaptation

Shapiro, and J. Stoyva (Eds.), *Biofeedback and Self-Control: An Aldine Reader on the Regulation of Bodily Processes and Consciousness* (Chicago: Aldine-Atherton, 1971).

of "Eastern" modes of spiritual discovery, ascesis, and development.[13]

1) The best-known example of the first kind of development is probably psychosynthesis, a methodology of therapy and education originated by Robert Assagioli. Assagioli is a medical doctor and psychiatrist who became convinced that the human unconscious was inhabited not only by repressed instincts and emotions but by a superconscious as well. Assagioli does not deny the "reality" of the "lower" unconscious but has sought ways of helping clients to gain access to, to become conscious of the "higher" unconscious as well in growing toward fuller self-realization and self-actualization. The methods of psychosynthesis include meditation, inner dialogues, guided imaginative fantasies, and interpersonal encounter. These methods are unified around the notion of a higher self at the core of each individual that can direct the harmonious development of all aspects of personality. Beyond personal synthesis lies access to creativity, transpersonal experience, and spiritual development.[14]

2) The second kind of methodology is more difficult to illustrate with one example. Yogin techniques and techniques from Zen Buddhism have found their way fragmentarily into various approaches to stimulating and supporting personal growth. In its more fully developed forms, it often embodies a radical disjunction between the individual "ego" which involves individuals in falsely ascribing "reality" to sensate and material objects and events that are inherently "illusory" and "Self" which is achieved through union with a transpersonal principle that is inherently "real." The approach of the ARICA Institute and its founder, Oscar Ichazo, may be taken as representative of this latter point of view.[15]

II. The Small Group as Medium and Target of Changing

It is not accidental that the small, face-to-face group has come to occupy a strategic place as a *medium* of planned changing in recent years. This is true for several reasons. The small group is a link between the individual and the larger social system of which he or she is a part. This is readily apparent in a formal organization, e.g., an army. The individual soldier belongs to a small group, a squad or a tank or bomber crew. This is, social-psychologically, his or her link to the larger army. And similarly with the student in a classroom which links him or her with the school-building system and in turn with the larger school system. The same is usually true, though not so obviously, of an individual's linkage with less formally organized systems like communities and racial and ethnic groupings. Thus the small group is potentially a medium for influencing both the persons who are its members and the larger system of which their group is a part.

Larger social systems ordinarily depend on small groups in formulating and maturing their policies and programs, whether the small group is a committee, cabinet, or board. Thus, change in the composition and functioning of such a

[13] Some attention has been given to developing a distinctively indigenous American way of gaining access to the transpersonal dimension of human life. This is illustrated by interest in the ethnographic reports by Carlos Castaneda on the spiritual powers of the Amerindian wise man Don Juan. See, for example, Carlos Castaneda, *Journey to Ixtlan: The Lessons of Don Juan* (New York: Simon and Schuster, 1972).

[14] See Roberto Assagioli, *Psychosynthesis: A Manual of Principles and Techniques* (New York: Viking, 1971).

[15] Sam Keen, " 'We Have No Desire to Strengthen the Ego or Make It Happy': A Conversation About Ego Destruction with Oscar Ichazo," *Psychology Today*, July 1973.

strategic small group may produce change also in the wider social system which is dependent upon that group for guidance and direction.

Human individuals develop value orientations originally through internalizing the norms of small groups on which they depend, notably families. Changes in value orientations of individuals may be accomplished by their seeking and finding significant membership in a small group with norms that are different in some respects from the normative orientation these individuals bring to the group.

Finally, whatever else it is, a small group is an organized social system. Individual members can learn about the general characteristics of social systems directly and experientially by becoming aware of the social system characteristics of a small group to which they belong.

a) For all of these reasons, the small group, as its structure and dynamics have recently become an object of psychological study and research, has come to be a strategic contemporary medium in programs both of personal and of social changing. It can, therefore, be argued that a core part of the training of change agents, whatever their specialized target of changing—person, organization, community, or macrosystem—is training in the diagnosis and management of small group processes. Such training takes two principal forms in contemporary America.

1) The first, the T-group, has been discussed in the preceding section as a methodology of individual changing. It was noted in that discussion that the T-group was originally used as a medium for learning experientially about the formation, processes, and development of small groups. And it is still used for this purpose in the training of change agents. In such training programs T-group experiences are ordinarily supplemented by conceptual seminars and skill-practice sessions, in which skills of group diagnosis

and intervention are practiced, followed by feedback of observed effects, and analysis and evaluation.[16]

2) The second form of group training follows what is frequently called the "Tavistock Model." This model for developing awareness and understanding of group structures, cultures, and processes has its intellectual roots in the psychoanalytical work of Melanie Klein and W. W. Bion. It is ordinarily conducted in a conference setting with from 50 to 70 participants. Participants experience group and organizational processes and structures in small study groups of 9 to 13 members, in the total conference group, and in an intergroup exercise. Their experiences are interpreted by the use of Bion's categories of emotional group states and other psychoanalytic and sociological concepts. The goal is an understanding of group behavior and of the influence of structure on behavior rather than the development of change-oriented strategies as in the T-group.[17]

b) Both forms of training just discussed create temporary groups under "laboratory" conditions in order for group members to learn experientially about small group formation and functioning. But ongoing groups with an indefinite life tenure may also be taken as targets of changing. Blake and Mouton, in their D/D matrix, discuss such change efforts as they occur in organizational development under the name of "team-building." "Team-building" may be applied to various work units, staffs, and boards in formal organizations. And similar team-building efforts

---

[16] For a discussion of skill practice and development see Eva Schindler-Rainman and Ronald O. Lippitt, "Awareness Learning and Skill Development," chapter 9, in Benne, Bradford, Gibb, and Lippitt, op. cit.

[17] See W. W. Bion, *Experiences in Groups* (London: Tavistock Publications, 1961), and Boris Astrachan, "The Tavistock Model of Laboratory Training," chapter 14, in Benne, Bradford, Gibb, and Lippitt, op. cit.

are used in planning councils, committees, commissions, and task forces at the community and macrosystem level as well.

1) A distinctive approach to group changing is represented by Virginia Satir's work with families. Family members are induced to objectify and analyze patterns of interaction in the functioning of the family as a small group. They are supported in trying out and evaluating alternative patterns where established patterns are seen to lead to unsatisfactory effects.[18]

III. Planned Changing at the Intergroup Relations and Community Level

Many Americans carry an ideal image of local community in their heads which may becloud a clear view of the realities of the contemporary community—urban, suburban, or rural. The ideal image is of a relatively undifferentiated neighborhood, with people, who know each other and who talk the same language, getting together periodically in a New England town meeting or its equivalent to thrash out differences about the public business, to levy taxes on themselves, and to select leaders from among themselves to carry out their mandates and to account for their stewardship to the people at their next public meeting.

Now, all of us "know" that local communities are no longer like that, even small-town and rural communities. We know also that the idealized image of the ways people can get together to direct and handle their public business is not practicable under contemporary conditions. Yet the values implicit in the ideal image, values that account for its hold on the

mentalities of many Americans, may still be valid, though the ways in which they can be translated into practice must be much more complicated and vastly different from the pattern of a town meeting and of selectmen directly responsive and responsible to that meeting.

These values are easy to state, however difficult they are to actualize in public practice. People affected by public policies and plans should participate in making them and in evaluating their consequences as they are acted upon. People should be informed about public issues and prepared to make intelligent choices and decisions with respect to them. Conflicts in interest among people should be confronted publicly and worked through to a viable and acceptable "trade off," if not consensus. Public officials should be responsible and accountable to the people who have endowed them with their authority. The initiation of changes should come from "volunteers" as well as from professionals and technicians, however much "volunteers" may need the services of professionals and technicians in converting their ideas for change into actuality. These, if I am not mistaken, are the values that lie behind most programs and projects in community development in America today.

We can get a mental hold on the complexity of contemporary communities, especially urbanized communities, by noting that they are differentiated both areally and functionally. A community, by definition, has spatial boundaries, though these may be difficult to define for purposes of planning and development. For example, the public safety of a community may be in the hands of a number of separate police forces—city, metropolitan, state, and federal. The boundaries of educational, public health, and judicial districts rarely coincide. Within its spatial boundaries, subareas may be specialized for particular kinds of land use under zoning laws and regulations—industrial, business, residen-

[18] Virginia Satir, *Conjoint Family Therapy* (Palo Alto, Calif.: Science and Behavior Books, 1967).

tial, and so on. Residential subareas are often differentiated by race, by ethnicity, and by social class.

Students of local communities recognize various lines of functional differentiation as well. These include religious, educational, recreational, welfare, health (physical and mental), political, economic, mass media, public safety, and cultural subcommunities. Each of these subcommunities is more or less separately organized. And indeed some subcommunities are divided by many separate internal organizations, for example, the religious subcommunity.

Efforts to actualize the values inherent in community development programs and projects must take these social-psychological realities of areal and functional differentiation into account.

a) It helps to map the kinds of planned changing going on in contemporary communities to recognize that much community development is organizational development. It is easy to recognize that the functional subcommunities do their many kinds of work through organizations. Some organizations are governmentally controlled and supported, others are privately supported and funded, others draw funding from both nongovernmental and governmental sources. And other organizations follow areal lines—neighborhood improvement associations, area planning councils, and so on.

And just as business and industrial organizations, confronted with the challenges of changing personnel, changing markets, and turbulent and unpredictable environments, have been seeking and, in some measure, finding ways of planning for change in their internal and external relations, so have nonbusiness and nonindustrial community organizations. All of Blake and Mouton's 25 varieties of organizational diagnosis and development are probably being tried here and there by welfare departments, churches, temples, schools, hospitals, Campfire Girls, Junior Leagues, area planning councils, labor

unions, television stations, political parties, War Resisters' Leagues, police forces, etc., etc., as well as by business and industrial organizations. Methodologies, of course, need to be adapted to differing organizational sizes, purposes, traditions, and degrees of sophistication. Blake and Mouton's analysis serves admirably in mapping this organizational aspect of community development.

b) But how does community development differ from organizational development, more particularly when a community change project or program requires interagency, interareal and interprofessional collaboration, as most significant change projects and programs do? Eva Schindler-Rainman has specified seven differences between community development and organizational development:[19]

> 1. In the community, the process is always *intergroup*, that is, between groups and organizations who must collaborate on given projects, while in the organization the process is within one organization. . . .
>
> 2. The second difference has to do with *loyalty*. Within the geographic community there are many loyalties to be dealt with, loyalties to several different organizations; often loyalty to the geographic community itself; loyalty to subcommunities; and loyalty to a variety of causes. In the organizational context there may be loyalty to the organization, and perhaps to one's department or superior, but it is a different kind of thing than the many different "loyalty hats" people wear within a community.
>
> 3. A third factor is the *commitment* factor. In an organization, part of the commitment, if an employee has it, is due to the fact that he is paid in money for his services. Commitment to community causes is often of a different variety. There may be strong religious, ethical, or philosophical commitments to particular causes or particular projects.
>
> 4. Another difference is that in the

[19] Eva Schindler-Rainman, "Community Development," chapter 19 in Benne, Bradford, Gibb, and Lippitt, op. cit., pp. 447–448.

community one almost always works with both *professionals and volunteers*, while that is not true in most organizations.

5. Also, the *multiple agenda* of communities need to be considered. While there might be the question of child care centers and improved education within the community, there are many other agenda. There will be many other kinds of things equally important to various people, all the way from urban-suburban planning to passing the bonds for the water district, to electing new board of education members, to rapid transit plans. Within the organization, though there may be multiple agenda, their extent is not nearly so vast or complicated as those of the total geographic community.

6. Another difference is that often in community development projects the *efforts* of people, both professioinal and volunteer, *are voluntary*; that is, people can be asked, requested, but not required, to come to meetings, and participate in a planning or action process. But in an organization it is possible for management to require participation of employees. The participation may or may not be willing, but it can be required. This is much harder to do in a community setting.

7. Another possible difference is that in community development there is a maximum effort to include *different sectors* of community population, and this is probably a more various group to draw from than would be found in any organization, even if all the different sectors of an organization were included in the development and . . . planning processes.

I will comment on current methodologies of changing in relation to two of the differences which Schindler-Rainman has identified and in relation to another aspect of current community development practice which she has not discussed.

1) "In the community, the [developmental] process is always intergroup." And among the intergroup relations that must be dealt with and handled are relations between racial groups, ethnic groups, and religious groups. These relationships are often marked by strong feelings of fear and hostility and by historically imbedded stereotypes. As we noted in "Planned Change in America" in Chapter I, boundaries between ethnic and racial groups became more sharply articulated in the 1960s in America. Identification with such groups became more closely intertwined with the personal identities of many of their members.

Rational collaboration in community planning and action between such groups and their members is virtually impossible unless methodologies can be found to develop understanding of these nonrational factors within the members and leaders of such groups. We discussed Max Birnbaum's clarification group earlier as a way of helping individuals to rediscover and affirm their own distinctive "social selves" and in the same process to understand and appreciate the distinctive and different social selves of members of other groups. This methodology has shown promise in training both professionals and volunteer, indigenous leaders who live and work in racially, ethnically, and religiously mixed community settings. For this purpose, clarification group training is conducted in a residential, "community development laboratory" with a mixed intergroup population. Clarification group experience is supplemented by conceptual inputs and by community diagnostic and planning activities.

Clarification group experiences have also been used successfully, in modified form, in actual community settings torn by interracial and interethnic conflicts, in laying the groundwork for intergroup participation in resolving the conflicts.[20]

2) "Another difference is that in the community one almost always works with both professionals and volunteers." The "ideal image" of community life with

[20] See Thomas J. Cottle, "Strategy for Change," *Saturday Review*, September 20, 1969, for a description and evaluation of one such use of the methodology.

which we began this section, stressed the *voluntary* character of the initiation, control, and evaluation of community changes by the people of the community. While this image is idealized, it reflects an historical reality in American life. Local problems were probably solved more by volunteer local citizen initiative and effort in small-town and rural America than in any other nation. There was less dependence on centralized initiatives and directives to induce and direct changes in local community life than in other nations.

While this tradition of volunteer effort never died completely in America, it was more and more restricted as various public services came increasingly to be delivered to people through the agency of complex and bureaucratized organizations and as the management and control of these organizations were increasingly turned over to paid and specially trained professionals. This was the trend in education, in churches, in the delivery of health services, in the distribution of public welfare, and in public safety. Volunteers tended to work more and more under the control of technically trained professionals, even in many of the volunteer boards and councils which were nominally in control of community agencies and organizations.

Some public-spirited citizens who were committed to the value of voluntary initiative and effort in American community life documented, deplored, and criticized this trend. But it was the populist protest movements of the 1960s which decelerated and perhaps (it is too early to say) reversed the trend. The unresponsiveness of established agencies and organizations to client and consumer needs, the "elitist" attitudes of professionals toward clients, the lack of popular participation in the direction of agencies on which people's lives depended were charges leveled against schools, churches, health and welfare agencies, and police forces among others. Some changes in structural arrangements to facilitate popular participation in community agencies and organizations have been made in response to protests and demands—decentralized "community" schools, "community" controlled health clinics, lay councils in churches, citizens' review boards for police forces, etc., etc.

But if such structural arrangements are to be maintained, extended, and made to work, programs of training and re-education for both volunteers and professionals in new, collaborative ways of working and relating must be planned, carried through, evaluated, and replanned. Such efforts are currently under way in many communities and under many auspices, though few would say that they are now adequate to their difficult task.[21]

3) I have suggested the multiplicity of community organizations which currently complicate processes of community-wide planning and action but which do serve as channels for getting a hearing for their members' interests and viewpoints into the councils of the community. But with all this multiplicity of organizations, there are numbers of people in most communities whose interests and views are not articulated or organized and who exert virtually no proactive influence in processes of community policy-making and planning, even though their lives are affected by the policies and plans which others make. Such people are the poor, members of racial and ethnic minorities, homosexuals and other deviates, and sometimes women, the old and the young. They have often internalized majority attitudes toward themselves as incapable of participating actively and openly in

[21] See Eva Schindler-Rainman and Ronald Lippitt, *The Volunteer Community: Creative Use of Human Resources* (Washington, D. C.: Center for a Voluntary Society, 1971), for a discussion of current methodologies for empowering volunteer efforts of various sorts and for re-educating professionals to support and collaborate with volunteer initiative and assumption of responsibility.

public decision-making. They feel power-less to influence other people or their environments in any significant way. We noted earlier the effort of liberation movements to alter the attitudes of such persons by supporting them in defining and publicly asserting their own needs and worth and in altering their self-defeating images of themselves.

IV. Planned Changing in Macrosystems

The uses of methodologies of planned changing, as we have defined it, in macrosystems—for example, in changing national policies or cultural patterns or in resolving issues between nations—are very much less frequent and, therefore, less differentiated than in change programs and projects targeted to persons, small groups, organizations, and local commu-nities.

This may be in part due to the preference of practitioners of planned changing for a clinical model of applied social science over an engineering model, to use Gould-ner's distinction.[22] It is easier to work "clinically" with even a large organization or community than with a nation or an international complex.

But I doubt if the limited penetration of planned changing into macrosystems is mainly due to the preference or orientation of change agent practitioners. Organiza-tional development programs have been conducted in a number of departments and agencies of national government in the U.S.A. and in other nations as well. And methodologies of planned changing are widely used in in-house training and consultation programs of staff develop-ment in many units of state and federal

governments. Most of these uses have been undertaken in efforts to improve internal communications, work satisfac-tion, and productivity. They have not led to differentiations of methodologies be-yond those noted in Blake and Mouton's matrix and in my survey. And they have not penetrated into processes of crucial policy and decision-making.

I suspect that the limited access of our sort of agents of planned change to crucial national and international meetings is rather due to deeply entrenched traditional attitudes and practices of governmental and intergovernmental policy-makers. Their strategies of changing tend to be power-coercive, rather than normative-re-educa-tive, to use Chin and Benne's distinction. Law and administrative and judicial decree are traditionally power-coercive instru-ments. Those who influence the making of laws and decrees work from carefully prepared positions. The process of ex-change between "positions" tends to follow an adversary model of attack and defense. And the outcome, if the power behind various "positions" is fairly equal, is at best a compromise, not a creative synthesis which involves the meeting and merging of minds and interests into some new common view which is commonly acceptable and which could not have been formulated by any member or representa-tive in advance of meeting and delibera-tion. It is the *mutually re-educative* processes out of which creative syntheses emerge upon which normative-re-educative strat-egists of changing basically depend. The use of such strategies requires of partici-pants openness, trust, and a willingness to make themselves vulnerable to the influence of those who oppose them. The entrenched methodologies of governmen-tal and intergovernmental policy-making are premised upon a distrust of those very qualities of exchange. Until the tragic wastefulness of human resources implicit in and consequent upon present processes of policy-making comes home to those in

[22] Alvin W. Gouldner, "Explorations in Applied Social Science," *Social Problems*, Vol. 3, No. 3, January 1956, pp. 173–181.

government, there will be little openness to seeking and developing alternative processes.

1) Meanwhile, it has been found that persons can experience and gain insight into the dynamics and development of macrosystems under laboratory conditions. This can be accomplished by setting conditions in a conference which lead to human phenomena analogous to, if not isomorphic with, those that develop historically in nations. Those who experience the phenomena can reflect upon their experiences and extract learnings from them that are applicable to their choices and functioning as citizens within the politico-economic scene. "History" can be put upon a humanly encompassable and observable stage.

Max Pages has described and analyzed the experiences that developed in a human relations laboratory in France when the usual initial structures of subgroupings were not provided and participants and staff accepted the task of building a miniature society from the ground up and of extracting learnings from their experiences.[23] Comparable experiences have been conducted in Denmark, in England, and in the United States. Perhaps a strategic step would be to recruit persons high in positions of governmental and intergovernmental policy-making for participation in such laboratories.[24]

2) Some attempts to use methods of planned changing in actual situations of transnational conflict have been reported. One of these was a study of groups of representatives of Ethiopia and Eritrea, who met with applied behavioral scientists in trying to settle a long-standing dispute about national boundaries and to try different and, hopefully, more effective ways of settling such disputes. Methods of collaborative management of conflict, developed in organizational development studies, were employed.[25]

Another reported experiment was to test the applicability of and results of T-group methods in an extended meeting in Israel of a group composed of Israeli and Arab members.[26]

Although the results of such experiments are in no way definitive, and though they have led to no differentiations in methods of practice, they are promising enough to warrant further efforts to extend methodologies of planned changing into the international field.

---

as a way of anticipatory try-out, practice, and revision of plans where a try-out in the "real" situation is seen as too costly or dangerous. See Wiliam A. Gamson, *SIMSOC: Simulated Society* (New York: Free Press, 1969), for a discussion of simulation methodologies.

Simulation is, of course, akin to psychodramatic and sociodramatic methodologies which were pioneered in psychotherapy and action training by J. L. Moreno. In these methodologies, human situations and difficulties are not only talked about but are dramatically acted out to provide rich "inner" and "outer" behavioral data, which, when analyzed, often lead to vivid, convincing, and applicable insights and learnings for the participants. See J. L. Moreno, *Psychodrama* (Beacon, New York: Beacon House, Inc., 1946). For a concise survey of current developments in psychodrama, sociodrama, and role-playing, see Hilarion Petzold, 'Psychodrama and Role-Playing," chapter 16 in Benne, Bradford, Gibb, and Lippitt, op. cit.

[23] Max Pages, "The Flexible Structures Laboratory," chapter 17 in Benne, Bradford, Gibb, and Lippitt, op. cit.

[24] Such experiences are analogous to simulation techniques which have been developed for research and training purposes in organizational and community settings not accessible for field experimentation. Simulation can also be used

[25] Richard E. Walton, "A Problem-Solving Workshop on Border Conflicts in Eastern Africa," *The Journal of Applied Behavioral Science*, Vol. 7, pp. 453—489.

[26] Martin Lakin, in collaboration with Jacob Lomrantz and Morton S. Lieberman, *Arab and Jew in Israel* (Washington, D.C.: NTL Institute, 1969).

II

Diagnostics of Planned Change

3
Systems

"Systems analysis" is a tool of the mind for observing, diagnosing, and intervening in the complex web of interdependencies which must be taken into account in processes of planned change. The articles in this chapter represent the technical use of the concept of system; they avoid the error of reification, that is, making "the system" into an active causal or resisting agent in the social dynamics of change.

Systems vary in size, complexity, and concreteness. The unit size may be an individual, a small group, an organization, a community, a nation-state, or indeed the world. As we become more acquainted with a given system and as more and more diagnostic frameworks of analysis are forged by the theorist, researcher, and practitioner, the limitless complexity of more and more elements and aspects to take into account in a system analysis has to be cut back to the practitioner's ability to handle no more than a few at a time.

The concrete organizational systems encountered in industry, in education, in health and social services, and in justice are treated as similar in systems dynamics; yet there are major differences between them and unique characteristics of each. In comparing or locating a system we suggest six dimensions representing differences that determine the system analysis:

(1) The "goals" of organizational systems can be assessed for the degree of their clarity-ambiguity, simplicity-diversity, and localization-diffuseness of responsibility. For example, school systems, compared to industrial systems, have ambiguous, diverse, and diffuse goals, with attendant consequences for evaluation of the effectiveness of the school system. The specificity of methods and means for achieving the goals are also relatively ambiguous, diverse, and diffuse. Social service systems too vary along similar dimensions.

(2) The degree of interdependence of parts of the system varies greatly. Industrial organizations, and the human body as a system, have a relatively high degree of interdependence of the parts, and an identifiable relationship to the environment. On the other extreme of loose interdependency, there is the despairing wail by an exasperated college president: "The college is a collection of rugged individualists held together by a common struggle over parking spaces." The processes of resource allocation, budgeting, and the exercise of influence, power, and authority may be diffuse and not differentiated in location of responsibility.

(3) The degree of internal structural differentiation may vary from simple role differentiation to highly complex and hierarchical functional segregation of jobs and specialities. The processes of a face-to-face small group as the ideologically preferred way of functioning have been applied to organizations as part of the struggle in creating and maintaining organizational systems embodying human values. The use of the small group analysis has led to blind spots about hierarchies and segmentation.

These dimensions have led to the label of the sociotechnical systems, or the sociotechnical approach to systems. In this approach the issues of goals, the means most appropriate for achieving these goals, and the human and social relationships suffusing these technical activities have become the mode of analyzing industrial organizations, with attempts to apply these to educational, mental health and social service systems as well. Although once used to indicate the necessity of human beings obeying the rational dictates of the technical systems, there are now efforts to give primacy to how the human and social systems can affect the creation of the technical systems not only of its means but also of its goals.

Decentralization into subsystems, creation of parallel and highly autonomous systems within the larger system, such as alternative schools or satellite operations in industry, and the creation of new interstitial systems such as coordinating councils, or new consortia, collaboratives or cooperatives for accomplishing tasks are new forms of systems.

(4) The degree of vulnerability to outside pressures varies significantly. Vulnerability is highly characteristic of public and secondary educational systems, and social service systems. These systems incorporate the ideologically valued form of client and community control. There is required a response to short-run demands or pressures which may be incompatible with the long-range goals of the system.

(5) Time perspective. Systems vary in the degree to which they are fixed in their dynamics around periodicity of activities and processes. Educational systems have been rigidified with the time calendar and its attendant processes. In addition, each system's development and growth over time phases and periods vary according to distinctive system properties and to historically differentiated institutional systems.

(6) Stability and resistance to change. Practitioners approach a system in terms of its readiness or resistance to change. The degree of interdependence, differentiation, and boundary vulnerability are bases for the analysis of stability and resistance to change.

Systems analysis may also be applied to the analysis of selected segments of a concrete system, such as the communications, power, or value subsystems.

Practitioners have increased need for understanding and coping with the environment of the system as interdependence has increased and rigid boundaries have loosened. Essay 3.1, "The Utility of Models of the Environment of Systems for Practitioners," shows the ways in which the environment of a system may be viewed and what particular structures of the environment are of use to the practitioner. Managing the environment of systems is an increasingly difficult task. Chin shows how the turbulent environment and the future perspective toward the environment may be differentiated into an articulated turbulent environment. The essay points to the importance of doing so lest agents of planned change plan only for reactions to turbulent, unpredictable, and swooping forces. Terreberry's article "The Evolution of Organizational Environments" (6.2) also details the concept of turbulent environment in Chapter 6.

Klein's article, 'Some Notes on the Dynamics of Resistance to Change: The Defender Role," offers a perspective on resistance to change. He suggests that what the practitioner sees as resistance to change may well be the testing of the thrust of the change by members of the system. After all, not all proposed changes are equally valuable, and some persons must perform roles in the system as the gatekeepers of standards of acceptability. Klein reminds us that the change agent may often define change in such ways that those who do not agree are seen as blind resisters of change. It is as if the change agent is saying, "We have values; the clients have psychological mechanisms." It seems more appropriate to view the occasion as an opportunity of working with the internal roles of the system, including those who defend the status quo, to foster mutually desirable change.

The ways in which practitioners see how constituent elements of a human system are put together shape the approaches to dealing with forces and expected resistances to change. It is proposed here that practitioners may find an economical set of ideas and concepts which organizes a number of perplexing and disorderly cacophonies, alters the mind-set of the change agent (which itself could well be the most major intervention possible) and points up bases for evaluating the effects of contemplated interventions. With such conceptual schemas seemingly useful for all occasions and all settings and which mold the reality of the perceiver and function in judging the actions to be undertaken, we do need some caution. Systems concepts comprehend stability of what exists and thus guide the approaches to change and changing. Do such functional approaches to system dynamics tend to be conservative and justificatory of the status quo? We don't think so when systems analysis is used to uncover the tensions of goals and realities and do not preclude or hide the normative evaluations which must be made by the members of the systems and by the change agent as well.

3.1 The Utility of Models of the Environments of Systems for Practitioners

Robert Chin

Organized models for the analysis of the environment of a system are increasingly necessary for the rapidly changing and interdependent world of the practitioner of planned change. Policy-makers, front-line practitioners, strategists, futurists, systems theorists, and planners regularly do make use of conceptions of environment because the operations of a system are intermeshed with the features of its environment. (*Illustrations:* "The person's high ego strength will cope with whatever social pressures he encounters." "The school board exists in a hostile environment." "Our organization must not only react, but must anticipate the social revolutions in its environment." "Our markets are shifting." "Change the environment, not the person." "Future shock." "We must train teachers to teach kids to live in a world 80 years off.") The social environment is forcefully impactful, and must be reacted to in deliberate ways. Are there different models of the environment,

models with common dynamics? What are some of the useful models that can guide the observations, diagnoses, and possible interventions about the environment and its impacts on the systems called individual, group, organization, or community?

The first part of this article reviews the system-environment relationships; the second examines conceptual models of what I shall call textures of and clusterings in the environment; the third identifies selected contents of environments; and the last part suggests some ways for practitioners to use the proposed conceptions.

I. System-Environment Relations

Contemporary systems feel anguish over the loss of control of the "outside" forces. Worse yet, these outside forces are confusing and changing and arise from very distant and at times unknown origins. Impacts strike unexpectedly, frequently, and are unaccompanied by clear alternatives of problem-solving or adaptive responses by the system. In short, the environment causes turbulent and acute effects on the individual, group, organization, and community. The supercharged reality of these dynamics is a constant theme of social commentators. The responses of a planned change practitioner, whether internal or external manager or facilitator-consultant to a system and its environment, require an organized set of models of types, structures and dynamics, and conceptions for managing the environment and its relation to a system in order to develop rational approaches. An effective strategy and thought model for planned change is dependent upon several factors: the selection of the target unit as a system (person, group, organization, community); the location of the boundary defining what is a part of the system and what is in the environment; the ability to analyze the environment in orderly fashion; the intervention theory, practices, and needed professional competencies for changing the system or the environment; the models used for the system—its interrelations and its development, direction, and form—and the assumed directions of flow of causal forces of the system and of its environment.

The operational definition of a boundary of a system—the demarcation fencing in that which contains greater commerce within than across the demarcation— conceptually separates a system from the environment—a definition in terms of the system's internal interdependency. Tackling the issue of the demarcation from the stance of the environment can restate what to include or exclude from a system conceptually. The boundary between the environment and the system, between internal and external factors, is always somewhat arbitrary, as is the choice of the size of unit forming the system. Convenience and utility are the main bases for these deliberate decisions in forming either a discipline of knowledge or a discipline of practice.

What have been some models of conceptualizing the environment-system relations?

The front-line practitioner's typical procedure for deciding what factors to place in the environment is usually determined by answers to two questions: Does the factor make a difference in achieving the system's objective? Can I do anything about this factor? If the factor is seen to make a major difference in achieving some objectives of the system and nothing can be done about it directly or immediately, then the factor is placed in the environment. The environment is thus conceptually used as a reserve category of factors to be taken into account later or as conditional to the actions to be undertaken but not directly attended to for intervention.

As interdependency of the parts of a system and its environment became both a recognition of reality and a crystallized value of practitioners, closed and open system models have been drawn upon for their convenience of thought for observations, diagnostics, and interventions. In focusing on systems theory for the analysis of the individual, group, organization, and community, the practices have tended to focus on the internal characteristics of parts, and the relationships of parts to other parts of the system. In contrast, "open systems" theory (Bertalanffy, Emery, and Trist)[1] pointed up the responses of the system to its environment, such as the system's open commerce across a boundary while still maintaining the integrity and avoiding the dissolution of the system, the proactive relation of the system to its environment, the equally effective multiple pathways available to a system to achieve

---

[1] See Terreberry (6.2) in this volume.

its goals (namely equifinality), and the adaptive responsiveness of a system to the changes in the environment. (*Illustrations:* counseling or consulting, training, organizational development, fact-gathering research and the internal climate supporting the problem-solving, planning, decision-making capabilities and flexibilities.) The theory and practice are focused to enhance the adaptive survival and growth of the system.

In intersystem theory, interdependency is broadened to describe and analyze the structured relations of a system to an organized part of the environment, namely another system. (*Illustrations:* "The social environment of the child is the family." "The committee must deal with another committee to get the job done." "Alternative schools, as an organization, must maintain relationships with the administrators of the regular school system and to the various constituencies of students, parents, teachers, and to the changing social scene.") Each of these depicts the interdependency of a system (an individual, group, organization) and another system—an intersystem model. There is a need for extending the analysis of the interdependency of a system and its environment to encompass more of the essential features of the environment than intersystem theory permits.

Planning and embodying the future in the present require some differentiated models of the environment of the system. The fearsome blob of the future, often experienced as undifferentiatingly overwhelming and catastrophic, can be focused, or at least brought under conceptual control, if more specific models of the future environment are used in the analysis. The emergent field of futurism—its approaches, values, and technologies for envisioning the future and reconstructing its possible shape, is presently based upon using known and specific variables of the environment. (*Illustrations:* The social indicators of the population and the state

of societal trends in youth rebellion, housing, or psychological ideals in humanistic psychology or in self-actualization.) But there is a trap in the practices of futurology, because the specific factors to be encountered in the future may indeed be substantively different from those seen as important in the present environmental phenotypes. Concrete planning for middle- and long-range futures is thus handicapped without models for examining the genotypic or underlying features of the environment.

There is a set of existing models to describe the features and dynamics of the system-environment relations. A common analogue is similar to the forces and their operations in the physical universe. Factors arising from the sun, planets, stars, meteors, and other events impact on the earth; the earth is a "spaceship" with an enclosed system acting as an environment for man. In this metaphor there is a postulated order and a regularity. Unexpected events are merely knowledge gaps, the limitations of the time-span to take into account. The causal forces scientifically are understood as system dynamics. In addition, man has used astrology and geomancy as ways of fitting conceptions of man's nature and behavior as affected by the forces of the physical universe.

The environment of an animal or species of animal is conceived of as consisting of a balance of forces plus an occasional major upheaval or a cataclysmic event such as a flood or a forest fire. This ecological model is that of a shifting balance of food in the environment and numbers within each and among the varieties of species forming an equilibrium. More recently, this equilibrium has been recognized as upset by man in his ruthless alterations and wanton activities, such as the consumption of resources in the environment without undertaking the restorative or recycling process to replace resources or the tipping of the balances between forces thus permanently upsetting the equilibrium. This model of the environment for a biological system is the basic balance of a steady state, with predictable transformations of resources and processes, and with the disastrous intrusion of exogenous directional forces. The environment is treated as a macrosystem or ecosystem occasionally disrupted by catastrophic forces. Basically the intrinsic nature of a particular system is fixed (by genes, or "human nature"), with the environmental forces selecting survivals.

The metaphors for man-made or social environments center around conflict and control. Research psychologists have struggled with the polarity of heredity versus environment in the formation of behavior patterns. Situationalists in social psychology and sociology have demonstrated the utility of concentrating upon the setting and its field of forces as governing behavior and action. Perception of the environmental field of forces (Lewin's psychological environment, subjective environment) and phenomenological analysis of the individual or group have dominated these research approaches. Practitioners in the applied social sciences have developed wide-angle conceptions to take account of "what's really out there" and its actual, potential, and perceivable impact.

A common metaphor is that the environment is composed of supernatural forces. Daemonic forces, some positive and some evil, abound. Halfway between the deities and man, the daemons act willfully and are a bit more fathomable and placable than gods, but still in essence not under man's control. In the contemporary scene in America, the revival of the exploration of inner states of man and the techniques of shamans, witch doctors, faith healers, and seers are intended to bring these daemonic forces into the service of man's desires to shape the environment.

Metaphors of social environments tend to be anthropomorphic (complex forces are personified as person or group actions), full of perceived causal attributions of the motivations of other individuals or groups (they are conspiratorial, they intend willfully some outcome), restrictive or repressive (individuality is suppressed by society) and focused upon the possibilities of bringing the environment under control. The environment is to be conquered (man over nature) or altered by deliberate effort (reconstruction, normative re-education, social change, socialist construction). In other cultural assumptions, man fits into nature (Taoism).

These conceptions tend to focus on the system with notions of the environment of the system treated as relatively undifferentiated. When the environment is studied, it is seen as a system, thus jumping to a different-sized unit directly. Can we derive concepts of the environment as environment? I propose to examine models of the textures of and clusterings in the environment and then some selected aspects of the environment as environment of a system.

II. Models of Textures of and Clusterings in the Environment

The *texture* of the environment of a system may be seen as having varying amounts of organization, pattern, and/or clustering. A simple conception of the texture of the environment is that of a plain and featureless ground in which the system exists as figure. No clusterings or salient features exist in the environment. Impacts on the system from the environment are random in time, place, and effects. Illustrative instances might be an infant without a differentiated environment, or an isolated prisoner-of-war camp with all-powerful and randomly behaving guards. Such a conception of the environment is also implicit when the focus of conceptualization is on the system and its input—

an input that is itself isolated, contextless, and without necessary meaning or regularity. Such a system does not have any predictability about the environment. Experimental researches using single stimulus variables often take on the characteristics of isolated inputs from the environment. The individual, group, organization, or community, however, rarely is in this simple an environment, except under pathological conditions. Furthermore, such systems will tend to create some image of what their environments are and will attribute some regularity and causal efficacy to the forces impacting from the environment.

Thus, a second model of the environment is that it is composed of a single bold and salient cluster of knowable probabilities of effects. The cluster in the environment may or may not be sufficiently organized internally to be treated as a system with its own internal dynamics. The impacts of this environment on a system arise directly from the cluster. Intersystem theory is applicable in treating the environmental parts and dynamics of the interacting system. (*Illustrations:* husband as a system with wife as the other system in the environment engaged in mutually reinforcing or interactive neurotic dynamics; a team as a system in interaction with another group in its environment in intergroup competition where intragroup activities of one system of individuals affect the intragroup dynamics of the other system's individuals.)

The third model of the texture of environment is when the environment is composed of several interlinked clusters and systems. Effects of the environment's clusters and systems result from the characteristics of each of the clusters and/or from the interactive nature of the clusters and systems with each other. (*Illustrations:* husband as a system with wife and children as environment, with the interactional dynamics of children and mother resulting in impacts separate from the individual impacts of the wife or child; a team with another team and a supervisory group in an organization.)

A word of caution: These three models of the environment are differentiated by the degree of clustering represented and by conceptions of the dynamics of the clusters, with varying predictability of the environmental systems. They are not solely defined by the number of elements contained in the environment. The focus is on the kinds of interactions of the parts of the environment with each other.

The fourth model of the texture of the environment which reflects the complexity of the environment is often called a turbulent environment (Emery and Trist).[2] A turbulent environment has multiple clusters and multiple systems, each with its own dynamics interacting with the other dynamic processes arising from the field of the environment itself, as well as from the interactive forces of the multiple systems. In this model the environment is a "field" of forces. It is rapidly changing in both its structures and its dynamics. Each part of the system of the environment is a source of change, with its interactive processes producing new forces for the system. This conception avoids an oversimplified linear determinism of impacts on the observing system. The stability of the impacts is seen through some second-order concepts (the rate of change, the speedup or slowdown of growth, the narrowing and widening of boundaries of the field of forces). The unforeseeable consequences of these interactions from time to time create a new field of forces. Under these conditions the environment as a total system will "step-jump" into new levels of functioning, forming new levels of steady state or balance. The noticeable tendency is for these step-jumps to occur more frequently in a given present than they did in the past. Revolutions in and of the structure and organization of

---

[2] See Terreberry (6.2) in this volume.

the environment become commonplace. In the long run, it is possible to expect these step-jumps to have some limits. A set of principles for analyzing the dynamics of these processes of a turbulent environment is not at hand; rather attention is paid to how the system can learn to adapt to a turbulent environment. (*Illustrations:* new levels of consciousness for future shock, the process emphasis for managing of change, the flexible structures of organizations for proactive management of new problems.)

Such fluid processes, in this conception of the environment, alter the channels of commerce across the boundaries: new ones will develop, and old ones will diminish in importance. These interactions, which are the essence of the complex and turbulent environment, do not appear to have the characteristics of steady-state or even stable relationships. The step-jumps in the equilibrium and the structures of the systems forming the environment interrelate with more and more distant systems, interpenetrating with more and more layers of the environment. The result is a conception stretching the limits of its useful properties. Is a new conception of these structures and dynamics of the environment called for?

A fifth model, the articulated turbulent environment, identifies the nodules, envelopes, and layers in the environment which organize, channel, and process the turbulent forces and information about them for the system. These special clusters and/or systems in the environment select, organize, focus, filter, dampen, amplify, translate or transform the forces in the turbulent environment. These articulations exist in the environment and are different from those parts of the system which perform essentially the same functions for the system internally. (*Illustrations:* credibly wise or trusted informants, such as parents, teachers, and advisors; news and information media, technical consultants; social indicators; research assessments,

"intelligence activities"; early warning systems.) These sources for transmission to the system may in turn become a dynamic part of the field of forces. For example, the mass media have progressed beyond being a passive conduit or messenger, as research reports hopefully can become. As such, they themselves become an interactive and dynamic cluster in the environment.

Articulating the turbulent environment has also been accomplished by the active and participative creation by systems of special temporary systems in the environment as an integral phase of planned change. These special temporary systems are constructed as a contrived arrangement in the environment of the system which is "not for real." The system reaches beyond its own boundaries in creating with others in a cultural island a try-out of a different way of managing in relating to its turbulently changing environment. This articulated temporary system in the environment (and not "in the system") is temporary; an alternative to regular ways of performing; a pattern of partial commitment and emotional investment; experimental; and, oriented to data and data collection on how the new ways relate to the turbulent environmental forces, fits, and produces effects and longer-range consequences. (*Illustrations:* for the individual, the cultural island of a training group such as the T-group; for the small group and organization, the simulation and/or pilot programs, or alternative organizational patterns.) Some dilemmas and conflicts do arise in the active creation of these temporary systems. First, the main system is viewed to be "inauthentic" in creating the temporary system in the environment which is not part of the system. The system does not seem to invest energy and make "real" commitments. Another dilemma is the condition of irreality and play acting deemed useful for experimenting artificially and creating potentially valued alternatives, as compared to dealing with the practical realities of the system and its environment. The transfer of the implications to the system of the trying out of new ways in the temporary system in the turbulent environment has been another dilemma. In reference to these dilemmas, some practitioners of planned change have abandoned the practice of constructing temporary systems and have developed practices aimed at direct change in the system, losing the virtue of concretizing and trying out the new visions of managing the turbulent environment. The practices for a model of the articulated turbulent environment allow for more experimentation, a major virtue and response to the dynamics of a turbulent environment.

These models of textures of the environment are descriptive of general features of environments. The next section identifies selected contents of environments.

III. Contents of the Environment

Five content aspects of the environment are selected for their relevance to planned change: (1) the means in the environment for transforming the environment; (2) the patterns that structure power and authority environment relations to the system; (3) the resources that I shall call nutriments because they serve functions of the system; (4) the available information in the environment for the system; and (5) the structures representing potential feedback loops to the system.

The means existing in the environment for transforming the features of the environment are a powerful source of social change. Technologies, physical and social, are increasingly present to alter the environment of systems. These crucial technologies are an exploding and accelerating source of change in the environment itself, and breed additional environment-alteration means.

Social technologies, such as re-educative techniques, knowledge-building techniques, the transformation of the nature of man's impulses, have not been as consequential as the means for transforming the physical environment. Yet the recognition of the necessity for making better use of the social technologies is constantly thrust forward as even more crucial than the physical means.

Practitioners have been concentrating upon these innovations in social technologies and assessing their impacts with the use of models of a plain or cluster environment.

Structures of authority and power are in the environment. The balances or ratios of dominance/subordination in influence of clusters or forces in the environment are defined for the system. The ratios of influence as perceived by the system become psychological issues of whether locus of control over the system is within the system or in the environment of the system. Materialistic determinists, along with fatalists, share a conviction that places power and influence over the individual, group, organization, or community system in key factors in the environmental structures. In addition to directly exercising authority and power, these structures also provide information for the system about its potentials and limits with respect to influence, control, and countercontrol.

Power, influence, authority, and control in turbulent environments are shifting and unstable coalitions in the environment, creating an intolerable condition for the system. A frequent reaction of the system is to attempt to apply a simpler conception of texture, to see a "power structure" even when such conceptions are not realistic. Applying an articulated turbulent model can lead to discovering the specific clusters and nodules which can or do mediate the environment's total influence relationships and which also create conditions to examine untested information about influence or lack of influence.

The next aspect of the environment we will examine is the resources in the environment. These resources are reviewed by us as nutriments with objects, functions, and dynamics involved in them (e.g., money, food, jobs, services, and psychological need fulfillment). These resources become nutriments supplying the system insofar as the system's survival and development are dependent upon the regular input of the resources as nutriments. Nutriments are promotive of repair and of growth.

The dynamics of the environmental structures for the delivery of nutriments for any given individual, group, organization, or community are often assumed to be based on a win-lose competition for limited or depleting supplies. This view is usually called a "zero-sum" assumption; that is, gains for one system require an equal loss for another system; the sum of the gains-losses equals zero; the size of the pie to be divided is fixed. (*Illustrations*: money, food supply, number of jobs, love from parents, intergroup striving for power and influence, an industrial firm's share of the market for its products.) Another possible assumption is that resources are expanding or expandable by transforming the conditions and resources, so that gain for one system can be accompanied by gain rather than loss for another system.

The social and psychological nutriments range (probably hierarchically) from the physiological to the psychologically based need for actualization of self. The analysis of the availability of these nutriments in the environment has to indicate how the texture shapes the nutriment structures of the environment. The individual, group, organization, or community cannot draw upon the environment unless the supplies are present, or in increasing supply, or are potentially expandable. (*Illustration*: a highly stressed unemployed parent can't easily be warm and supportive to a child.)

The environment is teeming with signals, symbols, and events as potential information to a system. This potential information in the environment may not ever be translated or organized as information for a system. (Some theorists of systems have restricted the term "information" to that which actually makes a difference in the actions of the system. Here we are treating information as that content in the environment which has the potential of altering the deliberate processes, strategies, and plans of the system.) Information is by symbols and codes to be scanned and decoded by the system. Clarifying the processes of communications in the environment and between system and environment are key approaches for practitioners in dealing with how as well as what is communicated.

The information may exist in a plain environment, and be thus conceptually managed as an input to the system, a convenience for researchers and theorists, but hardly a sufficient model for the practitioner. Clustered information, both by content, source, and by an organized structure of some coherency, may exist.

The conflict of the reliability and validity of information clusters (credibility), areas of distortions, the double-bind, the paradoxical action cues and demands, and risks of the consequences of undertaking action, become criterial for the work of temporary systems in an articulated turbulent environment.

Lastly, the identification of the available feedback sources and their dynamics in the environment are necessary to the activities of the practitioner. Feedback has been conceptualized as a characteristic of the system of the individual, group, organization, or community. The identification of the potential feedback arrangements of the textured *environment* of a system provides a setting for the analysis, diagnosis, and improvement of the internal feedback processes.

In summary, the models for analysis of the environment of systems directly deal with conceptions of how the environment is organized and what is in the environment.

IV. Utility of Conceptions to Practitioners

Conceptions of the texture and aspects of the environment are of use to the practitioner for diagnosing and intervening for planned change. The type of use depends upon the approach to change and the role of the agent of the change, whether as a technical or process consultant, facilitator, trainer, or action researcher in the laboratory mode of planned change, or as a policy-maker, advocate, or engineering consultant.

Three fundamental approaches to changing the relationships of a system to its environment are possible: (1) change the properties of the environment of the system; (2) change the interrelationship of the system to the environment; and (3) change either the internal characteristics of the system such as its awareness, perceptions, and images of the environment, or its internal responsiveness to the changing environment.

1. Changing the properties of the environment of the system involves acting directly to change the features of the environment. These changes of the environment are not necessarily made by the target system, the ultimate beneficiary of the changes of the features of the environment.

2. Changing the intersystem relationships between the system and its environment involves moving the boundary in or out, or establishing direct links between features of the environment and parts of the system, in order to regulate and manage the channels of relationship between the system and the environment, or lessening the disjunctive connections between the system and the environment.

3. Changing the internal characteristics of the system as related to the environment typically works to improve the system's scanning and sensing mechanisms, such as the individual's ability to see and hear; to create more roles in groups and organizations for scouting and researching the environment (survey research, market research); or to clarify the mechanisms and roles for transforming acquired information into action implications (Research and Development centers), thus clearing up the noisy channels of the inputs of the system. Improving the feedback mechanisms internal to the system to gather data about the effects, or consequences, of a system's actions on the environment is one of the most strategic and valued procedures for a normative-re-educative approach. Additionally, efforts to alter the attributed dynamics and causes have been central to the changing of the internal characteristics of a system. (*Illustrations*: feedback scanning by an individual; use of a process observer by a committee or by an organization.)

In order to illustrate the utility of the presented notions of the texture of the environment for these approaches, we will make use of a grid which interrelates somewhat mechanically the conceptions of texture with aspects of the environment. The grid itself opens the possibility of strategizing and selecting the conceptual model for planned change. For example, my suggestion is that the practitioner might begin with the assumptions of a turbulent environment for diagnosis of the case and its context. For more dissection, he could move to analyze the texture of the environment as multiclustered and then move to a cluster analysis. And for planned change, the practitioner could make use of the conceptual model of an articulated turbulent environment. The first set of activities shapes the diagnosis; the latter suggests the ways of managing the turbulent environment. Each practitioner probably evolves his/her own strategy and process of fitting together a set of

Textures of E	(M) Means in E for Environment Transforming	(A) Patterns of Authority and Power in E	Contents in E (N) Nutriments and Resources in E	(I) Potential Information in E	(F) Feedback System in E
(P) Plain E	P-M	P-A	P-N	P-I	P-F
(C) Cluster E	C-M	C-A	C-N	C-I	C-F
(M) Multicluster E	M-M	M-A	M-N	M-I	M-F
(T) Turbulent E	T-M	T-A	T-N	T-I	T-F
(AT) Articulated Turbulent E	AT-M	AT-A	AT-N	AT-I	AT-F

conceptual models for the purposes of planned change of the environment of a system. And, practitioners may locate how he/she typically does approach an analysis of the environment.

There are uses of the conceptions in each cell. For example, the cell M-A, multicluster patterns of authority and power in the environment, suggests the analysis of how the multiclusters manage their definitions of self and other with each other, and eventually with the system. The pattern of several teams in an organization in relation to top management is the clustered pattern of authority (environment for a manager (system) in one section. Intervening can be directly into the environment by consultation techniques with top management, or can be on the reporting relationships or management techniques of supervision, or can be consultation or training the manager and how he perceives and relates to authority and power. The techniques for facilitating change in the multicluster environment may well be different.

The cells are probably not of equal importance. Practitioners may train themselves to use each of these conceptions for the mindholds about the environment. Each conception can be intertwined with applied and basic social science, on the one hand, and the accepted role, agency policy, and the procedures of planned change.

In conclusion, a focus on the environment brings to saliency as figure that which has been treated as background to the figure of a system. Practitioners of planned change are increasingly attending to the texture and aspects of the environment as a wider definition of the discipline of planned change.

Methodologically, this essay has presented models of the environment. Models represent organized conceptual schemas, the abstract tools with which concrete theories are built. My emphasis on models is because practitioners can use this form of social science for the many disciplines of social practices as first-line practitioners as well as second-order practitioners who are generalizing, theorizing, and researching.

3.2 Some Notes on the Dynamics of Resistance to Change: The Defender Role

Donald Klein

The literature on change recognizes the tendencies of individuals, groups, organizations, and entire societies to act so as to ward off change. Though it is generally acknowledged that human beings have a predilection both to seek change and to reject it, much of the literature has isolated the latter tendency for special emphasis. In fact studies of change appear to be taken from the perspective or bias of those who are the change agents seeking to bring about change rather than of the clients they are seeking to influence. It seems likely, therefore, that our notions of change dynamics are only partially descriptive. It is interesting that Freud used the term "resistance" to identify a phenomenon which from his point of view, had the effect of blocking the attainment of his therapeutic objectives. One wonders whether patients would use just this term to refer to the same sets of interactions between themselves and their therapists.

Freud, of course, emphasized that resistances were a necessary and even desirable aspect of the therapy. He pointed out that without resistance patients might be overwhelmed by the interventions of the therapist, with the result that inadequate defenses against catastrophe would be overthrown before more adaptive ways of coping with inner and outer stimuli had been erected.

Reproduced by special permission from *Concepts for Social Change*, "Some Notes on the Dynamics of Resistance to Change: The Defender Role," Donald Klein, Cooperative Project for Educational Development Series, Vol. 1, National Training Laboratories, Washington, D.C., 1966.

Desirability of Opposition

It is the objective of this paper to suggest that, as in patient-therapist dyads, opposition to change is also desirable in more complex social systems. It is further suggested that what is often considered to be irrational resistance to change is, in most instances, more likely to be either an attempt to maintain the integrity of the target system to real threat, or opposition to the agents of change themselves.

Opposition to Real Threat

Change of the kind we are considering consists not of an event, but of a process or series of events occurring over a period of time, usually involving a more or less orderly and somewhat predictable sequence of interactions. Though it involves the reactions of individuals, it also entails reorganization of group, organizational, or even community behavior patterns and requires some alteration of social values, be they explicit or only implicitly held.

Few social changes of any magnitude can be accomplished without impairing the life situations of some individuals or groups. Elderly homeowners gain little and sometimes must spend more than they can afford for new public school buildings or for the adoption of kindergartens by their communities. Some administrators may lose their chances for advancement when school districts are consolidated to achieve more efficent use of materials and resources. Other examples of real threat could be cited from public health, urban renewal and other fields. There is no doubt that some resistance to change will occur when individuals' livelihoods are affected adversely or their social standings threatened.

However, there are more fundamental threats posed by major innovations. Sometimes the threat is to the welfare of whole social systems. Often the threat is not clearly recognized by anybody at the time the change occurs; it emerges only as the future that the change itself helped shape is finally attained.

For example, the community which taxes property heavily in order to support kindergartens or costly educational facilities may very well be committing itself to further homogenization of its population as it attracts young families wealthy enough to afford the best in education and drives out working class groups, elderly people, and those whose cultural values do not place so high a priority on education. The community which loses a small, poorly financed local school in order to gain a better equipped and perhaps more competently staffed district facility may also be committed to a future of declining vigor as its most able young people are as a result more readily and systematically siphoned off into geographically distant professional, industrial and other work settings.

It is probably inevitable that any major change will be a mixed blessing to those undergoing it in those instances when the status quo or situation of gradual change has been acceptable to many or most people. The dynamic interplay of forces in social systems is such that any stable equilibrium must represent at least a partial accommodation to the varying needs and demands of those involved. Under such circumstances the major change must be desired by those affected if it is to be accepted.

Maintenance of Integrity

Integrity is being used here to encompass the sense of self-esteem, competence, and autonomy enjoyed by those individuals, groups, or communities who feel that their power and resources are adequate to meet the usual challenges of living. Unfortunately such integrity sometimes is based on a view of reality that is no longer tenable. When changes occur under such circumstances they force us to confront the fact that our old preconceptions do not fit present reality, at least not completely. Dissonance exists between the truths from the past and current observations. In some cases relinquishing the eternal verities would resolve the dissonance but would also entail a reduction of integrity. However irrational, the resistance to change which occurs in such cases may have as its fundamental objective the defense of self-esteem, competence and autonomy.

In our complex, changing world the assaults on individual, group and community integrity are frequent and often severe. The field of public education is especially vulnerable to such assaults. So much so, in fact, that one sometimes wonders whether there are any truly respected educational spokesmen left who can maintain the self-esteem, sense of competence, and necessary autonomy of the schools against all the various changes which are being proposed and funded before they have been adequately tested.

Resistance to Agents of Change

The problem is further complicated by the growing capacity, indeed necessity, of our society to engage in massive programs of planned change and by the development of ever-growing cadres of expert planners capable of collecting and processing vast bodies of information, of organizing such information into designs for the future apparently grounded on the best available expertise, and of marshalling arguments capable of persuading great numbers of political, business, and other civic leaders that action should be taken. The difficulties which arise stem from the very magnitude of the changes being projected, from the rapidity with which such changes can occur, and from the troubling realization that these changes often are irreversible as well as far reaching, thus ensuring the prolongation of error as well as of accuracy.

Most important of all, however, as a generator of defense would appear to be the frequent alienation of the planners of change from the world of those for whom they are planning. The alienation is one of values as much as it is one of simple information. It exists in many fields but is perhaps most apparent in the field of urban renewal, where planners have yet to devise mechanisms whereby they can adequately involve their clients in the planning processes. Many examples can be cited. Health professionals feel that matters of the public health should be left in the hands of the experts most qualified to assess the facts and to take the necessary action. They often decry the involvement of the public in decisions about such matters as fluoridation through referenda or other means. Educators, too, are often loath to encourage the development of vigorous parent groups capable of moving into the arena of curriculum planning, building design, or other areas of decision making.

Few expert planners in any field are prepared to believe that their clients can be equipped to collaborate with them as equals. What can the lay person add to the knowledge and rationality of the technical expert? And is it not true that the process of involving the client would only serve to slow down if not derail the entire undertaking? The result is that each planning project proceeds without taking the time to involve those who will be affected by the planning until such a point when it is necessary to gain the client's consent. And if decisions can be made and implementation secured without involving his public, the planner's job is greatly simplified.

It is little wonder, therefore, that planners typically do not engage in collaborative planning with clients on specific projects. It is costly, time consuming, irritating, frustrating, and even risky.

However, the failure of planners to work collaboratively with those for whom they plan contributes to the well known American mistrust of the highly trained, academically grounded expert. Under the most benign circumstances, the client may be skeptical of the planner's recommendations. Given any real threat to livelihood or position, or given any feared reduction in integrity, clients' skepticism may be replaced by mistrust of planners' motives and open hostility towards them.

The motives of innovators are especially apt to be suspect when the planning process has been kept secret up until the time of unveiling the plans and action recommendations. By this time the innovators usually have worked up a considerable investment in their plans, and are often far more committed to defending than to attempting to understand objections to them. They are not prepared to go through once again with newcomers the long process of planning which finally led them to their conclusions. And they are hardly in the most favorable position to entertain consideration of new social data or of alternative actions which might be recommended on the basis of such information. The result often is that opposition to the recommended change hardens and even grows as the ultimate clients sense that their reactions will not materially influence the outcome in any way short of defeating the plan in open conflict.

Defense as Part of the Process of Innovation

Studies in such fields as agriculture and medicine have helped clarify the sequence of processes involved in successful innovation of new practices. Even in such technical fields where results can be more or less objectively judged in terms of profit, recovery rates, and the like, successful innovation occurs only after initial resistances have been worked through.

Innovation in any area begins when one or more people perceive that a problem exists, that change is desirable and that it is possible. These people then must decide how best to go about enlisting others to get the information needed to assess the problem further and to develop the strategy leading to implementation of a plan of action. However, we know that those people who are prepared to initiate change within their own groups, organizations or communities are often in a very unfavorable position from which to do so. In stable groups especially it is the marginal or atypical person who is apt to be receptive to new ideas and practices or who is in a position where he can economically or socially afford to run the risk of failure.

Thus it has been found necessary to carry out sustained efforts at innovation in which experimentation with new ideas can be followed by efforts at adapting or modifying them to fit more smoothly into existing patterns until finally what was once an innovation is itself incorporated within an altered status quo.

The Importance of Defense in Social Change

Up to this point, this paper has touched on some of the factors contributing to the inevitability of resistance to change and has presented but not developed the major thesis, which is that a necessary prerequisite of successful change involves the mobilization of forces against it. It has suggested that just as individuals have their defenses to ward off threat, maintain integrity, and protect themselves against the unwarranted intrusions of other's demands, so do social systems seek ways in which to defend themselves against ill-considered and overly precipitate innovations.

The existence of political opposition virtually ensures such defense within local, state and national government to the extent that the party out of power is sufficiently vigorous. The British system of the loyal opposition perhaps even more aptly epitomizes the application of the concept of necessary defense in the area of political life.

In more implicit ways, nongovernmental aspects of community life have their defenders. These latter individuals and groups constitute the spokesmen for the inner core of tradition and values. They uphold established procedures and are quick to doubt the value of new ideas. Their importance stems from several considerations:

First, they are the ones most apt to perceive and point out the real threats, if such exist, to the well-being of the system which may be the unanticipated consequences of projected changes;

Second, they are especially apt to react against any change that might reduce the integrity of the system;

Third, they are sensitive to any indication that those seeking to produce change fail to understand or identify with the core values of the system they seek to influence.

The Defender Role

The defender role is played out in a variety of ways depending on such factors as the nature of the setting itself, the kind of change contemplated, the characteristics of the group or individual seeking to institute change, and the change strategy employed. In a process of orderly and gradual change, the defender role may be taken by a well established, respected member of the system whose at least tacit sanction must be gained for a new undertaking to succeed. In a situation of open conflict where mistrust runs high the defender role may be assumed by those able to become more openly and perhaps irrationally vitriolic in their opposition. These latter are often viewed by the proponents of change as impossibly intractable and are dismissed as "rabble rousers" or "crackpots." This was frequently the attitude on the part of pro-fluoridationists toward the anti's.

Though crackpots may emerge as defenders under certain circumstances, it is suggested here that, so long as they are given support by a substantial segment of the population even though it may be a minority, they are expressing a reaction by all or part of the target system against real threat of some kind. In one community, I observed a well educated group of residents vote overwhelmingly against fluoridation at town meeting even though (as I viewed it) the small body of antifluoridationists expressed themselves in a highly emotional, irrational way. In later conversations it appeared that many who voted against actually favored fluoridation. They were influenced not by the logic of the defenders but by other dynamics in the situation which presumably the defenders also were reflecting. Some of those who voted "no" were unprepared to force fluorides on a minority; others pointed out that those presenting the case for fluorides had neglected to involve the voters in a consideration of the true nature and extent of the problem of tooth decay; and a third group wondered why the health officer and others fighting for the change were so insistent on pushing their plan through immediately rather than asking the town through the more usual committee procedure to consider the problem at a more leisurely pace. The pro-fluoridationists, on the other hand, were discouraged by the vote, felt rejected by fellow townspeople, and had grave doubts about bringing the issue up

again in view of the fact that "they don't want to protect their children's teeth."

In the instance of fluoridation the defenders usually have been drawn from the ranks of those who do not hold public office and who do not consider themselves to be members of the Establishment. This is not always the case, however. In civil rights controversies the change agents typically are the disenfranchised; the defenders occupy public office or appear to be close to the sources of existing power. But no matter whether the innovation comes from top down or bottom up, in each situation the defenders are representing value positions which have been important not only to themselves but to larger groups of constituents, and presumably to the maintenance of the culture itself.

In the Boston controversy over de facto school segregation the School Committee Chairman was elected by an overwhelming vote of those who, however bigoted many of them may be, believe they are defending their property values, the integrity of neighborhood schools, and their rights to stand up against those who are trying to push them around. If any of us were faced in our neighborhoods with the prospect of a state toll road sweeping away our homes, we, too, might convince ourselves that we could properly rise up in defense of the same values. The point is not whether the schools should remain segregated; they should not. Rather as change agents we must be concerned with the values held by the opposition and must recognize that, to a great extent, their values are ours as well. Moreover, it would help if we could grant that, in upholding these values, the defenders—however wrong we believe they are in the stands they take and the votes they cast—are raising questions which are important in our society and which we must answer with them. It is far too easy to dismiss neighborhood schools as a reactionary myth or to hold that they are unimportant in face of the larger objective of reducing intergroup barriers. The issues become far more complex, however, when we grant that neighborhood schools were established because in the judgment of many educators and citizens they had merits apart from the current controversy over segregation. Once having granted this, the problem becomes one of seeking solutions which can minimize the losses in respect to such merits and maximize the gains in respect to integration. I would predict that, if it were possible for the change agents to consider seriously the concerns of the defenders in the case of school integration, many of the latter would no longer feel so embattled and would no longer require the kind of leadership which in Boston has been renominated overwhelmingly for the School Committee.

But what about the motives of those who lead the opposition to good causes? Are they not apt to seize on virtuous issues simply as ways to manipulate opinion and to rally more support? No doubt this is true. Nonetheless, I think the point still holds that the virtues are there to be manipulated. They can be used as a smoke screen by demagogues only so long as those who follow them are convinced that the agents of change are themselves unscrupulous, unprincipled, and unfeeling. Therefore, we add to the anxieties and opposition of those who are being rallied by the demagogues if we dismiss the latter and fail to come to grips with the concerns of those who uphold them.

Of course, demagogues and rabble rousers do more than articulate the values of their followers. They also dare to give voice to the frustrations and sense of helpless rage which these followers feel but usually cannot express. Those who are the targets of change usually do not feel it is safe to give vent to their true feelings. The man who is a demagogue in the eyes of his opponent is usually a courageous spokesman to the follower whom he is serving as a defender.

How the Change Agent Views the Defender

Thus an important implication for the change agent is that the defender, whoever he may be and however unscrupulously or irrationally he may appear to present himself and his concerns, usually has something of great value to communicate about the nature of the system which the change agent is seeking to influence. Thus if the change agent can view the situation with a sympathetic understanding of what the defenders are seeking to protect, it may prove desirable either to modify the change itself or the strategy being used to achieve it. In certain situations the participation of defenders in the change process may even lead to the development of more adequate plans and to the avoidance of some hitherto unforeseen consequences of the projected change.

It is important, therefore, for those seeking change to consider the costs of ignoring, overriding, or dismissing as irrational those who emerge as their opponents. To ignore that which is being defended may mean that the planned change itself is flawed; it may also mean that the process of change becomes transformed into a conflict situation in which forces struggle in opposition and in which energies become increasingly devoted to winning rather than to solving the original problem.

Outcome of the Defender Role

What happens to the defender role during a period of change is no doubt a function of many factors, such as the nature of the issue, previous relationships between opposing sides, and the various constraints of time, urgency of the problem, and the like. We are all familiar with situations in which defenders and protagonists of change have become locked in fierce conflict until finally the defenders have either won out or been shattered and forced to succumb. Frequent examples can be found in the early history of urban renewal when entire urban neighborhoods, such as the West End of Boston, were destroyed and their defenders swept away as a consequence. It is also possible for conflict to continue indefinitely with neither side able to gain the advantage, to the extent that both sides contribute to the ultimate loss of whatever values each was seeking to uphold. Labor-management disputes which shatter entire communities are instances where the interplay between innovative and defensive forces ceases to be constructive.

Often in communities the defenders of values no longer widely held become boxed in and remain in positions of repeated but usually futile opposition to a series of new influences. The consensus of the community has shifted in such a way as to exclude those who may once have been influential. In their encapsulation these individuals and groups are no longer defenders in the sense the term is being used here; for they no longer participate meaningfully in the changes going on around them.

Finally, as has already been suggested, the defenders may in a sense be co-opted by the change agents in such a way as to contribute to an orderly change process.

School Administrator— Defender or Change Agent

Within school systems the balance between innovation and defense must always be delicate, often precarious. The history of education in this country is full of examples of major innovations accomplished by an outstanding superintendent which, no matter what their success, were immediately eliminated by his successor. Sometimes disgruntled citizens who have been unsuccessful in opposing innovations are better able to mobilize their opposition when no longer faced with powerful professional leadership. Sometimes teachers and staff members who have conformed to but not accepted the changes feel more secure to express their opposition to the new superintendent.

It has been pointed out by Neal Gross and others that the superintendent of a public school system faces the almost impossible task of mediating between the conflicting demands of staff, community, and other groups. He is almost continuously confronted with the opposing influences of innovators and defenders, not to mention the many bystanders within the system who simply wish to be left alone when differences arise. Under the circumstances it may well be that one of the most important skills a superintendent can develop is his ability to create the conditions wherein the interplay between change agents and defenders can occur with a minimum of rancor and a maximum of mutual respect. As we have seen in New York City and elsewhere, however, controversies do arise—such as civil rights—wherein the superintendent seems unable to play a facilitating role.

In situations that are less dramatic and conflict laden, the superintendent and other school administrators are usually in a position where they can and indeed must be both change agents and defenders. In the face of rapid social change they face the challenge of learning how to foster innovation, while at the same time finding the most constructive ways in which to act in defense of the integrity of their systems. It is also important that they learn how to differentiate between change which may pose real threat and change which is resisted simply because it is new and feels alien. Perhaps most important of all, they have the opportunity of educating the change agents with whom they work, either those inside their systems or those who come from the outside, to the point where the change agents perceive, understand, and value the basic functions and purposes of the schools.

The Force Field of the Defender

In human relations training we have frequently used Lewin's force field model as a way to introduce learners to the objective analysis of the forces driving towards and restraining against a desired change. Here, too, we have tended to view the change field through the eyes of the protagonists. I think it would be illuminating in any study of educational innovation to attempt to secure analysis of the force field from defenders as well as change agents at several stages of the innovative process. Comparative analysis of the views of protagonists and defenders might help illuminate the biases of the former and clarify more adequately the underlying origins within the target system of the opposition. It also should provide us with a better understanding of the dynamics of the defender role and how it can be more adequately taken into account in programs of social innovation.

4

Utilization
of Knowledge

The use of valid knowledge is the crux of planned change. What is valid knowledge, its processes of generation and creation, forms, tests, and transformation for utilization? Some of the common types of valid knowledge are those of the social and behavioral scientists (including the researcher); the applied first-order and second-order social and behavioral practitioners; the learners in a variety of settings; and the potential knowers who are now suppressed or oppressed. The purpose of this chapter is to raise some selected issues of utilization of knowledge in planned change.

In some sense, our treatment of knowledge, including theory and fact, is focused around three questions. First, what exists in the conditions or case under study; second, how is it changing; and third, how can planned change be brought about intentionally. Chin and Downey ("Changing Change," *Handbook on Research in Teaching*, 2d Edition, chapter 17) warn about the elusive nature of the primitive and superficial definitions of change. The attainment of general valid knowledge about planned change and its utilization requires in instances clear families of different concepts for system and structural change, innovation-focused installation, and process-based definitions of change and changing.

For the social and behavioral scientist, *valid* knowledge is contained in the theories and empirical findings which emerge from obeying the rules of the scientific method. The underlying commitment is to the experiment and its basic language of proof. Issues of reliability and validity are the key tests of knowledge. These rules are applied both to the internal conditions of a study and to the external arrangements to assert the generalizability of the findings of the particular study of the particular sample. The method of work is to focus on the reduction of the probability of plausible alternative explanations so as to enhance the "true" explanations. These ideas, explanations, and theories, then, form the basis of knowledge seen as the "selectively retained tentatives," an evocative phrase proclaiming the evolutionary process of science and science-making. A more empirical thrust is embodied in the use of information, data embodied in files and records, and macro or aggregate information. Social policy processes are increasingly dependent upon these data treated as social indicators of the state of the society or its sectors. Utilization of knowledge for the first-line practitioner can be based upon these types of valid knowledge when suitably transformed into the specific case or instance in which the action and planned action is to be undertaken.

The first-order practitioner on the firing line of action builds up a body of "valid" knowledge of selectively retained tentatives embodied in practices and is guided by feedback as practices form. The second-order practitioner is explicitly evaluating these formulations, practices, and programmatic efforts and their summative outcomes to build a case for a discipline intending to tie in with the knowledge of what exists and how it changes. Evaluation research models have the challenge of expanding their boundaries to encompass issues of utilization for first- and second-order practitioners as well.

The learners in transmissive and experiential settings (academic and field) accept and build valid knowledge. Field experiences, apprenticeships, internships create a learning setting in which subjective knowledge becomes intersubjective with appropriate sets of rules for testing these tentatives.

And, in the world of liberation of the suppressed and oppressed, whether of minorities, peasants, workers, or groups such as women, socialized members of groups, organizations and communities, proponents claim valid knowledge is generated and tested. Indeed for Mao Ze-Dong, theory and practice in tandem and combined is the sole basis of valid knowledge. For him, without Marxist *praxis*, there is no valid knowledge.

Underlying processes of the utilization of knowledge is what Argyris and Schön (4.1) point to as a discrepancy between espoused theories and theories-of-action-in-action. Espoused theories based on ideology and social science must give way to the formulation of the implicit and, at times, explicit theories-in-action, the theory of intervention. For theories-in-action tend to create a behavioral world that constrains or frees the individual. Argyris and Schön pick out criteria for the examination of theories-in-action: internal consistency, congruence between espoused theory and theory-in-use, effectiveness, testability, and valuation of the world created by the theory-in-use. They offer a pragmatic solution to the dilemmas and paradoxes occurring in the theory-in-action held by practitioners, and suggest ways in which these have been or could be sustained in a dialectic process. By their focus on theories-in-use, they offer a way to build an adequate behavioral examination of what theories-in-use create in the behavioral world.

Benne, in his article on the utilization of knowledge in field experiences (4.2), moves beyond the usual scientific definitions of valid knowledge and evaluated practice to show how a certain type of valid knowledge is created in field experiences of the learner. Valid knowledge for the learner is present when the experiences encountered are elevated to more general meaning by the person engaged in field experience. Most important, Benne points to the epistemological principles which justify these processes of creating valid knowledge.

4.1 Evaluating Theories of Action

Chris Argyris   Donald A. Schön

To consider the interaction of theories-in-use and their behavioral worlds, we must look at their tendencies rather than at their cross-sectional properties at any instant in time. Whether theories-in-use tend to create a behavioral world that constrains or frees the individual depends on answers to the following questions: Are the theories-in-use and espoused theories internally consistent? Are they congruent? Are they testable? Are they effective? Do we value the worlds they create? The relationships among these criteria are expressed in Figure 1.

From Chris Argyris and Donald A. Schön, *Theory in Practice: Increasing Professional Effectiveness* (1974). Reprinted by permission of Jossey-Bass, Inc., Publishers.

Internal Consistency

In a very simple sense, *internal consistency* means the absence of self-contradiction. But in the domain of theory of action, its meaning becomes more complex.

The most important kind of consistency lies not between propositions in the theory ("This man is generous," "This man is stingy") but among the governing variables of the theory that are related to assumptions about self, others, and the behavioral setting. For example, a theory of action might require two propositions—"Keep people calm" and "Encourage participative government"; if participative government can come about only through heated action, the theory is internally inconsistent,

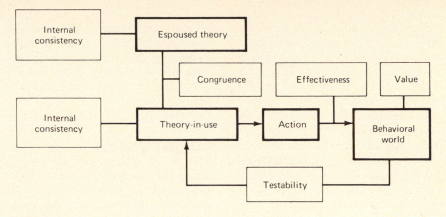

FIGURE 1

although not logically inconsistent. It is not self-contradictory, as saying a horse is and is not white would be. However, efforts to achieve the governing variables would interfere with one another.[1]

Each of these variables has a range that is acceptable; within that range, there are levels of preference. As long as calmness does not rise to the point of inertness, we may prefer to have things as calm as possible. As long as participation does not rise to the point of anarchy, we may prefer to have as much of it as possible.

If two or more such variables are internally incompatible in a particular context, one cannot achieve as high a level of preference for both of them taken together as one can for each of them taken separately.[2] If we call such a relationship

incompatibility, we can reserve the term internal inconsistency for the special case in which one variable will fall out of its acceptable range if the other is brought into the acceptable range.

Whether governing variables are incompatible or internally inconsistent depends on a number of factors.

1. Other governing variables—for example, variables related to self-protection, courtesy, or protection of others—may limit the means for achieving some variables.
2. The array of actions envisaged in the theory-in-use may be too narrow. Outside of that array, there may be some means for achieving one variable without dropping the other variable out of its acceptable range.
3. The acceptable range of each variable may be broadened or narrowed so as to make the two variables more or less incompatible.
4. The assumptions in the theory-in-use may be altered so as to make the governing variables more or less incompatible. For example, the assumption

[1] We might have chosen to speak of two inconsistent values. But remembering our earlier discussion of the field of constancy, there is a much larger set of variables for which under a given theory-in-use one strives toward keeping values within a desired range. It is among larger subsets of these that relations of consistency or inconsistency hold.

[2] Not all governing variables need behave this way. For some, perhaps, there may be no question of degrees of achievement. One either achieves them or does not; they are binary. Perhaps justice or truth-telling can be taken to be such variables. When two such variables in a given behavioral context interfere with one another, they exhibit internal inconsistency. Given the behavioral context, the injunctions to achieve these two values are in relation to one another very much like a logical contradiction.

"People cannot address the problem of self-government without becoming excited" may be absent from theory-in-use but may be valid in the situation; in this case, the agent would find that he cannot reach acceptable levels of both variables, but he would not understand why.

5. The protagonist may act on his world so as to make it take on characteristics that are either conducive or resistant to the internal consistency of his theory. His behavior may somehow affect people's sense of responsibility in a way that enables participation in self-government without disruption. Or, his behavior may have the opposite effect. Since this behavior is itself a reflection of other aspects of the theory-in-use, theories-in-use may tend to make themselves internally consistent or inconsistent. In the worst case, increasing one's efforts to achieve governing variables decreases one's chance of achieving them; in the best case, increasing one's efforts increases the chance of achieving them.

If two or more governing variables in a theory-in-use are internally inconsistent, then, for given settings or ranges, arrays of strategies, assumptions about the situation, constraining variables, and influences of action on the behavioral world there is no way of falling into the acceptable range for one value without falling out of the acceptable range for the other.

It is important to notice the relationship between internal consistency and constancy. Theory-in-use may be regarded as a program for action designed to keep the values of certain variables constant within acceptable ranges. It is analogous to a computer program for an industrial process that is designed to keep conditions such as temperature and pressure within acceptable limits. The program's internal consistency and the acceptable limits of the variables determine one another. The internal consistency of the theory-in-use conditions the ability of the theory-in-use to achieve the desired constancies; the nature of the desired constancies partly determines the internal consistency of the theory-in-use.

Congruence

Congruence means that one's espoused theory matches his theory-in-use—that is, that one's behavior fits his espoused theory of action. A second (and much-used) meaning of *congruence* is allowing inner feelings to be expressed in actions: when one feels happy, he acts happy.

These two meanings are complementary and show an integration of one's internal (what one who is aware of my feelings and beliefs would perceive) and external (what an outsider who is aware only of my behavior would perceive) state. Lack of congruence between espoused theory and theory-in-use may precipitate search for a modification of either theory since we tend to value both espoused theory (image of self) and congruence (integration of doing and believing).

The caricature of a politician shows him advocating what looks like an espoused theory for the benefit of others, feeling no uneasiness over that theory's incongruence with his theory-in-use. Such an individual probably does not believe in the theory he is advocating although he does have an espoused theory he believes; incongruence between the latter theory and his theory-in-use may very well cause uneasiness and trigger a change in theory.

The degree of congruence varies over time. One's ability to be himself (to be what he believes and feels) may depend on the kind of behavioral world he creates. A behavioral world of low self-deception, high availability of feelings, and low threat is conducive to congruence; a behavioral world of low self-esteem and high threat is conducive to self-deception and incongruence. If one helps create situations in which others can be congruent, his own congruence is supported.

There is no particular virtue in congruence, alone. An espoused theory that is congruent with an otherwise inadequate theory-in-use is less valuable than an adequate espoused theory that is incongruent with the inadequate theory-in-use, because then the incongruence can be discovered and provide a stimulus for change. However, given the importance of congruence to a positive sense of self, it is desirable to hold an espoused theory and theory-in-use that tend to become congruent over the long run.

Effectiveness

A theory-in-use is effective when action according to the theory tends to achieve its governing variables. Accordingly, effectiveness depends on: the governing variables held within the theory; the appropriateness of the strategies advanced by the theory; and the accuracy and adequacy of the assumptions of the theory. A strong criterion of effectiveness would require that governing variables stay in the acceptable range once they have been achieved. Some theories-in-use tend to make themselves less effective over time. For example, if an agent tends to become more effective in ways that reduce the effectiveness of others, he may increase the dependence of others on him and make it more and more difficult for himself to be effective. Long-run effectiveness requires achieving governing variables in a way that makes their future achievement increasingly likely. This may require behavior that increases the effectiveness of others.

Long-run effectiveness requires single and double-loop learning. We cannot be effective over the long run unless we can learn new ways of managing existing governing variables when conditions change. In addition, we cannot be effective unless we can learn new governing variables as they become important.

Note that long-run effectiveness does not necessarily mean that action becomes easier. One may respond to increased effectiveness by addressing himself to new governing variables for which he begins by being less effective; progress in effectiveness may be reflected in the sequence of governing variables one tries to achieve.

Testability

Theories of action are theories of control, like the theories involved in engineering, in clinical medicine, or in agricultural technology. They are testable if one can specify the situation, the desired result, and the action through which the result is to be achieved. Testing consists of evaluating whether the action yields its predicted results. If it does, the theory has been confirmed; if it does not, it has been disconfirmed. This tests the effectiveness of the theory.

Special problems regarding testability stem from two related characteristics of theories of action: theories of action are normative (they set norms of behavior) and they are theories of the artificial (they are about a behavioral world that they help to create). There are three basic problems.

1. How can one test theories that prescribe action? How can norms or values be tested?
2. Given that theories-in-use tend to make themselves true in that world, how can they be tested?
3. In a situation of action (particularly in a stressful situation), we are required to display the stance of action—that is, confidence, commitment, decisiveness. But in order to test a theory, one must be tentative, experimental, skeptical. How can we, in the same situations,

manifest the stance of action and the experimental stance?

Simple prescriptions ("Don't go near the water!") are not testable because they do not predict results, but if . . . then . . . prescriptions ("If you want to avoid catching a cold, stay away from the water in winter!") are testable. Testing may not be straightforward because assumptions, often hidden, accompany such if . . . then . . . prescriptions. It is assumed here, for example, that you will not expose yourself to other risks of catching cold. Only if we make such assumptions explicit and control for them can we interpret the failure or success of the experiment.[3]

A more challenging problem has to do with the testing of norms of values themselves. Can we test governing variables such as "stay healthy"? In one sense, the answer to this question must be no, because governing variables are not if . . . then . . . propositions and make no predictions. But if one looks at the entire range of variables—the entire field of constancy involved in a theory-in-use—it is meaningful to ask whether, over time, these values will become more or less internally consistent, more or less congruent with the governing variables of espoused theory, and more or less effectively realized. For example, a set of governing variables that includes "stay healthy," "disregard advice," and "seek out dangerous excitement" may turn out to become increasingly incompatible. In this sense, one may test the internal consistency, congruence, and achievability of governing variables. But one may do so only in the context of a theory-in-use in interaction with its behavorial world over time.

The second basic problem of testing

theories of action is their self-fulfilling nature. Here are two examples. A teacher believes his students are stupid. He communicates his expectations so that the children behave stupidly. He may then "test" his theory that the children will give stupid answers to his questions by asking them questions and eliciting stupid answers. The longer he interacts with the children, the more his theory will be confirmed. A second example involves a manager who believes his subordinates are passive, dependent, and require authoritarian guidance. He punishes independence by expecting and rewarding dependence with the result that his subordinates do behave passively and dependently toward him. He may test his theory by posing challenges for them and eliciting dependent responses. In both cases, the assumptions turn out to be true; both theories-in-use are self-fulfilling prophecies because the protagonist cannot discover his assumptions to be mistaken or his theory as a whole to be ineffective. The so-called testing brings the behavioral world more nearly into line with the theory, confirming for all concerned the stupidity of the students and the dependence of the subordinates. We call such a theory *self-sealing*.

An outsider may find that the teacher's and the manager's theories-in-use are incompatible with the outsider's perception of the situation. But the outsider operates on a theory-in-use of his own that is different from that of the protagonist. The protagonist himself cannot discover that his theory-in-use is mistaken unless he can envisage an alternative theory and act on it.

The protagonist may find that over the long run his theory becomes less consistent, less congruent, and less effective. This will depend on the stability of conditions under which he operates, the other values that make up his field of constancy, and other factors. As time goes on, the protagonist is less able to get

---

[3] In nonlaboratory situations, the concept of experiment is not rigorously applicable; it is not usually possible, for example, to institute strict controls. But a similar sense of experiment is applicable. . . .

information from others (students or subordinates) that might disconfirm his theory-in-use. Others become less willing to confront, to display conflict, to reveal feelings. In this sense, the protagonist's self-sealing theory becomes progressively less testable over time.[4]

Consider those affected by the protagonist's theory-in-use. The students, for example, may deceive their teacher about their real feelings and beliefs and still remain open to others who reveal that the teacher's assumptions are inaccurate; after all, the students live in many behavioral worlds, not only in the world of the school. But perhaps the students have no behavioral world free of these assumptions. If so, others could not discover real feelings and beliefs different from those that confirm the teacher's theory. Deception of others would have been converted to self-deception. In the behavioral worlds created by such theories-in-use, there would be no way to discover that the teacher's theory is self-sealing. For this, outside events would have to cause the theory-in-use to fail, or someone with a different theory-in-use would have to expose the students to a different behavioral world long enough to recover their awareness of feelings and beliefs different from these expected by the teacher.

The interaction of theory-in-use and behavorial world has a political as well as an experimental dimension. The continued exercise and confirmation of a theory-in-use can be seen as a political process that proceeds from suppressing certain kinds of behavior and information to creating conditions in which others repress both elements. The theory has then made itself true and, by its own lights, effective. Orwell in *1984* and Laing in *The Politics of Experience* both describe such political processes. There need be no conscious construction of theory and reality on the part of a powerful protagonist; one might say that the theory constructs its own reality.

The third basic problem of testing theories of action concerns the stance we should take toward our theories-in-use. One must regard any theory as tentative, subject to error, and likely to be disconfirmed; one must be suspicious of it. However, one's theory-in-use is his only basis for action. To be effective, a person must be able to act according to his theory-in-use clearly and decisively, especially under stress. One must treat his theory-in-use as both a psychological certainty and an intellectual hypothesis.

The apparent paradox is heightened in unstable situations of action where one is overwhelmed by information and unable to develop a grounded theory of what is going on. Here, norms for behavior substitute for knowledge. One need not know precisely what is going on because, independent of such knowledge, norms provide a basis for action.

An interventionist is a man struggling to make his model of man come true. In an unstable and uncertain world that nevertheless demands action, he puts a normative template on reality. All the more paradoxical, then, the demand that theories-in-use be treated as hypotheses.

Hainer (1968) described this existential stance as one of "affirmation without dogmatism." He considers the here and now to be both prior to and more fundamental than one's theory about it, treating theories as perspectives on reality

---

[4] . . . [It can be argued that] the testability of theories-in-use is essential to their effectiveness over the long run because effectiveness over the long run depends on double-loop learning. There is no learning without testability.

If there is no requirement for double-loop learning, the argument falls. But we will argue further that circumstances of progressive change—the loss of the stable state—make testability and double-loop learning an essential feature of theories-in-use. Otherwise, the protagonist cannot discover ahead of time the changes in conditions that will influence his effectiveness; and, when such changes have occurred, he will not be able to discover in a differentiated way the aspects of his theory that have failed him.

that are also bases for action. Operationally, we are ready to discover that our theory is mistaken and to change it; yet we are reluctant to make such a change since change implies unsteadiness or flightiness that would themselves be a basis for failure. The commitment to focus on the here and now lets us encounter the unpredictable and lets us deal with the next piece of reality when we encounter it, modifying our theory-in-use as events require.

Our ability to take such a stance and to be conscious of taking it (as a part of an ethic for situations of uncertainty) is a model of such behavior for others, reducing their need for here-and-now certainty and allowing them to be freer to test their own theories without giving them up as a basis for action. Their doing so, in turn, further encourages us to do so.

Values for the World Created by Theory

Because theories-in-use are mutually interdependent with their behavioral worlds, it is relevant to ask not only "Is your theory effective?" but also "How do you value the behavioral world created by the theory?"

One cannot and should not clearly separate the questions of knowledge applicable to the construction of the theory and the questions of value applicable to the construction of reality. For, as we have seen, these processes determine one another.

Should a protagonist's theory meet all of the criteria we have described, one can still ask, "How do I value the world he has created?" Even if the theory-in-use is effective for its own values, successfully repressive of all others to the point that testability has no meaning, one may still ask this question.

The manager in our earlier example may become more and more convinced that all of his subordinates are passive and that all initiative in the organization must come from him. But he may also come increasingly to dislike the behavioral world of his organization in which expanding demands on him are accompanied by expanding resentment and distrust.

In short, the criteria so far elaborated provide a basis for judging theories of action, but they do not substitute for the evaluation of the world created by the theory.

It is clear how an outsider, with an independent theory-in-use, could engage in such an evaluation. If the protagonist, himself, is to do so, however, he must begin to make a connection between his own theory-in-use and those features of his behavioral world he most dislikes; otherwise his negative evaluation will have no bearing on this theory. And other governing variables than those contained in his theory-in-use must be alive, or becoming alive, for him; his ability to ask such a question implies that he is able to envisage, even to some small extent, a behavioral world different from the one he has created.

Brief Review

We have so far described a conceptual framework for considering theories of action, their structure and role, their status as tacit knowledge, their interaction with the behavorial worlds in which they function, and the criteria that apply to them.

Theories of action are theories that can be expressed as follows: In situation S, if you intend consequence C, do A, given assumptions $a_1 \ldots a_n$. Theories of action exist as espoused theories and as theories-in-use, which govern actual behavior. Theories-in-use tend to be tacit structures whose relation to action is like the relation of grammar-in-use to speech; they contain assumptions about self, others, and environment—these assumptions constitute a microcosm of science in everyday life.

Theories-in-use are vehicles for achieving and maintaining governing variables within acceptable ranges; the governing variables constitute the field of constancy in which deliberate behavior takes place. Building theories-in-use involves learning about managing variables and learning about changing variables. Theories-in-use are theories of the artificial; they help to create as well as describe the behavorial worlds to which they apply. Hence, theory-construction and reality-construction go together. The constancy of theories-in-use is considered as valuable as the constancy of the behavioral worlds created by those theories.

The concept of theory-building or theory-learning, particularly the kind of learning that requires change in governing variables, involves a paradox. The impetus toward constancy of theories-in-use and behavioral worlds impedes change in governing variables.

Theory-Building Process and Dilemmas

How, then, do theory-building and learning occur? Some theory-building is a linear increase of building-blocks of experience; new microtheories that extend the application of old governing variables probably develop in this way. However, the kind of theory-building that involves both change in the governing variables and double-loop learning tends to be convulsive, taking the form of infrequent, discontinuous eruptions that are initiated by dilemmas. This pattern of change probably derives from the nature of dilemmas and from the characteristic patterns of response to them,[5] which will be described next.

[5] The concept of dilemmas and their role in precipitating change in values is not a new one. For example, Rokeach (1968) offers the following

Dilemmas consist of conflicts of requirements that are considered central and therefore intolerable. The dilemmas that are important to the development of theories-in-use may be organized around several criteria that apply to the relationship between theories-in-use and the behavioral world.

Dilemmas of incongruity arise out of the progressively developing incongruity between espoused theory (on which self-esteem depends) and theory-in-use. For example, a politician who sees himself as believing in participatory democracy is disturbed by the manipulative, rough-shod tactics he uses in his career. Another agent's espoused values of warmth and sensitivity turn out to be incompatible with the pain he finds himself inflicting on others.

In order for such conflicts to become dilemmas, the elements of espoused theory must be central to the protagonist's self-image, and events must emphasize the conflict between espoused theory and theory-in-use in ways that overcome normal attempts to avoid noticing the conflict. A potential dilemma may exist long before it surfaces.

Dilemmas of inconsistency arise when the governing variables of theory-in-use become increasingly incompatible. For example, one person finds it increasingly impossible, in the behavioral world he has helped to create, both to win and to

view: "The greatest pay-off should come about by bringing into an inconsistent relation the most central elements of the system. . . . Attention is thus drawn especially to . . . an inconsistent relation between two or more terminal values . . . since these terminal values are the most centrally located structures; having many connections with other parts of the system, we would expect inconsistencies which implicate such values to be emotionally upsetting . . . to dissipate slowly, to be long-remembered, to . . . *lead to systematic changes in the rest of the value system*, to lead to systematic changes in connected attitudes, and finally, to culminate in behavior change" (pp. 21–22).

contain the hostility of others when he wins. But the person values both the winning and the repression of hostility. Another person finds it increasingly impossible, in the world of the family he has helped to create, to do his duty regarding his children by punishing them and to maintain their respect. This person needs both to do his duty and to retain the respect of his children for doing his duty regarding them (derived from Laing, 1970).

Dilemmas of effectiveness arise when governing variables, in a theory-in-use/ behavioral-world interaction, become less and less achievable over time, finally reaching the point at which they fall outside the acceptable range. For example, a person seeks to keep others calm and controlled by suppressing conflict; the hostility engendered by the suppression reaches an unavoidable boiling point so that no one is calm and controlled. Another person values a strategy of combat because it is familiar, because he knows how to use it, and because its use carries high status with it. But conditions change (others become aware of the strategy) so that the strategy becomes less and less effective.

Dilemmas of value arise when the protagonist comes increasingly—and, finally, intolerably—to dislike the behavioral world his theory-in-use has helped to create. For example, the protagonist values trust within his own group and also values the progress of the group. To achieve this progress, the protagonist is devious and manipulative toward outsiders. Group members, who act as though they expect people to be generally consistent in their behavior, progressively mistrust the protagonist, and the atmosphere within the group becomes progressively more manipulative and devious.

Dilemmas of testability arise when the protagonist, who values his ability to confirm or disconfirm his assumptions, finds that he is eventually completely cut off from the possibility of doing so by the behavioral world he has helped to create. For example, a manager finds that his subordinates and peers, conditioned by the mistrust they have come to feel for him and by the punishment they feel they have received when they "leveled" with him, no longer give him any valid information at all.

These kinds of dilemmas are not mutually exclusive; for example, a dilemma of effectiveness may also be a dilemma of testability, depending on the perspective taken. However, all dilemmas share certain characteristics: there is conflict between some element of the prevailing theory-in-use and some criterion applicable to the theory. The protagonist experiences this conflict as a central one—that is, the values he places on the elements of theory-in-use and the criterion are central rather than peripheral; in the cycle of interactions between theory-in-use and behavioral world, the conflict gets progressively worse.

The dilemmas may be created suddenly, as conditions shift in the behavioral world, or they may emerge gradually through the cycles of interaction. In either case, change in the governing variables of theory-in-use tends to be convulsive because of a characteristic pattern of response to dilemmas.

The responses to emerging dilemmas are not characteristically efforts to effect substantive change in governing variables. We value the constancy of our theories-in-use and our behavioral worlds. Hence, theories-in-use tend to be self-maintaining. We tend to adopt strategies to avoid perceiving that data do not fit, that behavioral reality is progressively diverging from one's theory of it, that one's theory is not testing out.

The repertoire of devices by which we try to protect our theories-in-use from dilemmas displays great imagination. Some of the more striking devices follow.

We try to compartmentalize—to keep our espoused theory in one place and our theory-in-use in another, never allowing them to meet. One goes on speaking in the language of one theory, acting in the language of another, and maintaining the illusion of congruence through systematic self-deception.

We become selectively inattentive to the data that point to dilemmas; we simply do not notice signs of hostility in others, for example.

The protagonist adopts a political method of suppressing the offensive data; for example, he succeeds in frightening others enough so that they will not reveal their mistrust of him.

The protagonist acts, sometimes violently, to remove the offending elements or himself from the situation. He either gets the trouble-maker fired or—his behavioral world having become unbearable—he moves to California. Or he may resolve to break off relations with his son.

The protagonist acts in subtle ways to make a self-sealing, self-fulfilling prophecy of his threatened theory-in-use—like the manager or teacher in our earlier examples—by using his authority to elicit the desired behavior from others and to cause the rest to be suppressed.

The protagonist introduces change, but only into his espoused theory—leaving his theory-in-use unchanged.

The protagonist introduces marginal change into his theory-in-use, leaving the core untouched.

These devices and others like them, individually or in combination, tend to maintain theory-in-use in the face of the emerging dilemma. Therefore, even if the signs of the dilemma have appeared gradually, the eventual change in governing variables tends to be convulsive. By the time the conflict becomes intolerable, the protagonist tends to have exhausted his stock of defenses; he is well into an explosive situation.

All of these dilemmas are, in a fundamental sense, dilemmas of effectiveness. If the protagonist finds intolerable the inconsistency of his governing variables or his inability to confirm or disconfirm his assumptions, it is because inconsistency and lack of testability also mean inability to achieve minimum realization of governing variables. If incongruity is intolerable, it is because the protagonist finds that he cannot realize the central governing variables of the espoused theory on which his self-esteem depends. If there were no need for effectiveness, there would be no dilemmas.

Hence, the basic dilemma is one of effectiveness and constancy. The protagonist strives to be effective and to keep constant his theory-in-use and the behavioral world he has created. When, finally, he cannot do both in spite of his full repertoire of defenses, he may change the governing variables of his theory-in-use. This dialectic shapes the theory-building process. . . .

References

Hainer, R. "Rationalism, Pragmatism, Existentialism." In M. W. Shelly and E. Glatt (Eds.), *The Research Society*. New York: Gordon and Breach, 1968.

Laing, R. D. *Knots*. New York: Pantheon, 1970.

Rokeach, M. "A Theory of Organization and Change within Value-Attitude Systems." *Journal of Social Sciences*, 1968, 24 (1), 21–22.

4.2 Educational Field Experience as the Negotiation of Different Cognitive Worlds

Kenneth D. Benne

In the decade just past, the boundaries between schools, colleges and universities and nonscholastic institutions in their environments have become more permeable. One evidence of this change is the growing educational use of student field experiences as a supplement, adjunct or sometimes as a coequal partner to academic instruction. Field experiences have, of course, been an established part of many programs of vocational and professional education for a generation and more in medicine, nursing, social work, engineering, preaching, teaching, and various vocational trades. But, in the past decade, field experiences have found their way into programs of general education and liberal arts as well. Attempts to incorporate nonacademic experiences for students into academically sponsored courses and programs of instruction have been perhaps most frequent in departments centered in behavorial studies of human beings and human systems—psychology, sociology, political science, and anthropology. At any rate, it is these uses of field experiences with which this paper is concerned.

Students engaging in a combination of academic instruction with field experiences may be seen as *living out* a process of knowledge utilization. They are maintaining simultaneous memberships in a scholastic institution, professedly devoted to

This article is part of a longer report which grew out of a research into educational field experiences, conducted at Boston University under a National Institute of Education grant (DHEW-NIE-3-1756, Robert Chin, principal investigator) on Learning to Utilize Knowledge and Experience.

the production and/or dissemination of "basic" knowledge, and a practice institution or action setting in which knowledge and know-how are used in performing a social function or in meliorating a human condition. The student is placed in the position of a linking or bridging agent in two distinct social systems within the knowledge utilization chain. The quality of learnings achieved by the student will depend upon how adequately he or she understands and manages this dual membership, upon how well he or she integrates the discrepant and sometimes conflicting demands of the two social settings upon his or her thought, conduct, and expenditure of energies.

Field experiences for students in pre-professional and vocational education have frequently been marked by conflicts between academic and field supervisors. For academic supervisors, students are in the field to augment, widen, and deepen their learning of professional knowledge and skills. For field supervisors, learnings by students are subordinated to maintenance of quality service to clients (patients for student nurses, occupational therapists, and physical therapists in hospitals, pupils for student teachers in schools, congregants for student preachers in churches, etc.). The student is at a point of conflict between priority objectives in the two institutions in which he or she is involved in his or her field experience. For example, the academic supervisor wants greater responsibility in working with pupils for the student teacher than the field supervisor can willingly permit, in light of the hazards to pupil learning and to the public relations of the school which might result from the "mistakes" of a student teacher, even though the "mistakes" might furnish excellent opportunities for professional learning. Or, if the field supervisor guides the student teacher into "safe," routine tasks in the school, the academic supervisor may feel that the student teacher is being exploited by being required to work for the school with little or no possibility of learning from such work.

Such conflicts do occur in preprofessional field experiences where academic and field supervisors belong to the same profession and where both institutions have a stake in "good" education for prospective professional members. The possibility of conflict, and the actuality too, are greater where students are undertaking field experience in order "better" to learn psychology, sociology, anthropology, or political science. For here the common professional bond between academic and field supervisors, and the student too, is missing. And the discrepancy between the norms of the two social systems, e.g., a university department of sociology and urban police department, concerning appropriate thoughtways and behaviorways for their "members" is much wider.[1]

[1] I realize that educational field experiences may be undertaken by students and their academic advisors with various learning objectives in mind. In fact, the staff of the research project, out of which this report came, was able to identify ten different models of field experience in current use. The different models emphasize various "product" and "process" learning objectives for students engaged in field experiences: Product models—Socialization model, Pre-professional model, Service model, Change agent model; Process models—Actualization model, Dialogic model, Inquiry model, Embedded model, Multiple membership model, Responsibility model. I am concerned here with two aspects common to all these models. First, field experience involves students in a process of "knowledge utilization." Second, field experiences place students in a linking relationship to social systems with discrepant norms concerning knowledge—its nature, its uses, and its validation.

It is common, within academic circles, to attribute conflicts which students encounter in field experiences to differences between the norms and attitudes which operate in practice and field settings and the norms and attitudes characteristic of the academic setting, with resultant conflicting expectations as to how the student should invest his or her time and energy in work and learning. The fact that conflicts do occur for students in preprofessional and vocational field experiences, as noted above, indicates that such an explanation of the conflicts is partially true. For here, academic and field supervisors, and students too, hold a generally common view of the knowledges and skills which aspirants to professional status should acquire. The conflicts can be explained in some large part by *noncognitive* factors operating within and between the academic and nonacademic social systems involved.

But, in field experiences utilized for purposes of general education of students in the behavioral sciences, we have noted another important dimension in the conflicts. This conflict focuses in the cognitive area itself. The student confronts different notions concerning the nature of knowledge and the ways in which knowledge claims are to be tested and validated. The conflicts which students encounter are grounded in *epistemological as well as normative and attitudinal* differences in the social systems which students are expected to bridge and link.

It is often difficult for persons in academic settings to accept the notion that people in practice and action settings possess and use "knowledge" in informing their choices and decisions and in guiding and evaluating their actions unless that "knowledge" is akin in form and organization to the "knowledge" which they build and test and communicate in their academic enterprises. And it is difficult for actionists and practitioners in field settings, especially when they have been schooled in academic ways of "knowing" and academic definitions of "ideal knowledge" to defend and affirm their practical "knowledge" as an alternative, in some respects at least, to the "knowledge" professed by academics.

A short detour into the history of epistemology, the science of knowing, may help to illuminate this difficulty. Traditionally, epistemology has been studied and taught as a part of philosophy. The goal of epistemological studies has been seen as normative or prescriptive, in the sense that the goal of true knowing is to see or to comprehend a universal reality which somehow underlies or transcends everyday experience. "Knowledge" has been distinguished from the "opinions," "beliefs," and "notions" by which those engaged in practice and action make sense, individual or common sense, of their often chaotic worlds and by which they guide and justify their decisions and actions.

The normative models for "real knowledge" have been drawn from the processes and products of the efforts of persons who specialize in "knowing." These are scholars and basic researchers who are abstracted socially from the pushes and pulls of practical affairs and who are supported by one set of sponsors or another in pursuing their central purpose of adding to and refining the cultural stockpile of disinterested "knowledge." Western epistemologists, working for the most part, in modern times, in universities, have not drawn their models of valid "knowing" from the methods and products of thinking of men and women of action who guide, direct, and conceptualize the practical "makings" and "doings" of culture and society.[2]

The failure of Western epistemologists convincingly to demonstrate or exemplify their ideal of *absolutely* valid knowledge has evoked various criticisms of their ideal over the centuries. One notable recent example of such criticism is the work of John Dewey and other American pragmatists.[3] They sought to refocus epistemological studies in several ways which are relevant to our present discussion. They shifted their definition of "knowledge" from the products to the processes and methods of knowing, in their attack on "knowledge" as an unconditioned vision or comprehension of "reality." The subject matter of epistemological studies becomes the processes by which human knowers confront the confused and problematic in experience and seek to restore clarity and

---

[2] This is not to say that Western civilization has been devoid of "sages" or "technologists" among their men of knowledge, to use Znaniecki's distinction (F. Znaniecki, *The Social Role of the Man of Knowledge* [New York: Columbia University Press, 1940]). Plato might be taken as an archetype of the first and Leonardo da Vinci of the second. In brief, "technologists" cultivate knowledge of how to

fit and organize means and energies effectively and efficiently into processes of achieving ends without focal or responsible concern for the validity or "rightness" of the ends served. "Sages" are concerned with the "rightness" or "wrongness" of ends to be served through collective action and only secondarily with the "truth" or "error" of the evidences and arguments which they use to justify the "rightness" of the ends they recommend or the "right" ways to achieve those ends. The role of "scholar" or "basic researcher" has been defined in the West as different from the roles either of "sage" or "technologist." The "scholar" or "basic researcher" seeks, tests, and refines disinterested "knowledge" of the ends and means of human cultures without developing or recommending more powerful and refined means to be employed or without attempting to justify "right" ends and means and to condemn "wrong" ones. It is the "scholar" or "basic researcher" who has furnished grist to the mill of the Western epistemologists in their search for canons and criteria of valid knowledge. It has been noted and argued that *traditional Chinese* epistemology drew its canons and criteria of valid knowledge from the functioning of the "sage" rather than the Western model of "basic" scholar or researcher. See, e.g., I. A. Richards, *Mencius on the Mind* (New York: Harcourt, Brace, 1932).

[3] Out of a wide range of possible examples, John Dewey, *How We Think* (Boston: Heath, 1933), may be taken as typifying this shift in emphasis.

direction to experience. Inquiry, problem-solving, hypothesizing, verification became the focal concern of epistemologists. While the study of knowing processes in basic research and scholarly disciplines was not neglected by the pragmatists, Dewey and others included within the scope of epistemology "knowing" as it operates in practical judgments—planning, deciding, valuing. Dewey sought to formulate a generalized method of coming to know, which while differentiating processes of knowing in various research disciplines and in "basic" and "applied" researches, sought to identify formal elements of a generalized method of inquiry common to all these ways of knowing.

Dewey's approach to learning and knowing has not been accepted universally either in academia or in nonacademic settings, but it has been influential in both. It has helped to release and empower *empirical* studies of knowing processes by both psychologists and sociologists. The idea of knowledge as an unconditioned vision of a universal "reality" has been widely abandoned by scholars and basic researchers themselves, not alone due to Dewey's and others' criticisms of the idea but also to comparative studies of ways of knowing in various human cultures with various views of "reality." Psychologists have emphasized both organic and environmental *conditions* which affect the development of cognitive organization and functioning in and by persons.[4] And sociologists have explored the relations between social organization, social movements, and social change and various forms and functions of knowledge.[5]

We may summarize the historical shift I have been describing in the focus of epistemological studies in the table below.

This brings us back to our exploration of the epistemological differences in field and in academic settings from which we departed in our brief historical detour. Two things should now be clear. First, the prevailing contemporary viewpoint in epistemological studies lends credibility to the search for differences in established ways of knowing in academic settings and in established processes of knowing in practice and action settings. Second, the history of epistemology suggests why, where the traditional assumption that academic ways of knowing are inherently closer to "reality" than other ways has not been surrendered or lost, learning situations involving encounters between academic men and women and men and women of action and practice are frequently defined hierarchically, with proponents of the "academic" definition of "knowledge" in the superior position.

Without specifying some of the typical differences in epistemological orientation between members of academic organizations and members of action and practice organizations, which I will attempt to do later, a few general principles concerning the conditions of optimum learning by students in field experiences may now be stated. The student should be oriented to think of his acquisition of "knowledge" through field experience as a two-way not a one-way flow. He or she should not expect merely to find concrete examples in the field to illustrate and clarify the "knowledge" he or she has acquired through instruction in academia—be it in psychology, sociology, anthropology, or political science. Nor will the student be able to report, summarize, and evaluate his or her cognitive learnings from field experiences fully or adequately in terms and concepts congenial to the academic disciplines. Rather the student should be oriented to explore two cognitive worlds and to clarify the differences and overlaps between these two worlds. The student is

[4] See, for example, Jean Piaget, *Psychology and Epistemology: Toward a Theory of Knowledge* (New York: Viking, 1971).

[5] See, for example, Karl Mannheim, *Ideology and Utopia* (New York: Harcourt, Brace, 1936), and F. Znaniecki, op. cit.

From Emphasis On:	To Emphasis On:
Products of cognitive behavior	Processes of cognitive behavior
Retrospective reference to accumulated knowledge	Prospective reference to needed knowledge
Some *one* favored *ultimate* context of knowledge production and verification—the role of scientist, scholar, technologist, seer or sage	Acceptance of *plural proximate* contexts in which knowledge claims are initiated, formulated, and variously tested
Devotion to a criterion of certainty and verbal defensibility	Various criteria—usefulness, fruitfulness, illumination (insight), consensus of some validating community
Sharp separation between processes of knowledge building and verification and processes of knowledge application and utilization	Blurring of distinctions between knowledge building and knowledge application—between the "pure" and the "applied"

oriented to *utilize* the "knowledge" he or she finds and acquires in the field to confront relevant academic "knowledge" and to understand the strengths and limitations of both. This is in addition to the more familiar *utilization* of academic "knowledge" to illuminate processes of practice and action in the field.

Of course, students will not be fully empowered to engage in such fruitful inquiries, unless their supervisors, academic and nonacademic, share this conception of knowledge utilization as a two-way flow and support students in taking advantage of their opportunity for epistemological inquiry. In fact, a good way to facilitate such sharing and support is through seminars in which students, academic supervisors, and field supervisors participate. Such seminars may not only facilitate learning by students but build mutual understandings and appreciations by academic and nonacademic people of their different yet overlapping cognitive worlds as well. In such seminars, *noncognitive* blocks to communication will need to be faced and worked through—stereotypes one of another, status differentials between the two kinds of people and knowledges involved, and fears of exposure of inadequacy and incompetence.

But the assurance that there is "knowledge" to be gained by all parties to the exchange gives point and substance to the explorations.

Now let me suggest some of the typical differences which have been discovered to date in the form and organization of knowledge between academic persons and persons in practice and action settings. I hesitate to do this because a typology may be used by students and by academic and nonacademic supervisors to "stereotype" persons in the two worlds and to foreclose the *fresh* inquiries which need to be made by students and supervisors in each field and academic setting that is being used educationally. It is the inquiry which reveals the *actual* cognitive worlds that are involved and the actual learnings that may be derived from creative negotiation of these worlds. I trust that a partial typology (pp. 123–124) may guide and open up processes of inquiry and learning rather than foreclose or eliminate them.

I have, of course, emphasized differences between "scientists" and "practitioners" in my typology. My construct is of two "ideal types." Actual persons in academia or in field settings may and do incorporate complex mixtures and integrations of both types in their actual behavior

The Cognitive Worlds of Behavioral Scientists	The Cognitive Worlds of Social Practitioners and Action Leaders
1. People and human systems which they study are not of interest as particular cases but as instances to confirm or disconfirm generalizations about people and human systems. Knowledge is organized around verbally (and/or mathematically) articulated generalizations.	1. People and human systems are clients or constituents. The social practitioner and action leader are concerned with particular cases, situations and practical difficulties in order to help, improve or change these. Knowledge is organized around kinds of cases, situations, and difficulties and takes the form of effective ways of diagnosing and handling them.
2. The occasion for inquiry is some gap or discrepancy in a theory or conceptual scheme. "Success" in inquiry is measured by attainment of more warrantable statements of variable relationships which fill the gap and/or obviate the discrepancy.	2. The occasion for inquiry is some difficulty in practice, some discrepancy between intended results and the observed-consequences of actions or excessive psychic and/or financial costs of established ways of working. "Success" in inquiry is measured by attainment of ways of making and/or doing which are more effective in fitting means to ends and/or in reducing costs of operation.
3. Scientists try in the course of their researches to reduce or to eliminate the influence of extraneous values (values other than "truth" value) from the processes of collecting data and determining and stating the meaning of the data within the research context. Their knowledge is relatively independent of the uses to which it may be put.	3. Practitioners and action leaders try to find and interpret data which enable them to serve the values which they are committed to serve—"productivity," "health," "learning (growth)," and, in more political contexts, the "power," "freedom," and "welfare" of their "clients" or "constituents." Their knowledge is consciously related to use for some purpose or set of purposes.
4. Scientists set up their researches to reduce the number of variables at work in the situations they study, by controlling the effect of other variables. Experimental results take the form of statements about the relationships of abstracted and quantified variables.	4. Practitioners and action leaders (like historians and anthropologists) work in field settings where multiple and interacting variables are at work. Their understanding of situations tends to be holistic and qualitative, though they may of course use quantitative methods in arriving at their "estimate of the situation." Unlike historians and anthropologists, they do not *attend* to all the variables involved in the *full* understanding of a situation but rather to variables which are thought to be influential and accessible to their manipulation in handling the situation in the service of their chosen values.

The Cognitive Worlds of Behavioral Scientists	The Cognitive Worlds of Social Practitioners and Action Leaders
5. Time, in the form of pressing decisions, does not influence their judgments and choices so directly as it does those of practitioners. They can reserve judgment, waiting for the accumulating weight of evidence. A longer time perspective operates in their judgments of what needs to be done now and later. Their statements of what they know are more qualified, less impregnated with their own hunches and insights as to what incomplete evidence means for purposes of action.	5. Time presses the practitioner to decide and act—judgments cannot wait. He or she must judge in order to meet deadlines, whether the evidential basis for judgment is "complete" or not. They must depend on their own hunches and insights in attributing meaning to incomplete or contradictory evidence. Their knowledge is impregnated with their own hunches and values. It is more personal, more dependent on their own ability to read a situation than the more impersonal knowledge which the scientist professes and communicates.

and communication. In fact, the educational goal of field experiences, as I have analyzed these, is for students to attain consciousness and appreciation of the two forms of knowing and to integrate these into their cognitive repertoires. Students should be able to act appropriately, in one mode of knowing or the other, as their role and situation require it. And, as already suggested, academic and nonacademic supervisors should acquire the same understandings and flexibility of response.

Collaboration between academic persons and practitioners and action leaders is possible and often desirable. But effective collaboration requires recognition and affirmation of epistemological differences on both sides of the social divide, not denial of differences on the ground that we are both persons of good will or polarization of differences into an impassable gulf between "theoretical" persons and "practical" persons.

My typology, in its emphasis on differences, is thus not formulated in the interest of thwarting but rather of furthering collaboration. It does suggest some of the kinds of differences which students in field experiences might explore in actual situations. It is such actual differences which students can use in negotiating discrepant cognitive worlds and in learning experientially and academically about the utilization of behavioral knowledge.

5

Emerging Perspectives on Planned Organizational Change

Over the past decade, planned organizational change has undergone some profound, and altogether salutary changes. At least there are signs here and there; certainly at the mythic "leading edge" where the seminal minds can be found, planned organizational change has taken on a new maturity. If not found yet at Erik Erikson's eighth stage of human development, it is certainly beyond the adolescent's acne and pubescent antics.

There is an emerging, new perspective regarding planned organizational change, one which casts some doubt on a number of assumptions more or less characteristic of somewhat older versions. For example, most previous writing:

1) Took organizations as a single class: instrumental, large-scale, science-based, international bureaucracies, operating under conditions of

rapid growth. Service industries and public bureaucracies, as well as non-salaried employees, were generally excluded, like the "underclass" they actually were.

2) Paid practically no attention to the social ecology of interinstitutional relationships or to the boundary transactions of the organization. It was as if organizations were positioned in an environmental void, not unlike what Emery and Trist would call a "placid, random environment."

3) The *management* of conflict was emphasized, whereas the *strategy* of conflict was ignored.

4) Underplayed power of all types, while the role of the leader as facilitator—"linking pin"—using an "agricultural model" of nurturance and climate building was stressed.

5) Implied a theory of change based on gentle nudges of growth coupled with a "truth-love" strategy; that is, with sufficient trust and collaboration and with valid data, organizations would "get it together," progress monotonically (and even monotonously) toward some vaguely defined vivid utopia where openness, risk-taking, self-actualization, and democratic values would triumph.

Nowadays, John Cage said not long ago, everything seems to happen at once and our souls are conveniently electronic or omniattentive. And it seems very difficult to solve our organizational problems because they infect, reflect the malaises of the greater society, and before you know it, our institutional lives. Very much like the way Machiavelli analyzed bad, unwise political judgments or any bad, fatal decision. He likened these to diseases. Those diseases, like TB for example, that are extremely easy to cure during the onset and first stages but almost impossible to diagnose then, are in their later stages all too easy to diagnose, but almost impossible to cure.

This is the consequence of living in an age that appears through a flickering TV screen that goes in and out of focus as it is expressed through the new, less familiar media, the strikes, injunctions, overnight shortages, disruptions, bombings, kidnappings, and other demonstrations which befuddle and often numb our responses or lead us into a messy metaphysical pathos.

In his *Report to Greco*, Nikos Kazantzakis tells us of an ancient Chinese imprecation: "I curse you; may you live in an important age." So be it. Our organizations are damned, encumbered, buffeted, and burdened by some new forces and some badly understood old forces making Planned Organization Change more challenging and perplexing than we thought it to be. Or want it to be.

What we discern about the nature of society says something about the deficiencies of some contemporary approaches to planned organizational change. In general, these have tended to be primarily oriented to the internal dynamics of organization, aimed at contributing to the established (and increasingly questioned) ethics and goals of economic and organizational growth (rather than quality), and relatively unconcerned with affected constituencies (within) and pivotal constituencies external to the organization.

Yet, what we detect is that there are increasing pressures in the political-cultural-economic environment of our institutions which call for new forms of planned change, new, still undiscovered strategies that will generate more responsiveness to external forces and interest groups. And to complicate matters even more, the internal governance, tasks, and divisions of labor will have to be confronted in ways that we are only beginning to understand. New strategies of power and politics have changed the rules of the game. The signs of this challenge are now inherent in the revolution of values discussed by such authors as Philip Slater, Charles Reich, Saul Alinsky, Martin Luther King, and others.

The message in this for those of us involved in the field of planned organizational change is that our paradigms of planned change (or organizational development) desperately need to be broadened to account for the needs, aspirations, anger, and concern of outside interest groups and internal pressure groups and caucuses and to incorporate models of change which are more innovative and far-reaching in their definitions of who governs the organization. We seem to be living through a period when two dilemmas that confront almost every human institution have to be answered: First, how do we establish new forms of power when "nobody seems to be in charge"? And, secondly, how do we get everybody in the act and still get some action? We have also to better understand the only basic questions, according to Tolstoy, that interest human beings: How to live? What to live for?

Without such an effort, which we believe is based upon a realistic image of the forces of change now present in the environment, the contemporary organization will no doubt be forced to change anyway—but in ways it will find odious and even more intolerable—like Machiavelli's last phase of disease, painfully easy to diagnose, impossible to cure.

The articles included in this chapter do take into account many of the societal forces, and if we think about them as a conceptual collage, they tend to represent a new stage of organizational development.

Harrison (5.1) in the first article finds some lessons from the processes of conscious evolution of organizations relevant for leadership and strategy for a New Age.

The paper by Mohrman and Lawler (5.2), which examines the spread of the "quality of work life" movement, makes explicit a shift in paradigm. A similar shift in paradigm is in fact implicit in the other paper as well.

The authors represented in this chapter seem less chary of getting into questions of power, politics, and dissensus. They seem to understand—more than our so-called liberal politicians—what some politicians understand and exploit: that there may be an interesting (and potentially dangerous) shift away from an emphasis on race and ethnicity to economic *class*.

Taken as a whole, the articles examine (and sometimes career away from) threats to the legitimacy of authority, the growing tension between populist and elitist solutions, baffling forces which undermine the conditions under which democracy flourishes—fear.

These papers, in all fairness, are not fully evolved. On occasion their reach exceeds their grasp. And yet we like them, erratic and unfinished as they are. Perhaps we like them more because they are unfinished.

For surely, they accurately reflect Jefferson's notion of the "American way," America, always, as "an unfinished revolution." And one that is unlikely ever to cease unless those forces that manage to intervene and mysteriously disarm our collective intelligence fail to be better understood.

5.1 Strategies for a New Age

Roger Harrison

During the last few years of my career as a management consultant, I have been impressed with the apparent intractability of organization problems. I ask myself why our attempted solutions so often produce no effect, or else exacerbate the problems they are designed to solve.

As we look around at business organizations, we see that decades of human relations training have made managers and supervisors more skillful and sophisticated about relationships. Why is it that we do not, therefore, have committed and happy workers? We have better information systems than ever. But do we make decisions more easily—or significantly better? We have sophisticated models and programs for planning and strategizing, and yet the environment seems more turbulent and out of control than ever. How is it that organizations seem so unmanageable just when we have learned so much about the arts and sciences of management?

As ever, hope is just over the horizon. The Japanese seem to have solved vexatious problems of productivity and quality. In this country, new plant experiments have shown that workers are able to manage themselves and produce superior

Human Resource Management, Fall 1983, Vol. 22, Number 3, pp. 209–235 © 1983 by John Wiley & Sons, Inc. Roger Harrison is with Harrison Associates, Berkeley, California.

quality and quantity with less supervision than we used to think necessary.

Peters and Waterman have made "excellent companies" a national catch-phrase for the 1980s that perhaps rivals the evocative power of Sputnik in the 1960s. The word "leadership" is back in favor, even among the academics who consigned it to oblivion for its vagueness and softness a few decades ago. Recent interest in "high performance" at both the individual and the organizational levels has produced considerable insight into the ways in which high-performing systems differ from their more mediocre competitors.

Where should we look for the key to improving organizations and management? Should we emulate the Japanese? Do we study "excellent" companies and try to be more like them? Should we start anew so as to do it right at the beginning, leaving existing organizations to limp along or decline?

I do not know. An ancient story tells of a man who sees his neighbor looking under the streetlamp. The seeker says he dropped the key to his door and is trying to recover it. Asked if he dropped it under the streetlamp, he replies, "No, I dropped it while trying to open my door, but there's more light here." This article is written for those managers, consultants, and academics who feel that in our efforts to improve organizations we have perhaps made some basic error which dooms us to repeat both our mistakes and our successes, but not move beyond them. It is an attempt to move beyond the circle of light given by our current concepts and methods.

Faced with a plethora of choices, I find myself drawn toward an ideal of *balance* and *harmony*. For a couple of hundred years we as a nation have been in the forefront of progress, of improvement, and of innovation. As managers and consultants we have focused on fixing problems and making things better. We have ignored the Hippocratic maxim, "First do no harm," and we have created organizations which are chronically unbalanced, internally and externally. In consequence, we face increasing difficulty in maintaining control and autonomy. We shall explore how attempts to achieve desired levels of control destabilize and unbalance the systems we are endeavoring to improve. By endeavoring to maintain an *illusion* of autonomy and control, we exacerbate the problems we are trying to solve and find ourselves running ever faster just to stay even.

We shall consider two approaches to the integration of organizations other than direct control: *alignment* and *attunement*. By the first is meant the voluntary "joining up" of individual members of the organization, finding fulfillment in the larger purpose of the organization. By attunement is meant the support of the individuals by one another and by the larger whole which comes about through a sense of mutual responsibility, caring, and love. Organizations which become and remain healthy, vital, and productive over long periods of time embody both alignment and attunement in their values and cultures, and in their structures and systems. Building and maintaining alignment and attunement in healthy tension is a major function of leadership. When either becomes dominant, organizations become unbalanced and destructive.

The effective leader keeps the forces of attunement and alignment in balance within the organization and also within him- or herself. According to this concept, the "new age leader" is both visionary and steward: visionary in the forging of the dream and in keeping the flame alight; steward in caring for and nurturing the organization and its human parts.

Among leadership tasks a special place is reserved for vision and the power of thought. We shall explore the part which intuition has to play in organization learning and decision making. We shall also consider what sorts of management tasks and activities might constitute the beginnings of a "technology of attunement."

Finally, we shall look at strategic planning in the light of our concepts of attunement and alignment. We shall attempt to apply the concepts of harmony and balance to the relationships of the organization with its environment: customers, suppliers, competitors, and communities.

Leadership and Organization Alignment

Interest has been awakening in the concept of leadership through vision, purpose, and intention. We are becoming aware that trying to improve productivity and quality through systems of rules, regulations, checks, and controls is not only costly but ineffective. The low trust and depersonalization that are engendered by ever more elaborate attempts at control further reduce the voluntary motivation to contribute, and a vicious circle of control and alienation perpetuates itself.

There is hope that the visionary leader (as opposed to the mere manager) can revitalize organizations through giving people meaning, purpose, and a sense of higher values in their work. By articulating common purpose and exciting future possibilities, the leader lines up the organization members behind a shared dream or vision, and they all march forward into the future.

Both within organizations and in our private lives, many of us hunger for purposes higher than mere career success,

and seek a nobler vision in which we can enroll. We await the emergence of charismatic figures who will lift us from our apathy. The concept of "organization alignment" expresses our wish for meaning and purpose and tells us how we may achieve them in our work settings.

Alignment occurs when organization members act as parts of an integrated whole, each finding the opportunity to express his or her true purpose through the organization's purpose. According to Kiefer and Senge (1982), the individual expands his or her purpose to include the organization's purpose. An organization is "aligned" when the parts choose voluntarily to act fully as members of the whole.

Organization alignment is seen by its advocates as different from the situation where an individual sacrifices his or her own identity to the organization. It is rather the *expansion* of the individual's identity and sense of purpose to include the organization and its purpose. I believe, however, that there is a shadow side to the benefits.

Organization alignment behind visionary leadership must involve the merging of the individual's strength and will with that of the collectivity, along with a willingness to be directed by the leadership. In high-performing organizations animated by noble purpose this may not feel like much of a sacrifice. It is a bit like being a member of a fine symphony orchestra. Instead of playing in their own tempo, volume, and style, the members "line up" behind the conductor in the service of his vision of the ideal rendition of the noble and aesthetic qualities of the piece being played. By doing so, each is able to be a part of an achievement which no one could aspire to alone. Much of the time it must be a satisfying experience.

The trouble is that even organizations animated by noble purposes have their inhumanities. The symphony conductor may inspire the orchestra to perform at its best, but he may also be dictatorial, may humiliate members who fail to perform to his standards, may have scant regard for the personal needs of orchestra members, and so on. Nobility of aim is no guarantee of an open heart.

Nor is the inhumanity of high-performing organizations confined to the leadership. In my own work with plant startup (Harrison, 1981), I have documented how peer pressures develop that cause people to exploit themselves in the service of the cause. People burn themselves out; they sacrifice their personal lives and family relationships; and they ostracize those who do not share their commitment. Tracy Kidder's *The Soul of a New Machine* (1981) describes both the light and the dark sides of the aligned organization in fascinating detail. It illustrates the tendency of aligned organizations to demand and receive total commitment of their members toward purposes that are actually rather narrow.

It is not inevitable that alignment must be exploitative of individual members. But the tendency is there. It is no accident that many of our most exciting tales of high-performing, closely aligned organizations are referred to as "war stories." War is the ultimate expression of unbridled will in the pursuit of ends believed to be noble.

Organizations and the Daimonic

Rollo May's (1969) concept of the *daimonic* is extremely useful in seeking to understand the tendencies of organizations of all sorts to become unbalanced and inhumane. The daimonic is that aspect of man that seeks to express itself no matter what the cost or consequences. May describes it as follows:

> The daimonic is *any natural function which has the power to take over the whole person.* Sex and eros, anger and rage, and the craving for power are examples. The

daimonic can be either creative or destructive and is normally both. . . . The daimonic is the urge in every being to affirm itself, assert itself, perpetuate and increase itself. The daimonic becomes evil when it usurps the total self without regard to the integration of that self, or to the unique forms and desires of others and their need for integration. It then appears as excessive aggression, hostility, cruelty— the things about ourselves which horrify us most, and which we repress . . . or, more likely, project on others. But these are the reverse side of the same assertion which empowers our creativity. All life is a flux between these two aspects of the daimonic.

Our hopes for finding meaning and purpose in the workplace easily blind us to the daimonic dark side of aligned organizations and charismatic leadership. In our enthusiasms and hopes for a new order or renaissance in business, it is easy to create daimonic organizations. Business and government are full of examples of the daimonic: the narrow paternalism of a Henry Ford; the expansive dreams of an entrepreneur like John DeLorean; the limitless personal ambition of a Richard Nixon; the zealous invasions of privacy of the "sensitivity trainers"; and the short-sighted dedication to the "bottom line" of the dedicated careerist or "Gamesman" (Maccoby, 1976).

We must remind ourselves that an organization need not be dull, hidebound, and bureaucratic in order to be inhuman. High ideals and disregard of the individual frequently go hand in hand. Witness Hitler's SS, the Japanese kamikaze squadrons, the elite troops of every nation, willingly sacrificing every moderating human value to the nation, to brotherhood, and to victory. In our pursuit of the ideals of high performance and control, it is easy to forget that in a balanced system, neither the whole nor the parts dominate. The idea that we can achieve perfect integration between the needs of the people and the purposes of the organization is fatally flawed.

High Performance and the Illusion of Control

In our attempts to manage and improve organizations, we have overlooked the fundamental connectedness of things. Charles Perow's new book (forthcoming) tells how minor and unimagined errors in tightly coupled complex systems combine in unpredictable ways to create major catastrophes, which he calls normal accidents. These result because we try to fix the parts of systems in isolation from one another, without appreciating their interdependencies.

This article is not the place for an essay on the ultimate interconnections of all to all, but it is important to illustrate by a few examples what happens when we enter into illusions of autonomy and control.

The Illusion of Autonomy and Control

The implicit belief in autonomy is so pervasive in our society that it is difficult to step outside of it. It is, however, fundamentally wrong. A friend described a conversation with her Japanese host in Tokyo. Noticing the throngs of unlocked bicycles parked on the streets, my friend asked if theft were a problem. "Of course not," responded her host. "Anyone would know that to steal a bicycle would be the same as taking it from himself." If we somehow came to believe that we were so totally dependent on others, and they on us, that we experienced our actions as reflexive, how would we behave differently?

When we disposed of our waste products and pollutants, we would experience them as landing in *our* environment, not someone else's. When we "leaned down" our organizations by "getting rid of dead wood" we would experience the unused human resources, the decline in living standards, and the hopelessness and despair of those who lost their jobs as our own loss. When we put shoddy merchandise on the market or cut a sharp and not too honest deal, we would feel the disappointment and diminished trust as our own. When we acquired the best and brightest employees for our own department and found a way to transfer out the less competent and motivated ones, we would experience the decrement in performance of the receiving department as our own. When we negotiated a fat and juicy budget for ourselves, and another group had to limp along on meagre resources as a consequence, we would experience their shortage of resources as well as our surplus. In short, we would know and believe that a part cannot remain healthy in a system which is sick, and that the whole cannot thrive when its parts are suffering.

Most of us realize that we are more intimately interconnected than we allow for in our plans and actions. Because we share a mechanical, atomistic view of the world, it is hard for any of us to live our daily lives in continuous appreciation of our dependence on others and theirs on us. We cannot take into account our connections with other individuals, groups, organizations, nations, and global systems because we do not experience them directly and continuously. We are in a real sense prisoners of our perceptual frames. In a curious way our illusion of autonomy only frees us to wander in the dark, tripping over the unseen bonds which connect us to others.

The illusion of autonomy causes us to ignore our connections with others. The illusion of *control* leads us often to do violence to the systems of which we are parts, in our attempts to manage, repair, and improve them. We love to experiment, to tinker with things, to fix them when they are broken and improve them when they are not. We are driven to produce, to create, to innovate, to build, and to expand. We want the good things of life.

To build, to create, and to solve problems so that they stay solved for a while requires that we have *control*, that we be able reliably to produce the consequences we intend, and that the unintended consequences of our actions do not nullify our gains. We do not always realize that without autonomy we cannot have control; we can only have reciprocal interaction in which we are as much acted upon and affected as we are impacting on others. Our lack of appreciation of the interconnectedness of things leads us to attempt to solve many problems which we cannot solve, because we cannot know and manage the connections of the parts we act upon with the larger systems of which they are members.

At global and national levels our failures are glaring and obvious: attempts to manage the economy, to stamp out poverty, to solve population problems, to rid ourselves of insect pests, all have been more or less undone by unanticipated consequences of our actions, or by unappreciated connections which stabilized the systems we tried to change. Many, viewing recent history, argue for a "return" to *laissez faire*. These, however, have not really given up the illusion of control; they still believe that, freed of interference, business organizations can be controlled by their managers, and individuals can be autonomous in their own lives.

When we turn our attention to the organization, we have not far to look for examples of unanticipated consequences of attempts at control and problem solving. General Motors established a highly automated plant at Lordstown at least partly to gain greater control over the human element in production. Lordstown suffered from crippling wildcat strikes because people hated working there.

Banks have turned to automatic data processing in an attempt to reduce errors and cut costs. But partly because the job of teller is now both deskilled and low paying, teller turnover has become and remained a serious problem.

"Sociotechnical" and "open systems planning" approaches to plant design have succeeded in creating within large organizations "islands" of high performance, productivity, motivation, and worker satisfaction. After the startup phase, when the new plant becomes more closely integrated into the host organization, the productivity often suffers. Attempts to redesign existing plants along the lines of the experimental facilities have generally been unsuccessful.

It would be easy to overstate my case. There are indeed many counterexamples of organizations that have been changed and improved significantly, of problems that have been solved successfully, and of companies that have been well managed consistently over many years. We have become ingenious in diagnosing difficulties and solving problems during the years in which capitalism and science have flowered hand in hand. Most of us would agree, though, that it is not getting easier. It requires more knowledge, more information provided more rapidly, more management attention and skill, and more hard work to manage organizations successfully than it used to. The proliferation of training programs in stress reduction, negotiation, and conflict management tell us what we knew already: that stress, tension, and disagreement are on the increase within organizations, and between them and their environments.

The point of this review is not to sound another note of doom and gloom; it is to suggest that we are unlikely to find the key to our dilemmas by continuing to search in the circle of light cast by management science, analytical problem solving, job design, operations research, management information systems, strategic planning, and the like.

We should not just abandon these tools for newer methods, but rather we must do something much harder: change our minds, expanding and altering the mind-sets of perceptual frames that produced the tools that are now diminishing in effectiveness. We need to stretch in two directions. The first is to move beyond the realm of facts and analytical thinking into that of vision and intuition. The second, more difficult one will be to move beyond our preoccupations with purpose and action into a realm of being and harmony.

The Need for Vision, Intuition, and the Power of Thought

It is interesting that while the established core of business and bureaucracy has been a bastion of rationality, ideas about the "power of positive thinking" have cropped up with great regularity in sales training and in books for some would-be entrepreneurs. Organizations as successful as Matsushita and Toyota in Japan and IBM, Tupperware, and Mary Kay Cosmetics in the U.S. have not been ashamed to motivate their employees by group singing and highly emotional celebrations. Successful entrepreneurs in business have often been known for their intuitive hunches and impulsive decision making, as have the "deal makers" who make the running in merchant banking.

Because of our rational-analytical bias, we do not support people in business organizations in learning to use such intuition and Pied Piper motivation. The chances are that we are only fractionally as powerful in intuitive thinking as we could be if we supported one another.

A major barrier to legitimizing intuitive thinking in organizations is that many of us have trouble distinguishing high-quality intuition from sloppy, wishful thinking. Obviously we would like to install the former in our "new age organizations" and avoid the latter. We should *add the power* of what we loosely call right brain thinking to our already formidable talents for assembling, organizing, and reasoning with data. Intuition is not a substitute for facts, for experience, or for logic. It is a way of building on and going beyond facts and experience.

Studies of high-performing individuals in many fields have shown that successful people tend to visualize the results they want in their lives and work, and to affirm to themselves that they can accomplish their goals. They create a clear and conscious *intention* as to the desired outcomes, and allow their actions to be guided by that frequently affirmed intention. Rather than planning in detail what they will do and how they will go about it, they start by creating an intensely alive mental representation of the end state. That representation then works through the individual's intuition and subconscious perceptual processes as she or he makes the multitude of everyday decisions which bring the goal ever nearer.

Purpose and intention are far more powerful than plans. Never in my years as a consultant have I seen an organization changed in any fundamental way through rational planning. The leaders I have seen deeply influence their organization's characters and destinies have always operated out of intuition, guided by strongly held purposes and drawn on by a vision of a better future. They communicated their intentions verbally to others who could share their vision, and they communicated it daily to others through their "real time" actions and decisions. In due course, enough people shared the vision and the intention to reach "critical mass," and the dream became reality.

Some people believe that when we create our own future through vision and intention, we are tapping into spiritual powers and energies, that there is an almost supernatural quality to it. Louis Tice (1980), in his program "New Age Thinking," has a more rational explanation. Tice says that when we establish and affirm an intention and create a vision of the end state, we "program" our subconscious minds to selectively perceive anything which could help us achieve our purposes. Thus, although we may begin with no idea of how to achieve our goal, we will begin to see the means we need through the filter we have set up which will selectively bring to our attention events, people, and other resources which could be useful to us. Conversely, Tice cautions, we must avoid words and thoughts about failure, because these program us to see barriers and difficulties, and indeed to engage in actions which will bring about the negative ends we have visualized.

Warren Bennis tells a story that supports such a view. Observing that the successful leaders he has interviewed are more than ordinarily reluctant to talk about the possibility of failure, he links that trait to the superstition among high wire artists against speaking about the possibility of accident. Bennis goes on to describe how the great Kurt Wallenda upset his family a few days before his death by talking about falling, and then describes the missteps and hesitancies which later led to his fall from a high wire into a street in San Juan, Puerto Rico. Our visions, it would seem, program us for life and death, as well as for success and failure.

Sports psychologists report similar findings in their programming of athletes to concentrate on doing the right things instead of focusing on not doing the wrong things. Their experiences are supported by the literature on attribution—people who see themselves in a negative light attribute failure to themselves, but attribute success to outside forces beyond their personal control.

Louis Tice points out that our subconscious "programs" can be charted by observing our "self-talk," the commentary we make on ourselves and the world as we go about life. Negative self-talk includes, "It's not like me to do so well." "Some people have all the luck!" "I never seem to be able to. . . ." "That's not one of my strengths." Positive self-talk includes such affirmations as, "I'm specially good at. . . ." "I'm learning how to. . . ." "Every time I try this I do it better." "I'm going to find a way to. . . ."

Organizations have self-talk, too. It can be heard in the organization's myths and rituals, as Joanne Martin reports in cognitive social psychology. The "war stories" about heroes and villains tell us where an organization has been *and where it's going*. They tell us whether it is programmed for success or decline. When leaders want to prepare the organization for levels of performance beyond its self-image, they have to create new stories, myths, and rituals which will program the organization's collective consciousness for success. As Peters says, they have to create a series of "small wins," each of which is a sign and signal of positive change. It is not enough to articulate a vision of a hoped-for-future; that is necessary but not sufficient. Organization members have to be given new stories to tell, stories that point toward the successful achievement of the vision. The leadership's ability to conceive and create dramatic events, both large and small, is critical to changing the self-talk of an organization. A new achievement in quality, a promising innovation, a better safety record, these are the "small wins" that can be dramatized to form the basis for new stories. They lead to the big wins, such as Lee Iacocca's recent announcement that Chrysler has just paid off its government loans.

We may make fun of the group singing of Toyota and Tupperware, but they appear to sing all the way to the bank. Mottos such as "Better Things for Better Living, through Chemistry," and "Progress Is Our Most Important Product" may seem a little dated to us now, but both the songs and the mottos have been important parts of the self-talk of highly successful organizations. Purpose, vision, intention: When we venture into the turbulent waters of the unknown future, it gives us heart to have songs to sing and stories to tell, and a talisman to guide us. Our mythmaking may not be rational, but neither are the hopes and dreams that spur us on to success. Both spring from the human spirit.

Attunement: The Search for Harmony in Organizations

The concept of organization alignment speaks to us of human *will*, driving toward the fulfillment of vision and purpose. I believe that the counterbalancing force is to be found in the operation within organizations of human *love*, expressed as empathy, understanding, caring, nurturance, and support.

The potency of love in organizations is largely denied and repressed. We experience the same fear of it that we previously did with sex and power. Love has its daimonic side, and we are not wrong to be wary of it. There is a very real danger in encouraging people to look to the organization for the satisfaction of needs for nurturance which are frustrated due to

the fragmentation of family and community. And there are real limits on how much trust we can permit ourselves in the competitive and conflict-ridden cultures of many organizations.

I propose only that we allow ourselves to become aware of the reality of love. We shall not get rid of love by ignoring its operation in organizations, any more than we can avoid power by looking the other way. By refusing to examine love in organizations, we only prevent ourselves from accessing its healing, supportive, and creative influences. And these we do need.

Love is made necessary by the fact that there is no such thing as independent life. It arises from the recognition of our fundamental connectedness. Thus, its denial is part of the illusion of autonomy, and makes us vulnerable to the daimonic side of our needs for power and control. An understanding and acceptance of the power of love in organizations makes healing possible. It does not end conflict and competition, but it can bring grace and restraint into the dance of the warriors, and bind the wounds of both victor and vanquished.

As Kahlil Gibran wrote in *The Prophet* (1969), "Work is love made visible. And if you cannot work with love but only with distaste, it is better that you should leave your work and sit at the gate of the temple and take alms of those who work with joy."

Or, as a recent Delta Airlines ad put it, "When people love their work, it shows. . . . Our people are happy. Because they love what they do and who they do it for. When people feel that way, they simply have more to give."

Perhaps they do. They gave a Boeing 747 airliner to their company not long ago.

By the concept of attunement in organizations is meant a resonance or harmony among the parts of a system, and between the parts and the whole.

When we are attuned, we become more receptive to the subtle energies that connect us with one another. We become open to one another's needs and to our own sense of what is worthy of reverence in the work we do. Where alignment channels high energy and creates excitement and drive, attunement tames and balances the daimonic qualities of our quest by opening us to each other and to the messages from our hearts.

If an aligned organization is like a symphony orchestra, then attunement is represented by a jazz combo improvising. The members are alert to what each other player is doing and they support and build upon one another. Space opens for those who have solos to play. There is a sense of flow between the players which is unforced and uncompetitive. The essence of attunement is that the purposes of the parts are served by the whole and by the other parts. Each member's individual needs are respected and served by the organization and by the other members.

Alignment and attunement are both processes for achieving integration and unity of effort among the differentiated parts of a system. We need more integration, because we have created a world in which many of us are highly oriented to meeting our personal needs, often at the expense of the maintenance of our organizations and institutions. We have a lot of personal freedom; it is difficult to obtain needed integration through coercion or through rules and systems.

Neither alignment nor attunement is sufficient by itself. Organizations that are aligned but not attuned tend to be high-performing systems, which exploit their members and which may expend vast quantities of human energy and economic resources for dubious ends. They become daimonic warriors, so busy fighting the good fight that they forget what the battle was about. Organizations that are attuned but not sufficiently aligned tend to enjoy and support one another but do not get much done. They may be so oriented to caring for one another's needs that they cannot make and implement task decisions. They are not viable in a highly competitive environment. The leaders we need now are those who have the balance, the vision, and the heart to create both alignment and attunement in their organizations.

In the past, leaders we call "great" have often been very strong, ruling through fear and respect, or very charismatic, releasing and focusing the daimonic for their followers. Neither is appropriate to the balance between purposive thrust and nurturing harmony which I believe makes for sustainable performance in organizations.

Michael Maccoby (1981) has looked at the emerging character of the workforce and has identified the leadership traits which fit the emerging culture. Maccoby's new leader is seen as having a caring, respectful, and positive attitude toward people, and a willingness to share power. S/he is open and nondefensive regarding his or her own faults and vulnerabilities and avoids the use of fear and domination. The picture is of a secure and mature individual who can articulate values and high principles that give organizational life meaning, but who is more receptive and self-aware than we normally expect visionary leaders to be.

The new leader shares the characteristics which Joseph Campbell (1949) discusses in *The Hero with a Thousand Faces*. He or she is *called* by a mission and accepts the sacrifices and hardships of the task because s/he must. The hero does not only overcome barriers and obstacles, but is personally transformed in the process. The hero follows his or her *daimon* but is humanized by the challenges and difficulties of the journey.

There is something of the hero in all of us. The hero is not always strong, but is tempted, attacked, often overcome. S/he responds to an inner call, but is not independent. S/he receives help along the way, without which the journey would end in failure. The hero is often torn between inner forces of love and will, and he or she embodies and expresses both.

The hero's journey purifies the individual to a degree from the passions of the ego. Thus liberated from the daimonic, the individual is able to approach his or her role in the spirit of *stewardship*: leadership as a trust exercised for the benefit of all. As a steward, the leader serves the followers, guided by a vision of the higher purposes of the organization.

The organization is animated by and aligned with the sense of its own higher purpose. The leader focuses the attention and consciousness of the members on those purposes. But the leader also knows that the parts have legitimate purposes of their own which are not completely expressed by the purposes of the whole, and s/he facilitates the attunement processes by which organization members can come to know, respect, and care for one another's needs and individual purposes. The flow of human energy is not one way, from the members to the organization, but the uniqueness of each part is also preserved and nourished by the whole.

Leaders such as those described above are not numerous. Most of us do not embody equally the forces of love and will, nor have we been so purified by our own hero's journey that we are able to act for long periods of time without selfish interest. Also, leaders are shaped by the organizational cultures in which they develop, socialized by the myths, war stories, and rituals of that culture. An organization of "gamesmen" is likely to produce winners and losers, not heroes.

Processes of social change always seem to have a spiral quality: The times and circumstances bring forth the leaders, and the leaders influence the times. If we wish to facilitate such a process, we can look for the leaders, and we can in part alter the circumstances in which they develop. Creating such a climate for the development of the hero-cum-steward involves two aspects: finding and strengthening the sense of higher purpose in the organization, and creating processes that harmonize and integrate through attunement.

Strategic Thinking and the Creation of Meaning

We turn now to the leader's task in creating a sense of purpose and meaning in the organization. Partly, of course, this is a question of having values and acting consistently according to them. But that is a hallmark of integrity, not necessarily of leadership. It is in the creation of value-loaded *meaning* that leadership focuses and channels human energy.

As Peters and Waterman (1982) have argued so convincingly, effective leadership begins with action, followed by *labeling*. It is by labeling that we create meanings. The actions do not have to be large or dramatic in order to shape a sense of direction and purpose. Indeed, it is the series of "small wins" appropriately labeled and interpreted that weaves the fabric of stories, myths, and memories out of which we create the meaning in our organizational lives.

We usually think of strategy as the art of predicting the future, and then planning how to change the organization so that it will perform well in future time. It is a frustrating business, not least because the organization is thus always defined as wanting, when compared with the strategic ideal. Add to that the fact that the most dramatic events of the future are those which are least predictable. It is little wonder that some managers are losing their taste for strategic planning.

We seem to do more planning in organizations, as planning becomes less effective in a desperate attempt to make the future behave. It is, perhaps, an outgrowth of our preoccupation with maintaining the illusion of control. In fact, planning can only help us to deal with conditions and variables which we already know or suspect to the important. Planning defines what we know and don't know within a given context. Any future changes in context (variables and events not thought to be probable or important when the planning was carried out) will more or less invalidate our plans (Davis, 1982). Planning can estimate the risk of a downturn in the economy based on known historical factors such as inflation, interest rates, leading economic indicators, and so on. We can use that estimate to judge whether or not this is the right moment to launch a new product. But planning cannot tell us anything about either the likelihood or the impact on our marketing plans of unforeseen events such as the sudden rise of a new cult religion, the discovery of a major new oil field in China, or the development in Russia of a successful inoculation against cancer.

Most of us seem to be aware that unforeseen events are looming over our futures. We know that we do not know. We imagine wars, economic disasters, cataclysmic natural events, but we do not believe we can predict their likelihood by reference to historical data trends, so we cannot plan for them. If we could assign a probability to these events, we should still find it difficult to plan, because the events we imagine are so sharply discontinuous with our current experience as to paralyze both mind and will. Because we cannot plan for the future we fear and imagine, we plan instead for the future we hope for, one in which even the projected

negative events possess a comfortable familiarity.

But how can such an approach best prepare our organizations and ourselves for the future? Barry Stein (1983) says that instead of relying on strategic planning, the organization must learn to *adapt* to a condition of continuous change. ''The old managerial cry, 'I don't want any surprises' will have to give ground. Managers need to understand that they absolutely will have surprises and that they and their subordinates . . . will have to learn to handle them, and handle them well.''

Peters and Waterman report that their ''excellent companies'' are animated by a strong set of cultural values that give meaning to events occurring in the environment and guide people at all levels in the organization in making decisions that are consistent with the thrust of policy and purpose. At the same time, these companies are in a dialog with their customers and are so oriented to the marketplace by their ''appreciation systems'' that they quickly find meaning in and take action on the feedback they receive.

In our terms, these organizations are aligned behind a sense of mission and purpose. They are also attuned, but not only in the sense that the individual is valued and supported: They are in resonance with the marketplace as well, engaged in a continuous process of mutual influence and support with their customers.

Effective as it has been, this concept of attunement to the environment must be radically expanded in order for organizations to remain excellent, or indeed viable, in the future. Being sensitive to the marketplace is simply too narrow a connection with the world. It implies a degree of autonomy from events in the wider environment that simply does not exist.

Seen from a global viewpoint, the organization exists only as part of a larger reality, supported and nurtured by the larger system on which it depends: the nation, its culture, and many interest groups, the world economic and political system, and the physical and biological planet itself. To the extent that an organization acts in ignorance of the connections that link it to other parts, and to the whole system of the global environment, it will tend to experience surprise and shock at unanticipated events originating in the larger system. It will experience such events as deficient in meaning, and hence as a threat to its sense of reality and its own identity.

Long-range and strategic planning are one approach which organizations have taken to predict and control events in the wider environment and so experience fewer surprises. Because the web of causality is so complex, and because the larger system is *evolving* rather than simply operating as a steady-state system, such efforts must be unsatisfying. The error is not so much in the operations we use as in a mistaken *definition* of the organization as an autonomous entity, and were we to approach strategy from the point of view of endeavoring to *discover* the place of the organization in the larger systems of which it is a part and on which it depends, we would do far better.

From such a viewpoint, organization purpose is not simply decided by its members, but is in large part "given" by its membership in the larger system. The process of discovery is partly internal to the organization, involving an inner search for values and meaning. It also has an external aspect, that of discovering meaning through the transactions of the organization with its environment. Viewed in this way, a primary task of the leadership is the discovery of the organization's place and purpose in the world. And every event in its history can be viewed as part of a lesson.

Adopting such a point of view requires a fundamental change in one's orientation to goals and to the success and failure of one's plans. Most business organizations strive to succeed, to win against their competitors, against the government, sometimes against their suppliers and customers as well. The tougher conditions become, the harder they strive. Since conditions are increasingly tough, there are a lot of people out there striving. They experience a lot of failure in the difficult conditions, and they experience blame from others and from themselves. They experience high stress, as can be seen from the ever-increasing popularity of alcohol, drugs, and stress management courses.

A lot of that stress comes from seeing ourselves and our organization as autonomous. We deny our dependency on larger systems and events, and then we blame ourselves when our inharmonious actions do not lead to the achievement of our goals.

When we are striving to achieve goals, our learning is oriented to *means*. We learn more and more about what to do or not do in order to achieve the goals we have chosen. The excitement and stress often prevent us from questioning the goals themselves, or from seeking to read the lessons that our successes and failures are sending us about our place and purposes in the larger system.

When goals become very difficult to achieve, and it begins to seem as though the environment is hostile and unsupportive, it is typical of our culture to engage in problem solving—to identify the barriers to success and to work and plan to overcome them. We can, however, take the point of view that our organization has an appropriate place in the larger system, and that our task as managers and leaders is to attune our organization to its environment in order to discover what our part is and play it. The difficulties we experience are interpreted as signs and signals from the environment that we are somehow out of resonance with our true role. We read events as messages, rather than as judgments. We shall then expend less energy striving, and we shall move in harmony with the ebb and flow of events. If at some point we find that there is no longer joy in the struggle, that we are burning ourselves out in the effort to survive and succeed, then that will stimulate us to reevaluate our purpose and the meaning of our work. According to this point of view it should not be *difficult* for an organization to survive and thrive, if it is attuned to its part in the larger system, any more than an organ in a healthy body has to work especially hard to survive. When it plays its part, it receives the nourishment it needs.

The Search for Meaning

From a systems point of view, then, strategic thinking is a search for meaning, rather than a search for advantage. It is rational in its search for signs and signals from the environment and in its intentional search for relevant feedback. It is intuitive in the process of *appreciating* events and examining the activities and goals of the organization against the criteria of the heart.

In approaching strategy from the point of view of purpose, our aim is differential rather than positional in a market domain. Our endeavor is to forge a shared view of reality that will serve the organization members as a base for day-to-day decision making and direct the leadership thrust of the dominant coalition.[1]

[1] I am indebted to my colleague, David Nicoll, for this view of the strategizing process.

The activity is definitional in that we are attempting to penetrate the forms of the organization in its internal and external relationships in order to discover its essence. Our belief is that when the forms (systems and structures) and processes (doings) of the organization flow from its essential qualities (being), the organization will become energized and integrated, and will become attuned with its environment. Therefore, it will prosper.

The questions we ask in order to determine the essential qualities of the organization are simple, though the process of answering them may be difficult.

We may ask ourselves what we experience of *energy* and *meaning* in our work:

Does the production of goods and services enliven us, giving value and meaning to life?
Do we strive joyously, or with desperation?
Do we feel that we are net contributors of value in our work in the world?

We may ask questions about our organization's identity and special characteristics:

Who are we; how would we describe our core being?
What are our "gifts," our distinctive competences and resources; what have we to contribute which is unique and valuable?
What do we value and believe in? What constitutes integrity for our organization? Can we as organization members fully identify with the values?

We may ask what we are being "called" to do in the world:

What messages do we receive from customers about their needs?
What are we hearing from government, from the public, from financial markets,

from special interest groups? What do these messages tell us about how we are positioned with our many stakeholders?

What do developments in technology and resource availability tell us about our mission and purposes?

As we look farther afield in the world, what messages do we read in global trends and events about our calling?

As we search within ourselves, what needs in the world do we want to meet? What activities and processes have "heart" for us? What are the ways in which we love to work? What is it like when we are performing at our best?

We may examine our "core processes," the technology and systems we use to transform inputs into outputs:

How do our core processes link us to the rest of the world and structure our relationships with our stakeholders?

Are the relationships created by our core processes consistent with our values and with what we see to be our mission in the world?

Do our core processes provide us with the degree and kind of "energy flow" we need to survive and thrive (money, natural resources, people, "strokes").

Such questions are difficult to answer and test the commitment of leaders to the strategizing process. However, such a strategizing process is not without precedent, and those wishing to undertake it need not proceed entirely without guidance. The questions we pose above are similar to those addressed by the Open Systems Planning processes introduced in the early 1970s by Will McWhinney, Charles Krone, and James Clark (1983). Practitioners of the approach have developed techniques for leading organizations through a strategizing process, but for too

long they have been communicated almost entirely through an oral tradition.

Work by Jerry Fletcher (1983) suggests another approach, equally compatible with our point of view. Fletcher works with individuals and groups to find their "high-performance pattern." He asks clients to recall a series of episodes, in each of which high performance came easily, flowing in harmony with inner purpose. In such a state, barriers in the environment are not experienced as limitations, but simply as part of the dance. Fletcher has found that everyone can recapture such experiences, and that a common pattern runs through all such experiences of a single individual.

Fletcher's approach embodies the idea that high performance does not flow simply from an inner sense of purpose. An essential part of each individual's high-performance pattern is a specification of the environmental conditions that must exist for the person to "catch fire" and jump to that level of performance in which he or she is perfectly in tune with and supported by the environment. The search for the key to high performance places an emphasis on harmony with the environment, which is as strong as the weight given to the skills and values of the individual.

Following Fletcher's approach, organizations can examine their memories, myths, and war stories to find their high-performance pattern, and to learn what constitutes the attunement to the environment which releases high performance for that organization or subunit.

This strategizing process may or may not result in specific plans. Fundamentally, it has two aspects: *focusing* and *appreciating*. The appreciating process results in internal and external "mapping" of the organization in its environment. It is an expression of the members' shared beliefs about the nature of reality. Focusing results in a statement of the mission or purpose of the organization, and of the values that underpin it. Together, the "reality maps" and the mission statement form the basis for a projection of the organization into the future.

David Nicoll refers to such a projection as the "willed future." It is a statement of the organization's state of being at a later time when its essence will have been realized in its structures and processes, and it will be making its maximum contribution to the common good.

A statement of the willed future becomes the basic policy document of the organization, to which all lesser plans and decisions are related, and upon which the *intentions* of the organization members are focused. In this way the power of thought to create reality is brought into play.

The statement of the willed future becomes a center of the self-talk of the organization. By consulting the willed future at points of uncertainty and endeavoring to keep plans and decisions in conformity with its statement of intentions, the organization aligns its efforts, its "doings" with the strategy.

Evaluating the Strategizing Approach

How shall we evaluate our approach to strategy? We are told to know who we are, and to appreciate and understand our dependence on the environment. Out of these two flow both our sense of purpose and our high-performance pattern. Once so grounded, we can apparently "act according to our hearts, and trust in the Lord."

Many of our most successful enterprises were built by people who had just such a sense of who they were and what they were to contribute. Because such individuals did see more clearly than most their right relationship to the environment, they succeeded, and they put the stamp of their visions and values firmly on reality.

But of what utility is our approach in the established modern organization? There are real obstacles in most organizations to the establishment of a sense of common purpose, a unified appreciation of the meaning of events in the environment, and a vision of the willed future. If, as is common, it is difficult to keep coordinated planning going between, say, the production and marketing people, what shall we say of the chances of their agreeing on ultimate values and the meaning of organizational life?

The idea of establishing consensus around values with one's business associates implies a high degree of *mutual* commitment between the individual and the organization. The individual has to be there not just for what he or she can take, but for what he or she can create together with others to develop greater value. And the members must trust that their willingness to give will not be exploited or misused.

Then, too, there are questions of personal style. Sitting around and talking about our values and our relationship to the environment is exciting to those who like to think, but it can be exceedingly frustrating for those who prefer doing. Using one's intuition to go beyond the actual to a vision of the possible is a meaningful activity for those who trust their intuitions, but to more concrete, data-oriented people it can seem no more substantial than building castles in the air.

Whether we like it or not, we are being nudged by events to change our consciousness. Our old ways of seeing ourselves in relationship to the world no longer produce reliable satisfactions. We can struggle harder to change the world to accord with our perceptions, or we can allow ourselves to change internally.

The seeds of those changes are in all of us; we each need to experience conditions which support the growth of those seeds. One way to create those conditions is through the strategizing process. We need to stretch our whole brains if we are to live comfortably and competently in a world in which causal connections are increasingly tenuous, and in which data became dated almost as soon as they are collected. Becoming more intuitive does not mean becoming less rational. It means knowing the limits of rationality and being comfortable in venturing beyond the data.

Modest Beginnings

No matter how grand our flights of fancy, our visions of a New Age, we each have to start where we are. Usually that is in a situation of mixed threat and promise, our hopes approximately balanced by our cynicism and our fears. This final section is written for people who wish to make a start in such directions, but who wish to test the water before committing themselves in a very visible way. In the sections that follow are some suggestions for applying intuitive thinking and the idea of attunement in organizations.

Many of us mistrust intuition, because it seems not to be grounded on data. We see others parading their wishes as intuitive truths, and we do not wish to join them. There are two questions we may ask ourselves to ensure that we do not confuse our wishes and hopes with true intuition. Have we collected as much data as is practical in the situation? Are we showing respect for the data and using it to check our hunches and intuitions? By showing respect for the "negative case," we can often improve our intuitive performance.

If we can affirm that we are using intuition to both work with and go beyond the data, then we shall be able to benefit from the power of intuition, while avoiding its excesses. We can begin to introduce

and make legitimate the use of intuition in organizations which pride themselves on being practical, realistic, and tough minded. A few suggestions follow.

In conducting meetings, distinguish explicitly between what Neil Rackham calls *filter* and *amplifier* meetings. A *filter* meeting is (much like a brainstorming session) conducted to sift through a number of options for action, and to choose the best one. An *amplifier* meeting is one in which divergent thinking is encouraged. The idea is to *generate* possibilities, not to choose among them. Appropriate behavior is supportive and stimulative: recognizing contributions and giving credit for ideas; building on the contributions of others; drawing others out; summarizing, and testing for understanding and agreement. Criticism is deliberately withheld or turned into a "how to?"

The supportive and free-flowing atmosphere of an amplifier meeting encourages intuitive thinking. The competitive and abrasive qualities of the more prevalent filter meetings discourage it.

Ask subordinates to go beyond the data. Ask them to stretch their imaginations and support them in doing so. Ask, "What might be going on here that we're missing? Are there possible explanations we haven't thought of?"

Imagine the future. With colleagues, use techniques of the futurists to build alternate scenarios for your business, your technology, your markets, the society we live in.

Show people the whole picture. It is hard to be creative and imaginative about one's small part unless you can see how it fits the whole. Ask people to be aware of and think about the whole enterprise. Encourage them to cross boundaries and use their imaginations on operations other than their own.

Value the results of imaginative activities. Separate the selection of ideas to be acted on from your appreciation of the effort and mind stretching which has gone into their development.

When it comes to the "technology of attunement," we will find useful precedents from Japanese management, from Quaker practice, and from our own early history.

Lessons Already Learned

The development by Japanese management of Quality Circles is clearly an example of the practice of attunement. When a team from Lockheed went to Japan in 1973 to study these small groups of employees who met on company time to discuss quality and other work-related problems, they reported two key factors in their success. One was the uniquely cooperative and participative attitude on the part of Japanese supervision, an attitude which has since become something of a legend. The other was that the emphasis is not on improving productivity, but on improving the quality of working life by making the job better for the employee. Subsequent attempts to apply the Quality Circles approach in the United States have consistently demonstrated that they do not work unless they are experienced by employees as a genuine expression of these attunement values. Workers have proven hard to fool in this regard.[2]

Early American communities provide us with many examples of the means of attunement: structures and customs that expressed the responsibility and caring of the community and of each member to each other. The town meeting was a forum in which the viewpoint and concern of each interested member could be heard on any issue of the day. The responsibility community members took for individual members is seen in the "raising bees" in which everyone pitched in and helped a family put up the frame of a barn or house. The practical expression of love can be seen in the practice of taking turns sitting with the sick of other families, and in the community participation in laying out the dead and providing for the funeral supper. These customs gave concrete expression to the basic value of attunement: that the whole community had the responsibility to take account of and respond to the viewpoint, the concerns, and needs of each of its constituent parts. We may ask what are some of the ways in which we in modern organizations can and do actualize this same value.

At the heart of the process of organizations attunement is *knowing and being known*, not in the sense of exchanging mere information, but in the sense of what Geoffrey Vickers has called *appreciation* (the dictionary definition of which is "sensitive awareness," implying deep understanding rather than favorable evaluation). For attunement to occur, the parts of the organization must know and appreciate the whole and must be known and appreciated by it and by one another.

The innovative approaches to new plant design, which are variously called "sociotechnical," "open systems planning," and the like, all emphasize processes which result in knowing and being known. Process design and redesign may be conducted by creating a visual representation of the productive process, which is contributed to and revised by each member. The process invariably results in surprises to management, who have no idea of the multitude of modifications to the system and interconnections among the parts that have come into being over the system's life. Then, when changes are to be made to the system, all participate in mapping the connections and consequences that an alteration to one part will have for the others. The trust of all this communication is for the system to be known as a whole by its members, and

---

[2] I am indebted to Beverly Scott of Foremost-McKesson for this historical note.

for each member to be known as a unique individual.

Appreciation promotes trust. Workers in the new plants are frequently permitted unsupervised access to the plant site and are given a large measure of responsibility for the selection (and deselection) of their fellow workers. They exercise their freedom responsibly.

Sometimes attunement begins in stillness, as in the Quaker business meeting which begins with silence and returns to it whenever the discussion becomes confused or overly contentious. The result, according to a British colleague, David Megginson, is that an extraordinarily high proportion of Quaker meeting verbal behavior are "builds": that is, they take account of what the previous speaker has said, and add to it, rather than disagreeing or going off on an unrelated tangent.

Attunement may begin in discord, as in David Nicoll's use of the "discussion arena." Discussion arenas are like an organization town meeting, except that no decisions are taken. All parties interested in a problem or proposed change are invited to a meeting to present their viewpoints and hear those of the others. No decisions are taken at the meeting. Its purpose is solely to widen the appreciation by the participants of the concerns and needs of the various "stakeholders" in the problem, so "you don't have to fight if you don't want to."

Debriefing and "premortems" are attunement exercises if they are conducted in a "no fault" climate dedicated to increasing understanding and not to assigning blame. Both are used extensively in the military and defense establishments to bring to bear the accumulated experience and knowledge of both participants and experts around complex, expensive experiments such as space shots and nuclear tests. A "premortem" is a process whereby a proposed test procedure is reviewed exhaustively by a multidisciplinary group of specialists. The object is to predict in advance all things that might go wrong.

The processes of iterative decision making that are widely used in Japanese management as well as in many of our own informal political systems, are also examples of attunement. A proposal is circulated; each recipient comments on it; it is revised by the originator to take account of the comments; it is recirculated, and so on.

The costs and requirements for attunement are time and the willingness to be responsible. No technique can work unless there is at least a wish on the part of the participants to take account of and give weight to one another's concerns and needs, and those of the organization. Where people are highly competitive, the requirement of responsibility is difficult to meet.

We have become a nation of time misers. We give our time grudgingly, and we seem more willing to give it to tasks than we are to people. The Japanese have shown that the investment of time in gaining commitment, understanding, and appreciation can pay economic dividends. We must become convinced that putting time into the development of connectedness will ultimately be of value, if the idea of organization attunement is ever to become more than an interesting theory. By making the required investment, we can develop "Organization Appreciation Systems" which will outperform the Management Information Systems on which we now rely in order to control organizations from the top.

In thinking about attunement, it is perhaps useful to make a historical link to a style of management which has nearly disappeared as a coherent philosophy in large organizations, benevolent autocracy. Though the style is no longer dominant, it still survives to a degree in the great enterprises where it once flourished, companies such as Proctor & Gamble, Eastman Kodak, J. C. Penney, and Eli

Lilly. The business leaders who articulated and practiced philosophies of benevolence toward their employees were moved by deep caring and a sense of personal responsibility. They did not take care of their employees primarily because they thought it was good business to do so; rather, it became good business because they did it with heart. Because the employees perceived love behind the policies, they responded with loyalty and commitment, building strong emotional ties between individuals and the organization which have proven remarkably resilient even in these latter days. The reaction against benevolent autocracy seems to have been part of a general drive in our society toward autonomy and personal power. It was the autocracy we were unhappy with, not the benevolence.

We shall not succeed through the use of techniques, in the absence of heart. We have learned that through years of experimentation with participation, with human relations training, and with Quality Circle. We shall not succeed in establishing a network of support and caring while we are engaged in internal power struggles and cut-throat competition. Attunement does not require equality any more than love does, but it does need a climate of mutual respect, and a measure of peace in which to grow.

What then is the role of competition in the attuned organization? Must we, as some new age thinkers contend, make an evolutionary leap into a new age of love and light, in which we shall no longer experience fear, anger, and the drive to power? Perhaps, but it is hard to imagine a world without fear and power. In the real world, we can see successful social groupings of all kinds and sizes: couples, families, work groups, organizations. In these organizations, as in all nature, there is a balance of love and will, of support and competition. In the best such social systems, each person is a valued part, no matter what place they occupy. People feel valued and cared for for themselves, not merely for their instrumental skills, abilities, and personal characteristics.

One can experience in such organizations the difference between personal competition and depersonalized conflict. It is the latter, not the former, which creates the horrors of war and of industrial and commercial exploitation. Then the daimonic which is so often repressed in our individual lives as members of organizations, communities, and families finds expression in corporate acts of callous inhumanity. Conflict that takes place within a framework of responsibility and mutual respect may be fierce, indeed, mortal, but the dance of the warriors is not inhuman. We can look to the rituals of combat among Native Americans, or those observed by the samurai and by chivalrous combatants in our own past, to see ways in which the competitive daimon can be bounded and given a human face. Concepts such as honor, responsibility, and integrity may have an old-fashioned ring to them, but without them in the foundation, our "new age leaders" will be unable to build anything lasting to contain and channel the daimonic forces of both love and will.

First Steps

We each need experiences that support the growth of understandings, especially when those understandings are new, uncertain, and somewhat countercultural. One way to create those experiences is through forming or joining a small discussion group. In small groups we can experience that combination of mutual support and forthright confrontation which we need in order to test our insights and visions. We all need to be reminded occasionally that reality is changing, and we also need to be understood and accepted in our struggles to come to terms with that change. A small group composed of people who basically respect and feel good will for one another can provide the right balance of conditions, nudging us to change through exposing us to differing views of reality, while creating a climate of mutual support, which transcends differences of belief and opinion.

For those who wish to explore applications of "new age thinking" to work, I suggest meeting regularly with a few others you trust and respect. Spend enough time at it to create the conditions for sharing your hopes and fears a little more deeply than you would ordinarily feel comfortable in doing. Here are some basic questions you might address:

Do we use intuition to make decisions? For what kinds of decisions? How can reason and intuition support one another in our decision making?

Can we change reality with thought? What is the rate of intention in bringing about the results we achieve? Do we visualize our desired results? What would happen if we shared a common vision?

Do we see love at work in our organization? What are the pros and cons of seeing and talking about it?

What "daimonic" tendencies and processes do we see in our organization or in our own work? How does it express itself? In what ways do we suppress the daimonic, and how does it then come out?

What does the idea of stewardship mean to us? Can we identify genuine heroes we have known as leaders? What kind of leadership does our business need? What kinds of leaders do we regard as worthy of following?

What is our organization's purpose? What is its driving thrust, what its distinct competences? What are its values? How do these relate to our own purposes and values?

Of what larger systems is our organization a part? Can we intuit our organization's purpose from its place in these larger systems? Does such a concept as global or planetary purpose have any meaning for us in our work lives?

What messages do we attend to from the environment and what messages do we consistently ignore or consider illegitimate? What would happen if we listened to them?

With respect to goals, are we for the most part *pushed* by events, or *pulled* by our vision of a desirable future outcome? Do we experience more stress when we are reacting to events than we do when we are "on purpose"?

What is the relationship between our stated strategy and what we do? If our strategy doesn't determine our actions, what does?

As an organization, can we identify a "willed future"? How does it focus our efforts? If we don't have one, would it make a difference if we did?

What do we hope and fear from the future? Can vision, purpose, and attunement contribute to the realization of our hopes, and the avoidance of what we fear?

It is possible that if we give ourselves the opportunity to open our hearts and minds to one another, we will discover levels of attunement and common purpose that we didn't know existed. Perhaps together we will find our way home.

References

Campbell, Joseph. *The Hero with a Thousand Faces*. Princeton, NJ: Princeton University Press, 1949.

Davis, S. M. Transforming Organizations: The Key to Strategy is Context. *Organizational Dynamics*, Winter 1982.

Fletcher, J. L. *Achieving Sustained High Performance*. Los Angeles, CA: J.P. Tarcher, Inc., 1983 (in press).

Gibran, Kahlil. *The Prophet*. 85th ed. New York: Alfred A. Knopf, 1969.

Harrison, Roger. Startup: The Care and Feeding of Infant Systems. *Organizational Dynamics*, Summer 1981, 5–29.

Kiefer, Charles, and Senge, Peter M. "Metanoic Organizations in the Transition to a Stable Society." Paper presented at the Woodlands Conference, August 1982.

Kidder, Tracy. *The Soul of a New Machine*. Boston: Little, Brown, 1981.

Maccoby, M. *The Gamesman, the New Corporate Leaders*. New York: Simon and Schuster, 1976.

Maccoby, M. *The Leader*. New York: Simon and Schuster, 1981.

May, Rollo. *Love and Will*. New York: Norton, 1969.

McWhinney, W. The Transformative. Chapter 5 in *Resolving Complex Issues (A Work in Progress)*. Venice, CA: Enthusion, Inc., 1983.

Perrow, Charles. *The Normal Accident*. New York: Free Press, 1984.

Peters, T. J., and Waterman, R. H. *In Search of Excellence*. New York: Harper & Row, 1982.

Stein, Barry. *Goodmeasure Notes*. Cambridge, MA: Goodmeasure, Inc., Spring 1983.

Tice, Louis. *New Age Thinking for Achieving Your Potential*. Seattle, WA: The Pacific Institute, Inc., 1980.

5.2 The Diffusion of QWL as a Paradigm Shift

Allan M. Mohrman, Jr.   Edward E. Lawler III

The QWL "Movement"

There are a number of movements worldwide that represent challenges to the established, conventional views of management and organization. Quality of Work Life (QWL) is one of them. QWL has many precursors, components, and related movements. Some have been around for decades. They include sociotechnical approaches, joint labor-management problem-solving, co-determination, industrial and shop floor democracy, participative management, quality circles, organization development philosophies and techniques, job enrichment, employee ownership, worker involvement, Scanlon and other gainsharing plans, autonomous

Based on a paper presented at the Academy of Management Annual Meeting San Diego, California, August, 1981.

and self-regulating workgroups, and "new design plants." The picture they give of QWL is not one of a well-defined set of concepts and practices but a "hodgepodge" of bits and pieces, threads that are slowly being woven and rewoven in the attempt to achieve a coherently patterned fabric. The weaving process is underway but the fabric is not and may never be complete. For convenience we will call this yet-to-be-completed tapestry QWL but we could just as well have called it participative management, employee involvement, organization-employee integration, or some other general term.

The QWL tapestry, if achieved, will not be yet another item in a list of management approaches. Rather it will be a set of mutually compatible organizational philosophies, theories of organization, systems of values and beliefs, practices and techniques, concrete examples, empirical descriptions of those efforts and their results, and a social network for communicating and reinforcing these. It has been called a movement partially because many of these things have reached a critical mass in our collective consciousness and practices so that they are constructively reinforcing one another. This constructive reinforcement is being carried out by various communication media, networks of proponents, and centers for action and research which traffic in the substantive content of QWL. When successful, this constructive reinforcement creates the belief that there are new, more effective and projective ways to design and manage organizations, based on different assumptions about people and backed up by design techniques and principles. When fully successful these beliefs are played out and reinforced in new organizational forms and practices.

Whether or not there is a movement and whether or not it is growing or forming or spreading is subject to debate. The purpose of this paper is to present a framework with which we can both enter into the debate and comment on it. While there are a number of signs that there is a gathering QWL movement there are also signs that it is dissipating. Because we are aligned with a QWL view of the world we would like to understand these dynamics on the chance they may be turned to its use.

Imagery like "the weaving of threads into a tapestry" and terms like "constructive reinforcement" are only useful to a point. We need a conceptual framework that allows us to deal with the phenomenon in the complex, wholistic, and dynamic way implied above. The ideas of paradigm and paradigm shift do this (Kuhn, 1970; Imershein, 1977; Pfeffer, 1982). In the next two sections we present the concepts of paradigm and paradigm shift. Each section does two things: it explains what is meant in general by paradigm and paradigm shift

and it applies the concepts to the particular case of QWL.

Paradigm: Components and QWL Examples

The term "paradigm" refers to an entirety. A paradigm has a number of facets or components but is not a paradigm unless all are included. When we use the term we mean it to include three major facets. First, a paradigm has a way of looking at the world (Pfeffer, 1982). Second, a paradigm has a way of doing things (Pfeffer, 1982). Third, neither of the first two can take place without human agents, so a paradigm must include, and extends only as far as, the social matrix or network that adopts and practices it (Kuhn, 1970).

As we define paradigm below and illustrate with "QWL" examples, remember that we are using "QWL" to refer to a very broad range of activities and ideas that have not (yet) been linked into a paradigm. Whether or not they will be is the issue of this paper. Therefore our "QWL examples" below are, in part, conjectures about what the potential paradigm might be. Whether or not our conjectures are accurate, the point of this section is to define and illustrate "paradigm." We do admit, however, that in this section we seek to help the creation of a QWL paradigm as one more step in our encouragement of a paradigm shift.

Social Matrices

"Ways of looking at the world" and "ways of doing things" assume human agents. The initial component necessary to create a paradigm is the social network, community, or group that adopts its ideas and practices. The extent of this social matrix determines the extent of the paradigm. But more than simply having ideas and practices in common, the members of the paradigm's social matrix interact with one another. Both the content and the process of these interactions serve to solidify and perpetuate the paradigm socially. The existence of the paradigm at any level requires a social matrix, whether we speak of QWL at the societal, organizational, plant, or work group levels. Certainly in plants and work groups that operate according to a QWL paradigm the social matrices are probably synonymous with the populations of the units. In large corporations, one can sometimes see formal and informal networks that lace through the corporation to connect the QWL elements, as is currently true in General Motors and Cummins Engine.

Often, however, pockets of QWL endeavors must rely on networking external to the corporation such as the networks in the U.S.A. of "high involvement" plant managers. In the United States some industries are showing signs of a social matrix across the industry. In the automobile industry, for instance, Ford has instituted an "Employee Involvement" program that represents many of the same ways of looking at the world and doing things as the GM QWL program. Both efforts are, in part, responses to Japanese entries in the industry. The paper industry in the U.S. also has a large number of QWL endeavors, out of proportion to U.S. organizations in general.

We have found that our colleagues, and we assume the readers of this paper, have a tendency to assume that "paradigm" is a concept reserved for the beliefs and practices of the broadest communities. This probably accurately reflects its common usage and certainly was fostered by Kuhn in that he dealt with the paradigm of entire scientific communities or disciplines. We see no reason that the concept cannot also be used to refer to beliefs and practices of more limited social matrices. Imershein (1977), for instance, applied the concept to an organization to understand technology change as a paradigm shift.

We feel the idea is equally applicable at any level of social aggregation, from work groups and families to international networks. Since a paradigm does not exist separate from its social matrix, we will be careful to state the social matrix and level of aggregation in our examples.

Extending the social matrix of a paradigm is equivalent to its diffusion. But each addition to the social matrix changes the paradigm not only in scope but also in content. As the social matrix is extended the paradigm must be redefined to allow revisionist incorporation of the past beliefs and practices of the group added.

There are a number of networks and assemblages that are potentially building an international social matrix for QWL. One recent example is the creation of *Network Notes*, a "transnational" mimeographed communication medium to extend participatory democracy. Another is the September 1981 international conference on the quality of working life, "QWL and the 80's," held in Toronto.

The National Commission on Productivity and Quality of Working Life, the American Center for the Quality of Working Life, and the Work in America Institute are examples of national organizations in the United States that have actively pursued such networking. Other countries have networked in various ways, each peculiar to the particular context and history in that country. For instance, diffusion of the Japanese developments in participation and job redesign were heavily influenced by the Japan Federation of Employer's Associations and the Japan Union of Scientists and Engineers among others (Cole and Walder, 1981). In Sweden union-management experiments in shop floor governance were assisted by networks such as the Swedish Employer's Confederation, the Central Organization of Salaried Employees, and the Swedish Trade Union Confederation (Cole and Walder, 1981).

A Way of Looking at the World

Three subcomponents have been identified as belonging to this aspect of a paradigm: an image of the subject matter, beliefs in particular theories and models, and values (Kuhn, 1970; Ritzer, 1975).

An Image of the Subject Matter

Any paradigm is concerned with only a small part of all the world's phenomena. The various versions of a QWL paradigm all focus on the organizing of people into productive enterprise in ways that also meet the needs of the people.

The most salient aspect of QWL in the U.S. has been the human being and his or her welfare. For instance, Suttle (1977:4) defines QWL as ". . . the degree to which members of a work organization are able to satisfy important personal needs through their experiences in the organization." However, this is somewhat misleading. The individual's needs have been stressed in QWL because that is the element believed to *not* belong to the paradigm currently dominating management and organizational practice.

The emerging QWL paradigm, as we see it, stresses a balance between, or an integration of, the individual and the organization. In this paradigm, the center stage is occupied by attempts to resolve the dilemma of how to both satisfy the organization's needs for "predictability, stability, and coordinated effort" *and* the potentially great variety and ". . . variability of individual needs, interests, and motives" (Katz and Kahn, 1978:286). A current manifestation of this integration of organization and individual as the central focus in the emergent paradigm is the frequent coupling of "productivity" and "QWL" (e.g., Lawler and Ledford, 1982).

Beliefs in Particular Theories and Models

Paradigms encompass a number of characteristic theories or models that explain and relate the variables defining the subject matter. Most of the theories and models stemming from humanistic psychology and the human relations school are within the emergent QWL paradigm (Burrell and Morgan, 1979). In the case of QWL a number of theoretical approaches exist and have been used in various combinations. Among the more prominent are Likert's System 4 (1967), sociotechnical systems approaches (Cummings and Molloy, 1977), and various theories relating task characteristics and motivation (Hackman and Suttle, 1977). Recent texts in organizational behavior are essentially compendia of these and many other models and theories that can potentially be included in the QWL paradigm. The emerging QWL paradigm contains the belief that individual-organization integration is best achieved by participative governance; eg. industrial democracy, participative management, union/management cooperation (Cummings and Molloy, 1977; Garson, 1977). The basic emergent belief is that both organizational and individual needs can be met when attended to simultaneously rather than alternatively.

Values

The QWL paradigm is permeated by a set of values. These include a humanistic belief in the worth of the individual and, therefore, the importance of individual needs which should not and need not be traded off for reasons of technical efficiency and organizational effectiveness. Further, the QWL writings contain statements about employee rights and entitlements in such areas as participation, due process, privacy, and dignity (e.g., Walton, 1974).

A Way of Doing Things

There are two components that express ways of doing things that are characteristic of a paradigm: its methods and instruments, and its exemplars (Kuhn, 1970; Ritzer, 1975).

Methods and Instruments

The most frequent characterization of the QWL paradigm are its methods, techniques, instruments, and approaches. These are increasingly visible in our current "practitioner" literature (e.g., Burck, 1981; *Business Week*, 1981). QWL methods are identifiable because they stress individual needs as well as organizational effectiveness *and* they involve the employee in decision-making and problem-solving (Nadler and Lawler, 1982). These include: gainsharing plans, autonomous work teams, QC circles, worker ownership, worker councils, flexible benefits, joint union-management committees, co-determination, work restructuring, and realistic job previews (Lawler, 1981).

It is through these particular methods and instruments that QWL as a paradigm goes beyond its ideological and conceptual content. It is through the use and practice of these methods that people gain a "tacit knowledge" of the paradigm not communicable through theoretical abstractions (Kuhn, 1970; Imershein, 1977). In this sense the paradigm is only completely learned by doing.

Exemplars

Exemplars of a paradigm are those examples that are frequently and repeatedly used to illustrate it in use. While methods and instruments help concretize the paradigm, it is the unifying thread provided by common exemplars that ties together the various models, values, and methods composing the QWL paradigm. The role of exemplars as part of a paradigm is often overlooked (as it was by Burrell and Morgan, 1979); but the absolute necessity of exemplars in the existence of a paradigm has been repeatedly stressed (Kuhn, 1970; Ritzer, 1975; Imershein, 1977; Eckberg and Hill, 1979).

Common QWL international and na-

tional exemplars are the Volvo plant at Kalmar, Sweden; the General Foods plant at Tarrytown. Moreover, smaller social matrices like organizations and work groups often develop their unique exemplars from their own history and experiences, another work group or another plant in the same organization or in the same industry, for example. Over and over again these exemplars are invoked to illustrate one or the other of the elements of the QWL paradigm. Beyond illustrating the elements, these exemplars illustrate how the various components fit together to create a gestalt that at once captures the essence and reality of the entire paradigm.

Paradigm Shifts

The diffusion of a paradigm means an enlargement of the social matrix. The social matrix expands by adding new matrices that previously looked at the world and did things according to another paradigm. Each addition must therefore go through a process of shifting from one paradigm to another. Kuhn (1970) presented three broadly defined stages of paradigm shift: First, the shift is sandwiched between periods of normalcy in which the primary activities are "puzzle solving" within the prevailing paradigms. In a period of normalcy a shift is fueled by the emerging presence of anomalies, or novelties of fact, that do not conform with the prevailing paradigm. Such anomalies are always present and are usually taken care of by adjustments within existing models. The second stage occurs when anomalies accumulate and result in a growing state of crisis, accompanied by a strong insecurity felt by those practicing under the existing paradigm. Finally, there is a point of large-scale paradigm destruction and its replacement by a new paradigm. According to Kuhn, no shift is made until a new paradigm actually exists to replace the old. When the shift occurs the entire gestalt must shift; a new normalcy occurs, characterized by major shifts in its problems and its techniques. At the time the shift seems revolutionary. In retrospect the gradual accumulation of anomalies seems more evolutionary in nature, gradually and logically leading to the new paradigm.

Having characterized a paradigm shift in the abstract let us turn to its particular QWL embodiments.

Normal Practice

Normal practice prior to the shift consists of the conventional rules of organization as presently practiced. It has many embodiments and defies precise explication (as does QWL). It might be characterized as "management" practice to emphasize its hierarchical, unilateral, control-oriented nature. It is scientific management, theory X, bureaucracy, and mechanistic organization theory, among others. It is driven by functional logic and emphasizes planning, organizing, staffing, directing, coordinating, etc. Its exemplars and its methods are present everywhere in our everyday life and give rise to an extensive tacit knowledge of the paradigm of which we often are not cognizant. Indeed, we are not even aware of the degree to which we accept its practices, values, and ideas as correct.

Within their paradigms of normal management practice, organizations and researchers have for decades engaged in considerable puzzle solving. Many of these puzzles are efficiency-related and are solved within the paradigms by, say, industrial engineering and operations research models. Other examples of puzzle solving are the search for greater validity in performance appraisals and the rationalization of compensation practices and selection systems. They represent efforts to shore up the traditional paradigm and to make it more effective.

Anomalies and Crises

Many crises involve whole societies: shortages of labor, shortages of managerial expertise, shifting values and expectations in the labor markets, increasingly uncertain and ambiguous environments, drops in sales, drops in productivity, and competition that uses other approaches. These can lead to a questioning of the established practices. For instance, does increased fractionalization of human jobs necessarily lead to increased efficiency and higher quality as predicted? Why do our well-constructed plans sometimes lock us into paths to failure rather than ensure success? Why do highly paid employees fail to show up for work and fail to do their work?

Contingency approaches to management are supposed to attend to some of these anomalies; but not only do these approaches threaten to break by their own weight and complexity (specifying contingencies increases complexity geometrically), they more and more seem wrong in their assumption. For instance, even as managers try to match jobs to individual needs to obtain maximum "fit" they find that both jobs and needs are subject to change and redefinition by the individual and social unit so that they only "fit" when personal and social constructions so determine (e.g., Salancik and Pfeffer, 1977).

Paradigm Destruction and Replacement

Conceptually and ideologically the potential destruction of the current management paradigm has been underway for some time. Some of the attack has been pressed by humanists, and the human relations theorists. Others have challenged the basic assumptions of rationality, objectivity, and cause-effect in the dominant paradigm. They see organizational realities as being primarily constructed by political and various other social constructionist and enactment processes (see Pfeffer, 1981; Weick, 1979).

On the practical front, the dominant paradigm is threatened by real problems that seem intractable under its framework. Union-management conflicts are one example. Inability to respond to international competition is another. Not having adequate human resources to meet organizational needs is yet another. No matter to what degree the dominant management paradigm is discredited, however, there will be no shift until a new paradigm exists as a replacement. The process of paradigm shift consists of the dual processes of destruction of the old and construction of the new.

The period of paradigm shift, or attempted paradigm shift, amounts to competition between the two alternatives. The competition involves social, political, and aesthetic processes, rather than "scientific" or rational ones. On the surface the competition compares the rival paradigms in terms of their ability to lead to understanding and accomplishment. It is a process of selecting the most viable; for verifying one while falsifying the other. At a deeper level, however, the rivals are, by definition, incommensurate. They define the world and its problems in completely different ways. Each attempts to validate itself and invalidate the other on its own terms that the other can neither accept nor allow, since to do so would be to accept the underlying elements of the opposing paradigm. The battle cannot be resolved by proofs. This incommensurability also means that there are no such things as incremental or transitional shifts; the shift, when and if it occurs, must be all at once, a complete gestalt switch. Nevertheless the switch is preceded by incremental accumulations of anomalies in the old paradigm.

Kuhn (1970:151), quoting from Max Planck, specified one way paradigms triumph: ". . . a new scientific truth does not triumph by convincing its opponents and making them see the light, but rather because its opponents eventually die, and a new generation grows up that is familiar with it." A paradigm shift does not require the physical death of the opposition. There can be social and political "death" also, but there must be death.

This abstract scenario can be illustrated with QWL examples. Nehrbass (1979), for instance, berated those academics who espouse QWL approaches for allowing themselves to be blinded by their humanist values and ignoring the research that, he claimed, fails to substantiate their claims. Sometimes the same data points, e.g., the General Foods plant at Topeka, have been used as supporting evidence for both paradigms. For example, depending on one's point of view and choice of criteria Volvo's Kalmar plant can be seen as more effective, less effective, only as effective, or just as effective as other approaches to car manufacturing.

Examples can be found regarding the degree of diffusion of QWL also. Lawler (1978) sees a snowballing trend, while others (e.g., Cole, 1981) see no evidence for making such a claim. Without getting concerned with which is right these examples serve the purpose of showing how incommensurability precludes the possibility of deciding the competition with evidence. In this regard, it is interesting to note that in instances where a version of the QWL paradigm has been rather well accepted (e.g., Japan and various European examples) few felt compelled to validate the paradigm they chose.

Induction of a New Paradigm

Now that we have reviewed the stages that are involved in a paradigm shift, we are in a position to consider how is it that people are converted to the new paradigm.

Many of the influence processes by which this is done are well documented in the social sciences (Rogers and Shoemaker, 1971; Zimbardo, Ebbeson, Maslach, 1977). Of more concern to us are the characteristics of the paradigm that influence conversion.

It is necessary, but not sufficient, for the new paradigm to solve the problems facing the paradigm in crisis. The reason that it is not sufficient is that the prevailing paradigm also may be capable of handling the crisis with appropriate adjustments. A current example illustrates the point: One of the problem areas facing the current management paradigm has been articulated as worker alienation. Some theory and research indicate that alienation is due to a poor fit between individual needs and job characteristics. The prevailing management paradigm responds to these findings characteristically by seeking to improve fit by using traditional selection practices and redesigning jobs to bring both personal and job characteristics into line. Although such sensitivity to individual needs sometimes goes under the label of QWL, the QWL paradigm we see emerging would put the job design process jointly into the hands of the organization and its members and would also make the selection process a joint decision of informed choice, such as a realistic job preview (Wanous, 1980).

What are some additional characteristics of new paradigms that facilitate conversion? Kuhn suggests that when new paradigms can lead to phenomena or achievements entirely unsuspected or unattainable under the old paradigm, or when the new paradigm offers more aesthetic appeal, perhaps in the form of simplicity and straightforwardness, we tend to develop a *faith* that the new paradigm will be successful. In addition, a successful appeal to widely accepted values, such as democracy, can facilitate conversion. Anyone attending QWL conventions must be struck by the almost religious fervor exhibited by many of its adherents. In the United States one of the unanticipated "side effects" of allowing participation has been instances of dramatic improvement in productivity and other "bottom line" relevant criteria. Such examples have certainly led to larger scale embracing of the QWL paradigm. Most byproducts of QWL are not easily verified as such but are resolutely believed to be a result of QWL efforts.

When rival paradigms are in competition their incommensurability prevents verification of one over the other. Each paradigm, however, offers its own way of dealing with the crisis faced. Within its own terms each sees its own approach as progress. During shift, however, no progress is possible because there is no common definition for it and each rival invalidates the criteria of the other. After paradigm shift, however, progress is perceived not only in the subsequent accomplishments of normal puzzle-solving activity within the paradigm but in the reinterpretations of the new paradigm historical events are no longer perceived as disruptive social and political revolutions, but as sensible incremental stages of process toward the present state of knowledge and practice. Progress is measured in the paradigm's terms as development *from* prior states and not in terms of approach *toward* an ideal. We are more and more frequently hearing organizations set forth rational system-wide accounts on their past QWL efforts that are in stark contrast to more piecemeal and limited activities we remember a few years ago.

International Illustrations of QWL Paradigm Shift

In this section we sketch the acceptance of the QWL paradigm as it has occurred in several countries. We draw on secondary sources in these illustrations. In a real sense, therefore, we are dependent on the degree to which the original sources have interpreted their observation in a manner compatible with the concept of paradigm shift. These comments are meant to be illustrative only. They are necessarily incomplete.

Crises

An analogy used by Kuhn (1970:76) can be directly reversed. "As in manufacture, so in science—retooling is an extravagance to be reserved for the occasion that demands it. The significance of crises is the indication they provide that an occasion for retooling has arrived." The historical accounts of the societal shifts toward QWL type practices in Yugoslavia, China, Japan, Sweden, and West Germany (e.g., King and van de Vall, 1978; Garson, 1977; Cole, 1981; Cole and Walder, 1981; Tsuda, 1981) point to a prominent period of crises as the critical point.

These crises take a number of forms. In Japan and Sweden, for instance, the crisis took the form of severe labor shortage (Cole, 1981; Cole and Walder, 1981; Tsuda, 1981; Garson, 1977) especially in blue-collar jobs that were least desirable due to such factors as working conditions and routinization. In China and West Germany societal commitment to participative systems took place in response to severe lack of management expertise (Cole and Walder, 1981; Garson, 1977). Workers needed to assume the responsibility. In Yugoslavia economic blockade and large military expenditures during ideological conflict with Russia put severe pressure on an inefficient centralized management system and forced decentralization to the commune and a system of worker management (King and van de Vall, 1978). These were all crises for management that forced it to go to the resources provided by the worker and attend to the needs of the worker.

Components of Replacement Paradigms

Each country's history of the QWL movement has led it to look different places to develop its QWL paradigm. Germany, for instance, could look to its pre-Nazi days for examples and methods of participation that were incorporated after the war into its co-determination legislation (Garson, 1977). China could not, and literally created its exemplars and methods through actions necessitated by crisis. These, in turn, drove a rethinking of ideology, helping to create the break with Russia (Cole and Walder, 1981).

Japan borrowed heavily from U.S. human relations theorists for the conceptual underpinnings of the paradigm that allowed continuity with the paternalism of prewar management style. The QC circle technique also is attributable to U.S. sources (Cole, 1980). Similarly, Sweden found the socio-technical approaches developed in Great Britain to be of great use in their emerging paradigm. In turn, pressures from the common market resulted in British labor organizations turning to Germany's co-determination model as an exemplar (Garson, 1977).

An obvious generalization from these few observations is that there has been considerable cross-fertilization internationally regarding the components of the QWL paradigm. Paradigm development is facilitated by the presence of externally created components and exemplars. Cross-fertilization makes an international paradigm possible.

Politics of Paradigm Shift

According to the theory of paradigm shift, during the shift there should be political activity of one form or another by which competition between rival paradigms is carried out. In many European countries the predicted political activity has taken the form of legislation and union activity.

In Sweden, for example, the whole issue of the meaning of work was debated nationally as a result of a strike in a nationalized industry. The strike was as much against centralized union and governmental policy toward work as it was against its particular management. This resulted in a union stance for decentralization and experiments in local "shop floor" control. Shop floor democratization, such as at Volvo, did not change the basic paradigm of management networks and the experiments tended to be "encapsulated"—not diffused. This spurred union activity toward legislation of worker participation at all levels and beyond the initial experimenting sector (Cole and Walder, 1981; Garson, 1977).

In Japan the changes which occurred (e.g., QC circles) took place without much political activity. Evidently the changes were completely under management control and accepted as extensions of a paternalism and spirit of "common destiny" (Tsuda, 1981) and as a societal need. There appears to be no paradigm shift at this point. It could be argued that the shift really took place after the war when the Japanese society had to work out a system of company unions in reaction to a system of external unions imposed during the occupation.

A Paradigm Shift in the United States?

Now that we have outlined and illustrated the conditions which are hypothesized to lead to paradigm shift we are in a position to ask whether this is about to occur in the United States. In our view, the hypothesized conditions are in place for a paradigm shift to take place and, thus, should occur if the theory of paradigm shifts articulated here is correct.

First, as was mentioned earlier, QWL has rapidly developed recently, and has all the components for a complete paradigm.

Second, the United States is experiencing a crisis which is calling the old paradigm into question. The crisis has a number of different dimensions and outcroppings, but fundamentally is a crisis of organizational effectiveness that has in part been brought on by increasingly tough international competition. Whether or not the current crisis is objectively worse than others preceding it is not as important as the fact that it has received considerable attention and has been pointed to as a major symptom of paradigm failure. So far the existing paradigm has not responded well to the crisis. Productivity growth has been minimal to nonexistent, and in some markets U.S. goods are high-priced and low-quality. There is now increasing recognition that if this continues, the standard of living in the U.S. will drop (indeed it did during 1980). This crisis along with the development of the QWL Paradigm has pushed the United States to the point where a national debate is taking place between the traditional and QWL paradigms. This debate, which is taking place in the national media (see, e.g., NBC White Paper, 1980) as well as in workplaces, seems to signal the beginning of the third phase of paradigm shift—destruction and replacement.

Finally, the QWL paradigm has many of the characteristics which are needed for it to replace the existing one. First, it promises to solve the organizational effectiveness problem by better human resource utilization and motivation. Particularly in the last few years, instances of superior productivity, quality, flexibility, freeing up the managers, etc. have been claimed to result from QWL efforts (for instance in 1981 we heard in several public contexts representatives of both General Motors and the United Auto Workers claim that an increasing number of local agreements being finalized prior to the national bargaining agreement were the result of

QWL efforts). This has added an important dimension to a movement which, in many people's minds, was primarily identified with humanist concerns. In the eyes of its adherents, the emerging QWL paradigm certainly has a beauty in its synergistic balancing of the individual and organizational needs that inspire a faith that presently intractable problems, such as maximizing selection of the right people, quickly balancing out a line of workflow at time of product change, adjusting to down times in economic and production cycles, etc., can be eventually resolved by involving those affected. Finally it appeals to values which are fundamental in the United States: democracy, equity, personal growth, human dignity, and due process.

In summary, the QWL paradigm has not yet replaced the traditional one in the United States, but our analysis suggests it may be about to. But why now? The concepts in QWL certainly are not new. In our view, what is new is the organizational effectiveness crisis *and* the growing belief that QWL can solve it. The condition has not been present before and, as a result, the traditional paradigm has not been displaced. This crisis is relatively new and, indeed, unless it continues it may not be sufficient to dislodge the old paradigm, particularly if the old paradigm can be altered in some way to solve it (Hackman and Oldham, 1980). However, if it continues and if the paradigm shift model is valid, then the QWL paradigm should eventually replace the existing one. In essence, this means that a test of the shift model in the United States will be taking place over the coming years. However, the experiences from other countries and a few U.S. organizations illustrate the idea that the QWL paradigm can replace the traditional one during a period of crisis.

Conclusion

The theory of paradigm shifts and our reviews of diffusion in several countries suggest some intriguing conclusions about the diffusion of QWL. First, diffusion requires many necessary components— crises, exemplars, social networks, etc. The timing of the creation of these components does not appear to be critical. What is critical is that they are all brought together simultaneously. Second, contrary to the tendency of many to think so, diffusion is not a process that can be settled in a rational manner, although the comparative seductivity of the rationality offered by each side plays a large part. Finally, the nature of diffusion is such that once it occurs it will no longer appear to be radical. In situations where QWL has been completely diffused, those having adopted the new paradigm will not see major discontinuities from the past, since they will now be looking at the past from a framework which successfully incorporates it. While still in the past paradigm, however, the rival paradigm represented a completely foreign approach to the enterprise. If the theory is correct, one day managers in the United States may soon see the QWL paradigm not as a radical approach, but as the only way to operate. Right now this would represent a radical break with the past, but one which seems due.

References

Argyris, Chris. *Integrating the Individual and the Organization*. New York: John Wiley, 1964.

Burck, Charles G. "What Happens When Workers Manage Themselves." *Fortune*, July 27, 1981, 62–69.

Burrell, Gibson, and Gareth Morgan. *Sociological Paradigms and Organizational Analysis*. London: Heinemann, 1979.

Business Week. "Moving Beyond Assembly Lines." July 27, 1981, 87, 90.

Business Week. "The New Industrial Relations." May 11, 1981, 85–98.

Cole, Robert E. "Learning from the Japanese: Prospects and Pitfalls." *Management Review*, 5.1 (1980), 22–42.

Cole, Robert E. "Organizational Change and the Diffusion of Participatory Work Structure: The Cases of Japan, Sweden, and the United States." A paper presented at the Conference on Organizational Change, Carnegie-Mellon University, Pittsburgh, Pa., May 19–20, 1981.

Cole, Robert E., and Andrew G. Walder. "Structural Diffusion: The Politics of Participative Work Structures in China, Japan, Sweden, and the United States." Working Paper No. 226, Center for Research on Social Organization, University of Michigan, 1981.

Cummings, Thomas G., and Edmond S. Molloy. *Improving Productivity and the Quality of Work Life*. New York: Praeger Publishers, 1977.

Eckberg, Douglas Lee, and Lester Hill. "The Paradigm Concept and Sociology: A Critical Review." *American Sociological Review*, 44 (1979), 925–937.

Garson, G. David. "Paradoxes of Worker Participation," in *Worker Self-Management in Industry: The West European Experience*, G. David Green (ed.). New York: Praeger, 1977, 214–230.

Hackman, J. Richard, and Greg R. Oldham. *Work Redesign*. Reading, Mass.: Addison-Wesley, 1980.

Hacman, J. Richard, and J. Lloyd Suttle. *Improving Life at Work: Behavioral Science Approaches to Organizational Change*. Santa Monica, Calif.: Goodyear Publishing Company, Inc., 1977.

Health, Education, and Welfare Special Task Force. *Work in America*. Cambridge, Mass.: MIT Press, 1972.

Imershein, Allen W. "Organizational Change as a Paradigm Shift." *The Sociological Quarterly*, 18 (Winter 1977), 33–43.

King, Charles D., and Mark van de Vall. *Models of Industrial Democracy: Consultation, Co-determination and Worker's Management*. The Hague, Netherlands: Mouton Publisher, 1978.

Kuhn, Thomas S. *The Structure of Scientific Revolutions*. Chicago: University of Chicago Press, 1970.

Lawler, Edward E., III. "The New Plant Revolution." *Organizational Dynamics*, Winter 1978, 3–12.

Lawler, Edward E., III. "High Involvement Work Organizations: Design and Change Theory." Mimeo, prepared for a conference at Carnegie-Mellon University, May 19–20, 1981.

Lawler, Edward E., III, and Gerald Ledford. "Productivity and the Quality of Work Life." *National Productivity Review*, Winter 1981–82, 23–36.

Likert, Rensis. *New Patterns of Management*. New York: McGraw-Hill, 1961.

Likert, Rensis. *The Human Organization*. New York: Wiley, 1967.

MacGregor, Douglas. *The Human Side of Enterprise*. New York: McGraw-Hill Book Company, Inc., 1960.

Nadler, David A., and Edward E. Lawler, III. "Quality of Work Life: Perspective and Directions." *Organizational Dynamics*, 11.3 (Winter 1983), 20–30.

Nehrbass, Richard G. "Ideology and the Decline of Management Theory." *Academy of Management Review*, 4:3(1979), 427–431.

NBC White Paper. "If Japan Can . . . Why Can't We?" National Broadcasting Company, Inc., 9:30 p.m. EDT, June 24, 1980.

Ouchi, William G. *Theory Z*. Reading, Mass.: Addison-Wesley, 1981.

Pfeffer, Jeffrey. *Organizations and Organization Theory*. Pittman Press, 1982.

Ritzer, George. "Sociology: A Multiple Paradigm Science." *The American Sociologist*, Vol. 10 (August 1975), 156–167.

Roethlisberger, F. J., and W. J. Dickson. *Management and the Worker*. Cambridge, Mass.: Harvard University Press, 1939.

Rogers, Everett M., and F. Floyd Shoemaker. *Communication of Innovations: A Cross-Cultural Approach*. New York: The Free Press, 1971.

Salancik, Gerald R., and Jeffrey Pfeffer. "An Examination of Need Satisfaction Models of Job Attitudes." *Administrative Science Quarterly* 22 (September 1977), 427–456.

Suttle, J. Lloyd. "Improving Life at Work—Problems and Prospects," in *Improving Life at Work*, J. Richard Hackman and J. Lloyd Suttle, eds. Santa Monica, Calif.: Goodyear Publishing Company, Inc., 1977, 1–29.

Tonda, Masumi. "The Roots of the Uniqueness of Japanese Management." *Dentsu Japan Marketing/Advertising*, 18 (January 1981), 4–7.

Walton, Richard E. "Improving the Quality of Work Life." *Harvard Business Review*, May-June 1974, 12 ff.

Wanous, John P. *Organizational Entry: Recruitment, Selection and Socialization of Newcomers*. Reading, Mass.: Addison-Wesley, 1980.

Weick, Karl E. *The Social Psychology of Organizing*, 2d ed. Reading, Mass.: Addison-Wesley, 1979.

Zimbardo, Philip G., Ebbe B. Ebbeson, and Christina Maslach. *Influencing Attitudes and Changing Behavior*, 2d ed. Reading, Mass.: Addison-Wesley, 1977.

Zwerdling, Daniel. *Democracy at Work*. Washington, D.C.: Association for Self-Management, 1978.

6

Organizations: Internal and External Environments

During the closing years of the nineteenth century, "social Darwinism" was a popular ideology in entrepreneurial circles and among apologists for *laissez faire* capitalism. Its use as an ideology was to justify cutthroat competition among organizations as an instrument of "cosmic" selection of those most fit to survive the buffetings of history.

"Social Darwinism" has declined since that time as an ideology as mergers and cartels have become more popular than market competition among men of business. But Darwinian concepts, especially the concept of "environment," has had a rebirth in popularity as an explanatory and diagnostic device in organizational and social theorizing during the past two decades.

Terreberry, the second author in this chapter, in her "The Evolution of Organizational Environments," specifically acknowledges her debt to Darwinian thought: "Darwin published *The Origin of Species by Means of Natural Selection* in 1859. Modern genetics has vastly altered our understanding of the variance upon which natural selection operates. But there has been no conceptual breakthrough in understanding *environmental* evolution which, alone, shapes the direction of change. Even today most theorists of change still focus on *internal* interdependencies of systems—biological, psychological or social—although the external environments of these systems are changing more rapidly than ever before."

Actually there has been a conceptual breakthrough in understanding external environment as a determinant of organizational form, function, and management, a breakthrough acknowledged by Terreberry and most other authors in this section of the book. This breakthrough came in "The Causal Textures of Organizational Environments," an influential article by Emery and Trist published in 1965. Terreberry's argument is that Emery and Trist's fourth class of organizational environments, the turbulent field, is constituted by the unconditional influences of other formal organizations in the environment of any "focal organization."

The first author in this chapter focuses on the internal environment of an organization as a principal source of stability and change, wellness, and illness, in organizational life. He argues that this internal environment has not typically been seen or conceptualized correctly by managers or students of management and change. The correct view of the organization's internal environment is that of a "culture," in the anthropologists' sense of that term—"the system of norms, beliefs and assumptions, and values that determine how people in the organization act—even when that action may be at odds with written policies and formal reporting relationships."

Since "culture" is a "holistic" concept, Snyder's attempt is to identify leverage points in an organization's culture which can be identified and manipulated effectively by managers and agents of organizational change.

The third author in this chapter, Kurt Motamedi, seeks linkages between the internal and external environments of an organization in the interest of organizational survival. The two types of linkage he names "adaptability" and "copability." "Adaptability" is the capacity of an organization to sense and understand its internal and external environments and to take actions to produce a better fit or balance between the two. "Copability" refers to the capacity of a social system to maintain its identity and integrity as a living system while making necessary adaptations to its changing external environment.

These pieces demonstrate that it is useful to bring Darwinian concepts, especially that of "environment," to bear meaningfully upon the diagnosis and management of organizational problems.

6.1 To Improve Innovation, Manage Corporate Culture

Richard C. Snyder

Overview

In recent years, much attention has been focused on the decline of innovation in American industry, and our concomitant loss of productivity and competitive standing in the international marketplace.[1]

As recognition of these problems has grown, and the search for solutions increased, managers have found their vocabularies growing by leaps and bounds. Recent additions include such phrases as "new worker values," "reindustrialization," "double-digit inflation," and the somewhat mysterious "paradigm shift." Perhaps the most interesting of all is the phrase "corporate culture," which many observers believe to explain much of the success of certain Japanese firms and well-managed American companies that consistently distinguish themselves in the marketplace, take the lead in technical and managerial innovations, and satisfy the hearts, minds, and pocketbooks of their workers.[2]

Although almost unheard-of ten years ago, the phrase "corporate culture" has become so current that most managers would probably agree that their organizations have distinctive cultures—and that those cultures have dramatic impact on innovation, productivity, and morale. Perhaps more important, though, *very few managers have any experience in systematically managing those cultures or their impact.* Some, in fact, would deny that it can be done.[3]

Although organizational cultures are pervasive, tenacious, and decidedly "hard to get your arms around," I believe that they can be defined, assessed, and—to a certain extent—managed. And I also believe that in managing such cultures lies one of the keys to improved organizational performance and innovation. Furthermore, in the past few years, we have learned a great deal about the characteristics of several dozen of the most innovative, best-managed companies in the U.S. and in Japan, and the "levers" they use to impact their cultures. It is this new learning that forms the basis of this paper.

What Is Corporate Culture?

Corporate culture is the system of norms, beliefs and assumptions, and values that determine how people in the organization act—even when that action may be at odds with written policies and formal reporting relationships. Much more than any formal statement of rules or structure, it determines who says what to whom, about what, and what kinds of actions then ensue.

The author would like to acknowledge and thank Jim O'Toole, Judith Blumenthal, and Larry Greiner for their contributions to this paper. © 1982 by Richard C. Snyder.

[1] See, for example, "Innovation: Has America Lost Its Edge?" *Newsweek*, June 4, 1979; "The Sad State of Innovation," *Time*, October 22, 1979, pp. 70–71; O'Toole (1981b).

[2] Ouchi (1981); Pascale and Athos (1981); O'Toole (1981b).

[3] According to Robert F. Allen, who has done much of the work available on culture changes, this is the standard reaction of managers before undertaking culture change programs. See Allen (1980b).

Although "culture" is a term well known to anthropologists, it has until recently been almost totally ignored by organization theorists and managers alike. Lately, however, the impact of culture has gained considerable attention in the business press and among management experts.[4] The reason? It's a powerful force in determining the success of mergers and acquisitions, organization development efforts, and the implementation of corporate strategic plans. For example:

In 1968, when marketing-oriented Rockwell International merged with aerospace engineering wizards at North American, managers and analysts alike expected a synergistic reaction.

Rockwell, looking for new technologies and new products for commercial markets, saw North American as a place where 'scientific longhairs' threw away ideas every day that could be useful to Rockwell. North American, in turn, was attracted to Rockwell's commercial manufacturing muscle.

Rather than supporting each other, however, the basic values of the firms collided.

As then-CEO Robert Anderson lamented, the aerospace people weren't used to commercial problems. "We kept beating them on the head to diversify, but every time they'd try it they'd spend a lot of money on something that, when all is said and done, there was no market for, or they overdesigned for the market." The world views of the two firms, as it turned out, were radically different: 'Rockwell's company culture looked at the world as a rough-and-tumble place where profit margins dominate decision-making. North American's environment was more noble. Some 60 well-paid Ph.D.'s, for example, spent only 20% of their time on company business and were free to devote the rest as they chose on basic research. *This was not*

compatible with Rockwell's obsession about controlling costs and margins.'[5]

Thirteen years later, "executives are still trying to improve the cultural fit of the two firms."[6]

Another example illustrates the impact of corporate culture on innovative programs designed to improve executive health:

American corporations—concerned with employee health and rising health care costs—are on a health-buying spree, installing fitness centers, building gyms, and buying health programs. Thus far this flurry of activity has done little good. Illness rates and illness costs continue to soar, and the evidence shows that few people maintain even the changes in health practices that they are able to make. *The chief reason for the failure of business health programs appears to be that the organizational culture, filled with negative health norms, overrides whatever changes the individuals try to make.* Where companies have begun to treat health as a cultural as well as an individual problem, they find hope for long-lasting change in their employees' lives and considerable savings in the company health bill.[7]

Two further examples demonstrate the cultural bases of market failures and other neglects of consumer needs in the U.S. auto industry:

Henry Ford's "give them any color they want as long as it's black" philosophy so pervaded Ford Motor Company, and became a part of its culture, that, even today, the firm is slow to respond to demands in the marketplace, and has maintained a consistent second place among domestic auto makers.

Likewise, the culture of GM "led the corporation to market a car they knew was unsafe (the Corvair), and to engage in the subsequent seamy episode of trying to

---

[4] See "Corporate Culture: The Hard-to-Change Values That Spell Success or Failure," *Business Week*, October 17, 1980; also Schwartz and Davis (a,b).

[5] Schwartz and Davis (a), p. 15.

[6] Schwartz and Davis (b).

[7] Allen (1980a).

prove that Ralph Nader was a homosexual when he called the public's attention to the Corvair's safety problems. The myopic and self-deceiving culture of GM also led to enormous wasted investments in the Wankel engine, the catalytic converter, and air bags."[8]

Dealing Strategically with Culture

These examples point out the importance of culture, and, I believe, make the case that we must learn to deal strategically with our corporate cultures. At this point, it seems logical to ask:

1. What are the characteristics of organizations that successfully manage their cultures?
2. What tools, if any, do they use?
3. How can managers understand the culture of their own organizations?
4. What—if anything—can they do about these cultures?

Fortunately, there are at least partial answers to each of these questions. Recent research on Japanese businesses,[9] American organizations that share Japanese traits[10] (known as theory Z organizations), well-managed U.S. companies,[11] and the characteristics of innovative organizations[12] provides a number of clues to the first two questions, and these will be summarized later in the paper. Although by no means exhaustive or final, some answers to the second set of questions come from recent organizational and consulting experience, and from the adoption and adaptation of tools useful for the study of organizational cultures.

The big lesson of both research and consulting experience appears to be: great companies pay exquisite attention to the systematic management of their cultures and the socialization of their people into those cultures, and they design and use a variety of culture supports—devices that support and maintain those cultures.[13]

Furthermore, they appear to develop a fit between all of these culture supports that results in culture and systems congruency, such that on the whole, the organization gives much the same message to all of its parts.

The Management of Culture

Discussing the management of culture is a bit like talking about managing artists. While undoubtedly both artists and culture *can* be managed, the images called up by the word "managing" may be out of sync with reality. Culture is based strongly in nonverbal and intuitive dimensions,[14] is somewhat elusive, and resists efforts to control and change its nature.

From a logical standpoint, the management of culture can be divided into several phases:

1. Understanding the nature of the culture and its effects on the organization;
2. Assessing the forces that support the present culture and those that call for change;
3. Deciding what, if any, changes in the culture (or in other aspects of the organization) are necessary and feasible;
4. Using the levers available for culture change.

---

[8] O'Toole (1981b), p. 119.
[9] Pascale and Athos (1981).
[10] Ouchi (1981).
[11] Waterman et al. (1980); Peters (1980).
[12] Rothman (1974); Quinn (1978); Kanter (1981).

[13] Waterman et al. (1980), p. 16; Pascale and Athos (1981).
[14] Hall (1959, 1966, 1976).

Understanding the Nature of an Organization's Culture

A number of methods exist for understanding an organization's culture. These include:

1. Direct observation of the culture by an outsider;
2. Survey research using questionnaires and interviews (these may be aimed at past and present employees, as well as knowledgeable outsiders);[15]
3. Examination of organizational documents;
4. Direct assessment of the organization's culture by its members.

Although each of the first three methods has its own advantages, I believe that it would be unwise to use any of them without also involving the organization's own members in the assessment. All too often, studies performed by outsiders wind up on the organizational shelf, where they collect dust. Use of the fourth approach, particularly when it involves those affected and those that have the power to make change, seems strongly advisable.

Regardless of the method of study chosen, the types of questions to be answered include:[16]

1. What does it take to get ahead at this company?
2. What type of people succeed here?
3. What does it take to get fired here?
4. What type of people do badly here?

[15] A recent culture study using this approach was conducted by Larry Greiner and Chuck Maxey of U.S.C. Allen (1980a) contains a sample questionnaire, as does O'Toole (1981b).

[16] Many of these questions were suggested by Larry Greiner of U.S.C., in a personal interview. Others were derived from Levinson (1972); Hall (1976); McCaskey (1979); Mitroff and Kilmann (1966); O'Toole (1981a); and various works of Robert F. Allen and his associates (listed in the attached selected bibliography).

5. What are the most critical events of the organization's history?
6. What stories are told about those events, who tells them, under what circumstances are they told, and what impact do they have on behavior?
7. When people succeed here, what strategies do they use?
8. When people got into trouble here, what, specifically, did they do?
9. Why do people leave the organization?
10. In what ways has the organization changed in recent years, and how has it stayed the same?
11. What are the major strengths of the company?
12. What are the major weaknesses of the company?
13. What are your hopes for the future?
14. What are your fears for the future?
15. Who are the heroes of the organization?
16. Who are the villains?
17. What types of offices, furniture, spatial arrangement, etc. exist in the organization, and how do these affect behavior?
18. What types of policies, strategies, structures are used by the organization, and how do these affect behavior?
19. What topics, if any, are "taboo" in the organization?
20. Which rituals, if any, are obligatory in the organization?

Determining the Effects of the Culture on the Organization

Obviously, the answers to the questions listed above will give insight both into the nature of the culture and its impact on behavior. But I believe that it is very important for people in the organization to assess the impact of the culture on them, and on their strategies, and would therefore recommend that the following questions[17] be explored in groups composed of managers and staff members of the organization under study:

1. How compatible with the strategy and objectives of the organization is each aspect of the culture; and
2. How important is each aspect of the culture?

To simplify this process, it would be possible to chart the various aspects of the organization's culture in a matrix, as follows:

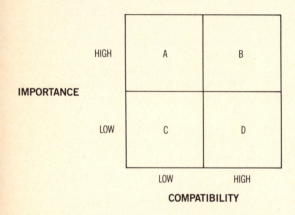

After placing these aspects of culture in the matrix, further examination of these culture elements would be in order. The two that are of the most importance are quadrant A and quadrant B. Important questions to be explored then would be:

How are these culture elements maintained?
What impact do they have on us?
How long have they been in the organization?
Is there any evidence that they are growing more or less pervasive in the company?

A systematic approach to the first question would be to use force-field analysis, coupled with a checklist of culture

supports. This would yield a diagram as follows:

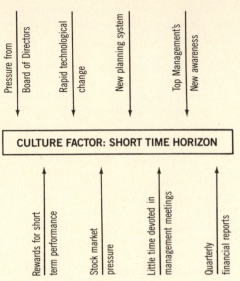

This would be done for each of the key culture elements, and would lay the base for the next phase of the process.

Deciding What to Do

At this point, management has a number of choices with regard to each culture pattern.[18]

A. Ignore it
B. Attempt to strengthen it
C. Manage around it
D. Change the organization's objectives, strategies, systems, etc. where they are incompatible with the culture
E. Attempt to change the culture pattern

Strategy A is not recommended. All too often, it results in unused MIS, failures of leadership, and the problems reported at the beginning of this article.

Strategy B may be extremely important for those desirable elements of culture that are not as pervasive as they should be.

---

[17] These questions are modified versions of those raised by Schwartz and Davis (a,b).

[18] Ibid.

This occurs often in firms that have a history of excellence, and which are growing rapidly. Hewlett-Packard, for example, is reported to be examining techniques for formally socializing their new employees into their culture.

Strategy C involves determining ways to get desired results that may replace present approaches that are culturally incompatible.

Strategy D reminds us that sometimes our expectations are unrealistic or our strategies ill-formed. In those cases, it may be necessary to reformulate goals and strategies, redesign systems, etc., to make them compatible with culture.

Strategy E may be the toughest of all. It takes a long time to develop a culture, and may take even longer to change it. Nonetheless, there is some evidence that elements of organizational cultures may be changed.[19] Due to the great amount of energy necessary to change culture, it is very important to focus on the elements that are most critical.

In the remainder of the paper, I will focus on some possible levers for culture change, and then show how some high performing companies use these levers to create organizational *culture systems* that support innovation and excellence.

The Levers of Culture Change

Culture is the pattern that connects virtually all aspects of organizational life. As such, it is the result of many different forces inside and outside the organization, not the least of which is history. As a result, it is a *systemic* phenomenon. And as we have all too often learned, "systemic problems require systemic solutions."[20]

Although this may appear obvious, many of the early efforts at culture change were carried out by behavioral scientists, who tended to focus only on the human aspects of organizations and often ignored structure, strategy, systems design, choice of technology, and so on. As a result, there have been few historic examples of planned organizational development efforts that produced systemic culture change.[21] To go beyond this single-factor approach, I propose that culture change efforts examine the following forces, and then choose those that are most readily implementable. Among the levers available for culture change are the following:[22]

1. *Superordinate Goals* (the guiding vision and philosophy of the organization)
2. *Management Style and Action*
3. *Human Resource Management*
4. *Organization Structure*
5. *Administrative and Control Systems*
6. *Planning*
7. *Information and Communication*
8. *Strategy*
9. *Physical Design and Setting*
10. *External Relations*

In reality, the top managers, or the organization's culture change agents, have an incredible variety of levers available. These levers will obviously be more or less appropriate depending on the nature of the problem and the nature of the existing culture. In some cases, certain aspects of organizations are "sacred" and may not be changed without enormous costs. In other cases, changes may be made easily. Thus, the culture-sensitive manager is advised to look for "corridors of indifference,"[23] and focus early change efforts in those corridors. It is extremely important to note that employees are both amazingly

---

[19] See Allen (1980a,b); Allen and Silverzweig (1977); Allen and Higgins (1979); and Silverzweig and Allen(1976).

[20] O'Toole (1980a), p. 5.

[21] Greiner (1981).

[22] Derived in part from the McKinsey & Co. 7-S framework described in Pascale and Athos (1981), p. 81.

[23] Wrapp (1967).

observant and often cynical about the management "fad of the month." As a result, they are inclined to disbelieve efforts at culture change that, for example, claim to promote a long-term time horizon, but leave reward systems, management information systems, and the content of management meetings untouched. Thus while it is possible to approach change efforts with a variety of tools, it is also possible to sabotage well-publicized efforts through the use of only a few of them. *Caveat mutator.*

How These Levers Are Used in Innovative Organizations

Within the past few years, several researchers have shed light on the management and organizational practices of many of the world's best-managed, most innovative organizations. Among these are McKinsey & Company's recently completed "excellent company" study,[24] William Ouchi's study of Japanese and American firms,[25] Rosabeth Moss Kanter's not-yet-completed study of innovations in organizations and how they are accomplished,[26] and Richard Tanner Pascale and Anthony Athos' study of Japanese firms and their counterparts in American industry.[27] In addition to these, several other studies shed light on the process of innovation under a variety of circumstances.[28]

From these studies, and from observations of my own, I have listed a number of ways that excellent (and other) organizations have used the "levers" of culture to promote innovation and managerial

excellence. While many of these approaches have been touted as cure-alls, I must caution the reader that one organization's pheasant may be a turkey to another. That is, while many of these innovative approaches to organization and management may work brilliantly in one setting, they may fall flat on their face in another—particularly if the organization is not ready for them. Therefore, the following list is neither a "design for the ideal organization" nor a prescription for change. Rather, it is a menu of a number of design choices that are available to "social architects" who wish to build innovative organizations.

Some Characteristics Frequently Found in Innovative and Well-Managed Organizations

1) Superordinate Goals

Clearly articulated[29]
Disseminated through all levels of the organization[30]
Demonstrated by consistent managerial action[31]

2) Management Style and Action

Clear and consistent communication of values through words (including slogans) and symbolic action[32]
Behavior and role modeling[33]
Participative, collaborative style[34]

---

[24] Parts of which are reported in Waterman et al. (1980) and Peters (1980).
[25] Ouchi (1981).
[26] Kanter (1981)
[27] Pascale and Athos (1981).
[28] Rothman (1974); Quinn (1978); Lehr (1979); Walton (1979); Kelly and Kranzberg (1978); Kingston; Lawler (1980); and Lawler and Drexler (1980).

[29] Ouchi (1981); Quinn (1978).
[30] Ouchi (1981).
[31] "Corporate Culture," *Business Week*, October 27, 1980.
[32] Bennis (1981); Waterman et al. (1980).
[33] This has been cited in virtually every piece I have seen on corporate culture, well-managed companies, etc.
[34] Ouchi (1981); Lawler (1980).

Active promotion of innovation[35]
Support and empowerment of others[36]
— Backing champions of innovation
— Providing necessary resources (time, money, access to people)
  Running interference and "managing the press"
— Demonstrating commitment publicly
— Cutting off losing projects[37]
Providing punishments and rewards[38]
— Recognition for outstanding performance (pay, manager's time and attention, public acknowledgement)
— Sharing rewards among those responsible for accomplishments
— Opportunity to pursue future projects
— Opportunity to fail without drastic punishments (at least for "good failures")[39]
— Strong emphasis on results
Persistence and consistency[40]

— Great attention paid to recruiting and hiring
Training and development[43]
— Greatly emphasized: substantial opportunity for employees to pursue in-house training and outside educational programs
— Attention to interpersonal as well as technical/functional skills
— Often includes orientation to culture and values of company
Orientation and early socialization[44]
— Almost obsessively attended to
— "Hands-dirty" first assignment
— Early opportunity to attend to driving areas of the firm
Promotion and assignment
— Dual career ladders (technical and managerial)[45]
— Rotation through various functions, staff and line (multiple careers)[46]
Job security[47]

3) Human Resource Management

Strong "people orientation"[41]
Recruitment[42]
— Carefully selecting employees that match the culture
— Giving prospective employees a clear description and feeling for the culture and asking them to determine how they would fit in, rather than simply "selling" the company to them

4) Organization Structure

"Structural looseness," "simultaneous loose-tight controls"[48]
Simple structures[49]
Lean staff[50]
Staff as advisors[51]
Temporary systems[52]
— Parallel structures
— Task forces/project teams
— "Skunk works"
Minimal sign-off requirements for new project approval[53]

[35] Rothman (1974), p. 466.
[36] Bennis (1981); Kanter (1981); Quinn (1978).
[37] Because innovative projects have a high failure rate, it is essential to cut off losing projects before they terminally drain the resources of the company. See Peters (1980).
[38] Lawler and Drexler (1980); Kanter (1981).
[39] Kingston, p. 148.
[40] Bennis (1981); Peters (1981).
[41] Virtually universally cited.
[42] Ouchi (1981); Walton (1979).

[43] Ouchi (1981); Waterman et al. (1980).
[44] Waterman et al. (1980); Peters (1980).
[45] Lehr (1979).
[46] Kanter (1981); Ouchi (1981).
[47] Ibid.
[48] Peters (1980); Rothman (1974).
[49] Peters (1980).
[50] Ibid.
[51] Lawler and Drexler (1980).
[52] Waterman (1980); Kanter (1981).
[53] Lawler and Drexler (1980).

Slack resources[54]
Encouragement of lateral relations[55]
Multiple power centers with budgets[56]
Decentralization ("small within large")[57]
— Separate divisions for new products[58]
— Small plants
Not organized along narrow functional lines[59]
Size is not critical[60]
— Small organizations better at concept formulation and prototype phase, large better at full-fledged development[61]
— When size is associated with slack resources, innovation increases[62]
— When size is associated with centralization, innovation decreases[63]

5) Administrative and Control Systems[64]

Simplicity
Minimal sign-off requirements
Flexibility

6) Planning

Systematic environmental scanning[65]
Relatively few objectives[66]
Long time horizon[67]
Bias toward action[68]

7) Information and Communication

Emphasis on lateral communication[69]
Temporary, problem-centered channels of communication[70]
— Task forces
— Project teams
Good news swapping[71]
Informality[72]
Random, free flow of information[73]
Company slogans[74]
Recognition programs[75]
Close to consumers[76]
Open to criticism and proposals for change[77]

8) Strategy[78]

Stick to basics
Avoid diversification in areas outside of company base of excellence
Close attention to customer needs
— Major source of new product innovations
— Direct contact with customers ("warm-armpit marketing")
Simplicity is power

9) Physical Design and Setting

Use of "open" office designs
Tend to be located near Universities or in areas of high innovation[79]

---

[54] Rothman (1974); Kanter (1981).
[55] Kanter (1981); Ouchi (1981).
[56] Kanter (1981).
[57] Virtually universally cited.
[58] Peters (1980).
[59] Waterman et al. (1980).
[60] Rothman (1974); Kelly and Kranzberg (1978).
[61] Kelly and Kranzberg (1978).
[62] Rothman (1974).
[63] Ibid.
[64] Peters (1980).
[65] Glueck (1980) contains a summary of the literature linking strategic planning to superior performance.
[66] Peters (1980).
[67] Quinn (1978); Ouchi (1981).
[68] Peters (1980).

[69] Kanter (1981).
[70] Peters (1980).
[71] Ibid.
[72] This is based on an unpublished study by McKinsey & Co., and on the author's own observations at Hewlett-Packard and several other innovative organizations.
[73] Kanter (1981).
[74] Peters (1980).
[75] Peters (1980).
[76] Peters (1980) cites the McKinsey study's observations as well as those of MIT's Eric Von Hippel, which indicate that customers are a major (if not *the* major) source of new product ideas.

Production systems that use newer designs which enhance worker participation and quality control[80]

10) External Relations

Top management devotes substantial time to external relations[81]

Strong emphasis on corporate social responsibility and ethical action[82]

Open "system boundaries"[83]

The Next Steps

After assessing the culture of the organization, and choosing among the many strategies for culture management and the levers for culture change, the problem of implementing the desired strategy still remains. This seems particularly problematic in the case of organizations whose present cultures are dramatically misaligned with their environments. While the topic of conducting large-scale culture change efforts is beyond the scope of this paper, there are indications that such efforts are—given sufficient managerial commitment, time and other resources, and well-managed change efforts—both possible and replicable in a variety of settings.

Perhaps the most promising work in this area has been carried out by Robert Allen and his colleagues at the Human Resources Institute in Morristown, New Jersey. Using a systematic approach to culture change based in part on methods similar to those discussed in this paper, HRI has conducted over 100 culture change programs, in situations ranging from litter and vandalism reduction and the promotion of executive health to the systematic development of culture in a new plant start-up and the financial turnaround of a two-year history of no profit in a fast-food sales district.[84] Based on their own reports, the results are quite impressive. It remains to be seen, however, whether such methods can be widely diffused and successfully used by others.

Another organization that has recently undertaken a systematic culture change effort was mentioned earlier in this paper—Rockwell International. Perhaps as a result of the awareness generated by cultural difficulties encountered in their merger with North American, Rockwell has recently undertaken a "culture analysis" of their automotive operations division. This analysis examines a number of aspects of the division's culture as they were in the mid-70's, lists the company's improvement efforts to date, assigns a numerical "grade" to the success of their present efforts, and points the direction for the future. Unlike many other organizations who treat such information as confidential,[85] Rockwell has made the results of their culture audit available to the public.[86]

Conclusion

The approach to the management of organizational culture presented in this paper is not intended to be an all-purpose solution to the problems of innovation in

---

[77] See the Intel "Informal Culture" statement in Ouchi (1981), p. 251.

[78] Peters (1981); Waterman et al. (1980); Pascale and Athos (1981).

[79] Kanter (1981); Kelly and Kranzberg (1978), p. 58.

[80] Walton (1979); O'Toole (1981a).

[81] Ouchi (1981).

[82] Ouchi (1981); O'Toole (1981a).

[83] Rothman (1974).

[84] See Allen (1981b); Allen and Silverzweig (1971); Silverzweig and Allen (1976); and the other works by Allen listed in the bibliography.

[85] Greiner (1981).

[86] See Ouchi (1981), pp. 149–154 for a discussion of the culture audit at Rockwell, and pp. 242–249 for a copy of the published results.

America. I do hope, however, that it will help to remind us all that:

A. We are constantly influenced by our cultures;

B. Without knowledge of those cultures, we are apt to be led astray in our efforts to manage and change our organizations;

C. With such knowledge, we will be in a much better position to strategically "invent the future"[87] of those organizations; and, finally,

D. While the job of culture management and change is certainly not a simple task, there are an increasing number of tools available to make the job easier. It is up to us to use these tools—and, whenever possible, to improve them. Failing that, we can expect to find ourselves further enmired in the problems of painfully slow culture change in times that demand rapid response.

[87] To quote a phrase used by George Steiner.

Selected Bibliography

Allen, Robert F. and Murphy, Richard. "Getting Started: The Case of the New Company." *Business*, July–August 1979, pp. 26–34.

Allen, Robert F. *Beat the System!* New York: McGraw-Hill, 1980(a).

Allen, Robert F. "The Corporate Health-Buying Spree: Boon or Boodoggle?" *S.A.M. Advanced Management Journal*, Spring 1980(b), pp. 4–22.

Allen, Robert F. "The Ik in the Office." *Organizational Dynamics*, Winter 1980(c), pp. 26–41.

Allen, Robert F. and Higgins, Michael. "The Absenteeism Culture: Becoming Attendance Oriented." *Personnel*, January–February 1979, pp. 30–39.

Allen, Robert F., and Pilnick, Saul. "Confronting the Shadow Organization: How to Detect and Defeat Negative Norms." *Organizational Dynamics*, Vol. 4, No. 1 (Spring 1973), pp. 3–18

Allen, Robert F., and Silverzweig, Stanley. "Changing Community and Organizational Cultures." *Training and Development Journal*, July 1977, pp. 28–34.

Baker, Edwin L. "Managing Organizational Culture." *Management Review*, July 1980, pp. 8–13.

Bennis, Warren. "The Five Key Traits of Successful Chief Executives." *International Management*, October 1981, p. 60.

"Corporate Culture: The Hard-to-Change Values That Spell Success or Failure." *Business Week*, October 27, 1980, pp. 148–160.

Ginsburg, Lee. "Strategic Planning for Work Climate Modification." *Personnel*, November–December 1978, pp. 10–20.

Glueck, William F. *Business Policy and Strategic Management*. New York: McGraw-Hill, 1980.

Greiner, Larry E. University of Southern California. Interview, December 2, 1981.

Hall, Edward T. *The Silent Language*. New York: Doubleday, 1959. Anchor Books, 1973.

Hall, Edward T. *The Hidden Dimension*. New York: Doubleday, 1966. Anchor Books, 1969.

Hall, Edward T. *Beyond Culture*. New York: Doubleday, 1976. Anchor Books, 1977.

Hayes, Robert H., and Abernathy, William H. "Managing Our Way to Economic Decline." *Harvard Business Review*, July–August 1980, pp. 67–77.

"Innovation: Has America Lost Its Edge?" *Newsweek*, June 7, 1979, pp. 58–68.

Jelinek, Mariann. *Institutionalizing Innovation*. New York: Praeger, 1979.

Kanter, Rosabeth Moss. "Power and Enterprise in Action: Conditions and Strategies for Entrepreneurial Accomplishments among Corporate Middle Managers." Lecture given at University of Southern California Business School, November 18, 1981.

Kelly, Patrick, and Kranzberg, Marvin, Eds. *Technological Innovation: A Critical Review of Current Knowledge*. San Francisco: San Francisco Press, 1978.

Kingston, William. *Innovation*. London: John Calder (n.d.).

Lawler, Edward E. "Creating High Involvement Work Organizations." Los Angeles: USC Center for Effective Organizations, 1980.

Lawler, Edward E., III, and Drexler, John A. "The Corporate Entrepreneur." Los Angeles: USC Center for Effective Organizations, 1980.

Lehr, Lewis W. "Stimulating Technological Innovation—The Role of Top Management." *Research Management*, November 1979, pp. 23–25.

Levinson, Harry. *Organizational Diagnosis*. Cambridge, Mass.: Harvard University Press, 1972.

Mansfield, Edwin. "The Economics of Industrial Innovation," in Patrick Kelly and Melvin Kranzberg, Eds., *Technological Innovation: A Review of Current Knowledge*. San Francisco: San Francisco Press, 1978, pp. 199–214.

McCaskey, Michael B. "The Hidden Messages Managers Send." *Harvard Business Review*, November–December 1979, pp. 135–148.

Mitroff, Ian I., and Kilmann, Ralph H. "Stories Managers Tell: A New Tool for Organizational Problem Solving." *Management Review*, July 1975. Reprinted in Harold J. Leavitt, Louis R. Pondy, and David M. Boje, *Readings in Managerial Psychology*, 3d ed. Chicago: University of Chicago Press, 1980, pp. 666–676.

Nadler, Leonard. "The Organization as a Micro-Culture." In Chip R. Bell and Leonard Nadler, *The Client-Consultant Handbook*. Houston: Gulf Publishing Co., 1979, pp. 144–154.

O'Toole, James. "The Failure of Success: Personal Observations on the Future of Innovation." Los Angeles: USC Center for Futures Research, 1981(a).

O'Toole, James. *Making America Work*. New York: Continuum, 1981(b).

Ouchi, William. *Theory Z: How American Business Can Meet the Japanese Challenge*. Reading, Mass.: Addison-Wesley, 1981.

Pascale, Richard Tanner, and Athos, Anthony. *The Art of Japanese Management*. New York: Simon and Schuster, 1981.

Peters, Thomas J. "Putting Excellence into Management." *Business Week*, July 21, 1980, pp. 196–205.

Quinn, James Brian. "Technological Innovation, Entrepreneurship and Strategy." *Sloan Management Review*, Spring 1979, pp. 19–29.

Rothman, Jack. *Planning and Organizing for Social Change*. New York: Columbia University Press, 1974.

"The Sad State of Innovation." *Time*, October 22, 1979, pp. 70–71.

Schwartz, Howard, and Davis, Stanley A. "Matching Corporate Culture and Business Strategy." (Letter size.) Cambridge, Mass.: Management Analysis Center, (n.d.), (a).

Schwartz, Howard, and Davis, Stanley A. "Matching Corporate Culture and Business Strategy." (Small leaflet.) Cambridge, Mass.: Management Analysis Center, (n.d.), (b).

Silverzweig, Stanley, and Robert F. Allen. "Changing the Corporate Culture." *Sloan Management Review*, Spring 1976, pp. 33–49.

Townsend, Robert. *Up the Organization*. New York: Knopf, 1970.

Truell, George F. "Tracking Down the 'Around-hereisms'—Or, How to Foil Negative Orientation." *Personnel*, July–August 1981, pp. 23–31.

Walton, Richard E. "Work Innovations in the United States." *Harvard Business Review*, July–August 1979, pp. 88–98.

Watermann, Robert H., Jr., Peters, Thomas J., and Phillips, Julien R. "Structure Is Not Organization." *Business Horizons*, June 1980, pp. 14–26.

Wrapp, H. Edward. "Good Managers Don't Make Policy Decisions." *Harvard Business Review*, September–October 1967, pp. 91–99.

6.2 The Evolution of Organizational Environments

S. Terreberry

Darwin published *The Origin of Species by Means of Natural Selection* in 1859. Modern genetics has vastly altered our understanding of the variance upon which natural selection operates. But there has been no conceptual breakthrough in understanding *environmental* evolution which, alone, shapes the direction of change. Even today most theorists of change still focus on *internal* interdependencies of systems—biological, psychological or social—although the external environments of these systems are changing more rapidly than ever before.

Introduction

Von Bertalanffy (1956) was the first to reveal fully the importance of a system being open or closed to the environment in distinguishing living from inanimate systems. Although von Bertalanffy's formulation makes it possible to deal with a system's exchange processes in a new perspective, it does not deal at all with those processes in the environment *itself*

that are among the determining conditions of exchange.*

Emery and Trist (1965) have argued the need for one additional concept, 'the causal texture of the environment'. Writing in the context of formal organizations, they offer the following general proposition:

> That a comprehensive understanding of organizational behavior requires some knowledge of each member of the following set, where L indicates some potentially lawful connection, and the suffix 1 refers to the organization and the suffix 2 to the environment:
>
> $$L_{11} \quad L_{12}$$
> $$L_{21} \quad L_{22}$$
>
> L_{11} here refers to processes within the organization—the area of internal interdependencies; L_{12} *and* L_{21} to exchanges between the organization and its environment—the area of transactional interdependencies, from either direction; and L_{22} to processes through which parts of the environment become related to each other—i.e. its causal texture—the area of interdependencies that belong within the environment itself (p. 22).

We have reproduced the above paragraph in its entirety because, in the balance of this paper, we will use Emery and

Originally published in *Administrative Science Quarterly*, March 1968, Vol. 12, No. 4, pp. 590–613. Copyright © 1968 by Administrative Science Quarterly.

References and footnotes in edited portions of this paper have been deleted.

* [Editors' Note: Chin's paper, selection 3.1 in Chapter Three of this volume, proposes conceptual models for the textures of the environments of systems and discusses the utility of such models for practitioners of planned change.]

Trist's symbols (i.e., L_{11}, L_{21}, L_{12} and L_{22}) to denote intra-system, input, output, and extra-system interdependencies, respectively. Our purpose in doing so is to avoid the misleading connotations of conventional terminology.

Purpose

The theses here are: (a) that contemporary changes in organizational environments are such as to increase the ratio of externally induced change to internally induced change; and (b) that *other* formal organizations are, increasingly, the important components in the environment of any focal organization. Furthermore, the evolution of environments is accompanied—among viable systems—by an increase in the system's ability to learn and to perform according to changing contingencies in its environment. An integrative framework is outlined for the concurrent analysis of an organization, its transactions with environmental units, and interdependencies among those units. Lastly, two hypotheses are presented, one about organizational *change* and the other about organizational *adaptability*; and some problems in any empirical test of these hypotheses are discussed.[1]

Concepts of Organizational Environments

In Emery and Trist's terms, L_{22} relations, i.e. interdependencies within the environment itself, comprise the 'causal texture' of the field. This causal texture of the environment is treated as a quasi-independent domain, since the environment cannot be conceptualized except with respect to some focal organization. The components of the environment are identified in terms of that system's actual and *potential* transactual interdependencies, both input (L_{21}) and output (L_{12}).

Emery and Trist postulate four 'ideal types' of environment, which can be ordered according to the degree of *system connectedness* that exists among the components of the environment (L_{22}). The first of these is a 'placid, randomized' environment: goods and bads are relatively unchanging in themselves and are randomly distributed, e.g. the environments of an amoeba, a human foetus, a nomadic tribe. The second is a 'placid, clustered' environment: goods and bads are relatively unchanging in themselves but clustered, e.g. the environments of plants that are subjected to the cycle of seasons, of human infants, of extractive industries. The third ideal type is 'disturbed-reactive' environment and constitutes a significant qualitative change over simpler types of environments: an environment characterized by similar systems in the field. The extinction of dinosaurs can be traced to the emergence of more complex environments on the biological level. Human beings, beyond infancy, live in disturbed-reactive environments in relation to one another. The theory of oligopoly in economics is a theory of this type of environment.[2]

These three types of environment have been identified and described in the literature of biology, economics and mathematics.[3] 'The fourth type, however, is

[1] I am particularly grateful to Kenneth Boulding for inspiration and to Eugene Litwak, Rosemary Sarri and Robert Vinter for helpful criticisms. A Special Research Fellowship from the National Institutes of Health has supported my doctoral studies and, therefore, has made possible the development of this paper.

[2] The concepts of ideal types of environment, and one of the examples in this paragraph, are from Emery and Trist (1965, pp. 24–6).

[3] The following illustrations are taken from Emery and Trist (1965). For random-placid environment see Simon (1957, p. 137); Ashby (1960, sec. 15/4); the mathematical concept of random field; and the economic concept of classical market.

new, at least to us, and is the one that for some time we have been endeavouring to identify' (Emery and Trist, 1965, p. 24). This fourth ideal type of environment is called a 'turbulent field'. Dynamic processes 'arise from the *field itself* and not merely from the interactions of components; the actions of component organizations and linked sets of them 'are both persistent and strong enough to induce autochthonous processes in the environment' (p.26).

An alternate description of a turbulent field is that the accelerating rate and complexity of interactive effects exceeds the component systems' capacities for prediction and, hence, control of the compounding consequences of their actions.

Turbulence is characterized by complexity as well as rapidity of change in causal interconnections in the environment. Emery and Trist illustrate the transition from a disturbed-reactive to a turbulent-field environment for a company that had maintained a steady 65 per cent of the market for its main product—a canned vegetable— over many years. At the end of the Second World War, the firm made an enormous investment in a new automated factory that was set up exclusively for the traditional product and technology. At the same time post-war controls on steel strip and tin were removed, so that cheaper cans were available; surplus crops were more cheaply obtained by importers; diversity increased in available products, including substitutes for the staple; the quick-freeze technology was developed; home buyers became more affluent; supermarkets emerged and placed bulk orders with small firms for retail under super-

For random-clustered environment see Tolman and Brunswick (1935); Ashby (1960, sec. 15/8); and the economic concept of imperfect competition.

For disturbed-reactive environment see Ashby (1960, sec. 7); the concept of 'imbrication' from Chein (1943); and the concept of oligopoly.

market names. These changes in technology, international trade, and affluence of buyers gradually interacted (L_{22}) and ultimately had a pronounced effect on the company: its market dwindled rapidly. 'The changed texture of the environment was not recognized by an able but traditional management until it was too late' (Emery and Trist, 1965, p. 24).

The first question to consider is whether there is evidence that the environments of formal organizations are evolving toward turbulent-field conditions.

Evidence for Turbulence

Ohlin (1958, p. 63) argues that the sheer rapidity of social change today requires greater organizational adaptability. Hood (1962, p. 73) points to the increasing complexity, as well as the accelerating rate of change, in organizational environments. In business circles there is growing conviction that the future is unpredictable. Drucker (1964, pp. 6–8) and Gardner (1963, p. 107) both assert that the kind and extent of present-day change precludes prediction of the future. Increasingly, the rational strategies of planned-innovation and long-range planning are being undermined by unpredictable changes. McNulty (1962) found no association between organization adaptation and the introduction of purposeful change in a study of their companies in fast-growing markets. He suggests that built-in flexibility may be more efficient than the explicit reorganization implicit in the quasi-rational model. (*Dun's Review* 1963, p. 42, questions the effectiveness of long-range planning in the light of frequent failures, and suggests that error may be attributable to forecasting the future by extrapolation of a noncomparable past.) The conclusion is that the rapidity and complexity of change may increasingly preclude effective long-range planning. These examples clearly suggest the emergence of a change in the environment that is suggestive of turbulence. . . .

The following are examples from two volumes of the *Administrative Science Quarterly* alone. Rubington (1965) argues that structural changes in organizations that seek to change the behavior of prisoners, drug addicts, juvenile delinquents, parolees, alcoholics [are] . . . 'the result of a social movement whose own organizational history has yet to be written'. Rosengren (1964) reports a similar phenomenon in the mental health field whose origin he finds hard to explain: 'In any event, a more symbiotic relationship has come to characterize the relations between the [mental] hospitals and other agencies, professions, and establishments in the community.' He ascribes changes in organizational national goals and technology to this inter-organizational evolution. In the field of education, Clark (1965) outlines the increasing influence of private foundations, national associations, and divisions of the federal government. He, too, is not clear as to how these changes have come about, but he traces numerous changes in the behavior of educational organizations to inter-organizational influences. Maniha and Perrow (1965) analyse the origins and development of a city youth commission. The agency had little reason to be formed, no goals to guide it, and was staffed by people who sought a minimal, no-action role in the community. By virtue of its existence and broad province, however, it was seized upon as a valuable weapon by other organizations for the pursuit of their own goals. 'But in this very process it became an organization with a mission of its own, in spite of itself.'

Since uncertainty is the dominant characteristic of turbulent fields, it is not surprising that emphasis in recent literature is away from algorithmic and toward heuristic problem-solving models (Taylor, 1965); that optimizing models are giving way to satisficing models (March and Simon, 1958); and that rational decision making is replaced by 'disjointed incrementalism' (Braybrooke and Lindblom, 1963). These trends reflect *not* the ignorance of the authors of earlier models, but a change in the causal texture of organizational environments and, therefore, of appropriate strategies for coping with the environment. Cyert and March (1953) state that 'so long as the environment of the firm is unstable—and predictably unstable—the heart of the theory [of the firm] must be the process of short-run adaptive reactions' (p. 100).

In summary, both the theoretical and case study literature on organizations suggests that these systems are increasingly finding themselves in environments where the complexity and rapidity of change in external interconnectedness (L_{22}) gives rise to increasingly unpredictable change in their transactional interdependencies (L_{21} and L_{12}). This seems to be good evidence for the emergence of turbulence in the environments of many formal organizations. . . .

In the short run, the openness of a living system to its environment enables it to take in ingredients from the environment for conversion into energy or information that allows it to maintain a steady state and, hence, to violate the dismal second law of thermodynamics, i.e. of entropy. In the long run, 'the characteristic of living systems which most clearly distinguishes them from the nonliving is their property of progressing by the process which is called evolution from less to more complex states of organization' (Pringle, 1956, p. 90). It then follows that to the extent that the environment of some living system X is comprised of *other living systems*, the environment of X is *itself* evolving from less to more complex states of organization. A major corollary is that the evolution of environments is characterized by an increase in the ratio of externally induced change over internally induced change in a system's transactional interdependencies (L_{21} and L_{12}). . . .

In the case of formal organizations, disturbed-reactive or oligopolistic environments require some form of accommodation between like but competitive organizations whose fates are negatively correlated to some degree. A change in the transactional position of one system in an oligopolistic set, whether for better or worse, automatically affects the transactional position of all other members of the set, and in the opposite direction, i.e. for worse or better, as the case may be.[4] On the other hand, turbulent environments require relationships between dissimilar organizations whose fates are independent or, perhaps, positively correlated.[5] A testable hypothesis that derives from the formal argument is that the evolution of environments is accompanied, in viable systems, by an increase in ability to learn and to perform according to changing contingencies in the environment.

The evolution of organizational environments is characterized by a change in the important constituents of the environment. The earliest formal organizations to appear in the United States, e.g. in agriculture, retail trade, construction, mining (See Stinchcombe, 1965, p. 156) operated largely under placid-clustered conditions. Important inputs, such as natural resources and labor, as well as consumers, comprised an environment in which strategies of optimal location and distinctive competence were critical organizational responses (Emery and Trist, 1965, p. 29). Two important attributes of placid-clustered environments are: (a) the environment is itself *not* formally organized; and (b) transactions are largely initiated and controlled by the organization, i.e. L_{12}. . . .

When the environment becomes turbulent, however, its constituents are a multitude of other formal organizations. Increasingly, an organization's markets consist of other organizations; suppliers of material, labor and capital are increasingly organized, and regulatory groups are more numerous and powerful. The critical response of organizations under these conditions will be discussed later. It should be noted that *real* environments are often mixtures of these ideal types.

The evolution from placid-clustered environments to turbulent environments . . . can be summarized as a process in which formal organizations evolve: (a) *from* the status of systems within environments not formally organized; (b) *through* intermediate phases, e.g. Weberian bureaucracy; and (c) *to* the status of subsystems of a larger social system. . . .

Inter-Organizational Analysis

It was noted that survival in disturbed-reactive environments depends upon the ability of the organization to anticipate and counteract the behavior of similar systems. The analysis of inter-organizational behavior, therefore, becomes meaningful only in these and more complex environments. The interdependence of organizations, or any kind of living systems, at less complex environmental levels is more appropriately studied by means of ecological, competitive market, or other similar models.

The only systematic conceptual approach to inter-organizational analysis has been the theory of oligopoly in economics. This theory clearly addresses only disturbed-reactive environments. Many economists admit that the theory, which assumes maximization of profit and perfect knowledge, is increasingly at odds with empirical evidence that organizational behavior is characterized by satisficing and bounded rationality. Boulding (1965) comments that 'it is surprisingly hard to make

---

[4] Assuming a non-expanding economy, in the ideal instance.

[5] Emery and Trist argue that fates, here, are positively correlated. This author agrees if any expanding economy is assumed.

a really intelligent conflict move in the economic area simply because of the complexity of the system and the enormous importance of side effects and dynamic effects' (p. 189). A fairly comprehensive search of the literature has revealed only four conceptual frameworks for the analysis of inter-organizational relations outside the field of economics. These are briefly reviewed, particular attention being given to assumptions about organization environments, and to the utility of these assumptions in the analysis of inter-organizational relations in turbulent fields.

William Evan (1966) has introduced the concept of 'organization-set', after Merton's 'role-set' (pp. 177–80). Relations between a focal organization and members of its organization-set are mediated by the role-sets of boundary personnel. 'Relations' are conceived as the flow of information, products or services, and personnel (pp. 175–6). Presumably, monetary and legal, and other transactions can be accommodated in the conceptual system. In general, Evan offers a conceptual tool for identifying transactions at a given time. He makes no explicit assumptions about the nature of environmental dynamics, nor does he imply that they are changing. The relative neglect of inter-organizational relations, which he finds surprising, is ascribed instead to the traditional intra-organizational focus, which derives from Weber, Taylor and Barnard. His concepts, however, go considerably beyond those of conventional organization and economic theory, e.g. comparative versus reference organizations and overlap in goals and values. If a temporal dimension were added to Evan's conceptual scheme, then it would be a very useful tool for describing the 'structural' aspects of transactional interdependencies (L_{21} and L_{12} relations) in turbulent fields.

Another approach is taken by Levine and White (1961, p. 586) who focus specifically on relations among community health and welfare agencies. This local set

of organizations 'may be seen as a system with individual organizations or system parts varying in the kinds and frequencies of their relationships with one another'. The authors admit that interdependence exists among these local parts only to the extent that relevant resources are not available from *outside* the local region, which lies beyond their conceptual domain. Nor do we find here any suggestion of turbulence in these local environments. If such local sets of agencies are increasingly interdependent with other components of the local community and with organizations outside the locality, as the evidence suggests, then the utility of Levine and White's approach is both limited and shrinking.

Litwak and Hylton (1962) provide a third perspective. They too are concerned with health and welfare organizations, but their major emphasis is on coordination. The degree of interdependence among organizations is a major variable; low interdependence leads to *no* coordination and high interdependence leads to merger, therefore they deal only with conditions of moderate interdependence. The type of coordinating mechanism that emerges under conditions of moderate interdependence is hypothesized to result from the interaction of three trichotomized variables: the *number* of interdependent organizations; the degree of their *awareness* of their interdependence; and the extent of *standardization* in their transactions. The attractive feature of the Litwak and Hylton scheme is the possibility it offers of making different predictions for a great variety of environments. Their model also seems to have predictive power beyond the class of organizations to which they specifically address themselves. If environments are becoming turbulent, however, then increasingly fewer of the model's cells (a 3 × 3 × 3 space) are relevant. In the one-cell turbulent corner of their model, where a large number of organizations have low awareness of their complex and unstandardized interdependence, 'there is little chance of coordination' (p. 417), according to Litwak and Hylton (1962). If the level of awareness of interdependence increases, the model predicts that some process of arbitration will emerge. Thus the model anticipates the inter-organizational implications of turbulent fields, but tells us little about the emerging processes that will enable organizations to adapt to turbulence.

The fourth conceptual framework available in the literature is by Thompson and McEwen (1958). They emphasize the interdependence of organizations with the larger society and discuss the consequences that this has for goal setting. 'Because the setting of goals is essentially a problem of defining desired relationships between an organization and its environment, change in either requires review and perhaps alteration of goals' (p. 23). They do not argue that such changes are more frequent today, but they do assert that reappraisal of goals is 'a more constant problem in an unstable environment than in a stable one', and also 'more difficult as the "product" of the enterprise becomes less tangible' (p. 24).

Thompson and McEwen outline four organizational strategies for dealing with the environment. One is competition; the other three are subtypes of a cooperative strategy: bargaining, co-optation, and coalition. These cooperative strategies all require direct interaction among organizations and this, they argue, increases the environment's potential control over the focal organization (p. 27). In bargaining, to the extent that the second party's support is necessary, that party is in a position to exercise a veto over the final choice of alternative goals, and thus takes part in the decision. The co-optation strategy makes still further inroads into the goal-setting process. From the standpoint of society, however, co-optation, by providing overlapping memberships, is an important social device for increasing the

likelihood that organizations related to each other in complicated ways will in fact find compatible goals. Co-optation thus aids in the integration of heterogeneous parts of a complex social system. Coalition refers to a combination of two or more organizations for a common purpose and is viewed by these authors as the ultimate form of environmental conditioning of organization goals (Thompson and McEwen, 1958, pp. 25–8).

The conceptual approaches of Levine and White and of Litwak and Hylton therefore appear to be designed for nonturbulent conditions. Indeed, it may well be that coordination *per se*, in the static sense usually implied by that term, is dysfunctional for adaptation to turbulent fields. . . .

Integrative Framework

Model

It is assumed that the foregoing arguments are valid: (a) that organizational environments are increasingly turbulent; (b) that organizations are increasingly less autonomous; and (c) that other formal organizations are increasingly important components of organizational environments. Some conceptual perspective is now needed, which will make it possible to view any formal organization, its transactional interdependencies, and the environment itself within a common conceptual framework. The intent of this section is to outline the beginnings of such a framework.

A formal organization is a system primarily oriented to the attainment of a specific goal, which constitutes an output of the system and which is an input for some other system (Parsons, 1962, p. 33). Needless to say, the output of any living system is dependent upon input into it. Figure 1 schematically illustrates the skeletal structure of a living system. The input

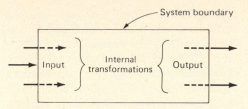

FIGURE 1   Structure of Living Systems such as a Formal Organization

and output regions are partially permeable with respect to the environment which is the region outside the system boundary. Arrows coming into a system represent input and arrows going out of a system represent output. In Figure 2, rectangles represent formal organizations and circles represent individuals and *non*-formal social organizations. Figure 2 represents the *statics* of a system X and its turbulent environment. Three-dimensional illustration would be necessary to show the *dynamics* of a turbulent environment sche-

matically. Assume that a third, temporal dimension is imposed on Figure 2 and that this reveals an increasing number of elements and an increasing rate and complexity of change in their interdependencies over time. To do full justice to the concept of turbulence, we should add other sets of elements even in Figure 2 below, although these are not yet linked to X's set. A notion that is integral to Emery and Trist's conception of turbulence is that changes outside of X's set, and hence difficult for X to predict and impossible for X to control, will have impact on X's transactional interdependencies in the future. The addition of just one link at some future time may not affect the super-system but may constitute a system break for X.

This schematization shows only one-way directionality and is meant to depict energic inputs, e.g. personnel and material, and output, e.g. product. The organization provides something in exchange for the inputs it receives, of course, and

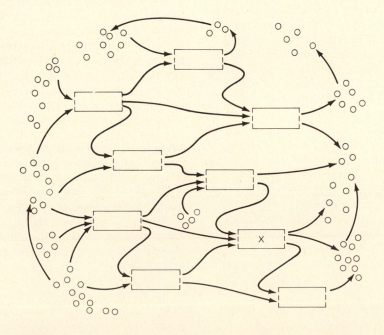

FIGURE 2   Illustration of System X in Turbulent Environment

this is usually informational in nature—money, most commonly. Similarly the organization receives money for its product from those systems for whom its product is an input. Nor does our framework distinguish different kinds of inputs, although the analysis of inter-organizational exchange requires this kind of taxonomic device. It seems important to distinguish energic inputs and outputs from informational ones. Energic inputs include machinery, personnel, clientele in the case of service organizations, electric power, and so on. Informational inputs are not well conceptualized although there is no doubt of their increasing importance in environments which are more complex and changeable. Special divisions of organizations and whole firms devoted to information collecting, processing and distributing are also rapidly proliferating, e.g. research organizations, accounting firms, the Central Intelligence Agency. . . .

Our simplistic approach to an integrative framework for the study of organizations (L_{11}), their transactional interdependencies (L_{21} and L_{12}) and the connectedness within their environments (L_{22}), gives the following conceptual ingredients: (a) units that are mainly formal organizations, and (b) relationships between them that are the directed flow (Cartwright, 1959) of (c) energy and information. The enormous and increasing importance of informational transaction has not been matched by conceptual developments in organization theory. The importance of information is frequently cited in a general way, however, especially in the context of organizational change or innovation. Dill (1962) has made a cogent argument on the need for more attention to this dimension.

The importance of communication for organizational change has been stressed by Ohlin (1958, p. 63), March and Simon (1958, pp. 173–83), Benne (1962, p. 232), Lippitt (1958, p. 52), and others. Diversity of informational input has been used to explain the creativity of individuals as well as of social systems (see, e.g. Allport, 1955, p. 76, Ogburn and Nimkoff, 1964, pp. 662–70). The importance of boundary positions as primary sources of innovative inputs from the environment has been stressed by March and Simon (1958, pp. 165–8, 189) and by Kahn *et al.* (1964, pp. 101–26). James Miller (1955, p. 530) hypothesizes that up to a maximum, which no living system has yet reached, the more energy a system devotes to information processing (as opposed to productive and maintenance activity), the more likely the system is to survive. . . .

Summary

The lag between evolution in the real world and evolution in theorists' ability to comprehend it is vast, but hopefully shrinking. It was only a little over one hundred years ago that Darwin identified natural selection as the mechanism of evolutionary process. Despite Darwin's enduring insight, theorists of change, including biologists, have continued to focus largely on internal aspects of systems.

It is our thesis that the selective advantage of one intra- or inter-organizational configuration over another cannot be assessed apart from an understanding of the dynamics of the environment itself. It is the environment which exerts selective pressure. 'Survival of the fittest' is a function of the fitness of the environment. The dinosaurs *were* impressive creatures, in their day.

References

Allport, F. H. (1955), *Theories of Perception and the Concept of Structure*, Wiley.

Ashby, W. R. (1960), *Design for a Brain*, Chapman & Hall, 2nd edn.

Benne, K. D. (1962), 'Deliberate changing as the facilitation of growth', in W. G. Bennis *et al.* (eds.), *The Planning of Change*, Holt, Rinehart & Winston.

Boulding, K. E. (1965), 'The economies of human conflict', in E. B. McNeil (ed.), *The Nature of Human Conflict*, Prentice-Hall.

Braybrooke, D., and Lindblom, C. E. (1963), *A Strategy of Decision*, Free Press.

Cartwright, D. (1959), 'The potential contribution of graph theory to organization theory', in M. Haire (ed.), *Modern Organization Theory*, Wiley, pp. 254–71.

Chein, I. (1953), 'Personality and typology', *Journal of Social Psychology*, vol. 18, pp. 89–101.

Clark, B. R. (1965), 'Inter-organizational patterns in education', *Administrative Science Quarterly*, vol. 10, pp. 224–37.

Cyert, R. M., and March, J. G. (1953), *A Behavorial Theory of the Firm*, Prentice-Hall.

Dill, W. R. (1962), 'The impact of environment on organizational development', in S. Mailick and E. H. von Ness (eds.), *Concepts and Issues in Administrative Behavior*, Prentice-Hall, pp. 94–109.

Drucker, P. F. (1964), 'The big power of little ideas', *Harvard Business Review*, vol. 42, May.

Emery, F. E., and Trist E. L. (1965), 'The causal texture of organizational environments', *Human Relations*, vol. 18, pp. 21–31.

Evan, W. M. (1966), 'The organization-set: toward a theory of inter-organizational relations', in J. D. Thompson (ed.), *Approaches to Organizational Design*, University of Pittsburgh Press.

Gardner, J. W. (1963), *Self-Renewal*, Harper & Row.

Hood, R. C. (1962), 'Business organization as a class-product of its purposes and of its environment', in M. Haire (ed.), *Organizational Theory in Industrial Practice*, Wiley.

Kahn, R. L., *et al.* (1964), *Organizational Stress*, Wiley.

Levine, S., and White, P. E. (1961), 'Exchange as a conceptual framework for the study of inter-organizational relationships', *Administrative Science Quarterly*, vol. 5, pp. 583–601.

Lippitt, R. (1958), *The Dynamics of Planned Change*, Harcourt, Brace & World.

Litwak, E., and Hylton, L. (1962), 'Inter-organizational analysis: a hypothesis on coordinating agencies', *Administrative Science Quarterly*, vol. 6, pp. 395–420.

Maniha, J., and Perrow, C. (1965), 'The reluctant organization and the aggressive environment', *Administrative Science Quarterly*, vol. 10, pp. 238–57.

March, J. G., and Simon, H. A. (1958), *Organizations*, Wiley.

McNulty, J. E. (1962), 'Organizational change in growing enterprises', *Administrative Science Quarterly*, vol. 7, pp. 1–21.

Miller, J. G. (1955), 'Toward a general theory for the behavorial sciences, *American Psychologist*, vol. 10, no. 9, pp. 513–31.

Ogburn, W. F., and Nimkoff, M. F. (1964), *Sociology*, Houghton Mifflin, 2nd edn.

Ohlin, L. E. (1958), 'Conformity in American society', *Social Work*, vol. 3, p. 63.

Parsons, T. (1962), 'Suggestions for a sociological approach to the theory of organizations', in A. Etzioni (ed.), *Complex Organizations*, Holt, Rinehart & Winston.

Pringle, J. W. S. (1956), 'On the parallel being learning and evolution' *General Systems*, vol. 1, p. 90.

Rosengren, W. R. (1964), 'Communication, organization and conduct in the "therapeutic milieu" ', *Administrative Science Quarterly*, vol. 9., pp. 70–90.

Rubington, E. (1965), 'Organizational strain and key roles', *Administrative Science Quarterly*, vol. 9, pp. 350–69.

Simon, H. A. (1957), *Models of Man*, Wiley.

Stinchcombe, A. L. (1965), 'Social structure and organization', in J. G. March (ed.), *Handbook of Organizations*, Rand McNally.

Taylor, D. W. (1965), 'Decision making and problem solving', in J. G. March (ed.), *Handbook of Organizations*, Rand McNally, pp. 48–82.

Thompson, J. D., and McEwen, W. J. (1958), 'Organizational goals and environment', *American Sociological Review*, vol. 23, pp. 23–31.

Tolman, E. C., and Brunswick, E. (1935), 'The organism and the causal texture of the environment', *Psychological Review*, vol. 42, pp. 43–72.

Von Bertalanffy, L. (1956), 'General system theory', *General Systems*, vol. 1, pp. 1–10.

6.3 Adaptability and Copability: A Study of Social Systems, Their Environment, and Survival

Kurt Kourosh Motamedi

Introduction

Through observation of individuals, groups, organizations, and other social systems,[1] two significant processes emerge as key factors in a system's effectiveness and survival—adaptability and copability. The aim of this paper is to outline and contrast the distinct sets of processes associated with adaptability and copability. By acknowledging that adaptability and copability are separate but interacting states, the contingency approach becomes useful to assess the relevant set of critical variables with which a system is faced. This will allow the individual, the consultant, and the manager/leader to gain insight into the particular set of problems confronting him before making the needed interventions.

A recent consulting experience with the top management team of a rapidly growing

The author would like to cordially thank professors Craig Lundberg of USC, William McKelvey of UCLA, and Warren Schmidt of USC for their helpful comments. Kurt Motamedi is Professor of Management at Pepperdine University.

[1] The term "social systems" is used throughout the paper to include individuals, dyads, groups, and organizations.

firm in the Middle East stimulated the author to think about copability and adaptability. In a team development session, two managers shared the concern that although the organization was doing quite well in relation to its competitors and the environment, it was falling apart internally. Others in the team acknowledged the problem and jointly began to search for and identify the internal problems and ways of dealing with them. The process was difficult and took many months because the range of problems was broad and included social as well as technical variables. It became evident that a great number of internal problems, stresses, strains, and disharmonies had been caused directly or indirectly by efforts to adapt to rapidly changing external environmental conditions and the inability to cope with them internally. The organization, with its rapid growth rate and turbulent environment (Emery & Trist, 1965; Terreberry, 1968), outwardly had gained the confidence of its relevant publics, achieved the impossible overnight, and expanded its task environment, but this had created unbearable conditions internally. Continuous need for overtime work, limited skills of lower-level managers, and importation of a large number of technical experts from Europe, the United States, and Japan had created cultural and communication tangles that had seldom been experienced by organizations in that particular country.

A similar case in the early Sixties involved a California firm whose president became interested in the application of the behavioral sciences in his organization. He invited a number of scholars and consultants in behavioral sciences and management to help improve the work processes for a higher quality of working life and productivity. As expected, experimentation and interventions led to improvement in both areas. *Business Week* (1973) reported that between 1960 and 1965, production jumped 30 per cent. Workers' productivity increased, as behaviorists predicted that it would. As the experiments continued and greater internal integration was achieved, more of the top managers' energies and efforts were spent on dealing with the needed internal changes. Consequently, managers paid less attention to the company's external environment—the state of the economy, the relevant publics and markets, and the competitors' advances in technology. The president reported that "the experiments caused him to lose touch with what was happening to his company." During the recession of 1970, the company was unable to adapt to its environment. Inventories had grown too large with obsolete components at noncompetitive prices; the cash position was weak, and the firm was on the verge of insolvency.

After reflecting on these and similar organizational, group, and personal experiences, the author concluded that surviving well requires a balance between *adaptability*, which relates to a social system's ability to deal with its external task environment and to remain environmentally relevant, and *copability*, which reflects a system's ability to deal with and

maintain a viable internal environment. Although neither process can exist in isolation, the distinction is necessary and helpful. A skillful manager or leader often is aware of these two sets of processes, consciously or unconsciously, and facilitates the appropriate processes at the appropriate time and place.

Discussions of relationships between systems and environment generally assume that adaptation is basic to any social system's success (survival) in dealing with its environment (Kast & Rosenzweig, 1976; Katz & Kahn, 1966; Thompson, 1967). Few discussions also mention coping as a necessary adjustment process for an effective system (Allport, 1961; Kroeber, 1964; Schein, 1969; Schein & Bennis, 1965). Unfortunately, because the distinction has not been made clear in the literature, the potential to use these concepts in understanding social systems has gone unrealized by many scholars and practitioners. A conceptualization encompassing adaptability, copability, and the relationship between them is presented in this paper.

Adaptability

To survive, social systems deal with changes and conditions in their environments by adaptation. Piaget (1932) defined adaptation as the equilibrium toward which the organism moves as the result of the interaction between itself and the environment. According to Piaget, adaptation consists of movement away from total egocentric orientation and the development of internalized operations. Fromm (1941) classified adaptation into two types: static and dynamic (a more detailed discussion of the difference will follow).

> By static adaptation we mean such an adaptation to patterns as leaves the whole character structure unchanged and implies only the adoption of a new habit. An example of this kind of adaptation is the change from the Chinese habit of eating to

the Western habit of using fork and knife. A Chinese coming to America will adapt himself to this new pattern, but this adaptation in itself has little effect on his personality; it does not arouse new drives or character traits.

By dynamic adaptation we refer to the kind of adaptation that occurs, for example, when a boy submits to the commands of his strict and threatening father—being too afraid of him to do otherwise—and becomes a "good boy." While he adapts himself to the necessities of the situation, something happens in him. He may develop an intense hostility against his father, which he represses, since it would be too dangerous to express it or even to be aware of it. This repressed hostility, however, though not manifest, is a dynamic factor in his character structure. It may create new anxiety and thus lead to still deeper submission; it may set up a vague defiance, directed against no one in particular but rather toward life in general. . . . This kind of adaptation creates something new in him, arouses new drives and new anxieties. (pp. 15–16)

Katz and Kahn (1966) refer to similar phenomena as an adaptive function, directed toward the survival of the social system outwardly and providing environmental constancy. A social system may attain control, via adaptive function, over the external environment or modify its internal structures to meet the requirements of the changing external environment. In other words, adaptability is the system's ability to interact with the environment in such a way as to ensure its own survival.

Adaptability involves a social system's ability to change (1) the external environment, (2) the internal environment to meet external environment demands, or (3) both internal and external environments simultaneously for a fit. Adaptability involves sensing and understanding both internal and external environments (the total environment) and taking action to achieve a fit between the two. There are at least four groups of actions (tactics) that social

systems can undertake to achieve adaptation in a given circumstance:

Conforming is accepting the change requirement and implementing the necessary changes.

Controlling refers to an active determination on the part of the system to influence (a) the source of change, (b) the flow (speed) of change, or (c) the direction (favorability) of the change, (e.g., a company lobbyist in Congress seeks to control a change in the environment by preventing unfavorable legislation, promoting favorable legislation, influencing the rate of these changes, or keeping the sources of change inactive).

Resisting means reluctance on the part of the system to respond to the needed changes by deliberate or unintentional delays and procrastination (organization routines or red tape tend to retard change efforts). Resisting reflects a doldrum or quasi-stationary (Lewin, 1972) situation in which a delicate balance of counteracting forces is in existence.

Opposing is the outright rejection of change implementation; it may lead to major conflicts that may involve confrontation and competition—a situation in which a social system shows inflexibility by not compromising or collaborating to resolve certain change problems in its environment.

In this context, the concept of long-range planning advanced by Steiner and Minor (1977) is an adaptive process applicable to any social system. Long-range planning provides systems with adaptability by controlling major internal and external variables over a period of time. Dynamic homeostasis (Katz & Kahn, 1966) is another example of adaptability that involves maintaining a system's stability by establishing a constant set of interactions with the external environment. The adaptability of a system is reflected in its "relevancy" with its external environment.

Copability

Copability is a social system's internal ability to maintain its identity and overcome the problem of change. The essence of copability is the ability of a system to conserve its integrity and distinct characteristics—"to hold one's own." It is a systemic property of any social system that brings the system's subunits into a functioning, cohesive whole. In Gestalt theory (Koffka, 1935), a similar notion is *prägnanz*, which corresponds to unity, uniformity, good continuation, simple shape, and closure. Bradley and Calvin (1956) refer to Le Chatelier's principle to decribe a similar phenomenon in terms of forces that tend to restore the system as closely as possible to its original state. Festinger (1957) labels this internal stabilization "dissonance reduction" forces, which deal with any change and disruption of the internal component parts and reduce the effect of change imposed by internal stress, strain, and disharmony. Copability also consists of the system's ability to deal with the change of its own self-concept, core cognitive processes (Kolasa, 1969), and accompanying emotions.

Copability is a social system's ability to diagnose the internal change-induced problems related to structure, processes, technology, values, needs, and purposes; to feel disharmonies within and among the subparts; and to take action to resolve, arrest, stall, or repress the problem. There are four groups of coping activities (tactics):

Resolution occurs when the internal change problem is identified, confronted, and alleviated. It is a condition of coming to terms with self.

Arresting is to identify the problem, locate points of stress or strain, and take actions to stop the growth of the problem and the associated pain. In this process, the problem is not totally removed and efforts are limited.

Stalling is to delay action or procrastinate to deal with a specific internal problem. The system is aware of the pain or disharmony, but it decides not to deal with it until a later time. An organization facing a major copability problem may stall and delay dealing with minor aches until a later time.

Repressing is a system's action to deal with an internal problem by refusing to acknowledge that a problem exists. Repressing may be useful if the problem is temporary and not significant enough to disrupt the internal core processes. In such situations, the costs associated with dealing with the problem may not exceed the benefits. However, when major problems are repressed, serious long-term and short-term consequences may arise.

A Comparison

Adaptability involves conscious efforts to relate with the external environment and copability consists of efforts (conscious or unconscious) to maintain an internal environment. A comparison of the two is presented in Table 1.

The relationship is complex and poses a dilemma. As a system becomes more relevant to its external environment, it may face identity diffusion and identity problems (including crisis). It may become differentiated (Lawrence & Lorsch, 1967) to an extent that its functioning is impaired seriously. Although the changes are purposeful and deliberate, the associated pain, stress, strain, and disharmony can reach unbearable levels. If the system is unable to cope with the imposed but necessary internal changes needed for adaptation, it will fall apart. There are also situations in which a social system becomes so inward looking, self-centered, and self-conscious that it loses sight of its task-environment requirements. The habits, attitudes, needs, folklores, myths, and beliefs that relate to the system's identity may become so fixed that they result in an inability to cope.

TABLE 1   A Comparison between Adaptability and Copability

Adaptability	Copability
Leads to a greater relevancy and better match with external environment.	Leads to a stronger identity and better integration within the internal environment.
Involves boundary expansion and contraction.	Involves boundary conservation.
Directed to achieve deliberate, conscious goals and objectives. Determined by external environment and others.	Directed to achieve conscious and unconscious needs.
Involves trans-boundary changes (import and export change).	Determined by internal environment and self.
Search is outward and extrospective.	Involves intra-system changes.
Time thrust (temporal orientation) is from future to now.	Search is inward and introspective.
Temporal emphasis is on the "future."	Time thrust is from now to the future.
Spatial emphasis is about "there."	Temporal emphasis is on the "present."
Consciousness function is dominated by sensory feeling and empirical thinking (Jacobi, 1973; Mitroff & Kilmann, 1976).	Spatial emphasis is about "here."
	Consciousness function is dominated by intuitive feeling and intuitive speculative thinking (Jacobi, 1973; Mitroff & Kilmann, 1976).
Thrust is toward change of the external environment or change of the internal environment to fit the external conditions.	Thrust is toward maintenance, integration, and retention of the internal parts as a whole.

It is helpful to distinguish between *dynamic* and *static* adaptability and copability. In Fromm's example of dynamic adaptation involving a father and his son, the focal system is the son relating to his environment—the father. The boy adapts to the strict and threatening demands of his environment by conforming and becoming a "good" boy. However, his forced conformity may create internal disharmonies and unpleasant feelings with which he must deal. His ability to cope with the internal disharmonies will determine how well he will survive in this and future situations. His adaptability requires a significant level of copability and is *dynamic*. However, the Chinese adaptation to the Western custom of using knife and fork creates little or no internal tension or disharmony. The adaptation necessitates little or no copability and is *static*. The dynamic adaptation, then, accompanies a much greater disruption of the internal system and necessitates a greater copability than static adaptation.

It is also true that dynamic coping calls for a greater need for adaptability than does static coping. For example, Litwin and Stringer (1968) describe a person with a high need for achievement as one who spends his time doing his job better, accomplishing something unusual and important, or advancing his career. The "achiever" copes *dynamically* with his feelings of inadequacy and internal disharmony by acting out and relating actively to the environment. This requires a greater adaptability. However, a person with a high level of anxiety may choose to cope *statically* by thinking and reflecting, meditating, daydreaming, or sleeping. These activities are not environmentally focused. They are inner or self-directed, represent static coping, and require little adaptability.

Implications for Organizations

To make appropriate organizational interventions, managers and practitioners must understand the nature of the environment and the adaptability and copability of the units that they work with. Koontz and O'Donnell (1972) define management as "a process of designing and maintaining the internal environment for organized effort to accomplish group goals." This definition primarily deals with the design and maintenance of the internal system for internal purposes and reflects a strong copability bias. Raia's view of management (1974), on the other hand, tends to include both the adaptability and copability concepts. He states:

> Management must not only create and maintain the organizational structure, but must understand and learn to deal with the resulting complexity of the total environment, one that is becoming more and more turbulent every day. (p. 4)

This notice emphasizes the importance of maintaining both organizational identity and environmental relevancy. Managers and practitioners must create and maintain a fit or balance between the internal organizational needs and external environmental requirements that will determine how well the organization will survive. A manager or an OD practitioner can facilitate the development of processes that will lead to organizational adaptability, copability, and their balance or "centeredness." Self-analysis to determine needs, weaknesses, and strengths and environmental analysis to determine task requirements, opportunities, and threats are important facilitative actions. The study of the social system's adaptability and copability is of crucial importance in any meaningful organization development or facilitative effort.

The degree and type of adaptability and copability required for survival are contingent upon the environmental characteristics of a social system. Emery and Trist's classification of four environments (1965) illustrates the point. The four environment types and related adaptability and copability levels are as follows:

1. *A placid, randomized environment* is the simplest environment in which resources, goals, and values are relatively unchanging and are distributed randomly (with constant frequency). A survival requires little change in knowledge and processes; as a result, adaptability and copability efforts in such environments tend to be low.

2. *A placid, clustered environment* is more sophisticated and may be described as one in which resources, goals, and values are relatively unchanging but are found in clusters. Survival in these environments requires knowledge, technologies, and processes that are specialized and fitted to deal with different clusters. The associated adaptability and copability levels of effort tend to be statically high but dynamically low. An organization with relatively stable but segmented markets, products, and suppliers must develop special competencies to deal with the unique but different types of requirements.

3. *A disturbed, reactive environment* involves many social systems of the same kind dominating the environment. Each social system affects the survival of the others via linear causal chains of consequences temporally and spatially. Survival depends on knowledge about other social systems' reactive behavior and their domain of environmental influence (resources, goals, and values). The associated adaptability and copability efforts tend to be statically low but dynamically high.

4. *A turbulent field environment* is the most complex. In these dynamic environments the causal chains of consequences are nonlinear and dependent on properties of the field itself. The field is dominated by motions on motions. Survival in such environments involves sophisticated knowledge about the environmental characteristics and the ability to bear the induced emotional strains and stresses. A system's efforts to survive require a high level of both static and dynamic adaptability and copability.

A summary of these four types of environment and the related adaptability and copability mix is presented in Table 2.

Managers and practitioners must consider the impact of the environment on their client systems. As the environment becomes more turbulent and less predictable, systems require a greater degree of dynamic adaptability and copability. The external fluctuations and uncertainties that turbulent field systems encounter have great potential for disrupting vital internal processes that then must be dealt with through greater copability. Of course, not all systems can develop appropriate adaptability and copability to survive in all situations. A system with low adaptability and copability in a highly demanding situation may need to be helped to find a niche in an environment in which its abilities appropriately fit its circumstances. Lorsch and Morse (1974) stated that "in those situations where the characteristics of individuals do not fit environmental and organizational conditions, placement and selection are important factors in achieving an improved balance between man and organization."

Readiness to move toward adapting or coping can be of great importance for survival in a given situation. A system confronting a situation that requires high adaptability or copability may not be ready to respond appropriately, in which case facilitation for system readiness may become the primary goal of the practitioner. The system may need to become more aware of its circumstances and more cognizant of the tactics and actions it undertakes (or lacks) for adapting and coping.

An understanding of the internal characteristics of the system is helpful to achieve an improved balance between the system and its environment. Each system has its own unique way of processing information and making decisions. A practitioner and researcher can assess many of the system's internal attributes, such as: identifying its dominant modes of perception and judgment (Jacobi, 1973; Myers, 1962); tolerance for ambiguity and frustration (Adorno et al., 1950); needs (Murray, 1938); Machiavellianism (Christie & Geis, 1970); and competence (White, 1963, 1967). This assessment will be useful to determine possible weaknesses in adaptability and copability.

Much research remains to be done on adaptability and copability. For example, although much of the research on organization change and development has been

TABLE 2   A Contingency Table of Adaptability and Copability in Different Environmental Types

	Required Level of							
	Copability				Adaptability			
	Static		Dynamic		Static		Dynamic	
	Low	High	Low	High	Low	High	Low	High
Turbulent Field		X		X		X		X
Disturbed Reactive	X			X	X			X
Placid Clustered		X	X			X	X	
Placid Random	X		X		X		X	

concerned with system adaptation and adaptability, there has been little attention, if any, paid to coping and copability. More needs to be known about the characteristics of people and groups in organizations that do have high adaptability and copability in different types of environments. A study of systems that confront sudden changes is necessary. For example, Kubler-Ross (1970) has classified the stages that a terminally ill patient experiences as anger, bargaining, depression, acceptance, and hope, which reflect different modes of adaptability and copability. Such studies yield valuable insight into personal and system adaptability and copability in rapidly changing environments.

The study of the interactions among environmental types, organizational forms, and members' differences for adaptability and copability is a challenge. Perhaps as a greater environmental turbulence (with more crises and scarcities) is experienced, these issues will become more important to both scholars and practitioners.

Summary

Adaptability refers to a social system's ability to sense and understand both internal and external environments and to take actions to achieve a fit or balance between the two. Adaptability brings about greater system relevance; copability is a social system's ability to conserve (maintain) its identity and overcome the problem of change internally. If the system is unable to adapt, it will not remain operative; if the system is too inward looking and self-centered, it will lose touch with the outside world and will become ineffective. The dilemma facing all systems is to find the point of balance between the two processes.

Each of the processes may exhibit static or dynamic characteristics. Static adaptability involves a low level of associated coping; dynamic adaptability requires a high level of coping because the accompanying internal disharmonies are great. Static copability requires little or no dealings with the environment; dynamic copability involves a great deal of interaction with the external environment. The mixture of these four types of processes is contingent on the conditions of the organization's external environment, organizational form, and members' characteristics. Organizations in turbulent field environments frequently face major changes and require a great deal of adaptability and copability. In placid environments, changes tend to be less significant and require lower adaptability and copability.

In our society, as the rate of change increases, the environment becomes more turbulent, resources become scarce, and the economy slows down, managers will need to understand and take into account the adaptability and copability characteristics of the organization (or subsystem) that they manage. Further assessment of systems' adaptability and copability seems vitally important.

References

Adorno, T. W., Frenkel-Brunswick, E., Levinson, D. J., & Sanford, R. N. *The authoritarian personality.* New York: Harper & Row, 1950.

Allport, G. W. *Pattern and growth in personality.* New York: Holt, Rinehart and Winston, 1961.

Bradley, D. F., & Calvin, M. Behavior: Imbalance in a network of chemical transformations, *Yearbook of the Society for the Advancement of General System Theory,* 1956, *1,* 56–65.

Burns, T., & Stalker, G. M. *The management of innovation.* London: Tavistock, 1967.

Christie, R., & Geis, F. I. *Studies in*

Machiavellianism. New York: Academic Press, 1970.

Emery, F. E., & Trist, E. L. The causal texture of organizational environments. *Human Relations,* 1965, *18,* 21–32.

Festinger, L. *A theory of cognitive dissonance.* Palo Alto, Calif.: Stanford University Press, 1957.

Fromm, E. *Escape from freedom.* New York: Holt, Rinehart and Winston, 1941.

Jacobi, J. *The psychology of C. G. Jung.* New Haven, Conn.: Yale University Press, 1973.

Kast, R. E.., & Rosenzweig, J. E. *Organization and management: A systems approach.* New York: McGraw-Hill, 1976.

Katz, D., & Kahn, R. L. *The social psychology of organizations.* New York: John Wiley, 1966.

Koffka, K. *Principles of gestalt psychology.* New York: Harcourt, Brace and World, 1935.

Kolasa, B. J. *Introduction to behavioral science for business.* New York: John Wiley, 1969.

Koontz, H., & O'Donnell, C. *Principles of management: An analysis of managerial functions.* New York: McGraw-Hill, 1972.

Kroeber, T. C. The coping functions of the ego mechanism: In R. While (Ed.), *A study of lives.* New York: Atherton Press, 1964.

Kubler-Ross, E. *On death and dying.* New York: Macmillan, 1970.

Lawrence, P., & Lorsch, J. *Organization and its environment.* Boston, Mass.: Division of Research, Graduate School of Business Administration, Harvard University Press, 1967.

Lewin, K. Quasistationary social equilibria and the problem of permanent change. In N. Marguilies & A. P. Raia (Eds.), *Organizational development: Values, processes and technology.* New York: McGraw-Hill, 1972.

Litwin, G. H., & Stringer, R. A. *Motivation and organizational climate.* Boston, Mass.: Division of Research, Graduate School of Business Administration, Harvard University, 1968.

Lorsch, J. W., & Morse, J. J. *Organizations and their members.* New York: Harper & Row, 1974.

Mitroff, I., & Kilmann, R. H. On organization stories: An approach to the design and analysis of organizations through myths and stories. In R. H. Kilmann, L. R. Pondy, & D. P. Slevin (Eds.), *The management of organization design.* New York: North-Holland, 1976.

Murray, H. A. *Explorations in personality.* Oxford: Oxford University Press, 1938.

Myers, L. B. *Manual: The Myers-Briggs type indicator.* Princeton, N. J.: Educational Testing Service, 1962.

Piaget, J. *The moral judgment of the child.* New York: The Free Press, 1965. (Originally published, 1932.)

Raia, A. P. *Managing by objectives.* Glenview, Ill.: Scott, Foresman, 1974.

Schein, E. H. *Process consultation: Its role in organization development.* Reading, Mass.: Addison-Wesley, 1969.

Schein, E. H., & Bennis, W. G. *Personal and organizational change through group methods.* New York: John Wiley, 1965.

Steiner, G., & Minor, J. *Policy & strategy.* New York: Macmillan, 1977.

Terreberry, S. The evolution of organizational environments. *Administrative Science Quarterly,* 1968, *12,* 590–613.

Thompson, J. D. *Organizations in action.* New York: McGraw-Hill, 1967. Where being nice to workers didn't work. *Business Week.* Jan. 20, 1973, pp. 80–100.

White, R. W. Ego and reality in psychoanalytic theory. *Psychological Issues,* 1963, *3,* 33–41.

White, R. W. Competence and the growth of personality. *Science and psychoanalysis,* 1967, *11,* 42–58.

III
Interventions for Planned Change

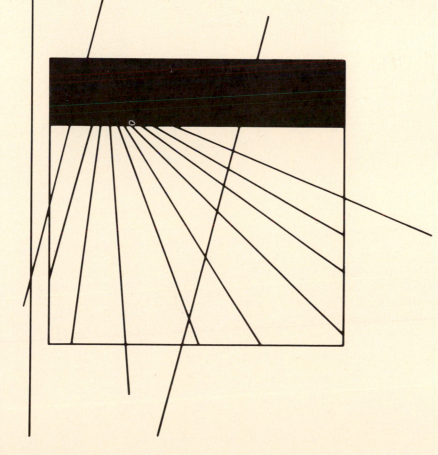

7
Planning Structures and Processes

Planning is an abstraction, one that all too often bounces off the eye, especially the eye of anyone whom the planning is supposed to affect. Planning for change, notwithstanding the abstract nature of the business, is also multifaceted, complex, ill-defined, and highly personal. As Churchman has one of his bogus characters say in his piece (7.5):

> You know what may be the real truth after all? A problem is something you personally can do something about, and a solution is something that pleases you to do about it. Problem and solution are forms of self-gratification.

And it's more than that, as the following papers demonstrate. Paul Nutt's paper is the most concise, up-to-date piece we have seen. Using a "transactional model," he is able to make plain the steps, phases, and components of the planning process, a process that can be applied to units of any size, from the small group (or dyad) to multinational organizations to communities.

The Mason and Mitroff paper explains "open system planning": how organizations can influence their stakeholders. William Dunn takes "knowledge" as the central feature of change and provides a long-sought-after rationale for the uses of knowledge in change endeavors.

The last three articles are unusual—even unique—in their approaches and are perhaps among the most intriguing papers in the vast literature of "social change." Both Schön and Churchman come out of the context of epistemology and show how the arcana of philosophy can help illuminate the darkness of change processes. Each arrives at "wisdom" in his own way: Schön confronts an "ill-defined" problem and concludes with some compelling ideas about "reflection" and "conversation"; Churchman introduces "conversation" as a means to induct the reader into the complexity and fascination of the almost ineffable "systems approach."

The Grabow and Heskin piece is the only "holdover" from our last edition and "holds up" remarkably well. Chapter 9, its earlier location, will be dealing with some of the issues "radical planning" raises.

These readings reflect the influence of the applied behavioral sciences over the past decade. The selections recognize that planned change is both a personal and an organizational phenomenon; they also attempt to include the environmental aspects of planned change, something our earlier editions did not highlight as much as the present volume aims to do. Each reading, by itself, provides an element or building block of planned change. Taken as a whole, they can be useful for identifying structure among the essential processes of planned organizational/social change.

7.1 The Study of Planning Process

Paul C. Nutt

Introduction

Planning is one of several responses that managers make when performance falls below norms, and both performance and norms are clear (March and Simon, 1958; Nutt, 1979). Planning methods are tools used by planners (with given amounts of support) to transform an undesirable state to a better one. The norm acts as a goal to guide the effort (Backoff, 1976). The current problem state is recognized by haphazard urban development or declining sales. Norms specify attributes of a land use plan

or a target sales level. The difference between performance and norms is called the performance gap (Downs, 1967). Planning is used to devise or revise an organization's policies, products, services, or internal operations seeking to close the performance gap by improving performance factors such as client satisfaction, costs, or quality.

Despite their importance, little is known about the merits of planning methods. A particularly neglected aspect is process. To get at process, case studies will be used to explore the practice of planning. The processes used will be compared to processes that theorists contend should be applied to carry out planning. This paper seeks to identify process features which can influence planning results and suggest a research program for their study.

Prepared for "Nontraditional Approaches to Policy Research," conference sponsored by the Graduate School of Business, University of Southern California, November 11–13, 1981. © Paul C. Nutt, 1983.

Planning Methods and Their Features

A review of the literature suggests that planning methods have two distinguishing features: process and technique (Nutt, 1981). The typical planning method has several interrelated stages. *Process* spells out the sequence or order in which these stages are to be carried out. *Technique* is the approach used to deal with the issues raised in each stage of the process. A planning method can be fully defined in technique and process terms. For instance, the "Program Planning Method" identifies five stages: problem exploration, knowledge exploration, priority development, program development, and program control and evaluation (Delbecq and Van de Ven, 1971). The "nominal group" is the technique used to identify problems in stage one and possible solutions in stage two.

The Planning Morphology

Generic process stages were identified by reviewing a large number of planning methods. The processes used by these methods were distilled until five stages (formulation, conceptualization, detailing, evaluation, and implementation) and three steps (search, synthesis, and analysis) emerged. These stages and steps define a "planning morphology," as shown in Table 1.

Planning Stages

The *formulation* stage is used to clarify the problem stipulation provided by the sponsor (Levine et al., 1975). These stipulations are often described in terms of discrepancies between an existing state and an ideal or desirable state (Pounds, 1969). Planning techniques are used to refine the definition of existing states and to describe "ideal" states, thereby verifying the existence and nature of the performance gap. Techniques like exception reports, Stakeholder Analysis (Mitroff et al., 1979; and Emshoff, 1980), the Nominal Group Technique (Delbecq and Van de Ven, 1971), Brainwriting (Gueschka et al., 1975), Function Expansion (Nadler, 1970), or Delphi surveys (Dalky, 1967) can be used to specify current or ideal states.

The *concept* stage of the planning process is used to develop a model which captures the planning problem. The model reduces ambiguity by breaking the problem into smaller, easier-to-understand components which are attacked one at a time in stage three. Model construction can be holistic and reductionist. Morphology (Zwicky, 1969) and Scenarios (Quade and Boucher, 1968) illustrate holistic techniques. Reductionist models are based on careful analysis of problems in operating systems. Techniques like Block Diagram (Wilson and Wilson, 1970), input-output (Hall, 1962), and Relevance Trees (Warfield, 1976) are used.

In the *detailing* stage, various representations of potentially viable solutions are developed. To sketch the operating features of a plan, "constructive" techniques, such as Systems Matrices (e.g., Nadler, 1970), General Systems Theory (e.g., Weinberg, 1975; Klir, 1972), or current system models (Quade and Boucher, 1968) are applied. To refine the plan, "interrogative" techniques, such as Interpretative Structural Modeling (Warfield, 1972), Simulation, or mathematical techniques (e.g., waiting lines and Dynamic Programming) are used to reveal ways that the plan can be improved.

The *evaluation* stage is used to identify the costs, benefits, acceptance, and other factors that influence the adoptability of each solution alternative. The evaluation information provides the basis to select

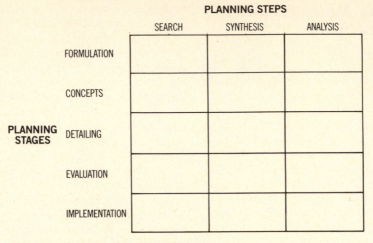

TABLE 1   The Planning Morphology

Planning Steps

among the alternative solutions or to rule out all of them as unacceptable. Evaluation information can be provided by Decision Trees, Simulation, queuing models, multi-attribute utility models (Huber, 1974; and Fisher, 1979), field experiments (Wholey et al., 1971; and Suchman, 1967), and quasi-experiments (Cook and Campbell, 1979). Operations Research techniques merge or couple stages three and four. Critics of operations research approaches contend that they emphasize evaluation at the expense of model construction.

Strategies to gain plan acceptance are considered in the *implementation* stage. Some implementation techniques stress cooptation and partial involvement of clients and/or sponsors (e.g., Delbecq and Van de Ven, 1971). They are applied as an integral part of the earlier stages. OD theorists approach implementation as an overlay to the first four process stages. For example, Lewin (1958) calls for a "change agent" who acts as the plan sponsor and guides users through a process which alters their objectives, social ties, and self-esteem and reinforces the positive aspects of the new plan.

Search is used to gather information for process stages. For instance, search procedures are used to identify or refine problem stipulations in stage one or possible solutions in stage three. Group processes such as Synectics (Gordon, 1972) and NGT (Delbecq and Van de Ven, 1971) illustrate techniques that stimulate the information sources of people.

In the *synthesis* step, techniques are used to assemble or put together ideas identified during search into a relational format. For example, morphological expansion (Zwicky, 1968) permutes elements of system components in novel ways and generic system components can be used to specify solution concepts (Nadler, 1970).

Analysis is applied to study or test stage results. At each stage of the process some form of ranking and sorting must be used to prune ideas to a manageable number. For example, paired comparisons can be used to select among objectives or prioritize problem lists in stage one (Nutt, 1981). In stage four the analysis step may require something as elaborate as a research strategy, to verify cause-and-effect relationships in proposed solutions.

The Transactional Model

Views of Process

Some planning methods keep the planning mode distinct from the decision mode as shown in Table 2. Such processes are called "planner-driven." The decision mode consists of a diagnosis, based on problem recognition (Nutt, 1979). When performance falls below expectations, conflict results, which leads to a problem stipulation. The stipulation of a performance gap activates the planning process. After activation, many (but not all) planning theorists prefer, and even try, to keep the sponsor at arm's length as the planning process unfolds. The loop shown for planning in Table 2 describes the path often preferred by planners: an orderly procession from one stage to the next terminating in some form of a field test. The sponsor must wait to see if the performance gap has been closed until information from field performance or a pilot test is presented.

Churchman (1979), Ackoff (1974), and many others contend that administrators should beware of accepting the planner's version of what can or cannot be done. As a consequence, planning processes can seldom unfold independently of sponsor involvement. In practice, sponsors often see the danger in waiting until the process unfolds before questioning the results. Some planning theorists also recognize the need for sponsor involvement (e.g., Churchman, 1979), but few articulate the nature of the transactions that should occur. In the discussion which follows, these "dialogues" are identified, which helps to prescribe ideal information exchanges between planner and sponsor.

A comparison of the planner-driven and sponsor-driven planning illustrates fundamentally different approaches to process. A "sponsor-driven" view of planning, shown in Table 3, calls for a transactional approach. Note that the

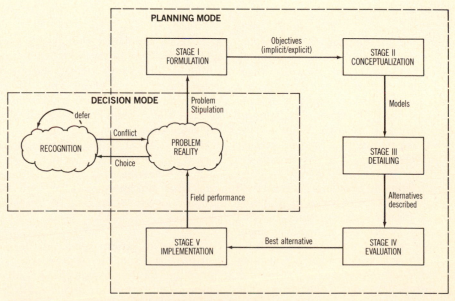

TABLE 2 The Planner-Driven Planning Process

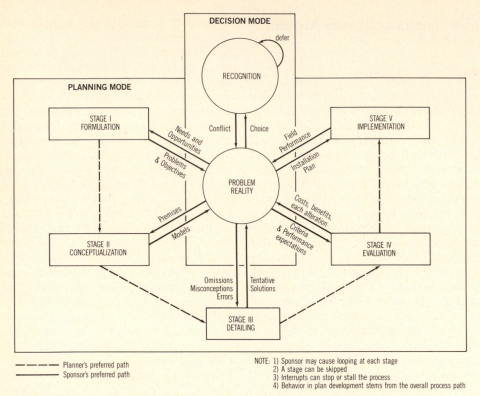

TABLE 3   The Transactional Model: Sponsor-Driven Planning Process

sponsor and the planner are expected to maintain a dialogue throughout planning (Churchman, 1971). This dialogue forces the planners to provide information to a decision-making process which is external to the planning process. The sponsor makes decisions in each stage of the process. The nature of these dialogues for each process stage is described below.

Formulation   The sponsor is faced with the problem: the frustrations of declining sales or profits, unacceptable hospital occupancy rates, or complaints about ineffective agency operations. The sponsor stipulates needs and/or opportunities that are interpreted by the planner using one or more planning techniques to provide problems and/or objectives. The sponsor

tests these stipulation changes by examining their ability to deal with factors (e.g., profits or occupancy rates) which motivated the planning effort. This dialogue may result in considerable redefinition or cycling. The sponsor can make unrealistic demands which may delay or distort the planning process. Too little stipulation can also create difficulties. Planners, left to their own devices, may have little insight into what can or should be done and propose overly restrictive or unrealistic objectives.

Conceptualization   Once an objective has been selected, the sponsor provides "premises" for the conceptualization phase. These premises provide notions of causality and/or interventions that sponsors believe can be helpful in dealing with the performance gap. Limits to the scope of inquiry are also provided. Armed with the definition of the planning arena and some solution concepts, the planner attempts to construct a model to represent the problem. The planner's model may change the arena or suggest a solution tact which challenges the premises initially offered. The sponsor may reject the model because it does not incorporate a sufficient number of premises. A model can be resisted when it does not include cause-effect or producer-product relationships implicit in the sponsor's premises. And, the sponsor should allow the planner to formalize his or her implicit propositions in concrete terms to permit modeling. This dialogue often leads to cycling. Cycling occurs when the model is progressively altered to incorporate the sponsor's objections. This dialogue may serve to stimulate high-quality solutions or may degenerate into an acrimonious controversy.

Detailing   The detailing phase is expected to provide a tentative solution. The sponsor tests the solution for omissions, misconceptions, and errors. Following widely held views of planning, the planner should attempt to introduce several competing solutions for the sponsor to consider (e.g., Simon and Newell, 1970; Mitroff et al., 1977). However, as Mintzberg and his colleagues point out, the typical project develops very few alternatives with distinct features (Mintzberg et al., 1976). The dialogue between the sponsor and the planner typically focuses on the merits of a single alternative. When a set of competing alternatives is introduced, the sponsor may see only the difficulties in sorting out a preferable plan and not the benefits that come from competing ideas.

Evaluation   In the next stage, each proposed solution is subjected to an evaluation. The sponsor identifies criteria (e.g., costs, benefits, and acceptance) to determine the best solution alternative. The evaluation determines how each alternative meets each criterion. The sponsor compares performance levels to his or her expectations. When these expectations are not met, cycling results. First, the evaluation is repeated to confirm the sponsor's norms or to verify the accuracy of the evaluative information (Nutt, 1979). If the options continue to be unacceptable, the sponsor may require that the project revert to an earlier stage to revise the solution. After several such cycles, the sponsor's norms may change (March and Simon, 1958) or the sponsor may adopt the alternative that has powerful proponents (Cyert and March, 1963). Cynical views of the sponsor's motives result. Planners who question a sponsor's motives may attempt to control the decision process by pruning and distorting evaluation information.

Implementation   In stage five the planner develops a strategy to install the plan. Performance factors like cost and satisfaction are gleaned from actual operations in the field and used to measure success. Performance measurements are monitored by the sponsor until the plan is functioning properly. Poor performance may cause a revision of the plan. Legitimate reasons for a new plan or revised plan may develop, but may be considered "sensitive" by the sponsor. Thus, the needs for refinement may be distorted (by the sponsor) or misunderstood (by the planner). Communication between the planner and the sponsor can break down and conflict may result.

Describing Planning Processes with the Morphology

Normative Processes

Tables 4 and 5 illustrate how the morphology can be used to summarize the *process*

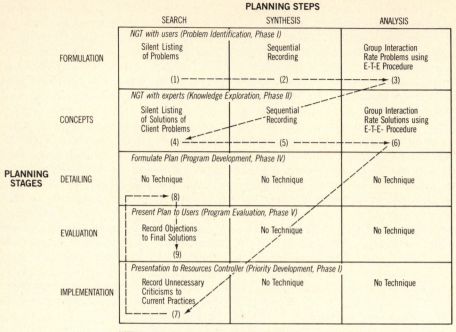

PLANNING STEPS

	SEARCH	SYNTHESIS	ANALYSIS
FORMULATION	*NGT with users (Problem Identification, Phase I)* Silent Listing of Problems (1)	Sequential Recording (2)	Group Interaction Rate Problems using E-T-E Procedure (3)
CONCEPTS	*NGT with experts (Knowledge Exploration, Phase II)* Silent Listing of Solutions of Client Problems (4)	Sequential Recording (5)	Group Interaction Rate Solutions using E-T-E- Procedure (6)
DETAILING	*Formulate Plan (Program Development, Phase IV)* No Technique (8)	No Technique	No Technique
EVALUATION	*Present Plan to Users (Program Evaluation, Phase V)* Record Objections to Final Solutions (9)	No Technique	No Technique
IMPLEMENTATION	*Presentation to Resources Controller (Priority Development, Phase I)* Record Unnecessary Criticisms to Current Practices (7)	No Technique	No Technique

(left label: **PLANNING STAGES**)

NOTE: Iteration, repeating stages and steps, often occurs. One iteration is described.

TABLE 4   The Planning Morphology for PPM

proposed by two planning methods. In Table 4 the morphology has been applied to describe the planning process used by the program planning method or PPM (Delbecq and Van de Ven, 1971). PPM applies the Nominal Group Technique (NGT) in planning groups made up of users or clients, content experts, and administrators who control resources. The results from each group are passed to the next group by representatives. Clients articulate priority problems to the experts, who, in turn, aid clients in presenting possible solutions to resource controllers.

Nadler (1970) has a systems orientation. Techniques are used to generate "what should (or could) be" a new scheme. A ten-step process is used, defining a hierarchy of objectives and selecting one to guide the definition of a system, using generic system elements and dimensions.

Solution quality is emphasized, which can be contrasted with the emphasis on acceptance in PPM. Table 5 describes the *process* used by this planning method. Note that the steps unfold linearly, moving through each stage and performing the steps required in that stage sequentially.

Comparisons of Normative Processes

Comparing Tables 4 and 5 reveals several interesting process differences. First, the sequence of stages and steps is markedly different. PPM sets the stage for detailing, which is the last activity in the process. Detailing is perceived to be relevant only when the ramifications of several types of solutions to priority client problems have been explored and tacitly approved by

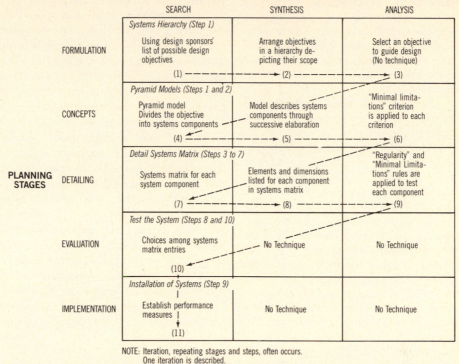

TABLE 5   The Planning Morphology for the Systems Approach

resource controllers. The systems approach stresses solution development with the planner in a leadership role. Implementation is the final stage in the process. Both methods have insightful and interesting processes and techniques and both ignore and treat superficially the requirements of several other stages.

Research Issues Posed by Normative Processes

Comparisons of planning methods find that diversity in process and stage skipping are typical. Some methods skip the formulation stage. A problem definition is needed to activate this type of planning process. In other planning methods, the responsibility for implementation is retained by the sponsor. Such methods skip stage five. Some methods (Asimov, 1962) unfold sequentially, moving through each process stage by performing search, synthesis, and analysis, or a similar set of activities. In contrast, the Delphi approach (Dalky, 1967) places great emphasis on search, providing few rules to synthesize or analyze the information gleaned from the survey. Thus, planning methods move through the stages and steps in the morphology by following *unique paths*. These paths, which identify the order of planning activities, define the process used by a planning method. Some processes may be more effective than others.

Behavioral Processes

Case studies of planning which summarize the order that planning techniques were used, give indications of the process from a behavioral perspective. Two case studies are described.

In the first, a hospital finds that an hourly employee is designated to cash payroll checks on pay day and returns each Friday with large sums of cash. The administration, fearing theft, decides to establish a branch bank in their lobby.

The planning process employed is summarized in Table 6, using the morphology. The planning problem was triggered by employee behavior. An interactive discussion among the executives was used to verify the dimensions of the problem, such as the frequency of occurrence and the sums of money involved. This led to a discussion of other potential benefits, such as service to physicians. The planner used a modified Delphi survey to get local bankers to make a proposal. The executive group selected a few proposals for further development. Stages two and three were delegated to the bankers. They used a branch bank concept (a "historical model") and their stock market analysis package to detail the branch bank concept. The planner checked the proposals for errors and used a MAU model (Huber, 1974) to evaluate the proposals. A contract was submitted to the board of trustees for ratification, which led to an interrupt. A local banker, who was also a board member, rejected the choice, claiming that his bank made the most competitive proposal. This led to a stalemate which aborted the project in its current form.

In the second case, a large organization was plagued with grievances filed by its PBX telephone operators about workload. The organization then assigned a planner

PLANNING STEPS

		SEARCH	SYNTHESIS	ANALYSIS
	FORMULATION	(1) Brainstorming identify behavior and its frequency of occurrence	(2) Delphi Bankers asked to offer suggestions	(3) Prioritize select objective
	CONCEPTS	(4) Off-the-shelf Planning model used by banks		
PLANNING STAGES	DETAILING	(5) Market Analysis By the bank	(6) Combine market data and suggest an automated teller (by the bank)	(7) Simluation check for errors
	EVALUATION	(6) Select criteria and establish criteria weights	(7) List attributes of each proposal and assess via criteria	(8) MAU model select a winner
	IMPLEMENTATION	(9) Draw up a contract		

Interrupt

TABLE 6   Branch Bank

to rectify the situation with a constraint: changes must not hike operating costs.

Table 7 summarizes the process used. The PBX operator grievances came through normal channels in the organization. To verify the facts, a Bell Telephone consultant was contacted. The consultant reported that workloads were well below Bell standards. This led to an objective of eliminating grievances without increasing operating costs. The planner skipped stage two and coupled stages three and four by using a queuing model. The operators were asked to identify schedules with the understanding that any schedule could be adopted as long as it did not increase costs. The queuing model was used to represent and evaluate the cost of each proposed schedule. After several meetings, a schedule was found that was acceptable and met the cost constraint. This schedule was implemented. No attempt was made to find the least cost (optimal) schedule. The implementation strategy was coopta-

tion, because the operators were allowed to select the solution. After the new schedule was implemented, the grievances stopped.

Research Issues Posed by the Behavioral Processes

The case studies summarized in Tables 6 and 7 and others like them suggest that the planning process is a composite, that stages and steps are often skipped, and that much planning is done informally. The planning process is made up of techniques drawn from several sources. Pure processes identifiable in the literature are seldom, if ever, applied. This may be due to gaps in these processes, where they fail to deal with important issues like evaluation, or because the planner has become adept at extracting and synthesizing planning ideas. A synthesized process may evolve and may even become contin-

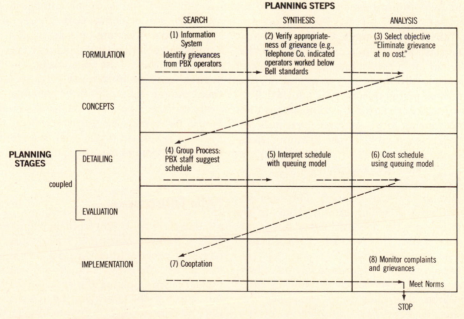

TABLE 7   PBX Staffing

gently based, where different techniques are used to deal with certain types of problems. If so, the implicit stages that are emphasized and the behavioral decision rules used by expert planners may offer important insights into the design of a contingency-based planning system.

It is also possible that planning practices stem from repertoires which are limited because few practitioners have a very wide exposure to planning theory. Even the most respected practitioners may have counterproductive preferences and outright biases, making it essential to compare processes focused on the same problem using success measures.

Not all stages and steps are carried out. Stages and steps may be deleted because they are seen as unnecessary for particular applications, or for all applications. Time pressure and limits on budget may also cause stage skipping. The stages skipped, or dealt with informally, suggest that the planner believes they lack importance, or at least lack priority when deadlines must be faced. Stages early in the process (one and two) and implementation seem to be skipped more often. The importance accorded these stages by the literature suggests that either education of the planner or a reexamination of the techniques is in order.

Much planning activity is informal. The information required by some stages and steps stems from sponsor demands or requirements, not formal planning techniques. For instance, many planning efforts are activated by a sponsor's stipulation which contains or implies a solution. Such a stipulation can mislead. The sponsor describes a solution, often in detail, in an attempt to be specific about needs or opportunities. In other cases, the sponsor's ideas are introduced by way of the stipulation. Some sponsors, in their commitment to processes with rapid closure, describe the plan (e.g., an operating system or policy) as a template which the planner is expected to adapt. It is hard for the sponsor to imagine that the adaptation can be both time-consuming and costly, which is often the case. Such stipulations eliminate stages one and two. Implementation is seldom formal. Sponsor decrees are often used when more subtle techniques are called for. Most planning theorists would argue that planning results would be improved if formal techniques were used more often.

The merits of composite processes, stage skipping, and informal v. formal techniques require study.

Describing the Dialogue with the Planning Path

When the sponsor draws the planner into the problem reality, as shown in the transactional model, they may emerge in any stage. The sponsor may apply tests that have little to do with the results the planner seeks to report. For instance, the planner may define the project's objective only to find the sponsor unwilling to reconcile the objective with needs and opportunities, insisting on a description of a proposed solution. If the planner fails to offer a solution, the pet ideas of the sponsor may be introduced. The planner then moves to stage three or four to evaluate the sponsor's idea. A model (stage two) may be constructed or the problem redefined (stage one), depending on the outcome of this evaluation.

Path Interrupts

Mintzberg et al. (1976) find that dynamic factors, called "interrupts," also cause a planning process to move from one stage to another. Interrupts stem from environmental factors, forcing the sponsor to halt the project to consider the views of important patrons, benefactors, or constituents. The project must pause to take in this information. Interrupts also occur when the sponsor attempts to understand the results from any stage or when the planner tries to overcome failures. Time pressure may also truncate the process. Sponsors with a "crises orientation" force planners into short cuts (stage skipping).

Tracing the Planning Path with the Transactional Model

The transactional model of planning (Table 3) can be used to trace the planning path. The branch bank and PBX case studies are used to illustrate two classic paths found in practice.

The branch bank project is profiled in Table 8. The sponsor recognizes a need

(check-cashing behavior) which is formulated by verifying the existence of a quick solution. This led to a delegation of planning responsibility, hoping to obtain a ready-made solution. The planning process was carried out by the local banks. No dialogue during this phase of planning occurred. Each bank proposed an automatic teller. These proposals were reviewed to determine misconceptions, omissions, and errors. One was found. The administrator would not allow an automatic teller to be located in the hospital lobby, commenting, "It makes the place look too commercial." The banks preferred this location, because they hoped to stimulate the lucrative business of physicians. This led to several cycles in stage three. Several of the bidders dropped

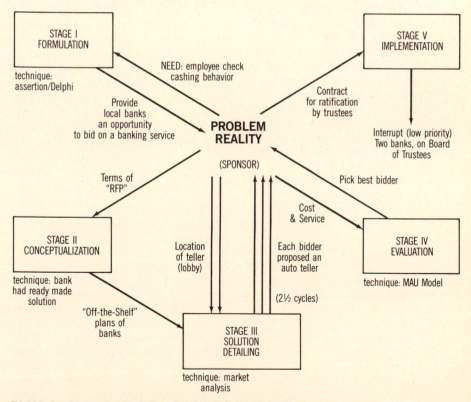

TABLE 8   Planning Path for the Branch Bank Project

out because of the location constraint. Those that remained proposed an alternative site and were evaluated using cost and service attributes. The optimal proposal was selected using these criteria. A contract was prepared and submitted to the board of trustees for ratification. One board member, the CEO of a bank that dropped out over the lobby location, claimed that they had not dropped out and pointed out that their bid was lower than the bank with which the hospital proposed to contract. (The decision to drop out had been made by a subordinate based on the standard operation procedures written by the bank CEO.) In discussion, it became clear that this bank was not the overall low bidder and that the low bids were predicated upon getting physician business. Other trustees became put off by the commercial nature of the discussion. The trustees, unable to reconcile these conflicting facts, called the project low-priority and tabled it.

The PBX case has a totally different path (Table 9). The need recognized by the sponsor was the union's grievance over workloads. In formulating the problem, the sponsor found that the grievances lacked merit and assigned a planner to eliminate the grievance without an increase in operating cost. At the planner's request, the sponsor delegated the choice of the terms of work to the PBX operators. The planner asked the operators to suggest a work schedule. The schedule was evaluated to determine its cost, using a queuing model. Seven cycles were required before a schedule with acceptable levels of both cost and satisfaction was found. The new schedule was put into place reluctantly by a disgruntled supervisor, who was not involved. Grievances stopped, ending the planning process.

Path Implications

The nature of these paths and others like them raises several issues about the process of planning. Sponsors seem to have more interest in some stages than others. In particular, sponsors seem to be more concerned about solution details and evaluation findings than objectives or models. The "pragmatic" and concrete nature of the discussion in stages three and four appeals to "hard-headed" administrators. Stages one and two seem to be viewed as esoteric and the sponsor leaves them to the planner. This practice is a striking contrast with the claims of planning theorists who view formulation and conceptualization as the most critical steps in planning.

Some Process-Related Research Issues

Path Orderliness

Planning projects appear to follow a chaotic path, quite unlike the orderly process described by the planning literature. But, as Mintzberg et al. (1976) point out, there is considerable logic to following a process which takes the project through distinct stages. The orderliness in the planning effort as it moves through stages of a process may improve results. The degree of order, imposed by particular planning processes, may be positively associated with superior plans.

The Merits of Truncated Processes

Sponsors behave as though some stages are unnecessary. In particular, the formulation and conceptualization stages are often skipped or treated superficially by sponsors (Mitroff et al., 1974). Sponsors try to move directly from the problem reality to defining omissions and errors, instructing a planner to pursue programs that rectify these errors. Such a sponsor prefers ready-made programs (like the automatic teller). They offer the sponsor a

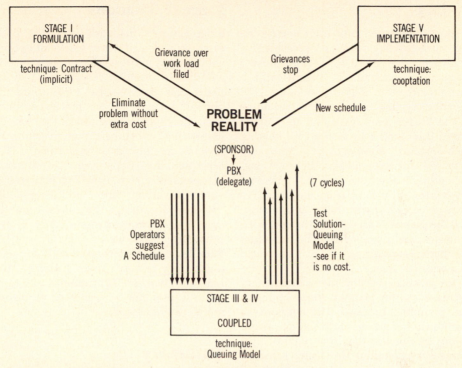

TABLE 9   Planning Path for the PBX Staffing Project

cheap and timely, if not innovative, response for many planning problems. According to Cyert and March (1963), a plan that *appears* to overcome perceived errors and omissions is promptly implemented. Thus, sponsors may prefer a process which consists solely of stages three and five. Only when the ready-made solution fails is a more extensive process authorized (Thompson, 1967).

In varying degrees, controversy surrounds the merits of each stage. Shortening the process seems sensible to sponsors who seek to control planning costs, demand fast answers, and have little tolerance for activities they perceive as esoteric. To cope with this type of sponsor, planners may skip stages or treat them superficially. A better understanding of

the value of each stage relative to its cost will be a convincing argument against such tactics.

In other instances, some stages are not necessary, as pointed out in the PBX case. Clearly, the merits of each stage should be assessed. Compulsively carrying out all five stages increases cost and lengthens the time necessary to produce a result. Certain types of problems may be amenable to a truncated process (stages two, three, and four). More complex problems may require the addition of stage one and stage five. Others contend that all planning problems should be restipulated and that success hinges on a formal implementation strategy. Problem factors, such as complexity, are important intervening variables when exploring the merits of stages.

Cycling

A sponsor who demands extensive reporting causes cycling within a process stage. The cycles define the number of times a planner is required to consult with a sponsor when in a particular stage. For instance, cycling occurred in stage three in the branch bank case and in coupled stages three and four in the PBX case. In each instance, solutions were compared with sponsor expectations. In stage one, the project objective can be redefined several times by comparing the objectives with perceived opportunities and in stage two the planner's model and the sponsor's premises are juxtaposed. The optimum number of loops for each stage is suggested as a research issue.

In practice, cycling may increase or decrease as the planner moves through the planning process. The amount of cycling that occurs in early stages (formulation) may be less than that required by a sponsor as solutions are being screened and evaluated. For complex problems, cycling may be greater in the formulation stage and then decline. Fatigue, a decline of sponsor interest, a false sense of security by the sponsor, and the like, may account for this decline.

Cycling may stem from personality factors. Both planners and sponsors have a preferred format for reporting results. Kilmann and Mitroff (1976) find that sponsors who like intuitive information, drawn from personal judgments, prefer narrative reports. Data-laden presentations are preferred by those who rely on factual reports. When the report is incompatible with the sponsor's preferred format, cycling may be stimulated and vice versa. Studies are needed to determine the amount of checking best for each stage of the planning process and how personality factors act to stimulate cycling which focuses the review on particular issues.

Multiple Solutions

Independently managed planning processes, as well as nurturing several options within each process, have been recommended to improve results (e.g., Abernathy and Rosenbloom, 1969). Initiating several planning teams for a particular project is thought to stimulate the competitive instinct in planners, particularly when rewards are linked to performance. For example, the Department of Defense independently commissioned two prominent consulting firms to design the "military hospital of the future." In this case, the recommendations made by the consulting firms were strikingly similar. This suggests that the costs of multiple plans may exceed their benefits. The marginal benefits of multiple solutions against costs, for a variety of problems, merits careful study.

Summary

Planning is a complex and, as yet, little-understood mode of inquiry. The complexity stems in part from the difficulty of making comparisons. It is hard to visualize how planning methods differ, let alone prescribe which should be used. In an attempt to breach these problems, a generic model of planning was proposed as a way to compare the processes used by various planning methods. A model with five stages, (formulation, conceptualization, detailing, evaluation, and implementation) and three steps for each stage (search, synthesis, and analysis) was used to define a planning morphology.

The morphology provided a basis to compare the processes proposed by planning theorists and to illustrate the processes used to plan in practice. These comparisons suggested that planning theorists proposed dramatically different processes that ignore several stages and steps.

Perhaps because of these oversights, case studies of planning projects found that planning processes actually used tend to be a composite of stages and techniques drawn from several sources.

The case studies also found that stages and steps were carried out selectively, emphasizing pragmatic issues (solutions and their merits). Hybrid planning processes are typical, many with a stage three/stage four form. Others appear to change with each project, suggesting that an implicit contingency framework may be operating in the mind of the experienced planner. Finally, much planning activity seems informal. Rather than using a formal technique, the sponsor makes demands or draws conclusions which are taken as given by the planner.

A transactional model of planning was developed to illustrate how sponsors influence and control the process. The planning path was defined as the route traced through the transactional model by a particular project. Using case studies, the path was found to skip the early stages, also suggesting that planning process is a key research issue.

The Research Approach in Brief

The morphology defined several process variables. These include formality (number of techniques applied), comprehensiveness (the number of morphology cells covered), hybrid process types (e.g., stages three-four), delegation (planning done by external agents), and use of "historical" or "off-the-shelf" models in stage two. These process variables would be correlated with an assessment of the plan's quality and whether it was adopted, rejected, or tabled.

The transactional model defines path in patternlike terms with orderliness and various pattern classifications as basic process variables to be related with plan outcome. Other process-related research variables include the ideal starting and stopping points, the values of multiple solutions, the merits of particular stages, and the merits of cycling (repeated review in a given stage).

In such studies, several intervening factors should be controlled. These include the sponsor's activation strategy, the number of key actors involved, plan scope (strategic, operational, or tactical), plan focus (policy, internal operations, product, or service), plan's perceived importance, managerial strategy used by the sponsor, sponsor's perception of the planner's skill, time pressure, and resources made available to the project.

Fifty case studies of planning have been profiled with the morphology and the transactional model. The next step is to compare the patterns in these processes with plan outcomes, controlling for the intervening factors.

References

Abernathy, W. J., and R. S. Rosenbloom, "Parallel Strategies in Developmental Projects." *Management Science*, June 1969.

Ackoff, R. L. *Redesigning the Future*. New York: Wiley, 1974.

Ackoff, R., and Emery, F. *On Purposeful Systems*. Chicago: Aldine-Atherton, 1972.

Asimov, M. *An Introduction to Design*. Englewood Cliffs, N.J.: Prentice-Hall, 1962.

Backoff, R. W. "Organizational Design: Problem Formulation." OSU Mimeo, 1976.

Churchman, C. W. *The Systems Approach*, rev. ed. New York: Dell, 1979.

Churchman, C. W. *The Design of Inquiring Systems*. New York: Basic Books, 1971.

Churchman, C. W., *The Systems Approach and Its Enemies*. New York: Basic Books, 1979.

Cook, T. D., and D. T. Campbell. *Quasi-Experimentation Design and Analysis Issues for Field Settings*. Chicago: Rand McNally, 1979.

Cyert, R. M., and March, J. G. *A Behavioral Theory of the Firm*. Englewood Cliffs, N.J.: Prentice-Hall, 1963.

Dalky, N. *Delphi*. Santa Monica, Calif.: The Rand Corporation, 1967.

Delbecq, A., and A. Van de Ven. "A Group Process Model for Problem Identification and Program Planning." *Journal of Applied Behavioral Science*, 1971.

Downs, A. *Inside Bureaucracy*. Boston: Little Brown, 1967.

Emshoff, J. R. *Managerial Breakthroughs: Action Techniques for Strategic Change*. New York: AMACON, 1980.

Fisher, G. W. "Utility Models for Multiple Objective Decisions: Do They Accurately Represent Human Preferences?" *Decision Sciences*, Vol. 10, No. 3 (July 1979), 451–479.

Gordon, W.J.J. *The Metaphorical Way*. Cambridge, Mass.: Porpoise, 1972.

Gueschka, H., et al. "Modern Techniques for Solving Problems," in *Portraits of Complexity*. Battelle Monograph Series, 1975.

Hall, A. D. *A Methodology for Systems Engineering*. New York: Van Nostrand, 1962.

Huber, G. "Multi-Attribute Utility Models: A Review of Field and Field-like Studies." *Management Science*, Vol. 20, No. 10 (1974).

Kilmann, R., and I. I. Mitroff. "Qualitative Versus Quantitative Analysis for Management Sciences: Different Forms for Different Psychological Types." *Interfaces*, Vol. 6, No. 2 (Feb. 1976).

Klir, G. J. (ed.). *Trends in General Systems Theory*. New York: Wiley Interscience, 1972.

Levine, C. H., R. W. Backoff, A. R. Cahoon, and W. J. Stiffen. "Organizational Design: A Post Minnowbrook Perspective for the New Public Administrator." *Public Administration Review*, July–Aug. 1975.

Lewin, K. "Group Decision and Social Change," in *Readings in Social Psychology*. New York: Holt, Rinehart and Winston, 1958.

March, J. G., and H. Simon. *Organizations*. New York: Wiley, 1958.

Mintzburg, H. "Planning on the Left Side, Managing on the Right." *Harvard Business Review*, July–August 1975.

Mintzburg, H., D. Raisinghani, and A. Theoret. "The Structure of Unstructured Decision Processes." *Administrative Science Quarterly*, Vol. 21 (1976), 246–275.

Mitroff, I. I., F. Betz, L. Pondy, and F. Sagasti. "On Managing Science in the Systems Age: Two Schemes for the Study of Science as a Whole Systems Phenomenon." *Interfaces*, Vol. 4, No. 3 (May 1974).

Mitroff, I. I., V. P. Barabba, and R. H. Kilmann. "The Application of Behavioral and Philosophical Technologies to Strategic Planning: A Case Study of a Large Federal Agency." *Management Science*, Vol. 24, No. 1 (1977), 44–58.

Mitroff, I. I., J. R. Emshoff, and R. H. Kilmann. "Assumptional Analysis: A Methodology for Strategic Problem Solving." *Management Science*, Vol. 25, No. 6 (1979), 583–593.

Nadler, G. *Work Systems Design*. Homewood, Ill.: Irwin, 1970.

Nutt, P. C. "Hybrid Planning Methods." Commissioned paper, AUPHA Conference on Health Planning, Washington, D.C., August 1981.

Nutt, P. C. "Comparing Methods to Weight Decision Criteria." *Omega, The International Journal of Management Science*, Vol. 8, No. 2 (1980), 163–172.

Nutt, P. C. "Calling Out and Calling Off the Dogs: Managerial Diagnosis in Organizations." *Academy of Management Review*, 1979.

Pounds, W. "The Process of Problem Finding." *Industrial Management Review*, Fall 1969, pp. 1–19.

Quade, E. S., and W. I. Boucher. *Systems Analysis and Policy Planning*. New York: Elsevier, 1968.

Simon, H. A. *Sciences of the Artificial*. Cambridge, Mass.: MIT Press, 1969.

Simon, H. A., and Newell, A. "Human Problem Solving—The State of the Art in 1970." *American Psychologist*, February 1970.

Suchman, E. A. *Evaluation Research: Principles and Practice in Public Service and Social Action Programs*. New York: Russell Sage, 1967.

Thompson, J.D. *Organizations in Action*. New York: McGraw-Hill, 1967.

Warfield, J. N. "Structuring Complex Systems." Battelle Monography, Number 4, April 1972.

Warfield, J. N. *Societal Systems: Planning Policy and Complexity*. New York: Wiley, 1976.

Weinberg, G. M. *An Introduction to Systems Thinking*. New York: Wiley, 1975.

Wholey, J. S., et al. *Federal Evaluation Policy: Analyzing the Effects of Public Programs*. Washington, D.C.: The Urban Institute, 1971.

Wilson, I. G., and M. E. Wilson. *From the Idea to the Working Model*. New York: Wiley, 1970.

Zwicky, F. *Discovery, Invention, Research through the Morphological Approach*. New York: Macmillan, 1969.

7.2 A Teleological Power-Oriented Theory of Strategy

Richard O. Mason   Ian I. Mitroff

Introduction

It is commonplace to say that the field of strategic planning necessitates a marriage of behavioral science and economics. It is still far from being commonplace, however, to recognize that the field requires the marriage of many more diverse disciplines as well. This paper argues that not only are behavioral science and economics indispensable to the field of strategic planning, but that also ethics and epistemology are as well. Even further, we argue that a concept of aesthetics is also absolutely indispensable.

These "nontraditional" concerns pose

Prepared for "Nontraditional Approaches to Policy Research," University of Southern California, November 1981.

the most severe challenge the field has to face. It is clear that the unification of such a wide array of disciplines and concerns cannot be accomplished by traditional means, such as by mathematical, statistical, or structural models alone. Instead, a new concept and meaning of unification is called for.

The paper points to a new concept of unification. It is based on the fact that social systems are fundamentally teleological in the sense that they are composed of teleological entities. Teleological systems are characterized by uncertainties in our ability to know the entities which compose such systems and in our ability to describe accurately the properties of the components themselves. If the attainment of certainty is a precondition for strategy-making our task is doomed to failure unless we can develop a concept of strategy making that is found on the clear appreciation, recognition, toleration, and use of uncertainty. We offer a teleological power-oriented theory in response to their need.

A Concept of Strategy

Strategies are plans for acquiring power. Power, in this context, refers to the human control of the energies necessary to achieve human purposes, whatever those purposes may be—survival, profitability, prestige, growth, efficiency, equity, or social responsibility. This kind of organizational power includes power over other human beings, exercised with or without their consent, with or against their "will" and with or without their knowledge or understanding. Thus, the power harnessed by a strategy may be used either for good or for evil. Ethical strategies, of course, are those which employ power in morally justifiable ways.

This power-oriented definition of strategy has much in common with the more traditional definitions which, drawing on notions of organizational Darwinism, define strategy as the "basic characteristics of the match an organization achieves with its environment" (Hofer and Schendel, 1978, p. 4). By biological analogy the successful organizations are those whose strategies insure the "survival of the fittest." These surviving organizations find nourishing niches in their environment. That is what fitness and, hence, power are all about.

Power is also the fundamental construct underlying some of the practical methodologies for making strategy. For example, the typical evaluation of the internal strengths and weaknesses of an organization as they relate to the external opportunities and threats has implicit in it the question "Does this organization have enough power—excess of strengths over weaknesses—to ward off its threats and avail itself of its opportunities?"

So, if this power-oriented definition of strategy is so similar to the other definitions, what is its advantage? The principal advantage is that it shifts the focus of the strategist's attention away from responsive behavior toward proactive behavior. That is, the responsive process of *matching* is replaced by the anticipatory process of creating *enabling* conditions. Power is a logical prerequisite to positioning. Once an organization is enabled with power it can become an effective matchmaker.

This subtle psychological shift also yields some fruits in analysis. The concept of power can be analyzed in terms of a means/ends schema; which, in turn, has direct application to the development and execution of a strategy. Drawing on the philosophy of Singer (1959), Churchman (1971, 1979), and Ackoff and Emery (1974), we propose that the enabling conditions of organizational power and, hence, of an effective strategy are:

A. The ability to change purposes (ends) and create new purposes. (Aesthetic Dimension)
   We refer to this as the "Change and Creativity" dimension

B. The ability to acquire and mobilize adequate resources (means). (Political, Economic Dimension)
   We refer to this as "Business—Political and Economic Function"

C. The ability to discover and develop resources and to allocate the right resource, in the right amounts, to the right organizational component at the right time; that is, the ability to relate means to ends effectively. (Knowledge, Information Dimension).
   We refer to this as "Information and Communication"

D. The ability to sustain cooperation and to eliminate conflict among all stakeholders so that the purposes are achievable (Ethical-Moral Dimension)

We refer to this as "Ethical, Moral, Cooperative"

In essence these four criteria describe a successful strategy as one which provides for good goals and objectives, adequate resources, effective management information and scientific information and cooperative efforts among the people involved. Notice that if a strategy fails by one of these four criteria it will be unsuccessful. Thus, each criterion is necessary for success. Moreover, satisfactory performance on all four criteria implies success for the strategy as a whole. Thus, collectively the satisfaction of these criteria is sufficient. Any strategy that satisfies these four criteria augments the power of an organization and therefore will be successful.

Organizational power for us is a teleological concept because power is defined in terms of the purposes that are to be achieved. Consequently we describe the enabling conditions for power as they relate to the teleological entities—we call them *stakeholders*—which compose a teleological system. Our teleological theory of organizations and strategy may be summarized by eleven key propositions.

Eleven Key Propositions

1. An organization is a collection of internal and external *stakeholders*.
2. A stakeholder is a distinguishable entity which has resources, its own purposes and "will," and is capable of volitional behavior. That is, it has vitality.
3. There is a network of interdependent *relationships* among all stakeholders. Some relationships are *supporting* in that they provide movement toward the organization's purposes. Some relationships are *resisting* in that they serve as barriers or encourage movement away from the organization's purposes.
4. A new strategy changes one or more of these stakeholder relationships.
5. A strategy results in more power for

the organization when it provides for a greater flow of purposeful achievement through the supporting relationships than flows through resisting relationships.
6. Relationships with each stakeholder may be changed in one or more of the following ways:
   a. *Convert* (change) the stakeholder by means of:
      (1) *Commanding* him through the exercise of power and authority
      (2) *Persuading* him by appealing to reason, values and emotion
      (3) *Bargaining* with him by means of exchange
      (4) *Negotiating* with him to reach "give and take" compromises
      (5) *Problem Solving* with him by means of sharing, debating, and arriving at agreed upon mutual conversions
   b. *Fight* the stakeholder and *politic* to overpower him by means of:
      (1) Securing and marshaling the organization's resources
      (2) Forming coalitions with other stakeholders
      (3) Destroying the stakeholder
   c. *Absorb* aspects of the stakeholder's demands by incorporating them in a process of *cooptation* which impart changes in some of the organization's goals.
   d. *Coalesce* with the stakeholder by forming a *coalition* with joint decision-making powers.
   e. *Avoid* or *ignore* the stakeholder.
   f. *Appease* the stakeholder by giving in to some of his demands.
   g. *Surrender* to the stakeholder.
   h. *Love* the stakeholder by forming an emotional bond and union with him.
   i. *Be* or *become* the stakeholder by transforming the organization into the stakeholder through merger, imitation, idolatry or role modeling.

Strategies must be implemented through one or more of these change-oriented activities. Hence, all strategies presuppose the presence of the power necessary to employ the relevant methods of bringing about change.

7. The state of the organization at time T will be the result of confluence of the behavior of all the organization's stakeholders as it flows through the network of relationships from the beginning up to time T.
8. Therefore a strategy undertaken at time T in order to achieve outcomes in time T + t is based on one or more assumptions about (a) the properties and behavior of the stakeholders, (b) the network of relationships which binds them to the organization, and (c) the organization's power to change relevant relationships.
9. *Leaders* are those stakeholders who create new strategies for an organization.
10. *Managers* are those stakeholders who allocate resources among the set of stakeholders and control their employment so that the purposes of the strategy are achieved.
11. *Operators* are those stakeholders who perform the tasks necessary to achieve the purposes of the strategy.

All stakeholders are operators to some degree. Which stakeholders are leaders and/or managers depends on the pattern of authority and responsibility relationships established within the organization. A dictatorship has a single leader. In a pure democracy all stakeholders function as leaders.

Having asserted these basic propositions, we next propose the enabling condition for strategic power based on the means/ends schema described earlier. In parenthesis following each condition are some of the key management concepts which relate to that condition.

Enabling Conditions for Strategic Power

A. Change and Creativity

1. The leaders of the organization must have the *inspiration* and creativity necessary to reevaluate the organization's current missions, purposes, objectives, and goals and to conceptualize new purposes.
(Leadership, Statesmanship, Goal-Setting, Missions, MBO)
2. The managers must have *capability* for translating new purposes into programs of action.
(Innovation, Creativity, Management of Change, Organizational Change, Invention, Patents, Copyrights, Flexibility, Changeability)
3. All stakeholders must have the *spirit*, *dedication*, and *commitment* necessary to secure the new purposes.
(Motivation, Incentives, Satisfaction, Promotions, Careers, Personal Values, Renewal, Catharsis, Energy, Drive)

B. Business—Political and Economic Functions

1. The total resources held by the collection of stakeholders must be adequate to accomplish the purpose.
(Capital Availability, Recruitment, Capital Budgeting, Finance, Purchasing, Energy, Mergers, Acquisition, Plant Location, Working Capital, Cash Flow, Inventory, Dividend Policy)
2. The managers must reallocate the resources from stakeholder to stakeholder so that each receiving stakeholder possesses the amount of resources necessary to carry out its tasks at the right time and place.
(Budgeting, Decision Making, Resource Allocation)
3. The stakeholders must employ the resources they have effectively and

efficiently when executing their tasks in order to insure that the maximally useful output is produced.
(Productivity, Production, Work Assignment, Organization Structure, Materials Handling, Design of Jobs)

4. The managers must distribute the output effectively to all relevant stakeholders.
(Marketing, Sales, Distribution, Sales Force, Sales Training, Advertising, Customer Relations)

C. Information and Communication

1. The collection of stakeholders must have the capacity to acquire or produce basic knowledge—scientific, industrial and operations—about the organization's products, technology, operations, finances, markets, and customers.
(R&D, Accounting, MIS, Market Research, Operations Research, Corporate Intelligence, Planning, Library)

2. The managers must insure that the right information is transmitted to the right stakeholder at the right time.
(Communications, Organization, Reporting, Dissemination, Education, Training, Advertising, Public Affairs, Auditing, Storage and Retrieval, Telecommunications, Teleconferencing)

3. Each stakeholder must have the capacity to use the knowledge and information he receives to make effective decisions.
(Management Systems, Knowledge Utilization, Applied Research, Participation, Boards of Directors, Policy-Making Structure, Authority, Responsibility, Accountability, Cognitive Style, Intuitive Decision Making, Decision Processes)

D. Ethical, Moral, Cooperative

1. Each stakeholder must have the peace of mind within himself to be fully effective in his organizational life and all other aspects of his life.
(Mid-Life Crisis, Quality of Work Life, Human Potential, Satisfaction, Health and Safety, Stability, Fringe Benefits, Stress, Psychic Energy)

2. There must be a minimum of conflict between the internal stakeholders—individuals, groups, departments—that function within the organization.
(Organization Development, Role Clarification, Conflict Resolution, Leadership, Dissension, Goldbucking)

3. There must be a minimum of conflict between the organization and its external stakeholders such as governments, public interest groups, social activists, unions, and competitors.
(Public Relations, Government Relations, Labor Relations, Ethics, Morality, Social Responsibility, Product Safety, SEC, EPA, EEOC, OSHA, OPEC, Issues Management, Freedom of Information, Antitrust)

Methodology

What methodologies, then, are appropriate for the process of strategy making if one accepts their power-oriented theory of strategy? How is the strategist to define the strategic problem, to study it and to forge an action plan? The key we believe lies in proposition number 1, namely, the assumption that "an organization is a collection of internal and external *stakeholders*." As we describe in our recent book *Challenging Strategic Planning Assumption* (Mason and Mitroff, 1981) the first step in the strategic planning process is to identify the full range of relevant stakeholders.

Stakeholders are woven together in a producer/product web. The outcome—that is, *effect*—of the strategy will be the result of the collective behavior of all the stakeholders—that is, *cause*. No one stakeholder acting alone can *cause* the outcome to result. However, a stakeholder's actions can be necessary, although not sufficient, for achieving the desired result. The more power a stakeholder has—in terms of purposes, resources, knowledge and co-operation—the more influential its contributory role in achieving the outcome. An illustration will help make this point clearer.

Some years ago Heublein, Inc. embarked upon a strategy intended "(1) to make Smirnoff the number one liquor branch in the world; (2) to continue a sales growth of 10% a year through internal growth, acquisitions, or both; and (3) to maintain Heublein's return on equity above 15%" (Steiner and Minor, 1977, p. 541). The achievement of these goals will depend upon the collective actions of Heublein's stakeholders—customers (largely relatively prosperous, young adults), competitors, suppliers, stockholders, creditors, employees, franchisors and distributors, salesmen, labor unions, local communities, investment bankers, government agencies, the corporate management and staff and a host of others. Each of these stakeholders' supportive behavior is necessary to the accomplishment of the goals. Any one of them can "pull the plug" as it were by withdrawing support. However, each of these stakeholders also has its own purposes, its own strategy, its own power position; that is, its own vitality. By definition, not all of its goals will be consistent with those of Heublein. Some of each stakeholder's goals will reflect its own unique existence. This difference in purposes between Heublein and its stakeholders means that some stakeholder behavior will be nonsupportive, resisting, or opposing to Heublein's strategy. Thus, Heublein functions in a field of stakeholder forces which are unavoidable and to some extent uncontrollable. This leads us to the conclusion that the success of Heublein's strategy for achieving its three goals depends inevitably on the assumptions it makes about its stakeholders and their behavior.

The strategic assumption surfacing and testing technique (SAST) we have developed (Mason and Mitroff, 1981), is designed to help organizations identify their stakeholders and to ferret out the assumptions they are making about them in their strategy. The task, of course, is formidable due to the immense number of stakeholders any organization has. Indeed, the task would be overwhelming were it not for one key notion. Stakeholders and the assumptions being made about them—like Orwell's animals—are not all equally significant. Some stakeholders' assumptions are more crucial to the success of the strategy at any point in time than are others.

John R. Commons had a great insight into this problem. He classified stakeholder forces as either complementary—generally supportive of the goals—or limiting. "The limiting factor is the one whose control, in the right form, at the right place and time, will set the complementary factors at work to bring about the results intended" (Commons, 1961, p. 628). For any given strategy there are relatively fewer limiting factors—let us call them *strategic assumptions*—than there are other forces in the stakeholder force field. Strategic power consequently depends on having purposes, resources, knowledge and cooperation necessary to control the limiting factor. For this reason, the SAST process forces the strategist to rate the stakeholder on a scale of *importance*.

Heublein, for example, made the crucial assumption that the relatively prosperous young adult market would buy vodka. They acted on that assumption by advertising Smirnoff intensively in this market, including the portrayal of women in its advertisements and the launching of the Smirnoff Mule for the discotheque set, and their strategy paid off. Ford made similar assumptions about young adults' willingness to buy the Edsel and, of course, it failed. Clearly Ford's assumption was important but it was wrong.

So, SAST requires that a second question be asked of any assumption. How *certain* are you of the validity of this assumption? The strategist is required to rate each assumption on a scale of *certainty*. The result of the two ratings—importance and certainty—is a two-dimensional plot that reveals the strategic status of each assumption at the point in time it was plotted.

There are some important concerns that flow from having rated an assumption as to its certainty, especially if it is an important assumption. The basic concern is "what is our current state of knowledge about this assumption?" We have found that an effective way to respond to this question is to submit the assumption to argumentation analysis. We have drawn on and modified the work of Toulmin (1958) and Rescher (1976) to create a model of argumentation analysis for strategic decision-making. Its basic questions are:

1. What is your best judgment as to the assumption to make about a stakeholder and the ratings of importance and certainty you assign to that assumption? The response is treated as a *conclusion* in an argument.
2. What *facts* do you base your judgment on?
3. What *warrants*—interpreting assumptions—are required to interpret the facts as supporting evidence for the conclusion?
4. What are the *rebuttals*—conditions under which your conclusion does *not* hold?
5. How *plausible* are your conclusions, facts, warrants, and rebuttals?

The answers to these questions may be processed through a logical mechanism to determine their relative epistemological status (Mason and Mitroff, 1981).

As a strategist considers a potential limiting factor assumption, the results of argumentation analysis take on additional significance. If the strategist's knowledge is inadequate and time permits, he may want to engage in business intelligence and management information systems activities in order to improve his knowledge and understanding of the assumption. In an article entitled "Creating the Manager's Plan Book" (Mason, Mitroff, and Barabba, 1980) we identified three modes of inquiry that might be used at this stage:

1. empirical, scientific, and other research methods,
2. dialogue, reflection, and other intuition and judgment supporting methods, and
3. monitoring methods.

The effective use of any of these methods will increase the power of the organization to achieve its goals, especially if the inquiry effort is directed toward limiting factors.

Monitoring takes on special significance throughout the strategic history of an organization. Strategic assumptions tend to have a "half-life." Through time stakeholders flow in and out of the relevant network. The forces they exert in the field change. And, of course, the purposes and goals of the organization change as well. By dint of new external forces or the successful management of a limiting factor, the force field shifts. Some new stakeholders and the assumptions being made about them emerge as crucial; others move down to a less compelling status. Consequently, we recommend that the importance/certainty rating graph be updated periodically and that strategic information systems be instituted to provide the necessary background data. These systems need to report on the current state of power of each stakeholder in the relevant force field in terms of its purposes, resources, knowledge, and degree of cooperation. All strategic assumptions made about stakeholders ultimately relate to the power they potentially can exert in the organization's force field, that is, within the relevant network of stakeholders.

This leads us to the final stage in strategy—action-taking, or in the language of strategic planning, implementation. SAST provides guidance for action-taking by focusing attention on the limiting factors and the stakeholders who control them. These stakeholders have power, so does the organization, and their forces interact through a relationship of mutual dependency. A new strategy inevitably requires changing one or more of these power-based stakeholder relationships. The planning of change then as Warren Bennis and his associates reminded us years ago (Bennis, Benne, and Chin, 1961, 1969) is fundamental to the successful implementation of strategy. In principle, a strategy should have an action plan for each stakeholder although in practice, the major emphasis should be directed towards those stakeholders controlling the limiting factors in the force field. The planned change involves the processes of converting, destroying, absorbing, coalescing, avoiding, appeasing, surrendering, loving and becoming as outlined in Proposition 6 above. The processes that are finally chosen depend on the power profiles of the organization and the stakeholder involved.

It should be noted that this broad stakeholder force field analysis subsumes many contemporary approaches for analyzing industries such as Michael Porter's *Competitive Strategy* (1980) approach. Concern with such factors as threats to entry, intensity of rivalry, product substitutability, product complementary, buyers' power, suppliers' power, and the like all relate to the kinds and direction of power that a stakeholder might exert within the stakeholder force field. The strategist must assess that power and develop an action plan accordingly. Distinctive competence in this context refers to the class of purposes an organization's power permits it to achieve.

All of the foregoing indicates why the aspects of power identified in the section of the paper above "Enabling Conditions for Strategic Power" are so important. These are the crucial dimensions of organizational power in a strategic situation. An organization's power and hence its ability to achieve its purposes is based on the four key components identified—ability to change, resources, knowledge, and cooperation. Each of these four components has three or four logical subdivisions which help define their scope. Collectively, these enabling conditions form a skeletal framework for evaluating an organization and its stakeholders at any point in time and for guiding the development of a successful strategy. Also based on the theory of teleological systems and ends/means scheme we propose that the set of conditions is necessary and sufficient for success. One need only take this broad set of conditions and apply it in more refined detail in conjunction with SAST and argumentation analysis to the strategic problem at hand.

References

Ackoff, R. L., and Emery, F. *On Purposeful Systems*. Chicago: Aldine-Atherton, 1974.

Bennis, W. G., Benne, K. D., and Chin, R. *The Planning of Change*, 1st ed. New York: Holt, Rinehart and Winston, 1961.

Bennis, W. G., Benne, K. D., and Chin, R. *The Planning of Change*, 2d ed. New York: Holt, Rinehart and Winston, 1969.

Churchman, C. W. *The Design of Inquiry Systems*. New York: Basic Books, 1971.

Churchman, C. W. *The Systems Approach and Its Enemies*. New York: Basic Books, 1979.

Commons, J. R. *Institutional Economics*. Madison: University of Wisconsin Press, 1961.

Hofer, C. W., and Schendel, D. *Strategy Formulation: Analytic Concepts*. St. Paul: West Publishing, 1978.

Mason, R. O., and Mitroff, I.I. *Challenging Strategic Planning Assumptions*. New York: John Wiley & Sons, 1981.

Mason, R. O., Mitroff, I. I., and Barabba, V. P. "Creating the Manager's Plan Book," *Planning Review*, July 1980.

Porter, M. E. *Competitive Strategy*. New York: The Free Press, 1980.

Rescher, N. *Plausible Reasoning*. Amsterdam: Van Gorcum, 1976.

Singer, E. A. *Experience and Reflection*. Philadelphia: University of Pennsylvania, 1959.

Steiner, G., and Miner, J. B. *Management Policy and Strategy*. New York: Macmillan, 1977.

Toulmin, S. E. *The Uses of Argument*, Cambridge, England: Cambridge University Press, 1958.

7.3 Usable Knowledge: A Metatheory of Policy Research in the Social Sciences

William N. Dunn

This paper outlines a metatheory of policy research in the social sciences, that is, an organized set of propositions about existing theories of usable knowledge. By outlining the main contours of a metatheory of policy research I seek, first, to counter the regrettable present trend towards conceptual entanglement that now characterizes much theoretical work on the uses of social research in public policymaking. Second, by engaging in a process of reflective theory-building I hope to uncover and raise to a level of explicit consciousness many unexamined assumptions and hidden standards of assessment that now impair or corrupt our understanding of the role of policy research in social problem solving. Finally, I want to supply a metatheoretical structure that promotes at least marginal improvements in our capacity to understand and planfully shape the production of usable knowledge.

My major substantive claim is that the understanding and conduct of policy research may be improved by adopting propositions and principles of "critical constructivism," a metatheory of knowledge use with eclectic multidisciplinary origins. In making this claim I should state at the outset that I am not interested in siding with any particular theory; nor do I propose to provide a quick "paradigmatic fix" that will suddenly heal some ailing worldview. My aim, rather, is to create a metatheoretical structure that permits and even compels a more reflective posture towards the role and limitations of policy research in the social sciences.

Arguments offered in support of my claim are organized in four sections. In the first section I compare and contrast alternative *definitions* of knowledge use, arguing that a division of phenomena-to-be-explained (explananda) into "subjective" versus "objective" properties represents a suitable starting point for sorting existing theoretical perspectives. The struc-

Portions of this paper were prepared under Grant Number NIE-G-81-0019 from the National Institute of Education, Research and Educational Practices Program, U.S. Department of Education. The author would also like to acknowledge the support of Ian I. Mitroff and Richard O. Mason, who organized the conference where parts of this chapter were originally presented, and the contributions of Marija G. Dunn to the design of the last section.

ture of the second section is similar to the first, except that here I compare and contrast alternative *explanations* of knowledge use, arguing that a division of explanations (explanantes) into "imposed" versus "generated" phenomena provides an appropriate additional basis for distinguishing theoretical perspectives. The third section creates, on the basis of the intersection of explananda and explanantes of knowledge use presented in the first two sections, a fourfold typology of theoretical perspectives. These perspectives are then further differentiated according to characteristics of three media (knowledge, users, and social systems) through which imposed versus generated explanations of knowledge use operate. The product is an expanded typology that captures many of the most important theoretical claims and assumptions about the role of policy research in producing usable knowledge. Finally, the fourth section outlines propositions and corollaries of "critical constructivism." The argument is that this particular metatheoretical posture not only helps uncover and explore complementary features of existing perspectives; it also provides norms for developing new and more appropriate theories of policy research that enlarge the domain of usable knowledge—that is, knowledge that enhances our collective learning capacities.

Knowledge Use: The Criterion Problem

One of the most basic questions about any field of inquiry surrounds the criteria used to define its subject matter. At present it is difficult to bound the field of knowledge use in meaningful and persuasive ways, chiefly because the field is highly fragmented and conceptually "soggy" (Weiss, 1977:11). As Ganz (1981:186) observes, there has been a "continued adherence to an 'iron triangle' between creation, diffu-

sion, and utilization without reference to the complex interactions among these activities, institutional arrangements, and social change . . ." Researchers have tended "to think of themselves as working—or at least concentrating—on knowledge creation, knowledge diffusion, or knowledge utilization. As a result, these three subfields in the study of knowledge have evolved relatively independently of each other" (Rich, 1981a:7). Thus far, there is no plausible theoretical foundation that links these three subfields, while the "tangled literature" (Nelson and Winter, 1977) of the field as a whole reflects the absence of a minimal set of criteria for defining knowledge use as a dependent variable or phenomenon-to-be-explained (Zaltman, 1980; Dunn and Holzner, 1981).

Under such conditions several alternatives are available to those who wish to impart more structure and coherence to the field. Along with Lindblom and Cohen (1979), Wildavsky (1979), and Knott and Wildavsky (1980) we can elevate our present difficulties to the status of an ontological principle, announcing that the "nature" of the policy-making process or of knowledge itself imposes essentially unalterable constraints on the creation of usable knowledge. Here we run the risk of attributing properties of "irrationality" to social systems when, in fact, (ir)rationality is a property of the constructs we ourselves offer to explain them. Alternatively, we may acknowledge the complexity of knowledge use in contexts of practice, arguing that contextually determined definitions of knowledge and of use are unique indexical expressions (Knorr, 1981). Here we risk the abandonment of knowledge use as a "pseudo-problem" when, instead, it is an authentic problem whose generalizable dimensions we are simply unable to penetrate with the tools at hand. A third alternative is to develop a loosely organized multidisciplinary strategy, appropriating whatever insights may be available in existing social science disciplines (sociology, political science, economics, psychology, anthropology) and their many subfields (sociology of knowledge, economics of information, cognitive psychology, applied anthropology) and hybrids (planned social change, communication of innovations, information sciences, artificial intelligence). Here the major risk is an unreflective brand of eclecticism and a diffuse labeling process that may further entangle or even knot orientations in the field.

Another alternative is to begin with the field as it is, taking theoretical diversity and conflict as a datum or problematic situation which we might organize in more plausible and productive ways. Here we aim not at "solving" the problem—for example, by employing a favored discipline-based model or hybrid which yields explanations that shun the very complexity we wish to make intelligible—but at "structuring" the problem as a necessary prelude to eventual solutions. To do so, however, requires that we systematically uncover competing theoretical perspectives of knowledge use and their underlying assumptions.[1] In this way we may discover complementarities as well as conflicts among different perspectives, avoiding any mistaken impression that a single theory adequately represents the role of policy research in producing usable knowledge.

The discussion that follows attempts to classify or sort theories of knowledge use according to answers provided to two questions:[2] (1) How is knowledge use *defined*? (2) How is knowledge use *explained*? The first question leads us towards alternative assumptions about knowledge use as a phenomenon-to-be-explained (explanandum), while the second yields assumptions about classes of phenomena which explain knowledge use (explanantes). By pursuing both questions at once we may avoid the kinds of difficulties that arise when two or more perspectives which are based on a common definition of knowledge use—and, thus, which may be viewed as theoretical cohorts—also propose fundamentally different explanations. The same situation arises in reverse when two or more perspectives are based on a similar explanation of entirely different phenomena. Accordingly, the plethora of conflicting research findings and conclusions that characterizes the field is not due so much to an *absence* of definitions of "utilization," or even of multiple outcome measures (Larsen, 1981:151), but to the *presence* of conflicting and/or mixed definitions and explanations of knowledge use, however implicit or ambiguous these might be.

Existing definitions of knowledge use seem to share at least one property in common: Knowledge use is a cognitive relation among two or more purposively behaving actors. By specifying that knowledge use is a "cognitive" relation we mean that the accompaniment of one actor's behavior by that of another is somehow affected by the act or faculty of knowing. Indeed, it is this cognitive stipulation, and perhaps this alone, that differentiates knowledge use from disciplines or fields that investigate other types of relations based, for example, on power, status, or exchange.[3]

---

[1] By theoretical perspective I mean a loosely organized set of claims and underlying assumptions that provide not only a "way of viewing" knowledge use, but also a commitment to define and explain the phenomenon in specific ways. I thus avoid, for reasons that will become clear, more restrictive definitions of theory as a systematically organized and logically connected set of propositions designed to explain or predict some class of phenomena. The terms "theory," "theoretical perspective," and "perspective" are used interchangeably in the first three sections of the paper.

[2] These questions, along with the methodology used to compare and contrast theories (or theoretical perspectives), are based on Walter Wallace's fine attempts to map the domain of sociological theory (Wallace, 1969; 1971).

[3] Specialized fields devoted to the study of

By stipulating that the behavior in question is purposive we call attention to the teleological character of knowledge use. The striking common feature of otherwise conflicting definitions of knowledge use is their dependence on assumptions about the motives, intentions, or purposes of "producers" and "users." In one of the broadest classifications available, Machlup (1962, 1980), for example, extends Scheler's threefold classification of knowledge (intellectual, instrumental, spiritual) by providing a teleological contrast among intellectual, practical, spiritual, pastime, and unwanted knowledge. Classifications of use—for example, "conceptual," "instrumental," and "symbolic" uses of knowledge (Rich, 1975; Caplan, 1979; Knorr, 1977)—follow a similar pattern of teleological reasoning. Indeed, it is difficult to formulate a satisfactory definition of knowledge or of use that does not hinge on the purposes of "knowers" or "users" (see Churchman, 1971).

Agreement on this abstract definition of knowledge use begins to dissipate when we consider specific features of existing perspectives. While knowledge use may be a cognitive relation among purposively behaving actors, this cognitive relation may be defined in two fundamentally different ways: one type of definition emphasizes *objective*, observable, and overt cognitive relations among purposively behaving actors, while the other stresses *subjective*, non-observable, and covert cognitive relations.[4] The difference between these definitions, as Wallace (1969:6–7) observes of social relations in general,

> corresponds to the difference between the Newtonian and Weberian definitions of "action." Newton's definition of mechanical action was entirely in terms of external observables. . . . Weber took exactly the opposite view by asserting that bodies' social action is so far distinguishable from mechanical action as to be definable *only* in terms of their internal states.

Although there may be and often is considerable overlap between these two types of definitions in particular theories of knowledge use, it remains possible to characterize theories in terms of their *emphasis* on one type of cognitive relation rather than the other. Thus, for example, while Machlup includes in his definition of knowledge use both the "process of informing" (an objective cognitive relation) and the "message or knowledge conveyed" by this process (a subjective cognitive relation), he nevertheless defines the use of *knowledge* as a subjective cognitive relation:[5]

> If one wants to be consistent in keeping separate the process of informing and the

cognitive relations have also grown out of several disciplines, including the sociology of science (Merton, 1973), the sociology of knowledge applications (Holzner and Marx, 1979), qualitative sociology (Schwartz and Jacobs, 1979), cognitive psychology (Hayes, 1978), and the psychology of science (Fisch, 1977).

[4] The objective-subjective behavior distinction is, of course, somewhat ambiguous. One source of ambiguity, as Wallace (1969:7) observes, is the technical difficulty of directly observing subjective behavior (e.g., knowledge, attitudes, values). An equally important source of ambiguity (one Wallace does not mention) is the technical difficulty of determining whether objective behavior does or does not reflect particular cognitive properties—for example, knowledge of particular policy recommendations or the findings of program evaluations. For this reason Merton (1949), Suchman (1972), Weiss (1977), and Rein and White (1977) have called attention to the "latent" goals of policy research. In short, it is even more difficult to make inferences about "knowledge use" from objective behavior than it is from subjective behavior. A solution for this problem may be found in a metatheory that posits a dialectical relation between behavior now distinguished as "objective" versus "subjective," "conceptual" versus "instrumental," "intellectual" versus "social," and "cognitive" versus "interactive" (see Section 4 below).

[5] Machlup's definition of knowledge use as a subjective cognitive relation leads him to conclude (erroneously, I think) that "Operational definition of use is practically impossible . . ." (1979:64).

message or knowledge conveyed by that process, one would be well advised to avoid altogether speaking of "uses" of information, except if one wishes to refer to choices among alternative modes of information. . . . use of a mode of information should not be confused with the use of the message or knowledge conveyed (Machlup, 1979:65).

The definition of knowledge use as a subjective cognitive relation is evident in many other perspectives. House (1981:12–13), for example, recommends that investigations of knowledge use in education be "directed at the different 'meanings' produced by the change efforts rather than at the change itself," citing an example where an unsuccessful attempt to introduce PPBS was accompanied by extensive culture conflict (see Wolcott, 1979). Similarly, Aaron (1978:159) stresses that the use of research and experimentation on poverty, while it is seemingly unconnected to specific overt changes in the behavior of policymakers, nevertheless "corrodes the kind of simple faiths on which political movements are built." In the same vein, Patton's work on utilization-focused evaluation defines knowledge use in terms of "more penetrating perspectives, increased capabilities, and greater commitments to action" (Patton, 1978:290). Caplan, while acknowledging the importance of objective cognitive relations associated with "instrumental" use, stresses the importance of subjective relations found to characterize "conceptual" use among high-level policy makers confronted by macro-level problems of high complexity (Caplan, 1979:465).

In contrast to an emphasis on subjective cognitive relations we find those who stress objective, observable, and overt cognitive relations. Here there is no apparent reference to underlying purposes, motivations, or intentions. Thus, for example, knowledge use has been viewed as an overt process of adopting and implementing research-based innova-

tions (National Institute of Education, 1978), or as a change in the structure and functioning of a social system (Rogers, 1973). These definitions of knowledge use, which emphasize directly observable consequences of acting on knowledge—that is, an objective cognitive relation—assume that use occurs when an entire set of recommendations is implemented in a form suggested by researchers (Larsen, 1981: 150).

Perhaps the clearest example of a definition of knowledge use in terms of objective cognitive relations is provided in a study of the use of evaluation research in criminal justice (Larson and Berliner, 1979). Noting that "evaluation is a process that produces information to assist in the allocation of resources," the authors go on to define use in terms of the "decision-consequential impact" of research on decisions involving "an irrevocable allocation of resources" (Larson and Berliner, 1979:2). Quoting Howard (1966), the authors contend that "a decision is not a 'decision to make a decision,' but rather the concrete action implied by the decision" (Larson and Berliner, 1979:23n).[6]

The distinction between subjective and objective cognitive relations, while it provides a suitable basis for comparing and contrasting the explananda of theories of knowledge use, fails to acknowledge several additional distinctions. For example, alternative distinctions involving macro and micro levels of use have been employed by Caplan (1979), while more differentiated classifications of types of use are available in the literature (e.g., Larsen

---

[6] This quotation, and others like it, should be sufficient to convince the doubting reader that the term "objective cognitive relation" is not a self-evident contradiction. While we may disagree with such definitions it is important to recognize that many observers assume (most often implicitly) that objective, observable, and overt behavior is indicative of some cognitive relation—namely, one that is based on the subjective act or faculty or knowing.

et al., 1976; Weiss, 1976; Hall and Loucks, 1977; Dunn, 1980; Knott and Wildavsky, 1980; Zaltman, 1980; Rich and Goldsmith, 1981). The most appropriate position towards these alternative distinctions is simply to argue that the subjective-objective distinction captures many of the most important definitions current in the field. Indeed, the subjective-objective distinction uncovers and clarifies behavior now treated in these classifications as if it shares some single underlying property. For example, Knott and Wildavsky (1980:546) propose a sevenfold typology of "standards of knowledge utilization," some of which (e.g., cognition and reference) conform to what we have defined as a subjective cognitive relation, while others (e.g., implementation and impact) are instances of objective cognitive relations.

Finally, the use of the subjective-objective distinction to differentiate explananda of theoretical perspectives omits distinctions based on ordinary and scientific knowledge (Lindblom and Cohen, 1979), frames of reference (Holzner and Marx, 1979), truth tests and utility tests (Weiss and Bucuvalas, 1980), and policy sectors, arenas, and institutional contexts (Rich, 1979; J. Weiss, 1979). This omission is deliberate, since it is these and similar distinctions that permit us to differentiate the explanantes of theories of knowledge use.

Knowledge Use: The Problem of Explanation

Apart from their different emphases on subjective and objective cognitive relations, available theories also offer different classes of phenomena to explain knowledge use. Theories which adopt a common definition of knowledge use as a subjective cognitive relation (e.g., "conceptual" use) frequently advance different explanations of this same phenomenon—for example, explanations

derived from knowledge-specific, policy-maker constraint, or two-communities theories of knowledge use (see Caplan, Morrison, and Stambaugh, 1975). A similar situation sometimes exists in reverse, since authors who share the same explanatory schema—for example, an interactive, pluralistic, and incremental theory of policy-making—may hold fundamentally different definitions of knowledge use. Thus, while Lindblom and Cohen (1979:12) affirm that "knowledge is knowledge to anyone who takes it as a basis for action," Wildavsky (1979:27–28) and Knott and Wildavsky (1980) reserve the term "knowledge" for

> . . . theories relating policy variables to effects where the principles are confirmed by the empirical test of repeated decisions. . . . When policy makers are *certain* that manipulating these variables will produce the expected effects—that is, if "x" is done, "y" will follow with a known probability—then they have knowledge (547, 546; emphasis supplied).

Whatever else one may say about interactionist explanations of knowledge use, in this case their authors hardly share a common or cohesive theory—they are attempting to explain entirely different phenomena.

The principal phenomena offered to explain knowledge use may be grouped into two main classes: conditions that are *imposed on* users by the given nature of knowledge, of users themselves, or of the social systems in which they interact; and conditions that are *generated by* users as they create knowledge, their own standards for assessing knowledge, or the social systems of which they are members. The first type of explanation implies that knowledge use is "natural," determined," or "imperative," while the second suggests that knowledge use is "artificial," "self-determining," or "constructed."[7]

[7] Wallace (1969:11–13) juxtaposes the terms "determined" versus "free-willed," while others (e.g., Rein, 1976) reintroduce the classic "nom-

Theories of knowledge use which provide explanations stressing imposed phenomena are sometimes offered by those concerned with the nature of social science knowledge and its effects on research utilization. For example, Bernstein and Freeman (1975), observing that "there have been few cases of actual effective utilization of evaluation research for expected purposes" (5) offer an imposed explanation based on assumed characteristics of "quality" research and the attendant failure of federal agencies to ensure production. "Quality" research is defined as research that conforms to standards of experimental and quasi-experimental design (100–101), while the failure to enforce such standards is described in the following terms:

> . . . there is neither a federal evaluation policy nor a set of requirements and guidelines regarding what constitutes an appropriate evaluation. This lack has severe consequences. It results in a failure to enforce any standardized set of evaluation requirements, even when present in legislation (Bernstein and Freeman, 1975:6).

Whereas this and related perspectives (e.g., Yin *et al.*, 1976) seek to explain decision processes and other objective cognitive relations primarily in terms of imposed knowledge-specific characteristics, others stress imposed explanations based on assumptions about the nature of users or their environing social systems. For example, Mitroff and Mitroff (1979) employ Jungian personality theory, which assumes given underlying personality structures or traits, to explain patterns of interpersonal communication among knowledge users and producers. Whereas this imposed explanation focuses on user-specific characteristics, others stress

phenomena that operate through social systems. For example, the weight of arguments offered in support of theories of a "post-industrial" society (Bell, 1973) is borne by explanations that stress conditions which are imposed by social system-specific characteristics—particularly, the proposition that the growing interdependencies, complexity, and pace of change of contemporary society make existing knowledge obsolete, thus increasing the demand for new forms of policy-relevant knowledge (see Straussman, 1978).

Theories of knowledge use are also based on explanations that emphasize phenomena which are generated by users as they create knowledge, their own standards for assessing knowledge, or the social systems of which they are members. For example, Carol Weiss outlines three classes of generated conditions which parallel distinctions among knowledge-specific, user-specific, and social-system-specific characteristics: knowledge-driven, decision-driven, and interactive models of knowledge use (C. Weiss, 1977: 11–14). In her own work Weiss has offered explanations based primarily on phenomena generated by users—specifically, the truth tests and utility tests that constitute the frames of reference of decision makers (Weiss and Bucuvalas, 1980). Whereas Lindblom and Cohen (1979) are concerned with knowledge-specific characteristics in general—that is, with relations between "ordinary" and "scientific" knowledge— Weiss and Bucuvalas specifically address knowledge as a product of user-specific frames of reference. That they are not principally interested in social system-specific characteristics is evident in their description of their enterprise as a classical sociology of knowledge "turned upside down" (see Holzner, 1978:8):

> Whereas the classical sociology of knowledge was concerned with the social bases of intellectual productions, a sociology of knowledge application would be concerned with the social bases of intellectual produc-

---

othetic-idiographic" distinction. Strasser (1976), in distinguishing "social-technological" and "social-emancipatory" explanations, provides a more powerful and conceptually rich schema that addresses the role of critical or reflective properties of explanantes of theories.

tions, a sociology of knowledge application would be concerned with the social consequences of knowledge. . . . [there is a] need for understanding the multiple frames of reference with which actors perceive knowledge and the discrepancies between the frames of reference of knowledge producers and knowledge users (Weiss and Bucuvalas, 1980:302).

Finally, other explanations place primary emphasis on phenomena generated by social systems. Janet Weiss argues that attention to "relationships between the structures of policy making and the avenues by which social science may participate in policy debates permits analysis of both the overall level of social science use that sectoral arrangements seem to support and the particular kinds of use that sectoral arrangements encourage" (J. Weiss, 1979:439). Caplan provides a similar but more general explanation by stressing generated phenomena that also operate through social systems. In Caplan's words, "social scientists would be well advised to pay particularly close attention to the utilization theories that stress the lack of interaction between social scientists and policymakers as a major reason for nonuse" (Caplan, 1979:461; see also Caplan, Morrison, and Stambaugh, 1975, and Poppen, 1978).

A Typology of Theoretical Perspectives

The intersection of definitional and explanatory dimensions outlined in the preceding sections yields a basic typology for classifying theories of knowledge use (Table 1). The product of the typology is four ideal types that capture basic properties of contemporary theories. In Table 1 these ideal types have been labeled with terms that describe the essential features of competing definitions (explananda) and explanations (explanantes), as these have been discussed so far, rather than the

disciplinary orientations (e.g., "philosophy of science" or "sociology of knowledge") or preferred metaphors (e.g., "two-communities theory") of their authors. By treating these four theoretical perspectives as ideal types, and by attaching labels that describe their most basic theoretical properties, we may circumvent some of the conceptual entanglements that now characterize the field.

One major ideal-typical theory of knowledge use may be designated "interactional imperativism," since it defines knowledge use in primarily objective (interactional) terms and offers explanations that stress phenomena that are imposed on users (imperative). The work of Knott and Wildavsky (1980) closely approximates "interactional imperativism," as we have characterized this perspective, since their theory of dissemination and knowledge use holds that the overt and observable utilization behavior of policymakers is a function of the availability of "authentic" knowledge provided through "natural" processes. Specifically,

. . . premature dissemination in the absence of knowledge contributes to information overload, thus making dissemination a cause of underutilization rather than a cure. Dissemination should not substitute for supply when natural processes are cheaper and more effective. . . . Three difficulties stand out: pretensions to knowledge, which make many dissemination efforts premature; artificiality (or the Newcastle syndrome) substitutes unnecessarily for the natural spread of knowledge; and the Mathew effect in which those policy makers who are the most in need of dissemination are also the ones who are the least able to process and apply what is sent (Knott and Wildavsky, 1980:573, 574).

A second ideal-typical perspective, "cultural imperativism," defines knowledge use in essentially subjective (cultural) terms and provides explanations that stress phenomena that are imposed on users (imperative). An impressive recent treatise

TABLE 1   A Basic Typology for Classifying Theories of Knowledge Use

The Principal Phenomena that *Explain* Cognitive Relations Are:	The Principal Cognitive Relations that *Define* Knowledge Use Are:	
	Objective (Interactional)	Subjective (Cultural)
Imposed on Users (Imperative)	Interactional Imperativism	Cultural Imperativism
Generated by Users (Constructed)	Interactional Constructivism	Cultural Constructivism

on knowledge and knowledge production (Machlup, 1980) approximates cultural imperativism, as we have defined it, since the emphasis is on a "knowledge industry" constituted by given structures of production and occupational specialization which create new and diverse forms of knowledge. While "for most parts of the production of knowledge no possible measure of output can be conceived that would be logically separate from a measure of input" (Machlup, 1980:225), the class of imposed phenomena used to explain knowledge and its use are based on

> an industry approach to the total value of the output of all firms, agencies, departments, etc., that generate or disseminate knowledge, and an occupation approach to the amount or value of the input of knowledge producing labor (Machlup, 1980:227).

A third ideal-typical perspective, "interactional constructivism," defines knowledge use in primarily objective (interactional) terms and supplies explanations that stress phenomena that are generated by users (constructed). Interactional constructivism is evident in explanations that stress "the symbiotic relationships among policy actors, knowledge, and the political and institutional context of policy making" (J. Weiss, 1979:456–57). The use of knowledge by policymakers

cannot be understood independently of the processes for making public policy. These processes provide the critical organizational and political contexts that shape policy makers' needs for outside expertise; create organizational channels of information flow that routinely bring (or fail to bring) ideas and evidence to policy makers' attention and define problems, decision situations, policy alternatives, and solutions in ways that determine which evidence is considered to be relevant (J. Weiss, 1979:439).

The fourth and final perspective in our basic typology is "cultural constructivism," an ideal-typical theory best represented by the work of Knorr (1981). Cultural constructivism defines knowledge use in essentially subjective (cultural) terms and offers explanations that stress phenomena that are generated by users (constructed). For Knorr, contexts of practical action are radically underdetermined by generalizable standards or rules. As such, practical action is indexical:

> . . . rules and decision criteria, and more generally definitions of the situation, are interpreted in context . . . it is the concrete, local translation of rules or decision criteria which determine the selections that are made, and which subsequently shape the outcomes of these selections (Knorr, 1981).

Clearly, these four ideal-typical theories are highly general and abstract; they do not capture particular assumptions, propositions, or hypotheses put forth in alternative theories of knowledge use. For this reason it is desirable to differentiate the basic typology into additional subclasses of explanations (Table 2). This yields an expanded typology based on additional distinctions among knowledge-specific, user-specific, and social system-specific properties of imposed and generated explanations. The product of this expanded typology is twelve ideal-typical perspectives of knowledge use. These twelve perspectives are illustrated below with statements drawn from the work of leading contributors to theory and research on knowledge use.

Psycho-Interactional Imperativism

Psycho-interactional imperativism defines knowledge use primarily in objective (interactional) terms and provides explanations that stress phenomena which are imposed on users (imperative) via given psychological properties of users themselves. Mitroff and Mitroff (1979) exemplify psycho-interactional imperativism insofar as their effort to define and explain knowledge use in terms of transactional analysis (TA) and Jungian personality theory, respectively, is based on an "external" explandum and an "internal" explanans. In order that effective knowledge utilization occur

it is desirable that the parties be as *different* on their Jungian profiles as possible. On the other hand, it is critical that they come as close as possible to functioning in the adult mode [posited by transactional analysis]. Difference is called for in Jungian terms so that both parties can challenge their assumptions about what form and type of knowledge is needed so that they can broaden their perspectives . . . . adult

TABLE 2   An Expanded Typology for Classifying Theories of Knowledge Use

The Principal Phenomena that *Explain* Cognitive Relations Are:		The Principal Cognitive Relations that *Define* Knowledge Use Are:	
		Objective	Subjective
Imposed on users via properties of:	Users	Psycho-Interactional Imperativism	Psycho-Cultural Imperativism
	Knowledge	Epistemo-Interactional Imperativism	Epistemo-Interactional Imperativism
	Social Systems	Socio-Interactional Imperativism	Socio-Cultural Imperativism
	Users	Psycho-Interactional Constructivism	Psycho-Cultural Constructivism
Generated by users via properties of:	Knowledge	Epistemo-Interactional Constructivism	Epistemo-Cultural Constructivism
	Social Systems	Socio-Interactional Constructivism	Socio-Cultural Constructivism

functioning is required so that they can benefit from their differences (Mitroff and Mitroff, 1979:214).

Psycho-Cultural Imperativism

Psycho-cultural imperativism defines knowledge use primarily in subjective (cultural) terms and supplies explanations that emphasize phenomena which are imposed on users (imperative) via given psychological properties of users themselves. Campbell's "evolutionary epistemology" comes very close to psycho-cultural imperativism insofar as this "descriptive epistemology"—that is, an epistemology descriptive of man as knower—seeks to explain the evolution of science and other cultural artifacts in terms of psychobiological processes of adaptation and natural selection. In Campbell's words,

> . . . man has evolved from some simple unicellular or virus-like ancestor and its still simpler progenitors. In the course of that evolution, there have been tremendous gains in adaptive adequacy, in stored templates modeling the useful stabilities of the environment, in memory and innate wisdom. Still more dramatic have been the great gains in mechanisms for knowing, in visual perception, learning, imitation, language and science. At no stage has there been any transfusion of knowledge from the outside, nor of mechanisms of knowing, nor of fundamental certainties (Campbell, 1974:413).

Epistemo-Interactional Imperativism

Epistemo-interactional imperativism defines knowledge use primarily in objective (interactional) terms and offers explanations that emphasize phenomena which are imposed on users (imperative) via given epistemological properties of knowledge. This perspective has already been illustrated with references to the ideas of Bernstein and Freeman (1975), Wildavsky (1979), and Knott and Wildavsky (1980). A

variation of this perspective—but one that assumes the ubiquity of "knowledge" rather than its scarcity or nonexistence—is the "bureaucratic power" model of Rourke: "Bureaucratic power thus reflects the technological revolution and the growing influence of specialized knowledge in modern civilization" (Rourke, 1972).

Epistemo-Cultural Imperativism

Epistemo-cultural imperativism defines knowledge use primarily in subjective (cultural) terms and supplies explanations that stress phenomena which are imposed on users (imperative) via given epistemological properties of knowledge. Toulmin's evolutionary theory of scientific development, based on the analogue of population genetics, explains the growth of knowledge in terms of competing intellectual variants (e.g., theories) carried by scientists in a process characterized by selective diffusion, selection, and retention (Toulmin, 1972). Popper's evolutionary epistemology, which posits a natural trial-and-error process of selecting theories whose epistemological properties make them more or less fit to solve empirical puzzles, also exemplifies epistemo-cultural imperativism (Popper, 1972; Campbell, 1974:436).

Socio-Interactional Imperativism

Socio-interactional imperativism defines knowledge use primarily in objective (interactional) terms and offers explanations stressing imposed phenomena that operate via given characteristics of social systems. Among the many illustrations of socio-interactional imperativism is the "bureaucratization of inquiry" model put forth by Rich (1979, 1981). In contrast to perspectives that stress characteristics of knowledge as a key factor in knowledge use, the bureaucratization of inquiry perspective assumes that

> the characteristics of knowledge are a necessary but not sufficient condition in accounting for the application and utilization of scientific knowledge. This view of the problem stipulates that the bureaucratization of the knowledge inquiry system— the production, process, and use of information—is the critical variable for understanding levels of utilization and nonutilization. . . . "Bureaucratization" refers to issues of internal agency control and ownership as superseding all other considerations. . . . Thus, according to this perspective, one would affect change in the knowledge inquiry system by influencing bureaucratic rules and procedures—not knowledge and/or policy/sector specific characteristics (Rich, 1979:328-329; Rich, 1981).

Socio-Cultural Imperativism

Socio-cultural imperativism defines knowledge use primarily in subjective (cultural) terms and supplies explanations that stress phenomena which are imposed on users (imperative) via given characteristics of social systems. An appropriate illustration of socio-cultural imperativism is Wilensky's treatise on "organizational intelligence" (Wilensky, 1967). Addressing "institutional threats to the reasoned use of knowledge," Wilensky explains variations in organizational intelligence by emphasizing phenomena imposed on users via given characteristics of complex organizations and their environments: "The more an organization is in conflict with its social environment or depends on it for the achievement of its central goals, the more resources it will allocate to the intelligence function and the more of those resources will be spent on experts . . ." (Wilensky, 1967:10).

Psycho-Interactional Constructivism

Psycho-interactional constructivism defines knowledge use primarily in objective (interactional) terms and offers explanations that emphasize phenomena which are generated by users (constructed) via dynamic psychological properties of users themselves. Etheridge's recent overview (1979) of theory and research on government learning outlines, among other perspectives, a dynamic "bureaucratic dependency theory":

> Dependent people tend to be fearful of, and to resist, change. . . . They may have a greater need for leaders to define reality, lead, and think for them . . . be more prone to stress, complain without being constructive, tend to wait for other people to solve problems. They may also be prone to symbolic politics rather than substantive problem-solving. . . . dependency can be induced and sustained by bureaucracies and need not be solely a personality trait (Etheridge, 1979:38–39).

Psycho-Cultural Constructivism

Psycho-cultural constructivism defines knowledge use primarily in subjective (cultural) terms and supplies explanations that stress phenomena which are generated by users (constructed) via dynamic psychological properties of users themselves. The definition of government learning proposed by Etheridge (1979:4), while it includes "behavioral effectiveness" as an objective (interactional) property of knowledge use, emphasizes "increased intelligence and sophistication of thought. . . ." In offering explanations of knowledge use as "government learning" Etheridge relies heavily on theories of active learning created within developmental psychology:

> Developmental theorists . . . see people as fundamentally seeking for—and often achieving—further qualitative personal growth or development, an achievement which is partly facilitated or blocked by their environment. This developmental, so-called rationalist, tradition holds an active, constructionist view of learning, believes there are innate capacities and predispositions of the mind to make independent sense out of the world, capacities for active internal processing, self-reflection, and

qualitative transformation of understanding and competence autonomous from external hedonistic incentive systems (Etheridge, 1979:27–28).

Arguing that organizational learning can be indexed to individual learning—mainly by focusing on "the intelligence and sophistication of thought which informs decisions, policies, and programs"—Etheridge nevertheless punctuates several special requirements of government learning: adequate internal learning systems; consultative and adversarial procedures involving external critics; organizational memory; and "the embodiment of new understandings or revised policies in the action and understanding of people throughout the organization" (Etheridge, 1979:9–10).

Epistemo-Interactional Constructivism

Epistemo-interactional constructivism defines knowledge use primarily in objective (interactional) terms and provides explanations that stress phenomena which are generated by users (constructed) via dynamic properties of knowledge. Weiss' platform for a new social sociology of knowledge applications—that is, a sociology of knowledge "turned upside down" (see Holzner, 1978:8)—is principally concerned with the effects of frames of reference on decision making (Weiss and Bucuvalas, 1980:25). Identical or closely related perspectives are evident in work on "knowledge systems" (Holzner and Marx, 1979), "theories-in-use" (Argyris and Schön, 1974; Zaltman, 1977), "strategic assumptional analysis" (Mason and Mitroff, 1981), and "reforms as arguments" (Dunn, 1981).

Epistemo-Cultural Constructivism

Epistemo-cultural constructivism defines knowledge use primarily in subjective (cultural) terms and provides explanations that emphasize phenomena which are generated by users (constructed) via dynamic properties of knowledge. Laudan's theory of scientific progress approximates the meaning of epistemo-cultural constructivism insofar as its principal focus is on the development of new scientific theories as a consequence of competing rational standards or rules for certifying and challenging the adequacy of knowledge claims (Laudan, 1977). While scientific theories are underdetermined by data, this does not entail the conclusion that knowledge claims are properly explained solely or even primarily in terms of externally imposed "sociological" factors (Laudan, 1981).

Socio-Interactional Constructivism

Socio-interactional constructivism defines knowledge use primarily in objective (interactional) terms and provides explanations that stress phenomena which are generated by users (constructed) via dynamic properties of the social systems of which users are members. Lindblom and Cohen (1979) equate knowledge use with "social problem solving," that is, "processes that are thought to eventuate in outcomes that by some standard are an improvement on the previously existing situation. . . . For us, 'solve' does not require an understanding of 'the problem' but only an outcome . . ."(4). "Problem solving" defined in this way is then explained primarily in terms of social processes that are interactive, pluralistic, and incremental (see Lindblom, 1980). In their words:

> Information and analysis constitute only one route among several to social problem solving. . . . a great deal of the world's problem solving is and ought to be accomplished through various forms of social interaction that substitute action for

thought, understanding, or analysis. Information and analysis are not a universal or categorical prescription for social problem solving. In addition, PSI [Professional Social Inquiry] is only one among several analytic methods, because other forms of information and analysis—ordinary knowledge and casual analysis foremost among them—are often sufficient or better than PSI for social problem solving (Lindblom and Cohen, 1979:10).

Socio-Cultural Constructivism

The last ideal-typical perspective yielded by our expanded typology is socio-cultural constructivism. Socio-cultural constructivism defines knowledge use primarily in subjective (cultural) terms and provides explanations that stress phenomena which are generated by users (constructed) via dynamic properties of social systems. This perspective is evident in much research on "conceptual" uses of social science knowledge by policymakers (see C. Weiss, 1977:15–16), including so-called "enlightenment" models of knowledge use (e.g., Rose, 1977; Cohen and J. Weiss, 1977) and those which stress "ideology" in the classic sense of false consciousness (Mills, 1959; Habermas, 1970; Gregg et al., 1979). Representative expressions of socio-cultural constructivism, as that perspective is characterized here, may be found in Rein and Schon's overview of problem setting in policy research (1977) and in general treatises on the role of social science in public policymaking (e.g., Rein, 1976; Rein and White, 1977). Rejecting a narrow and instrumentally oriented conception of problem solving, Rein and Schon propose instead that the process of policy development

is essentially about a process of *problem setting*; it is concerned with developing new purposes and new interpretations of the inchoate signs of stress in the system that derive from the past.

Policymakers use research as an instrument to legitimate action in perpetual striving for consensus of belief and for organization of the fine structure of government action; policy may influence the research agenda more than research influences the direction of policy (Rein and Schon, 1977:235, 236).

In summary, there are at least twelve ideal-typical perspectives of knowledge use now available to enhance our understanding of the role of policy research in social problem solving. Each of these twelve perspectives, it should again be emphasized, is an "ideal" or "extreme" type in the sense that it represents a one-sided accentuation of a particular set of standards for assessing knowledge use which is part of a wider universe of diverse and frequently conflicting views about knowledge and its practical uses. While the basic and extended typologies described above are artificial entities, as indeed all intellectual constructs must be, they capture many of the most important perspectives now prevalent in the field.

The contributions of different theorists have been used to illustrate each ideal type; ideal types, therefore, are not intended as methodological generalizations about theorists whose own research typically evidences a great deal more complexity than a given ideal type can possibly capture. Nevertheless, this process of strategic typification is a reasoned one that deliberately circumvents unproductive disciplinary labels (e.g., "political," "economic," "sociological," "philosophical"), prematurely specified distinctions (e.g., "conceptual" versus "instrumental" use), and doubtful hypothesis and empirical generalizations (e.g., "knowledge use is a function of the 'quality' or 'authenticity' of knowledge and its availability to policymakers"). Instead, the basic and extended typologies are intended to uncover and raise to a level of explicit consciousness the most basic theoretical properties of an emerging but understandably complex and tangled field.

Critical Constructivism: A Metatheory

The twelve theoretical perspectives outlined in the last section may be investigated in several different ways, depending on what standards of assessment we wish to employ in appraising them. One investigative strategy is to assess theories in terms of their empirical content, for example, by aggregating or otherwise reviewing available research findings that seem to oppose or support their claims, underlying assumptions, and hypotheses (see Rogers and Shoemaker, 1971; Rothman, 1974; Bernstein and Freeman, 1975; Yin and Heald, 1975; Dunn, 1980). This strategy, while useful for some purposes, is likely to prove highly unsatisfactory as a vehicle for improving theories of knowledge use. We are likely to find that available studies are essentially incommensurable (see Larsen, 1981), not only or even primarily because there are discrepancies in procedures for measuring or "calibrating" variables, but because available studies reflect unresolved basic theoretical conflicts among those who have conducted them. Under these circumstances it would come as no surprise that we are presently unable to generalize *any* contemporary theories of knowledge use or planned change (Berman, 1981).

Another investigative strategy is to assess theories in terms of their logical properties, for example, by examining their scope, simplicity, consistency, determinacy, and level of abstraction (Wallace, 1971; Popper, 1961; Merton, 1967). While the logical properties of theories are indeed important, this strategy is inappropriate under conditions where we do not know what to explain—that is, where we have

not yet decided how to define knowledge use itself. Indeed, this formal logical strategy, when combined with empirical standards for assessing theories, is itself a theory of knowledge use that parallels in most respects what has been described as "epistemo-cultural imperativism." An interest in empirically confirmed and logically consistent propositions reflects a special technical definition of knowledge and our own preferred mode of explaining why we will (or will not) use knowledge conveyed by a given theory.

A third strategy of investigation might involve some combination of historical and social-psychological analysis. Here we might focus on the sociohistorical or psychological bases of theories, or the wider research traditions of which they are part—for example, by examining the professional incentive systems that promote and retard the acceptance of given perspectives or the psychological traits of theorists themselves. Apart from the present impracticality of this alternative, we should recognize that this strategy would also commit us to particular theories of knowledge use—that is, we would necessarily be applying standards of assessment that fall within the scope of "imperativist" perspectives that emphasize social system-specific explanations.

The point is that each of the four basic perspectives and their differentiated subtypes may be used to derive standards of assessment for appraising all other perspectives, including the reflexive application of a theory to itself. While this observation may seem unnecessarily abstract or convoluted, it also yields an important practical insight: *Each theoretical perspective may be viewed as a theory-in-use that actually affects the behavior of diverse knowledge users.* Thus, we can take each perspective as a "datum" that constitutes a frame of reference and component underlying standards for assessing "usable knowledge" (see Zaltman, 1981; Holzner and Fisher, 1979; Dunn, 1981). Here we will focus on the different ways that theorists themselves "construe" knowledge use, rather than on external conditions that may seem to make theories imperative. Yet if we wish also to assess or evaluate theories, that is, reflect critically on their underlying assumptions, we require standards of assessment that are not also part of the class of standards intrinsic to the theories themselves: "Whatever involves *all* of a collection must not be one of the collection" (Whitehead and Russell, 1910:101; Watzlawick *et al.*, 1974:6). In short, what is required is a metatheory of knowledge use, a "theory of theories" that is not itself one of the collection.

The remainder of this section outlines the main contours of "critical constructivism," a metatheory whose eclectic multidisciplinary origins lie in the sociology of knowledge applications (Holzner and Marx, 1979; Weiss and Bucuvalas, 1980), the psychology of personal constructs (Kelly, 1955), the politics of interactive decision making (Lindblom and Cohen, 1979), and the philosophy of argumentation and practical discourse (Toulmin, 1959; Toulmin, Rieke, and Janik, 1979; Willard, 1980; Mason and Mitroff, 1981). In pursuing this aim I shall economize by presenting a series of propositions and corollaries that are specified in terms of users, knowledge, and social systems, that is, according to the three main subdivisions of the extended typology of theories presented in the last section.

Users

1. *Knowledge use is a systemic cognitive relation structured by the ways that users anticipate events* (Kelly, 1955).[8] Knowledge

[8] This subsection draws heavily on personal construct psychology and the theory of "constructivist alternativism" (Kelly, 1955). Some of Kelly's corollaries have been excluded from this presentation. For extensions and interpretations of Kelly's work, including research applications in mental health, marketing, and other areas, see Frost and Braine (1967), Bannister and Mair (1968), and Stringer and Bannister (1979).

use is systemic in the sense that cognitive relations between two or more actors are interdependent. Interdependency renders such terms as knowledge "transfer" (Glaser, 1973) and "translation" (Lazarsfeld and Reitz, 1975) inappropriate; the term "transaction" captures the essence of cognitive interdependency (Zaltman, 1979). Interdependency is nevertheless a property of cognitive relations, that is, of joint occurrences based on the act or faculty of knowing. For this reason "production" metaphors that yield distinctions among producers, disseminators (linkers), and users are at best misleading. Cognitive relations are seldom based on spatiotemporal proximity, since "enlightenment" (Cohen and J. Weiss, 1977) is rarely bound by overt behavioral relations and motor interaction. Yet cognitive relations "are not formless but structured, the structure both facilitating and restricting a person's range of activities" (Bannister, 1962:105; Kelly, 1955). The anticipation of events is purposive or teleological, oriented towards the construction of future reality (cf. Holzner, 1968).

1.1. *Users differ from each other in their construction of events (Individuality Corollary).* Users differ "not only because there may have been differences in the events which they have sought to anticipate but also because there are different approaches to the anticipation of the same events" (Kelly, 1955). The distinction between "objective" and "subjective" behavior—between "externally" imposed and "internally" generated realities—is unnecessary and redundant. As a "unit act" knowledge use is constituted by a dialectical conjunction of subject and object; objective behavior relations alone are never representative of knowledge use. Theories of "instrumental" use, when they exclude the construction of events, are not theories of *knowledge* use; theories of "conceptual" use, when they exclude events that are constructed, are not theories of knowledge *use*.

1.2. *Users evolve for their convenience in anticipating events a construction system or frame of reference embracing ordinal relationships among constructs (Organization Corollary).* Users differ not only in their constructions of events but also "in the ways they *organize* their constructions of events" (Kelly, 1955). Organized construction systems or frames of reference may be characterized in terms of their internal consistency and hierarchical complexity. What are called "reality tests"—that is, standards for assessing the adequacy, relevance, and cogency of knowledge claims (Holzner and Fisher, 1979; Weiss and Bucuvalas, 1980; Dunn, 1981)—reflect complex ordinal relationships among constructs.

1.3. *Users choose for themselves constructs through which they anticipate the greater possibility for the definition and extension of their frames of reference or construction systems (Choice Corollary).* "Definition is the name given to the system's becoming more explicit and clear cut in constructing elements already subsumed; extension is the name given to the system's becoming more comprehensive so that it may subsume new elements" (Bannister, 1962:107). A researcher's decision to maximize internal and/or external validity (Cook and Campbell, 1979) is an illustration of the difference between definition and extension, respectively, as is the distinction between "micropositive" and "macronegative" policy research (Williams, 1971).

1.4. *A construct is convenient for the anticipation of a finite range of events (Range Corollary).* Users may construe "effective" policies versus "ineffective" ones, but will not find it convenient to construe "effective" versus "ineffective" research findings, since re-

search findings are typically outside the range of convenience of the construct "effective-ineffective."

1.5. *A user's construction system or frame of reference changes as he successively construes replications of events (Experience Corollary).* The constructions one places upon events are "working hypotheses" which are put to the test of experience. A user's "anticipation or hypotheses are successively revised in the light of the unfolding sequence of events a construction system undergoes . . ." (Kelly, 1955). For this reason, policy problems do not stay solved; they are redefined and even "unsolved" (Ackoff, 1974).

1.6. *The change in a user's construction system or frame of reference is limited by the permeability of the constructs within whose range of convenience the changes lie (Modulation Corollary).* "A construct system is free or determined with respect to its permeability" (Bannister, 1962:108). The more permeable a user's superordinate constructs—for example, those associated with underlying assumptions or a worldview—the more likely he will be able to change subordinate elements of a construct system or frame of reference. Permeable and impermeable constructs may be illustrated by considering the relatively great flexibility of theories, as distinguished from hypotheses, and of policy problems as compared with policy alternatives or the decision rules used to select them. This distinction is also evident in contrasts between ill-structured and well-structured problems (e.g., Raiffa, 1968; Mitroff, 1974) and problem-solving and problem-setting models of policy research (Rein, 1976; Rein and Schön, 1977).

1.7. *Users may successively employ subsystems of constructs that are incompatible (Fragmentation Corollary).* Incompatible subsystems of constructs are evident only when they are directly compared; incompatibilities disappear when a subsystem is linked to a superordinate system. For example, policy researchers may contend that the provision of more jobs to the unemployed will lead to riots and other civil disturbances. The appearance of self-contradiction is based on an inference from a single subsystem according to which more jobs create more satisfied people. Once jobs and riots are linked to the superordinate construct of "relative deprivation" (the perceived gap between rising expectations and fixed capabilities) the apparent incompatibility disappears. Single subsystems of constructs, including various "reality tests," are unreliable predictors of subsequent action unless we also know the superordinate construct systems of which they are organized components—namely, assumptions matter (Mason and Mitroff, 1981).

1.8. *To the extent that one user's construct system or frame of reference is similar to that employed by another his cognitive processes are similar to those of the other user (Communality Corollary).* We should expect similarities in cognitive processes between users with similar construct systems, even when they experience different events, rather than expect similarities in cognitive processes between users experiencing the same events. Thus, what we experience as policy problems are products of thought acting on external events or environments (Ackoff, 1974), such that the communality or conflict among users' frames of reference governs the structure of policy problems.

1.9. *To the extent that one user construes the construction process of another he may play a role in a social process involving the other user (Sociality Corollary).* To construe the construction processes of another is not necessarily to use identical constructs, or employ the same frame of reference, but "to possess constructs which assume another's within their range of convenience" (Bannister, 1962:110). Thus, for a social scientist to play a role in the social processes of a policymaker who believes that the enforcement of law and order will reduce crime does not involve the social scientist in simply adopting and translating these constructs into a researchable problem, but requires the social scientist to employ constructs that subsume those of the policymaker—for example, by showing that poverty subsumes law and order and crime.

Knowledge

2. *Knowledge is a cultural artifact established through transactions among construing users.* Although knowledge is knowledge to anyone who takes it as a basis for some commitment to action (Lindblom and Cohen, 1979), knowledge is structured by the construction systems or frames of reference of different users. To the extent that users construe the construction processes of other users they are involved in a transactional cognitive relation where two or more parties reciprocally affect, through argument and persuasion, the acceptance and rejection of knowledge claims. Thus, knowledge is not "exchanged," "translated," or "transferred," but transacted among users who constructively negotiate the truth, relevance, and cogency of knowledge claims (Dunn, 1981). Hence, to "use" knowledge is to anticipate events by construing their replications.

2.1. *The adequacy of a knowledge claim is a function of its assimilability within a user's superordinate construction system (Adequacy Corollary).* The adequacy or "truth" of a knowledge claim depends on the extent to which it may be assimilated within a superordinate construction system, that is, a construction system that warrants a claim as plausible by virtue of subordinate status within the construct system (cf. Toulmin, Rieke, and Janik, 1979). Superordinate construction systems may be causal, teleological, empirical, pragmatic, ideological, ethical, or authoritative (Dunn, 1981). "Reality tests" (Holzner and Marx, 1979) are particular types of superordinate construction systems.

2.2. *The relevance of a knowledge claim is a function of its range of convenience to users in anticipating events (Relevance Corollary).* Knowledge claims, apart from their adequacy, may lie outside a user's range of convenience in anticipating events. Thus, a causal claim about the effects of early childhood education on subsequent achievement may be assimilable within a superordinate construct system (e.g., a theory of achievement motivation), but lie outside the range of convenience of users who anticipate socioemotional development of children. "Relevance" and "utility" tests (Holzner and Fisher, 1979; Weiss and Bucuvalas, 1980) are particular representations of a user's range of convenience.

2.3. *The cogency of a knowledge claim is a function of the requisite force expected of a construct system in anticipating particular events (Cogency Corollary).* Construct systems vary in the degree to which they anticipate events. When claims are construed as adequate by virtue of their assimilation into a superordinate construct system, the construct system may lack the requisite force expected in anticipating certain events. Particular events may evoke "conservative" or "liberal" expectations about the requisite force of a construct system in anticipating events. For example, physicians and lawyers differ in their presumptions about sickness and guilt and the need to treat or protect clients. "Cogency tests" establish the requisite force expected of a construct system in anticipating events.

Social Systems

3. *Social systems are artificial entities whose creation, maintenance, and transformation is a function of knowledge transactions.* The social systems in which knowledge use takes place are dialectical entities: "Society is a human product. Society is an objective reality. Man is a social product" (Berger and Luckmann, 1967:61). For this reason explanations of knowledge use that stress imposed or generated social phenomena are one-sided and incomplete representations of one or another complementary property of social systems. What we know as "markets" and "bureaucracies" are artificial entities whose consequences are nevertheless real or natural for those who participate in their creation, maintenance, and transformation through knowledge transactions (Knott and Wildavsky, 1980). Similarly, what we know as "social experiments" or an "experimenting society" (Campbell, 1971) are symbolically mediated change processes involving the transaction of new social arrangements, rather than the discovery of experimental outcomes that are independent of the preferences of investigators. Reforms, therefore, are better visualized as arguments (Dunn, 1981) than experiments (Campbell, 1975, 1979). Arguments are naturally occurring corollaries to research contexts; every user conducts his own research act (Willard, 1980).

3.1. *The performance of social systems in achieving collective goals is a function of the degree to which shared construction systems or frames of reference successfully anticipate events (Rationality Corollary).* Rationality is a property of the construction systems and behavior of individual and collective users; there are as many types of rationality as there are construction systems in society. Attributions of rationality, irrationality, or non-rationality to social systems (Lindblom, 1980; Wildavsky, 1979) are products of the construction systems of analysts rather than those of users about whom analysts generalize. It is in this sense that rationality is "situated" (Simon, 1976) or "indexical" (Knorr, 1981).

3.2. *The success of social systems in anticipating events is a function of the hierarchical complexity, permeability, and integration of collectively shared construction systems or frames of reference (Capacity Corollary).* The successful anticipation of events depends on the number of superordinate constructs in a construct system, their permeability, and integration. Whereas rationality is a property of self-construed effective behavior or performance in anticipating events, collective learning capacity (e.g., government learning) is a structural property of shared construction systems. In this sense "increased effectiveness cannot, by itself, index increased learning" (Etheridge, 1979:5).

3.3. *The freedom to make collective choices that successfully anticipate events is a function of collective learning capacities (Emancipiation Corollary).* Collective construction systems or frames of reference are constituted, in part, by theories—that is, "higher order abstractions by which we gain freedom from the particularities. . . . The theories comprise prior assumptions about certain realms of the events. To the extent that these events may, from these prior assumptions, be construed, predicted, and their relative courses

charted, men may exercise control, and gain freedom for themselves in the process" (Kelly, 1955:22). Accordingly, a "rational" society (Habermas, 1970), or one where social scientists contribute to "enlightenment" (C. Weiss, 1977; Cohen and J. Weiss, 1977), is an emancipatory one. In the last analysis knowledge use is about freedom and human control; the "dependent variable" or phenomenon-to-be-explained is not instrumental rationality, or even collective learning capacities, but emancipation.

Conclusion

In an attempt to untangle the field of knowledge use I have constructed an extended typology designed to capture the most basic properties of present-day theories of knowledge use. Rather than side with any particular theory, or an ideal-type of which it is an illustration, I have instead attempted to take each theory as a "datum." Since most theories are internally fragmented or underspecified it is difficult to explore their assumptions (propositions, hypotheses) with the aim of uncovering complementarities or new opportunities for synthesis that arise from theories themselves.

The analysis therefore shifted to a metatheoretical level where three propositions and fifteen attendant corollaries serve as bases for making statements about ideal-typical theories as a whole. This procedure satisfies the condition that "whatever involves *all* of a collection must not be one of the collection" (Whitehead and Russell). The most important conclusion is that the "dependent variable" or phenomenon-to-be-explained is not instrumental rationality, or even collective learning capacities, but emancipation.

References

Aaron, H. J. (1978). *Politics and the Professors: The Great Society in Perspective.* Washington, D.C.: Brookings.

Ackoff, R. L. (1974). *Redesigning the Future: A Systems Approach to Societal Problems.* New York, N.Y.: Wiley.

Argyris, C., and D. A. Schön (1974). *Theory in Practice: Increasing Professional Effectiveness.* San Francisco, Calif.: Jossey-Bass.

Bannister, D. (1962). "Personal Construct Theory: A Summary and Experimental Paradigm." *Acta Psychologica,* 20:104–120.

Bannister, D., and J.M.M. Mair (1968). *The Evaluation of Personal Constructs.* London: Academic Press.

Bell, D. (1973) *The Coming of Post-Industrial Society.* New York: Basic Books.

Berger, P. L., and T. Luckmann (1967). *The Social Construction of Reality.* Garden City, N.Y.: Doubleday Anchor.

Berman, P. (1981). "Educational Change: An Implementation Paradigm." In R. Lehming and M. Kane (eds.), *Improving Schools: Using What We Know.* Beverly Hills, Calif.: Sage.

Bernstein, I. N., and H. Freeman (1975). *Academic and Entrepreneurial Research.* New York: Russell Sage Foundation.

Campbell, D. T. (1979). "A Tribal Model of the Social System Vehicle Carrying Scientific Knowledge." *Knowledge: Creation, Diffusion, Utilization,* 1, 2:181–202.

Campbell, D. T. (1975) "Reforms as Experiments." In E. B. Struening and M. Guttentag (eds.), *Handbook of Evaluation Research.* Vol. 1. Beverly Hills, Calif.: Sage, pp. 71–100.

Campbell, D. T. (1974). "Evolutionary Epistemology." In P. A. Schilpp (ed.), *The Philosophy of Karl Popper.* LaSalle, Ill.: Open Court Press, pp. 413–463

Campbell, D. T. (1971). "Methods for the Experimenting Society." Paper delivered to the American Psychological Association, Washington, D.C., September 5.

Caplan, N. (1979). "The Two Communities Theory." *American Behavioral Scientist,* 22:459–470.

Caplan, N., A. Morrison, and R. J. Stambaugh (1975.) *The Use of Social Science Knowledge in Policy Decisions at the National Level: A Report to Respondents.* Ann Arbor: Center for Research on Utilization of Scientific Knowledge. Institute for Social Research. University of Michigan.

Churchman, C. W. (1971). *The Design of Inquiring Systems.* New York: Basic Books.

Cohen, D. K., and J. A. Weiss (1977). "Social Science and Social Policy: Schools and Race." In C. H. Weiss (ed.), *Using Social Research in Public Policy Making.* Lexington, Mass.: D.C. Health

Cook, T. D., and D. T. Campbell (1979). *Quasi Experimentation.* Chicago: Rand McNally.

Dunn, W. N. (1981). "Reforms as Arguments." *Knowledge: Creation, Diffusion, Utilization,* 3, 2 (forthcoming).

Dunn, W. N. (1980). "The Two Communities Metaphor and Models of Knowledge Use: An Exploratory Case Survey." *Knowledge: Creation, Diffusion, Utilization,* 1, 4:515–536.

Dunn, W. N., and B. Holzner (1981). "Knowledge Use and School Improvement Conceptual Framework and Study Design." Working paper KU-01. Knowledge Use and School Improvement Project. University Program for the Study of Knowledge Use.

Etheridge, L. S. (1981). *Government Learning: An Overview.* Prepared for publication in Samuel Long (ed.), *Handbook of Political Behavior.* New York: Plenum.

Fisch, R. (1977). "Psychology of Science."

In I. Spiegel-Rosing and D. deSolla Price (eds.), *Science, Technology, and Society: A Cross-Disciplinary Perspective.* Beverly Hills, Calif.: Sage, pp. 277–318.

Frost, W. A., and R. L. Braine (1967). "The Application of the Repertory Grid Technique to Problems in Market Research." *Commentary*, 9, July:161–175.

Ganz, C. (1981). "Linkages Between Knowledge Creation, Diffusion and Utilization." In R. Rich (ed.), *The Knowledge Cycle.* Beverly Hills, Calif.: Sage, pp. 185–206.

Glaser, E. M. (1973). "Knowledge Transfer and Institutional Change." *Professional Psychology*, 4:434–444.

Gregg, C., T. Preston, A. Geist, and N. Caplan (1979). "The Caravan Rolls On: Forty Years of Social Problem Research." *Knowledge: Creation, Diffusion, Utilization*, 1, 1:31–61.

Habermas, J. (1970). *Toward a Rational Society.* Boston: Beacon.

Hall, G. E., and Loucks, S. F. (1977). "A Developmental Model for Determining Whether the Treatment Is Actually Implemented." *American Educational Research Journal*, Summer, 14 (3):263–276.

Hayes, J. R. (1978). *Cognitive Psychology: Thinking and Creating.* Homewood, Ill.: Dorsey Press.

Holzner, B. (1978). "The Sociology of Applied Knowledge." *Sociological Symposium*, 21:8–19.

Holzner, B. (1968). *Reality Construction in Society.* Cambridge, Mass.: Schenkman.

Holzner, B., and E. Fisher (1979). "Knowledge in Use: Considerations in the Sociology of Knowledge Application." *Knowledge: Creation, Diffusion, Utilization*, 1, 2:219–244.

Holzner, B., and J. Marx (1979). *Knowledge Application: The Knowledge System in Society.* Boston: Allyn and Bacon.

House, E. R. (1981). "Three Perspectives on Innovation: Technological, Political, Cultural." In R. Lehming and M. Kane (eds.), *Improving Schools: Using What We Know.* Beverly Hills, Calif.: Sage.

Howard, R. A. (1966). "Decision Analysis: Applied Decision Theory." In D. B. Hertz and J. Melese (eds.), *Proceedings of the Fourth International Conference on Operations Research.* New York: Wiley.

Kelly, G. A. (1955). *Psychology of Personal Constructs.* Vols. I and II. New York: W. W. Norton.

Knorr, K. D. (1981). "Time and Context in Practical Action. On the Preconditions of Knowledge Use." Paper prepared for a Conference on Knowledge Use. University Program for the Study of Knowledge Use. University of Pittsburgh, March 18–20.

Knorr. K. D. (1977). "Policymakers' Use of Social Science Knowledge: Symbolic or Instrumental?" In C. H. Weiss (ed.), *Using Social Research in Public Policy Making.* Lexington, Ma.: Lexington.

Knott, J., and A. Wildavsky (1980). "If Dissemination Is the Solution What Is the Problem?" *Knowledge: Creation, Diffusion, Utilization*, 1, 4:515–536.

Larsen, J. (1981). "Knowledge Utilization: Current Issues." In R. Rich (ed.), *The Knowledge Cycle.* Beverly Hills, Calif.: Sage, pp. 149–167.

Larsen, J. K., *et al.* (1976). *Consultation and Its Outcome: Community Mental Health Centers.* Final report. Palo Alto, Calif.: American Institutes for Research.

Larson, R. C., and L. Berliner (1979). "On Evaluating Evaluations." Working paper. Operational Research Center. Massachusetts Institute of Technology.

Laudan, L. (1981). "Overestimating Undetermination: Caveats Concerning the Social Causes of Belief." Unpublished paper. Pittsburgh: Center for History and Philosophy of Science. University of Pittsburgh.

Laudan, L. (1977) *Progress and Its Problems: Towards a Theory of Scientific Growth.* Berkeley and Los Angeles, Calif.: University of California Press.

Lazarsfeld, P., and J. Reitz (1975). *An Introduction to Applied Sociology.* New York: Elsevier.

Lindblom, C. E. (1980). *The Policy Making Process*. Englewood Cliffs, N.J.: Prentice-Hall, Inc.

Lindblom, C. E., and D. Cohen (1979). *Usable Knowledge: Social Science and Social Problem Solving*. New Haven, Conn.: Yale University Press.

Machlup, F. (1980). *Knowledge and Knowledge Production*. Princeton, N.J.: Princeton University Press.

Machlup, F. (1979). "Uses, Values and Benefits of Knowledge." *Knowledge: Creation, Diffusion, Utilization*, 1, 1:62–81.

Machlup, F. (1962). *The Production and Distribution of Knowledge in the United States*. Princeton, N.J.: Princeton University Press.

Mason, R. O., and I. I. Mitroff (1981). "Policy Analysis as Arguments." Symposium on Social Values and Public Policy. W. N. Dunn (ed.). *Policy Studies Journal*. Special Issue. No. 2:579–584.

Merton, R. K. (1973). *The Sociology of Science*. Chicago: University of Chicago Press.

Merton, R. K. (1967). *On Theoretical Sociology*. New York: Free Press.

Merton, R. K. (1949). *Social Theory and Social Structure*. New York: Free Press.

Mills. C. W. (1959). *The Sociological Imagination*. New York: Oxford University Press.

Mitroff, I. I. (1974). *The Subjective Side of Science*. New York: Elsevier.

Mitroff, I., and D. Mitroff (1979). "Interpersonal Communication for Knowledge Utilization." *Knowledge: Creation, Diffusion, Utilization*, 1, 2:203–217.

National Institute of Education (1978). *Reflections and Recommendations*. Fourth Annual Report of the National Council on Educational Research. Washington, D.C.

Nelson, R. R., and S. G. Winter (1977). "In Search of Useful Theory of Innovation." *Research Policy*, 6(1).

Patton, M. Q. (1978). *Utilization—Focused Evaluation*. Beverly Hills, Calif.: Sage.

Poppen, P. (1978). "Social Scientists' Attempts to Influence Public Policy." *SPSSI Newsletter*, 48:10–12.

Popper, K. R. (1972). *Objective Knowledge*. Oxford: Clarendon Press.

Popper, K. R. (1961). *The Logic of Scientific Discovery*. New York: Science Editions.

Raiffa, H. (1968). *Decision Analysis*. Reading, Mass.: Addison-Wesley.

Rein, M. (1976). *Social Science and Public Policy*. Baltimore, Md.: Penguin.

Rein, M., and D. A. Schön (1977). "Problem Setting in Policy Research." In C. H. Weiss (ed.), *Using Social Research in Public Policy Making*. Lexington, Mass.: D.C. Heath.

Rein, M., and R. White (1977). "Policy Research: Belief and Doubt." *Policy Analysis*, 4, 2:239–271.

Rich, R. (ed.). *The Knowledge Cycle*. Beverly Hills, Calif.: Sage.

Rich, R. F. (1981). *The Power of Social Science Information and Policy Making*. San Francisco: Jossey-Bass.

Rich, R. F. (1979). "Editor's Introduction." *American Behavioral Scientist*, 22, 3:327–337.

Rich, R. F. (1979). "Systems of Analysis, Technology Assessment and Bureaucratic Power." *American Behavioral Scientist*, 22:393–416.

Rich, R. F. (1975). "Selective Utilization of Social Science Related Information by Federal Policymakers." *Inquiry*, 13(3).

Rich, R. F.., and N. M. Goldsmith (1981). "The Utilization of Policy Research." In S. S. Nagel (ed.), *The Encyclopedia of Policy Studies*. New York: Marcel Dekker, Inc.

Rogers, E. M. (1973). "What Are the Opportunities and Limitations in the Linking of Research with Use?" Presented at the International Conference on Making Population/Family Planning Research Useful. Honolulu.

Rogers, E. M., and F. Shoemaker (1971). *The Communication of Innovations*. New York: Free Press.

Rose, R. (1977). "Disciplined Research and

Undisciplined Problems." In C. H. Weiss (ed.), *Using Social Research in Public Policy Making.* Lexington, Mass.: D.C. Heath.

Rothman, J. (1974). *Planning and Organizing for Social Change: Action Principles from Social Science Research.* New York: Columbia University Press.

Rourke, F. (1972). *Bureaucratic Power in National Politics.* Boston: Little, Brown and Co.

Schwartz, H., and J. Jacobs (1979). *Qualitative Sociology: A Method to the Madness.* New York: Free Press.

Simon, H. A. (1976). *Administrative Behavior: A Study of Decision-Making Processes in Administrative Organization.* 3d ed. New York: Free Press.

Strasser, H. (1976). *The Normative Structure of Sociology: Conservative and Emancipatory Themes in Social Thought.* London and Boston: Routledge and K. Paul.

Straussman, J. (1978). *The Limits of Technocratic Politics.* New Brunswick, N.J.: Transaction.

Stringer, P., and D. Bannister (eds.) (1979). *Constructs of Sociality and Individuality.* London: Academic Press.

Suchman, E. (1972). "Action for What? A Critique of Evaluation Research." In C. H. Weiss (ed.), *Evaluating Action Programs.* Boston, Mass.: Allyn and Bacon.

Toulmin, S. (1972). *Human Understanding.* Princeton, N.J.: Princeton University Press.

Toulmin, S. (1959). *The Uses of Argument.* Cambridge, England: Cambridge University Press.

Toulmin, S., R. Rieke, and A. Janik (1979). *An Introduction to Reasoning.* New York: Macmillan.

Wallace, W. (1971). *The Logic of Science in Sociology.* Chicago: Aldine.

Wallace, W. (1969). *Social Theory.* Chicago: Aldine.

Watzlawick, P., J. Weakland, and R. Fisch (1974). *Change: Principles of Problem Formation and Problem Resolution.* New York: W. W. Norton.

Weiss, C. H. (ed.) (1977). *Using Social Research in Public Policy Making.* Lexington, Mass.: D.C. Heath.

Weiss, C. H. (1977). "Introduction." In C. H. Weiss (ed.), *Using Social Research in Public Policy Making.* Lexington, Mass.: D.C. Heath.

Weiss, C. H. (1976). "Research for Policy's Sake." Presented at a Symposium on Applied Sociology: Patterns and Problems. Case Western Reserve University, Cleveland, Ohio.

Weiss, C. H., and M. J. Bucuvalas (1980). "Truth Tests and Utility Tests: Decision Makers' Frames of Reference for Social Science Research." *American Sociological Review,* 45, 2:302–312.

Weiss, J. (1979). "Access to Influence: Some Effects of Policy Sector on the Use of Social Science." *American Behavioral Scientist,* 22, 3:417–436.

Whitehead, A. N., and B. Russell (1910). *Principia Mathematica.* 2d ed. Vol. I. Cambridge: Cambridge University Press.

Wildavsky, A. (1979). *Speaking Truth to Power: The Art and Craft of Policy Analysis.* Boston, Mass.: Little, Brown and Co.

Wilensky, H. (1967). *Organizational Intelligence: Knowledge and Policy in Government and Industry.* New York: Basic Books.

Willard, C. A. (1980). *A Theory of Argumentation.* Unpublished manuscript. Pittsburgh, Pa.: Department of Speech. University of Pittsburgh.

Williams, W. (1971). *Social Policy Research and Analysis: The Experience in the Federal Social Agencies.* New York: Elsevier.

Wolcott, H. F. (1977). *Teachers vs. Technocrats.* University of Oregon. Center for Educational Policy and Management.

Yin, R. K., and K. Heald (1975). "Using the Case Survey Method to Analyze Policy Studies." *Administrative Science Quarterly,* 20 (September): 371–381.

Yin et al. (1976). *A Review of Case Studies of Technological Innovations in State and Local Services.* A Report. Santa Monica, Calif.: Rand Corporation.

Zaltman, G. (1980). "Construing Knowledge Use." Presented at the Conference. The Political Realization of Social Science Knowledge. Institute for Advanced Study. Vienna, Austria: June.

Zaltman, G. (1979). "Knowledge Utilization as Planned Social Change." *Knowledge: Creation, Diffusion, Utilization*, 1, 1:82–105.

Zaltman, G. (1977). "Towards Theory of Planned Social Change: A Theory-in-Use Approach." Paper prepared for the second meeting of the network of consultants on Knowledge Transfer. Denver, Colo.: December 11–13.

Zaltman, G., K. LeMasters, and M. Heffring (1982). *Theory Construction in Marketing: Some Thoughts on Thinking*. New York: J. Wiley.

7.4 Conversational Planning

Donald A. Schön

In the course of one of his visits to MIT's Division for Study and Research in Education, Sir Geoffrey Vicker's "backroom boys" caused him to muse on the subject of dialectic. Having long since noted that practical inquiry ought not to be evaluated solely or mainly in terms of its effectiveness (for effectiveness must be measured in terms of objectives, and practical inquiry includes the appreciative processes through which objectives are formulated), Sir Geoffrey came to the idea of dialectic as he searched for an account of design, planning, and policy-making which would include both the shaping of objectives and the attempt to achieve them. In this brief essay, I shall explore his idea of dialectical inquiry in the specific context of planning.

Any such exploration ought to begin with the dominant, Instrumentalist view of practical rationality. On this view, rational practice is a form of technical problem-solving in which the inquirer begins with clear and explicit objectives and alternative means for achieving them. His problem is always one of choosing the means best suited to the achievement of intended objectives in the face of con-

straints and fixed parameters of the environment. The best solution is the decision to adopt the least-cost means most likely to achieve the objective function. Effective action implements such decisions.

Instrumentalism, whose origins go back at least as far as Aristotle, continues to dominate contemporary approaches to policy analysis, planning, program evaluation, and professional education.[1] Critics of Instrumentalism have focused attention on the difficulty of the distinction between means and ends, and on the particular stance toward inquiry which is implicit in the technical point of view. In the early decades of this century, John Dewey pointed out that the distinction between means and ends is easily confounded. What is a means in one context may be an end in another. Even in one and the same context, it may be impossible to make a clear distinction between means and ends.[2] And even when ends are clearly named

Essay in Honor of Sir Geoffrey Vickers

[1] See, for example, the writings of policy scientists such as Howard Raiffa, Frederick Mosteller, and Richard Zeckhauser; Herbert Simon's *Sciences of the Artificial* (MIT Press, 1974) and Edgar Schein's *Professional Education* (McGraw Hill, 1976).

[2] John Dewey, *Human Nature and Conduct*.

as ends, they are often problematic, vague, shifting, and mutually conflicting. In actual practice, ends are not unambiguously "given" with the problem to be solved but must be discovered or constructed in the course of inquiry. And what is true of ends is also true of means. They, too, are seldom given with the problem but must be invented and reinvented in the course of inquiry. Before we can decide whether to do this or that, we must discover what to do.

For all of these reasons, it is seldom that we are presented in actual practice with instrumental problems that are, in Herbert Simon's phrase, "well-formed."[3] Even when problems are clearly stated at the beginning of an episode of practice, they often come apart later on as problem-solving produces unintended outcomes which lead to a rethinking of suitable ends, appropriate means, constraints and fixed parameters of the environment. In short, what the inquirer usually confronts is not a problem but a problematic situation.[4] In situations that are confused, puzzling, irritating, troubling, problem-setting must precede problem-solving. But the work of problem-setting cannot be understood within the framework of Instrumentalism. We cannot evaluate problem-setting in terms of the achievement of intended objectives when it is through problem-setting that objectives are constructed. On the contrary, problem-setting is a necessary antecedent condition for instrumental inquiry.[5]

Instrumentalists have dealt in various ways with the problem of setting the problem. Some of them have spoken of the need to make an "arbitrary choice" of ends, and have referred to personal preference, aggregated social choice, politics, or the "client's decision"—all of which leave the choice of ends outside the boundaries of rational inquiry. Some of them have claimed that practical inquiry takes place within the context of a hierarchy of ends, so that the choice of any particular end can be seen as instrumental in relation to higher-order ends. But it has not seemed possible to construct a hierarchy of ends which is consensual among inquirers, or even stable in the practice of an individual inquirer. At best, such a hierarchy may be constructed, after the fact, to account for a particular episode of inquiry; once made, it is of little use in accounting for the next such episode.

Vickers has opened up a more promising approach to practical rationality with his notion of dialectic inquiry, a notion closely linked to the idea of *stance* toward inquiry. He has pointed out that on the Instrumentalist view of practical inquiry as technical problem-solving, the inquirer is seen as a spectator/manipulator. In the name of disinterested objectivity, the spectator/manipulator places himself outside the problem he seeks to solve. From this distant position, and in accordance with his objectives, he tries to analyze and control the situation. Vickers has observed, however, that we are always *in* the situation about which we inquire, whether or not we take cognizance of that fact. Constructing the reality of our situations, acting from our constructions, changing the situation through our actions, transformed by our apprehensions of the changes we have wrought, we are "agents experient."

According to this profoundly ecological view, we understand ourselves as inquirers within a larger system of entities which are both parts of our environment and agents in the environment of which we are parts. A farmer, for example, functions as a technical problem-solver insofar as he decides what crops to plant, what fertilizer to use, what methods of pest control to

[3] Herbert Simon, op. cit.

[4] John Dewey, *Logic: The Theory of Inquiry*.

[5] See Martin Rein and Donald A. Schon, "Problem-Setting in the Formation of Public Policy," in Carol Weiss, ed., *Using Social Science Research in Public Policy Making* (Heath and Company, 1979).

employ. But, along with his fellow farmers, he is a creator of problems insofar as he depletes the soil and alters the ecology of his region. Seeing himself as an agent/experient, a farmer might try to understand himself as a part of the larger problem that he also tries to solve.

With this notion of the inquirer as an ecologically embedded agent/experient, we have a way of making sense of the "side effects," "externalities," and "counterintuitive consequences" which we have learned, sometimes reluctantly, to find characteristic of practical inquiry—namely, that

—our problem-solving often gives rise unpredictably to new problems;
—we can never make a move which has only the consequences intended for it;
—when we try to solve the problems created by our solutions, we often make them worse;
—in the course of inquiry, we often discover new purposes at stake in our action which fall outside the boundaries of our original intentions;
—these purposes turn out, not infrequently, to be mutually incompatible or even inconsistent;
—when we attend to the history of efforts to achieve the purposes we now see as conflicting, we often become aware of a pattern of "hitching on" to earlier problems or of pendulum swings from one horn of a dilemma to another (for example, in the twists and turns of housing and youth corrections policies, and in the oscillations between centralization and decentralization[6]).

Such observations as these become understandable when we think of the inquirer not as a technical problem-solver

(a view which appears plausible only when we abstract a small chunk of inquiry from its context) but as an agent/experient in conversation with the situation of which he is a part. On the basis of an appreciation of his situation, the inquirer takes action, to which the situation responds by "talking back," revealing new problems, surfacing new and sometimes conflicting purposes. As in all good conversations, the backtalk is only partly predictable.[7]

On this view, it is clear that we can no longer judge the success of practical inquiry solely or primarily in terms of its effectiveness. For when we see inquiry as a conversational process in which problem-solving is interwoven with problem-setting, we see that the objectives by which we judge effectiveness are also products of inquiry. How, then, should we evaluate "conversational" inquiry? What ought we to mean by "good dialectic"?[8]

When we consider this question in the context of planning, it is complicated by the fact that planners may engage, in two senses, in a conversation with their situations. Consider, for example, a transportation planner, charged with assessing the transportation network of a city. He may see the need for a new road. As he develops proposals for the road, complete with the maps and statistics of which planners are so fond, and as the road is built, people (the "planned-for") may respond in a number of ways. These may be similar to or different from the expectations suggested by the planner's

[6] Martin Rein has discussed this point in his *Social Science and Public Policy* (Penguin Books, 1978). See also Kenneth Geiser, "Reform School Reform," Ph.D. Thesis, MIT Department of Urban Studies and Planning, 1978.

[7] "Backtalk" and "feedback" are not equivalent terms. In the latter, a message of "match" or "mismatch" of outcome to expectation is fed back to the agent. In the former, a change in the situation, produced by an earlier move, is apprehended; and that change may yield a restructuring of the problem to be solved.

[8] Chris Argyris and I have addressed the question of "good dialectic" in our study of organizational learning, *Organizational Learning* (Addison-Wesley, 1978).

origin-destination studies. As Jay Forrester has pointed out, for example, the very existence of the road may create an unexpected demand for additional travel.[9] We can think of the building of the road as the planner's move in a conversation with people in the situation, who respond with an unexpected increase in their demand for travel.

But when we recognize that people in the situation are capable of forming their own appreciations, constructing their own meanings for the planner's moves, and taking action on the basis of their appreciations and interpretations, then the planner's conversation with the situation can be understood in a more nearly literal sense. What the planner sees as "counter-intuitive consequences of action" we can understand in terms of the meanings the planned-for attach to the planner's moves—meanings that may be incongruent with the planner's intentions. The responses of the planned-for, which seem perfectly natural to them, may seem odd to the planner. The ensuing miscommunication has its parallel in the familiar miscommunications of everyday talk, and might be remedied by reciprocal reflection on the meanings constructed for the messages sent and received.

Thus the planner's moves and the responses of the planned-for may be seen, metaphorically, as a conversation. But the context of planning is one in which planners and planned-for might literally talk with one another (communicating or miscommunicating, as the case may be) concerning the meanings they have formed for their own and the other's moves. The historical unfolding of a planning sequence can be seen and analyzed, in both of these senses, as a conversation.

Edward Popko has provided a very nice example of such an analysis in his recent study of squatter settlements and sites-and-services programs in Colombia.[10] His study provides a context in which to explore the meanings of "good dialectic."

Squatter settlements are the hodge-podge accumulations of shacks and jerry-built structures which poor migrants from the countryside construct for themselves in nearly all cities of any size in the developing world. In Latin America these *invasiones*, or *favellas*, were at first regarded by the city fathers as illegal takeovers of land, criminal invasions of property, public health hazards, forms of dirt. But as often as the city fathers would attempt to clear away the shacks, the squatters would pop up somewhere else. They remained in the cities, surfacing now in one place, now in another, their numbers often augmented by new arrivals from the countryside.

From a very different point of view—one advocated by planners like John Turner[11]—the squatters had a right to land. As they constructed their own dwellings, they were demonstrating initiative and independence. Their settlements were sites for social learning. As the new settlers entered into the life of the city, they gradually improved their bamboo and tarpaper shacks, so that a walk from the outer edge of a settlement to the oldest parts of it revealed a transition to solid, elaborately constructed brick and cement structures equipped with utilities skillfully filched from the city's service system. The squatter settlements were systems in which, with minimal investment of capital, the poor could engage in self-help.

As this counter-view began to come into good currency, some public agencies launched programs of "aided self-help," offering squatter families access to materials, capital, and technical assistance. Still later, "sites-and-services" programs were

[9] Jay Forrester, *Urban Dynamics* (MIT Press, 1969).

[10] Edward Popko, *Squatter Settlements and Housing Policy*, Ph.D. Thesis, MIT Department of Urban Studies and Planning, 1980.

[11] John Turner, *Housing by People* (Pantheon, 1977).

initiated in which municipalities made available chunks of land, divided into individual parcels, graded and prepared for the construction of housing. They provided basic services such as water, sewage, roads, and electricity. Community associations were given the task of selecting settlers, allocating construction loans, and distributing building materials. Individual families would then construct their own dwellings. The municipality attempted to work with rather than against the squatters, to harness and support the squatters' initiative and skills, and to provide what the squatters were least able to provide for themselves. By the mid-seventies, most of the World Bank's housing loans to developing countries specified sites-and-services.

Popko has studied the historical sequence of housing intiatives in Colombia—squatter settlements, aided self-help, and sites-and-services. He has tried to understand how public officials understood and planned for their interventions, how settlers interpreted and responded to public actions. He found a rather systematic incongruity between, on the one hand, the intentions and assumptions of the planners and, on the other, the interpretations and responses of the settlers.

Public officials believed that settlers would purchase sites to house their own families, would build their own homes, and would need construction-oriented technical assistance. They believed the poorest of the poor would take advantage of sites-and-services programs. Popko found, on the contrary, that fully 30 percent of the settlers bought sites as investments and used structures either for commercial enterprises or for rental housing. Many settlers did not build their own housing but hired contractors to do so. When the traditional bamboo, tarpaper and polyethylene had been cheap and readily available, settlers had found it economic to build their own shacks. But when these materials became scarce, the

settlers turned to bricks and concrete, which they considered too expensive to use in amateur self-help. They chose, instead, to rely on professional contractors. (Nor did they do this because they valued their time more highly in income-producing jobs than in self-help construction; often they remained on the site while the work was going on, to make sure that the contractors refrained from stealing materials.)

The Colombian planners were disappointed with their sites-and-services projects because they did not produce the expected results. Not only did settlers often use the projects as sources of income rather than as housing for themselves, they often bypassed sites-and-services projects altogether and went instead to unserviced pirate *barrios*, new squatter settlements which had sprung up at the edge of the town. But Popko believes this had a great deal to do with the way in which the planners had laid out the parcels of land. Most of the prepared lots were small, suited to the needs of an individual family. But settlers who had rental housing in mind tended to prefer the large lots they could find (unserviced) in the new invasion *barrios*.

The planners found that many of the users of sites-and-services projects were not members of the lowest-income group, but were among the more affluent poor. In Popko's view, it was precisely this group which had the enterprise, the knowledge, and the resources to develop the sites as sources of additional family income. These people were investors, even though they had very little capital to invest, and they tended to behave as economic men. They even set rent levels very much as prevailing techniques of time-preference analysis would suggest they ought to do. It made economic sense for them to prefer larger to smaller lots, to hire contractors rather than to engage in self-help. Like prudent investors, they wanted to minimize the risks of construction; they had no need of the technical assistance offered by the public agencies.

Popko recommends, in his conclusions, that housing planners in Colombia ought to learn from these findings to rethink their target groups, their strategies for site selection and layout, and their criteria for construction loans and technical assistance. But the evidence suggests that the Colombian planners, discouraged with project performance, have decided to discontinue sites-and-services programs. They seem to be returning to the principle of fully built housing.

Popko's story of the Colombian experience suggests a conversation of planners and planned-for in which both parties constructed different and incongruent meanings for one another's utterances and were unaware that they did so. Each party acted on the basis of his own understanding, to the surprise and puzzlement of the other. The planners' disappointment with project outcomes stemmed from their misunderstanding of the project's changing environment and of the meanings the project had for its intended beneficiaries. The settlers, self-selected from among the urban poor, saw the project as an opportunity for investment, and acted accordingly.

What would it mean for such a conversation to become a good dialectic? Clearly not that the planners would achieve their initial purposes. On the contrary, a principal lesson of the sites-and-services experience seems to be that the initial project goals were ill-conceived. What then? I suggest that in a good dialectic the planners would reflect on their conversation with the planned-for. They would literally talk with the settlers in the attempt to discover and test the meanings their moves had for the settlers. And they would restructure both their goals and their strategies of action to accommodate their new understandings.

Such a reflective conversation would depend on a number of conditions, of which these are some of the more important:

1. It would be necessary to remember the sequence of events which make up the story of the conversation. There would need to be an institutionalized memory capable of surviving the turnover of project personnel—here, a memory of the sequence of squatter settlements, aided in self-help and sites-and-services programs, of the intentions and assumptions underlying them, and of the responses to them. As the planners attempted to make sense of their present situation and design their next moves, they would need to take account of their history.

2. It would be necessary to recognize that the meaning of the situation, and the actions taken in it, may vary greatly from one party to another. Such awareness would have to be accompanied by an inclination to inquire into the other's meanings and by skill in doing so. As everyone knows who has ever gotten stuck in a circle of miscommunication, it is no easy matter to get unstuck. Miscommunication tends to be one of those problems we make worse in the attempt to solve it. Indeed, effectiveness in listening for and testing others' meanings often requires a set of values, strategies, and assumptions very different from those normally brought to conversation.[12]

3. In the context of such a search for understanding, planners would need to be aware that the planned-for may be in some respects quite different from, and in some respects quite similar to, themselves. Squatters living on the thin edge of survival may nevertheless be economic men able to calculate the best ways of using their capital.

[12] Chris Argyris and I have written about these skills, which we describe in terms of interpersonal theories-in-use, in *Theory in Practice* (Jossey-Bass, 1974).

4. Planners would need to be attentive to changes in the context which might falsify assumptions previously valid. A change in the market for building materials can make the difference between economically rational and economically irrational self-help.
5. Planners would need to cultivate a habit of attending to the ways in which their own values and purposes may conflict with one another—a nose for dilemmas. Those families best able to manage the building of their own dwellings, for example, may not be those most in need of shelter. A reflective conversation with the planned-for is likely to surface such dilemmas and to call for inquiry into the reframing of conflicting values.

When planners become participants in a reflective conversation with the planned-for, they become more vulnerable to learning from the previously counterintuitive consequences of their own (and their predecessors') interventions. They are more likely to become aware of the need to restructure the theories underlying their earlier moves. They are more likely to recognize dilemmas which demand reframing or choice. They are more likely to become aware of ways in which their interests may conflict with the interests of their intended beneficiaries (the more reliably we communicate with others, the more clearly we may perceive our disagreements!); and such conflicts of interest will require negotiation and/or joint inquiry. Finally, the planners are likely to discover that they must manage the paradoxical task of committing now to policies and values which will have to be restructured as the conversation unfolds.

In all of these respects, planners will be including in their inquiry the shaping of objectives, the setting of problems, which the Instrumentalist view of practical rationality ignores.

7.5 Perspectives of the Systems Approach

C. West Churchman

My apologies for the particular style of this paper, but I've found that the usual expository method is becoming (for me) more and more ineffective. The difficulty lies in what I perceive to be a very deep lack of communication about the so-called systems approach. There are radically different opinions about how men should try to understand social systems, but the arguments usually proceed at the superfi-

This research was supported in part by the National Aeronautics and Space Administration under General Grant #NGL 05-003-404 under the University of California. (Reprinted from *Interfaces* August 1974. Vol. 4, No. 4)

cial level. The humanist cries out that we shouldn't try to quantify everything. To the systems analyst this complaint is altogether irrelevant, because of course he isn't trying to quantify everything, since at best such an effort is hopeless. From his point of view, the humanist's complaint amounts to trying to formulate all problems in a ridiculously vague way to justify the humanist's inability to reason precisely. So each side talks and neither listens. To the systems analyst models do provide a reasonable way of describing reality, whereas to the humanist they do not. But *why* each feels this way is rarely explained by either. I've never heard anyone who works with models explain why they are reasonable approaches to reality, although common sense would seem to argue that anyone who approaches society systematically would have to defend his own inquiring system. But then a very peculiar thing about many systems analysts is that they do not consciously include themselves in the system being studied.

One of the difficulties is that in the usual expository paper the issues are not presented dramatically enough. And it's not easy to find the dramatic format for stating them. Recently I was chairing a conference which was discussing the design of an international ecological university. It was clear that there were two opposing points of view about the systems approach to ecological problems, but after each remark by one of the participants, a person on the other side would say "we don't disagree at all," and proceed to deliver a short speech to establish the agreement. This was thoroughly frustrating, like a dream in which you are trying to go deeper in the water, but something keeps pushing you back to the surface. Finally, I got my dramatic clue for stopping the agreement-game. We were talking about the need for an interdisciplinary or even "transdisciplinary" approach to ecology. One side was talking about how to put the physical, biological and social "together" for more effective solutions to problems of pollution. The other side was objecting that pollution is not a physical, or biological, or social problem, to which the first side kept responding that they agreed, and hence the need to merge the disciplines. Finally, I saw my chance. "What the other side is saying," I said to the first side, "is that there is no such thing as the 'biological' aspect, or the 'economic' aspect of a social problem; problems should not be broken into disciplinary segments and then solved by a blender operation. To do so is to destroy the essential meaning of the problem." At

least this statement stopped the agreement-game. It had never occurred to the first side that there was any other way to look at social problems except through the spectacles of one or more disciplines. *They* thought their innovation was the invention of a multidisciplinarian pair of spectacles, whereas their opponents were objecting to the raw materials out of which the spectacles were to be made.

I don't know whether the other side really believed that there is no "economic aspect" of a social problem, because they all grew up in the disciplines and could hardly escape their bondage to tradition. At most they were expressing a hope that in the new university there would be a withering away of respect for the disciplines as such, so that the new generation of students wouldn't see themselves as economists, biologists, and the like. But the hope of this side of the debate did create a dramatic shock that stopped the debilitating agreement-game. Drama does not thrive on unblemished reasonableness: tragedy is disturbingly unreasonable. When one of the participants exclaimed, "You mean to tell me that there is no biological aspect of the pollution problem," his exclamation implied "what an unreasonable belief!" but it also indicated that for the first time he had come to realize that his own reasonable world view could be wrong.

So I'm going to take the very risky course of dramatizing the debate about the systems approach. This will be a conversation between three characters who find themselves together in a highly dramatic situation. They are sitting in the lounge of a Boeing 747 which is now bound for Cuba, having just been hijacked off its expected journey to New York. It is the hijacker's intention to keep some of the passengers as hostages. The characters are first a Mr. Action, who is a very busy and successful executive, formerly on his way to several very important and critical meetings in New York, but now, in good managerial style, stoically waiting out the situation. The second is Mr. C. S. Temm, a very well-known systems expert, who has astutely taken this golden opportunity to sell Mr. Action on the importance of the (Mr. Temm's) systems approach to his (Mr. Action's) problems. As in all good approaches to systems by systems experts, there will be no mention of contracts or money at this stage. But Mr. Temm's opportunity is threatened by the third character, who in gadfly fashion is constantly buzzing around the smooth flow of Temm's remarks. He is Mr. S. R. Teez, known to his friends as "Sock Rat," a not so well-known professor of philosophy, of morals and metaphysics, who is intensely interested in approaches like Temm's to social and ethical problems. There is also a fourth but largely silent character who from time to time comments on the conversation with four-letter expletives; but he is clearly in the process of getting drunk and his judgments are therefore thoroughly unsound.

Mr. Temm has been explaining to Mr. Action the clear need to perceive social problems in the context of many interacting sectors. "The correct systems approach," he says, "is analogous to the design of a machine. There is no such thing as *the* perfect wheel, or cog, or connection; the excellence of any of these 'sectors' of the machine depends on how they are interlinked."

"It also depends," says Mr. Action, "on the people involved. That's where you systems people go wrong. You assume that an organization is just a lot of cogs and wheels, whereas any successful manager realizes that his main role is leadership, helping people in the organization to do the right job at the right time."

"I agree with you wholeheartedly," Temm rushes in to say. "Of course organizations are not merely machines. We use the machine analogy to help explain the need to model interconnections of sectors. But we do try to measure personal qualities as well, so that we can get an accurate description of each sector."

At this point Mr. Teez bounces in. "I've been wondering," he says, "about the ontological status of this thing you systems analysts call a 'problem.' " As his listeners stare at him blankly, he hurries on to explain, "What I mean is, how do you know that a problem really exists? How do you know there are problems, like you know, for example, that there are chairs and tables?"

Mr. Action mutters "Good God!" Mr. Temm for once is completely silenced, while the fourth character mutters his first expletive.

"Well look," says Teez to Action. "You were on your way to New York to attend some meetings where you expected to consider and solve some problems. Hence you've sacrificed some of your valuable time because you believe these problems really exist. Now why? Why do you believe this?"

"My God," says Action, anxious to get the agenda of the conversation changed as quickly as possible. "What kind of a question is that? I'll tell you why I'm going—was going—to New York. They've got a strike of garbage men on their hands, and I'm going—was going—to help them settle it as quickly as possible. If you'd been walking around New York and smelt and seen those piles—and then claimed they had no problem!"

Temm sees his chance to score: "I agree that the strike is a symptom of a problem, just as a sore throat is a symptom of a disease. But the real problem is much deeper, and perhaps settling the strike as quickly as possible isn't the right answer. We ought also to consider how the sanitation sector is linked to other sectors of the City."

Action is about to reply, but Teez is a professor and knows how to handle his class. "So," says the professor, "Action here believes that problems exist because there is a mess which anyone can see, and

Temm believes that prolems exist if we can conceptualize them in a certain way. 'Esse est percipi' or 'Esse est cognosci' are the Latin versions, I believe. But I still don't understand. Here we are in a mess, on our way to Cuba perhaps to be held hostages. But I personally don't feel that a problem exists, because there is nothing I can conceivably do about it. So Action means that the problem of garbage exists because he with others can solve it. But this reasoning doesn't help because it lands us in another question just as difficult as the first, namely, how do we know that a solution exists? And I don't see Temm's idea either. Surely people have problems even though they don't think about them or think about them well.''

Action and Temm are both ready to bounce in, but Action, the leader, makes it by a split second. ''I don't understand all this abstract stuff,'' says Action. ''Temm here is bad enough with all his sectors that he wants to consider while the city rots in its sewage. But you want us to sit back and contemplate nirvana amid the rosy smell of garbage. Christ, there's only one practical way to handle a mess like this, and that's to go to the source of the trouble and remove it. It's like—'' and here Action slips for a moment on the slippery surface of the abstract—''it's like surgery. That's it! When your appendix ruptures, the doctor opens you up and removes it. That's what a solution is: finding the source of the trouble and removing it! By God, that's a good one! I never thought of it that way, but that's right!'' Like anyone who lives his reality in the concrete, Action is really pleased with this refreshing slide into the abstract. He's already got the theme of his next speech before the Conference Board, because this idea of a solution's being the removal of the trouble can be repeated a dozen times, each time sounding like a new idea. And it fits into Action's basic idea of the importance of leadership, too.

He's gone into a kind of reverie, and scarcely hears Temm's monologue.

''Surgery *is* a good example,'' says Temm, ''because a surgeon would be negligent if he operated without first checking on the patients' general condition, his blood pressure, heart, and the like. I'm not denying the urgency of problems like garbage or ruptured appendixes. Actually, systems science recognizes the degree of urgency as an important aspect of a solution. Thus we who practice the art recognize the need to distinguish between a one-day, one-week, one-year 'solution.' In the shorter time solutions, we obviously can't build elaborate models and collect accurate data. But the methodological principles remain the same. I'm saying for example that if you decide to stop the garbage strike by some sort of a compromise on wages and fringe benefits, then, no matter how short the time you ought to consider how this decision will affect other sectors of the city, policemen's wages, for example, because all 'solutions' are simply part of a feed-back loop.''

''This,'' thinks Temm to himself, ''is really the best shot I've had. I've really shown Action how he fits into the broader picture of things. We need his leadership to implement the results of systems science, but the really basic need is for a comprehensive grasp of the relevant features of the system.'' But Action has heard very little of Temm's remarks, because he's marveling at the glory of the phrase ''leadership grasps the root of the problem, and tears it out like a common weed.''

Teez sees that his class has gone to sleep on him, each dreaming about his own admirable properties. So he has to try to jolt them.

''You know what may be the real truth after all? A problem is something you personally can do something about, and a solution is something that pleases you to do about it. Problem and solution are forms of self-gratification, that's all. Action here is gratified when he leads. So he creates or searches around for situations where he can exert his leadership. When he finds such a situation, it becomes a 'problem' for him, and his leadership behavior is the 'solution.' Temm is gratified when he can build a model or conceptualize all of a problem in terms of interacting sectors. So he creates or searches around for situations which he can model, and when he finds one it becomes a 'problem,' and his model is a 'solution.' "

Teez, a normally timid man, realizes he never would make such a remark back on the campus, primarily because he doesn't really believe it, secondarily because it is (to him) a rude frontal attack. He doesn't believe it, because he hates the philosophy of relativism with a passion; it's the most simpleminded cop-out he can imagine, to say that a solution depends on the person. Action and Temm are both very complicated systems, and it's thoroughly misleading to regard them as simple entities who are "gratified"; this smacks of the very worst of "aspiration level" psychology or economic utility theory which so naively assume that human beings are single-minded aspirers or wanters. But here he is, 35,000 feet up in the air going God knows where, and so live dangerously, say shocking things.

Teez doesn't believe in his remarks, dispassionately, but his companions—including the drunk—disbelieve in anger.

"This hogwash is what we pour our taxes into higher education for," trembles Action in rage. "I'd just like to see you do a decent day's work sometime, and then come blubbering around about your home-made abstractions."

Temm is more reasonable though fed up. "I don't get you at all, Teez. You sound like a sophomore philosophy student. I always thought that philosophers were seeking for the Good and the True, and so am I. Plato in his *Republic* tried to put all the sectors together in a reasonable way. He was seriously wrong and of course technically handicapped (he had no knowledge of differential equations, for example). But I always thought philosophers respected his basic ideal of rational planning, which we're still struggling to improve on. Plato was wrong in thinking that 'solution' means one final 'best' city state, because we recognize that 'problem-solution' is an ongoing process, a learning or adaptive process which is basically justified in terms of human ideals like resources, education-health, cooperation. I think philosophy can play an important role—and" (looking at Action) "deserves some bite of the tax money. But you seem to be making hash out of sincerity."

"I know what you mean," says Teez contritely, talking now mainly to Temm. "But I was forced to take the backward step I did to remind us of another human quality besides the rational, namely, humility. I don't like relativism any more than you do, but I think we have to keep passing through its perspective of reality to gain a richer insight. I admire your and Action's perspectives of social reality, but they're not the only ones. To me the eye-opener of the Third World Movement is that a black person—say—can recognize that he has a perspective of social reality that is different from yours but just as refined, just as educated, just as justified."

"I appreciate the wish of the black man to assume an equal role in our society," says Action, who has become a bit calmer, "but what is required is leadership, and I don't mean white leadership either. We—the white men—have to help the black community to develop their own leadership. Without it, the black man will continue to flounder."

"I agree with you that leadership is essential," concedes Temm, "but leadership is simply the action part of thought. Uncontrolled leadership, as we saw in Nazism of the 1930s, can be as dangerous as floundering."

"You've got it the wrong way round," says Action. "Of course thought and reason are important aspects of good leadership, just as much as a good sense of where the trouble is and how to root it out is. I use talents like yours, Temm, in our organization all the time: economists, personnel experts, the whole bunch. But useful as these guys are, they're not the ones who decide on policy, on funding, on how things go. They're the staff of the central command.''

By this time Temm realizes that Action has not been listening at all, and that this was no time for a sales pitch anyway. So, like Teez earlier, he decides on the frontal attack: ''I'd be happy to concede that leadership is important if it weren't that leadership has landed the world in such a mess: into tragic wars, starvation, pollution, hopelessly inadequate education, and on and on. The shocking state of so-called criminal justice is a pure case of leadership into social immorality, all because the leaders decide that the only cure for crime is incarceration. It's like believing the only cure for a common cold is to cut off the nose. The nose is the root of the problem of the cold, so root it out!'' he jeers.

Action has become quite red in the face again, but is speechless for the moment. If he'd had one of his staff along, he would have been advised to stay out of this debate altogether; you can't win in the battle of pedantic words.

But Teez has been thinking, which, to the good Hegelian philosopher he is, means searching for a synthesis. ''I think I see a new perspective of the systems approach,'' he says. ''What both of you have been struggling to do is to subsume the other into your own world view. Action wants to make Temm's modeling an essential part of the total leadership function, so that he can 'swallow' Temm into his larger world view. Temm wants to make Action's leadership an essential sector of the total system, so that he too can 'swallow' Action into *his* larger world view. The black man sees both Action's leadership and Temm's models as the white man's subtle form of racism, so that he 'swallows' both of you into *his* larger world view. Now the hated relativist wants to stop here, and tell us that there can be no true perspective of society. No matter what information or evidence is brought forward, Action can always show that it 'proves' his idea of the fundamental importance of leadership, just as Temm can 'prove' that the evidence supports the need for comprehensive modeling. The old pragmatists tried to go beyond relativism by suggesting 'experimentation.' They were wrong if they meant that an experiment decides between two or more hypotheses, because as I say, no data ever will ever destroy a viable picture of social reality. But experiments can help us develop our world views in greater and greater depth and significance. So this may be the synthesis: the systems approach means enabling every man to appreciate as fully as possible his own view of social reality by listening seriously to other views. This is where our explorations should begin. But what is happening? The plane seems to be banking in a steep turn!''

At this point the pilot announces that the hijackers have ordered them to New York to dump the passengers.

''But why?'' cry all the debaters in unison.

''Because,'' says the fourth man, in a somewhat slurred voice, ''I'm one of the hijackers. At first we figured to rob the U.S.A. of some of its high-powered talent. But after listening to the lot of you, it's obvious you'll do harm wherever you are with your constant talk, talk, talk! So we're taking you home. Revolution is the only way the oppressed people can win, and revolution will win while you're all busy debating world views.''

''Oh dear,'' murmurs Teez as the hijacker disappears.

''Don't worry,'' says the stewardess.

"He was really quite drunk. But then he had a point, you know. After all, none of you men ever once included a woman in your so elegant and comprehensive systems."

7.6 Foundations for a Radical Concept of Planning

Stephen Grabow　　　　　　　Allan Heskin

Not only the goals of planning, but its internal structure as well needs changing. At present, it perpetuates elitist, centralizing, and change-resistant tendencies. A new paradigm rising to challenge the "rational-comprehensive" model of modern planning is based on systems change and the realization of a decentralized communal society that facilitates human development in the context of an ecological ethic by evolutionary social experimentation. Planning in the radical sense is the facilitation of this change through a dialectical synthesis of rational action and spontaneity. . . .

Modern Planning

At the core of modern planning, of our only existing concept of planning, is the "rational-comprehensive" model: the establishment of an objectively defined set of goals; the statement of all possible alternate courses of action to attain these goals; the evaluation of those courses of action in terms of their efficiency; the selection of that alternative which most nearly optimizes the set of goals; and

Reprinted by permission of the *Journal of the American Institute of Planners*, Vol. 39, No. 2, March 1973.
　　Footnotes in edited portions of this paper have been deleted and remaining footnotes renumbered.

finally, the assessment of that action, once implemented, in terms of its actual effects upon the overall structure.

While many planners follow this structure and even try to extend its applications[1] it is well known that the rational-comprehensive model itself is an unattainable "ideal" (Bolan, 1967). Nevertheless, almost all current theory is an attempt to modify the model in order to cope with both "political reality" and the perceived limits of human rationality.[2] These attempts do not change its internal structure at all because they do not question the fundamental assumptions upon which it is based.

The distinctive feature of the rational-comprehensive model, in its original and "modified" forms, assumes knowing in advance the probable outcome of any course of social action (that is, it is predictive). Both modern planning and its technique—the rational-comprehensive model—exist within the context of objec-

[1] For example, see articles in May 1965 issue of the *Journal of the American Institute of Planners*.

[2] For example, some well-known modifications include: describing the structure to be nonlinear; correlating action with governmental policy formulation; encouraging "citizen participation" in the formulation of goals; and integrating "intelligence systems" and computer-aided techniques within the process of generating and assessing alternate courses of action. See also: "Bounded Rationality" in Herbert Simon (1957); Charles Lindblom (1959); and Amitai Etzioni (1967).

tive consciousness: "a state of consciousness cleansed of all subjective distortion (and) all personal involvement." (Roszak, 1969: 208). The predictive nature of the rational-comprehensive model calls for this objective state of mind, one which evaluates alternative futures by objective means. This objectivity, this attempt at being rationally comprehensive, is at the heart of our critique of modern planning.

Critique Of Modern Planning

Modern planning, objective planning, has elitist, centralizing, and change-resistant tendencies.

1. Modern planning is elitist in that it sets the ostensible "planner", the rationally comprehensive advisor, apart from the world he or she is to "plan." It sets up what Theodore Roszak calls an "invidious hierarchy":

> As soon as two human beings relate in detachment as observer to be observed, as soon as the observer claims to be aware of nothing more than the behavioral surface of the observed, an invidious hierarchy is established which reduces the observed to a lower status. (1969: 222).

In *I and Thou*, Martin Buber captured this critique in his distinction between *using* the world ("I-It") and *relating* to the world ("I-Thou"). Planning as it exists today calls only for the use or manipulation of others, of nature, of the world; it foregoes a meaningful relationship *with* the world.

2. Modern planning is centralizing. The outcome of the attempt to know in advance results in preordained behaviorism or self-fulfilling prophecy, whether consciously—as the philosopher Herbert Marcuse (1969) would have us believe—or unconsciously—as the psychoanalyst Erich Fromm (1967) would have us believe. Modern planning,

planning in the objective, manipulative sense, requires the monitoring and control of all observed activity. This type of control necessitates centralized authority. Again, Roszak provides us with an explanation:

> . . . the social environment—the body politic—must be brought as completely under centralized, deliberate control as the physical body has been brought under the domination of the cerebrum. Unless the order of things is readily apparent to a command and control center—in the individual, it is the forebrain; in society, it will be the technocracy—and available for manipulation, it cannot be respected as order at all. (1969: 226).

3. Modern planning is change-resistant. The final result of the attempt to know in advance, to control outcome, is the eventual elimination of all but preprogramed social change. Unpredictable change is uncontrollable and is considered synonymous with undesirable change. All attempts are made to suppress it. But history has taught us that significant change is always unique, unpredictable and unrepeatable: change is an open-ended creative process; in the rational-comprehensive model, it is precisely the creative sources of social change that are not and cannot be taken into account (Dunn, 1971: 125).[3]

Perceptions of Duality

From this critique of modern planning, several dichotomies suggest themselves: elitism versus anarchy, manipulating ver-

---

[3] While Dunn and others have been able to get at the core of modern planning in their critique of its internal inconsistencies and malfunctioning, our critique goes further: we maintain that, even if modern planning *could* work on its own terms, it is incompatible with human freedom. For a convincing discussion of why planning *can't* work as it is presently conceived, see Dunn (1971); and Hasam Ozbekhan (1969:47–155).

sus relating, centralization versus decentralization, control versus chaos, programing versus creativity, objectivity versus subjectivity, and rationality versus irrationality. In the original debate over planning, these or similar dichotomized issues were presented. In 1959, John Friedmann stated that this debate was now closed:

> We no longer ask: Is planning possible? Can planning be reconciled with a democratic ideology? But: How may existing planning practice be improved? The problem of planning has become a problem of procedure and method. (1959)

From our perspective, Friedmann spoke too soon. In the crisis of the 1960's the debate has been reopened.[4] There are today two principal methods for resolving this new debate, most simply stated as the dichotomy between planned action and spontaneity. These two methods grow out of different perceptions of duality: dominance and balance. A third view, dialectic, constitutes the foundation for a more radical perception of duality than either of these two. . . . [The] . . . third view, *dialectic*, sees the entities not as related opposites but as components of the same thing—only their immediate context causes them to appear contradictory. The dialectic acknowledges an unbearable tension, an incongruity in the context of presently perceived reality, and gives rise to forces which are wholly at odds with existence as we know it to be. It aspires to go beyond our present notions of "reality," redefining the meaning of existence in such a way that the contradictions between the specific instances of the duality disappear; everything is seen as a manifestation of the same thing. The process by which this transcendent state is attained is synthesis.[5] It is our intention in this essay to attempt that synthesis.

[4] It should be noted that Friedmann himself is in the forefront of this new debate. See this development in Friedmann (1959), (1966) and (1973).

[5] For a particularly vivid visual impression of

The New Paradigm

This synthesis, which constitutes the foundation for a radical concept of planning, is part and parcel of the emerging pattern of our time. We presently live under a world view consisting of the maintenance of a mass technocratic society governed by the myth of an objective consciousness, through the demands of the rational-comprehensive model, with emphasis on an accommodating economic growth. The paradigm rising to challenge this present concept of reality is based on *systems change and the realization of a decentralized communal society which facilitates human development by fostering an appreciation of an ecological ethic based on the evolutionary process: spontaneity and experimentation.*

Systems Change

The new paradigm recognizes the fragile nature of the present view of reality. It recognizes that when anomaly arises to seriously question the efficacy of the dominant world view, societies seek a new world view, a new reality, which deals with the anomaly and ends the crisis.[6] It

dialectical synthesis, see M. C. Escher (1971), especially his woodcut "Dag en Nacht," p. 11.

[6] See Thomas Kuhn's description of the rise and fall of scientific paradigms in his *The Structure of Scientific Revolutions* (1962). He traces the emergence and inevitable disintegration of competing explanations of the perceived universe: the competition for attention among alternate views; the arrival of consensus upon one view; the articulation and extension of that view to cover all perceptions of reality; the emergence of a phenomenon which calls the view into question; and the crisis in which alternate views again compete for attention to resolve the anomaly. It is by calling into question the principles of validation by which consensus comes about, as well as articulating the inevitability of the cycle, that Kuhn effects a profound loss of innocence.

also recognizes that societies to date have not looked upon this process of "paradigm shift" as being existential in nature and in the interest of human development: such change has been resisted. We believe that there is sufficient anomaly to demand revolutionary change. We further believe that the new paradigm must itself recognize the process of paradigm shift as a good and necessary component in the human learning process. Only in this way can society serve the *present* needs of both individuals and the world based on an understanding of the past and an open future.

The Decentralized Society

Decentralization is necessary to reduce the scale of joint activity. Mass society is alienating—its byword is efficiency. The byword of efficiency is control. If people are to be free—not, in the words of C. Wright Mills (1959), just "cheerful robots"—they must be free to form their own unity with the world. As Erwin Gutkind has said:

> Where is the firm basis on which we can build a new social structure? There are only two starting points—the individual human being and the unity of the world. Everything in between is of doubtful value. . . . artificial, a man-made incident of history—leaders, States, frontiers. All the abstract concepts attached to them are obstacles to the emergence of man into the full light of self-respectability and independence, of world consciousness and intimate social contact. (1953:20–21)

From this basis, society must be reorganized so that the maximum number of decisions possible can be within the effective reach of as many people as possible. Decisions affecting the mass can be made with the consent of the mass by

temporary organizations[7] called together by the mass: in our view organizational continuity is the first step to tyranny.

The collective is the primary organized unit of this society. The Canyon Collective speaks to the oft-asked question of the desirable size and organizing principle of these decentralized units:

> Size is a question of politics and social relations, not administration. The collective should not be bigger than a band. The basic idea is to reproduce the collective, not expand it. The strength of the collective lies in its social organization, not its numbers. The difference between expansion and reproduction is the difference between adding and multiplying; the first bases its strength on numbers and the second on relationships between people. (Canyon Collective, 1970: 9)

Decentralization is ecologically sound: complex, diversified organisms survive; specialized organisms perish.[8] The tendency of mass society is to cause the grouping of fewer and fewer units (that is, metropolitan centers) and by the weight of its very size prevent flexibility and demand conformity. However, the evolutionary future of human beings is bound up with the ability of their social organizations to cope with an ever-changing environment. Civilizations survive or perish in accord with this ability. Innovation and experimentation in social organization is therefore necessary for human development. Mass society inhibits social experimentation. The City—the locus of mass society—having served its purpose in the evolution of the demand for change, is no longer useful in its present form and only inhibits further evolution.[9]

[7] For a complete presentation of this idea, see Warren Bennis and Philip Slater (1968).

[8] See especially Peter Kropotkin's presentation of the ecological basis of decentralization in his *Mutual Aid*.

[9] For a more complete presentation of this idea, by an urban historian, see Erwin Gutkind, *The Twilight of Cities* (1952), and his *The Expanding Environment* (1953).

The Communal Society

The decentralized society is communal. By communal we mean socialist and "utopian": the organization of society and the division of labor to the advantage of all.[10] Our present society also professes this ideal. It promises that this ideal society will be achieved through competition. In recent years, a partial "balance" between the notions of competition and cooperation has been sought under the title of the "Welfare State." Its promise, however, has not been kept.[11]

In the dialectics of competition and cooperation, competition is seen as the frustration of cooperation. Our present society, then, is seen as artificially creating and nurturing this frustration to encourage competition (Slater, 1970). The denial of the material benefits of society by virtue of sex, race, or class; the exploitation and the accumulation of capital by some while others are forced to do alienating labor; the measuring of progress, achievement, and success in terms of power—all are manifestations of this artificial frustration that festers like a sore in our humanity.

Human conflict and struggle are, of course, inevitable as part of the "pain of being human" (Marcuse, 1969). They may even be psychologically necessary for human development (Maslow, 1968). But, the communal society does not nurture and enlarge this conflict. It rather is a society in which the struggles of human beings are devoted to resolving conflict between man and himself, man and man, and man and nature, to attaining symbiosis: living together for the mutual benefit of all. Most of all, a communal society is not a society which finds the value of togetherness only in a fight against an external and terrifying "them" (Laing, 1967: 91–94). . . .

The Facilitation of Human Development

Human development consists of social and economic development and should be contrasted to the present emphasis on economic growth. As René Dubos notes, "All societies influenced by western civilization are at present committed to the gospel of growth" (1968: 191). This desire for growth, sold to the people by the promise of economic well-being, has proven a hollow victory: the emphasis on economic growth has resulted in the alienation of individuals from themselves and from each other—as Marx claimed,[12] and from their environment—as Dubos claims (1968: 191–193).

Combining the ideas of both Marx and Dubos, we perceive that society must look not only to the attainment of a minimum *quality* of life but to the setting of a maximum quantity as well. If indeed the phenomenological world is finite, then setting the maximum has taken on the importance of attaining the minimum.

A major factor in the acceptance of the growth drive is the western concept of death. The fear of death and the concomitant desire for "extended" life has placed an almost unbearable pressure on the world.[13] It is ironic that the drive for extended life should result in so much death.

We accept a view of humanity which includes a desire for disequilibrium as well as a desire for equilibrium: in other words, individuals desire to risk their lives as well

---

[10] Buber describes such a society in *Paths in Utopia* (1968: 14, 80).

[11] See Michael Harrington's *The Other America*, the Report of the Kerner Commission, or the Pentagon Papers.

[12] See, for example, "The Meaning of Human Requirement," Karl Marx, *Economic and Philosophic Manuscripts of 1884* (1964).

[13] See, for example, Norman O. Brown, *Life against Death* (1959), especially pp. 105–109.

as to survive,[14] as Albert Camus has tried to tell us in many ways.[15] The present dominance in our society of the survival drive—sublimated into the drive for status—over the risk-taking drive may mean more than an "escape from freedom." It may mean the end of survival. The attainment of maximum equilibrium and minimum disequilibrium may mean total disequilibrium. Some level of economic well-being is necessary for people to exercise choice between survival and risk, but once attained, continued economic growth seems only to prevent further development of the individual.

The Context of an Ecological Ethic

The ecological ethic is simply stated as the merging of the development of the individual with the unity of the world.[16] While many writers have described it in part, it is not a wholly intellectual concept. Because of this, no one person, or group of persons, can realistically claim a special relationship to it. Each of us is born with knowledge of it.[17] Societies to date have mutilated that knowledge and have not allowed it to mature. Carl Rogers describes this knowledge as an "organismic value system,"[18] and Abraham Maslow describes

the mature state as self-actualization.[19] Martin Buber describes it as an "I-Thou" relationship with all that surrounds the individual—whether "thou" be a person, a cat, or a tree.[20] He also noted the difficulty one encounters in attempting a full description: as one approaches the true relationship, words fail, concepts disintegrate. Its totality is more than we have learned to rationally communicate. The science of Loren Eisley approaches that description but only metaphorically.[21] In the evolution of human consciousness, it appears as a merging of the unconscious, the self-conscious, and the object-conscious parts of the individual psyche.[22] Marx referred to it as the "species essence."

The ethic is being increasingly restated in many ways and in many forms. It encompasses the ecology "movement" itself as well as the themes of peace, love, and freedom. It is expressed in a growing awareness and interest in eastern theology and philosophy, such as described in the work of Alan Watts (1968). It finds expression in a striving for higher "syn-

---

[14] See, for example, Edgar Dunn (1971: 177–180).

[15] The existentialism of this quality is described in Albert Camus, *The Stranger* (1946) and *The Rebel* (1956).

[16] For the only comprehensive presentation of this concept in the West, see Pierre Teilhard de Chardin, *The Phenomenon of Man* (1965). The introduction by Julian Huxley is an essential part of the presentation.

[17] Trigant Burrow speaks of this as the "pre-conscious foundations of human experience" in this book of the same title (1964).

[18] See, for example, Carl Rogers, *Person to Person: The Problem of Being Human* (1967).

[19] See, for example, Abraham Maslow, *Toward a Psychology of Being* (1968).

[20] See, for example, Martin Buber, *I and Thou*. In this translation by Walter Kauffman, the word "you" is preferred to the archaic "thou" by which Buber really meant "HE is here now"—an essentially mystical translation.

[21] See, for example, Loren Eisley, *The Immense Journey* (1956).

[22] This is based on a "triad" theory, with modified correspondence to Jung's concept of the "collective unconscious," "the personal conscious," and the "personal unconscious." This is outlined in his "The Structure and Dynamics of the Psyche" (1927/1941) in vol. 8 of the collected works. See Carl G. Jung, *Memories, Dreams and Reflections*, edited and recorded by Aniella Jaffe (1961), especially pp. 324–326. This integration of the parts of the psyche paves the way for more possibilities of consciousness, what Maslow has called: ". . . transpersonal, transhuman, centered in the cosmos rather than in human needs and interest, going beyond humanness, identity, self-actualization, and the like" (Maslow, 1968: iv).

ergy" described by Hampden-Turner (1970: 54–56).[23] And finally, in an attempt to evolve an ecological theory of value described by Arthur and Stephanie Pearl (1971).

Although on numerous occasions in this essay we have referred to the development of the individual, it should now be understood that the emerging paradigm is not "individualistic" in nature.[24] In stating that the ecological ethic is the merging of the development of the individual with the unity of the world, we are stressing that people do not exist alone but rather, with each other, with nature and with the entire world. Society, no matter what the scale, socializes every individual; the ethic calls for a society that allows the "organismic value system" within the individual to mature rather than to be suppressed. It calls for human development on a scale not experienced to date. The fulfillment of the ethic requires "planning"—in a radical sense—of the nonrepressive society.

Modern planning has as its major theme the desire of man to control his own destiny. But the emerging paradigm is not man-centered. Consequently, the major theme of radical planning is every individual's organic desire to merge with the unity of the world. One is no longer striving to be master, only an equal participant in the totality of the world.

[23] See, for example, Charles Hampden-Turner, *Radical Man* (1970), especially Chapter 3: "A Model of Psycho-Social Development," pp. 54–56.

[24] In the introduction to *The Phenomenon of Man*, Julian Huxley writes: "A developed human being . . . is not merely a more highly individualized individual. He has crossed the threshold of self-consciousness to a new mode . . . and as a result has achieved some degree of conscious integration—integration of the self with the outer world of men and nature, integration of the separate elements of the self with each other. He is a person, an organism which has transcended individuality in personality" (Teilhard de Chardin, 1965: 19).

Lincoln said: "As I would not be a slave, so I would not be a master." Instead of controlling the flow of history, one attempts to join that flow.

Synthesis

In the process of dialectical synthesis, the two components critical to integration of contradictions in reality are consciousness and action. We have identified that consciousness as the organic unfolding of an ecological ethic, but what remains seems to be the question of appropriate *action*.[25] In relationship between consciousness and action, further synthesis is imperative. Each is related to and dependent upon the other. To value one over the other is to suggest a lesson of history: the incompleteness of all "revolutions" to date.

The action component of the emerging paradigm is an "existential leap" out of anomaly and crises, out of duality and contradiction. In Montgomery, Alabama, 1955, Rosa Parks, a black seamstress, sat down in the front of a bus in a seat reserved for whites and made that leap: she denied objective reality. Martin Luther King describes the moment:

> So every rational explanation breaks down at some point. There is something about the protest that is suprarational: it cannot be explained without a divine dimension. Some may call it a principle of concentration, with Alfred N. Whitehead; or a process of integration, with Henry N. Wieman; or Being-itself, with Paul Tillich; or a personal God. Whatever the name,

[25] Richard Flacks notes in "Strategies for Radical Social Change" (1971: 7–14) that the failure of Marxist Socialism was the failure of the working class to achieve that appropriate consciousness. Along with Marcuse, Roszak, and others, he makes a strong case for the "belated" emergence of that appropriate consciousness. But the problem now seems to be the question of appropriate "action" (e.g., "the long march").

some extra-human force labors to create a harmony out of the discords of the universe. There is a creative power that works to pull down mountains of evil and level hilltops of injustice. (1958: 69–70)

In the deep regions of "dialectic" there is this question: Do the material conditions of society determine consciousness—as Marx would have it—or does consciousness determine the material conditions of society—as Hegel would have it? Neither answer alone, it would seem, tells us much about Mrs. Parks. She was, as Dr. King says:

anchored to that seat by the accumulated indignities of days gone by and the boundless aspirations of generations yet unborn. She was a victim of both the forces of history and the forces of destiny. She had been tracked down by the Zeitgeist—the spirit of the time. (1958:70)

What of this leap? Of the synthesis of rational action and spontaneity? We have yet to describe the way in which we can all sit down, as it were, in the front seat of the bus.

Evolutionary Experimentation

The action component of the emerging paradigm we have chosen to call "evolutionary experimentation."[26] It is called evolutionary because it borrows much from what we know of biological evolution.[27] Biological evolution is a revolutionary process: these revolutions are called "mutations." The history of biological evolutionary processes is the history of the

successes and failures of these mutations.[28] Social evolution is the history of successful and unsuccessful attempts at social mutation. Humans have the ability to mutate—to change reality—not only in the sense of extending a trend but in the sense of a radical shift, one which, although it learns from the past, is wholly new.[29] To date, most have thought it impossible to plan revolution. If one uses "plan" to mean "predict," we would agree. But if one uses "plan" to mean "facilitate," we would disagree. The process of evolutionary experimentation, in full cognizance of the nature of change, is the engagement in social experimentation, the attempt of mutation, as a means of facilitating social evolution. In this sense, as Huxley says: "man discovers that he is nothing else than evolution become conscious of itself" (in Teilhard de Chardin, 1965: 221).

We see evolutionary experimentation as having three components: the ethic, social experimentation, and learning.

1. The ethic—the ecological—is the only constant in the process, although it appears to be changing as it unfolds and our knowledge of its implications ases.

2. To experiment is to act, to act without the necessity of certainty or probability of result: to take risks, but always with the purpose of learning. Experimentation in the social world rather than in the closed world of the laboratory entails a realization that situations rarely, if ever, reoccur: life is constantly in flux.[30] However, one is not attempt-

---

[26] We are indebted to Edgar Dunn (1971) for this term and for parts of its meaning.

[27] We use the term "borrows" because biology and social evolution have a number of significant dissimilarities. See Dunn (1971), pp. 105–109.

[28] Also see Thomas Kuhn (1962) for a general description of a similar process in regards to the rules of science itself.

[29] Also see Thomas Kuhn (1962) for a discussion of "normal" versus "extraordinary" science.

[30] Henri Bergson described this "flux" in relation to personality growth: "Each of its moments is something new added to what was before. We may go further: it is not only something new, but something unforeseeable." See his *Creative Evolution* (1944: 8).

ing to deduce "rules" from the experiment but rather, to acquire a facility to deal with complexity—to learn.

3. Learning includes the concepts of understanding, evaluation, and reformulation. Understanding means recognizing the present, the past, and the nature of change. Evaluation means deciding whether experimentation has brought us closer to or taken us away from the ethic. Reformulation is the reintegration of the individual's knowledge (or the group's knowledge) with that of society's into greater complexity. It is reformulation, as opposed to addition: it is, to acknowledge a concept from eastern philosophy, "karmic." . . .

Radical Planning

What we mean by planning is a *synthesis* of rational action and spontaneity: evolutionary social experimentation within the context of an ecological ethic.[31]

In this radical definition of planning, who is the planner? In our view, the planner is active: a radical agent of change. He or she is not, as are so many of today's professionals, a creature of divided loyalty,

---

[31] Marcuse calls this: "the union of the new sensibility with a new rationality: The imagination becomes productive if it becomes the mediator between sensibility on the one hand, and theoretical as well as practical reason on the other, and in this harmony of faculties . . . guides the reconstruction of society" (*An Essay on Liberation*, 1969: 37–38). Only in this sense are the basic problems of planning, as Roszak says, "questions of social philosophy and aesthetics" (1969: 230), or as Shulamith Firestone would have it: "The merging of art with reality." See, for example, *The Dialectic of Sex* (1971).

one who owes as much or more to the profession as to the people. Instead, the job is to facilitate social experimentation *by* the people. The radical planner is a nonprofessional professional: no longer one with a property right entitled "planning," but rather an educator and at the same time a student of the ecological ethic as revealed in the consciousness of the people. Such an individual strives for self-actualization of one-self and of the others with whom one lives. Finally, he or she is not apart from the people: the "planner" is one of us, or all of us.

The emerging paradigm will be realized by any, and the many, means necessary. This recognizes the need for experimentation, and it recognizes the manifold activity which makes up a unified revolution.[32] Change must take place in all realms: social, economic, technological and scientific, educational, religious, cultural, sexual, and political. It is no longer productive to argue which should come first. It is no longer productive to claim the right way to make a revolution. The answer will not be found in either the seizure of power or in the destruction of all power. We are all part of the same process in the evolution of human consciousness. The revolution is where you are, and it is what *we* are becoming: consciousness and action merge. Martin Buber was perhaps more eloquent:

> Just as I do not believe in Marx's "gestation" of the new form, so I do not believe either in Bakunin's virgin birth from the womb of revolution. But I do believe in the meeting of idea and fate in the creative hour. (1958: 138)

---

[32] The only limit we see is the ecological ethic itself, which seems to suggest that while an act may be necessary for the survival of humanity, it may not be necessary for humanity to survive.

References

Bennis, Warren, and Philip Slater (1968) *The Temporary Society*. New York: Harper and Row.

Bergson, Henri (1944) *Creative Evolution*. New York: Modern Library.

Bolan, Richard (1967) "Emerging Views of

Planning." *Journal of the American Institute of Planners* 33, no. 4 (July).

Brown, Norman O. (1959) *Life Against Death: The Psychoanalytic Meaning of History.* New York: Vintage.

Buber, Martin (1968) *Paths in Utopia.* Boston: Beacon.

——— (1970) *I and Thou.* New York: Scribner's.

Burrow, Trigant (1964) *Preconscious Foundations of Human Experience.* New York: Basic Books.

Camus, Albert (1946) *The Stranger.* New York: Vintage. (1956) *The Rebel.* New York: Vintage.

Canyon Collective (1970) "Communalism."

de Chardin, Pierre Teilhard (1965) *The Phenomenon of Man.* New York: Harper and Row.

Dubos, René (1968) *So Human an Animal.* New York: Scribner's.

Dunn, Edgar (1971) *Economic and Social Development: A Social Learning Process.* Baltimore, Md.: The Johns Hopkins Press.

Eisley, Loren (1956) *The Immense Journey.* New York: Vintage.

Escher, M. C. (1971) *The Graphic Works.* New York: Ballantine.

Etzioni, Amitai (1967) "Mixed Scanning: A Third Approach to Decision-Making," *Public Administration Review* 27 (Dec.).

Firestone, Shulamith (1971) *The Dialectic of Sex: The Case for Feminist Revolution.* New York: Bantam.

Flacks, Richard (1971) "Strategies for Radical Social Change," *Social Policy* (March/Apr.).

Friedmann, John (1959) "The Study and Practice of Planning," *International Social Science Journal* 11, No. 3:327–339.

——— (1966) "Innovative Planning: The Chilean Case," *The Journal of the American Institute of Planners* 35, no. 5 (Sept.)

——— (1973) *Transactive Analysis.* Garden City, N.Y.: Doubleday.

Fromm, Erich (1967) *Escape from Freedom.* New York: Avon.

——— (1970) *The Crisis of Psychoanalysis.* Greenwich, Conn.: Fawcett.

Gutkind, Erwin (1952) *The Twilight of Cities.* London: Watts.

——— (1953) *Community and Environment.* London: Watts.

——— (1953a) *The Expanding Environment: The End of Cities—The Rise of Communities.* London: Freedom Press.

Hampden-Turner, Charles (1970) *Radical Man.* Garden City, N.Y.: Anchor Books.

Harrington, Michael (1959) *Toward a Democratic Left: A Radical Program for a Majority.* Baltimore, Md.: Penguin.

Jung, Carl G. (1961) *Memories, Dreams and Reflections.* Aniella Jaffe, ed. New York: Vintage.

King, Martin Luther, Jr. (1958) *Stride toward Freedom: The Montgomery Story.* New York: Harper and Row.

Kropotkin, Peter (1955) *Mutual Aid.* Boston: Sargent Press.

Kuhn, Thomas (1962) *The Structure of Scientific Revolutions.* Chicago: University of Chicago Press.

Laing, R. D. (1967) *The Politics of Experience.* New York: Dell.

Lindblom, Charles (1959) "The Science of Muddling Through." *Public Administration Review* 19 (Sept.)

Marcuse, Herbert (1966) *One-Dimensional Man.* Boston: Beacon.

——— (1969) *An Essay on Liberation.* Boston: Beacon.

Marx, Karl (1964) *Economic and Philosophical Manuscripts of 1884.* New York: International.

Maslow, Abraham (1968) *Toward a Psychology of Being.* Princeton, N.J.: Van Nostrand.

Mills, C. Wright (1959) *The Sociological Imagination.* London: Oxford.

Montagu, Ashley (1962) *The Humanization of Man.* New York: Grove Press.

Ozbekhan, Hasam (1969) "Towards a General Theory of Planning," in Erich

Jantsch, *Perspectives of Planning*. Paris: Organization for Economic Cooperation and Development, pp. 47–155.

Pearl, Arthur and Stephanie (1971) "Toward an Ecological Theory of Value," *Social Policy* (May/June).

Rogers, Carl (1967) *Person to Person: The Problem of Being Human*. Walnut Creek, Calif.: Real People.

Roszak, Theodore (1969) *The Making of a Counter Culture*. Garden City, N.Y.: Anchor Books.

Simon, Herbert (1957) *Models of Man*. New York: Wiley.

Slater, Philip (1970) *The Pursuit of Loneliness*. Boston: Beacon.

Watts, Alan (1968) *The Book: On the Taboo against Knowing Who You Are*. New York: Collier.

8
Education and Re-education

This chapter is the heart of the normative re-educative approach to planned change. The selection of articles to appear was difficult and, to a large degree, arbitrary, because of the large number of articles, books, and pamphlets available. There is a burgeoning set of articles, collections of articles, handbooks, and volumes on the theory, research, approaches, and techniques of the laboratory education or normative re-educative strategies of planned change. *The Laboratory Method of Changing and Learning: Theory and Application* (Palo Alto, California: Science and Behavior Books, 1975), by Benne, Bradford, Gibb, and Lippitt, is an extensive survey and has bibliographies of other publications on the differentiated aspects of personal growth, T-groups, laboratory education designs, small group processes, and Organizational Development. The uses of survey research and evaluation research and training are omitted from this chapter because they are increasingly technical and voluminous. The emphasis here is on the processes underlying the normative re-educative approaches.

It is a pleasure to reintroduce Lewin through Benne's article, "The Processes of Re-education: An Assessment of Kurt Lewin's Views." Practitioners of planned change and applied behavioral scientists have long pointed to Lewin's role in the development of the field. By reviewing some of the original work by Lewin and Grabbe published in 1945, Benne shows the present continuity and modifications down to the seventies. For those concerned with their own intellectual rootage, this paper supplements the attributions typically made to Kurt Lewin's role and contributions as a social psychologist to an applied social science, namely the use of the small group, and force field analysis.

"Process Consultation" by Edgar Schein captures the concrete uniqueness of the set of activities on the part of the consultant which help the client to perceive, understand, and act upon the process events which occur in the client's environment. The client, that is, the manager in a work group, or the teacher-counselor with students, unfreezes values and perceptions, develops new diagnostic stances and skills, and creates new action structures in working with the processes in the work group or the school. Community mental health consultation (Caplan, "Types of Mental Health Consultation," in *The Planning of Change*, 2d Edition, 1969) has pioneered a parallel approach.

The article by Brickman *et al.* is another, relatively formal approach to consulting, one that stems from a purer form of the counselor/client relationship. The authors, drawing on their clinical experience, create a fascinating typology of "helping-coping models": enlightenment, moral, medical, and compensatory. Their models are particularly interesting in light of the subsequent article by Emory Cowen. "Help Is Where You Find It" summarizes and compares findings that show that people get help from the damnedest (and, on occasion, extremely effective) sources: hairdressers, bartenders, divorce lawyers, and work supervisors.

Kennedy's "Ruminations" is an eclectic article, focusing on methods and interventions capable of changing organizations. He covers the waterfront, from the role of communications to planning, passion, and policy. Finally, in the Schein and Bennis piece, we get closer to the actual process of learning, the basis for all planned change activities.

8.1 The Processes of Re-education: An Assessment of Kurt Lewin's Views

Kenneth D. Benne

Kurt Lewin was an inveterately hopeful man. Yet this hope was more than a general temperamental stance toward life and experience. It drew its substance from several deep value commitments. One of these was to science, not as a body of knowledge but as a way of life. Science, for Lewin, "is the eternal attempt to go beyond what is regarded as scientifically accessible at any specific time." "To proceed beyond the limitations of a given level of knowledge, the researcher, as a rule, has to break down methodological taboos which condemn as 'unscientific' or 'illogical' the very methods or concepts which later on prove to be basic for the next major progress." Lewin, following the lead of one of his philosophy teachers, Ernst Cassirer, saw science as an adventuring into poorly known yet important areas of experience and an inventing of ways to gain dependable knowledge of those hitherto unknown or vaguely known areas. He had ventured early in his Berlin days to bring the study of human will and emotion into the range of psychological experimentation. In doing this, he had struggled "against a prevalent attitude which placed volition, emotion and sentiments in the 'poetic realm' of beautiful words, a realm to which nothing corresponds which could be regarded as 'existing' in the sense in which the scientist

This essay is a shortened version of a paper read at the celebration of the 25th anniversary of the Connecticut State Workshop on Intergroup Relations conducted at New Britain, Connecticut, in the summer of 1946. It was here that the T-group was discovered or invented. Staff members were Kurt Lewin, Kenneth D. Benne, Leland P. Bradford, Ronald Lippitt, Morton Deutsch, Murray Horwitz, and Melvin Seeman.

uses the term. . . . Although every psychologist had to deal with these facts realistically in his private life, they were banned from the realm of 'facts' in the scientific sense."[1]

This same commitment to the spirit of science as a human enterprise, as intrepid inquiry, in which current scientific taboos are overcome through bold theorizing and creative research designs and methods, had led Lewin, in his Iowa days, to collaborate with Ronald Lippitt and Ralph White in bringing small group processes into the ambit of experimental inquiry. Lewin was a theorizer and researcher. But he saw theory not alone as a way into significant inquiry and research but as a practical guide to reconstructive work in social practice and action as well.

Lewin was thus a moralist as well as a scientist. But he was decidedly not a moralistic moralist, in the sense of one who seeks to impose the principles of any established moral tradition upon the realities of contemporary conduct in order to control it within the confines of that tradition. His was rather a morality of reality-orientation toward confronting contemporary situations in their tensions and conflicts, a morality of focusing the cooperative human intelligences of those within those situations upon inventing ways of managing and improving them. The values to which he was most basically committed were thus methodological values, combining values inherent in scientific and democratic processes and methods.

[1] All quotations from K. Lewin, "Cassirer's Philosophy of Science and Social Science," in Paul A. Schlipp (ed.), *The Philosophy of Ernst Cassirer* (New York: Tudor, 1949).

Lewin's hope for cooperative action research as a way for human beings to solve their problems and manage their dilemmas represents best this dynamic fusion of democratic and scientific values. In a real sense, the whole Connecticut workshop was a project in cooperative action research. Ronald Lippitt's book on the workshop makes this clear.[2]

Kurt Lewin was moved by fears as well as by hopes. He was a Jew who had been driven out of his homeland by anti-Semitism become an article of official state policy in Hitler's Third Reich. His mother died in a Nazi gas chamber. He found strong currents of anti-Semitism, of racism, of ethnocentrism in his adopted country, the United States. He felt the contradictions between America's professed democratic commitment to the nurture of self-directing personalities and the self-hatred and self-rejection which persons within oppressed minorities avoided or overcame only with great effort and suffering. He saw democratic institutions eroded by the perpetuation of racial injustice and threatened by mounting and unresolved intergroup conflicts. He feared that the seeds of totalism might grow to destroy democracy in the United States and in the world unless the forces of research, education and action could be united in the eliminating of social injustice and minority self-hatred and in the wise resolution of intergroup conflicts. Kurt's fears reinforced the vigor of his efforts to serve his hopes and commitments.

The lure of learning answers to unanswered questions was a passion in Lewin, the man, the scientist, and the moralist. My fondest memories of Kurt in the Connecticut workshop are of his deep engagement in discussing the problems which participants laid before him. He was prepared to learn along with anyone— he seemed to be unusually free of status

consciousness. He listened and questioned avidly. From time to time he would raise a finger of his right hand and say "Ah ha! Could it be this way?" And he would then propose a new conceptualization of the problem which more often than not opened up a new way of seeing it and new avenues toward solution. The lure of unanswered questions and of finding data which might lead toward better diagnoses and prognoses was strong in Kurt and in those who collaborated with him.

One central theme running through the concerns and curiosities of the mature Lewin and exemplified in the New Britain workshop is the theme of re-education. Through what processes do men and women alter, replace or transcend patterns of thinking, valuation, volition, overt behavior by which they have previously managed and justified their lives into patterns of thinking, valuation, volition, and action which are better oriented to the realities and actualities of contemporary existence, personal and social, and which are at once more personally fulfilling and socially appropriate? The processes are more complex than those of learning anew as any action leader, therapist, or teacher of adults knows from experience. They involve not extrinsic additions of knowledge or behavioral repertoire to the self or person but changes in the self, and the working through of self-supported resistances to such changes. And, since self-patterns are sustained by norms and relationships in the groups to which a person belongs or aspires to belong, effective re-education of a person requires changes in his environing society and culture as well.

About a year before the Connecticut workshop, Lewin, along with Paul Grabbe, formulated ten general observations on re-education.[3] These principles of re-educa-

---

[2] R. Lippitt, *Training in Community Relations* (New York: Harper's, 1949).

[3] K. Lewin and P. Grabbe, "Conduct, Knowledge and Acceptance of New Values," *The Journal of Social Issues*, Vol. I, No. 3, August 1945.

tion were not simple derivations from Lewin's field theoretical perspective on human conduct. They grew out of his attempt to interpret, out of that perspective, reports of a number of projects in re-education as various as Alcoholics Anonymous, a training program for police officers in intergroup prejudice, and a successful attempt to change a stereotype of older workers in an industrial organization.

What I propose to do is to assess these Lewinian generalizations in the light of the knowledge and know-how concerning re-education accumulated, in the twenty-five years of experience and experimentation with training, since their original publication. My assessment will, of course, reflect the limitations of my knowledge of these cumulative experiences in training and my own theoretical and value orientation.

Lewin's analysis assumed that effective re-education must affect the person being re-educated in three ways. The person's *cognitive* structure must be altered. And for Lewin this structure included the person's modes of perception, his ways of seeing his physical and social worlds, as well as the facts, concepts, expectations, and beliefs with which a person thinks about the possibilities of action and the consequences of action in his phenomenal world. But re-education must involve the person in modifying his *valences* and *values* as well as his cognitive structures. *Valences* and *values* include not alone his principles of what he should and should not do or consider doing—which along with his cognitive views of himself and his world are represented by his beliefs. They include also his attractions and aversions to his and other groups and their standards, his feelings in regard to status differences and authority, and his reactions to various sources of approval and disapproval of himself. Re-education finally must affect a person's motoric actions, his repertoire of behavioral skills, and the degree of a

person's conscious control of his bodily and social movements.

The complexities of re-educative processes arise out of the fact that they must involve correlative changes in various aspects of the person—his cognitive-perceptual structure, his valuative—moral and volitional—structure, and his motoric patterns for coping with his world(s). And changes in these various aspects of the person are governed by different laws and relationships. Thus re-education runs into contradictions and dilemmas. For example, a person's learning facts which run counter to his stereotypic attitudes toward members of an outgroup may actually lead to denial of this knowledge and increased guilt and more frantic defense of his stereotypes unless his valences and values are opened up, explored, and altered. And changed stereotypes may leave the person awkward in dealing with members of the outgroup, if his motoric skills have not been brought into line with his new cognitive and value orientation. This awkwardness may evoke responses in his trying to deal with members of the outgroup in new ways which reconfirm him in his old stereotypes or lead him to immobilization because of augmented inner conflicts. Re-educative experiences must be redesigned with the mutli-faceted aspects of behavioral change in mind and designed further to help persons become aware of and responsible for the dilemmas and contradictions which arise out of this inescapable complexity. I believe that experiences with re-education since Lewin's formulation have confirmed his assumption that the "whole person" must somehow be involved in processes of effective re-education.

Lewin's principles dealt with the complex interrelationships between changes in cognitive-perceptual orientation and value orientation. He did not deal with the involvement of motoric changes in their interrelationships with the other two. Experimentation with body movement and with behavioral conditioning in achieving behavioral change has thrived during the quarter of a century since Lewin wrote. And some of my supplementation of his principles of re-education arises from this fact.

1. Lewin stated his first principle as "The processes governing the acquisition of the normal and the abnormal are fundamentally alike." This principle breaks cognitively through the wall that has traditionally separated dealing re-educatively with persons manifesting "abnormal" behavior and with those who are seen as "normal" behaviorally. Behavioral abnormalities have been classified as pathological or as criminally or quasi-criminally deviant. Special personnel with special training, working in special settings with special techniques, have been developed to deal in segregated fashion with the therapy of the pathologically abnormal and rehabilitatively with the criminally deviant. "Education" for "the normal" has been sharply separated conceptually and institutionally from "therapy" for the pathological and "rehabilitation" for the deviant.

The wall between "education" on the one hand and "therapy" and "rehabilitation" on the other has been breached on many fronts—in mental health, in prison reform, and in converging movements between education and therapy. But the resistance to thinking about and dealing with re-education of persons as they are, normal and abnormal, and in the same processes is still powerful in the thinking and practice of most people. Probably, this is related generally to the persistence of class theoretical thinking as over against field theoretical thinking in the management of human affairs, a distinction with which Lewin, the philosopher of science, was much concerned. For people whose ways of thinking are class-theoretical, classifications devised as artifacts, as abstract tools of thought, not as representations of reality, "abnormal" and "nor-

mal" people, for example, are given the status of realities, with class membership constituting a difference of kind or substance for the individuals in the class. Field theoretical thinking about people and the processes of their re-education keeps a focus on the reality of concrete persons in their actual manifold relationships and situations and does not let abstract classifications of persons prescribe the mode or manner of their differential treatment. I see field theoretical thinking as highly desirable in contemporary analyses and management of human affairs. This Lewinian construction of a way of thinking about thinking seems to me both more conducive to the fuller actualization of humane values and to effectiveness in our policies and practices of education and re-education.

Controversies about what is "therapy" and what is "education" have dogged the development and extension of T-group practices since their inception. Actually, the lines between the two have become blurred in a number of ways, and rightly so in my opinion. Educational programs are slowly escaping the fetters of their traditional exclusive preoccupation with cognitive development and are taking responsibility for affective and volitional development as well. As this happens, expressive behavior which might once have been considered abnormal in educational settings is becoming legitimized as relevant to the idiosyncratic development of persons. In fact, we have discovered that behavioral manifestations in intensive group experiences which might once have been coded as pathological, and so to be avoided and repressed, are actually aspects, even necessary aspects, of processes of personal growth and self-discovery. The lines between the pathological and the growthful in behavior still need to be drawn. But training experiences, along with extensions from therapeutic practice into preventive mental health education, have shown that the lines are not easy to draw. As they are drawn, I hope they will be taken as practical judgments of re-education that persons require from time to time in their careers, not as a restoration of nonfunctional distinctions between the "normal" and "abnormal" which Lewin's first principle of re-education wisely repudiates.

2. The theory and practice of training is only beginning to catch up with Lewin's second principle—"The re-educative process has to fulfill a task which is essentially equivalent to a change in culture." Counseling and therapy have traditionally sought to facilitate changes in persons with little or no assumption of responsibility for facilitating changes in the cultural environment in which persons function outside the counseling or therapeutic setting. This tends to place the entire burden of behavioral adjustment or adaptation upon the individual. Changes in the cultural environment, which was involved in the dysfunctional behavior which brought the person to counseling or therapy, have not been focused upon in the re-educative process, which is ordinarily carried on in a specially designed setting apart from the social and cultural involvements of the person's ongoing life. There is now a tendency to involve significant other persons and their common culture in the process of reexamination, reevaluation, and commitment to change, along with the person who has felt the environmental stress most deeply—as in therapy for a family in place of or as adjunct to therapy for an individual family member; treatment of disturbed individuals in their home and work settings, not in segregated situations, and so forth. In training, work with what Gibb has called embedded groups—work staffs, entire organizations, whole families—has come to supplement or to replace cultural island training of persons drawn away from their home settings. This involves changes in culture that are ideally consonant with and supportive of changes in personal knowledge, value orientation, or motoric skill achieved through training.

At the same time as organizational development and community development approaches to personal-social-cultural changing have come into being and spread, personal growth training in settings designedly abstracted from the outside roles and institutional involvements of participants have been developing in various laboratory programs and growth centers. These seem to focus on personal re-education with little or no assumption of responsibility for changes in the culture, outside the center, in which persons live and function most of their lives. Do the successes claimed for such programs contradict Lewin's second principle of re-education?

I do not think that they do. A counterculture has grown up in the United States (and outside as well) with norms that are markedly different from those of established culture. This counterculture has found social embodiment in communes of various sorts, in Hippie gatherings, in various associations of drop-outs from established institutional life. The manifestations of counterculture are often closer to the norms cultivated and in various degree internalized by participants in personal growth laboratories and centers—living in the moment, suspicion of deferred gratification, guidance of the choices of life by feelings, authenticity of personal expression as the prime virtue, and so on.

What we are seeing in certain developments in the training field is not an abrogation of the principle that effective personal re-education involves correlative changes in culture. It is rather a difference in the subculture of our national culture for which training is being conducted. It may be more accurate to say that community and organizational development streams in human relations training are more hopeful about the possibilities of reconstructing and humanizing established organizations and institutions than are those who train for participation in the counterculture. Trainers who see training for personal growth without reference to correlative training for social and cultural change as a way of changing established culture are, I think, denying the reality embodied in Lewin's second principle of re-education.

3. "Even extensive first hand experience does not automatically create correct concepts (knowledge)." Lewin leveled his third principle against re-educators who, aware that lectures and other abstract ways of transmitting knowledge are of little avail in changing the orientations or conduct of learners, see experience as such as the way to personal changing, including cognitive changes toward correct knowledge, which are required by effective re-education. He pointed out that thousands of years of human experiences with falling bodies did not bring men to a correct theory of gravity. What was required was specially constructed man-made experiences, experiments, designed to reach an adequate explanation of the phenomena of falling objects, in order to achieve a correct theory. Lewin was convinced that re-educative experiences must incorporate the spirit of experimental inquiry and, insofar as possible, the form of experimentation, if correct knowledge is to be the result. I believe that Lewin is correct. It is important to recognize that the principle opens to question the effectiveness of traditional classroom practices which seek to induce students to learn about the results of other people's inquiries and do not involve them in processes of inquiry in areas where their own beliefs are recognized by them to be vague, conflicting, or somehow in doubt. It is important to recognize also that the principle equally throws doubt upon the effectiveness of training where trainers and participants confuse having an exciting and moving experience with the achievement of adequate and transferable learnings (cognitive changes).

In training, it takes time and effort for a group to learn a method of experimental inquiry where their own feelings, perceptions, commitments, and behaviors are the data to be processed in the inquiry. But this is the goal of responsible training. At least, experiences which have not been prehypothesized need to be reflected upon and conceptualized *post factum*, if valid learnings are to issue from the training process.

Actually this principle supports Lewin's advocacy of action research as a format for integrating personal re-education and social change into the same process. Action research when it is most valid achieves the form of field experimentation.

4. "Social action no less than physical action is steered by perception." The world in which we act is the world as we perceive it. Changes in knowledge or changes in beliefs and value orientation will not result in action changes unless changed perceptions of self and situation are achieved.

Developments in the training field since Lewin's day have reconfirmed this principle. And much of the development of training technology has been focused on ways of inducing people to entertain, try out and perhaps to adopt ways of perceiving themselves and their situations which are alternative to their habitual ways of perceiving. Openness to new knowledge and new valuations usually follows rather than precedes changes in perception. Habitual perceptions are challenged by open exchange of feedback between members of a group as they share their different responses to the "same" events. If a member attaches positive valence to other members of the group or to the group as a whole, he can accept different perceptions of other members as genuine phenomenological alternatives to his own ways of perceiving self and world. And he may then try to perceive and feel the world as others in his group perceive and feel it. In the process, his own perceptual frames may be modified or at least recognized as belonging to him and operating as one among many other constructions of social reality.

It is, I think, true that the most impressive developments in training technologies have been focused upon the inducing of perceptual change—more powerful forms of feedback, including the uses of audio and videotape, extending awareness of previously unnoticed processes and feelings, bodily and otherwise, as in Gestalt therapy, training in listening and in observation, psychodrama and fantasy experiences, experiences with the arts, and so on. These illustrate ways of cleansing, opening and refining the doors of perception, which have been developed over the years by practitioners and theorists of re-education. Lewin may have been a lonely phenomenologist among re-educators when he enunciated this principle twenty-five years ago. Most re-educators have become phenomenologists today.

5. "As a rule the possession of correct knowledge does not suffice to rectify false perceptions." This principle underlines the relative independence of processes of perception from processes of cognition and valuation in the organization of the person, a point already emphasized. Lewin did not recognize so fully as most trainers do today the close linkage between social perception and self-perception. Dynamically, I tend to see others in a way to support and maintain my image of myself. And I perceive myself in a certain way in order to justify myself to myself and to others. Only as the need to justify myself is reduced, as in a supportive, acceptant, loving social environment, can I freely experiment with alternative perceptions of myself and in turn with alternative perceptions of other people. Changes in self-perception and in social perception come about through "experimentation" in interpersonal relations at precognitive levels of experience.

6. "Incorrect stereotypes (prejudices) are functionally equivalent to wrong concepts (theories)." All of us who have studied prejudices in ourselves and others know how incorrect stereotypes can persist as ways of explaining the motivations and behavior of persons against the weight of evidence to the contrary. The story of the man who believed he was dead illustrates the point. His friends and his psychiatrist pointed out evidences to indicate that he was alive but the belief persisted. Finally, his psychiatrist got the man to admit that dead men don't bleed and gained his permission to prick his finger with a pin. When the blood came, the man, astonished, said, "Doctor, I was wrong. Dead men do bleed."

What Lewin was underlining here with respect to re-education of incorrect stereotypes was the inadequacy of experience as such to change a person's or group's theories of the world. Specially designed experiments which people design and carry out for themselves are required to instate new more adequate concepts in the place of those which they have held habitually. One condition of experimentation is for the experimenter to accept the fact of alternative conceptualizations of some event. The experimenter can then arrange experiences to furnish evidence for or against the alternative hypotheses in trying to determine which of the alternatives most adequately explains the evidence. In recognizing that an incorrect stereotype is functionally equivalent to a theory in his mental organization, the experimenter must develop and accept an ambivalence in himself toward the adequacy of his stereotype. Without ambivalence, the person sees no need to submit his stereotypes to an experimental testing.

Ambivalence toward one's habitual ways of explaining social events usually comes when consensual validation toward social events breaks down. Other people whose views he prizes explain the same event in ways different from his own. If he can acknowledge his ambivalence toward the stereotype, he can become active in gathering and evaluating evidence to disconfirm or confirm the stereotype or its alternative. Changes in stereotypes will ordinarily not occur until the person is involved as a self-experimenter with his own and alternative ways of explaining his social world. The self-experimenter must have an appropriate laboratory in which to work, both as a support to his persistence in arduous processes of self-inquiry and to furnish the data which the testing of his alternative hypotheses requires.

7. "Changes in sentiments do not necessarily follow changes in cognitive structures." Just as some of Lewin's earlier principles have urged the relative independence of processes of changing cognition and processes of changing perception, this principle stresses the relative independence of processes of cognitive change and changes in value orientation, action-ideology, or sentiment.

Lewin was quite aware that many re-educative attempts reach only the official system of values and do not involve the person in becoming aware of his own action-ideology, often nonconscious, which actually shapes his personal decisions and actions. Such superficial re-education may result in merely heightening the discrepancy between the superego (the way I ought to feel) and the ego (the way I actually do feel). The individual develops a guilty conscience. Such a discrepancy leads to a state of high emotional tension but seldom to appropriate conduct. It may postpone transgressions from the official ideology but it is likely to make the transgressions more violent when they do occur.

Subsequent training experience seems to bear out one factor of great importance in facilitating a person's reconsideration and reconstruction of his action-ideology, his sentiments or his value system. This is the degree and depth to which an individual becomes involved in seeing and accepting a problem with respect to the adequacy of his operating values. Lacking

this involvement, no objective fact is likely to reach the status of a fact for the individual, no value alternative is likely to reach the status of a genuine alternative for the individual, and therefore come to influence his social conduct.

8. "A change in action-ideology, a real acceptance of a changed set of facts and values, a change in the perceived social world—all three are but different expressions of the same process."

It was a part of Lewin's great contribution to an understanding of re-education to emphasize the intimate connection between the development of a value system by a person and his growth into membership in a group. An individual becomes socialized through internalizing the normative culture of the groups to which he comes to belong. His value system is his own putting together, perhaps in a unique way, the various internalized normative outlooks of the significant associations which have contributed to the building of his social self—family, religion, age group, sex group, ethnic group, racial group, and so forth. Re-education, as it affects action-ideology, value orientation, perception of self and social world, is a process of re-socialization or, as Lewin tended to prefer, a process of re-enculturation. Re-education of persons thus requires their involvement in new groups with norms that contrast in significant ways with those of the groups to which a person has previously belonged. The norms of the re-educative group must, as Lewin pointed out again and again, be those which support and require members to engage in experimental inquiry into their own socialization as it affects their present functioning and their development into the future. The norms of re-educative groups are thus not accidental. They are the norms of the social research community—openness of communication, willingness to face problems and to become involved in their solution, willingness to furnish data to facilitate own and other's inquiries, willingness to submit ambivalences and moot points to an empirical test, and so on. The material dealt with in the re-educative group is, of course, personal and social material. It is inquired into not alone in the interest of gaining more valid and dependable knowledge of interpersonal and social transactions in general but in the interest of rendering contemporary personal and social action more informed, more on target, more in line with clarified and chosen values, and in the further interest of narrowing the gap between internal intention and outer consequences in processes of decision and action.

Lewin's views of re-education helped the staff at New Britain to project out of their experience there the T-group as the prototype of the re-educative group. The T-group, as it developed, tended to focus on inquiry into interpersonal relationships between members and into the idiosyncratic aspects of member selves as they revealed themselves in T-group transactions. The typical T-group, whatever that may be, did not ordinarily explore directly the social selves of members, the effects of significant membership and reference groups upon members and their attempts to deal with each other in fruitful processes of inquiry and experimental action.

Max Birnbaum and I have been developing laboratory groups, which we call clarification groups, in which members are encouraged to inquire into their social selves.[4] The effects of memberships on action-ideology, value orientation, social perception, stereotypy are explored openly and directly. We like to think that this variation in laboratory training, which supplements rather than supplants T-groups and consultation with groups and group interfaces embedded within organizations and communities, is in line with Lewin's central interest in improving community and intergroup relations.

Lewin was quite aware of one dilemma which faces all re-educators. The principle of voluntarism, of free choice by persons to engage in self and social inquiry, is an important element in effective re-education. Yet the urgency of unsolved human problems leads all of us at times to force people into programs and processes of re-education. The maintenance of the principle of voluntarism is very difficult in field experiments in which entire social systems—schools, industries, community agencies—become involved. Lewin put the dilemma in this way— "How can free acceptance of a new system of values be brought about, if the person who is to be educated is, in the nature of things, likely to be hostile to the new values and loyal to the old?"

This, I believe, is a real dilemma. There is no neat solution to it. Training experience has indicated that two operating attitudes or stances of re-educators are very important in managing the dilemma. The first is an attitude of respect for resistance and a commitment to utilize the resources of the resistant in shaping plans for experimental action and its evaluation. The second is to seek ways of helping hostile rejectors to recognize that their stance of total rejection usually masks a genuine ambivalence and conflict within themselves. If they can accept this ambivalence within themselves, they are accepting the existence of a problem to be inquired into and so become candidates for voluntary involvement in the processes of its resolution.

9. "Acceptance of the new set of values and beliefs cannot usually be brought about item by item."

Lewin here points out the inescapable fact that a value system is a system. It must have an integrity of its own if it is to perform its function of helping persons maintain their identity and wholeheartedness in the choices which their conflicted

[4] See Max Birnbaum, "The Clarification Group," chapter 15, in Benne, Bradford, Gibb, and R. Lippitt (Eds.), *The Laboratory Method of Changing and Learning* (Palo Alto, Calif.: Science and Behavior Books, 1975).

environment thrusts upon them. Introducing new particular values which are not coherent with other values in the person's outlook on self and world may augument the inner conflict and compartmentalization, the reduction of which is a part of the motivation that brings persons into a process of re-education.

I think that many trainers, coming as many do out of indoctrination in social science which, however dubiously, claims value neutrality, avoid facing up directly to the dimension of inquiry into value orientation which is a necessary aspect of effective re-education. They may encourage participants to clarify feelings, to apply and test new concepts, and to practice skills of inquiry. They may avoid direct confrontation of differences among participants and themselves with respect to beliefs and ideologies. A piecemeal approach may be quite appropriate to skill development, expression of feelings, and even to conceptual clarification. It is, and here I agree with Lewin, inappropriate in the reconstruction of a value orientation. Some of us, in the training profession, have done some work in training for value inquiry. More work needs to be done.

10. "The individual accepts the new system of values and beliefs by accepting belongingness in a group." This insight of Lewin's into the indispensability of groups as media of effective re-education and its basis in the nature of human socialization has already been emphasized. This fact of life is resisted by many persons made impatient by the urgency of recognized needs for behavioral change in various areas of pressing social issue. They frequently try to bypass the group participation which is required for behavioral changes—put it on TV, write more popular books on psychiatry and applied social science, pass a law, require people to change their behavior. I am not against any of these as aspects of programs of social change. But, taken as adequate means for the humanization and person-

alization of relationships in our bureaucratized mass society and culture in which loneliness, alienation, personal confusion, impotence are the lot of many if not most people, the counsel seems a counsel of despair not of hope. The counsel of hope seems to me to involve reconstruction of our organized life of social action. And the reconstruction will come only as collaboration between researchers, educators, and actionists comes to replace the self-segregation and autistic hostility which now tend to characterize their relationships. This was Kurt Lewin's vision of a re-educative society and it is one in which I gladly share.

Lewin and the Grabbe's wise discussion of the implications of his tenth principle are worth quoting at length.

> When re-education involves the relinquishment of standards which are contrary to the standards of society at large (as in the case of delinquency, minority prejudices, alcoholism), the feeling of group belongingness seems to be greatly heightened if the members feel free to express openly the very sentiments which are to be dislodged through re-education. This might be viewed as another example of the seeming contradictions inherent in the process of re-education. Expression of prejudices against minorities or the breaking of rules of parliamentary procedures may in themselves be contrary to the desired goal. Yet a feeling of complete freedom and a heightened group identification are frequently more important at a particular stage of re-education than learning not to break specific rules.
>
> This principle of in-grouping makes understandable why complete acceptance of previously rejected facts can be achieved best through the discovery of these facts by the group members themselves. . . . Then, and frequently only then, do the facts become really *their* facts (as against other people's facts). An individual will believe facts he himself has discovered in the same way that he believes in himself or in his group. The importance of this fact-finding process for the group by the group itself

has been recently emphasized with reference to re-education in several fields. . . . It can be surmised that the extent to which social research is translated into social action depends on the degree to which those who carry out this action are made a part of the fact-finding on which the action is to be based.

Re-education influences conduct only when the new system of values and beliefs dominates the individual's perception. The acceptance of the new system is linked with the acceptance of a specific group, a particular role, a definite source of authority as new points of reference. It is basic for re-education that this linkage between acceptance of new facts or values and acceptance of certain groups or roles is very intimate and that the second frequently is a prerequisite for the first. This explains the great difficulty of changing beliefs and values in a piecemeal fashion. This linkage is a main factor behind resistance to re-education, but can also be made a powerful means for successful re-education.[5]

I would like now to comment briefly on an omission from Lewin's principles of re-education of which he was quite aware. You will recall that Lewin recognized three dimensions to effective re-education—cognitive and perceptual structures, values and valences, and motoric action—the individual's control over his physical and social movements. It was the third dimension which Lewin chose not to conceptualize. And it is the place of physical and social movements in processes of re-education which has become most controverted in the field of training and re-education generally in recent years.

I recognize three developments in which the motoric dimension of behavioral change has been focused upon and made the object of research and experimentation. The first arose within the Lewinian training movement itself. This was the attempt to define human relations skills and to devise opportunities for people to practice these skills for themselves with feedback near to

the time of performance—both through simulation under laboratory conditions and through field practice under reality conditions. This development thrived as an adjunct to T-group experience in early laboratory designs. Then as the T-group, often under the ambiguous name of sensitivity training, tended to be taken as the complete process of re-education by some trainers and by many participants, interest in skill practice as an important part of re-education declined. Lately, new interest in structured experiences in human relations training has been manifested, and a number of guidebooks for trainers and groups have been published, outlining skill practice exercises which have been developed and tested over the years in the emerging training profession. I think this revised interest is a healthy one and should be encouraged. Let me suggest two cautions. First, "putting participants through" exercises before they have, in Lewinian language, been unfrozen, before they have seen reasons to change their concepts, perceptions, ideologies, or skill will likely leave little lasting deposit in their behavioral repertoire. Or it may leave them with new bags of tricks which are not integrated with altered and better integrated values, concepts, or perceptions and so can be utilized only mechanically rather than organically in their life and work.

Second, I tend to distrust prescriptions by trainers which do not grow out of a joint diagnosis by trainers and participants of their needs for skill development. If they are used openly and frankly as a tool for furnishing diagnostic data to trainers and participants, such use may avoid the timing error of putting the cart before the horse.

The second use of movement as an aid to re-education has arisen within the field of applied humanistic psychology, to which, in one sense, Lewinian psychology belongs. But these developments draw heavily on the more organismic psychologies of Wilhelm Reich and Fritz Perls,

[5] Lewin and Grabbe, op. cit.

among others. These uses of movement draw heavily upon tactile and kinesthetic perception as a corrective to the more socialized and moralized visual and auditory perceptions and their chief tools of expression and communication—words. Experiences in nonverbal movement help to open up people to awareness of conflicts and discrepancies within themselves and between themselves and others in their social world. I believe that dissimulation and self-delusion is more difficult in tactile and kinesthetic perceptions than in verbalized reports of what people see and hear. And I have found nonverbal movements a useful tool to extend awareness to ordinarily nonconscious bodily processes, feelings, and emotional states. "Movement" can be effectively designed into overall programs and processes of re-education. I have two cautions which I would make about the use of experiences in nonverbal movement in training. First, it may increase the dependence of participants upon the trainer who knows the powerful technology which the participants do not know. It may thus, unwittingly, fail to develop the autonomy of participants in assuming more intelligent control of their own continuing socialization in the society in which they live. Second, the hesitation to verbalize the meaning of nonverbal experiences may

militate against the conceptualization of the meanings of the experience which is a necessary part of transfer of learnings beyond the laboratory. For words are the tools of valid conceptualization as well as tools of obfuscation and self-delusion as they are often used.

The third emphasis on motoric action in re-education comes out of behavior therapy and is based on the rather strict behavioristic psychology, particularly of Skinner. I do not doubt the evidence of behavioral changes accomplished through reconditioning processes. I have grave doubts about the effects of such re-education upon the "inner" processes of valuing, conceptualizing, willing, which, on their own assumptions, behavior therapists do not take into account in their experimentation or in the evaluation of its results. I have more faith in re-education which helps persons bring their inner and outer behavior into more integral relationships through a process in which participants play a responsible part as researchers, educators, deciders of and for themselves.

My reassessment of Lewin's views of re-education has, I hope, convinced you, as it has convinced me, of their continuing fruitfulness in guiding continuing developments in the training field and in applied social science more generally.

8.2 Process Consultation
Edgar Schein

Managers often sense that all is not well or that things could be better, and yet do

From Edgar H. Schein, *Process Consultation: Its Role in Organization Development* (Reading, Mass.: Addison-Wesley Publishing Company, 1969), pp. 4–9.

not have the tools with which to translate their vague feelings into concrete action steps. The kind of consultation I will attempt to describe . . . deals with problems of this sort. Process consultation does not assume that the manager or the organization knows what is wrong, or what is needed, or what the consultant should do. All that is required for the process to begin constructively is some *intent* on the part of someone in the organization to improve the ways things are going. The consultation process itself then helps the manager to define diagnostic steps which lead ultimately to action programs or concrete changes.

Process consultation is a difficult concept to describe simply and clearly. It does not lend itself to a simple definition to be followed by a few illustrations. Instead, I will . . . give some perspective by contrasting P-C with more traditional consultation models.

How Is Process Consultation Different from Other Consultation?

We do not have in the field of management a neat typology of consultation processes, but a few models can be identified from the literature . . . and from my own experience in watching consultants work.

The Purchase Model

The most prevalent model of consultation is certainly the "purchase of expert information or an expert service." The buyer, an individual manager or some group in the organization, defines a need—something he wishes to know or some activity he wishes carried out—and, if he doesn't feel the organization itself has the time or capability, he will look to a consultant to fill the need. For example: (1) A manager may wish to know how a particular group of consumers feel, or how to design a plant efficiently, or how to design an accounting system which fully utilizes a computer's capability. (2) The manager may wish to find out how he could more effectively organize some

group. This would require some surveying of their activities, attitudes, and work habits. (3) A manager may wish to institute a morale survey procedure for his production units, or an analysis of the quality of some complex product. In the first of the above examples, the manager desires *information*; in the latter two examples, he wishes to *purchase a service* from the consultant. In each of these cases there is an assumption that the manager knows what kind of information or what kind of service he is looking for. The success of the consultation then depends upon:

1. whether the manager has correctly diagnosed his own needs;
2. whether he has correctly communicated these needs to the consultant;
3. whether he has accurately assessed the capability of the consultant to provide the right kind of information or service; and
4. whether he has thought through the consequences of having the consultant gather information, and/or the consequences of implementing changes which may be recommended by the consultant.

The frequent dissatisfaction voiced by managers with the quality of the services they feel they receive from their consultants is easily explainable when one considers how many things have to go right for the purchase model to work.

Process consultation, in contrast, involves the manager and the consultant in a period of *joint* diagnosis. The process consultant is willing to come into an organization without a clear mission or clear need, because of an underlying assumption that most organizations could probably be more effective than they are if they could identify what processes (work flow, interpersonal relations, communications, intergroup relations, etc.) need improvement. A closely related assumption is that no organizational form is perfect, that every organizational form has strengths and weaknesses. The process consultant would urge any manager with whom he is working not to leap into an action program, particularly if it involves any kind of changes in organizational structure, until the organization itself has done a thorough diagnosis and assessment of the strengths and weaknesses of the present structure.

The importance of *joint* diagnosis derives from the fact that the consultant can seldom learn enough about the organization to really know what a better course of action would be for that *particular group* of people with their *particular sets* of traditions, styles, and personalities. However, the consultant can help the manager to become a sufficiently good diagnostician himself, and can provide enough alternatives, to enable the manager to solve the problem. This last point highlights another assumption underlying P-C: problems will stay solved longer and be solved more effectively if the organization solves its own problems; the consultant has a role in teaching diagnostic and problem-solving skills, but he should not work on the actual concrete problem himself.

The Doctor-Patient Model

Another traditionally popular model of consultation is that of doctor-patient. One or more executives in the organization decide to bring in a consultant or team of consultants to "look them over," much as a patient might go to his doctor for an annual physical. The consultants are supposed to find out what is wrong with which part of the organization, and then, like a physician, recommend a program of therapy. Often the manager singles out some unit of the organization where he is having difficulty or where performance has fallen off, and asks the consultant to determine "what is wrong with our —— department."

As most readers will recognize from their own experience, in spite of the popularity of this model it is fraught with difficulties. One of the most obvious difficulties is that the organizational unit which is defined as the patient may be reluctant to reveal the kinds of information which the consultant is likely to need in order to make his diagnosis. In fact, it is quite predictable that on questionnaires and in interviews systematic distortions will occur. The direction of distortion will depend upon the company climate. If the climate is one of mistrust and insecurity, the respondent is likely to hide any damaging information from the consultant because he fears that his boss will punish him for revealing problems; if the climate is one of high trust, the respondent is likely to view contact with the consultant as an opportunity to gripe, leading to exaggeration of problems. Unless the consultant spends considerable time *observing* the department, he is not likely to get an accurate picture.

An equally great difficulty in the doctor-patient model is that the patient is sometimes unwilling to believe the diagnosis or accept the prescription offered by the consultant. I suspect most companies have drawers full of reports by consultants, each loaded with diagnoses and recommendations which are either not understood or not accepted by the "patient." What is wrong, of course, is that the doctor, the consultant, has not built up a common diagnostic frame of reference with the patient, his client. If the consultant does all the diagnosis while the client-manager waits passively for a prescription, it is predictable that a communication gulf will arise which will make the prescription seem irrelevant and/or unpalatable.

Process consultation, in contrast, focuses on joint diagnosis and the passing on to the client of diagnostic skills. The consultant may recognize early in his work what some of the problems are in the organization and how they might be solved. He does not advance them prematurely, however, for two reasons. One, he may be wrong and may damage his relationship with the client by a hasty diagnosis which turns out to be wrong. Two, he recognizes that even if he is right, the client is likely to be defensive, to not listen to the diagnosis, to misunderstand what the consultant is saying, and to argue with it.

It is a key assumption underlying P-C that the client must learn to see the problem for himself, to share in the diagnosis, and to be *actively involved* in generating a remedy. The process consultant may play a key role in helping to sharpen the diagnosis and in providing alternative remedies which may not have occurred to the client. But he encourages the client to make the ultimate decision as to what remedy to apply. Again, the consultant does this on the assumption that if he teaches the client to diagnose and remedy situations, problems will be solved more permanently and the client will be able to solve new problems as they arise.

It should be emphasized that the process consultant may or may not be expert in solving the particular problem which is uncovered. The important point in P-C is that such expertise is less relevant than are the skills of involving the client in self-diagnosis and helping him to find a remedy which fits his particular situation and his unique set of needs. The process consultant must be an expert in how to diagnose and how to develop a helping relationship. He does not need to find an expert resource in those areas, finance, and the like. If problems are uncovered in specific areas like these, the process consultant would help the client to find an expert resource in those areas, but he would *also* help the client to think through how best to get help from such an expert.

Assumptions Underlying Process Consultation

Let me pull together here the assumptions stated thus far. I have said that P-C assumes that:

1. Managers often do not know what is wrong and need special help in diagnosing what their problems actually are.
2. Managers often do not know what kinds of help consultants can give to them; they need to be helped to know what kind of help to seek.
3. Most managers have a constructive intent to improve things but need help in identifying what to improve and how to improve it.
4. Most organizations can be more effective if they learn to diagnose their own strengths and weaknesses. No organizational form is perfect; hence every form of organization will have some weaknesses for which compensatory mechanisms need to be found.
5. A consultant could probably not, without exhaustive and time-consuming study, learn enough about the culture of the organization to suggest reliable new courses of action. Therefore, he must work jointly with members of the organization who *do* know the culture intimately from having lived within it.
6. The client must learn to see the problem for himself, to share in the diagnosis, and to be actively involved in generating a remedy. One of the process consultant's roles is to provide new and challenging alternatives for the client to consider. Decision-making about these alternatives must, however, remain in the hands of the client.
7. It is of prime importance that the process consultant be expert in how to *diagnose* and how to *establish effective helping relationships* with clients. Effective P-C involves the passing on of both these skills.

Definition of Process Consultation

With these assumptions in mind, we can attempt to formulate a more precise definition of P-C.

> P-C is a set of activities on the part of the consultant which help the client to perceive, understand, and act upon process events which occur in the client's environment.

The process consultant seeks to give the client "insight" into what is going on around him, within him, and between him and other people. The events to be observed and learned from are primarily the various human actions which occur in the normal flow of work, in the conduct of meetings, and in formal or informal encounters between members of the organization. Of particular relevance are the client's own actions and their impact on other people.

It should be noted that this definition brings in several new concepts and assumptions, relating in general to what one looks for in making one's *diagnosis*. The important elements to study in an organization are the human processes which occur. A good diagnosis of an organizational problem may go beyond an analysis of such processes but it cannot afford to ignore them. By implication, the process consultant is primarily an expert on processes at the individual, interpersonal, and intergroup levels. His expertise may go beyond these areas, but it must at the minimum include them. Improvement in organizational effectiveness will occur through effective problem finding in the human process area, which in turn will depend upon the ability of managers to learn diagnostic skills through exposure to P-C.

I am not contending that focusing on human processes is the *only* path to increasing organizational effectiveness. Obviously there is room in most organizations for improved production, financial, marketing, and other processes. I am arguing, however, that the various functions which make up an organization are always mediated by the interactions of people, so that the organization can never escape its human processes. . . . As long as organizations are networks of people, there will be processes occurring between them. Therefore, it is obvious that the better understood and better diagnosed these processes are, the greater will be the chances of finding solutions to technical problems which will be accepted and used by members of the organization.

8.3 Models of Helping and Coping

Philip Brickman
Jurgis Karuza, Jr.
Ellen Cohn

Vita Carulli Rabinowitz
Dan Coates
Louise Kidder

There are now two distinct bodies of literature on helping, one in social psychology and one in clinical psychology. The literature in social psychology focuses

Reprinted from *American Psychologist*, April 1982, Vol. 37, No. 4, 368–384.

on the question of when people try to help, on material or instrumental aid as the critical form of help, and on help in short-term relationships or experimental situations. Darley and Latané's (1968) work on group influences on bystander intervention is a prototypical example. The literature in clinical psychology focuses on the question of when attempts to help produce changes in recipients, on instruction and emotional support as the critical forms of help, and on help in long-term or ongoing relationships. The many studies evaluating the success of psychotherapy (see Smith & Glass, 1977) exemplify this research.

It is our belief that (1) a general theory of helping and coping must build a bridge between these two literatures; (2) the critical factor on which such a bridge must be built concerns the form people's behavior takes once they decide to help; and (3) the critical determinants of the form of their behavior are their attributions of responsibility for problems and solutions. Part of the reason the social and clinical literatures have not reached out to one another is that each, in its own way, has taken for granted the form people's behavior will take when they decide to help. In social psychological experiments, helping is typically constrained by the experimental situation; for example, if the response of interest is donating money, this is the only means of helping that subjects are allowed to exhibit. In clinical settings, choices of how to help are typically determined by professional training and institutional context.

What we are focusing on is how people decide whether material aid, instruction, exhortation, discipline, emotional support, or some other form of help is most appropriate and what the consequences of these choices are. We begin with a brief discussion of our view of responsibility and how this differs from past views in the field. We then derive four general models of helping and coping, review findings bearing on the consequences of the choice of models for help givers and help recipients, and present the implications of these models for research and practice in a variety of real-world settings.

Causal and Moral Elements in Attribution of Responsibility

Until recently, research on attribution of responsibility has presumed that people are primarily interested in arriving at an accurate understanding of the causes of events (cf. Fincham & Jaspars, 1980, for a review of this literature). Save for efforts to protect their own ego, the exact extent of which remains controversial (Zuckerman, 1979), people are presumed to assign responsibility for events in a way that best reflects this understanding. It is our contention, on the contrary, that people are less concerned about understanding the causes of events than about controlling behavior, both their own and other people's, to maximize desired outcomes. People control behavior by making rewards and punishments contingent on the occurrence of that behavior. They assign responsibility in order to notify others and themselves that this is the case. People who feel morally responsible in the eyes of others believe that others would feel entitled, and even obliged, to reward or punish them depending on how they acted and what happened (Hamilton, 1978). People who feel morally responsible in their own eyes believe that they would be entitled or obliged to think better or worse of themselves as a function of how they acted and what happened (Schwartz, 1977).

Furthermore, the question of moral responsibility can be conceptualized as involving two separate issues—blame and control (cf. Feinberg, 1970). We assign blame to people when we hold them responsible for having created problems. We assign control to people when we hold them responsible for influencing or changing events. In the language of causal attribution, blame and control are not spoken of directly. Blame arises as a concern indirectly in the question of whether an event was internally caused or externally caused. People are blamed for failing an exam if the cause of the failure was internal (lack of effort), but not if it was external (an impossibly difficult exam). Control arises as a concern indirectly in the question of whether a cause is stable or unstable. People are thought to be able to control an unstable cause (lack of effort, which could be increased in the future), but not a stable cause (lack of ability, which ordinarily cannot be increased).

But this causal representation of moral concerns quickly breaks down on closer inspection, as a number of authors (Kruglanski, 1975; Pettigrew, 1979; Weiner, 1979) have already recognized. There are internal causes, such as disease or lack of ability, for which a person is not blamed, and external causes, such as hostility by others or a car with faulty brakes, for which a person can be blamed (cf. Brickman, Ryan, & Wortman, 1975). There are unstable causes that a person is not held responsible for controlling, like bad luck, and stable ones that a person is supposed to be able to control, such as habitual carelessness or slovenliness. We need a conceptual framework that makes the questions of blame and control the explicit focus.

Fortunately, such a framework already exists in the language we use when talking about problems and solutions. Responsibility for the origin of a problem, generally responsibility for a past event, clearly involves the question of deserving and blame. Responsibility for the solution to a problem, generally responsibility for future events, clearly involves an assessment of who might be able to control events. The answers to these two questions are often correlated. If a person has no responsibility for a problem, we may be inclined not to assign them any responsibility for a solution. Thus we say, "You got yourself into this—now get yourself out," or "It's my fault—let me fix it." This may account for why the two have not been clearly

distinguished in the past. It is also, however, quite unfortunate because it leads people to think that looking for a solution to a problem means finding who is to blame for it, or that discovering who was at fault means that a solution will be found. It also leads people to think that the solution to a problem must necessarily be found on the same level as the origin of that problem (e.g., that a problem with a biological origin must have a biological solution)—or, if the variables producing that problem cannot be changed, that no solution is possible.

Four Models of Helping and Coping

Whether or not people are held responsible for causing their problems and whether or not they are held responsible for solving these problems are the factors determining four fundamentally different orientations to the world, each internally coherent, each in some measure incompatible with the other three. These different models of helping and coping exist in the minds of helpers, aggressors, and recipients of help or aggression. They are also embodied in social institutions that mete out help or punishment. The models are not always publicly displayed or acknowledged. People may not even be aware of the assumptions they have made about responsibility for problems and responsibility for solutions. But they cannot, as social actors, avoid making such assumptions, and the assumptions they make in turn have consequences both for their own behavior and for the behavior of others they influence. Each set of assumptions makes it easier to solve certain problems and harder to solve others. For example, the assumptions in most doctor-patient relationships facilitate the acceptance of information and instructions by the patient but make it hard for patients to assert their own opinions.

Our first task is to describe the nature and implications of these four models of helping and coping. Two of the models, the moral model and the medical model, involve attributing to the same person responsibility either for both the problem and the solution or for neither the problem nor the solution. The other two, the compensatory model and the enlightenment model, involve attributing responsibility for the solution to someone other than the party who is blamed for the problem. Because the moral and medical models are consistent in their attribution of responsibility, they are to some extent easier to keep in mind. They are also more familiar, as indicated by the very fact that familiar labels exist to designate them. It is our conviction, however, that the compensatory and enlightenment models are equally important to the organization of social behavior and that a full understanding of any one of the models can only come in the context of understanding all four.

It should be noted that all of our models specify the behavior expected of both a person labeled as coping with a problem and of other parties labeled as trying to help this person. However dependent people are, they are still held responsible for doing something more or less well, even if it is only being compliant and following instructions. However independent people are, they are still entitled to call on others for some form of help, even if it is only to cheer them on in their efforts to cope. Our models are thus concerned less with the question of whether helping or coping occurs than they are with the question of the assumptions that underlie different forms of helping and coping and the likelihood that the assumptions made by a party trying to help someone with a problem will coincide with the assumptions made by the party who is trying to cope with the problem. The implication of our

analysis is that if either helping or coping is to be understood, the two processes must be studied together rather than separately.

A number of our central hypotheses about the consequences of each model, discussed below, are summarized in Table 1.

Moral Model: People Are Responsible for Problems and Solutions

We call the model in which people are attributed responsibility for both creating and solving their problems the moral model. Clearly, morality is broader than the moral model, and there is a vital sense in which all models of attribution of responsibility are moral models. But the name *moral model* is the one people have used, historically, to indicate that others feel neither obligated to help (since everyone's troubles are of their own making) nor capable of helping (since everyone must find their own solutions). Under the moral model, for example, drinking is seen as a sign of weak character, requiring drinkers to exercise willpower and get control of themselves in order to return to sobriety and respectability. Over the last century we have gradually changed our treatment of alcoholics, homosexuals, and mental patients from a moral basis to a medical one (Albee, 1969; Gusfield, 1967). The gains and losses of this change, as we will see, are still under debate.

Under the moral model, we suggest, actors see themselves and are seen by others as lazy or as failing to make the critical effort that is the necessary and sufficient condition for their progress. The attribution to lack of effort is made despite the fact that the person may be working very hard and that strenuous effort or active striving is the dominant style of actors who apply the moral model to

TABLE 1   Consequences of Attribution of Responsibility in Four Models of Helping and Coping

Attribution to self of responsibility for problem	Attribution to self of responsibility for solution	
	High	**Low**
High	Moral model	Enlightenment model
Perception of self	Lazy	Guilty
Actions expected of self	Striving	Submission
Others besides self who must act	Peers	Authorities
Actions expected of others	Exhortation	Discipline
Implicit view of human nature	Strong	Bad
Potential pathology	Loneliness	Fanaticism
Low	Compensatory model	Medical model
Perception of self	Deprived	Ill
Actions expected of self	Assertion	Acceptance
Others besides self who must act	Subordinates	Experts
Actions expected of others	Mobilization	Treatment
Implicit view of human nature	Good	Weak
Potential pathology	Alienation	Dependency

themselves. However strenuous the effort, it is seen somehow as either not enough or misdirected, with the fault for the error again lying with the individual. Under the moral model, no one besides the individual must act for the individual to be able to change, if he or she wants to, although it may be helplful to actors if they have peers who exhort them to change and improve, as in self-help groups.

The helping that takes place within the moral model consists of reminding people of how responsible they are for their own fate and how important it is that they help themselves. Help of this sort is, of course, more likely to benefit people who have the resources to use it. Thus it is star players that are most likely to profit from moral exhortations from their managers—for example, the dispensation of either a kick in the pants or a pat on the back when such reinforcers are needed. Help in the moral model—help in the form of

rewards and punishments for appropriate behavior—is often not even called help and, thus disguised, can flow more readily to the advantaged. Brickman and Stearns (1978) have shown that subjects consider subsidies to the wealthiest group in a population fair if they are called incentives for investment rather than relief. It is in such forms—crop subsidies, urban renewal programs, tax write-offs, support for public institutions like universities, which are used mainly by the advantaged—that our own society helps the already well-off (Tussing, 1974).

The value of the moral model for coping is that it compels people to take an unequivocal stance toward their lives. If they do not like the way things are, they should recognize that they are responsible for changing them and should start changing them, rather than sitting around complaining or waiting for someone else to do something. If change does not seem worth the effort, they should accept the way things are—recognizing that they were responsible for creating them in the first place—and once again stop complaining or blaming others. The primary message of est training is that participants are totally responsible for everything they ever have been or will be and are fools (or worse) unless they realize this (Brewer, 1975; Frederick, 1974). It is understandable that something like est training might have great appeal to a generation that is struggling to reconcile the conventional adult roles they have moved into with their previous dreams of an alternative life-style. Est teaches them to resolve their ambivalence either by accepting what they are doing as their own personal choice— or (less likely) by breaking away and doing something different.

The potential deficiency of the moral model (a disorder adherents of this model can, but do not have to, fall into) is that it can lead its committed partisans to defend the idea that victims of leukemia chose their leukemia and victims of rape, at some level, chose to be raped (e.g., Schutz, 1979)—in other words, to take completely seriously the idea that the world is just (Lerner, 1980). Moreover, in leading people to believe that they are responsible for all things, it may lead them to believe that all things are possible. As Donald Campbell once said, however, in his seminar on religion for skeptics, the belief in one's own omnipotence is even more incredible than the belief in God. Out of such a belief come mathematicians who ruin their careers by staking them on the solution of an impossible problem and spouses who ruin their lives by staking them on the pursuit of an unworkable relationship (Janoff-Bulman & Brickman, 1982). The moral model is also conducive to a pathology of loneliness. Success is one's own doing, lack of success means that one was not in the right frame of mind. People are at most cheerleaders for one another.

Compensatory Model: People Are Not Responsible for Problems but Are Responsible for Solutions

We call the model in which people are not blamed for their problems but are still held responsible for solving these problems the compensatory model. People in this model see themselves, and are seen by others, as having to compensate for the handicaps or obstacles imposed on them by their situation with a special kind of effort, ingenuity, or collaboration with others. People who help others under the assumptions of this model likewise see themselves as compensating by their help for resources or opportunities that the recipients of the help deserve but somehow do not have. The responsibility for using this help, however, or the critical responsibility for determining whether this help is successful is seen to lie with the recipients.

Under the compensatory model, by our analysis, actors see themselves and are seen by others as deprived or as suffering, not from their own deficiencies, but from the failure of their social environment to provide them with goods and services to which they are entitled. To solve their problems, and perhaps to compel an unwilling social environment to yield the resources necessary to solve them, actors must be assertive. In this they may need the help of peers or subordinates. If they receive training, it is training designed to empower them to deal more effectively with their environment. A nurse or a therapist who approaches a patient in the spirit of the compensatory model says to the patient, in effect, "I am your servant. How can I help you?," rather than "Do what I say." The typical response of observers who assume the compensatory model is to mobilize on behalf of the deprived person—at least for a time, or until the missing resources have apparently been supplied and the person can (and should) be responsible for his or her own fate.

The Reverend Jesse Jackson has, in recent years, been forcefully articulating the spirit of the compensatory model with his repeated assertion to black audiences that "You are not responsible for being down, but you are responsible for getting up." The same message is carried in different words when he says, "Both tears and sweat are wet and salty, but they render a different result. Tears will get you sympathy, but sweat will get you change" ("Learning to Excel," 1978). Parents embody the compensatory model when they tell their children that they do not care who made the mess, they just want it cleaned up, and that they, the parents, often take responsibility for cleaning up messes around the house that they did not make. Wives adopt the compensatory model by seeing their husbands as the source of the problems that need to be solved in the marital relationship and themselves as responsible for finding the solutions (Madden & Janoff-Bulman, 1981).

The strength of the compensatory model for coping is that it allows people to direct their energies outward, working on trying to solve problems or transform their environment without berating themselves for their role in creating these problems, or permitting others to create them, in the first place. The compensatory model also allows help recipients to command the maximum possible respect from their social environment. They are not blamed for their problems, but are given credit for coming up with solutions. Bosses, superiors, and everyone else with the power to do so tries to make sure that any help they receive is received under the assumptions of the compensatory model—something they need in order to discharge their official duties rather than something they need because of personal deficiency.

The potential deficiency of the compensatory model lies in the fact that those who see themselves as continually having to solve problems that they did not create are likely to feel a great deal of pressure in their lives and to wind up with a rather negative or even paranoid view of the world. This seems to be the endemic form of disorder among political leaders, who are commonly given credit for solving problems they did not create and who also commonly come to see the world as a series of conspiracies against them. This kind of problem-solving orientation also appears to govern the Type A behavior pattern in which actors display a great sense of time pressure, competitive achievement striving, high expectations for control, hostility when thwarted—and a greater vulnerability to heart attacks (Friedman & Rosenman, 1974; Jenkins, 1971).

Medical Model: People Are Not Responsible for Problems or Solutions

We call the model in which people are not held responsible for either the origin of their problems or the solution to their problems the medical model because the practice of modern medicine is the most striking and familiar embodiment of these assumptions. Patients are collections of organs that can malfunction or become infected. Drugs, surgery, and other treatments can be aimed directly at the distressed organs, ignoring the patient as a person. Neither the illness nor the treatment is the person's responsibility. It should be noted, however, that our formulation of the medical model includes the practice of medicine only as a special case of a more general set of assumptions about human behavior. The medical model in our sense refers not only to cases in which people are thought to be victims of disease but to all cases in which people are considered subject to forces that were and will continue to be beyond their control. Thus a Skinnerian view of determinism (Skinner, 1971), that human behavior is determined by rewards and punishments in a way that makes it foolish to blame people for their problems or give them credit for solutions, is also a version of our medical model.

Under the medical model, individuals with problems see themselves, and are seen by others, as ill or incapacitated. They are expected to accept this state, which in turn involves exempting them from their ordinary social obligations and imposing on them the responsibility for seeking and using expert help (Arluke, Kennedy, & Kessler, 1979; Parsons, 1951; Segall, 1976). Unless the illness is chronic (Kassebaum & Baumann, 1965) or terminal (Lipman & Sterne, 1969), people are also expected to try to get well. The other actors believed necessary to bring about this change are experts (e.g., doctors) who have been trained to recognize what the problem is and to provide what service or treatment is available. Even when the solution is largely one that the person can or must carry out themselves, such as bed rest, the responsibility for prescribing this solution and for judging whether it has been successful rests with the expert.

The advantage of the medical model for coping is that it allows people to claim and accept help without being blamed for their weakness (they are not responsible for their problem and cannot be expected to take care of it by themselves). The same symptoms that would be punished under another model are entitled to treatment under the medical model. Nettler (1959) found that child care agents who believed that human behavior was determined by biological or environmental forces were less punitive toward children with problems. Mulford and Miller (1964) found that people who defined alcoholism as a disease, rather than as a moral weakness, were more likely to endorse supportive treatment for alcoholics. Valins and Nisbett (1971) suggest that there may be actual therapeutic benefits for people from attributing disturbing symptoms, such as apparent delusions or ostensible homosexual inclinations, to natural or biological causes

rather than psychological ones, especially if they can thereby discount the importance of these symptoms and relieve themselves of the worst of their anxieties.

The deficiency of the medical model is that it fosters dependency. The more psychiatric outpatients believe that their mental disorders are an illness rather than a problem in social learning, the more they feel dependent on mental health professionals (Morrison, Bushell, Hanson, Fentiman, & Holdridge-Crane, 1977). Once people are made to feel dependent on others, they may lose the ability to do even something they once did well (Langer & Benevento, 1978). Giving nursing home residents a larger role in caring for themselves and for others can prevent both psychological and physical deterioration (Langer & Rodin, 1976; Langer, Rodin, Beck, Weinman, & Spitzer, 1979; Rodin & Langer, 1977), and similar procedures can speed recovery of hospital patients (Taylor, 1979). Wack and Rodin (1978) argue that a large part of the helplessness in nursing home patients can be traced directly to medical procedures: Ordinary upsets are treated as symptoms; medication is freely prescribed; permission from doctors and nurses is required before patients can engage in any activity. Recipients of help under the medical model are unlikely to protest inadequate or coercive interventions, since they see no way of solving their problems by themselves. This is, or course, an attractive feature of the medical model for helping agents whose main interest is in controlling the behavior of those receiving help (cf. Szasz, 1960).

Enlightenment Model: People Are Not Responsible for Solutions but Are Responsible for Problems

We call the model in which people are blamed for causing their problems, but not believed to be responsible for solving them, the enlightenment model. This refers to the fact that in applications of this model, central emphasis is placed on enlightening participants as to the true nature of their problem (which they may not regard as something for which they should take responsibility) and the difficult course of action that will be required to deal with it. Representatives of all our models are, to some extent, concerned with instructing people to make the appropriate attributions of responsibility for the causes and solutions to their problems. In the enlightenment model, however, these attributions require people to accept a strikingly negative image of themselves and, in order to improve, to accept a strong degree of submission to agents of social control. Because people tend to resist this position, the emphasis on enlightening them or socializing them to accept it is especially apparent.

Under the enlightenment model, we suggest, actors see themselves and are seen by others as guilty or sinful, or at least as responsible, by their past behavior, for suffering or a problem that they must endure in the present. It is their own impulses—to eat, drink, lie, cheat, steal—that are out of control. To control these impulses, people must submit to the stern or sympathetic discipline provided by agents who represent the authoritative moral (and if necessary physical) force of the community. Since the solution to these problems lies outside the person, the solution can be maintained only so long as the relationship with this external authority or spiritual community is maintained. As testimony to this continuing relationship, past recipients of help under the enlightenment model (e.g., alcoholics; see below) often actively proselytize others to take the same steps that they have taken.

The enlightenment model is the basis of coping whenever people are unable to control what they experience as undesira-ble behavior on their part. When a drug addict or an alcoholic tells people, for the forty-second time, that he or she has turned over a new leaf and is about to change his or her life, this claim of future responsibility is treated with understand-able skepticism. With a repeated history of failures to change, addicts themselves may find it impossible to credit any more promises that rest on their own capacity for self-control. The "Who are you kid-ding?" response may be short-circuited, however, if the troubled person can point to a powerful and respected external agency—God, a religious cult, a new set of duties—as the source of change, especially if this attribution is supported by others who also believe in this agency. Thus Malcolm X, St. Paul, or Charles Colson may be able to make their claims of having changed more credible by pointing to an irresistible external force as the basis of change.

Alcoholics Anonymous (AA), one of the most successful examples of an enlightenment model organization, explic-itly requires new recruits both to take responsibility for their past history of drinking (rather than blaming it on a spouse, a job, or other stressful circum-stances) and to admit that it is beyond their power to control their drinking—without the help of God and the commu-nity of ex-alcoholics in Alcoholics Anony-mous (see Antze, 1976; Gartner, 1976). The group is familiar with all of the usual excuses for alcoholism, and the fate of all of the usual promises to reform, and makes short work of them when they are offered by a newcomer: "At the first meeting, I was asked to tell my story . . . I gave a detailed account of all the stresses that drove me to drink . . . and sat back to wait for compliments. The leader asked this neat Irish gal sitting next to me, 'Well, what do you think of his talk?' She said, 'It sounds like bull—— to me.' Everyone agreed with her" (Breo, 1978). Consistent with the assumptions of the enlightenment model, alcoholics who join Alcoholics Anonymous have been found to have a stronger sense of guilt and responsibility for their past troubles (Trice & Roman, 1970) and a higher need for affiliation and community (Trice, 1959).

The deficiency of the enlightenment model lies in the fact that it can lead to a fanatical or obsessive concern with certain problems and a reconstruction of people's entire lives around the behaviors or the relationships designed to help them deal with these problems. This is the criticism that has most frequently been leveled against AA (e.g., Cummings, 1979), against agencies for the blind that require participants to renounce the visual ability they have lost and become "born again blind men" (Scott, 1969), against cults and religious revival movements, and against what dieting means for so many dieters. Alcoholics Anonymous reorganizes people's lives so that they stay away from their old drinking places and drinking partners, but they retain their concern for drinking as an issue in their lives and spend much of their time at AA meetings with new AA friends. What is more serious, the enlightenment model can place great power in the hands of the agents who control what participants believe is their ability to cope with their lives. Converts are asked to repudiate their old, evil ways and to repeatedly perform acts that bear witness to this repudiation (Kanter, 1972; Lofland & Stark, 1965). All bad things are blamed on the residue of the old life and good things credited to the experience of the new (Proudfoot & Shaver, 1975). Under these circumstances enormous power lies in the threat to withdraw access to the new life and send people back to the old. In most of the foregoing examples, such as Alcoholics Anonymous, this power is diffused in the hands of a variety of friends and fellow sufferers. In some instances, however, it is concentrated in a single charismatic authority—a Charles Manson, a Jim Jones,

a Charles Dederich—who seeks increasingly extreme forms of commitment from followers, culminating in the acts of murder or suicide that shock the rest of the world.

The Models in Four Real-World Settings

Although real-world settings may often contain a mixture of the assumptions that characterize our various models, it would be most encouraging for our analysis to isolate settings that exemplify the models in relatively pure form. This is what Rabinowitz (1978) set out to do in her dissertation. To represent the moral model, she tracked down and interviewed 12 graduates of erhard seminars training (est); to represent the enlightenment model, she interviewed 12 members of a national evangelical group called Campus Crusade for Christ; to represent the compensatory model, she interviewed 12 participants in a job training program sponsored under the Comprehensive Employment and Training Act (CETA); and to represent the medical model, she interviewed 12 students seated in the waiting room of a college infirmary.

Consistent with the assumptions of each model, est participants and Campus Crusade for Christ participants rated themselves as more responsible for their problems and past lives than CETA participants or infirmary patients. CETA and est participants rated themselves as more responsible for finding solutions to their problems than did Campus Crusade members and infirmary patients. Furthermore (and all differences reported here are highly significant), est participants saw themselves as stubborn individuals who were themselves the essential agents of change. CETA participants saw themselves as deprived individuals who needed someone in the role of a tutor to assist them for a short period of time. Infirmary patients saw themselves as sick and needing the help of skilled professionals. Campus Crusade for Christ participants saw themselves as self-destructive and requiring guidance from others who have "been there" and subsequently come to grips with their problems. Clearly these results can only be considered preliminary. But they are highly encouraging to the notion that these models actually exist, in relatively coherent form, in a variety of real-world settings.

Consequences of the Choice of Models

In this section we will attempt to show that attribution of responsibility for problems has very different consequences from attribution of responsibility for solutions to those problems, for those who are the targets of such attributions and for those making such attributions; that, ironically, the assumptions made by help givers to justify their help often undermine the very effectiveness of this help; and, finally, that many of the problems characterizing relationships between help givers and help recipients arise from the fact that the two parties are applying models that are out of phase with one another.

Competence and Burnout

We hypothesize that models in which people are held responsible for solutions (the compensatory and moral models) are more likely to increase people's competence than models in which they are not held responsible for solutions (the medical and enlightenment models). It may also be beneficial not to hold people responsible for problems, though the evidence for this is less clear.

Data that bear on these hypotheses can be derived from a comparison of studies that have looked at the effects of attributing symptoms to external causes with studies that have looked at the effects of attributing progress or improvement to external causes (cf. Valins & Nisbett, 1971). The evidence on symptom attribution or attribution of responsibility for problems is equivocal. Some studies (Barefoot & Girodo, 1972; Rodin & Langer, 1980; Ross, Rodin, & Zimbardo, 1969; Storms & Nisbett, 1970) have found therapeutic gains when subjects are induced to believe that their symptoms (anxiety, insomnia, physical decline) have external rather than internal causes. Other studies have found that highlighting possible external causes for symptoms has no effects or negative effects (Bootzin, Herman, & Nicassio, 1976; Chambliss & Murray, 1979a; Singerman, Borkovec, & Baron, 1976). These contradictory results may be due to the fact that mentioning an external cause for symptoms relieves anxiety, but also undermines the degree to which subjects give themselves credit for any subsequent improvement. Results in any particular experiment would depend on which of these two factors was stronger.

With regard to attribution of responsibility for improvement, on the other hand, benefits derive from making internal rather than external causes salient (to use the causal language employed in past studies), and the evidence for this is quite clear. In the same study of smoking reduction in which they found no effects of what subjects were told about the causes of their symptoms (like irritability), Chambliss and Murray (1979a) found that informing subjects that their gains (reduced smoking) were due to their own efforts, rather than a drug, did indeed help subjects to reduce their smoking. Earlier, Davison and Valins (1969) found that subjects who believed that a solution (an improvement in their ability to tolerate painful shocks) was due to them rather than to a pill they had taken were better able to endure shocks in the future. Working with psychiatric outpatients, Liberman (1978) found that members of a group induced to attribute improvement to medication (actually a placebo) were significantly less likely to maintain these changes three months later than were members of a group induced to attribute improvement to their own efforts. Chambliss and Murray (1979a, 1979b) have reported, however, that self-efficacy manipulations were less effective for subjects classified as external on Rotter's (1966) scale than for subjects who believed in their own ability to control reinforcements.

Attributing responsibility for a solution to external agents is most likely to result in temporary, rather than permanent, improvement, that is, improvement that is maintained only so long as the external agent is salient (Kelman, 1958). Thus Miller, Brickman, and Bolen (1975) found that second graders who were persuaded by their teacher that they should keep their classroom neat and tidy decreased their littering for a while but then returned to a baseline rate. Only children who had been convinced that they were neat and tidy people, and who attributed their newfound cleanliness to themselves, maintained the improvement over subsequent months. Likewise, Nentwig (1978) found that subjects who were led to attribute their reduction in smoking behavior to a deterrent drug (actually a placebo) showed substantial short-term gains but lost most of these by the time of a six-month follow-up. At this point, a group whose treatment had emphasized the importance of their own actions was significantly more successful in controlling smoking behavior. Jeffrey (1974) found a comparable superiority in the maintenance of weight loss by subjects who were induced to reward themselves for this loss as compared to subjects who were rewarded for the loss by the experimenter (cf. also Dienstbier & Leak, Note 1). The general argument that people tend to persist more in the pursuit of behavior that they see as intrinsically determined rather than determined by external forces, like pay, is developed by

deCharms (1968), Deci (1974), and Lepper and Greene (1978).

Similarly, in the literature on attribution, achievement, and helplessness, subjects who believe that they can control their own outcomes are more likely to persist in the face of difficulties and less likely to show debilitating effects of stress (e.g., Dweck, 1975; Seligman, 1975). According to Burgess and Holmstrom (cited in Bennetts, 1978), a rape victim who has behavior she can blame and change (e.g., gullibility in listening to a fast-talking stranger) is likely to cope better than a victim who has no behavior she can blame (e.g., someone attacked while she was asleep in bed). The advantage of believing one is responsible for future solutions appears to hold regardless of whether people attribute problems to a cause for which they are not responsible (bad luck) or a cause for which they are responsible (lack of effort). As in the case of psychiatric symptoms, attribution of responsibility for progress or for a solution appears to be more important than attribution of responsibility for the problem. Like people with high self-esteem or high expectations for success (Janoff-Bulman & Brickman, 1982), high-status actors are more likely to assume responsibility for solving problems and to take the kind of active role in exploring and structuring these problems that makes solutions more likely. Alkire, Collum, Kaswan, and Love (1968) showed that sorority seniors were better able to decode messages sent by sorority freshmen than vice versa, largely because the senior recipients took a more active role in questioning the transmitter about points in the message that they did not understand.

The Dilemma of Helping

All this leads us to recognize a trap that we call the *dilemma of helping*. The very label *help* implies that recipients are not responsible for solving a problem (as in the medical or the enlightenment models) and that help givers are. When people say that someone deserves help, they may mean only that this individual is not to be blamed for their problems—an important determinant of the willingness to help (cf. Barnes, Ickes, & Kidd, 1979). But, unwittingly or not, they also imply that this individual is not in control of and cannot be held responsible for solutions. When people fail to distinguish between attribution of responsibility for a problem and for a solution, they must choose between two unsatisfactory alternatives: holding actors responsible for both problems and solutions and thus not giving help; or holding actors responsible for neither problems nor solutions and giving help on terms that undermine actors' sense of competence and control and their ability to make effective use of the help itself. Thus, in a series of studies of the elderly, Karuza, Zevon, and their colleagues (Karuza, Zevon, Rabinowitz, & Brickman, in press) found the elderly preferred to apply the medical model, perhaps as the one justifying the most substantial form of help, yet were better off (in terms of positive affect and self-perceived coping) when other models were applied. Our preference for the compensatory model rests on our conviction that it is the only one that resolves this dilemma of helping— justifying the act of helping (since recipients are not responsible for their problems) but still leaving help recipients with an active sense of control over their lives (since they are held responsible for using this help to find solutions).

Ironic support for the value of the compensatory model comes from evidence that help givers (who assume that they are responsible for solving a problem they did not create) often benefit from helping even when the recipients of that help (who are not attributed responsibility for a solution, whether or not they are blamed for the problem) do not. School children who are in trouble academically have been found to profit from being given the responsibility for tutoring a young child (Allen, 1976). Zajonc (1976) has shown that the pattern of IQ development in families, as revealed by a number of national surveys, requires the assumption that all children except the last born profit intellectually from having a younger sibling whom they can teach. Bargh and Schul (1980) have shown that people learn more effectively when they anticipate having to teach someone else in the future, and new college professors are commonly impressed with how much more they learn from preparing a course than from taking one. On an affective level, college students working to help mental patients (Holzberg, Gewirtz, & Ebner, 1964) or troubled boys (Goodman, 1967) showed significantly more positive change in their self-acceptance than control groups not involved in such helping. By the testimony of members, a major reason for the success of Alcoholics Anonymous is that participants not only try to solve their own problems (which, as we have seen, they can do in this context only by accepting the discipline of the organization) but increasingly take responsibility for helping other members with their drinking problems.

There is, however, a further irony in this one-sided state whereby the assumptions in helping may benefit the helper more than the recipient of help. Helpers generally want to succeed in being helpful, just as people want to succeed in anything they do (cf. Weiss, Boyer, Lombardo, & Stich, 1973). Among professional helpers, liking for clients is consistently correlated with the belief that clients have improved or will impove (Doherty, 1971; Thompson, 1969; Wills, 1978). Moreover, by the social definition of their role, therapists are supposed to be helpful. If they choose the wrong model, however, they will not be, because the assumptions they make will undermine the success of their very effort to help; and in the long run, their own sense of competence and self-esteem will decline along with those of their clients. This decline in self-esteem and involvement has been observed in numerous populations of helping professionals—social workers, poverty lawyers, nurses, teachers—and has even been given a name, *burnout* (Freudenberger, 1974; Maslach, 1978).

Communication and Social Support

Since help threatens both a recipient's status and a donor's resources, it can also clearly be a threat to the solidarity of their relationship (cf. Brickman & Bulman, 1977). In general we hypothesize that help will contribute to the solidarity and stability of a relationship when it embodies assumptions that are congruent with the dominant assumptions of that relationship; it will undermine the stability of the relationship when it embodies assumptions that conflict with the dominant assumptions of the relationship. Thus unequal status relationships will be most stable when help in them flows from the superior to the inferior along the lines of the enlightenment and the medical models (the two models most likely to foster deference from the recipient) and from the inferior to the superior along the lines of the moral and the compensatory models (the two models least demanding of deference from the recipient). Accordingly, lower-class patients are more likely to continue in therapy with a high-status, middle-class therapist when the therapist is controlling and directive (along the lines of helpers in the enlightenment and medical models) than when the therapist is passive or nondirective (Duckro, Beal, & George, 1979). High-status parties are less likely to have help forced on them for minor infractions (Hollander, 1958) or when they do not want it (Rushing, 1969) and less likely to be seen as accepting coercive or

directive help (Thibaut & Riecken, 1955).

The literature on helping and coping has emphasized the positive aspects of having close personal relationships (Cobb, 1976). People with such relationships have been found to cope better with, among other things, problems of pregnancy (Nuckolls, Cassel, & Kaplan, 1972), physical disability (Smits, 1974), terminal illness (Weisman & Worden, 1975), and bereavement (Clayton, 1975). There are a number of recent indications, however, that this uncritical view of social support (the very label connotes something with positive effects) is too rosy. Pearlin and Schooler (1978) found that seeking help for marital and parental problems correlated with more, rather than less, distress, while Lieberman and Mullan (1978) found no benefits from use of a wide variety of both professional and nonprofessional sources of help. Wortman and her associates have described in compelling detail the difficulties experienced by cancer patients (Wortman & Dunkel-Schetter, 1979), rape victims (Coates, Wortman, & Abbey, 1979), and depressed people (Coates & Wortman, 1980) in trying to elicit a satisfactory response from others.

The problem with much social support, in our view, comes from the fact that people trying to be supportive apply the wrong model to victims or misunderstand the model that victims are trying to apply to themselves. The process of what we might call secondary victimization (the process by which victims are victimized once again by awkward or ineffective efforts to help them) appears to have two major phases. In the first phase, when counselors or friends hear rape victims blaming themselves (Janoff-Bulman, 1979) or paraplegics saying that their accident was the result of an activity they had chosen and would choose again (Bulman & Wortman, 1977), they are baffled by what appears to be the victims' tendency to blame themselves for something that was in no way their fault. Friends fail to understand that what may seem to be the victims' need for blame is actually their need for control and that victims' belief that they have been and will be in control of their lives is more vital than ever to them as they attempt to explain and adapt to the traumatic event (illness, rape, bereavement) that has just befallen them. The plight of the victim makes others anxious as well as sympathetic, and they express this ambivalence by a complex pattern of approach and avoidance that is in fact quite confusing to victims (e.g., Wortman & Dunkel-Schetter, 1979).

In the second phase, friends finally switch from trying to protect and take care of victims to wanting victims to again take over responsibility for their own lives. Now, however, victims are no longer ready to do this. Having never been able to fully share their feelings about the traumatic event with supportive others, they are not yet ready to relinquish thinking and talking about it. Having learned that others are masking ambivalent feelings, they are no longer confident of their ability to share feelings or to master their social environment. Friends, increasingly puzzled by and impatient with victims' seemingly inexplicable dependency, may now begin to blame them, for their current behavior if not for their initial victimization, in a way that they conspicuously avoided doing in the early days after the loss.

It is important here to understand that the group that victims may draw on for sympathy about their problem may be quite different from the group that they need to provide useful information and support for possible solutions to this problem. People may recognize that they have a problem by comparison with normal others, but need a group of similarly victimized others to determine who can realistically be held responsible for various possible solutions. Similarly, in the study of relative deprivation (cf. Crosby, 1976), we need to understand that people may determine that they are being unfairly treated by comparing themselves with one set of others (e.g., others apparently less qualified than they who are earning almost as much money) and yet look to an entirely different set of others to establish the feasibility of different possible solutions (e.g., other occupational groups who have coped with a similar status threat).

Implications for Research and Practice

We may have wrong models in place in a number of areas—and worse yet, the tendency to respond to trouble by prescribing larger doses of the same model, rather than considering a different one. Certainly we have many social programs that are not getting the intended results. McCord (1978) recently reported the results of a 30-year follow-up to the famous Cambridge-Somerville delinquency study, indicating that boys in the experimental group, who had been given counselors and support, appeared to be worse off on a variety of dimensions than did boys in the control group. Stebbins, St. Pierre, Proper, Anderson, and Cerva's (1978) analysis of the nationwide set of programs in compensatory education known as Follow Through found that children enrolled in such programs were less likely to do well on a number of variables than were comparable children not enrolled. At the very least we need to know exactly what models are in place in such social enterprises. In the following sections we discuss what we know and what we need to know about the models of helping and coping in a number of important areas of social practice.

Education

It seems reasonable to believe that the dominant model for student behavior changes as we move from elementary school to high school to college. In grade school, children's behavior is rather fully programmed by teachers, as in the medical model. Children learn to follow directions in elementary school. In high school students are socialized to take somewhat more initiative in solving problems they are confronted with, as in the compensatory model. Simply by coming to class regularly and turning in assignments on time they demonstrate the reliability that will later be valued highly in many routine jobs (cf. Bowles & Gintis, 1966). In college there is still less supervision of student activity. Students create and define their own problems—what projects to work on, whether to attend class—and provide (or fail to provide) their own solutions, as in the moral model. Here they demonstrate the kind of intrinsic motivation and internal control that will be of value in executives and bureaucrats (cf. the structure of work place control outlined by Edwards, 1979). The discipline of reform school, for those students unfortunate enough to fall into it, embodies the assumptions of the enlightenment model.

For reasons previously discussed, we tend to believe that either the compensatory or the moral model is the most favorable one for student performance. In a survey of 36 elementary school classrooms, Deci, Nezlek, and Sheinman (1981) found that teachers who used rewards to give students information, rather than to control them, had students who were more intrinsically motivated (curious, wanting to be challenged and to demonstrate mastery) and perceived themselves as more competent (cf. also deCharms, 1976; Dweck, 1975). In general, however, it is not posible to know from past research whether various treatments increased students' sense of responsibility for both problems and solutions, only problems, or only solutions, or how students and teachers apportioned responsibility for shared problems (cf. Gordon, 1974). Moreover, two cautions to the belief that it is

always good to hold students responsible for their learning must be registered. It may not be optimal for teachers to impute too much responsibility to students, if this leads them to cut down the amount of instruction, support, or discipline to less than what students actually need to solve problems. Thus Swann and Snyder (1980) found that subjects who were induced to believe that ability emerges spontaneously from natural development of pupils' intrinsic capabilities provided pupils that they believed had high ability with inadequate instruction for performing the task in question (a card trick). Second, the same model may not be optimal for all students. Even though training people in achievement motivation and self-determination has led to substantially more productive behavior in a number of settings (McClelland & Winter, 1969), Kolb (1965) found that a sample of boys low in socioeconomic status actually did worse in school after such training than did a control group of similar status who did not receive this training.

Psychotherapy

Different forms of psychotherapy make different assumptions about the nature of the problem and the solution, assumptions that may be well suited to certain categories of patients and ill suited to others.

Rational-emotive therapy (Ellis, 1962) and existential therapy (Frankl, 1969) appear to embody the assumptions of the moral model. Ellis (1973) is quite clear that individuals' feelings of worthlessness do not come from the attitudes of a parent or a spouse, but from the individual's tendency to take these attitudes too seriously, and that individuals have the primary responsibility for recognizing this and for changing their distorted thinking. The therapist's role is to attack these distortions directly, vigorously, and persistently and to exhort the patient to change.

Psychoanalysis, at the other extreme, seems to embody the assumptions of the medical model. It is human nature, parental failures, and the rigid demands of civilized society that produce neurotic problems. Furthermore, since the dynamics of behavior lie hidden in the unconscious, unanalyzed patients cannot possibly know enough about themselves to solve these problems. The device by which change is to be produced is the patient's relationship with (and dependence on) the analyst, conceptualized as a transference of the major emotional patterns from the patient's previous life.

Therapeutic communities, like Synanon, Daytop Village, Overeaters' Anonymous, and Alcoholics Anonymous, appear to embody the assumptions of the enlightenment model, as described in our initial presentation of that model. Clients bring a problem, such as drug addiction, for which they feel responsible and yet without resources to cure. The discipline of the therapeutic community allows them to see the prospects for change as having a hopeful, external source that has apparently been successful with people even more down and out than they.

Finally, we are inclined to see cognitive behavior therapy as embodying the assumptions of the compensatory model. The role of the therapist is the limited but critical one of teaching clients how to alter maladaptive cognitive processes and environmental contingencies (Mahoney & Arnkoff, 1978). Once taught how to recognize and control these contingencies, clients are expected to set their own standards, monitor their own performance, and reward or reinforce themselves appropriately (Kanfer, 1977).

Future research can assess whether different models are actually more successful when applied to disorders in which they are congruent with the patient's or significant others' assumptions about who is responsible for what. Phobia, for example, is a state in which people are continually mobilized against what they feel is some external threat, whereas depression is a state in which people are preoccupied with themselves as the apparent source of insoluble problems. It may be no accident that behavior therapy has had its most striking success with phobias, while highly structured therapeutic communities, mood-elevating drugs, and perhaps psychoanalysis may be most successful for people who are unhappy with their lives in general and uncertain what to do about it.

Prisons

Although crime may have its ultimate cause in environmental conditions or in the fact that some segments of the population are denied access to legitimate means for achieving success (Merton, 1957), it is pointless to call for a compensatory model for treatment of offenders. The first demand of the law is that people be held responsible for their actions. The punishment that is administered to offenders, once they have been found guilty, is designed to reaffirm the validity of the rule that has been violated and to reassure onlookers that they will be protected against further violations in the future, either by the defendant (through incapacitation or rehabilitation) or by other potential offenders (through deterrence).

The medical model, like the compensatory model, suffers in the public eye as a basis for treating offenders in that it does not hold offenders responsible for their past actions. The medical model leads to the idea that offenders should be released when they are cured, however long or short a time this may take. Interestingly enough, this idea is also unpopular among offenders, because it compels them to participate in rehabilitation programs that they find worthless or demeaning and also deprives them of any firm knowledge of when they will be considered cured and released.

The enlightenment model, as we have seen, is generally the model that guides responses to offenders. Since offenders are responsible for a problem and—under this model—cannot be considered responsible for a solution, they must be isolated in a community that will provide them with the discipline and self-control they seem to lack. Unfortunately prisons, as they now exist, meet none of the requirements for an effective therapeutic community but, rather, create a situation in which offenders learn more about how to evade authority, in prison and in society, than about how to get what they want by legitimate means.

Under the remaining model, the moral model, offenders are both blamed for their past actions—as required by our sense of justice (cf. Lerner, 1980)—and yet are still held responsible for some behavior that would contribute to the solution of the problem they have caused. The essential feature of a moral model for offenders is the requirement that offenders make some form of restitution either to victims or to society, as a way of rebuilding respect both in their own eyes and those of others. Brickman (1977) has discussed at length how restitution stands as a more compelling principle of justice than either deterrence or rehabilitation and how many of the practical difficulties associated with restitution programs may be overcome (see also Forer, 1980). For example, restitution programs may operate by allowing offenders to do useful work while in prison, thus protecting society from contact with people it regards as dangerous while still allowing such people to contribute to the general welfare.

Welfare

Everyone appears to agree that the major problem with welfare is that it cuts people off from incentives for providing their own solutions. Usually the creation of this dependency is seen as the inadvertent by-product of a generosity whose implications have not been thought through. The Westerners who gave steel axes to Stone Age Australians, for example, may have been unaware that the replacement of stone axes with steel ones, which the tribes themselves could not create, would unravel a good part of the kinship and exchange structure of the culture (Sharp, 1952). In other analyses, however, the dependency and humiliation created by welfare is seen as the deliberate result of a strategy of social control designed to motivate workers to stay at their low-paying jobs while convincing them that the system cares about their struggles to support themselves (Piven & Cloward, 1972).

The dominant model for welfare, therefore, is either the medical model or the enlightenment model, both of which presume the recipient needs to be taken care of, though differing in the extent to which they blame the recipient for being in this predicament. The moral model is of little use for questions of welfare, since welfare usually involves providing recipients with some very specific resources that they need (such as food or shelter), not merely exhortation to work harder and to do better (though such sermons may, of course, accompany welfare to make clear to recipients the moral universe from which their dependency has excluded them). The remaining model is the compensatory model, with whose virtues we are already familiar. There is, interestingly enough, an outstandingly successful example of welfare that was run on the assumptions of the compensatory model: the G.I. Bill passed after World War II. Aid under this bill was given to people who were seen as entitled to it (veterans) for a specific purpose (education) and a limited period of time. It was not a gift or a privilege for which recipients had to be grateful. It was routinely available, not something recipients had to go out of their way to solicit (cf. Gross, Wallston, &

Piliavin, 1979). Moreover, it was clear that recipients had the right to refuse this aid, if they experienced it as unnecessary, and the ability to determine that it would be used by them in times, places, and quantities that they found suited to their own needs (cf. Gaylin, Glasser, Marcus, & Rothman, 1978).

Conclusion

We have used a distinction between attribution of responsibility for a problem and attribution of responsibility for a solution to derive four general models that specify what form people's behavior will take when they try to help others (or to help themselves) and what form they expect recipients' behavior to take. We have reviewed evidence from both social and clinical psychology indicating that these models are internally consistent, have significant consequences, and are reasonable descriptions of alternative approaches in education, psychotherapy, law, and welfare.

The derivation and description of these models is, however, only a beginning. We need research to establish what factors determine the choice of model by different agents and what factors determine the effectiveness of each model in given situations. For example:

1. Are some helping models (e.g., those that attribute responsibility for solutions to clients) uniformly better than others? Or are different models best for different clients?
2. Are client-provider teams using the same models more effective, or are clients better motivated by providers whose models are somewhat discrepant from the client's initial assumptions?
3. Is it better to apply one model to a help recipient consistently or to change models as the recipient becomes first more and then less involved in the helping relationship (e.g., to begin with models that imply little recipient responsibility and gradually increase the responsibility attributed to recipients; cf. Lemkau, Bryant, & Brickman, in press)?
4. Do help givers burn out less using some models than using others? Do congruent or consistently applied models reduce work stress for professional service providers?
5. How do organizational structures (cf. Lenrow, 1978) and professional role socialization determine the choice of helping model? How do the past experiences of recipient populations determine recipients' choice of models?
6. Has there been a historic evolution of the dominant models applied to different populations? Do new models arise out of the clash of older ones? For example, the prospective emergence of the compensatory model as the dominant one in childbearing situations (Cronenwett & Brickman, Note 2) may be seen as an evolving compromise between the competing claims of establishment medical models and natural childbirth movements intially taking the form of enlightenment models.

The answers to these and similar questions will add substantially to our understanding of what happens when people try to help and why they are successful at this enterprise less often than they would like to be.

Reference Notes

1. Dienstbier, R. A., & Leak, G. K. *Effects of monetary reward on maintenance of weight loss: An extension of the overjustification effect*. Paper presented at the meeting of the American Psychological Association, Washington, D.C., September 1976.
2. Cronenwett, L., & Brickman, P. *Models of helping and coping in childbirth*. Manuscript.

References

Albee, G. Emerging concepts of mental illness and models of treatment: The psychological point of view. *American Journal of Psychiatry*, 1969, *125*, 870–876.

Alkire, A. A., Collum, M. E., Kaswan, J., & Love, L. R. Information exchange and accuracy of verbal communication under social power conditions. *Journal of Personality and Social Psychology*, 1968, *9*, 301–308.

Allen, V. L. *Children as teachers: Theory and research on tutoring*. New York: Academic Press, 1976.

Antze, P. The role of ideologies in peer psychotherapy organizations: Some theoretical considerations and three case studies. *Journal of Applied Behavioral Science*, 1976, *12*, 323–346.

Arluke, A., Kennedy, L., & Kessler, R. C. Reexamining the sick-role concept: An empirical assessment. *Journal of Health and Social Behavior*, 1979, *20*, 30–36.

Barefoot, J., & Girodo, M. The misattribution of smoking cessation symptoms. *Canadian Journal of Behavioral Sciences*, 1972, *4*, 358–363.

Bargh, J., & Schul, Y. On the cognitive benefits of teaching. *Journal of Educational Psychology*, 1980, *72*, 593–604.

Barnes, R. D., Ickes, W., & Kidd, R. F. Effects of the perceived intentionality and stability of another's dependency on helping behavior. *Personality and Social Psychology Bulletin*, 1979, *5*, 367–372.

Bennetts, L. The type of attack affects rape victims' speed of recovery, study shows. *New York Times*, April 14, 1978, p. A16.

Bootzin, R., Herman, C. P., & Nicassio, P. The power of suggestion: Another examination of misattribution and insomnia. *Journal of Personality and Social Psychology*, 1976, *34*, 673–679.

Bowles, S. E., & Gintis, H. *Schooling in capitalist America*. New York: Basic Books, 1966.

Breo, D. AA equals RX for doctors whose lives get all bottled up. *Chicago Tribune*, Dec. 2, 1978, Section 1c, 1–2.

Brewer, M. Erhard seminars training: "We're gonna tear you down and put you back together." *Psychology Today*, August 1975, pp. 35–40; 82–89.

Brickman, P. Crime and punishment in sports and society. *Journal of Social Issues*, 1977, *33*(1), 140–164.

Brickman, P., & Bulman, R. J. Pleasure and pain in social comparison. In J. M. Suls & R. L. Miller (Eds.), *Social comparison processes*. Washington, D.C.: Hemisphere, 1977.

Brickman, P., Ryan, K., & Wortman, C. B. Causal chains: Attribution of responsibility as a function of immediate and prior causes. *Journal of Personality and Social Psychology*, 1975, *32*, 1060–1067.

Brickman, P., & Stearns, A. Help that is not called help. *Personality and Social Psychology Bulletin*, 1978, *4*, 314–317.

Bulman, R. J., & Wortman, C. Attributions of blame and coping in the "real world": Severe accident victims react to their lot. *Journal of Personality and Social Psychology*, 1977, *35*, 351–363.

Chambliss, C., & Murray, E. J. Cognitive procedures for smoking reduction: Symptom attribution versus efficacy attribution. *Cognitive Therapy and Research*, 1979, *3*, 91–95. (a)

Chambliss, C. A., & Murray, E. J. Efficacy attribution, locus of control, and weight loss. *Cognitive Therapy and Research*, 1979, *3*, 349–353. (b)

Clayton, P. J. The effect of living alone on bereavement symptoms. *American Journal of Psychiatry*, 1975, *132*(2), 133–137.

Coates, D., & Wortman, C. B. Depression maintenance and interpersonal control. In A. Baum & J. Singer (Eds.), *Advances in environmental psychology* (Vol. 2). Hillsdale, N.J.: Erlbaum, 1980.

Coates, D., Wortman, C. B., & Abbey, A. Reactions to victims. In I. H. Frieze, D. Bar-Tal, & J. S. Carroll (Eds.), *New approaches to social problems.* San Francisco, Calif.: Jossey-Bass, 1979.

Cobb, S. Social support as a moderator of life stress. *Psychosomatic Medicine*, 1976, *38*, 300–314.

Crosby, F. A model of egotistic relative deprivation. *Psychological Review*, 1976, *83*, 85–113.

Cummings, N. A. Turning bread into stones: Our modern antimiracle. *American Psychologist*, 1979, *34*, 1119–1129.

Darley, J. M., & Latané, B. Bystander intervention in emergencies: Diffusion of responsibility. *Journal of Personality and Social Psychology*, 1968, *8*, 377–383.

Davison, G. C., & Valins, S. Maintenance of self-attributed and drug-attributed behavior change. *Journal of Personality and Social Psychology*, 1969, *11*, 25–33.

deCharms, R. *Enhancing motivation: Change in the classroom.* New York: Irvington, 1976.

Deci, E. L. *Intrinsic motivation.* New York: Plenum, 1974.

Deci, E. L., Nezlek, J., & Sheinman, L. Characteristics of the rewarder and intrinsic motivation of the rewardee. *Journal of Personality and Social Psychology*, 1981, *40*, 1–10.

Doherty, E. G. Social attraction and choice among psychiatric patients and staff: A review. *Journal of Health and Social Behavior*, 1971, *12*, 279–290.

Duckro, P., Beal, D., & George, C. Research on the effects of disconfirmed client role expectations in psychotherapy: A critical review. *Psychological Bulletin*, 1979, *86*, 260–275.

Dweck, C. S. The role of expectations and attributions in the alleviation of learned helplessness. *Journal of Personality and Social Psychology*, 1975, *31*, 674–685.

Edwards, R. *Contested terrain: The transformation of the workplace in the twentieth century.* New York: Basic Books, 1979.

Ellis, A. *Reason and emotion in psychotherapy.* New York: Lyle Stuart, 1962.

Ellis, A. (E. Sagarin, Ed.). *Humanistic psychotherapy: The rational-emotive approach.* New York: Julian, 1973.

Feinberg, J. *Doing and deserving: Essays in the theory of responsibility.* Princeton, N.J.: Princeton University Press, 1970.

Fincham, F. D., & Jaspars, J. M. Attribution of responsibility: From man the scientist to man the lawyer. In L. Berkowitz (Ed.), *Advances in experimental social psychology* (Vol. 13). New York: Academic Press, 1980.

Forer, L. G. *Criminals and victims: A trial judge reflects on crime and punishment.* New York: Norton, 1980.

Frankl, V. E. *The will to meaning: Foundations and applications of logotherapy.* New York: New American Library, 1969.

Frederick, C. *Est: Playing the game the new way.* New York: Dell, 1974.

Freudenberger, H. J. Staff burn-out. *Journal of Social Issues*, 1974, *30*(1), 159–165.

Friedman, M., & Rosenman, R. H. *Type A behavior and your heart.* New York: Knopf, 1974.

Gartner, A. Self-help and mental health. *Social Policy*, 1976, *7*(2), 28–40.

Gaylin, W., Glasser, I., Marcus, S., & Rothman, D. J. *Doing good: The limits of benevolence.* New York: Pantheon, 1978.

Goodman, G. An experiment with companionship therapy: College students and troubled boys—Assumptions, selection, and design. *American Journal of Public Health*, 1967, *57*, 1772–1777.

Gordon, T. *Teacher effectiveness training.* New York: Wyden, 1974.

Gross, A. E., Wallston, B. S., & Piliavin, I. M. Reactance, attribution, equity, and the help recipient. *Journal of Applied Social Psychology*, 1979, *9*, 297–313.

Gusfield, J. R. Moral passage: The symbolic process in public designations of deviance. *Social Problems*, 1967, *15*, 175–188.

Hamilton, V. L. Who is responsible? Toward a *social* social psychology of responsibility attribution. *Social Psychology*, 1978, *41*, 316–328.

Hollander, E. P. Conformity, status, and

idiosyncrasy credit. *Psychological Review*, 1958, *65*, 117–127.

Holzberg, J. D., Gewirtz, H., & Ebner, E. Changes in moral judgment and self-acceptance as a function of companionship with hospitalized mental patients. *Journal of Consulting Psychology*. 1964, *28*, 299–303.

Janoff-Bulman, R. Characterologic versus behavioral self-blame: Inquiries into depression and rape. *Journal of Personality and Social Psychology*, 1979, *37*, 1798–1809.

Janoff-Bulman, R., & Brickman, P. Expectations and what people learn from failure. In N. T. Feather (Ed.), *Expectations and actions*. Hillsdale, N.J.: Erlbaum, 1982.

Jeffrey, D. B. A comparison of the effects of external control and self-control on the modification and maintenance of weight. *Journal of Abnormal Psychology*, 1974, *83*, 404–410.

Jenkins, C. D. Psychologic and social precursors of coronary disease. *New England Journal of Medicine*, 1971, *284*, 244–255; 307–317.

Kanfer, F. H. The many faces of self-control, or behavior modification changes its focus. In R. B. Stuart (Ed.), *Behavioral self-management*. New York: Brunner/Mazel, 1977.

Kanter, R. M. *Commitment and community*. Cambridge, Mass.: Harvard University Press, 1972.

Karuza, J., Jr., Zevon, M. A., Rabinowitz, V. C., & Brickman, P. Attribution of responsibility by helpers and by recipients. In T. A. Wills (Ed.), *Basic processes in helping relationships*. New York: Academic Press, in press.

Kassebaum, G. G., & Baumann, B. O. Dimensions of the sick role in chronic illness. *Journal of Health and Human Behavior*, 1965, *6*, 16–27.

Kelman, H. C. Compliance, identification, and internalization: Three processes of opinion change. *Journal of Conflict Resolution*, 1958, *2*, 51–60.

Kolb, D. A. Achievement motivation training for underachieving high-school boys. *Journal of Personality and Social Psychology*, 1965, *2*, 783–792.

Kruglanski, A. W. The endogenous—exogenous partition in attribution theory. *Psychological Review*, 1975, *82*, 387–406.

Langer, E. J., & Benevento, A. Self-induced dependence. *Journal of Personality and Social Psychology*, 1978, *36*, 866–893.

Langer, E. J., & Rodin, J. The effects of choice and enhanced personal responsibility for the aged: A field experiment in an institutional setting. *Journal of Personality and Social Ps</ology*, 1976, *34*, 191–198.

Langer, E. J., Rodin, J., Beck, P., Weinman, C., & Spitzer, L. Environmental determinants of memory improvement in late adulthood. *Journal of Personality and Social Psychology*, 1979, *37*, 2003–2013.

Learning to excel in school. *Time*, July 21, 1978, pp. 45–46.

Lemkau, J. P., Bryant, F. B., & Brickman, P. Client commitment to the helping relationship. In T. A. Wills (Ed.), *Basic processes in helping relationships*. New York: Academic Press, in press.

Lenrow, P. B. The work of helping strangers. *American Journal of Community Psychology*, 1978, *6*, 555–571.

Lepper, M. R., & Greene, D. *The hidden costs of reward*. Hillsdale, N.J.: Erlbaum, 1978.

Lerner, M. J. *The belief in a just world*. New York: Plenum Press, 1980.

Liberman, B. L. The role of mastery in psychotherapy: Maintenance of improvement and prescriptive change. In J. D. Frank, R. Hoehn-Saric, D. D. Imber, B. L. Liberman, & A. R. Stone (Eds.), *The effective ingredients of successful psychotherapy*. New York: Brunner/Mazel, 1978.

Lieberman, M. A., & Mullan, J. T. Does help help? The adaptive consequences of obtaining help from professionals and social networks. *American Journal of Community Psychology*, 1978, 6, 499–517.

Lipman, A., & Sterne, R. S. Aging in the United States: Ascription of a terminal sick role. *Sociology and Social Research*, 1969, 53, 194-203

Lofland, J., & Stark, R. Becoming a world-saver: A theory of conversion to a deviant perspective. *American Sociological Review*, 1965, 30, 862–874.

Madden, M. E., & Janoff-Bulman, R. Blame, control, and marital satisfaction: Wives' attributions for conflict in marriage. *Journal of Marriage and the Family*, 1981, 43, 663–674.

Mahoney, M. J., & Arnkoff, D. A. Cognitive and self control therapies. In S. L. Garfield & A. E. Bergin (Eds.), *Handbook of psychotherapy and behavior change*. New York: Wiley, 1978.

Maslach, C. The client role in staff burnout. *Journal of Social Issues*, 1978, 34(4), 111–124.

McClelland, D. C., & Winter, D. G. *Motivating economic achievement*. New York: Free Press, 1969.

McCord, J. A thirty-year follow-up of treatment effects. *American Psychologist*, 1978, 33, 284–289.

Merton, R. K. *Social theory and social structure* (Rev. ed.). Glencoe, Ill.: Free Press, 1957.

Miller, R. L., Brickman, P., & Bolen, D. Attribution versus persuasion as a means of modifying behavior. *Journal of Personality and Social Psychology*, 1975, 31, 430–441.

Morrison, J. K., Bushell, J. D., Hanson, G. D., Fentiman, J. R., & Holdridge-Crane, S. Relationship between psychiatric patients' attitudes toward mental illness and attitudes of dependence. *Psychological Reports*, 1977, 41, 1194.

Mulford, H. A., & Miller, D. E. Public acceptance of the alcoholic as sick. *Quarterly Journal of Alcohol Studies*, 1964, 25, 314–324.

Nentwig, C. G. Attribution of cause and long-term effects of the modification of smoking behavior. *Behavioral Analysis and Modification*, 1978, 2, 285–295.

Nettler, G. Cruelty, dignity, and determinism. *American Sociological Review*, 1959, 24, 375–384.

Nuckolls, K. B., Cassel, J., & Kaplan, B. H. Psychosocial assets, life crisis and the prognosis of pregnancy. *American Journal of Epidemiology*, 1972, 95, 431–441.

Parsons, T. *The social system*. New York: Free Press, 1951.

Pearlin, L., & Schooler, C. The structure of coping. *Journal of Health and Social Behavior*, 1978, 19, 2–21.

Pettigrew, T. F. The ultimate attribution error: Extending Allport's cognitive analysis of prejudice. *Personality and Social Psychology Bulletin*, 1979, 5, 461–476.

Piven, F., & Cloward, R. *Regulating the poor*. New York: Vintage, 1972.

Proudfoot, W., & Shaver, P. Attribution theory and the psychology of religion. *Journal for the Scientific Study of Religion*, 1975, 14, 317–330.

Rabinowitz, V. C. Orientations to help in four natural settings (Doctoral dissertation, Northwestern University, 1978). *Dissertation Abstracts International*. (University Microfilms No. 79-07,928)

Rodin, J., & Langer, E. J. Long-term effects of a control-relevant intervention with the institutionalized aged. *Journal of Personality and Social Psychology*, 1977, 35, 897–902.

Rodin, J., & Langer, E. J. Aging labels: The decline of control and the fall of self-esteem. *Journal of Social Issues*, 1980, 36(2), 12–29.

Ross, L. D., Rodin, J., & Zimbardo, P. G. Toward an attribution therapy: The reduction of fear through induced cognitive-emotional misattribution. *Journal of Personality and Social Psychology*, 1969, 12, 279–288.

Rotter, J. B. Generalized expectancies for internal vs. external control of reinforcement. *Psychological Monographs*, 1966, *80*(1, Whole No. 287).

Rushing, W. Two patterns in the relationship between social class and mental hospitalization. *American Sociological Review*, 1969, 34, 533–541.

Schutz, W. *Profound simplicity*. New York: Bantam, 1979.

Schwartz, S. H. Normative influences on altruism. In L. Berkowitz (Ed.), *Advances in experimental social psychology* (Vol. 10). New York: Academic Press, 1977.

Scott, R. A. *The making of blind men: A study of adult socialization*. New York: Russell Sage, 1969.

Segall, A. The sick role concept: Understanding illness behavior. *Journal of Health and Social Behavior*, 1976, 17, 163–170.

Seligman, M. E. P. *Helplessness*. San Francisco, Calif.: Freeman, 1975.

Sharp, L. Steel axes for Stone Age Australians. In E. H. Spicer (Ed.), *Human problems and technical change*. New York: Russell Sage, 1952.

Singerman, K., Borkovec, T., & Baron, R. Failure of a "missattribution therapy" manipulation to reduce speech anxiety. *Behavior Therapy*, 1976, 7, 306–313.

Skinner, B. F. *Beyond freedom and dignity*. New York: Knopf, 1971.

Smith, M. L., & Glass, G. V. Meta-analysis of psychotherapy outcome studies. *American Psychologist*, 1977, 32, 752–760.

Smits, S. J. Variables related to success in a medical rehabilitation setting. *Archives of Physical Medicine and Rehabilitation*, 1974, 55, 449–454.

Stebbins, L.B., St. Pierre, R. G., Proper, E. C., Anderson, R. B., & Cerva, R. R. An evaluation of Follow Through. In T. D. Cook, M. L. Del Rosario, K. M. Hennigan, M. M. Mark, & W. M. K. Trochim (Eds.), *Evaluation studies review annual* (Vol. 3). Beverly Hills, Calif.: Sage, 1978.

Storms, M. D., & Nisbett, R. E. Insomnia and the attribution process. *Journal of Personality and Social Psychology*, 1970, 16, 319–328.

Swann, W. B., Jr., & Snyder, M. On translating beliefs into action: Theories of ability and their application in an instructional setting. *Journal of Personality and Social Psychology*, 1980, 38, 879–888.

Szasz, T. The myth of mental illness. *American Psychologist*, 1960, 15, 113–118.

Taylor, S. E. Hospital patient behavior: Reactance, helplessness or control? *Journal of Social Issues*, 1979, 35(1), 156–184.

Thibaut, J. W., & Riecken, H. W. Some determinants and consequences of the perception of social causality. *Journal of Personality*, 1955, 24, 113–133.

Thompson, C. L. The secondary school counselor's ideal client. *Journal of Counseling Psychology*, 1969, 16, 69–74.

Trice, H. The affiliation motive and readiness to join Alcoholics Anonymous. *Quarterly Journal of Studies on Alcohol*, 1959, 20, 313–320.

Trice, H., & Roman, P. Sociopsychological predictors of successful affiliation with Alcoholics Anonymous. *Social Psychiatry*, 1970, 5, 51–59.

Tussing, A. D. The dual welfare system. *Society*, January–February 1974, 11, 50–57.

Valins, S., & Nisbett, R. E. *Attribution processes in the development and treatment of emotional disorders*. Morristown, N.J.: General Learning Press, 1971.

Wack, J., & Rodin, J. Nursing homes for the aged: The human consequences of legislation-shaped environments. *Journal of Social Issues*, 1978, 34(4), 6–21.

Weiner, B. A theory of motivation for some classroom experiences. *Journal of Educational Psychology*, 1979, 71, 3–25.

Weisman, A. D., & Worden, J. W. Psychosocial analysis of cancer deaths. *Omega: Journal of Death and Dying*, 1975, 6, 61–75.

Weiss, R. F., Boyer, J. L., Lombardo, J. P., & Stich, M. H. Altruistic drive and altruistic reinforcement. *Journal of Personality and Social Psychology*, 1973, 25, 390–400.

Wills, T. Perceptions of clients by professional helpers. *Psychological Bulletin*, 1978, 85, 968–1000.

Wortman, C. B., & Dunkel-Schetter, C. Interpersonal relationships and cancer: A theoretical analysis. *Journal of Social Issues*, 1979, 35(1), 120–155.

Zajonc, R. Family configuration and intelligence. *Science*, 1976, 192, 227–236.

Zuckerman, M. Attribution of success and failure revisited, or: The motivational bias is alive and well in attribution theory. *Journal of Personality*, 1979, 47, 245–287.

8.4 Help Is Where You Find It: Four Informal Helping Groups

Emory L. Cowen

Once upon a time, mental health lived by a simple, two-part myth: *Part 1*: People with psychological troubles bring them to mental health professionals for help. *Part 2*: One way or another, often based on verbal dialogue, professionals solve those problems and the people live happily ever after.

And sometimes the cookie does indeed crumble according to the myth. But events of the past several decades suggest that the "marriage-in-heaven" script is *not* nature's only, or even most frequent, way. In real life the idyllic myth breaks down at several key points.

Let's talk first, and only briefly, about Part 2: Heresy though it may have been 20 years ago, it is now permissible to say that not all problems brought to mental health professionals are happily adjudicated. How much of the shortfall is due to the imprecision of our professional "magic," or even to the lack of skill of our magicians, and how much to the selectively refractory nature of the problems that professionals see remains unclear. Much clearer is a sense of mounting dissatisfaction with the

reach and effectiveness of past traditional ways (Cowen, 1973; Cowen, Gardner, & Zax, 1967; Rappaport, 1977; Zax & Cowen, 1976), a dissatisfaction that has powered active new explorations toward a more promising tomorrow in mental health. Important recent developments in community mental health are born of exactly such skepticism.

Although those developments, the ferment behind them, and the conceptual and programmatic alternatives to which they direct attention are vital and timely issues (Cowen, 1980), this article focuses on Part 1 of the myth, that is, that people with psychological problems *bring* them to mental health professionals. As biased middle-class professionals, teachers, or students, that "regularity" (to use Sarason's [1971] term) is so much part of what we see, hear, and read about, what we teach and are taught, that we impute to it a universality that has little to do with the "out-there" reality. For the most part people do *not* bring their personal troubles to mental health professionals at *any* point in their unfolding, least of all in response to early, sometimes keenly important, signs of distress.

There are many reasons why that is so. Different ones apply to different people.

Reprinted from *American Psychologist*, April 1982, Vol. 37, No. 4, 385–395.

Some folks do not have the money to pay for costly services. For others, services are not available for geographic or logistic reasons. Some people's ideologies, belief systems, or stereotypes make services, as packaged, unappealing if not unacceptable. And even when such barriers do not exist, many troubled individuals prefer to talk with people who are known and trusted in more natural contexts—people who are willing to listen when they are ready to talk. Who those other people are varies with the individuals, the nature of their problems, and a community's resource system and ecology. But they are there, voluntarily or otherwise, involved at some level in the nitty-gritty of interpersonal helping. Some are professionals such as clergy, lawyers, physicians, educators, nurses, welfare and enforcement agents, knowledgeable on their own turfs but not trained in mental health. Those were the first "other-helpers" (to use Gershon & Biller's [1977] term) drawn, systematically, into the net of interpersonal involvement. Those were the prime targets for mental health consultation's initial surge (Caplan, 1970; Grady, Gibson, & Trickett, 1980; Mannino, MacLennan, & Shore, 1975). But there are others—natural care givers untrained in any professional discipline: neighborhood folk and those whose jobs put them into daily contact with personal troubles. In part because of the intrinsic nature of their roles and person interactions and perhaps in part because of their personal warmth and compassion, such individuals continually field interpersonal distress. Indeed, Collins (1973) has argued that among low-income groups with limited access to (or fondness for) the services of a predominantly middle-class mental health establishment, natural neighbors and informal care givers are the prime sources of help when personal troubles develop. That point was both recognized and harnessed, in the form of innovative program structures better attuned to the needs and realities of the inner-city poor (Reiff, 1967; Riessman, 1967; Riessman, Cohen, & Pearl, 1964).

There are ample data to indicate that society's formally anointed agents for engaging psychological distress field only a small fraction of such problems. Thus Gurin, Veroff, and Feld (1960), as part of the Joint Commission (1961) survey, established that less than one fifth of those who saw themselves as having psychological problems took those problems to mental health professionals. By contrast, more than two thirds brought them to their clergy or physicians. That message has since been confirmed many times and in many guises (Gottlieb, 1976; Roberts, Prince, Gold, & Shiner, 1966; Ryan, 1969).

Major de facto helping channels, besides professionals in other fields identified by those surveys and particularly by the recent President's Commission on Mental Health (1978), include natural support systems and networks (Caplan & Killilea, 1976; Gershon & Biller, 1977; Heller, 1979; Mitchell & Trickett, 1980; Sarason, Carroll, Maton, Cohen, & Lorentz, 1977) and informal care givers or urban agents (Caplan, 1974b; Collins, 1973; Collins & Pancoast, 1976; Kelly, 1964). Clinically and anecdotally, we become ever more aware that such mechanisms are woven inextricably into the fabric of human help giving. At the same time, the specific interpersonal help-giving behaviors of informal, natural care givers are among mental health's most seriously overlooked areas of potential knowledge and practical use. Asymmetrically, at least 95% of our current knowledge about the workings and effectiveness of helping processes is based on a special sampling of less than 5% of all interpersonal help-giving interactions, that is, socially recognized and sanctioned interactions in which the help agents are formally trained, credentialed, mental health professionals.

There is great need to redress that imbalance in a value-free, fact-finding context. Making no judgments about whether informal help giving is good or bad, right or wrong, it is an overriding reality that the mental health field has thus far shrugged off. What is the nature and extent of those processes? How do they differ across contexts and settings; that is, what is the *ecology* of informal helping? Such questions must be answered if we are to begin to address a challenge that Caplan (1974a) sounded 15 years ago, in speaking of informal care givers: "How can we make contact with [them] and how can we educate them so that they give wise counsel to those in crises who seek them out?"

The Studies

In an effort to answer those questions, we studied four groups known or suspected to be involved in interpersonal help giving: hairdressers, divorce lawyers, bartenders, and industrial supervisors (Cowen, Gesten, Boike, Norton, Wilson, & DeStefano, 1979; Cowen, Gesten, Davidson, & Wilson, 1981; Cowen, McKim, & Weissberg, 1981; Doane & Cowen, 1981; Kaplan & Cowen, 1981). This article describes that work, what we have learned from it, and what we think it means. At the time we started, we had two and a half broad purposes in mind. The first, by far the most important, was to document the basic facts and descriptive profiles of interpersonal help giving in the four contexts. A second was to identify cross-group differences in such behaviors and ecological factors that prompt such differences. And the "half purpose," if you will, was to see if we could develop training and consultation models for interested help givers to buttress and support their de facto help-giving roles.

Although the four studies are based on a common research paradigm, pragmatics and realities necessitated several procedural variations. It will be simplest, sanest,

and least disruptive of the further narrative to describe those variations now. All four studies were built around a detailed, structured interview or questionnaire that evolved from early, extensive pilot testing. As we began with each new group, we first made "ecologically appropriate" changes in the schedule and then did pilot testing to be sure that it was well adapted to the new context. A concrete example: It is one thing to ask about the interpersonal help giving of family-practice lawyers who have continuing in-depth contacts with an average of about 20 divorce clients per year and rather a different thing to probe the same area with bartenders, who have five times that many contacts in a single evening.

Hence the schedule's content (e.g., number and exact substance of items) and format (use of 3-, 4-, or 5-point rating scales) varied across groups. So did its form of administration. Hairdressers and bartenders were seen in face-to-face interviews while working. Those interviews were often marked by breaks in tempo and disruptions, which reached major proportions with some bartenders (Cowen et al., 1981). Information from family practice attorneys came from a mail survey conducted with the approval of the local bar association. Company preferences determined the format used with supervisors. In most cases survey forms and instructions for completing them were distributed by the company's personnel office, and respondents returned completed forms directly to us by mail. Forms submitted by lawyers and supervisors were checked for completeness and fidelity of response and, where necessary, were followed up promptly.

All respondents, whether interviewed or not, were volunteers. Overall, about 60% of those contacted agreed to participate in the studies. The final samples consisted of 90 hairdressers, 62 family-practice attorneys, 97 supervisors, and 76 bartenders.

The schedules used for the four groups included anywhere from 19 to 30 questions, many with subparts, which can be grouped into seven main clusters:

1. Information about the backgrounds, employment histories, and work patterns of respondents.
2. Descriptions of their clienteles and the frequency and nature of their contacts with them.
3. Summaries of verbal interactions with clients, particularly time spent dealing with their personal problems. For this critical item, an early, key distinction was made among three categories: plain talking time, versus talking about casual, minor everyday concerns, versus talking about moderate to serious personal problems. All of the surveys and this report focus exclusively on the last category.
4. Reports of the nature and frequency of specific personal problems raised by clients.
5. Descriptions of respondents' strategies for handling clients' personal problems.
6. Feelings about being called on to engage themselves with clients' personal problems and satisfaction with that role.
7. Respondents' perceptions of their effectiveness and their need for help in dealing with clients' personal problems.

Given that the raw data pool includes responses to 30 different items from 325 people representing four diverse groups, there is no gracious way to summarize all the data in this cross-sectional overview. The present report is thus limited to highlights, and even those are presented in transistorized form.

The Findings

Table 1 summarizes demographic and work characteristics of the four samples. Mean ages of the groups ranged from 34 (bartenders) to 44 (supervisors). Their sex composition was strikingly different. Hairdressers had the highest proportion of females (60%) and lawyers the lowest (1.5%). Both bartenders and supervisors were predominantly, but not exclusively, male groups. With respect to work characteristics, three groups (hairdressers, lawyers, and supervisors) were very stable, averaging 9–15 years in their respective fields and seven or more years in their current jobs. Bartenders were more mobile, averaging six years in that work and two and a half years in their present jobs. But the most striking differences among groups was their "flow of clientele." Hairdressers saw an average of 55 customers per week, averaging 46 minutes with each, of which 25 were spent talking. Lawyers worked with an average of only 20 divorce clients a year but had many in-depth contacts both in person and on the phone with each. Overseeing an average of 27 workers each, supervisors interacted with an average of three workers regarding moderate to serious personal problems, for a total of two and a half hours per week. Bartenders served an average of 104 customers per work session.

The survey's most basic question, in one or another form, concerned the number or proportion of clientele who raised moderate to serious personal problems. Those numbers varied. For lawyers the estimate approached 40%. In descending order the corresponding figures for the other groups were: hairdressers—33%; bartenders—16%; supervisors—7%. Those figures are both informative and misleading. Thus lawyers had interpersonal helpgiving contacts with relatively few, often very upset clients; those contacts were deep and extended over many sessions. Although bartenders fielded *proportionately* fewer serious problems, because they averaged 500 person contacts per week (many fueled by disinhibition), they saw more troubled people *absolutely* than any other group. Given the base-rate freneti-

TABLE 1   Demographic and Work Characteristics of Four Help-Giver Samples

	Group			
Variable	Hairdressers ($N = 90$)	Lawyers ($N = 62$)	Supervisors ($N = 97$)	Bartenders ($N = 76$)
M age	38	40	44	34
Sex Distribution				
M	37	61	88	53
F	53	1	9	23
M years in occupation	15	13	9	6
M years in current job	7½	7	7½	2½
M no. of clients served	55/week	20/year	3/week	104/day

Note. M = male; F = female.

cism of their work situations, however, most of those contacts were brief and superficial.

Personal Problems Raised

One key survey item listed a series of personal problems that people might raise with them. Those problems varied across groups, to reflect feedback from pilot work before each survey began. Respondents were asked to report a frequency of occurrence for each problem. Although the literal rating scales used (see Table 2) varied slightly across studies, subjects had the option of responding to each item along a continuum anchored at one extreme by never (lowest numbers) and at the other by very frequently (highest numbers). Table 2 summarizes responses on this item.

Allowing for variations in rating formats, lawyers and hairdressers reported higher frequencies of problem occurrence than did supervisors and bartenders. Moreover, somewhat different problems came up with the several groups. For hairdressers the "big three" were problems with children, health, and marriage, with depression and anxiety not too far behind. For bartenders marital, job, and money problems came up most often. Of passing

interest is the fact that sex problems, with consistently low frequencies for all other groups, occurred fourth most frequently at the bar. That less than profound finding merely confirms what many people have already learned from personal experience.

Frequently occurring problems visited on lawyers and supervisors differed appreciably from those that came to hairdressers and bartenders. They were more context-bound. Thus, for lawyers highest frequency problems included anger with spouse, depression, and problems occurring around immediate spouse contacts. And for supervisors they were problems with fellow workers, advancement opportunities, and job restlessness.

Salient summary observations for this body of data are as follows: (1) Overall, personal problems came up with substantial frequency in these four contexts, more so, however, for hairdressers and lawyers than for bartenders and supervisors; (2) problems raised, in the aggregate, were not strikingly different from those brought to mental health professionals; (3) the four groups exercised different "pulls" in terms of the types of problems most often raised with them.

Handling Strategies

Respondents in all groups judged (again, from never to very frequently) how often

TABLE 2 Problems Raised: Mean Scale Ratings and Rank Orders for Frequency of Occurrence

Problem	Hairdressers		Lawyers		Supervisors		Bartenders	
	M	Rank	M	Rank	M	Rank	M	Rank
Difficulties with children	3.78	1	2.10	4	1.24	5.5	1.53	7
Physical health	3.67	2	1.95	6	1.24	5.5	1.77	6
Marital problems	3.53	3			.92	8	2.53	2
Depression	3.34	4	2.39	2	.63	10	1.95	5
Anxiety, nervousness	3.31	5			.74	9	1.05	9
Jobs	3.17	6					2.77	1
Financial	3.09	7			1.26	4	2.43	3
Emotional/ psychological	2.81	8	2.07	5	.62	11		
Sex	2.52	9	1.36	16	.45	12	1.96	4
Drugs	1.59	10			.19	14	.81	10
Alcohol	1.34	11			.34	13	1.10	8
Anger with spouse			2.59	1				
Managing contacts with spouse			2.25	3				
Managing day-to-day affairs			1.92	7				
Guilt			1.88	8				
Confusion			1.86	9.5				
Loneliness			1.86	9.5				
Family reactions			1.71	11				
Worthlessness			1.58	12				
Fear of going crazy			1.53	13				
Loss of friends			1.42	14				
Problems with fellow workers					1.76	1		
Concern about opportunity for advancement					1.36	2		
Dissatisfaction with job					1.31	3		
Job security					1.18	7		

Note. Number of scale points (range): for hairdressers, 5 (1–5); for lawyers, 3 (1–3); for supervisors, 5 (0–4); for bartenders, 4 (0–3).

they used each of a series of handling strategies to deal with personal problems raised with them. The list included mental health "standbys," such as listening and proposing alternatives, and some "shamefully naive" practices to which many mental health pros would surely say "nyet," for example, changing the topic, telling people to count their blessings,

refusing to get involved. Table 3 summarizes the frequency of usage data for handling strategies. Hairdressers and bartenders reacted similarly. Their three most frequent tactics were "offering support and sympathy," "trying to be lighthearted," and "just listening"—in 1-2-3 order for hairdressers and 3-2-1 order for bartenders. Listening and supporting were also among super-

TABLE 3 Response Strategies: Mean Scale Ratings and Rank Orders for Frequencies of Occurrence

Strategy	Hairdressers		Lawyers		Supervisors		Bartenders	
	M	Rank	M	Rank	M	Rank	M	Rank
Offer support and sympathy	3.98	1	4.03	1	1.99	1.5	2.72	3
Try to be lighthearted	3.90	2	2.21	10	1.20	9	2.87	2
Just listen	3.73	3	3.10	7	1.99	1.5	3.47	1
Present alternatives	3.34	4	3.78	5	1.75	5	2.26	4
Tell person to count blessings	3.28	5	2.36	9	.91	11	1.63	10
Share personal experiences	3.17	6	2.52	8	1.52	6	2.25	5
Try not to get involved	3.13	7	2.14	11.5	.62	12	1.87	6
Give advice	2.97	8	3.82	4	1.39	8	1.84	7
Ask questions	2.72	9	3.92	2	1.92	3.5	1.71	9
Try to get person to talk with someone else	2.62	10	2.14	11.5	1.40	7	1.47	11
Try to change topic	2.59	11	1.52	13	.35	13	1.76	8
Point out consequences of bad ideas			3.88	3				
Help clarify feelings			3.59	6				
Suggest reading			1.78	12				
Get person to come up with alternatives					1.92	3.5		
Say that "I'm not right person to talk with"					.93	10		

Note. Number of scale points (range): for hairdressers, 5 (1–5); for lawyers, 5 (1–5); for supervisors, 4 (0–3); for bartenders, 5 (0–4).

visors' top frequency strategies. Not so, however, for lawyers. Although they also went for support and sympathy, their next preferred approaches were asking questions, giving advice, and pointing out the consequences of bad ideas.

Feeling Reactions

All respondents also judged the frequency of occurrence of a series of feeling reactions they might have (from not at all to very strong) when people raised personal problems with them. Those ratings are summarized in Table 4. Groups were more similar to each other on this dimension than the two preceding ones, with only slight cross-group variations. High-frequency feeling reactions for all groups were: sympathetic, encouraging, supportive, and gratifying. At the same time less

TABLE 4 Feeling Reactions: Mean Strength and Rank Orders

	Hairdressers		Lawyers		Supervisors		Bartenders	
Feeling	M	Rank	M	Rank	M	Rank	M	Rank
Gratified	2.51	1	1.44	4	1.29	4	1.29	4
Sympathetic	2.44	2	2.49	1	1.38	3	1.78	3
Encouraging	2.36	3	2.09	3	1.54	1	2.00	1
Supportive	2.29	4	2.46	2	1.46	2	1.83	2
Puzzled	1.63	5	1.18	7	.82	5.5	1.05	7
Helpless	1.49	6	1.33	5	.82	5.5	1.09	5.5
Uncomfortable	1.47	7	1.21	6	.75	7	.87	9
Bored	1.44	8	1.16	8	.37	9	1.03	8
Trapped	1.31	9.5	1.09	11	.32	10	1.09	5.5
Depressed	1.31	9.5	1.12	10	.24	12	.55	10
Angry	1.13	11	1.11	9	.25	11	.37	11
Frustrated					.69	8		

Note. Number of scale points (range): for hairdressers, 3 (1–3); for lawyers, 3 (1–3); for supervisors, 4 (0–3); for bartenders, 4 (0–3).

positive reactions, such as feeling helpless or puzzled, came up with some frequency.

Several other items also bear on this domain. All groups were asked how comfortable they felt when people raised personal problems with them. Although all landed on the comfortable side, hairdressers felt several JNDs more natural and comfortable than their confrères. Respondents were also asked to judge their own effectiveness as helpers. Although there was considerable intragroup variability, all four groups ended up in the moderately effective range, with hairdressers a bit higher and bartenders a bit lower than the others. With some oscillation here and there, the trend is for all of these "plumbers" to see themselves as doing a decent (but short of supersensational) job as interpersonal helpers.

Mental health consultation was described for two groups seen in face-to-face interviews—hairdressers and bartenders—and respondents were asked to rate their interest in it. Hairdressers were much more positively disposed to the possibility than bartenders, a fact later confirmed by the differential responses of the two groups to a concrete opportunity to take part in such a program.

In summary, then, the groups seemed more to enjoy than to dislike the help-giver role and to feel moderately comfortable in it. In fact, a number of respondents across samples stated that they saw helping others with their problems as a normal, indeed sometimes very important, aspect of their job. One hairdresser hit that point on the head when she said: "To be perfectly truthful I regard myself a B− hairdresser. But my business is booming. Mostly that's because I listen to people, care about their personal concerns, and try to be helpful. The guy down the street is really an A+ hairdresser—one of the best in town. But he's going to go out of business because he can't stand people and is incapable of listening sympathetically to *anyone's* problems." Another perspective on the issue came from a supervisor who said: "Personal problems are part of everyone's life at one time or another, and if a supervisor doesn't deal with this fact he will pay the price with high reject rates, repairs, and absentee problems."

Ecological Indicators

Several data bits already cited point to the possibility that the different ecological surroundings of the four groups pull differently for personal problems. Thus, hairdressers and lawyers, often with long-term, close, essentially private contacts with people, field heavier problems than bartenders and supervisors. Similarly, the special nature of the lawyer-divorce client and supervisor-worker relationships seems to attract personal problems related to the common-interest turf that brings those dyads together.

One can also ask whether differential characteristics of helper groups relate to how they handle appeals for help. Although the data on this point are spotty rather than systematic, several titillating findings can still be cited. Two groups, hairdressers and bartenders, were asked what they would like to do if they left their present occupations. All jobs mentioned by both groups were categorized as relating or not relating to interpersonal help-giving roles. About one third of the jobs mentioned by hairdressers were clearly help oriented; by contrast, such jobs were rarely mentioned by bartenders.

A related discovery: For three of the four groups, all except the lawyers, we compared the help-giving roles of men and women. Although those analyses were constrained by small female numbers in the bartender and industrial supervisor samples, important cross-group consistencies were found nonetheless. The overall sense of those findings was that females, compared to males, were more often called on to deal with personal problems; used more engaging, task-oriented handling strategies, and felt more at home in the interpersonal help-giving role. Women, it seems, are more socialized than are men to the role of engaging personal problems and do so more patiently and sympathetically.

One can also ask about possible cultural and ethnic differences in informal help giving. Collins and Pancoast (1976) have suggested that natural neighbors and informal care givers may be the prime sources of help available to poor people experiencing personal distress. Although the present data do not bear directly on that issue, a recent dissertation (Searcy, 1980) does. That investigation extended our initial hairdresser study to beauty shops serving middle- and low-income black and white clientele. A striking finding, consistent with Collins and Pancoast's (1976) observation, was that black, particularly low-income black, beauticians reported a significantly higher proportion of personal problems than did white beauticians.

Another ecological reality that shapes the kinds of interpersonal help giving that takes place is the environmental surroundings in which the contact occurs. For us, the bar was by far the most frenetic surrounding encountered. Bartenders have contact with over 100 customers in any single work session. Often they serve 8 or 10 customers at once; indeed their income may depend on the graciousness and efficiency with which they perform that balancing act. Accordingly, it is a bit of an understatement to say that conditions for engaging personal problems at the bar are less than idyllic. Small wonder that some bartenders do not want to hear about people's personal problems and most are lukewarm to consultation.

At the same time, the bartender sample provided a unique opportunity to explore one dimension of ecological surroundings. By sheer luck of the draw, the sample included identifiable subgroups working predominantly afternoon (i.e., before 6 p.m.) and evening (i.e., after 6 p.m.) shifts. The most important ecological differentiator between those groups is that the afternoon sample averaged 40 fewer customers per work session. Afternoon bartenders fielded twice as many moderate to serious personal problems, engaged those problems more patiently and sympathetically, and had fewer negative feelings when the problems came up. In other words, to the extent that extremely harsh environmental conditions at the bar relented, interpersonal help giving rose.

Overview and Implications

The rest of this article will back away from details of the component studies to reexamine, in the light of their findings, the complex issues they were designed to address. Before doing that, let it be said that we harbor no illusions about the technical elegance of the studies. To the contrary, with problems of sampling and variability of method, not to mention those involving veridicality of verbal report, the studies well exemplify some classic problems of research in the community cauldron (Cowen, Lorion, & Dorr, 1974). Nevertheless, the panoramic sweep of their findings offers a preliminary view of an important, heretofore largely uncharted, turf. However risky, it may be heuristic to use the data mass as a springboard to speculate about several larger questions such as: "What's going on in the world of informal, interpersonal help giving?" and "What challenges and caution points are suggested by the findings thus far?"

A first, striking finding, by way of overall impressions, is the fact that in all walks of life, lots of psychological, adaptive problems get dropped every day on sometimes willing, sometimes unsuspecting and perplexed, ears. Reexamining Table 2, one sees that the problems people raise, in the aggregate, are not unlike those fielded by the mental health establishment. Thus, to pick up on the opening metaphor, it would indeed be a myth to assume that mental health professionals are society's sole custodians of people's

psychological well-being. To do so would be, in Sarason's (Sarason, Levine, Goldenberg, Cherlin, & Bennett, 1966) idiom, an outstanding example of professional "preciousness."

Many years back we learned from Gurin et al.'s (1960) survey that only a small proportion of people's self-defined psychological problems ever come to mental health professionals. Clergy and pediatricians far outdistance us. That eye-opening datum was a stimulus for the rapid climb of mental health consultation. The present data raise an even more severe possibility—namely that the sum of *all* of the interpersonal helping activities of mental health professionals, *plus* duly recognized nonmental health surrogates, such as clergy and physicians, still comprises only a minor fraction of society's interpersonal help-seeking and help-giving commerce.

Many factors feed into that reality. Mental health professionals, sheltered by their special backgrounds, training, experiences, and biases, have an oversimplified mind's-eye view of how people resolve personal problems: "A body has a heavy personal problem, so it goes to a shrink!" The present data suggest clearly that such is not the way of the world. The need to talk, that is, to seek help and comfort when troubled, is nearly universal. How that need is met, however, is far from universal. Underrated (if not ignored) factors, such as dollars and cents, the people we know and trust, personal ideologies, belief systems and stereotypes, and the opportunities that a given situation offers, all powerfully shape people's help-seeking behaviors. Lots of people go lots of places with lots of problems. Although some may not like that reality, there is an ever-increasing need to recognize it.

Second, there *are* differences in the problems brought up with different helper groups. One thing that helps to explain those differences is the nature of the relationship between the helper and the recipient of help. Contacts that lawyers and hairdressers have with clients typically span considerable time periods and are embedded in natural, trusting relationships. Bartenders, by contrast, have briefer, less predictable, often crisis-oriented contacts with people less well known to them. Moreover the bar's hectic ecology constrains intimate personal conversations. Thus the present data suggest that special situational ecologies shape both the nature and extent of the personal problems that surface. That is a domain that surely warrants further study. We do not yet fully understand, even for the present four groups, the many human and environmental variables that color interpersonal help-giving interactions. Moreover, those arbitrarily chosen groups are by no means society's only informal help-giving outlets. Differential problem pulls could well be even more pronounced with as yet unstudied groups, such as cab drivers, adventitious travel partners, or other individuals with whom contacts occur in stranger-in-the-night, never-to-be-seen-again contexts.

The area of responding strategies used has unusual potential for touching exposed nerves. The facts are clear enough. Hairdressers, bartenders, and, to a lesser extent, supervisors use similar responding gambits. Lawyers, by contrast, have a different style and touch. Perhaps their bloodlines and training impel them to ask lots of questions and point out the consequences of bad ideas. Whatever the reason, there are real group differences in this sphere. The whole area is, to say the least, sensitive. Just talking about helping techniques that laypersons use is "fightin' words" for many mental health professionals. That is seen as their private turf, where they alone have (a) special knowledge and wisdom and (b) the right to judge the appropriateness of the words and deeds of anyone who has the temerity to put on interpersonal helping vestments. In that sphere, professionals are trigger-quick to identify foul-ups by "aliens." That

being the case, there are at least several schools of thought—some frankly vulgar—about how renegade survey data such as the present data, might best be used. Some would argue that laypersons are already "messing around" too much and that such behavior, like botulism, must be stamped out. Others, who see informal help giving as an inevitable aspect of reality, indeed one that fills a major social void, may be moved to join that reality. The word *joining*, however, is a bit of a Rorschach inkblot. To some it means, "Give the heathens a dash of truth and a smidge of technology." Others are appropriately wary about mental health wisdom or consultation's being unilateral goods. Gottlieb (1974) and Rappaport (1977), for example, argue that it may do more harm than good to impose rigid mental health "facts" where they do not fit or to shrug off hard-come-by street wisdom.

The missing link in these studies, indeed in the basic argument I am developing, is the absence of trustworthy data about *effectiveness* (i.e., actual helpfulness) of informal care givers. Although it is easy enough *in principle* to think of ways to collect such data (e.g., direct observation of helping interactions, helpfulness judgments by recipients), actually trying to *do* those things will raise complex, delicate tactical problems. In the absence of effectiveness data, mental health professionals should be humble and open in approaching care-giver training and consultation. Where we have facts, they can be shared; where we lack such facts, we should not be pulling rank.

The area of helpers' feeling reactions is, fortunately, less complicated than most of the other survey data. Beyond the Pete Seeger "ticky-tacky" disclaimer that *all* groups included individuals whose reactions to interpersonal help giving ranged from "I love it" to "I can't stand it," the main-effects finding was that respondents felt good about being asked to help others and accepted that calling as a natural part of their jobs. Most people, it appears, have at least a small "goody two-shoes" part to their self-concepts, and most live comfortably with that role. That is not to say, however, that they see themselves as professionals. Many are perplexed by the trying interactions they have had and at times feel over their heads. Their reflex, except perhaps for bartenders, is less to bail out of the helper role and more to look for input from mental health that might enable them to do a better job of it.

When asked for their opinions about their own effectiveness, the groups responded similarly: "We're coping and doing a decent job, but there are gaps, and we can use help." The spontaneous recognition of a need for help prompted us to offer separate (10 sessions) training and consultation programs for volunteer hairdressers (Weisenfeld & Weis, 1979) and lawyers (Doane, Note 1). Both programs were well attended, lively, task oriented, and well received by teacher-consultants and care givers alike. The hairdresser curriculum covered topics such as the nature of interpersonal help, from whom and in what forms people seek help, listening and attending skills, initiating responses, responding to feelings and meaning, the concepts of empathy and understanding, problem-solving strategies, and community facilities and referral mechanisms. Sessions provided ample time for case-material input from participants and for discussion. One goal was to elevate participants' consciousness with respect both to listening skills in general and to underused but potentially helpful techniques such as recognizing and reflecting feelings. To evaluate the program's impact, a multiple-choice measure was used consisting of 14 brief vignettes of typical personal problems that come up in the beauty shop. Each vignette was brought to a crucial choice point where the hairdresser had to respond based on specific options: (a) providing alternatives,

(b) reflecting feelings, (c) giving advice, and (d) telling the person to count his or her blessings. Although participants did indeed dramatically increase (i.e., from 5% to 70%) their choice of reflection responses after the program, that fact per se still does not answer the bread-and-butter question: "Did the change in technique help troubled customers to feel any better?" It is as hard to answer that question about informal helpers as it is about licensed clinicians.

A few final parting remarks: Pretty, the data *are not*. But they do tell us a few things: One, for sure, is that we must lay to rest the myth that people tie up their problems in neat packages with blue ribbons and hand them exclusively to certified mental health specialists. No way! Personal problems are matters of prime everyday concern to most people, who will seek, in whatever ways, to deal with them. For society at large, and even more in certain of its sectors, most distressed people look first toward accessible, parsimonious, well-understood, trusted sources of help that are minimally costly or stigmatizing. Those "specs" do not typically define mental health professionals; indeed, in most cases family, friends, neighbors, support networks, and informal care givers fill the bill much better. Accordingly, only a small fraction of interpersonal distress, biased toward entrenched, longstanding problems housed in fiscally solvent souls, ever enters the formal mental health system.

The present findings are really only teasers. The larger challenge that they spotlight—a complex one indeed—is to understand how people seek and get help for personal problems at all levels. Which people, which kinds of problems, what sources of help, what kinds of outcomes— that is the matrix framing the present informational lag. Although it is a tough matrix to fill, rational future planning in mental health requires that it be done. A much more precise knowledge of a society's de facto help-giving mechanisms is an essential precondition for upgrading its help-giving effort.

Reference Note

1. Doane, J. A. *A mental health training and consultation program for family practice attorneys*. Unpublished manuscript, University of California, L.A., 1977.

References

Caplan, G. *Theories of mental health consultation*. New York: Basic Books, 1970.

Caplan, G. Preventing mental disorders. In G. Caplan, *Support systems and community mental health*. New York: Basic Books, 1974. (a)

Caplan, G. *Support systems and community mental health*. New York: Basic Books, 1974. (b)

Caplan, G., & Killilea, M. (Eds.). *Support systems and mutual help: Multidisciplinary explorations*. New York: Grune & Stratton, 1976.

Collins, A. H. Natural delivery systems: Accessible sources of power for mental health. *American Journal of Orthopsychiatry*, 1973, 43, 46–42.

Collins, A. H., & Pancoast, D. L. *Natural helping networks: A strategy for prevention*. Washington, D.C.: National Association of Social Workers, 1976.

Cowen, E. L. Social and community interventions. *Annual Review of Psychology*, 1973, 24, 423–472.

Cowen, E. L. The wooing of primary prevention. *American Journal of Community Psychology*, 1980, 8, 258–284.

Cowen, E. L., Gardner, E. A., & Zax, M. (Eds.). *Emergent approaches to mental health problems*. New York: Appleton-Century-Crofts, 1967.

Cowen, E. L., Gesten, E. L., Boike, M., Norton, P., Wilson, A. B., & DeStefano, M. A. Hairdressers as caregivers: I: A descriptive profile of interpersonal help-giving involvements. *American Journal of Community Psychology*, 1979, 7, 633–648.

Cowen, E. L., Gesten, E. L., Davidson, E. R., & Wilson, A. B. Hairdressers as caregivers: II: Relationships between helper-characteristics and help-giving behavior and feelings. *Journal of Prevention*, 1981, 1, 225–239.

Cowen, E. L., Lorion, R. P., & Dorr, D. Research in the community cauldron: A case report. *Canadian Psychologist*, 1974, 15, 313–325.

Cowen, E. L., McKim, B., & Weissberg, R. P. Bartenders as informal interpersonal help-agents. *American Journal of Community Psychology*, 1981, 9, 715–729.

Doane, J. A., & Cowen, E. L. Interpersonal help-giving among family practice lawyers. *American Journal of Community Psychology*, 1981, 9, 547–558.

Gershon, M., & Biller, H. B. *The other helpers: Paraprofessionals and non-professionals in mental health*. Lexington, Mass.: Lexington Books, 1977.

Gottlieb, B. H. Reexamining the preventive potential of mental health consultation. *Canada's Mental Health*, 1974, 22, 4–6.

Gottlieb, B. H. Lay influences on the utilization and provision of health services: A review. *Canadian Psychological Review*, 1976, 17, 126–136.

Grady, M. A., Gibson, M. J. S., & Trickett, E. J. *Mental health consultation theory, practice and research: An annotated reference guide*. College Park, Md.: University of Maryland, 1980.

Gurin, G., Veroff, J., & Feld, S. *Americans view their mental health: A nationwide interview survey*. New York: Basic Books, 1960.

Heller, K. The effects of social support: Prevention and treatment implications. In A. P. Goldstein & F. H. Kanfer (Eds.), *Maximizing treatment gains: Transfer enhancement in psychotherapy.* New York: Academic Press, 1979.

Joint Commission on Mental Illness and Health. *Action for mental health.* New York: Basic Books, 1961.

Kaplan, E. M., & Cowen, E. L. The interpersonal help-giving behaviors of industrial foremen. *Journal of Applied Psychology*, 1981, 66, 633–638.

Kelly, J. G. The mental health agent in the urban community. In *Symposium No. 10, Urban America and the planning of mental health services.* New York: Group for Advancement of Psychiatry, 1964.

Mannino, F. V., MacLennan, B. W., & Shore, M. W. (Eds.). *The practice of mental health consultation.* New York: Wiley, 1975.

Mitchell, R. E., & Trickett, E. J. Task force report: Social networks as mediators of social support: An analysis of the effects and determinants of social networks. *Community Mental Health Journal*, 1980, 16, 27–44.

President's Commission on Mental Health. *Report to the President* (Vol. 1). Washington, D.C.: U.S. Government Printing Office, 1978. (Stock No. 040–000–00390–8)

Rappaport, J. *Community psychology: Values, research and action.* New York: Holt, Rinehart & Winston, 1977.

Reiff, R. Mental health manpower and institutional change. In E. L. Cowen, E. A. Gardner, & M. Zax (Eds.), *Emergent approaches to mental health problems.* New York: Appleton-Century-Crofts, 1967.

Reiff, R., & Riessman, F. The indigenous nonprofessional: A strategy of change in community action and community mental health programs. *Community Mental Health Journal*, 1965, 1 (Monograph No. 1).

Riessman, F. A neighborhood-based mental health approach. In E. L. Cowen, E. A. Gardner, & M. Zax (Eds.), *Emergent approaches to mental health problems.* New York: Appleton-Century-Crofts, 1967.

Riessman, F., Cohen, J., & Pearl, A. (Eds.). *Mental health of the poor.* New York: Free Press, 1964.

Roberts, J., Prince R., Gold, B., & Shiner, E. *Social and mental health survey: Summary report.* Montreal, Canada: Mental Hygiene Institute, 1966.

Ryan, W. (Ed.). *Distress in the city: Essays on the design and administration of urban mental health services.* Cleveland, Ohio: Case Western Reserve University Press, 1969.

Sarason, S. B. *The culture of the school and the problem of change.* Boston: Allyn & Bacon, 1971.

Sarason, S. B., Carroll, C., Maton, K., Cohen, S., & Lorentz, E. *Human services and resource networks.* San Francisco, Calif.: Jossey-Bass, 1977.

Sarason, S. B., Levine, M., Goldenberg, I. I., Cherlin, D. L., & Bennett, E. M. *Psychology in community settings.* New York: Wiley 1966.

Searcy, M. L. An investigation of the interpersonal help-giving involvements of black and white beauticians (Doctoral dissertation, University of Rochester, 1980). *Dissertation Abstracts International*, 1980, 41, 3199B.

Weisenfeld, A. R., & Weis, H. M. A mental health consultation program for beauticians. *Professional Psychology*, 1979, 10, 786–792.

Zax, M., & Cowen, E. L. *Abnormal psychology: Changing conceptions* (2nd ed.). New York: Holt, Rinehart & Winston, 1976.

8.5 Ruminations on Change: The Incredible Value of Human Beings in Getting Things Done

Allan A. Kennedy

The easiest thing to do with an organization is write about how it should work; much more difficult is actually to make the organization work differently. I see a lot of that syndrome as a consultant, since teams are always eager to write reports but seem to stumble miserably when it comes to actually wading in with the organization and making things happen. What is particularly unusual about this pathology is that things are happening all the time within any real organization and it would seem, in theory, to be a simple matter to channel some of that existing activity. Alas, we seem not even to have a reasonable way, i.e., a conceptual framework, for thinking about change.

Because of my profession, I have been spending considerable time of late trying to get a grip on this problem. This paper represents an artificial milestone in this never-ending journey in that it presents some perspectives and their possible implications but makes no pretense about being such a framework. Specifically, the paper covers thoughts related to (1) how human beings communicate, (2) how things get done in this world, and (3) implications for organization design. Perhaps to others this will begin to suggest at least the elements of a realistic framework for understanding and undertaking change.

Communication among Humans

Recently I have been reading a combination of Montaigne, Nietzsche and Lewis Thomas.

From *Exchange*: The Organizational Behavior Teaching Journal 1981, Vol. VI, No. 1, 4–11.

To my surprise, all three independently commented on an aspect of human beings that seems to me to be important in terms of understanding organizations and organizational change. Their independent observation was that the mind of a human being is much more capable of thought than the body of the human is capable of articulating or otherwise expressing the morass of fleeting thoughts as they occur—in effect a structural problem in the construct of the human animal. More specifically, at any point in time, virtually any awake human has going on in his/her head a continuous flow of activity that in some sense represents thought—e.g., "Should I phone Dave Lawrence now or should I wait for Larry to call and why should I bother writing another damned piece and Cheryl Tiegs really looks gorgeous . . ." and so on and so forth. Meanwhile we are only capable of writing at 50–100 words per minute or speaking at perhaps as much as 200 words per minute. As a result, only a teeny fraction of the incredible internal goings on ever sees the light of day . . . and just as well considering the sort of garbage floating around in my head.

Similarly in terms of listening. We must start from the premise that the person speaking (however articulately) is only conveying a teeny fraction of what he really "thinks" about the subject at hand. We add to that a phenomenon of selective listening running at perhaps 25–50 percent efficiency at best. We further add to that a comment on the process of listening—i.e., we don't really listen for precisely what the speaker/writer is saying; what we really do is listen for a hook (metaphor, story, image, idea) that triggers a response in our catalogue of private thoughts then instantaneously attribute our thoughts/feelings/etc. about the stored material to the speaker. Jimmy Carter invokes the Democratic tradition and millions of Americans stir to a sense of FDR, the WPA, and the Great Depression.

Add to this a third phenomenon which relates to communicating: While in the process of communicating, people take inputs from a very wide variety of sources—much wider than typically is the intent of the one trying to communicate. For example, if one tries to speak to another, the listener invariably "hears" more than the spoken word—e.g., body language, impressions of the speaker as a real individual, and as a symbolic individual. Moreover, typical communicatees further compound this already-confusing-enough circumstance by adding their own unspoken fears, anxieties, aspirations, and passions to the jumble of input to be processed by their minds. "What is this person really saying?" "What will he want next?" "What is he really up to?"

In short, the simple act of one human being "communicating" with another turns out to be outrageously complicated. I like to picture what goes on in a human head as shown on the exhibit: a quick and somewhat random search of an eclectically organized card file. The end result of this overall process—partial articulation, selective listening, intrusion of related distracting thoughts, a somewhat random search pattern to decode the message—is distortion: Humans rarely communicate precisely what they have on their minds. They, practically speaking, settle for far less.

Not to overcomplicate the art of communication, there are occasions (usually trivial cases—one stranger to another: "What time is it?") when people can dispense with all the inherent distractions and focus right on the point. Unfortunately, however, life is not always so simple. And often the more complex messages are indeed also the more important messages. "America needs reindustrialization" say some today. What in the world does that mean in and of itself? Just to articulate that elusive notion accurately would require volumes of print. And that says nothing about the difficulties of the listener in hearing the message. How very different the message of reindustrialization must sound to the president of a company specializing in industrial robotics compared to an unemployed welder from the auto industry. In short, as the importance and complexity of the message increases, the likelihood of serious interhuman distortion increases also. And this would seem to be nothing more nor less than a fact of life.

I would like to offer the hypothesis that the above paragraphs do—more or less—accurately convey the essence of human communication. And in the following paragraphs suggest why this may have some relevance in several areas:

1. Importance of Simplicity in Communications

Our recent research into the organizational characteristics of excellent companies found, somewhat to our surprise, that these companies were in many ways simple-minded about what they do. "More than two MBO objectives is no objective"—a quote from a leading electronics concern; fundamental adherence to one or two simple beliefs—a universal finding from all of the companies. Simple-mindedness in management to what end?

One form of simple-mindedness deserves another. And my simple-minded model of the communication process suggests that these simple-minded managers of excellent companies are right on the mark. If distortion is bound to occur, then for God's sake limit the potential scope of the distortion by keeping the message simple. Or as a former Managing

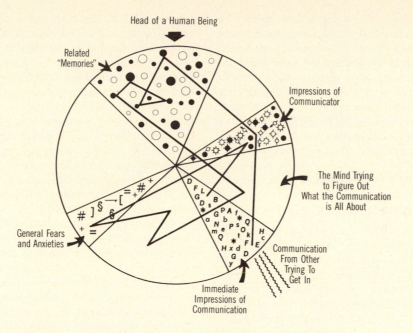

FIGURE 1   How a Human Being Processes a Communication

Director of McKinsey once said: The key management problem "is keeping the herd moving roughly west"; "the folks in the organization will figure out on their own how to ford the stream" (I added).

2. Role of Trust in Communications and Change

There is a considerable literature that suggests that communications are better in high-trust situations. My model of communication would suggest this is likely because:

Individuals who trust one another usually have more of a pool of shared experience/impression in their respective heads (what else, after all, is trust) that must aid them in decoding their mutual communications.

Individuals who trust one another may not communicate accurately but this may not be an impediment to their getting something done! Their trust

level may lead them *not to feel it necessary* to figure out precisely what the other is trying to say.

3. The Role of Authority in Communications and Change

The world, for better or worse, is a hierarchical world. This hierarchy, in turn, has a massive influence on communication. One aspect we have observed in virtually all of our client situations is the extraordinary degree to which people down the line attribute meaning to the actions and communications of their superiors. The simplest of statements get blown totally out of proportion and given meaning far beyond the intent of the speaker. Alternatively, good senior managers learn to accept their role as largely symbolic and deliberately orchestrate the symbols and patterns of their office to get their most fundamental message across.

This phenomenon occurs because virtually all of us carry around in our heads a residue of thoughts related to authority.

These thoughts (or more likely memories) may derive from childhood experiences; or may derive from seminal experiences in our adult organizational life. Whatever their origins, they dramatically influence what we take from any particular communication directed at us. It is, I would suggest, no surprise that top-down-driven change is often the most efficient of all organizational change processes.

4. Role of Repetition/ Reinforcement in Communications

Always when a change effort fails, we come back saying: "We should have spent more time explaining it." Similarly, allow me the observation that some superb managers are incredibly boring: they keep repeating the same things over and over. And add to that the observation that most well-managed companies/institutions are absolutely obsessive about the things they care about. You should work in IBM to understand the degree to which that whole organization harps away on the importance of customer service. What is going on in all these examples, and understandable in terms of the model of communication articulated above, is the building up of a residue of shared memories/perspectives around a common theme. Once this residue is firmly implanted in peoples' minds, it aids immeasurably in decoding communications. And in some instances it may also serve to lessen, or at least channel, the individual distortion that inevitably occurs.

There are probably other implications as well; these stand out in my mind as being the most important.

Role of People in Getting Things Done

Having dispensed with the vastly complicated subject of human communication in a few pages, let me now move on to a second topic of some importance: getting things done. Organizations, large or small, exist to get something done. More often than not, the something that needs doing requires communication among individuals. But the actual "getting it done" involves someone, a human being, doing something. Given the immense difficulty involved in communicating accurately, how in the world does this ever occur?

I would like to suggest that it is in the nature of human beings to take the random inputs and communications thrown at them, bounce these inputs against their own experience, indeed distort them mercilessly, and come out with the thing to be done—i.e., that humans are integral to getting things done. The absolutely incredible thing about human beings is their innate ability to modify, tailor, and apply these inputs to their own experience, and even at times to be creative in the process. Imprecise communications facilitates this uniquely human trait—indeed it is the imprecision itself which is essential for getting things done.

Consider a silly but nontrivial example: keypunching. Many organizations in today's world need to get data transferred from one medium to a machine-readable form. The art that does this is called keypunching. It is not one of the most endearing of human art forms because of the inherently dull and repetitive nature of the task.

Because there is so much data to be so transformed, the real need is to have these data transformed *accurately and productively*. Here's where people come in. There are clear limits to the physical abilities of human beings to hit the keys accurately and quickly. However, left to their own devices, there are almost no limits to the degree of productivity an individual keypuncher can achieve by taking full advantage of the capabilities of their instruments and organizing their own flow of work to best advantage. I have seen it with my own eyes so I know it is true. I am sure that most people have seen its analog in the equally prosaic confines of the typing pool. Every typing pool I have ever seen has one eccentric who manages to be twice as productive as everyone else around.

While the star of the typing or keypunching pool may be a phenomenon we have all observed in our organizational lives, it is surely a phenomenon given short shrift in organization literature and practice. I know of only one manager, Rene McPherson when he was at Dana Corporation, who explicitly acknowledged the phenomenon:

> Until we believe the expert in any job is the person performing it, we shall forever limit the potential of that person. Consider a manufacturing setting: Within their 25-square-foot area, nobody knows more about how to operate a machine, improve its quality, optimize the material flow, or keep it operating than the machine operators. Nobody!

McPherson, of course, made this philosophy operative while he ran Dana by radically decentralizing responsibility for productivity improvement down to the level of the people who could actually do something about it. He was rewarded by the No. 2 Fortune 500 ranking in return to investors and an annual productivity improvements far in excess of the rest of American industry.

We have found in our research on the organizational characteristics of excellent companies that other stellar performers— TI, Blue Bell, McDonald's (to take examples in widely different industry settings)—rely heavily on the individual people in their organization for their outstanding performance. But as a general rule, most organizations neither function nor even think that way about themselves. Strange, since again this phenomenon seems to be little more or less than a fact of life.

Again it seems to me there are some straightforward implications of this hy-pothesis that humans are integral to the process of getting things done, for example:

1. Role of Plans and Planning in Getting Things Done

I have spent many years of my life drafting "implementation plans" to facilitate getting things done. Consultants and practitioners both spend endless hours trying to design organizations that facilitate getting things done. The folly of all this is that most things worth doing in this world are far too complicated to spell out in perfect detail. The even greater folly is the failure to recognize that things worth getting done get done *because* there are real, live, distortion-prone human beings at the other end of the communications line. People make things happen—not plans, not processes, not organizational schema.

If any of the above makes sense, the only way to get nontrivial things done in this world is to design people into the process from the beginning. People with their unique ability to distort communications (for better or for worse) are the means of getting all-but-trivial things done in this world. And designing people into the process means giving them latitude to exercise their own discretion in what is to be done. In place of plans and planning, perhaps we need far greater emphasis on a process to capture the hearts and minds of the people we are trying to change. Of which more below.

2. Role of Communications in Getting Things Done

Organizational change is just a fancy way of saying getting a whole bunch of things done. As a management consultant, my business, if you will, is helping organizations change. Over the years, I have developed (or borrowed from others) some rules of change that I believe are universally operative in today's world.

Change occurs only when a real need for change exists.

Change occurs only when a clear plan exists for at least the first few steps of the change.

Change occurs only when an actionable consensus of people in the organization are behind the change.

Change occurs inevitably at its own pace.

Clearly (I think), communications is the process used to build the actionable consensus that seems always to be needed if change is to occur. (See my article in an earlier issue of *Exchange* [Volume IV, Number 3] which articulates this position.) But what is an "actionable consensus?"

Typically, by consensus we mean detailed agreement on a point. The model discussed above suggests this is a misdefinition (and in fact a misdirection).

True, total agreement is likely impossible since people inevitably distort all communication in light of their own feelings, experiences, histories, priorities.

Seeking to achieve such total agreement is likely to be counterproductive in that it would take away from that most unique of human traits: the ability to modify an idea to fit with circumstances as the individual uniquely perceives them.

What is likely needed is agreement in broad terms on a change goal or target—i.e., "west" or "east"—and a deliberate attempt to leave all other qualifying details to be worked out.

Moreover, what really may be needed to form a consensus is simply the illusion of an agreement with an actual change target/goal so diffuse as to be acceptable to all.

The key mechanism, therefore, for effecting change is a communication process that seeks first and foremost to establish such a general "heads of agreement" consensus about the direction in which change is to occur. (It seems also to me, in passing, that one of the unique strengths of the Japanese is their socially well-established sense of both the importance of such a consensus and the means of achieving it in the normal course of events.)

3. Structure of an Efficient Change Process

If the goal of a change process is to get something done and the means of achieving that goal is tapping into the innate ability of humans to adapt a general direction/communication to the world as they see it around them, then the structure of an efficient change process would be highly atomized. Just as Rene McPherson was willing to rely on his machine operator to figure out the best work flow around the machine, the intelligent change agent must be willing to rely on the individual people in the organization to design the changes that affect themselves.

This concept of an atomized organization for effecting change would not be such a potentially unique insight were it so seldom the practice today.

Much change today is still attempted by dumping voluminous reports on the desks of senior management—i.e., the subject of change is often not even addressed except under the guise of an implementation plan.

Even when the change process is seriously considered, the most common organization mechanisms proposed are either: (a) implementation "czars," or (b) task forces. Both notions, it strikes me, are inadequate for the task of effecting change.

—Czars are only useful in the sense of providing a focal point for consistency checking, but that is seldom the charter they are given.

—Task forces are most useful as a device for forming a consensus. As a device for actually effecting change, the inevitable homogenizing influence of the task force is self-defeating to the desired process of adaptation that should be under way.

As a substitute, a change process that simply puts the mantle on as many individual shoulders as possible—however chaotic that might seem—would be much preferred.

4. Role of Feedback and Management Forums

If an efficient change process is to be structured along the lines of having a thousand change agents out there doing their own thing in their own bailiwicks, how in the world would such a process be controlled? The answer to the question put that way is self-evident: through the careful use of feedback to individual change agents perhaps under the guise of structured management forums. What better way to control a change process than to have frequent reporting by individual change agents back to a group, the keeper of the change concept, which can serve the purpose of fine-tuning the detailed directions of changes proposed.

5. Importance of Rewards and Motivation

If as Rene McPherson suggests, the individuals in the organization are to be trusted to design their own changes as part of the overall change program, then the individuals must be motivated to take on the task. This suggests to me three elements that deserve careful forethought.

Early consensus-building efforts cannot stop only at agreement; they must strive for enthusiasm as well. It is not a chance occurrence that people who are enthusiastic about something really give it more effort (one need only watch the bench of a winning sports team to realize that). But how often is this factor seriously considered as an integral part of the serious process of effecting change?

Informal reward systems must reinforce the change process. Doing things differently is inherently difficult; all human beings would rather rely on precedent. But doing things differently is the heart of effecting change. And to get 1,000 change agents out there enthusiastically trying, requires that the flow of informal rewards must be carefully considered. I would suggest that the rubric for a successful change program must be one that allows the change agent to benefit directly from his/her own change—i.e., the charge to a change agent must be "go out there and make your life better." I would further suggest that this Pollyana objective is realistic: Improving organization effectiveness is not inherently a zero-sum game.

Formal rewards must be frequent, visible, and consistent for a change program to work. If you want change, put your money where your mouth is.

6. Role of Passion and the True Believer in the Process of Change

It is certainly no great insight to note that I too am bemused by that most chimerical of human afflictions—passion. Whether it is in its essence a left/right brain phenomenon or whether its origins are elsewhere, passion seems to be the most distracting of all human endeavors. Communications with the passionate true believer are virtually impossible: True believers hear only what they want to hear. Giving direction to them is useless; they will inevitably follow their own passion-driven sense of direction.

Passion, however, is not a negative force in the world by any means. Culturally we associate passion with most of the great artistic innovations of the ages. The notion of the passionate artist is virtually a cliche in our many languages. Similarly in politics, most major political changes are marked by extreme passion and it is arguably possible that it is indeed the passion of the true believers that made the upheaval occur. Passion, it turns out, is also a major factor in more prosaic arenas. Studies have shown, for example, that the key to new products in the industrial arena is a committed "product champion"—in effect, a passionate true believer in the value of the new concept. History and organizational literature are overrun with mythologies about autocratic, seemingly obsessed geniuses who built great institutions (one needs look no further than Tom Watson for a model of this kind). So somehow, passion is what shakes the cages of the world and makes things happen.

In my experience, successful change processes need zealots if they are to be successful. Far beyond the minimal requirements of fashioning a consensus, there is a need to allow people—some people, not all—to become so committed to an idea for change that they simply go off the deep end and cross the line from concurrence to zealotry. Quite honestly, I have no idea how to do this in the real world; I just know it is of paramount importance in the process of producing change.

There are likely other implications, but these strike me as the most important. What is further tantalizing is that these notions might begin to add up to a framework for change.

Suppose I really had the courage of my convictions and were given a freehanded mandate—e.g., from Ronald Reagan to dramatically change the role of the Federal Government from being profligate (or so he would say) to becoming frugal and cost conscious. How might I go about this task? I am tempted to suggest the following:

I would carve out a section of the government large enough to be roughly representative but small enough to be addressable in a lifetime. Let's say, for the sake of argument, the Post Office.

I would then spend a year or so conducting endless series of meetings throughout the organization about what this new mandate might mean. Each meeting would have no more than 10–15 people in them but I would have them going on everywhere—virtually ignorant of the possible short-term implications for productivity.

From these meetings I would attempt *ad hoc* to extract a number of elements:

A general theme that could be used as a rallying cry for the change process itself—one with which many people in the meetings seemed to concur.

A team of perhaps 100–200 "keepers of the change concept" who would be pulled out of their existing jobs, given lots of status and function as a sounding board downstream. The team would include some—but not all—of the true believers found in the course of the meeting.

A listing of *all* the true believers found so we could watch what they did later on.

With these three results achieved, I would then launch the next phase of the change process—a radical decentralization of the organization. Since this is only a theoretical exercise, let me be playful. My decentralization would abolish the entire hierarchy of the Post Office—i.e., all Post Office workers would become equal—except, of course, for my keepers of the change concept. In place of the existing hierarchy, I would substitute working groups of roughly 10 peers at all (previous) levels of the organization and ask them to design their own organization in keeping with the change concept. Their recommendations would be presented to a local committee of keepers of the change concept—say at biweekly intervals for a two–three-month period. At the end of this period, the local committees would make recommendations upward. Two rules to guide their recommendations:

They would have to approve at least 70 percent of the recommendations put to them by the local working groups.

They would have to approve *all* recommendations put forward by our secret group of zealots—however absurd their ideas.

The keepers of the change concept would then meet for 30 days in the woods of Minnesota to hammer out all other details of the new organizational arrangements for the Post Office.

Finally, for a three-year period (or until Ronnie got booted out for destroying the Postal Service), I would constitute the keepers of the change concept as watchdogs and process decision makers for the new organization.

Fantasies aside, my concern is that it might actually work.

Implications for Organization Design

For decades, managers, consultants, and academics have been exchanging views on how organizations work and how to make them better. The exchange of views would not be worrisome except for the fact that real live organizations of people are continually being tampered with in the process.

Two main items strike me as wrong about much of this dialogue and practice. The first is that it misses the point by focusing on the organization itself as an entity. A better view would be to see the organization as simply and totally a collection of people with the real problem being how to enable those human beings to get done a series of things related to the purpose of the organization as a whole.

The second is that our views of organization seem always to be based on a static view of the world when, in fact, an organization, however moribund, is nothing if not dynamic. It is rather like trying to figure out the workings of the hydrogen bomb with the benefit of Newtonian mechanics. Again these comments alone are surely not helpful, but there may be implications:

1. Organization Structures Have No Meaning except as Related to Enabling Human Beings to Get Things Done

There are endless books on the advantages/ disadvantages of functional versus divisional versus matrix structures. In some fundamental way, none of these arguments are relevant unless they explicitly address the question: "Will this structure help that person get his set of things done?" While it may be pushing the point too far, I would argue for these new principles of organization structure design.

All structures should be tailored to the individuals in the organization.

All structures should be dynamic (i.e., continually changing) to suit the changing needs of individuals.

Structural schema should be designed person by person for all the people in the organization (i.e., not top down to serve the needs of a few, senior management individuals).

2. Our Concepts of Decentralization Should Be Extended Downward—Much Lower in the Organization

Even though decentralization either to regional or local structures or into freestanding divisions has had a major impact on the effectiveness of organizations today (mostly for the good), I would like to offer the hypothesis that our thinking about decentralization has not gone far enough. Per my model of how the world works, you do not really begin to get the benefit of people's potential for initiative until you get down to groups of people no larger than 10–15 (I could be talked into 100 but would be skeptical at that size). Nowhere, to my knowledge, has anyone proposed methodologies for either constructing or managing organizations truly decentralized to this extent. But it is my belief that the real advantages of decentralization will only become apparent when we begin to reach this far.

3. Structural Schema Ought to Have in Them the Mechanism for Change

I, like probably many others, have struggled for years to understand Texas Instruments' OST concept. Basically, it is a formal mechanism for organizational regeneration. The "shadow" organization concepts now in place at Millipore have a similar purpose. I think that established mechanisms for ongoing reorganization such as these are easily as important as getting the organization structure right in the first place. Again it strikes me that I am unaware of any sensible literature dealing with this central area of organization.

4. Managers Should Have the Formal Responsibility for Tradeoffs That Fall between the Cracks of a Formal Organization Structure

The concept of a matrix structure was right as a way of dealing with the inherent complexities of today's world. But the concept was dead wrong in pushing this through the organization. Making these tradeoffs is what managers are there for. And if we are to tap their inherent ability to adapt, we must put managers into the

organization where real tradeoffs need to be made. In short, the key design requirement is to give managers real jobs to do too. This design principle is much more important than span-of-control, etc.

5. Management Information Systems Should Be Designed to Aid Real People in Getting Things Done

It is a truism that good system design starts with the user. But the truism breaks down when the system designer then imposes his/her logic on what the user should be doing. Rather, the end point of the MIS exercise should be to make available data to a person/user so that person/user can react to that data and do something different with it. That's how an organization can get the value of having the person there in the first place. Alas, few systems are now defined that way.

6. Management Processes Should Be Simple Conduits of Information Between People

Traditionally we think of management processes as control devices in an organization. "With the sales management system we can tell the salespersons how to spend their time." This view is consistent only with the pristine organization unpopulated by people. In an organization of people, a management system should attempt to convey meaningful information so that the people at either end of the communication channel can respond accordingly. Given the inherent difficulty in achieving clear communications, this in turn implies that management processes, to be effective, must be extraordinarily simple in design.

7. Much More Emphasis Should Be Placed on People Socialization Processes

If people are to make the organizational engine run, then they must have some idea of where it is heading. This occurs through interaction with other people in the organization—i.e., a socialization process. But few organizations we know today really pay the kind of attention they need to these processes.

8. The Nature of the Work Task Needs to Be Clearly Delineated at All Levels of the Organization

Today most jobs are defined by job descriptions, titles, reporting relationships, etc. These characterizations tend to be very light at all levels in terms of defining what that human being is actually supposed to be getting done in his/her job. MBO systems try to bridge this gap—but typically miss the mark by postulating vague generalities as objectives. A human-oriented organization does not necessarily mean a nonhierarchical organization; what it does mean is an organization where every individual has a real job with the discretion and latitude to carry it out.

Admittedly much of organization theory and practice seems to be heading in this direction; the question I would raise is one of pace and extent in light of the realities of real human organizations. While I cannot really integrate the above points into a pro forma for an effective organization, I am struck by pieces we all seem to be missing. For example, in my idealized organization, every single person would be required to spend one working hour a week and one working day a month redesigning his/her own job. To make sure this was really done I would require written—albeit simple—reports on how this time was spent and what resulted. And I would pay bonuses to those who did the best job. I think I could defend this practice theoretically with the arguments presented in this paper. But then why isn't anyone trying it?

8.6 Laboratory Education and Re-education

Edgar H. Schein   Warren G. Bennis

Introduction

We would now like to explain how learning really takes place. To do this, we will focus on those forces in the laboratory setting, culture, staff value system, and training design that initiate the first and most important attitude change—that of learning how to learn, of coming to value the meta-goals of laboratory training. Once

Reprinted from *Personal and Organizational Change through Group Methods* (New York: John Wiley & Sons, Inc., 1965).

this step has been accomplished, the learning process almost takes care of itself. The data are there, ready to be looked at and learned from. All that is really needed is the willingness to look at them and the ability to pay attention to them.

The residential laboratory has, from the outset, a social structure and a culture (normative system) that have been created largely by the staff and are imposed on the delegate.[1] This social structure in

[1] This imposed culture should not be confused with the particular norms and structures built by the groups as the laboratory proceeds,

combination with the training design creates the essential forces that make learning possible. These forces can be grouped into three major categories as follows:

Forces That Motivate Learning by Unfreezing the Delegate We have pointed out that unfreezing may begin with dilemmas and disconfirmations which occur in the organizational settings prior to entry into the laboratory. But the laboratory creates a whole new set of dilemmas and exposes the delegate to a new set of disconfirming cues which serve as powerful motivators for learning.

Forces That Enhance Willingness to Be Open and Authentic by Reducing Threat from Others All of the activities of a laboratory are built around the collection of observations and reactions of the delegates to the here-and-now events of the laboratory. Learning can occur only if delegates come to be willing to be open and honest about their observations, reactions, and feelings. What ordinarily militates against such openness and authenticity is fear of the reactions of others. To be open and honest is to expose oneself to *danger from others*. They may take advantage of the person, retaliate if they feel he has been hostile, or demean him by not taking him seriously. Consequently, to understand how the laboratory enhances learning requires us to examine those forces in it that reduce threat from others and promote openness and authenticity.

Forces That Enhance Willingness and Ability to Listen to and Pay Attention to the Reactions and Feelings of Others by Reducing Threat from Within The basic learning in a laboratory results from a

delegate discovering what impact he has on others, what impact others have on him, and what the consequences of the various reactions which members have are for group functioning. This learning requires that the delegate listen to the reactions of others and pay attention to them. What ordinarily militates against listening and paying attention is his own defensiveness or fear of his own reactions. To listen and to pay attention is to expose oneself to *danger from within oneself*. The delegate may learn things he does not wish to hear, he may become anxious or be overwhelmed by guilt, or he may lose self-esteem. Consequently, understanding how the laboratory enhances learning requires us to examine those forces in the laboratory which reduce threat from within and promote the willingness and ability to listen and pay attention to the reactions of others.

Forces That Motivate Learning by Unfreezing the Delegate

Isolation and Loss of Support for Accustomed Routines

The laboratory setting, particularly in a total residential laboratory, requires the delegate to become involved in a social system and to suspend for one or two weeks his membership in the back-home social system. The laboratory isolates him from co-workers, family, and daily work routines. Such isolation is a powerful unfreezing force because to a large extent our beliefs, attitudes, and values derive their stability from the daily confirmation which others provide us with. If we are removed from our usual pattern of relationships, we lose the support which others provide us with. Beliefs, attitudes, and values become less stable as the person is isolated from his normal routine and pattern of relationships.

---

although the interaction of the initial and emergent cultures is of obvious relevance to the full understanding of how and why people learn in a laboratory.

This process of loss of support through isolation is particularly acute in the area of self-concept or identity. Our beliefs about ourselves and our feelings of self-esteem are learned from and supported by the reactions of others. We learn to define ourselves partly in terms of the reactions we elicit in those others whose reactions we particularly value. Hence the loss of the daily feedback from bosses, co-workers, family, and friends, exposes the delegate to uncertainty about himself: who he really is and how much worth he should attach to himself. Whatever anxiety is generated by isolation is, of course, reinforced by the knowledge the delegate has that the laboratory may be a place where he will learn something about himself which he did not know before, where people will "tell him the truth about himself" or expose his weaknesses. Thus, the very transition to the laboratory social system is likely to be inherently a potent experience.

The isolation of the delegate from his back-home setting is usually reinforced by the immediate removal of what might be called "self-defining equipment." The delegate is told and shown by the example of the staff's informal attire that the laboratory is a highly informal place. Uniforms, business suits, and other external symbols of status are discouraged. Even clerics who attend a laboratory find themselves attending sessions without their collars or habits. Nothing is more surprising than to see, on the last day of the laboratory, the informal gathering of people who have learned to know each other in the T-group, donning their back-home clothes for the plane and train trips home.

In addition to the loss of identifying clothing, the delegate usually suffers the loss of his title and full name. In the pre-laboratory information folders, there is usually a card asking him to give his preferred nickname so that it can be put on his name tag. The name tag he is given

when he arrives bears this nickname and his last name, but no title, company affiliation, or other identifying information is shown. The delegate soon learns, through staff example, that regardless of relative age, status, formal rank, or personality attributes all members of the laboratory community address each other by first name. It is often quite traumatic for the person used to being called Mr., Dr., or Sir to find himself nothing more than Jim, John, or Teddy in a group of strangers. The laboratory imposes a surface intimacy which can be very upsetting to those not used to it.[2]

Reinforcing the loss of distinguishing clothing, formal titles, and organizational affiliations is the loss of privacy which results from sharing a room with one or more people, eating meals family style, and using public toilet and shower facilities. The delegate finds himself in a life situation where his daily needs are routinely taken care of, but where there are no established routines or status props behind which to hide. The person is suddenly on his own with respect to others, and there are not clearcut cues as to what sort of behavior is appropriate. His consciousness of himself is thus greatly heightened, as is the likelihood of his discovering in himself feelings and reactions which he did not know he had. In Goffman's terms, in the laboratory setting the front and back stages of life become

---

[2] The full import of this informal norm was only recently brought home to us through a program for M.I.T. graduate students and their wives (a group who had accepted two-year internship appointments in African nations). One of the wives found herself in a T-group in which the staff member was also an M.I.T. faculty member. This young woman admitted near the end of the laboratory, with obvious discomfort, that one of the most difficult aspects for her had been to call the trainer and other older members of the T-group by their first names. She was 20 years old and totally unused to such "disrespectful" behavior on her own part.

merged to a great extent, exposing the person more fully and increasing the probability of social anxiety or identity crises.

Thus far, we have pointed out how various aspects of the laboratory setting create for the delegate a situation in which his accustomed roles are not supported by any of the props and routines which are typical in the back-home situation. Instead, he encounters a number of forces which actually disconfirm certain of these roles and push him toward something which might be called the "learner role."

New Learning Norms

The process of learning new norms, particularly norms which pertain to the learning process itself, is most visible in the unstructured setting of the T-group. Basically what happens to the delegate is that he discovers that methods of handling other people and groups that have worked well in the back-home setting fail to work in the T-group. As most of the group members experience such failure, they are forced to re-examine and redefine their goals and their method of operation. Out of this process arise the norms which make learning possible.

For example, the person who has been successful as an aggressive leader in the back-home setting finds few followers in the T-group; the skillful manipulator finds that others can see through him and resent his manipulation; the silent observer finds others demanding to know what he thinks; and so on. The delegate finds that he does not have the protection of a formal power position; he cannot just adjourn the meeting at an appropriate moment, walk out rather than answer a question, or employ other strategies which he may have employed with success in his past interpersonal and group relationships. Often this leaves the delegate with a genuine sense of helplessness and forces him to seek other solutions.

As back-home norms fail to be con-firmed, new norms are confronted and worked on: "we are here to learn, i.e., to change or be influenced"; "the correct way to behave is to help the learning process along"; "we are all equal and all enjoy high worth in the eyes of the staff"; "success in the laboratory is defined by how much we learn, i.e., how much we change"; "we are here to test and re-evaluate our basic approach to ourselves, other people, and groups"; "learning is an important and valuable activity; if you are not willing to learn, there is something wrong with you and you should not be in the laboratory"; "we are on our own and have to manage our own learning; the staff will not be of much help."

In addition, the key norm, that anything which occurs in the group can be legitimately scrutinized and analyzed, is communicated in lectures and through trainer example. Thus, the decision which a minority railroaded through the group can be re-examined and undone; various roles and strategies which members exhibited can be focused on, discussed, and reacted to.

There is a definite moral overtone to all of these norms: being a successful learner is good; being unwilling or unable to learn is bad. No single activity communicates these messages to the delegate. Rather, they come out of the brochures, introductions, trainer remarks and behavior in the T-groups, and the pressure from other delegates who are already highly motivated to learn. There is little doubt that the laboratory exerts powerful conformity pressures on the individual who does not accept to some degree the norms about the learning process.

Somewhat related norms tend to develop in the T-group, are imposed in exercises, and are mentioned explicitly in theory sessions: "in order to learn you must be an *active* participant, you must *expose* to some degree your typical behavior"; "you must be interested in and *help* in trying to understand why you, others, and the group are behaving the way you or they are"; "you must be *willing to tolerate a certain amount of tension*, because learning usually provokes some tension"; and "you must initially *trust the basic method* of the laboratory and the staff."

Supporting these norms, particularly the one about equality and group responsibility, is the manner in which the staff present themselves to delegates. *First*, even though there is a formal staff structure with a laboratory dean and informally defined senior and junior staff, trainers tend to present themselves as professional equals unconcerned about hierarchical formal authority. The emphasis is on individual responsibility, getting the man most qualified for any particular situation, and on a "collaborative concept of authority."

Second, the staff attempts to communicate that "we are all in this together"; "we must collaborate and help each other to learn"; "no one of us has all the resources necessary"; "each of us has some of the resources we will need." In saying this to delegates, the staff is not being devious or dishonest. Rather, we must distinguish between norms that concern *how to learn*, and norms that concern *what will be learned*. The staff creates a setting which, in effect, *imposes norms of how to learn*, but such norms do not prejudge what will actually happen in the groups, what observations will be made, what feelings will be revealed, and therefore, *what will be learned*. Genuine collaboration is needed in maximizing *what will be learned*.

To reinforce the norms about learning and the image of staff-delegate equality, staff members attempt to exemplify the laboratory philosophy in their own interactions with each other. One extreme has been to invite delegates to observe staff meetings to see for themselves how the staff operates. A more common situation arises in theory sessions if staff members supplement each other's lecture material, raise questions, or disagree with each other. Extra efforts tend to be made in these situations to listen to and to deal constructively with the issues posed. When

staff members violate their own learning norms, it often has severe repercussions among the delegates.

In summary, the main thrust of the forces described thus far is toward (1) the destruction of norms associated with a formal hierarchical social structure, (2) the establishment of a more informal peer culture in which status is achieved based on acceptance of new norms, and (3) the acceptance of a learner role and learning norms which reflect the underlying values of laboratory training.

Summary

The unfreezing forces which are generated in a laboratory setting can be roughly classified into the following categories: (1) isolation from accustomed sources of support—colleagues, family, and regular routines; (2) removal of self-defining equipment, status, title, etc.; (3) loss of certain areas of privacy; (4) lack of confirmation or actual disconfirmation of roles which are appropriate in the back-home setting; (5) breakdown of hierarchical authority and status structures in favor of a kind of peer culture and informal status based on laboratory norms; (6) a set of laboratory norms about the value of the learning process and the method of learning; and (7) deliberately created lack of structure to heighten consciousness of self and to create unavoidable dilemmas.

It is these forces which motivate and initiate the learning process by unfreezing the delegate, by arousing social anxiety through disconfirmation, and by focusing the delegate on himself in his relationship to others.

Forces That Enhance Willingness to be Open and Authentic by Reducing Threat from Others

If learning is to occur in the laboratory setting, delegates must be willing and able to be open and authentic with each other. The primary barrier to openness and authenticity is the danger of being hurt by others. A person may be hurt in retaliation for something he has said or be punished because he has broken one of a number of cultural rules about not stating feelings openly.

Some of these norms, deeply ingrained in Anglo-Saxon culture, are:

1. *Norms designed to protect the feelings of another person*: "don't say anything if you can't say something nice"; "don't criticize if you can't provide a constructive alternative"; never talk about someone behind his back."
2. *Norms designed to increase self-protection*: "people who live in glass houses should not throw stones."
3. *Norms suggesting that feelings only cause trouble*: "let sleeping dogs lie"; "don't sir up a hornet's nest"; "don't rock the boat"; "when ignorance is bliss, it's folly to be wise."
4. *Norms suggesting that emotions are immature and should be masked*: "only sissies cry"; "keep a stiff upper lip"; "learn to take it on the chin."

In addition to such norms, there are a variety of informal "rules of the game" such as not criticizing people in front of others, never carrying tales out of school, and keeping feelings out of work relationships. Cultural norms in favor of openness, like "call a spade a spade," "shoot straight from the shoulder," and "call them as you see them," refer mostly to the area of work performance rather than to interpersonal feelings.

We are all overtrained culturally to accept others for what they are, not to tell them anything which conceivably might hurt them, and to give compliments whenever possible, even if they are not sincere. In order to maintain our self-esteem at the highest possible level, we present ourselves in the most favorable light possible. Others collude with us in whatever self-deception is involved by granting us whatever they feel they can. Only rarely do we get direct forthright reactions to our behavior.

The laboratory setting provides the delegates with an opportunity to obtain information about themselves and others which is ordinarily unavailable. Such information, the feelings and reactions of others, is essential for us to have if we are to understand why others behave toward us as they do. For example, one of the biggest discoveries which members of T-groups make is that the seemingly random events which occur in the group become highly understandable once the feelings of the members are brought out into the open.

For the laboratory setting to enhance learning at this level, it must help delegates suspend the norms *against* openness, reduce threat from others, and provide opportunities for building new norms *in favor* of openness. The laboratory must create a psychologically safe environment to minimize the risks of openness. A number of factors work in this direction: the temporariness and "game" quality of the laboratory, the learning method itself, psychological theory, and the presence of the staff. Let us examine each of these in detail.

The Laboratory as a Temporary Game

A number of conditions make the laboratory and its setting different from the usual back-home settings. *First*, it is clearly understood by all participants that the laboratory is a temporary and short experience. However traumatic it may be, it will not last forever. *Second*, it is highly informal and egalitarian. Those dangers which arise from direct formal authority and power are minimized. Staff members use only veiled sanctions, minimizing the use of any direct authority. *Third*, the laboratory is isolated and self-contained. The only witnesses to whatever goes on are fellow participants and staff. A clear norm is established early: Whatever happens at the laboratory is confidential. It will be learned by others only if delegates themselves tell about it. There is no outside audience; those inside the cultural island share the same fate. *Fourth*, there is no product to be manufactured or service to be performed for anyone else. All participants are there only for their own and each other's benefit. *Fifth*, none of the relationships formed during the laboratory are permanent or carry necessary implications for the back-home situation (except in the special case of team training). Delegates who come from the same organization or know each other well are generally put into different T-groups. *Sixth*, most of the basic needs for food and lodging are automatically taken care of by dormitory living, thus freeing the delegate from distracting choices and helping him focus attention on learning. *Seventh*, there is a clearcut routine of activities for each day that further minimizes choices. In short, the temporariness provides a culture which minimizes responsibilities while focusing on learning and change.

The atmosphere which these conditions create in the residential laboratory is not unlike that of an ocean cruise or retreat. The demands of real life are temporarily suspended, permitting people to concentrate on themselves and each other. Threats from others are reduced because the stakes for which people are playing are temporary. The person may get emotionally hurt in the laboratory but he does not lose his job or take a cut in salary. He can engage others in the context of a game and experiment with open communications in trivial ways before raising the stakes. Such experimentation permits him to feel out the others to see what kind of danger, if any, they represent. The fact that most delegates come to the laboratory with the

constructive intent of learning and helping each other reduces the likelihood that such experimentation will have disastrous outcomes.

The Learning Method as Protective

The learning method serves to reduce threat from others by promoting an emphasis on (1) here-and-now *specific* events and acts rather than people, (2) objective reaction and analysis rather than evaluation, and (3) the legitimacy of experimentation.

1. One of the major assumptions which the staff makes about effective learning is that it is safer and more productive to collect observations, reactions, and feelings about some *specific* group incident or *specific* member behavior than about a group member in general. For example, the trainer may respond or ask others to respond to "Harry's attempt to get his point across," not to a question such as "how do the group members feel about Harry in this group." Wherever possible, the trainer by example or direct suggestion focuses the group on the specific behavior of a member rather than on his total character or personality.

The major assumption which underlies this strategy is that it is easier both to give and to receive feedback on specific behavior because this feedback does not represent an evaluation of the person as a whole. If the feedback is too threatening, the person is offered the defense that the behavior was not really typical of him.

A second assumption which underlies this strategy is that by focusing on specific behavior the group members learn to be better observers of their own and others' behavior. From being forced to make more *precise* observations, they learn how easy it is to stereotype another member and to miss the important fact that his behavior may be highly variable.

A third assumption which underlies this strategy is that only by reference to specific behavioral data is it possible to compare, contrast, and accumulate reactions. If one person sees Harry as hostile whereas another sees him as supportive, it cannot be determined how to reconcile these observations without knowing which behavior of Harry's produced each of the reactions. The two persons may be reacting to the same behavior differently, or they may simply be focusing on different behavior which Harry has exhibited at different times.

2. By focusing on specific behavior rather than on the total person, it is also easier to establish a norm of *objectivity*. The trainer encourages by example and suggestion that observations and reactions be an accurate *description* of how the person felt or what he saw, not an *evaluation* of the other person's behavior. Of course, true objectivity is never possible where human interactions are involved. What we mean by objectivity in this context is the attempt to be as explicit as possible about what our feelings and reactions are and to distinguish these from judgmental evaluations of either our own or the other person's behavior and feelings. Being descriptive is an important aid in the achievement of this kind of objectivity. In general, it is easier to be descriptive in reference to some event than about the totality of impressions one has gained of another person, although eventually group members become skillful in giving objective feedback on general impressions as well.

As members achieve skill in objective reporting, the climate becomes safer for all concerned. For example, hostile reactions can be controlled and neutralized by being objectively analyzed—what triggered these reactions, what earlier feelings were present between the combatants? We do not mean to imply here that successful learning requires the elimination of direct outbursts

of feelings. Rather, we wish to underline that the norm of objectivity and the sanction to analyze any behavior that occurs, serves in the member's fantasy life as a safety valve. If feelings run too high, the group can use as a coping device an objective analysis of why feelings were high, how they were being handled, and how they might be handled in the future.

3. The norm of *experimentation* is also critical in promoting openness and authenticity. As group members, possibly under the goading of the trainer, try small experiments in being open, they usually discover that this leads to more mutual acceptance and support, not to rejection and hostility. The discovery that openness leads more often to acceptance than to rejection is one of the most powerful forces toward a re-examination of cultural norms about interpersonal relationships and communication. If group members experience success in trying to be open, they become more strongly committed to the laboratory norms about learning.

Psychological Theory as a Source of Protection

Theory sessions, staff behavior, and trainer comments all attempt to underline several basic points about emotions that, if understood, serve to protect the delegate psychologically from the threat of others: (1) emotions exist within all of us, whether we are aware of them or not; (2) all people have both tender, loving emotions and tough, aggressive emotions, although they may be more comfortable expressing one set or the other, (3) emotions generally have specific causes, though the causes may be multiple; (4) once the cause is identified, the emotions often are not as threatening to the person himself or others as they initially seemed; (5) emotions, even if quite violent, are normal, can be understood, and must be analyzed objectively if interpersonal and group relationships are to be understood. In short, every attempt is made to legitimize the existence and expression of feelings, to help delegates accept their own and others' feelings, not as something to be frightened of and retaliated against, but as something to be understood and learned from.

For example, a common incident in T-groups or exercises is some hostile remark by person A to person B that results in an open or veiled fight and raises the general level of tension in the group. If the group can stop the fight and analyze the prior events or feelings, it often turns out that person A was tense, not hostile, and that some behavior of B triggered A into showing his tension through hostility. The group can then explore further what the sources of tension were, an exploration that often reveals that A was not alone in being tense and that the group can do something constructive about its sources of tension.

The eventual outcome is that A's hostility is revealed to be something other than rejection of B. It may well have reflected a total group problem rather than some specific problem of A's. The group may also learn that hostility is generally a *symptom of tension*, even closeness (not necessarily of *malice*), and that hostility, therefore, need not be fearful or mysterious. As different kinds of feelings are brought under control and scrutiny, the environment becomes safer for the expression of new feelings, helping to make communication more open and authentic.

The Staff as a Source of Protection

It is difficult to assess the exact impact of the staff. On the one hand, staff members vary greatly in how they present themselves to the delegate population, and, on the other hand, delegate *fantasies* about the staff are as important as actual staff behavior. Such fantasies usually involve the attribution of omniscience and omnipotence to staff members. The staff does have some real power and authority. For example, their power to manage whatever dangers arise in the laboratory is communicated in a number of ways.

First, the staff clearly has a plan and a theory. Whether staff members say "we are all in this together as equals" or "we are here to help you learn," it is clear that they know what they are doing. They exhibit relatively little tension themselves, particularly in the presence of strong feelings. If they are tense they often are able to communicate that it is all right to feel tense and to demonstrate actual resources in dealing with situations when danger gets too high (e.g., the trainer will protect a group member who is getting attacked too strongly or will intervene in tense situations and help the group to analyze the source of the tension).

Second, the staff is professionally trained and is granted the authority of knowledge and experience. Whether this makes the individual staff member more competent to create a learning situation or not is less important than the *faith* that his experience and training elicit in the delegates. Their belief that the trainer has "been here before" and "will rescue us when the going gets too rough" is important in stimulating the taking of psychological risks by exposing feelings. The trainer may, in fact, not have experienced the kind of situation the group is in, and may feel completely inadequate on occasions. Nevertheless faith in his abilities is crucial for delegates to feel early in the laboratory. This faith is often evidenced by their reluctance to believe any statements on the trainer's part that he is in the dark or feels powerless. The fact that he exhibits some power and knowledge often leads to the fantasy that he has total power and omniscience.

Third, the staff member attempts by personal example to establish a norm of openness and authenticity. While there are many variations in trainer behavior, most trainers attempt by one means or another to demonstrate to group members that it is possible and profitable to reveal feelings and reactions, and that this can be done in a manner that minimizes threat.

Some trainers attempt to establish this norm by being completely open about their own feelings, not only in the T-group but in all contacts with delegates. At the other extreme, there are trainers who will withhold their *feelings* but be quite open about their *observations* of what is happening in the group. They may suggest the sharing of feelings but not necessarily set a personal example. In between lies a gamut of trainer styles—some trainers are more comfortable expressing tender emotions; some will express their feelings after other delegates have done so, others will initiate the process; some will blurt out their feelings almost as soon as they become aware of them, others will report their feelings at a later time. Whether the personal example turns out to be helpful to the group in achieving a safer psychological climate probably depends more on the trainer's authenticity than on his actual style. If he is unaware of his own feelings or distorts them in the process of communicating them, he probably does more damage than if he withheld them altogether. If he has strong feelings which are valid reflections of group process (in contrast to being primarily a reflection of his own needs) and fails to share them explicitly, he may be working against the norm of openness.

Fourth, the staff member attempts to demonstrate by example and by presentation of theory that feelings are always present and can be harnessed to aid the group in getting work accomplished when properly modulated and integrated. In other words, the sharing of feelings not only produces personal learning for the group members, but also enables the group to consider the question of how feelings can be integrated into work

activities. The staff member often plays a crucial role here in showing the role of *timing* in the expression of feelings, in showing how the *modulation* of strong feelings can make their expression less threatening and more constructive, and in showing how the group can alternate its activity from high *task* orientation to a high group building and *maintenance* orientation. He shows this by his personal example in how he times and modulates his own feeling expression and by pointing out examples of good timing and modulation when they occur in the group.

The problem for the group is to find a principle of appropriateness that supersedes the simple norm that authentic open communication is always a good thing. If learning is the only goal, the simple norm is probably valid for all times and all situations. Whether open authentic communication is useful when a group is trying to accomplish a task depends on some principles of appropriateness (when and how and about what to be open and authentic).[3]

One such principle of appropriateness would be that the expression of feeling must be relevant to the group or interpersonal situation. The staff member will encourage a group whenever it is ready to develop principles of appropriateness in terms of its own needs, anxieties, and concepts of relevance. Some groups will be conservative, others daring in the kinds of feelings they declare to be appropriate. The role of the trainer is not to set the limits personally but to help the group work out its own limits.

Fifth, every laboratory of any size

[3] In actual fact such principles have to be consciously or unconsciously applied even in the pure learning situation. We can never be open about all feelings at all times, partly because there are too many of them, partly because we always select and filter our communication in terms of the goals we are trying to accomplish and the norms operating in the situation.

designates one of its staff members as counselor for those delegates who feel the need of individual counseling. He is usually a psychiatrist or clinical psychologist hired explicitly for this purpose. His presence, alone, communicates a sense of security that all contingencies which may arise can be taken care of. His presence also heightens anxiety in some by communicating the possibility that someone may be sufficiently upset to need counseling.

A final point which must be made is that the very presence of the staff arouses feelings about authority figures that are imported from the larger culture. In some delegates, staff members arouse feelings of dependency, in others, feelings of counter-dependency, and in still others they arouse neither. For the delegate to learn fully from his experience, he must also come to recognize and analyze his feelings toward the staff authorities, particularly the T-group trainer. But the analysis of the role of the staff member and the feelings aroused by him and in him also make him less available as the omnipotent protector. Consequently, it is unlikely that the group will be able to face up to and discuss these feelings until enough of a climate of trust and safety has been built up to make the staff member less omnipotent.

Summary

We have argued that learning depends on some degree of openness and authenticity of communication. Openness and authenticity in turn depend upon the willingness of the participant to violate cultural norms that discourage such communication. The primary danger in openness and authenticity is that others will be hurt and will retaliate or that others will punish the person for violating cultural norms. In assessing how a laboratory setting stimulates openness and authenticity, it is necessary to examine forces that reduce threats from others and encourage new norms in favor of authentic communication.

Several sets of such forces or conditions are identified. *First*, the laboratory is temporary and isolated from the permanent back-home situation. It is a situation similar to a game in which the stakes are real but not as high as the stakes back home. The relationships formed are temporary and have no direct relation to back home. The laboratory is an artificial situation and not automatically governed by traditional norms.

Second, the learning method itself offers some protection and forces re-evaluation of traditional norms. The focus on specific incidents or pieces of behavior rather than on the person as a whole minimizes total rejection. The norm of objectivity permits even highly evaluative communications to be examined and reassessed. The norm that any incident or behavior is fair game for analysis and reconstruction permits better understanding of the feelings that have arisen and, if necessary, the clarification or the undoing of damage done by their expression. The analytical approach also provides a safety valve in giving the group a safe detour when feelings run too high to be handled directly. Finally, the norm of experimentation leads to the discovery that authentic communication leads to less hostility and rejection than nonauthentic communication—the more of it members do, the safer the climate becomes (partly because protective mechanisms also develop alongside the climate of openness).

Third, psychological theory offers protection in declaring that feelings are ubiquitous and normal, that everyone has both tender and tough emotions, that feelings have causes which can be understood, and once understood are not as threatening, and that the specific and seemingly isolated feelings of a given member are often merely symptoms of tensions which are more widely shared in the group.

Fourth, the staff is a source of protection both in reality and in fantasy. The existence of a planned set of learning experiences and a theory of learning reassures the delegate that the staff knows what it is doing and will not let anyone get really hurt. The staff tends not to be tense in the presence of strong feelings and to have ways of coping with such feelings. It is professionally trained and has the authority of knowledge and experience. It sets a personal example of openness and authenticity and thereby demonstrates its value for the learning process. It attempts to show by example and theory presentation that not only does feeling expression and authentic communication lead to more learning, but also that feelings can be integrated into work activities to the mutual enhancement of both. Finally, the staff helps the group define principles of appropriateness to integrate feelings into ongoing work situations.

Fifth, many laboratories designate a psychiatrist or clinical psychologist as counselor to help any delegate who develops personal problems during the laboratory.

Forces That Enhance Willingness and Ability to Listen to and Pay Attention to the Reactions and Feelings of Others by Reducing Threat from Within

The major forces that stand in the way of listening and utilizing feedback are the personal tensions which most delegates experience prior to and during the early parts of the laboratory. These tensions preoccupy the delegate and force him to cope; his attention is focused on reducing tension rather than on learning about himself.

The tensions have several different sources: (1) dilemmas created by the unfreezing forces—how to establish a viable identity in the group, how to control others, how to insure that the group goals will include his own needs, and how to keep the group discussion at an *appropriate* level of intimacy; (2) the heightened consciousness of self that brings with it the possibility of discovering something within himself that will prove to be unacceptable; (3) the actual possibility of getting honest reactions to himself from others, which have always been relatively unavailable and may prove to reveal unacceptable parts of himself or, worse, may prove himself to be entirely unacceptable; (4) defensive reactions to feedback already obtained, either because it was hostile and retaliatory, or because it was too threatening; (5) the belief or assumption that he may not be able to change behavior which is unacceptable to others (therefore it may be better not to learn about it in the first place); (6) the belief or assumption that feedback is always evaluative and always deals with inadequacies or with things that are wrong.[4]

Given this kind of initial constellation of forces, how can the delegate relax enough to be able to listen and utilize feedback? Let us look at the same set of factors we discussed in reducing external dangers: the laboratory as a temporary game, the learning method, psychological theory, and the role of the staff.

[4] Miles (personal communication) has suggested that this particular belief or assumption grows out of our childhood experiences where we received direct reactions to our own behavior only when we exceeded bounds or did something wrong. Even if feedback was positive, it was still evaluative. Most people, in other words, have no experience with objective feedback (nonevaluative reactions of others to one's behavior).

The Laboratory as a Temporary Game

The temporary nature of the laboratory experience, the fact that it is not for keeps, that the stakes are not as high as they would be back home, that many people share the same fate, and that there are no witnesses to whatever interpersonal disasters might occur, serves to reassure the person somewhat and to give him hope. In his own mind, he can liken the tension he experiences to the tension which he has experienced in other novel situations or in strange social situations to which he has been exposed. He can dismiss the tension as being irrelevant to his real self and can retreat to the safer assumption that the laboratory is some kind of human relations game dreamed up by academics. He might say to himself, "who wouldn't be tense in a situation where you sit around all day talking."

At the same time, the recognition that the situation is strange and is more like a game makes it easier to take an experimental attitude or a devil-may-care kind of philosophy toward the learning possibilities. The person can say to himself that because it is not for keeps and does not involve his real self anyway, he might as well get his money's worth and find out what others think about him. He generally knows that the situation is very much for keeps, but he can rely on the game culture as a defense if what he hears is too threatening. It may help therefore for the staff to support the fiction of the game in the early parts of the laboratory.

The fact that the laboratory is temporary and has unreal "as-if" qualities makes it easier for norms of mutual acceptance to be established. Not only do delegates have fewer cues about each other and confront each other in a more genuine sense, but also the temporary game quality makes it possible for delegates to extend themselves to other people in ways they would not ordinarily. In effect, they say, "I might not accept this guy back home or on the job, but I guess I can accept him and try to get to know him here since we are going to be together only for one or two weeks anyway." Here again the analogy to the isolated vacation spot or the ocean cruise is meaningful. To the extent that people engage each other only in terms of certain limited parts of themselves, and in a temporary context, they can suspend some of the evaluative reactions they might have if they knew the total person in his own setting.

The presence of a large heterogeneous population, combined with adequate recreation facilities and free time for informal get-togethers, also stimulates acceptance and a climate of mutual support. Even if the person loses some self-esteem in his T-group, or is too tense to play a role well in an exercise, or feels the trainer has rejected his ideas, he can always find at least one or two others in the total laboratory community who are having similar experiences and who will accept him unconditionally. Thus, in the community room, over drinks, or under a tree, pairs or trios are seen sharing their anxieties with each other, trying to make sense of the experiences of the day, working through some of their feelings about the feedback that they received during a T-group session, or just asking each other whether they are basically acceptable or not. In a real sense, delegates get together to test a wide set of assumptions and realities. They ask themselves questions like: "Do they really dare to listen," "Is there an island of escape for them if what they hear is too traumatic," "Is there someone who will help them work through the real meaning and import of what they have heard?" To the extent that each delegate can find at least one other person in the laboratory with whom to establish such a mutually accepting relationship, he can begin to listen and utilize feedback.[5]

[5] In a sense, these informal contacts create *new* temporary systems within the laboratory sys-

The Learning Method as Reassurance

Most of the points previously made about the learning method apply as much to reducing threat from within as they do to reducing threat from others. Once the delegate learns that feedback from others can be limited to certain of his behaviors, that it can be objective and nonevaluative, and that the reactions of others to his behavior will vary, he becomes somewhat reassured that he will not be traumatized by his laboratory experience. Once some of his tensions about what he may learn about himself are reduced, he becomes more ready to expose himself and to listen for reactions.

It is probably safe to say that, for most delegates, their fantasies of being rejected and criticized far outrun reality. Even if a delegate arouses a thoroughly negative reaction in others, it is likely that the group would have enough wisdom and sensitivity not to give direct threatening feedback in this area, until it felt that the person was prepared to hear such feedback. Therefore, the realities of the T-group and the laboratory are likely to be reassuring rather than threatening, once the initial tension of getting started has been mastered. Even if initial feedback is unequivocally negative, its *unambiguous* quality may result in some relief from tension. Often what has bothered the person is a history of receiving ambiguous feedback.

The learning method helps reduce threat from within in another way. Laboratories, as we have said, develop clear norms about the legitimacy of inquiry. We have already pointed out how these norms can help the group neutralize violent emotional issues. The norms also

tem. As T-groups and laboratory culture stabilize, the base for learning perhaps shifts to ever newly created temporary systems.

have a direct impact on the delegate's fantasies and fears about loss of self-esteem which result from revealing feelings that may be unacceptable to others. We believe that the primary impact of the climate of inquiry and analysis is the reassurance of the person. Analysis of feelings inevitably leads to their modulation and to mechanisms for shunting aside feelings that are too difficult to cope with. As each delegate witnesses how the group successfully manages the emotional expressions of others, he becomes more reassured about his own emotions. He learns that the environment is safe and that the group is strong enough to cope with his feelings.

We have examined how the learning method helps the delegate indirectly. It helps him to cope with those inner tensions which operate as preoccupiers and prevent him from listening to feedback. But the learning method also deals *directly* with the problem of listening, either by having structured exercises and theory sessions on the topic, or through interventions by the trainer when he observes conspicuous failure to listen.

Exercises, theory sessions, and interventions tend to be very helpful to the group primarily because most people assume they know all about listening and are convinced that they do it reasonably well. Once they understand and have demonstrated to them in their own behavior the distortions and failures in the listening process, they become more interested in listening to all aspects of the group process. They learn that listening is a much more active process than they had ever assumed, and that it involves getting into a helping relationship with others (helping others to communicate more clearly as well as to understand better). As they become more active in their listening, they find that this too reduces some of their tensions, particularly those revolving around the fear of loss of control.

We may cite one very simple but highly

effective exercise. The trainer suggests that the group introduce into its discussion the simple ground rule that, before a speaker makes his own point, he should repeat what the previous speaker said, *to the previous speaker's satisfaction*. As the group attempts to do this, individuals discover not only how little of a previous speaker's comments they have actually heard, but also that different people have heard different things. The listeners suddenly discover how preoccupied they are with their own next point, various tensions, irrelevant observations, and so on.

Psychological Theory about Problems of Listening

One of the most common topics covered in theory sessions is communication. No matter how long or short the laboratory, one or more sessions dealing with the problems of accurate sending and receiving of information and feelings are almost always found. The topic of communication is covered in many different sessions, but a common thread in most of them is the difficulties of listening. The major points which, if understood, would reduce threat from within could be stated as follows: (1) it is difficult to listen effectively because of various preoccupations of the listener and various filters he uses to sift out the incoming messages; (2) such preoccupations are primarily symptomatic of over-concern with oneself and one's own points, rather than a reflection of concern for the other person who is trying to communicate; (3) the filters used are primarily defensive in nature, designed to protect the person from disconfirming information; (4) the filters operate as implicit assumptions and may deprive the person of important information about himself; (5) the only way communication can be improved is for the person involved to become more consciously aware of the filters used both by sender and receiver, which in turn can

be accomplished only by a more active collaboration between the parties to the communication, thus, (6) both talking and listening are active complex processes requiring making an effort and checking out whether the message has gotten across or not.

Theory sessions dealing with this type of content serve to focus delegates on the communication process and thereby help them recognize and deal with some of their own defenses against feedback.

Most laboratories will also introduce specific theory on the problems of giving and receiving *feedback*. The difficulties of being objective and nonevaluative in *giving* feedback are contrasted with the difficulties of *hearing* it without immediately rejecting it or worse, retaliating if the feedback is seen as hostile. The problems of creating a climate conducive to feedback are talked about and brought into the open. The problem of timing and assessing the readiness of a potential receiver of feedback is analyzed. The tremendous difficulty of listening to and utilizing feedback is acknowledged as normal, not as insurmountable. By intellectual discussion of defense mechanisms, the groundwork is laid for helping people make explicit what they have been doing implicitly. Once the delegate can acknowledge his own defenses and accept them as normal, he can also begin to question their overall utility for him. Once he has asked himself how useful his defenses are, he has laid the groundwork for surmounting them.

The Staff as a Source of Protection

Just as the presence of the trainer protects members from each other (at least in the members' fantasies), so it also makes possible the fantasy that the trainer will protect each person from himself. Particularly in the early stages of the laboratory, it is important for delegates to believe in the omniscience and omnipotence of the staff because, for many of the delegates, identification with the staff serves as an important mechanism of borrowing strength for coping with the tensions generated within the delegates themselves. We are suggesting here a re-creation of earlier processes of identification with parents as a way of coping with uncontrollable impulses arising from within the person. The delegate can see that the trainer is not upset by his own feelings and can believe that the trainer can control any feelings that might arise in the group. Hence he can use the trainer as an absorber of and protector against his own feelings.

The importance of this mechanism can be seen if the trainer actually shows weakness, loss of control, or feelings which are incongruent with this powerful image. Those group members who have relied on him will become very tense, show great disappointment, and will tend to withdraw from further self-exposure in the group. Their ability to listen to feedback will drop proportionately because of new preoccupations. Other members will rejoice and attempt to step into the leader role themselves. If they have the requisite personal qualities, they may successfully reassure the more dependent members just as the trainer did.

The example which the staff member sets in how to deal with the person's own feelings and how to receive and utilize feedback is an important reality factor. By reality factor, we mean something which depends on the trainer's actual behavior rather than on delegate fantasies about him. Usually the trainer has little opportunity early in the group life to set an example of how to receive feedback because he gets very little. He can, however, set an example of how to give objective nonevaluative feedback when he shares his own reactions with the group, and can point up examples of such feedback when they occur among other group members. If the group has had

incidents both of evaluative and non-evaluative feedback, he can invite them to compare their reactions to the two types, and thereby help them build norms of appropriateness for giving as well as receiving feedback.

Norms about receiving feedback can also be built around incidents involving different reactions which members have had to how others were hearing and utilizing feedback. For example, some members deny the feedback and exhibit overt defensiveness; others look and act so hurt that they arouse guilt in the group; still others ask questions and attempt to explore the implications of what was said to them; still others listen silently but then attempt to experiment with other modes of behavior. Some reactions will leave the group much more comfortable and ready to proceed; others will block further communication. The trainer can help, by inviting an analysis of different incidents, to establish norms for future member behavior.

The presence of a staff member designated as counselor is a final source of support. If any delegate finds himself unable to cope with feelings welling up within him, he knows that he can seek professional help as well as informal support from his friends. Delegates do utilize the laboratory counselor as well as their T-group trainers in this manner and derive obvious benefit from it, as judged by their own reports and observations of their behavior.

Summary

We have argued that a major barrier to listening is the variety of personal tensions that preoccupy the person, particularly early in the laboratory. A second barrier is the pattern of defenses and filters the person sets up to screen out certain kinds of communications directed to him. A third barrier is the erroneous assumption which most people make that they are able to listen reasonably effectively, and therefore do not need additional knowledge or skills in this area. A fourth, and perhaps most important barrier of all, is the tendency to maximize *self*-esteem and to devalue, from the outset, what others attempt to tell us. This is an attitude that the group experience must change before effective listening can commence. These various barriers reflect primarily threats from within the person himself.

Many of the forces which were identified as reducing external threat also reduce threat from within by providing reassurance, support, and an atmosphere of unqualified acceptance. The temporary nature of the experience and the egalitarian atmosphere work toward such reassurance. The possibility of finding one or two close friends with whom to share problems is another force which the heterogeneous population and free time makes possible. The unreality or game quality of the laboratory makes it possible to rationalize a feeling as unreal and therefore not ultimately threatening.

The learning method with its emphasis on objectivity, nonevaluation, and focusing on incidents and behavior rather than total people, also operates to reassure the delegate and help him cope with inner feelings. For one thing, he learns that his fantasies about how horrible feedback would be are not borne out by the reality of what goes on in the group. The learning method also helps the delegate achieve greater knowledge about the problems of listening and, through exercises, increases his actual listening skills. Defenses can be made explicit and analyzed in the context of the exercise in which they are less threatened.

Psychological theory about the problems of listening, giving feedback, and receiving feedback supports exercises and trainer interventions. The assumption is made that the more the person can intellectually understand the process of threat and defense, the better his chances are of coping with his own feelings as they really operate.

Staff members help delegates cope with their inner threats partly by being available as powerful figures whose strength can be borrowed through identification and partly by setting an overt example of how to give and receive feedback. By their interventions, they can focus on incidents and help the group build norms appropriate to its members and their needs. The opportunity for individual delegates to obtain counseling help is a final source of support.

9

The New Age: Organizational and Political Factors of Planned Change

Ralph Waldo Emerson always greeted friends with the following question: "What's become clear to you since we last met?" What's become clear to the editors (since our last edition) is that the New Age is upon us and raises all sorts of questions about the political/organizational factors involved in planned change. While the issues of "equity," "justice," and "liberation" are still with us and remain unresolved—those were the issues the third edition raised—in this volume, we approach some of the major issues of the eighties: war and peace, how our paradigms of thought "frame" issues (and block the view of others), how cultural and political domains influence our models of change.

Not one of the readings included in this chapter was in the previous edition, and the reason is simple: America keeps changing. What's "become clear" to us since the last edition is that our society has undergone, and is still experiencing, a number of seismic changes, many of whose consequences are still unfolding.

John Naisbitt has been using an incredibly accurate method of probing sensitive changes in the attitudes and actions of the American public.[1] Among the trends he has detected, the following portend the most significance for planned change:

1. A shift from a predominantly industrial society to an *information society*. The principal role of information-gathering is to guide future actions and produce future results. An information society is unlike an agricultural society, for example, which tends to look to the past for patterns of sowing, reaping, harvesting, etc.
2. De-institutionalization. Many institutions are being dismantled and reshaped. This is best illustrated by the continuing evolution of what we once knew as the Post Office, the telephone system, the airlines, the health care system.
3. High tech/high touch. As technology interrupts or alters our social relationships we tend to either reject it or to find intensified human contact elsewhere.
4. Computer as liberator. Business organizations can now shift into smaller, less hierarchical groupings.
5. Biology as the dominant science. An unimagined emergence of new products and industries will result.
6. Multiple options.
7. Decentralization. For the first time in American history, decentralization is moving faster than centralization. According to Naisbitt, "The process of centralization, after reaching a high point in the 60s, is now declining rapidly. Problem solving, particularly in the field of energy, is becoming increasingly localized."

   The readings we chose to include in this fourth edition are those which, one way or another, take into account some of the central issues which the aforementioned trends alert us to. Ruth Katz examines how "programmed instructions," a code, directs responses to a recurrent set of problems. Seymour Sarason brings in a welcome historical note to a field which tends, on occasion, to blind itself with its ahistoricity. His is a cautionary tale which wonders aloud with questions about "intractable problems," problems that cannot be neatly circumscribed. Not an unusual state of affairs, by the way. David Bakan provocatively raises the question of how or why methodologies selected have (or may have) certain tendencies, that is, give impetus to politics, of war and peace. Finally, John Van Gigch tackles the issue of how various planning models, all claiming to be "democratic," offer their own brands of "freedom."

---

[1] Quoted in *The Tarrytown Letter*, Tarrytown Group, Tarrytown, N.Y., April 1982.

9.1 Societal Codes for Responding to Dissent

Ruth Katz

The fashionable concept of code, as applied to the social sciences, seems most usefully defined in terms of a set of "programmed instructions" directing social systems to respond to a recurrent set of problems in a particular way. The development of the notion of code has been accompanied by an effort at formalization and schematization of these directives using quasi-mathematics of information theory, structural linguistics and related fields. If the concept of code is to be of use—that is, if it is to add something that takes us beyond theories of the primacy of culture—it is to this formalization of hidden directives with their possible structural implications (Levi-Strauss, 1963; Piaget, 1970) and to the adequacy of their description of the processes of continuity and change in familiar social situations that we must look.

Perhaps the most fundamental problem to which to address an inquiry of this kind is the problem of dissent. History, sociology and anthropology are replete with examples of heresy, protest, schism, rebellion and expulsion, as well as alternative examples of merger, accommodation, cooptation and the like. Religion and politics are only the most obvious of the institutional areas in which such problems repeatedly arise. Groups, societies and institutions of all kinds are challenged in the same ways. The patterned set of social relations and rules for the mobilization of these relations to cope with threat, internal or external, are keys to the integrity and continuity of a culture over extended periods of time and wide varieties of ostensibly different situations.[1]

Acculturation studies contain many valuable observations concerning organized efforts to preserve culture—especially those aspects which a group values most highly—when the way of life of the group is threatened. For example, it has been emphasized often that the reactions to threat which Linton (1943) called "perpetuative-rational nativistic movements" are guided by "boundary maintaining mechanisms."[2] Taking this as his starting point, Freed (1957) made an important contribution to the idea of social codes long before the introduction of the actual word. He suggested "type societies" in acculturation studies. While we shall take issue with him at certain points, we shall make use of Freed's analysis of the two archetypical modes for the successful management of social continuity which he perceives in the *shtetl* culture of the Eastern European Jews, on the one hand, and that of the Pennsylvania Amish, on the other, demonstrating their applicability to a wide variety of groups.

Freed's analysis is limited to structural features, arguing that the social organization of a society and the way it organizes certain of its culture patterns are the critical factors in resisting disintegration. Thus, while all societies have, in one form or another, some boundary-maintaining mechanism, there are but a limited number of distinctive structural forms underlying these mechanisms and capable of contrib-

---

[1] Cf. Eisenstadt (1973) for a discussion of the persistence of such social codes and their reappearance in ostensibly changed situations. Also note the conflictful conditions under which codes are more likely to be invoked and articulated.

[2] For a relevant discussion on "mechanisms of limitation" see Buchler and Nutini (1969).

uting to continuity and containing potential deviation. Although we shall deal with it in detail below, it is worth noting here that while Freed's analysis is structural it is also static in the sense that it says nothing about the transformational processes which result from the successive application of such structural responses; in other words, it does not account for problems which have been raised under the heading of "evolutionary invariance" (Baum, 1975) or the "structural implications for derivatives" (Eisenstadt, 1973).

The questions we wish to put are three: (1) whether there are identifiable codes for responding to dissent; (2) whether these codes can be usefully outlined in transformational terms; and (3) whether the preconditions for the development of different kinds of codes can be specified.

Codes for Coping with Dissent

Societies are almost always concerned with their integrity and continuity, although not all to the same degree. As we shall argue below, certain groups are more concerned with preserving the integrity of their values, others are more concerned with their continuity as social organizations. Under unusual circumstances, certain groups may care rather little about either.

Societies, groups and organizations which do care—about their integrity, continuity or both—have to work at ensuring their institutions and have to be prepared continually to cope with the threat of dissent, deviance and innovation. There are two major responses to potential dissent: expulsion and incorporation. Note the similarity to Hirschman's (1970) concepts of "exit" and "voice."[3] Without

claiming to exhaust the list of other possible responses, this paper will pay particular attention to a third response which might be called "dispensation," or the licensing of certain individuals or groups to play deviant roles—not so much for their own sake, of course, but to contribute to the stability of the group.

To assume, however, that these responses present themselves as fixed alternatives from which to choose is simply not sound. Indeed, the choice itself is part and parcel of that structure which it serves as a protective mechanism. Moreover, assessments of the consequences of a choice may result in the "decision" to give one of the other alternatives a try. Indeed, oscillating between alternatives may be as much a part of systems which have built-in dilemmas—and there are many of these—as are the clear-cut choices. While characteristic of all groups, the labeling and relabeling of the same phenomena—a particular form of deviance, for example—may thus reflect different degrees of genuine transformation.

It is hardly necessary to provide examples of incorporation and expulsion of potentially deviant groups except for the fact that they may allow us to extrapolate the "schemes" in which motivation, action and consequences are bound. We have at hand, for example, a most telling case of the condemnation and expulsion by the Catholic Church of the Waldensians in 1181–4, and some thirty years later, the recognition and incorporation by the same Church of a rather similar group, the Franciscans (Leff, 1967). Peter Walde's group, "the poor men of Lyons," was founded about 1170 and preached the emulation of Christ the Man, insisting that the asceticism which that conception implies should be a binding

---

[3] Hirschman (1970) came to our attention after this paper was completed. His concern with exiting vs. protesting in response to dissatisfac-

tion is closely related to the argument of this paper. His primary emphasis is on individual rather than group behavior, and in most of his arguments the locus of power resides in the members rather than the organization.

precondition for membership in the Church. They called for Apostolic Christianity, where the Church itself must forgo wealth and privilege. The authority of the Church hierarchy was rejected, and the word of the Scriptures was invoked against the Church itself, which was no longer recognized as the instrument of God's will. Paradoxically, emphasis on Christ, the man, enabled each man to feel more of a God, and implementation of the wishes of the group would have meant, in fact, the dismemberment of the Church.

The Franciscans were inspired by the self-same apostolic ideas. Both groups rejected a mercantile life for one of wandering poverty. But whereas Walde and his group were condemned by the Bishop of Lyons in 1181 and then by Pope Lucius II in 1184, St. Francis' group was recognized by Pope Innocent III in 1210. "Although it is inconceivable," says Leff, "that St. Francis could ever have been a heretic it is more than possible that in different circumstances Walde might have remained within the Church. Conversely without the insight of Innocent III, St. Francis' and St. Dominic's groups might have been formed into new orders" (p. 419). The Waldensians set up as a splinter group, gaining adherents and surviving the Middle Ages by "bringing practice into conformity with precept" . . . denouncing the Roman Church and claiming to be the one true apostolic church.

Both Franciscans and Waldensians venerated Christ's poverty. But whereas the Waldensians insisted on the capitulation of the Church, St. Francis viewed the evangelical life as a revelation from God addressed to the individual believer. This distinctive emphasis of the Franciscans, while perhaps even more demanding than that of the Waldensians, made it possible for the Church to incorporate the Franciscans as a pious elite while condemning the Waldensians as heretics.

While the bases of the differential preference of the Church are clear, historically speaking, neither of the responses passed unpaid-for. The ultimate consequence of incorporating groups like the Franciscans and of allowing the growth of more pious enclaves within the Church increased internal differentiation and inevitably fostered the secularization of the Church as a whole. Conversely, by expelling groups like the Waldensians, the Church relinquished its control over the momentous growth of counter-sentiments which accumulated on the outside, unwittingly contributing to the egalitarian ethic and the recognition of common cause among the various dissenting groups.

The "Logic" of Formation and Re-formation

Yet, this inconsistency in the attitude of the Church to deviant and splinter groups may be consistent indeed, and can be described in terms of a code: Let B stand for "Bible," in the broad sense of writings which serve as legitimizing agents; D for "dogma," in the sense of a selected body of articles of faith; and O for "organization." Let the equilibrium between D and O ($D \leftrightharpoons O$) be our starting point, the point at which orthodoxy became defined and the authority of the Roman Church established.[4] If the structural relation $D \leftrightharpoons O$ stands for the Church ($D \underset{\longleftarrow}{\overset{B}{\rightleftarrows}} O$) as arbiter of God's will (B) on earth, the following "evolutionary invariants" of "Formation" and "Re-formation" will result from the patterns of incorporation and exclusion respectively; in other words, the successive application of each of the two response patterns will have a distinctive, and

---

[4] We shall not deal with dissent which became such only retrospectively by having failed to be accepted as orthodoxy, but rather with dissent which presented itself as a direct challenge to the Church following its establishment.

cumulative, structural effect over time (see Figure 1).

The cardinal numbers in the schema represent the number of changes undergone in cumulative fashion so that each triangle represents the state of affairs at a given moment in time. The reintroduction of B at each stage represents the renewed appeal to the authority of Scripture to legitimate the change.[5] The right-hand side of the scheme, representing the process which we propose to call Formation, reflects the situation of the Church as it incorporates the "pious" orders; these developments have their origin in O, the organizational element in the original triangle. The left-hand side of the scheme, under the original D, represents the dispersal of incompatible groups, expulsions or breakaways from the mother Church, which share, however, both the fate and attitudes of heretics. Strictly

speaking, both D and O are composites of ends and means, but whereas ends are emphasized over means in the former, means are emphasized over ends in the latter. Hence, the relationship between the Formation scheme and our original O, and the Re-formation scheme and the original D.

The signs minus ($-$) and plus ($+$) stand for concession and accretion, or weakening and strengthening, respectively. It will thus be observed that accretion and concession on the left-hand side forces "practice into conformity with precept" in the sense that O is diminished with each increase in D. The right-hand side, however, weakens precept (D) at the expense of practice (O). Ironically, by choosing what seems "best" for the preservation of their institution, we see the "policy-makers"—on the right-hand side—enabling those whom they reject to live up to their professed beliefs. Pragmatism breeds the Gods! Or, less poetically, one may say that institutionalization,

[5] It need not be limited to Scripture as we have stated before.

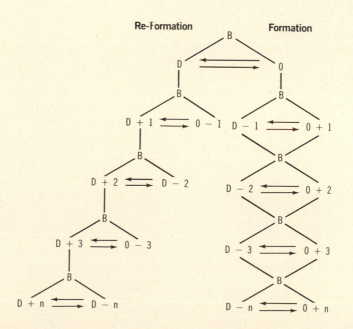

FIGURE 1 Cumulative Structural Effects of Incorporation and Exclusion

centralization, secularization and an orientation to here-and-now go well together, as do ideologization, looser networks of relations and an orientation either to a glorified past or to a utopian future. All of this is implicit in the scheme.

And although we have been referring to religious examples, it should be clear that the same processes apply to other institutions as well—political parties, for example. Troeltsch (1949) and Michels (1949) would be equally applicable here, for the "logic" of Formation and Re-formation stands for the dialectics between ideology and power, not only as manifested in universal religions but as it comes to the fore elsewhere as well.

If the analysis presented so far is correct, it suggests an hypothesis concerning the structure of Protestantism: it suggests that the macro-structure which we call Protestantism owes its origin to a "pre-history" of successive failures to become something resembling the mother Church. Rather than modeling itself on the principle of Formation by incorporating successive breakaway groups and incorporating its own dissidents, these sects appear to continue to pursue the exclusionist logic of Re-formation. Should this, in fact, prove to be the case, one may view the Protestant Reformation as an unanticipated consequence of the successive actions of the Catholic Church in breeding egalitarianism and nonconformisms which did not organize as a monolithic competitor but, rather, as a loose confederation of groups which came to recognize the common principle underlying their existence. The proposition, in short, concerns the mere dropping of a hyphen.

Exclusion as Social Code

The code implicit in the example of the Catholic Church is one which both excludes and incorporates, according to whether the deviant group gives enough leeway to the establishment to subsume it dogmatically and to relocate it organizationally. Of the two mechanisms, exclusion is the less favored, and indeed can be shown to have costly consequences.

Yet, there appear to be systems which prefer exclusion as a code, and viewed transformationally, may even be said to have prospered thereby. Economic systems based on free competition are a case in point.

Our argument may be restated as follows: Just as the Catholic Church excluded certain deviant groups which proved unsubsumable for one or another reason (including lack of imagination) so there may be other groups which exclude themselves. The argument is simple enough, but simply not enough without spelling out its transformational implications. For this kind of schism—whether in religion, politics or economics—leads to a competing church, party or enterprise. That is, the breakaway group establishes the very kind of organization from which it separated and internalizes the same set of "directives" leading to organizational elaboration with its attendant preference for subsuming dissenters, allocating them to a special place, while promoting the growth of oligarchy and centralization.

The case of Protestantism, we suggest, appears to be different. It did not create a competing church but rather a sort of federation of churches. The repeated history of exclusion and rebellion of different groups, equality for the individual and more direct experience through fundamentalism, appears to have been guided by the additional discovery of nonconformity *within themselves*. While exclusion weakens organization by definition, the experience of nonconformity makes room for the idea of the legitimacy of opposition. Taken together it means (1) leave us if you insist on disagreeing, but (2) remember that we, too, were rebels, and (3) our common rebelliousness creates a basis for loosely sticking together. In short, there may arise a pluralistic federation of rebels which together acts like a movement.

The code of exclusion which programs Protestant fundamentalism is illustrated by Freed's (1957) example of the Amish. Freed makes a point of emphasizing the egalitarian character of the group. The maintenance of the group's "nativistic movement" is not in the hands of specialists but is equally the responsibility of all of the adult members of the society. This absence of a group of specialists is correlated in the Amish type of society with strong means of social control (which are readily used) and the frequent expulsion of deviant individuals, and sometimes, of schismatic groups. These splinter groups may form over very minor points.

Clearly, Protestant churches behave in a variety of ways. Some, like the Amish, try to stay out of the world and have trouble relating to others, including—or especially—their own breakaway groups. Others have leaned more toward incorporation, having become—as one might have expected—large and rich and competitive, in many ways, with their Catholic forebears. But in an overall sense, it seems useful to think of Protestantism as "programmed" by exclusion, with the added recognition of commonality. This best-of-both-worlds code may have contributed to the recognition of the legitimacy of difference, and the rights of minorities—not inside the individual sect, which is exclusionist, but inside the broad domain of Protestantism and perhaps Western society at large. The separation of church and state and the awareness, often the acceptance, of individual and group difference may prove to be related.

Should this be the case, one may argue that Protestantism was not only expedient to the rise of capitalism, but also to the idea of pluralism in the West. Both relate to the democratization of society before the turn of the curve of diminishing returns.

The evolution of the kibbutz movement provides a parallel example. Its origin is in utopian socialism, emphasizing the desire to live the socialist dogma in person and here-and-now rather than by proxy and "after the revolution." The history of the kibbutz movement includes a series of successive schisms, expressed in the breakaway of groups of kibbutzim from their own kibbutz federations and the breakup of individual kibbutzim due to dogmatic and organizational infighting among their members. Yet, through all of this, the sense of commonality pervades the kibbutzim and the kibbutz federations. Despite all their differences—the differences which forced them apart—they are far the stronger as a result of their awareness of the need to remain together. They require dogmatic homogeneity within the group and recognize the legitimacy of dogmatic pluralism within the movement as a whole. Links of a similar sort sometimes characterize the relationships among splinter groups of other ideological organizations—movements for national liberation, for example—or among terrorist groups espousing a multiplicity of causes with ostensibly little common interest.

Dilemmas and the Dynamics of Codes

Perhaps these "exclusionists" furnish us with another clue to the workings of codes. If codes are directives for action which guide the responses of organizations in situations of choice, it appears that the situations among which they must choose have the character of dilemmas. But dilemmas, by definition, are insoluble; they do not permit a once-and-for-all choice. The dilemma at hand is a good illustration: one cannot continually choose for dogmatic integrity and still hope to remain an organization—any kind of organization. By the same token, one cannot repeatedly choose for organization and hope to remain with a coherent set of beliefs. Organization and dogma are horns of a dilemma, both of which require attention. Thus, by preferring to concern itself with organization, the code of incorporation threatens the *raison d'être*, while the exclusionist code threatens to empty the pews. Ostensibly, the simple solutions of incorporation and exclusion are both self-destructive.

The more subtle way of examining these codes, therefore, also requires attention to the ways in which each code copes with the "other" horn of the dilemma. The exclusionists do so by making certain—perhaps by having to make certain—that the excluded do not stray too far. Perhaps the idea of federation—among the Protestants or among the kibbutzim—is a typical exclusionist response to the other horn of its dilemma. Similarly, the incorporationists have to see to it that dogma is neither diluted beyond recognition nor so energized that it threatens organizational control. The creation of special orders within the Church for sectarians—so that they are appropriately visible and invisible, accessible at certain times and places, and out-of-reach at others—represents an example of attention to the other horn of the inclusionist dilemma.

Indeed, the challenge that sets the programmed instructions of the code into action is the very dilemma with which the code deals. Dissidence arises when parties seek to modify organization or authority in the name of dogma or dogma in the name of organization. Attending to organization, one invites challenges to authority often couched in the name of dogma. Similarly, attending to dogmatic coherence, one stimulates challenges to dogma often couched in the language of organization.

The Christian church is well experienced in such dilemmas. Its earliest and most continuous problem, perhaps, arises from the competing doctrines of preordination—whereby man's fate is a function of God's grace, which is unfathomable—and of freedom-of-will, whereby man's own choice affects his fate.[6] Augustine preached predetermination but his followers found that the doctrine provided little motivation to strive for the good. Pelagius insisted on the primacy of deliberate acts of will, which, rightly employed, will permit a man to perfect himself and merit the recognition of God. As unanticipated consequence, man dared to equate his own self-determination with God's. Shuttling between the horns of this dilemma is familiar Christian practice.[7] It has led to a multitude of codes, characteristic of the different churches. Calvin's solution—as explicated by Weber—is based on the idea that man's deeds on earth are a kind of quest for grace. In the modern church, says Passmore (1970, p. 100) the dilemma is addressed simultaneously: "the hymns may assume predestination, but the sermons are Pelagian."

Thus, while a code may favor one horn of a dilemma over the other, both horns require attention. And what is true for the dilemma within dogma is no less true for dilemma of dogma and organization. The dilemma generates the need for decision, but the decision can never be final. To the extent that a group favors one type of decision over another—that is, to the extent that the decision isn't simply random oscillation between solutions (between incorporation and exclusion, for example), we speak of codes. But it is misleading, as we have just seen, to think that leaning toward solutions on one side

---

[6] For the thorough discussion on which these paragraphs are based, see John Passmore (1970).

[7] Responding to his critics, Augustine himself—Passmore tells us—formulated the dilemma thus: "If then there is no grace of God, how does He save the world? And if there is no free will, how does He judge the world?" Kulandran (1964, p. 74) sees in this dilemma the struggle between rationalism and mysticism which pervades many religions.

exempts the group from attention to the other side of its problem. Hence codes must be closely examined for the ways in which they concern themselves—often simultaneously—with both sides of a dilemma.

We have had some insight into the ways in which the Catholic code of incorporation and the Protestant code of exclusion—which we have called Formation and Re-formation—look over their shoulders to the co-existence of another side of the dilemma for which they also have developed characteristic responses. We turn now to examine a third code, characteristically Jewish, which also addresses the dilemma of dogma and organization, as it repeatedly demands recognition and, by virtue of its own inherent contradictions, regularly reasserts itself.

Dispensation as Social Code

The sociology of religion—if not of politics—provides us with a third kind of mechanism which deserves attention, in addition to the basic ones of exclusion and incorporation. The key to this code is the idea that deviance may be anticipated and deviants may be "licensed" to carry on with their deviance, for their own good, and even more, for the good of the whole.[8]

This mechanism arises to solve a problem which lies in between the codes of incorporation and exclusion. As we have seen in the case of the Catholic Church, incorporation implies subsuming, and subsuming often requires the allocation of a specific place and role to deviants. The example of the institutionalization of

the Franciscan Order makes this clear. Thus, the code of incorporation, as has already been argued, implies differentiation. Exclusion, on the other hand, implies much greater equality both because of its fundamentalist and individualist tendencies and because of its basic suspiciousness of organization and hierarchy. Such sectarian movements are doomed to isolation and perpetual weakness unless they federate, we have argued.

The Jews provide the in-between example. On the whole, their code is inclusionist: every effort is made to keep deviants inside. In traditional orthodoxy, the threat of schism between *hasidim* and *mithnagdim* was overcome by subsuming. In modern Judaism, the schismatic appearances of Reform and Conservative movements have, on the whole, been retained by incorporation—by invoking, as a last resort, the rule of "a Jew, even though he has sinned, remains a Jew." And like inclusionist churches, parties and the like, we shall expect the Jews to have a differentiated social structure relevant to their perpetuative problems.

On the other hand, the Jews have some of the qualities of sectarianism: they are exclusive, at least insofar as religious contact is concerned. Yet, there is an ever-present concern with the surrounding world, both for reasons of internal security and for reasons of commitment to this-worldly achievement in intellectual and material terms. Their problem is how to preserve a traditional "sectarian" culture and yet partake of the world, how to be exclusive and inclusive at once.

Freed suggests that the Jews of the shtetl solved one aspect of this problem by differentiation. The learned—the "specialists" dedicated to the maintenance of the core of the culture—were permitted to continue to learn. This they did in relative isolation, protected by the society from disturbing influences, while the rich supported them materially, gaining prestige thereby. On the whole, the business world

---

[8] Hirschman (1970, p. 115) argues that loyalty sometimes induces high officials to remain at their posts even where "exit" would serve the body politic better. Such officials are then allowed to play their dissident roles from within.

was the province of the low and middle-class Jews, and of women, who had low status to begin with. Religious study, in other words, was the aspect of culture selected for perpetuation and special conditions were created to insulate and support its chief practitioners. Changes were accepted in peripheral areas of the culture while keeping the religious sphere uncontaminated. "The class structure," says Freed, "the prestige system, patterns of charity, isolation of religious scholars, and male superiority were integrated, maintaining and preserving the formal aspects of shtetl culture" (p. 56).

But Freed does not go far enough. For Jewish tradition makes room for certain kinds of contact with the outside world not only in peripheral areas of the culture, but in its religious sphere as well. In fact, one may argue that had this central focus not been also a pliable focus, the tradition could hardly have survived the challenges of a changing world. To be sure such pliability must be "programmed" if it is to ensure continuity in the face of change. It must be able to bridge between "particularistic revelation" and universal reason. This, we propose, is achieved through the code of dispensation.

Let H. C. stand for Holy Community, Ha for *halakha* (the authoritative Jewish *corpus juris*) and T for *torah*. The triangle

$$Ha \nearrow \overset{HC}{\underset{}{\leftrightarrows}} \nwarrow T$$

represents the core of Jewish tradition. Thus, the torah (T) was revealed to the holy community (HC), which is governed by the halakha (Ha), which is in accord with the torah (T). If pliability is to be made room for, obviously it must be located in the jurisdictional corner (Ha) of our triangle, leaving the revelational side untouched. The dispensation code is then structured in the following way:

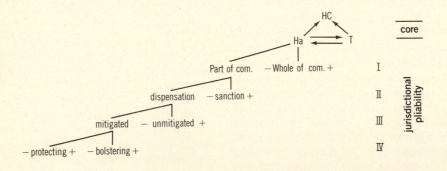

FIGURE 2   The Dispensation Scale

The above scheme is a composite of stages (I–IV). Whenever a challenge presents itself the whole of the scheme is invoked beginning each time at the top. Plus (+) and minus (−) represent "yes" and "no" answers to a series of questions as to who, under what conditions and why a proposed action may be performed when that action is not in obvious accord with the tradition. Not every proposed action requires invoking the entire scheme to its very bottom. How far down to go will depend on the nature of the challenge at hand. The stopping point, however, is invariably dictated by the reaching of a "yes" answer at any level save for the bottom stage (IV), which is decisive as to whether an adjustment could have been made altogether.

It needs to be emphasized, however, that the key point in our proposition is not the number of stages (which for all we know may not be exhaustive) but rather that they work in scalelike fashion, in a two-sided scale in fact, incorporating checks and balances. Thus, purpose or justification is the primary criterion in stage IV, qualification or delimitation in stage III, issue or topic in stage II, and whether it involves the entire community or only part of it in stage I.

Unlike the other two codes, each of which transforms in a unidirectional way with consequences which are irreversible (unless one switches codes), the dispensation code has, so to speak, built-in pliability. It must therefore be invoked as a whole, each time anew. It will be noticed that the orientation of the plus is inward with a double entendre, namely, "reinforcing" of the core values of the group, while the orientation of the minus side is outward, namely "protective" of the group against external threat.

An example will show how the scheme works. As is well known, throughout Jewish history secular studies presented a direct challenge—second to none—to religious studies, either because of their content or as competitors for time, or both. However, not all secular studies have been traditionally perceived as equally threatening to our so-called "specialists." For example, the study of philosophy may have been viewed as a greater threat than the study of biology. The latter, in turn, may have been considered as less "benign" than mathematics and so forth. The above attitudes can easily be projected onto our code. Philosophy will most likely find itself all the way at the bottom of the scale (if at all), farthest removed from the core because it presents the greatest threat to it. In other words, the license to study philoso-

phy would be granted only after the proposal had been sifted at each successive stage. Thus, in answer to the question at stage I, it would be decided that the study of philosophy was not intended for the community as a whole. If legitimate for only part of the community, the question at stage II is whether it is acceptable for all members of this part or whether it requires a special dispensation. If the latter, stage III asks whether the dispensation is unlimited or whether it is circumscribed or mitigated. If mitigated, stage IV asks what legitimates the mitigated pursuit altogether, and what defines the boundaries which circumscribe it: reinforcement of the inner-core of the tradition? protection against incursions from outside? or neither? The answer to all these will determine who may study philosophy and under what conditions.

Assuming that biology is a lesser threat, sifting would probably stop at stage III, while mathematics may well be satisfied by answering the question at stage II.

There have been different schools of thought concerning dispensation for secular studies both over time as well as contemporaneously. The possibility of differences both over time as well as at the "same time" is not so unusual-sounding save for the fact that in the present case such heterogeneity is legitimized by the dispensation code itself provided only that each proposal is processed through the scheme as a whole each time it emerges or re-emerges. It is the very strictness of the order, the immutable sequence of the steps which is the source of flexibility and legitimation. If the implications of the dispensation code for continuity and change are apparent, not so the possibilities it harbors for an undulating historical process. The dispensation code is pliable indeed!

Dispensation as a code (employing the very steps outlined above or other steps, but scalelike steps nevertheless) is not only at work in Judaism. The licensing of deviance is a widespread phenomenon, commanding a respectful place in the lives of individuals, in social interactions, social organizations and social systems. Again the kibbutz provides an apt and ready example since it faced and still faces a problem similar to the one discussed here concerning the licensing of higher education: it cannot afford to send everybody off to the university and not every subject is equally legitimate for study.

As we have seen, with respect to another issue, the kibbutz employed the code of exclusion, as we tried to show. Clearly, "when," "how," and "where" need to be specified, since they play a part in the decision to employ one code or another. Is the code then immanent in the issue, or inherent in the culture? This is *the* question.

Conditions for Different Patterns of Response

Three questions were posed at the outset: (1) whether there are identifiable codes for responding to the threat of dissidence, (2) whether these codes can be usefully outlined in transformational terms, and (3) whether the preconditions for the development of different codes can be specified. Two of these questions have already been dealt with. The third received only partial and nonexplicit treatment. However, the picture that emerges from our attempted answers to the first two questions is one that challenges the very posing of the third question in terms of "preconditions." For the codes themselves constitute part of those conditions, and there seems nothing that can be viewed apart from, or prior to, the conditions. In this sense they are to be viewed in terms similar to norms; they characterize that by which they are defined.

A comparison of different groups in relation to a specific problem may suggest some key variables relevant to the use of one code in preference to another. Bearing in mind the central concern of this paper with the management of continuity and change, consider the following dimensions in terms of which the several groups may be classified. Thus, with respect to each group, we ask: (1) Is the group stratified relative to the issue of continuity? (2) Does the group want contact with the outside world or is it inward-looking? (3) Does it seek converts or new members? (4) Does the group define itself and its membership as a different kind of people than non-members?

Though the variables are tentative in number and perhaps unequal in importance, they are by no means arbitrary. They characterize the groups in brushstroke fashion without attempting a comprehensive definition; indeed, we shall make a case for brushstrokes in the concluding section, below. At any rate, it is evident from the table that the "incorporationist" Catholics and the "exclusionist" Amish are indeed diametrically opposd to each other whereas the Jews occupy an in-between position—particularistic in parts and universalistic in others. The similarity between the Catholics and the Jews with regard to the first two dimensions should not be allowed to overshadow their differing social functions. Whereas the interest of the Church is centered around the preservation of the institution, that of the Jews focuses on the preservation of the group. The difference between the two with regard to the third and fourth variables highlights this variance in orientation.

The similarities between the Amish and the Jews should likewise be understood in terms of their somewhat different social functions which, again, are highlighted by the variables on which they differ. Thus, while the Jews and the Amish are primarily interested in the preservation of their

TABLE 1

	Catholic Church	Jews	Amish
Stratification relative to continuity	Yes	Yes	No
Want contact with outside	Yes	Yes	No
Want converts	Yes	No	No
Define selves as different	No	Yes	Yes

respective groups, the Jews, on the whole, stand for difference without separateness from the world, the Amish stand for both separateness and difference.[9]

Other Protestant churches may be classified in terms of these same dimensions. Thus, a chart of this kind may take us some distance toward differentiating among Protestant groups which, as already noted, run the range from "egalitarian" churches like that of the Amish to churches with institutional structures similar to Catholicism. More generally, our comparison suggests that whether or not a group considers itself exclusive and whether or not it desires contact with the outside effects the structure of the group and its patterns of response.

No less interesting is the fact that the different "combinations" reported in Table 1 seem to pertain also to (1) the degree to which the group is alert to the possibility of threat to its continuity, and (2) the

perception of the seriousness of such threat. Together, these factors combine to affect (3) the group's perception of its decision time for action. The "type" of response may perhaps be viewed, by extension, as an organic part of a "cyclican" chain reaction, so to speak serving both as consequence and cause. A comparison of the three groups along these lines might look as follows:[10]

Should careful historical investigation support the relatedness of code formations to the above, there is much to be learned from this three-dimensional comparison. To begin with, there seems to be direct relationship between awareness of potential threat, perception of threat as serious and decision time for action with respect to heresies. Thus, there are three different bases for response. Secondly, if we attach the codes to these three profiles we find the Catholic Church and not the Jews in

[9] It should be reiterated that we are discussing the core of Amish culture. In economic affairs, for example, the Amish allow themselves contact through preset intermediaries and are, in fact, very up-to-date farmers. This problem of the differential applicability of codes to central and peripheral aspects of a culture, or indeed the possibility that different codes co-exist with respect to different institutional areas, is an important one, and is related to the recent discussions of theories of institutional "convergence" and "nonconvergence." Seeking patterns across institutional areas, Kroeber (1963), for example, stressed convergence. Other scholars argue nonconvergence. By the same token,

different groups or classes may converge upon each other in certain institutional realms but not in others. A case in point is the convergence of upper and lower classes in the 19th-century waltz craze while maintaining much stricter boundaries in the field of economic behavior. Indeed, the ostensible convergence in the one area may give the false impression of convergence in the other. For data relevant to this historical case, see Katz (1973).

[10] "Awareness," "threat," "decision time for action," are variables often employed in political science in connection with crisis situations. For interrelationship of the three see Charles F. Hermann (1969).

TABLE 2

	Awareness		Threat		Decision Time for Action	
	Surprise	Anticipated	High	Low	Short	Extended
Jews		X		X		X
Amish	X		X		X	
Catholic Church		X		X		X

the "in-between" position. This suggests that the "dispensation" code is the most inclusionist of the three in that deviation is anticipated and planned for so as to minimize loss to the group.

Conclusion

The purpose of this paper was to suggest an approach to the unveiling of social codes by means of which organizations and communities chart their continuity. While examples have been introduced illustratively, the paper uses these cases as points of departure for the construction of ideal types and bold hypotheses rather than for detailed analysis. To conclude in the same spirit and even to go a step further—always assuming the validity of what has been said so far—we venture to suggest that codes seem to crystallize, morphologically, through a sifting process of actions and reactions, creating content-free dynamic structures.

Such organic growth does not necessarily imply organic use. Thus, one may "borrow" somebody else's code, so to speak, if the issue at hand seems to bear a resemblance to the conditions associated with the alternative code. Just as norms run the entire gamut from very private and personal use to values embracing the entire civilization, so do codes manifest themselves on the micro- and macro-levels. The larger the group to be

embraced, the fewer and more selective the codes become. Pardoxically, they gain in *symbolic* importance with each new selection which they survive by virtue of becoming less and less bound to specific situations. Thus a culture as a whole may be identified by an overriding code, with different codes for different subcultures as exemplified by systems and organizations of all kinds. Some of these, in turn, may borrow codes for managing certain issues from others and so on.

In other words, codes do not vary. Their number seems to be finite and probably relatively small. They appear, however, in a variety of different clusters of different combinations and with different hierarchical orderings. Some aspects of synchretism, levantinism, nouveau-richesse and above all of "cultural ear-marks" which come to the fore in processes of modernization, for example, can be explained in terms of borrowing of codes which offset the combinations of the cluster while maintaining the original hierarchical ordering. There is an obvious connection here to studies of diffusion and in particular to questions concerning differential rates of change of parts within a single system (Barnett, 1964).

The higher the code in the hierarchy, we have argued, the less specified the situation in which it is invoked and the more people it encompasses. Hence a code which is to affect everybody in a society, as in the case of innovation, must be accepted by everybody. It follows that (1) the higher the code the less transferable it becomes, and the less readily relinquished (since the more symbolic a code becomes, the more it sheds directives for action); and (2) the heterogeneity of a society facilitates "borrowing" by part but retards the acceptance of that which affects the whole. The relative stability of Western civilization and its unimpaired growth as well as the influence it was able to exert on other civilizations may be attributed certainly in part to its heterogeneity.

The question, then, of whether codes are immanent in the issue or inherent in the culture is a question about relevance, with regard to which issue and culture are interchangeable, depending on . . . issue and culture.

Bibliography

Barnett, H. G. "Diffusion Rates," in Robert D. Manners, ed., *Process and Pattern in Culture*. Chicago: Aldine Publishing Company, 1964, pp. 351–362.

Baum, Rainer C. "Authority and Identity: The Case for Evolutionary Invariants." *Sociological Inquiry*, 1975.

Buchler, I. R., and H. G. Mutini. *Game Theory in the Behavioral Sciences*. Pittsburgh: University of Pittsburgh Press, 1969, pp. 1–23.

Eisenstadt, S. N. *Tradition, Change and Modernity*. New York: John Wiley, 1973.

Freed, Stanley A. "Suggested Type Societies in Acculturation Studies." *American Anthropologist*, 1957, 59:55–67.

Geertz, C. *The Interpretation of Cultures*. New York: Basic Books, 1973.

Hermann, Charles F. "International Crisis as a Situational Variable," in James N. Rosenau, ed., *International Politics and Foreign Policy*. Glencoe, Ill.: The Free Press, 1969.

Hirschman, Albert O. *Exit, Voice and Loyalty*. Cambridge, Mass.: Harvard University Press, 1970.

Katz, R. "The Egalitarian Waltz." *Comparative Studies in Society and History*, 1973, 15:368–377.

Kulandran, Sabapathy. *Grace in Christianity and Hinduism*. London: Lutterworth Press, 1964.

Kroeber, A.Z. *Style and Civilizations*. Los Angeles: University of California Press, 1963.

Linton, Ralph. "Nativistic Movements." *American Anthropologist*, 1943, 45:230–40.

Leff, Gordon. *Heresy in the Later Middle Ages: The Relation of Heterodoxy to Dissent. 1250–1450*. New York: Barnes and Noble, 1967.

Lévi-Strauss, C. *Structural Anthropology*. New York: Basic Books, 1963.

Michels, Robert. *Political Parties*. Glencoe, Ill.: The Free Press, 1949. Reprinted in R. K. Merton *et al.*, eds., *Reader in Bureaucracy*. Glencoe, Ill.: The Free Press, 1952.

Passmore, John. *The Perfectability of Man*. New York: Scribner's, 1970.

Piaget, J. *Structuralism*. New York: Basic Books, 1970.

9.2 The Nature of Problem Solving in Social Action

Seymour B. Sarason

You cannot understand a past era unless it leaves some kind of record or evidence of what people said or did. We look back from a vantage point that allows us to scan for myriad evidence, a scanning impossible for anyone in that past era. We like to believe that our vantage point is high enough, that our vision is unclouded by all of those factors that put blinders on those who lived in that past era, and that we have the accrued knowledge, skill, and wisdom to explain not only what happened, or how forces were related to each other, but also the why of it all. And the why of it all almost always has to do with ways of thinking that give order and direction to daily living. What lends fascination to historical constructions and reconstructions is the process of deducing or intuiting what people in that era took for granted. But if the process is fascinating, it is inherently problematic. For one thing, there are many vantage points—so many, in fact, that it is literally impossible for one person or group to achieve them all. No less serious for those who have to believe that they are on the road to truth, and that the road has an end, is that reconstructions of the past always reflect what we from our present vantage points take for granted. Can you deduce what people in a far-off era took for granted without having what you take for granted affecting your conclusions in ways that you cannot know but that people in future eras will think they know? The process of historical reconstruction inevitably says as

much about the present as it does about the past. If history strikes so many people as uninteresting and irrelevant, it is, in part, because they do not understand that what we call history is literally manufactured by the present. When Henry Ford, that self-made sage, said "history is bunk" he was saying a good deal about himself and many others in our society, far more than he was saying about the past. That was obviously less true, but still true, in the case of Gibbon's *Decline and Fall of the Roman Empire*.

The social-historical stance has not been a dominant feature of American psychology. An amusing but illuminating example—back in the late forties the American Psychological Association began to accredit graduate programs in clinical psychology. An APA committee came for a site visit to Yale, and part of their time was spent talking with our graduate students. At the end of the visit I talked with one of the committee members, who expressed satisfaction with our program with one exception. He had asked one of our graduate students if he had read Köhler's (1925) *The Mentality of Apes*, and the reply was: "No one reads that any more. That's old hat." We both laughed, very uneasily. Both of us were pre-World-War-II-trained psychologists and very much aware that as a result of the war, the face of psychology was being changed. For both of us, the Henry Ford type of statement by the graduate student presaged something disquietingly new in psychology, but it was hard to put into words. The downgrading of the historical stance was not new, but if what this student said was at all representative of his generation of psychologists, the small place held by history in the field of psychology would shrink to near invisibility. If I had to say what bothered me, it would be that I placed a lot of weight in living on the sense of continuity, a belief not created or particularly reinforced by my training in psychology. Beyond that personal need, my unease had little conceptual substance. But something told me that what the student said was very important, and I have been trying ever since to make sense of it. The first conclusion I came to was that there was really nothing new in what the student said. By virtue (among other things) of psychology's divorce from philosophy and its marriage to science, history in psychology became a lot of narrow histories depending on the particular problem that interested you. That is, if you were interested in reaction time to a type of stimulus, you had the obligation to know what others in the past had done and found. This obligation served several purposes: to deepen your knowledge of the particular problem, to avoid repeating what others had done, and to increase the chances that what you were going to do would shed new light on the problem. This might be called the rational justification of the use of history. But, as is always the case, there were nonrational factors at work. In fact, justifying the use of history only on rational grounds, or describing it as a completely rational process, should have been warning enough that these justifications were incomplete and misleading. Behind these justifications were some beliefs and hopes. One of them was that you were going to add something new to an understanding of the problem precisely because you were building on knowledge provided by others from the past.

In the scientific tradition, knowledge is cumulative: You either add a new brick to the edifice of knowledge so that it looks different or, better yet, you destroy the edifice and present your colleagues with a foundation for a new and better structure.

One part of this tradition says that knowledge is cumulative, the other part says that your contribution is proportionate to how much past knowledge you have rendered obsolete. You use history, so to speak, with the hope of destroying its usefulness. This kind of attitude or hope is subtly but potently absorbed by young people entering scientific fields, and I believe it has been particularly strong in psychology, less because of psychology's youth as a scientific endeavor and more because of its self-conscious desire to identify with that endeavor. This has tended to produce still another belief: If a study was done 10 years ago, it is unlikely that you will learn much from it; if it was done 20 years ago, the chances are even smaller; and if it was done before World War II, don't forget it but be prepared quickly to do so. Put in another way, it would go like this: "We have come a long, long way in a relatively short period of time and there is not much from the past that is usable to us now. What is more worrisome than whether we are overlooking anything from the past is whether someone in the present is rendering what I am doing as wrong or obsolete." Köhler studied apes during World War I. Obviously, the odds are small that he has anything to say that is important to the here and now of psychology! Yes, he probably belongs in the Museum of Greats but you only go to museums when you are not working.

My purpose is neither to discuss nor question the implicit and explicit uses of history in scientific research. What I wish to suggest is that these uses (and, therefore, perceptions and conceptions of the past) have been very influential in shaping people's attitudes toward the significance of history in general. That is, among all those who think of themselves as scientists, there has been a noticeable tendency to view the social world as having been born a few days ago. This should not be surprising when one considers the status and functions society has given to science. Within the confines of its own traditions, science long has been on an onward–upward trajectory in the course of which it has displayed a seemingly boundless capacity to solve its problems. This did not go unnoticed by society as it saw that in solving its problems science could also contribute to the welfare of society. Scientists and the public came to agree that the deliberately impractical goals of science (knowledge for knowledge's sake) had very practical implications. No one ever said it, and perhaps no one ever thought it, but the agreement between science and society contained a "message": Society had problems *now* and science could be helpful in solving them *now* or *in the foreseeable future*. There was no disposition to recognize that the relatively ahistorical stance of science might be mischievously inappropriate to social problems. Put in another way, the pride that science took in rendering past scientific knowledge obsolete, the view of its past as more interesting than it was usable, the concentration on now and the future—these stances fatefully determined the degree to which, and the ways in which, society's problems would be placed in a historical context. This type of influence seemed proper and productive as long as the findings of science had two types of consequences: one was of the technological, thing-building or thing-creating variety, and the other was of the illness-prevention or the illness-curative variety. It may be more correct to say that the nature of the influence went unnoticed as long as there was near-universal social acceptance of what science seemed to be able to do. As long as society posed essentially nonhistorical questions for science, science came up smelling technological roses. Agriculture, industry, medicine, the military—they asked the kinds of here-and-now questions to which the findings of science could be applied.

It is hard to overestimate how total identification with science eroded whatever significance social history had for psychology. For one thing it seriously limited the capacity of the field to examine its past in order to illuminate its present, that is, to try to fathom how its view of the past (and its projections into the future) might be a function of the myth-making present. For another thing, it blinded psychology to the obvious fact that any field of human endeavor is shaped by forces beyond its boundaries and that its structure and contents can never be wholly explained by that endeavor's narrow history. For example, can one understand the history of behaviorism or psychoanalysis by restricting oneself to what behaviorists and psychoanalysts did and said? Boring did his best to sensitize psychologists to *zeitgeist*, but his efforts have been honored far more in the breach than in the practice. "The spirit of the times" is such an apt metaphor because it warns us that what we think and do, what we think we are, what we say the world will be—all of these in part reflect influences that are time-bound and hard to recognize. The word *spirit* (an uncongenial one in psychology), like the concept of the unconscious, reminds us that as individuals or fields we are affected by forces near and far, known and unknown, inside and outside.

At its best, social history serves the purpose of reminding us that we, like those of past eras, are very biased, time-bound organisms. We differ in all kinds of ways from those of past eras, but one thing we clearly have in common: We breathe the spirit of our times. If we use social history for the same purpose that we do a table of random numbers, we stand a little better chance of avoiding the worst features of uncontrolled bias. At the very least, sensitivity to social history makes it hard to ignore several things. First, despite all the diversity among human societies, past and present, each dealt with three problems: how to dilute the individual's sense of aloneness in the world, how to engender and maintain a sense of community, and how to justify living even though one will die. Second, each society defines and copes differently with these problems, and as a society changes, as it inevitably does, the nature of the definitions and copings changes. Third, these changes, more often than not, are not recognized until people see a difference between past and present definitions and copings. Fourth, the three problems are always here and there in the life of the individual and the society, but not in the sense that inanimate matter is here and there. Fifth, these are not problems that people have created, and they can never be eliminated or ignored. Sixth, any planned effort to effect a social change (as in the case of scientists who seek to apply their knowledge and skills for purposes of social change) that does not recognize and understand the history and dynamics of these three problems will likely exacerbate rather than dilute the force of these problems.

Applying scientific and technological knowledge and skills in social action is not like applying paint on a wall, except as both applications literally obscure what one may not like to look at. Scientists who enter the world of social action like to think themselves possessed of the basic knowledge and problem-solving skills of their science, and they often have a feeling of virtue because they are applying these to practical social issues. What they fail to see is that because science does not start with the three problems, because it in no explicit way recognizes or is controlled by them, science *qua* science has no special expertise to deal with them. Everyone knows the old joke about the graduate student who had learned about Latin-square design and was looking for a problem that fitted it. There is a way of looking at science and seeing some similarity between it and this student. Science has learned a lot about problem

solving, but when it looks beyond its confines to the arena of social problems, it has tended not to ask what the "basic" problems are there but rather to seek problems that fit its problem-solving style: clear problems that have unambiguously correct solutions. The separation of science from disciplines concerned with social history will always obscure from science that not all basic problems in nature can be molded to its problem-solving models.

Science and Solutions

Before World War II, academic psychology never quite made up its mind whether it was a social or biological science. The image of the laboratory was very attractive. After all, look at what had been discovered in laboratories, and wasn't society grateful? If psychology was to earn society's gratitude, and also be accepted by the older sciences, what was needed, among other things, was a certain kind of place where problems could be analyzed, dissected, and studied. A laboratory was a place where one solved problems. One could study problems outside of a laboratory but that meant that one had drastically reduced the chances of finding solutions to basic problems. In a laboratory one could manipulate variables, and, obviously, one could not arrive at rigorous solutions without experimental manipulation of variables. The image of the laboratory contained several features: physical isolation, clearly stated problems, experimentation, hard work, solutions. It was such an attractive image that few psychologists seriously questioned its appropriateness for their new field. There were psychologists for whom the laboratory was not an appropriate place to study problems, but they did not question the other features of the image. Their task, they would say, was the same but harder because experimental manipulation outside the laboratory was so difficult. They felt inferior, and were made to feel inferior, because it was so unlikely they could "really" solve any problem. The "real" general laws of human behavior were going to be found by studies done in certain ways and places. Science could not tolerate sloppiness of method and uncertainty of solution.

Take, for example, pre-World-War-II psychology's view of psychotherapy. My guess is that psychologists would not have been in favor of making the practice of psychotherapy illegal. They would have agreed that if people had personal problems there should be trained individuals to try to help them. But, they would have added, psychotherapy is an art, and a pretty poor one at that, and do not confuse it with science or technology derived from science. So, they could have been asked, what are *you* doing about it? The answer would have been that psychological science is seeking the basic laws of human behavior and not until the basic questions are clarified, studied, and solved in the most rigorous ways can a foundation be provided for truly effective psychotherapeutic practice. It's like building bridges: Basic science had to solve a lot of basic problems before engineers could build bigger and better bridges. It is, they said, going to take us time, and one of the worst things we could do would be to start studying an applied problem like psychotherapy to the neglect of more basic psychological issues. Let us not kill the goose that lays the golden eggs, as an eminent psychologist once said.

Now, if one knew something about social history and had the courage, one could have asked: "Is it possible that these problems are of a human and social nature and are not solvable by science? Is it not obvious that in the chasm between your scientific findings and solutions, on the one hand, and the realm of human affairs, on the other hand, there is a mine field of values for the traversing of which your science provides no guide? If we can build

magnificent bridges, or develop life-extending vaccines, is it only because of basic problem-solving research or is it also because society wanted those fruits from the tree of science? Just as technology depends on basic science, don't both depend on or reflect the wishes of the larger society? What will happen if and when the social world changes and the relation between society and psychology is altered so that psychology is asked and willingly attempts to solve social problems it never encountered, and never could encounter, either in the laboratory or through employment of any of its research strategies? Will psychology be found inherently wanting?

These were questions that could not be raised in psychology before World War II. Some of these questions were explicitly raised by one psychologist, J. F. Brown, in his 1936 *Psychology and the Social Order*, but no one paid him much mind. In the midst of a social catastrophe, the Great Depression, Brown saw the crisis in psychology. He was able to because social history in its Marxist version had become part of his conceptual framework. His was not a parochial mind—witness his attempt to bring together Marx, Lewin, and Freud. Lynd, a sociologist, raised similar questions in his 1939 book *Knowledge for What?* Having studied Middletown before and after the Great Depression, Lynd, like Brown, questioned the traditional directions of the social sciences and asserted their conceptual and moral bankruptcy.

In one crucial respect, Brown and Lynd were in basic agreement with an underlying assumption of science: All problems of society, like those in the rest of nature, had solutions. The problems might be of a different order, the ways of studying and controlling them might require new theories and methodologies, and their solutions might be a long way off, but they were solvable. Who would deny that the creativity and ingenuity that had unravelled the mysteries of the atom, exemplified in the work of Rutherford and Bohr, or that allowed Einstein to supersede Newton, would falter when faced with the problems of social living? But what if these problems were not solvable in the sense to which science was accustomed?

The concept of solution in science is by no means a clear one, and it is beyond my purposes to examine the different and overlapping meanings that concept has been given. In one respect, however, the lay and scientific understanding of a solution is very similar: A problem has been "solved" (a) when it does not have to be solved again because the operations that lead to the solution can be demonstrated to be independent of who performs them, (b) when the solution is *an* answer to a question or set of related questions, and (c) when there is no longer any doubt that the answer is the correct one. If there are competing answers, the problem has not yet been solved. So, when geneticists around the world were trying to "solve" the genetic code, they could agree on only one thing: Someone would find *the* answer. And the answer would be of the order of "four divided by two is two." There is or will be only one correct solution. There are times, of course, when the solution about which there is consensus is proved wrong, and then everybody is off and running to find the "really" correct solution. The correct solution always raises new questions, but at least the earlier question does not have to be solved again. The question was asked, the solution was found, and now for the next question.

Problem solving is a venerable and sprawling field in psychology. I wish to note two of its characteristics. The first is that almost without exception the human subject is presented with a problem that is solvable, although the correct answer may be arrived at in different ways. Indeed, how an individual arrives at a correct solution has been considered no less important than the fact that he or she got a right solution. One of the major

influences of the Gestaltists (Wertheimer, Koffka, Köhler, Lewin) on research in problem solving was in their emphasis on the psychological factors and processes (e.g., set, insight, perceptual reorganization) that preceded solution. The graduate student's opinion notwithstanding, Köhler's (1925) studies of problem solving in apes are still instructive reading, as is Wertheimer's (1959) classic *Productive Thinking*. The fact remains, however, that the distinctive emphasis of the Gestaltists had meaning in the context of solvable problems. It is not fortuitous that Wertheimer illustrates his ideas by a description of how Einstein solved problems with which physicists of the time had been grappling.

A second characteristic of the problem-solving literature is that the types of problems used in research almost defy categorization. It is an exaggeration to say that each researcher develops his or her own stimulus problem, but it is not a gross exaggeration. It would be understandable if someone concluded that when researchers used the words *problem solving*, they were far more interested in *solving* than they were in *problems*.

Let me illustrate the significance of these two characteristics of the problem-solving literature by asking this question: Why, for all practical purposes, is there nothing in this literature on how artists solve their problems? For example, what was the problem or problems Cézanne was trying to solve? This question has nothing to do with his personality, although it does with his times. What was the cognitive substance of the problem, how was he trying to solve it in a visual form, what made for such a long struggle, and did he solve the problem? Several answers could be given to these questions. One would be that we cannot be sure what the problem was, and even if he were alive we could not accept his version of the problem. How do you justify studying problems whose clarity and formulation you know ahead of time must be of dubious status and when there are no known ways of determining what the "real" problem is? If you are fuzzy about the nature of the problem, how can you ever state criteria by which to judge successful outcomes? And what would we do if Cézanne had said: "In this painting I solved the problem, in that one I did not." Do we accept his judgments, and what have we learned by doing that? And what do we learn from fellow artists who are awed by Cézanne's accomplishments? Their judgments permit no firm conclusions about the relationship between problem and solution. Besides, not every artist, then or now, agrees either about the substance of Cézanne's artistic problems or artistic solutions. A final answer might be: Cézanne is a great artist, but his problem-solving accomplishments cannot be understood and judged in the way the works of great scientists can be. In short, they would say Freud was right: Before the artist you throw up your hands. These are problems that are not science's cup of tea. There is problem solving that does not fit the researcher's requirements of a clear, manipulable problem and unambiguous criteria for the correct solution. So, science has always left that problem alone, albeit from a stance of superiority. The problems of social living were also left alone until the emergence of the social sciences, led by economics. Just as the natural sciences had developed laws about the nonhuman world, the social sciences would seek the laws of human society, not only for the purposes of explaining the workings of society but for controlling it. They would be the embodiment of Plato's philosopher-kings. Apparently they were not impressed with the fact that Plato saw the problems of social living as so difficult to understand and cope with, requiring of philosopher-kings such a fantastic depth of learning and wisdom, that one could not entrust social responsibility to them until they were well along

in years. And to my knowledge, Socrates infrequently answered a question and never solved a problem. He was too impressed with man's capacity for self-justification and self-deceit. Neither Plato nor Socrates ever assumed that the accomplishments of Greek scientists reflected a model of question asking and problem solving that was appropriate to the development of the good society. In the millennia that followed, there were many people who took a similar position. Science never really came to grips with them, least of all social science.

Social Action

Let us now turn to a moment in history when the workings of impractical science led to a most practical product, one that our scientists and society desperately wanted. It was a moment that simultaneously illustrated the fruitfulness of scientific problem solving and exposed its inappropriateness for solving social problems. I refer, of course, to the successful solution of all the problems, theoretical and technical, leading to the harnessing of atomic energy for military purposes. As soon as it became evident that a successful atom bomb was in the offing, some scientists began to ask themselves questions: Should it be used, how should it be used, and how could the seemingly endless uses of atomic energy be exploited for human welfare? They saw a problem, many problems, and as in the case of Cézanne, the substance of the problem was by no means clear. The end result of a successful solution seemed clear: a world in which the destructive uses of atomic energy were rendered impossible or nearly so and in which its uses for human welfare were maximized. But how do you go from here to there? What was the bearing of the scientific tradition on that problem?

As best as I can determine, none of the scientists thought they were dealing with a scientific problem. They recognized that they had been catapulted into a social world that was fantastically complicated, constantly changing, and seemingly uncontrollable. It was not even a maze, because that image conjures up entry points, stable pathways, and some kind of end point. The social world was not a maze. It was not even a cloud chamber, because that is a device rationally constructed to record and measure predictable events. It may be a world of facts and events but it is ruled by passions. It is ironic in the extreme that at the same time that the world saw these scientists as at the apogee of human achievement, the scientists saw themselves as angry, bewildered, impotent people. They became like most other people: passionate, committed, partisan, rhetorical, and irrational. Those are not characteristics foreign to scientific controversy and investigation, but the morality of science and the critical eyes of the scientific community are effective controls against the undue influence of these characteristics. If you suspect a fellow scientist of lying and cheating, or of just being a damn fool, you have ways of finding out and spreading the word. But that means there is consensus about the rules of the game. The social world is not the scientific world. As a physicist friend once said to me, "What the hell kind of world is it?" He used exactly the same tone of petulance-anger that Professor Henry Higgins uses in *My Fair Lady* when he asks why women can't be like men. My friend also went on to say (paraphrased), "I can't deal with a world where everybody has his own definition of the problem, where facts are an intrusive annoyance and of tertiary importance, where who you are is more important than what you know, and where the need to act is more decisive than feeling secure about what the consequences will be." And he concluded with this: "I will stick to my world where there are answers, and if I don't find them, someone else will."

When the atomic scientists entered the world of social action, that world could not be molded to fit the problem-solving strategies to which they were accustomed.

But, many social scientists thought, those were atomic scientists and one should not be surprised that when they left the world of minute matter and entered the world of human matters, they faltered. After all, they were not social scientists whose stock in trade was human matters. The fact is that up until World War II, the social sciences had contributed to our understanding of the social world, but, with one noteworthy exception, these contributions were mainly descriptive, or analytic, or historical. They were not contributions stemming from the social scientist's effort to participate in and solve social problems. Like the natural scientists, the social scientists were the dispassionate observers, and deliberately so, who sought to formulate clear questions to which clear answers could be obtained. They saw their task as understanding the social world, not changing it. The one exception was economics, which for decades had an intimate tie with the practical world of government, business, industry, and finance. Early on, economists not only described the world as they saw it but they drew conclusions about what should or should not be done. They were listened to, and they took responsible positions in the social arena. Heilbroner (1961) has aptly called them the "worldly philosophers." They lived, so to speak, in two worlds: the scientific problem-solving world, and the world of social action.

It was the Great Depression that really made the world of social action accessible to increasing numbers of economists. The underlying assumption, of course, was that economists had knowledge and skills that could inform public policy and action. If, during the thirties, the atomic scientists had developed firm friendships with their university colleagues in economics (unlikely events in the community of scholars), they would have learned much earlier than they did that scientific knowledge as power in the social arena is of a different order than it is in the research community; that in the social arena one is always dealing with competing statements of a problem and there is no time or intention to experiment in implementation with one or another of the formulations; that the choice of formulation has less to do with data than with the traditions, value, world outlooks, and the spirit of the times; that the goal of social action is not once-and-for-all solutions in the scientific sense but to stir the waters of change, hoping and sometimes praying that more good than harm will follow; that the very process of formulating a problem, setting goals, and starting to act not only begins to change *your* perception of problems, goals, and actions but, no less fateful, the perceptions of *others* related to or affected by the process in some way. *In the phenomenology of social action, problem changing rather than problem solving is figure, and you know what that does to solutions regardless of how you define them!*

World War II opened up many opportunities for social scientists to be in social action or policy-related roles. It was truly the first global war bringing us into contact with scores of different cultures and peoples. So, as never before, anthropologists became socially important people. And sociologists and psychologists were even in short supply. World War II forever changed the social sciences. They were exposed to new problems, and much that they thought they knew was proved either irrelevant or wrong. More important, they tasted the heady wine of influence and action and they liked it. Government needs us, they said, and government seemed to agree. At lease one noted psychologist (Doob, 1947) had his doubts and wrote a brief paper beautifully describing the naive scientist in the world of social action. Doob's paper is noteworthy in two other respects. First, his recognition that in

social action, the scientist *qua* scientist is like a fish out of water—dead.

> Where social science data are inadequate or where social science itself can provide only principles or a way of approach to a problem, the social scientist must hurl himself into the debate, participate on an equal or unequal footing with men and women who are not social scientists, toss some of his scientific scruples to the winds, and fight for what seems to him to be valid or even good. A strict adherence to the scientific *credo* in such circumstances leaves the social scientist impotent and sterile as far as policy is concerned. (Doob, 1947)

Second, the fact that Doob early on learned that if he responded seriously to his and others' needs for mutuality and community, even if some of those others were opponents, social action could be rewarding despite the fact that one never knew whether one was having an intended programmatic effect, that is, whether one was solving a problem.

In the aftermath of World War II, the government became both patron and employer of social science. After all, the argument ran, if the government respected and supported social science research, as it did research in the biological and natural sciences, the social atom might be split and its energies harnessed for the greatest good of the greatest number. For 20 years after World War II, the social sciences became, and with a vengeance, vigorous, quantitative, theoretical, and entrepreneurial. If you wanted to solve in a basic and once-and-for-all way the puzzles of individual and social behavior, you needed resources of the wall-to-wall variety. True, it would take time to learn to ask the right questions, to develop the appropriate methodologies, before you could come up with the right answers. What we were after were those bedrock laws of social behavior and process that would allow a society "really" rationally to diagnose and solve its problems. Give us time (and money) and you will not regret it. In the meantime, if you think we can be helpful to you with your current problems, please call on us. And call they did, and go they went. The results have been discouraging and shattering, discouraging because of the lack of intended outcomes, and shattering because they call into question the appropriateness of the scientific-rational model of problem definition and solution in social action. Nelson (1977), a noted economist, has summed it up well in his recent book *The Moon and the Ghetto*. (I am sorry he did not retain the original subtitle: *A Study of the Current Malaise of Rational Analysis of Social Problems*. The malaise is real, and, to my knowledge, Nelson is one of the few who has dared to articulate what others only think about.)

> The search for "the Great Society" entailed highly publicized efforts at turning the policy steering wheel. Broad new mandates were articulated—the war on poverty—and specific policies were designed to deal with various aspects of the problem. The histories of these departures clearly identify the key roles often played by research reports, social science theory, formal analytical procedures. More recent years have seen an increasing flow of proposals for organizational reform: vouchers for schools, health maintenance organizations, greater independence for the post office, a national corporation to run the passenger railroads, pollution fees, revenue sharing. It is easy to trace the intellectual roots of many of these ideas. The technoscience orientation has come later, and never has had the thrust of the others. Nonetheless the intellectual rhetoric has been strong, and has generated at least token efforts to launch the aerospace companies on problems of garbage collection, education and crime control, and programs with evocative titles like "Research Applied to National Needs."
>
> The last several years have seen a sharp decline in faith, within the scientific community as well as outside, regarding our ability to solve our problems through scientific and rational means. Those who want to get on with solving the problems obviously are upset about the loss of

momentum. It is apparent that many of the more optimistic believers in the power of rational analysis overestimated that power. There are strong interests blocking certain kinds of changes. Certain problems are innately intractable or at least very hard. But the proposition here is that a good portion of the reason why rational analysis of social problems hasn't gotten us very far lies in the nature of the analyses that have been done. John Maynard Keynes expressed the faith, and the arrogance, of the social scientist when he said, "The ideas of economists and political philosophers, both when they are right and when they are wrong, are more powerful than is commonly understood. . . . I am sure that the power of vested interests is vastly exaggerated compared with the gradual encroachment of ideas." But surely Abe Lincoln was right when he made his remark about not being able to fool all of the people all of the time.

> In addition to their clumsy treatment of value and knowledge (a problem that seems to infect analysts generally), analysts within each of the traditions have had a tendency to combine tunnel vision with intellectual imperialism. . . . Members of the different traditions have had a tendency to be lulled by their imperialistic rhetoric. This has often led them to provide interpretations and prescriptions that the public, and the political apparatus, rightly have scoffed at. Failure to recognize the limitations of one's own perspective has made analysis of problems that require an integration of various perspectives very difficult. Indeed a kind of internecine warfare obtains among the traditions over the turf that lies between them. (Nelson, 1977, pp. 16, 17, 19)

Nelson illustrates his position using day care, breeder reactor programs, and the SST.

Nelson argues that there are inherent limitations to the scientific problem-solving model as the basis for social action, and he also suggests that there are problems that are inherently intractable. The very word *intractable* is foreign to the scientific tradition. In science, problems may be extraordinarily difficult, but they can never be viewed as intractable, and if some fool says a problem is intractable it is because he or she is not posing the problem correctly or does not have the brain power to work through to the solution. In science, fools are people who say problems are intractable. In the realm of social action, fools are people who say all problems are tractable.

The Challenge of Intractability

Why is it so difficult for people, particularly scientists, to entertain, let alone accept, the possibility that many problems in social living are intractable, not solvable in the once-and-for-all-you-don't-have-to-solve-it-again fashion. I have already given one part of the answer: Science has been such a success in solving so many of the problems in nature that people became persuaded that the dilemmas and puzzles of the human social world would like-wise become explicable and controllable. In fact, people in Western society were so persuaded that it became an article of unquestioned faith. And when religion's hold on people's minds began to disappear and the scientific outlook and enterprise took its place, it tended to go unnoticed that one article of faith (the world is divinely ordered) had been supplanted by another (the world, animate and inani-mate, is ordered, knowable, and control-lable). And the tendency of science to be ahistorical in general, particularly in regard to social history, effectively obscured for people that the rise of modern science not only coincided with the Age of Enlighten-ment but was its major beneficiary. And few things characterized that age as did the belief in the perfectibility of man and society. As Becker (1932) so well described, the heavenly city of St. Augustine would be built on earth, not through divine inspiration but through human reason. Science could not recognize the possibility of intractable problems, and like the religions it supplanted, it purported to give clear direction and meaning to living.

What would happen if one accepted intractability, which is no less than to accept the imperfectibility of man and society? What would keep us going? How would we justify our individual strivings and our commitment to social action? What happens to the idea of progress? What will permit us to look forward to tomorrow? Do we seek, as some people do, new religious experiences that tell us we are not alone in this vast world, that there are solutions to the problems of living, and that mortality can open the door to immortality? And that last ques-tion, I submit, contains the substance of the real challenge of intractability to science in that it says that humans need to deal with three facts: they are inevitably alone within themselves, they need others, and they will die. These are facts that create problems, but they are not the kinds of problems that fit into science's problem-solving model. Leaving religion aside (although it is true for many believers), the problems created by these facts need to be solved again, and again, and again. At different times in our lives, the same problem has a different answer.

It has not gone unnoticed that the wonders of science and technology have had little or no effect on society's capacity to help its members feel less alone in the world, to enjoy a sense of community, and to help them cope with anxiety about death. Some would argue that the failure of science to start with and to be governed by these facts of human existence has exacerbated the pain associated with them. And when value-free science entered the realm of human affairs, it exposed its naivete, its ignorance of social history, its hubris, and its blindness to man's need to deal with his aloneness, to feel part of and needed by a larger group, and to recognize and not deny his mortality. This is what the atomic scientists learned, or should have learned.

There is a malaise in all the sciences. For the first time in modern science, as well as in modern Western society, people are questioning whether the fact that science and technology can accomplish a particular feat is reason enough to do it. In psychology we have been brought up short by the fact that as adherents of science we do not have license to conduct research in any way we want. We are accountable, and that means that we should feel and nurture the bonds of similarity and communality between ourselves and the people we study. It is the difference between *knowing* that you are studying people, like yourself, and not "subjects." Society does not exist for the purposes of scientists. It is arrogance in the extreme to look at society from a *noblesse oblige* stance, expecting that the gifts you give it will be responded to with gratitude, not questions or hesitations. Today, both among scientists and the public, there is the attitude that one should look a gift horse in the mouth.

What bearing does this have on social action? Well, let us talk about Norway. As you know, several years ago they found a lot of oil under the Norwegian Sea. Far from this being greeted with hosannas and visions of a bountiful future, Norwegian leaders reacted with a kind of fear. What could happen to their society if they plunged into the development of the oil fields and began to collect the billions of dollars from the sale of oil? What would be the consequences for Norwegian culture, for their sense of continuity with their past, for their sense of community? A decision was made to go as slowly as possible, to give priority to what they regarded as the important issue in living! The Norwegians know that they live in a world they cannot control, that they will be subject to pressures within and without their society to develop the oil fields

quickly and fully, that they may be unable to act in ways consistent with their needs and values. They may not be able to have it their way. Indeed, we can assume they will fall short of their mark. What will keep them going is what is wrapped in what a poet said: "Life takes its final meaning in chosen death." That may sound melodramatic but only to those who cannot understand that the fact of death informs the experience of living. We live each day as if we were immortal, although our rationality tells us how silly a basis for living that is. If our own rationality does not tell us, we can count on all sorts of events and experiences to shock us, not into the recognition of the fact that we will die, but into confronting how we justify why we have lived and how we planned to live (Becker, 1973; Sarason, 1977). And when scientists confront those questions, and each one does at one time or another, they frequently find that there was a lot they took for granted that they wish they had not. But that is the fate of everyone. At each vantage point in our lives we see our history differently.

As for the scientists who enter the arena of social action (and that may be in different roles), they would do well to be guided by the values they attach to the facts of living in much the same way that the amazing Norwegians are trying to do. This will present scientists with a type of problem (and transform their concepts of solution) for which their scientific models are inappropriate and may even be interfering. They will find themselves dealing in persuasion, not only facts; the problems will change before and within them; they will not be concerned with replicability because that will be impossible; there will be no final solutions, only a constantly upsetting imbalance between values and action; the internal conflict will be not in the form of "Do I have the right answer?" but rather "Am I being consistent with what I believe?"; satisfaction will come not from colleagues' consensus that their procedures, facts, and conclusions are independent of their feelings and values, but from their own convictions that they tried to be true to their values; they will fight to win not in order to establish the superiority of their procedures or the validity of their scientific facts, concepts, and theories but because they want to live with themselves and others in certain ways.

Most scientists who entered the arena of social action have left it bloodied, disillusioned, and cynical. They came with data and solutions, but even when they had neither, they assumed that their training and capacity for rational thinking and their ability to pose clear problems and find appropriate methods leading to solutions would establish their credibility as well as their right to an important role in rational social change. Most of them did not realize, if only for their lack of knowledge or respect for social history, that they were fully agreeing with Karl Marx, who had said that it was not enough to try to understand the world. You had to change it and in a scientific way! Marx considered himself a scientist, and the arrogance of scientism permeated his writings and actions. He had his theory, he stated the problems, collected his data, developed procedures, and had no doubt about the correct solution. And what scorn he had for his unscientific opponents! But Marx did not fool himself about what was behind his science, indeed prior to it. He saw man pathetically alone, separated from others, afraid of living and dying. Unfortunately, his dependence on his science led him to give priority to methods dictated by that science and not to what those methods meant *at that time* to man's plight. The solution to that plight was put off to the distant future. In the meantime, trust Marx's scientific theory and procedures. Look what it explained and promised!

The scientist is committed to seeking and saying his or her truths and must not be concerned with whose ox is being gored, an imperative that science has never questioned because to do so would be to destroy the enterprise at its foundation, which is, of course, moral in the sense of describing how scientists should live with each other. To the extent that they live together on the basis of that imperative, scientific problems can be solved. In the social arena, whose ox is being gored cannot be ignored. It can, of course, be ignored, but history contains countless examples of how bloody the consequences can be. And yet, there are times when one takes a position and acts, knowing that the oxes of other individuals and groups will be gored. But somewhere along the way one should be aware that as important as the desire to prevail over your opponents is, the need on both sides is to feel some bond of mutuality. Winning no less than losing can increase one's sense of loneliness and decrease the sense of belonging. In science, how you did something is no less important than what you say you found. Some would say that how is more important. There are hows in social action, but of a very different cast, so different that it becomes understandable why so many scientists who entered the arena of social action faltered. They could not unlearn fast enough to start learning that the nature of problem solving in the kitchen of social action bore no resemblance to what they had been accustomed to. It is not a kitchen for everyone. But as my favorite president liked to say: "If it's too hot in the kitchen, get the hell out."

Even if you can get out, you will still be dealing with the same issues in your personal life and social circle. But even as a scientist, a new problem has arisen. I refer, of course, to the growing sentiment, already reflected in certain legislation, that what science studies, and the ways it conducts its studies, will be determined by the larger society. And one of the diverse factors behind that determination is the feeling that despite our dazzling capacity to gain new knowledge and skills, to open new vistas for human experience, perhaps even to create new forms of life, we still feel alone, socially unconnected, unhappy in living and fearful of dying. It is a very hot kitchen, not one that the wonders of science and technology have been or will be able to air-condition.

What I have said is no excuse for inaction or pessimism, or any other attitude that only deepens the sense of aloneness, accentuates the lack of community, or makes facing the end an intolerable burden. Nor have I in any way intended to denigrate science or intellectual endeavor. There is a difference between science and scientism, between modesty and arrogance, between recognizing limitations and seeing the whole world from one perspective.

Social action takes on a very different quality when it is based on or controlled by certain facts and values. In a recent book, some colleagues and I (Sarason, Carroll, Maton, Cohen, & Lorentz, 1977) describe an effort over a 3½-year period to develop and sustain a barter economy network of relationships, the purposes of which were to deal more effectively with the fact that resources are always limited and people have a need for a sense of community. I should emphasize that it was an effort not only to increase people's access to needed resources but to do it in a way that also widened and deepened their sense of belonging. The members of this network range from high school students to researchers from different colleges and universities. It is an ever-expanding network of human relationships that makes it a little easier, and sometimes a lot easier, to cope with personal and intellectual needs. Central to the story we tell is a remarkable woman we call Mrs. Dewar, whose distinctive characteristic is the ability to scan her world to see and create opportunities whereby people unknown to each other are brought together because each has something the other person needs. There is resource but no money exchange, and people stay together and have call on each other.

The problem-solving literature is not helpful in trying to understand a Mrs. Dewar or several others like her that we describe. None of these individuals has dealt with solvable problems defined in the traditional scientific sense, but they have transformed their worlds. How they did it is no less important than why they did it, but their distinctiveness in social action lies in the way they put the whys and hows together. In these days when social scientists, suffering from the burnt-child reaction, are either retreating from the world of social action or scaling down their claims to credibility, they would be well advised to pay attention to people like Mrs. Dewar who are not burdened by the concept of "problems" but whose thinking and actions are explicitly powered by the concepts of "opportunities" and "matching," concepts in the service of a clear vision of what makes learning and living worthwhile.

References

Becker, C. L. *The heavenly city of the eighteenth century philosophers*. New Haven, Conn.: Yale University Press, 1932.

Becker, E. *The denial of death*. New York: Free Press (Macmillan), 1973.

Brown, J. F. *Psychology and the social order*. New York: McGraw-Hill, 1936.

Doob, L. W. The utilization of social scientists in the overseas branch of the office of war information. *American Political Science Review*, 1947, 41(No. 4), 649–677.

Heilbroner, R. L. *The worldly philosophers*. New York: Simon & Schuster, 1961.

Köhler, W. *The mentality of apes*. New York: Harcourt, Brace, 1925.

Lynd, R. S. *Knowledge for what? The place of social science in American culture*.

Princeton, N.J.: Princeton University Press, 1939.

Nelson, R. *The moon and the ghetto*. New York: W. W. Norton, 1977.

Sarason, S. B. *Work, aging, and social change. Professionals and the one-life-one-career imperative*. New York: Free Press (Macmillan), 1977.

Sarason, S. B., Carroll, C., Maton, K., Cohen, S., & Lorentz, E. *Human services and resource networks*. San Francisco: Jossey-Bass, 1977.

Wertheimer, M. *Productive thinking* (enlarged ed.). New York: Harper, 1959.

9.3 The Interface between War and the Social Sciences

David Bakan

The immediate cause of my involving myself in the question of war was an aim to provide myself with a methodological exercise in connection with psychology. As an academic, the thinking that I do with respect to psychology has rarely to meet the test of consequentiality. Thus, I asked, how does one think if one's thought has to meet tests of consequentiality? How would a person, whose major activity is thinking and for whom the thinking is consequential, think about things? What kind of a psychology might be appropriate for someone who must discipline himself or herself by such a criterion?

As an expedient I proposed three hypothetical personages about whom I could think in order to pursue such a line of investigation. I sought to sketch out the metaphysical views that they might have which might serve them in their particular projects. The first personage that I considered was the detective. That which is central to his or her thinking, the crime, is intrinsically unique and intrinsically unavailable to direct observation. The detective's technique is to gather data, imagine possibilities, choose among them,

From *Journal of Humanistic Psychology*, Vol. 22, No. 1, Winter 1982, 5–18. © 1982 Association for Humanistic Psychology.

and construct a coherent historical scenario. Perception, imagination, and ability to comprehend the logic of events, both forward and backward in time, are his or her major mental resources. The detective assumes that within physical actuality there is never any contradiction, while within human minds and tales contradictions—and therefore conflicts as well—may prevail. One of the detective's major techniques is to imagine contradictory possibilities and to bring actual data to bear in choosing among them. It was in my consideration of the detective that I became even more sharply aware of a limitation of the positivist view of science than I was before this exercise. It is possible to gain knowledge of that which is unique, not directly observable, and not replicable. The everyday assumption of the detective is that it is possible for the mind to apprehend that which is not apprehensible by the senses, if we may go back to that old platonic distinction.

My second personage was the inventor. He or she is a fashioner of possibilities, and one who brings possibilities into actuality. That with which the inventor is concerned does not exist—not in thought and not in physical actuality. Then he thinks it and subsequently fashions it. In considering the inventor, I coined a word that will have some use for us presently. The word is "anthropogenesic": made by humans. It was especially in the consideration of the inventor that I became more sharply aware of another limitation of positivism. Positivism tends to favor subject matter that is not anthropogenesic, as, for example, the laws of physics, which existed even before people evolved. Now, it seems to me that most of the interesting psychological phenomena are made by people. They are the products of culture, learning, and invention, including the various political, economic, and social inventions that constitute the major contexts of our psychological lives.

The third personage with which I thus concerned myself was the warrior. He turned out to be the most interesting of the three. If the warrior is to be successful, he or she must at least be a detective and an inventor. Furthermore, the criterion of consequentiality is more obviously critical, since success and failure are in terms of life and death, which may be the ultimate categories of consequentiality.

Thus the question, What shall the metaphysics of a warrior be? What does one take as the "real" when life and death depend on it? It was this question that brought me to consider the nature of warfare in detail.

On War in the Modern World and Positivism

In my reading and thinking about war, I could not for long maintain my role exclusively as methodologist. It became more than an exercise almost immediately. I soon realized that I was involved with these questions actively for myself and all of the human beings with whom I identify, and I realized that in these considerations I was not only thinking about some hypothetical warrior, but also had to be the warrior, since I share in the conse-

quentiality or the possibility of war. The danger of war is great. The consequentiality I had posed as a criterion for methodological purposes is itself very real for me, and for all those who currently dwell on this planet.

Thought failure can itself be among the causes of war. Any attitude that disparages thought is dangerous. What is not cognized may be or may contain or may generate great danger. There is some parallel—or even a deeper connection—with individual psychopathology: There is a tendency to press considerations of war out of consciousness as if that might eliminate the possibility of war. The avoidance of thinking about that which is dreaded often only increases the likelihood that that which is dreaded will pass from possibility to actuality. The convergence of Freud's death instinct and the failure of consciousness perhaps is best exemplified in the example of war.

Virtually every country is capable of waging extremely destructive warfare. The total military destructive power is greater than ever in history. Intentions to use this power are volatile. Friendship bonds seem sufficient for military alliances but not for the prevention of war.

If a war were to begin it would quickly take on a totally self-perpetuating character. Clausewitz, the writer of the great classic on war, had claimed, as he has been so often quoted, that "war is nothing but a continuation of political intercourse with the admixture of different means." At present, war would quickly become independent of the political conditions of its origin. All other ends would be absorbed into the ends of war itself.

The great and often-cited paradox with respect to war must be faced. It is argued that military preparation reduces the likelihood of war, and there is truth in that assertion. It is argued that military preparation increases the likelihood of war, and there is truth in that assertion. Resolving this paradox should be the major project of the human race at this stage in history. This project follows upon two other major historical human projects, the elimination of malnutrition and overwork. These problems have, however, at least *in principle*, been solved. We have sufficient resources and technology so that there is no need for any human being on this planet, ever again, to suffer from malnutrition or overwork.

It is my deepest belief that the resolution of this paradox of military preparation is within the orbit of the social sciences. The social sciences have, however, been inhibited by forces that themselves are associated with the history of war and war preparation. We now need to overcome these inhibitions. I believe that, by allowing the social sciences to flourish, even that they may better serve in connection with military preparation, the likelihood of war would be reduced. It would increase military capability—within the paradox. But it would also reduce the need to fight. For fighting is caused by lack of proper management in political, economic, and social spheres. Proper management in these spheres may be greatly advanced by better social sciences. And better solutions in these spheres would make war unnecessary.

Certain developments have taken place over the last several hundred years in connection with war, on the one hand, and in connection with science, on the other, each of which has served the other. A kind of self-sustaining system, which itself constitutes a danger, has thus been set up. Because of the role of science in weapon development, certain notions of science have become fixed, and the availability of science-facilitated weapon and defense technology has encouraged military strategy that persists in leaning on certain forms of human interaction, most notably hierarchy and obedience. Hierarchy and obedience are ancient social inventions that themselves may be anachronistic both civilly and militarily. Sci-

ence has tended to become increasingly positivistic within this complex. This positivistic trend has inhibited the development of the social sciences. Consequently, even military strategy, which might have benefited from more mature social sciences, is deprived of advantages it might win from them.

This is the major point of this article: Science has become increasingly positivistic. Positivism is an inhibitory force on the development of the social sciences. Society is deprived of the benefits of the social sciences, even for military strategy, but more significantly the solution of the political, social, and economic problems. With the solution of the latter, the question of military recourse would not even have to be reached.

The suggestion that there could be any relationship between positivism, on the one hand, and anything having to do with the conduct of war, on the other, must strain credibility. Let me give an example to indicate the ideological depths of this relationship, and to indicate some possible consequences. Military strategy must take account of *capability* and *intention* of a possible enemy. Danger is greatest when the possible enemy is both *capable* of conducting warfare and has the *intention* to do so. Danger is decreased with a decline in capability or intention or both. The assessment of capability and intention constitutes the major work of the various intelligence agencies of the world. A military strategist who would ignore capability and intentionality on the grounds that they are not properly scientific would do so at great peril.

And that is my point, of course. The concepts of capability and intentionality fare poorly in positivistic contexts. Neither is very "scientific": Capability deals with a war that has not even been fought, with weapons, strategies, skills, and techniques that may not even have yet been developed or designed. When faced with classes that do not even have a single extant member, probabilities based on relative frequency—the favorite view of probability within positivism—can have no foundation. The future war is an unknown from a positivistic point of view, for positivistic prediction is based on extrapolation from past concrete facts, rather than informed imagination of possibility and probability. The great curb that positivism characteristically puts on imagination makes it deficient. There is no way to assess capability simply on the basis of observed fact alone, or even by fact and scientific knowledge alone.

As far as intentionality is concerned, it is the classical rejectee of positivism. Teleology, purpose, design, goal direction, and the like may not be counted among causes or used as part of any explanation, the positivistic position insists. Indeed, this has been the primary target of positivistic criticism. The project of much positivistic science is precisely to demonstrate the existence of mechanistic, efficient causes. Whatever may appear to be the result of purpose or design is an illusion. The celebrated example for positivistic thought was Darwin's explanation of the development of biological forms as a result of the principle of natural selection; and the celebrated mechanism in the social sciences for the explanation of behavior, no matter how purposive it may appear, is the principle of reinforcement, the behavioral analogue of the principle of natural selection.

What has happened historically is that military strategists have been grateful to scientists when they have been able to deliver aid in connection with the development of technological advances, but otherwise the scientist's input is regarded with little enthusiasm. The fundamental relationship of science to government was firmly established when Charles II granted the founding charter to the Royal Society of London in the seventeenth century. In return for the charter, the king extracted an oath from its members that they would withdraw from involvement in politics. That was the birth of value-free science. That pattern has persisted to modern times. Most of the scientists who made the atom bomb did not even know what they were working on, and when they sought to have input with respect to policy after Hiroshima and Nagasaki, they were strongly discouraged.

Military Considerations

But there are intrinsic factors on the military side that have tended to favor such a positivistic science as well. In order to appreciate this it might be of value to review briefly the military history of the last few centuries.

It is virtually taken for granted in the Western world that military organization must be strictly hierarchical, and that, within the hierarchy, obedience must be total. There has been some ethical qualification to this in various war-crimes trials in which obedience to unlawful orders has been challenged. But for the most part, there has been no great challenge to the principles of hierarchy and obedience on grounds of effectuality in Western military circles. In spite of losses suffered fighting guerrillas, among whom hierarchy and obedience are far less significant—there is less reliance on orders, chains of command, fixed organization, established forms of behavior, and the like—militarists have not become aware of the essential weaknesses of the hierarchy-obedience form of organization. The *productivity*, if I may use such a term in this connection, of the military hierarchy-obedience model has not yet been adequately assesed.

Military organization has not always been authoritarian. It has been suggested that the very birth of democracy in ancient Greece was due to the fact that the style of warfare shifted from conflicts between individual heroes to conflicts between mass armies. From the moment that a man was armed and became skilled in fighting, rights had to be granted to him; otherwise he might use those very arms against the aristocrat who armed him. In modern warfare, where success increasingly depends on the direct and immediate local exercise of intelligence, rigid hierarchical structures and reflexive obedience are anachronistic. Centers of command and communication links, critical features of hierarchy, are extremely vulnerable. Secrecy is a major tool of hierarchy. However, secrecy has become so penetrable in the modern world that it, too, is quickly becoming anachronistic. Giving up dependence on secrecy also has the compensatory advantage of enlarging the diffusion of intelligence within one's own forces.

The modern emphasis on hierarchy and obedience may be said to go back to Frederick the Great, king of Prussia during most of the second half of the eighteenth century. He compiled detailed manuals of procedure, fixed hierarchical relationships, and imposed severe discipline. Training was aimed at developing rapid, mindless, reflexive obedience as ingrained habit. A soldier, he said, should be more afraid of his commanding officer than the enemy.

Napoleon, following in the footsteps of Frederick, added the concept of force as a central notion, much, as I shall presently indicate, as the concept of force became the central one in positivistic science. In Napoleon we have the great convergence of modern science with modern warfare. Physical force converged with the force of arms. Mass in physics converged with the mass of a military force. Napoleon indicated that "force equals mass times speed" was a basic feature of military strategy. However inexact his physics, physical force, as elaborated in the context of Newtonian physics, was his fundamental metaphor. War was based on ballistic force and mass, the latter including gigantic armies. The Blitzkrieg, thermonuclear bombs, and the carpet bombing of Vietnam descend directly from Napoleon.

Clausewitz, a teacher in the Prussian military college and a great admirer of Napoleon, expressed the basic mentality of Frederick and Napoleon in his compendious treatment of war, formulating in words the principles they had expressed in their military leadership. The huge armies in World War I, fighting gigantic mass against gigantic mass for many months, were consistent with Clausewitz, the textbook that the military leaders of both sides had studied. Hierarchy, bureaucracy, obedience in large armies, and reliance on technology's additions to the mass, acceleration, and accuracy of ballistic missiles were the dominant features of World War I.

We can categorize military strategies in accordance with their relative reliance on force or intelligence. The trend after Frederick, Napoleon, and Clausewitz was to rely on force, in spite of the great significance of intelligence to victory in the history of human conflict. It is interesting to note that in Clausewitz's book (1976) there is one short chapter (Book III, Chapter 10, p. 203) devoted to "cunning," and that is mostly to disparage it, especially for its negative relationship to "character."

World War II, interestingly enough, displayed somewhat greater use of intelligence, in connection with strategy. A good deal of the training of soldiers in World War II was devoted to overcoming "noble" ideas of character. Rommel's victories by the use of craft and cunning earned him the title The Desert Fox. The Japanese demolished Pearl Harbor with cunning. Guerrilla influences stemming from the American frontier fighting styles, the Spanish guerrillas against Napoleon, Lawrence's Arabian victories, and the Boer victories—the latter having been directly witnessed by young Winston Churchill in South Africa—all played their role in informing strategy in World War II. The Germans followed more on Frederick, Napoleon, and Clausewitz.

The most important demonstrations of

the deliberate uses of intelligence rather than force in this century were demonstrated, however, in Asia, with Mao, and with General Giap against the Americans in Vietnam. Mao, in his extensive writings on the conduct of war (Mao Tse-Tung, 1968), placed much greater stress on the human component in warfare than on the technology of warfare, which is so characteristic of the West. Within that, he stressed the significance of strategic intelligence. He was very aware of Lawrence's strategies. But in particular he cites and praises a book on the conduct of warfare from the fourth century B.C., written by one Sun Tzu (1977). Mao's thought on the conduct of warfare was very influential in Vietnam. Indeed, copies of the writings of Mao and Sun Tzu were widely distributed among the Vietcong and the North Vietnamese during the war.

Let me dwell briefly on this book by Sun Tzu, because it places in perspective alternative military modes of thought that we might otherwise take too much for granted. The essence of Sun Tzu's approach is intelligence: "Know the enemy and know yourself: in a hundred battles you will never be in peril" (1977: p.84). The major target is never something concrete, as the ballistic mode of thought of the West tends to take it. Rather, the target is the enemy's strategy. "What is of supreme importance in war is to attack the enemy's strategy" (p. 76). Instead of war involving a tradeoff with other values, there is a continuity between civil and military excellence: "Those who excel in war first cultivate their own humanity and justice and maintain their laws and institutions. By these means they make their governments invincible" (p. 88). One does not lean on those of lower rank: "A skilled commander seeks victory from the situation and does not demand it from subordinates" (p. 93). One does not depend on old habits. One does not even repeat that which was successful: "When I have won a victory I do not repeat my

tactics but respond to circumstances in an infinite variety of ways." One forms tactics on the basis of the situation at hand: "One able to gain the victory by modifying his tactics in accordance with the enemy situation may be said to be divine." War itself is already indicative of shortcomings, for "to win a hundred victories in one hundred battles is not the acme of skill" (pp. 100–101). And so on through this remarkably intelligent book. It is a book on the art of warfare, but in which the ultimate art is to transcend the need for warfare. It is dedicated to maximizing the use of intelligence and minimizing the use of force. In some very important ways, the war in Vietnam was a test of Sun Tzu versus Clausewitz, with the result being the worst military outcome in American military history.

There are connections between the use of intelligence as a primary strategy and nonauthoritarian forms of interaction. Intelligence does not grow well in authoritarian atmospheres. Intelligence, where it exists, does not readily submit itself to command, especially where the intelligence of the command is not commensurate. While fear may be useful in connection with the formation of simple motor habits, it is not useful in connection with the development of high skill and intellectual, imaginative, and creative mental processes. Furthermore, resistance by deliberate or semideliberate stupidity is one of the commonest forms of reaction to resented authoritarianism. The value of reflexive obedience may have been great in Frederick's army. But one cannot operate modern, complex, sophisticated equipment on the basis of reflexive obedience. In modern warfare, broad perspectives, freedom to take initiatives, considerable knowledge, considerable perceptual acuity, considerable wisdom, and considerable independence of judgment are required at all levels of hierarchy. These are so important that hierarchical structure often simply fades in operational conditions.

While in a certain sense these observations may be obvious, one would not know they are obvious from looking at modern military behavior, including the Vietnam fiasco.

Positivism

Having made these few remarks about the nature of the military situation, let me now turn to a consideration of positivism as a force determining the nature of the sciences, particularly the social sciences. I have indicated that positivistic social science is not even useful with respect to modern warfare, and I have suggested that the social sciences, freed from the inhibiting influence of positivism, could contribute to the solution of political, social, and economic problems to make war obsolete. I have already indicated how, at least on the points of capability and intentionality, intelligent military conduct and positivism diverge.

Positivism has a history as a school of philosophy, which characteristically chases, often breathlessly, after each new development in the physical sciences so as to pronounce on the nature of knowledge and the proper conduct of investigation.

Positivism also constitutes a code of conduct for research workers in the nonphysical sciences, the biological sciences, and the social sciences. While it may be possible to be exact about the meaning of positivism as the view of a small group of philosophers, such exactness is not possible for positivism as this cultural phenomenon. As a cultural phenomenon its role is as a standard of conduct, of honor, indicating what is scientific and what is not scientific, where the word "scientific" is a euphemism for "proper." I stress the cultural character of this so-called scientific attitude. It is yet to be shown that this attitude has had, or is likely to have, a demonstrable positive effect on the course of discovery beyond the physical sciences. Even within the physical sciences, positivism is not universally accepted and is not a dominant feature among the leading discoverers. In the social sciences, where the self-conscious advocacy of positivism is greatest, the benefits of positivism are very hard to find.

What is positivism? It is first an orientation that stresses *fact* as the object of knowledge. This, in and of itself, is not objectionable. However, positivism also denies that there can be any other object of knowledge besides facts. During its history, it has been associated with a variety of "isms" that have been connected with physics, such as atomism, reductionism, materialism, mechanism, and determinism. Positivism is "anti" many things. It is antimetaphysical, antitheological, antiteleological, anti-idealistic, antimystical, antisubjective, antivitalistic, antiholistic, anti-interpretive, anti-introspective, antispeculative, antihumanistic, and so on. Positivism is associated with various preferences. It prefers data to theory, and it prefers theory to speculation. It prefers data that are readily described physicalistically. Mentation and vitality—that is, mind and life—are not recognized. (Since life has no reality, killing and dying must have little significance.) Insofar as the positivist begrudging allows some mentation for scientists, it is largely restricted to logical and mathematical mentation, and inferences are made according to rule. It prefers formal to informal logic. It prefers data that come in the form of numbers. It prefers deduction to induction. It is suspicious of generalization. There are some among the positivists who totally disavow induction because it is too remote from fact. It prefers the objective to the subjective. It prefers the actual to the possible. Indeed, the possible, which characteristically is not factual, can have no existence. (This point is critical in connection with warfare, since warfare must entail the consideration of the possible as its central concern.) It prefers phenomena that tend to reoccur rather than that which is unique, and thus it demands replicability. One thing that follows from this is the positivistic theory of prediction, which is essentially a theory of prediction by extrapolation. (In warfare, of course, the theory of prediction by extrapolation is a disaster.) It prefers data from the laboratory rather than the field, and prefers field data that are similar to laboratory data, since it seeks phenomena characterized by their replicability. It prefers the molecular to the molar, the simple to the complex, intellectual frugality (called parsimony) to intellectual spending. It avoids all questions of human values, seeking a "value-free" science. It rejects final cause and formal cause, allowing only material and efficient causes (applying the Aristotelian categories), although under the influence of David Hume, who is particularly important in the history of positivism, even the reality of efficient cause is denied, making it out to be merely a weak inference from the observation of co-occurrence.

I would like to dwell a bit on the notion of force. As I have already suggested, force is a principal concept associated with the military. We speak of the armed forces. It is also the principal concept associated with the history of modern science. The giant step in the history of science was made by Isaac Newton in his explication of force, especially in the laws of motion. The convergence is considerably deeper than mere linguistic coincidence, for it is largely on the ground of Newton's explication of force that all of the subsequent development of the physical sciences took place. With it, historically inordinate physical forces, to be exerted at will, to be used to destroy structures and kill people, were placed into the hands of fighting men.

Now for positivism the only valid knowledge is that which is given by science, with physical science standing as its chief model. Physicalistic facts are the only valid objects of knowledge. The positivistic position denies the existence or intelligibility of any other forces but physicalistic ones. Anything else exceeds the boundary of fact and scientific law. Any form of thought or procedure of investigation that is not reducible to the scientific method thus conceived is illegitimate. In the social sciences, positivism expresses itself as behaviorism in psychology. It has also led to the redesignation of the social sciences as "behavioral" sciences. It leads to the denial of mind, the failure to study it, and ultimately to mindlessness in practical action, by denying the effectiveness of mind in the world. Positivism came into existence in the early nineteenth century when the industrial revolution was well under way. It came in the wake of the great optimism, which was associated with various developments in technology, a technology that also had dramatic consequences for the conduct of war. Science was raised up in prestige, and positivistic writers proclaimed its significance for all realms of human existence, including politics, ethics, and even religion. Science, according to Comte, was humanity's great achievement, to stand as our final view of the universe, after we had passed through our earlier and more primitive theological and metaphysical stages. Saint Simon, who coined the word "positivism," believed that both a great new spiritual power and a great new temporal power had thus finally evolved.

Great reinforcement of this positivistic vision came with, and especially after, World War II, in which science contributed variously to the war effort. The most notable and ultimate contribution of science was the atom bomb, giving more destructive force than had ever been dreamed of. Following the war there was a massive program of support of the sciences, including a major support program of basic research that was almost completely dominated by this positivistic vision.

Deeply locked into this vision is the assumption that science can serve only *through* its contribution to technology, and not in any other way. The Marxists, who took to heart the idea of studying society scientifically but did not accept the positivist strictures, and who quickly demonstrated their power in applied contexts, became anathema. So did some of those scientists who, after having played a role in the development of the atom bomb, sought to have a place in the determination of public policy. At the same time, the social sciences have been hobbled by the positivistic view of science, preventing them from adequately examining the political, social, and economic aspects of society so as to form a proper ground for action. Furthermore, and this is a major point of this article, the social sciences have not even been able to serve as an adequate basis for military strategy.

Positivistic Hobbling of Thinking: Military Strategy

Positivism's claim that fact is the only possible object of knowledge has several very severe implications for military conduct. We can make the position of positivism clearer by making a distinction between that which is actual and that which is not actual. Since matters of fact are all in the realm of the actual, positivism restricts knowledge to such actual matters of fact.

Now in military situations, the stress is characteristically on such things as capability and intentionality, which we have already mentioned, as well as vulnerability, capacity, tolerability, loyalty, dependability, resistance, flexibility, replaceability, interchangeability, and so on. All of these categories refer to reality that is not actual and hence not factual in the positivistic sense. They address the realm of *possibility*, which is never factual. Now, there is little

question but that intelligent people use the information from the actual to infer what is possible and to infer likelihoods. There is no denying that. But positivistic, on the one hand, and intelligent, on the other, are, I am afraid, not the same.

One of the ironies in intellectual history is that positivism, from its inception, has boasted that out of it would emerge the power to predict and control events. The latter boast was repeated by John B. Watson, the founder of American behaviorism, and became a favorite slogan of positivistic psychology and positivistic social science generally. But positivism, as such, has been associated with precious little in the way of actual prediction and actual control in the social sciences. The fantasy of such prediction and control has appeared regularly in the behavioristic literature, but not in fact, except under police conditions in which the control stems from the police conditions rather than the knowledge base.

The method of prediction that is characteristically espoused in the positivistic literature is, as has already been indicated, one or another form of extrapolation. Let's think of extrapolation in a warfare context. The method of extrapolation is based on the assumption of some kind of law of inertia with respect to facticity. Liddell Hart (1967), a military historian and analyst, has indicated that victories characteristically are associated with the development of some tactic or strategem that goes against the expectations of the enemy. If there is any inertia to facticity—which is probably more the case with nonvital and nonmentational events—then for sure the force of some new tactic or strategem can overcome it. It is an open question whether one should seek to enter into the future riding on the inertia of facticity or with an awareness of new forces that arise from intelligence, imagination, and creativity—that arise from life and mind.

The recognition that mind is a source

of force sharply differentiates the mentality of the warrior from the positivistic social scientist. The warrior simply cannot afford the luxury of ignoring the force of the human mind on events. It is patent that the human mind is a major force in world history. If we admit that culture itself is a major factor in the determination of events, we must also note that culture is the historical creation of people. Culture is also a major factor in determining strategies and expectations. Certainly, strategies and expectations play a role in the outcome of human conflict. Without allowing the force of mind, as well as the products of this force, as constituents of reality, one is doomed to be the loser in conflict.

Positivistically influenced social science literature characteristically disallows the existence of other minds. In the seemingly more sophisticated presentations, the existence of other minds is said to be simply an inference based on unreliable extrapolation from a single case; mind cannot be an object of scientific investigation because it is not publicly observable; observations of mind are not subject to replication; and the social sciences can only be pursued by the collection of facts of overt behavior. Not only is the mind not recognized as a force in events; its very existence is denied as a proper object of study. Avoiding the study of mind, positivistic social science is in little position to help the warrior to be able to know anything about the mind of the enemy.

The tendency to ignore mind as force arises also from the exaltation of physics in positivism. Within positivistic contexts, if mind has any reality at all, it is conceived as some kind of epiphenomenon of brain, and brain, being material, is ultimately the expression of the fundamental laws that characterize the material universe. Thus, at least in principle, the positivistic position urges that any study that would involve the study of mind is, at best, only provisional, waiting upon the more basic study of brain, and the materials that make it up. But such a view again downgrades the role of mind as a force in the world. Its force is seen simply as something derivative of physical forces, with the inhibiting thought always that physical force is best studied through the method of physics.

Let me dwell further on that which is created by humans. The laws of physics predate people and their creations. Among their creations we must include military strategems, among which are those yet to be created. The simple fact is that most of the things that are important to human beings during their lives on earth are the result of human actions—are the result of the force that people exert—rather than the laws that predate their very existence. The political, social, and economic structures, as well as each political, economic, and social event that transpires, has *anthropogenesic* factors. Now, the model science for the positivistic view, physics, tends to study what is not anthropogenesic. Indeed, one of the great efforts in positivistic science is to try to exclude anthropogenesic factors. The latter is one of the most important aims associated with the use of the experimental method, especially in the social sciences.

If the social sciences are to advance so that they might be of use to people—in the odd undesirable instance of military efforts, but, more important, for the general solution of political, social, and economic problems—anthropogenesis itself must become a major topic of investigation. Only through the proper understanding of human anthropogenesis will we be able to bring even our own anthropogenesis fully to bear to serve our ends. As long as the social sciences take the physical sciences as their model, the most critical thing associated with human beings, anthropogenesis, is systemically excluded.

To progress in our understanding of anthropogenesis, any number of concepts that have been ruled out of order by the positivistic orientation must be brought into focus: life, mind, purpose, intention, goal, will, imagination, design, planning, and the like. The intellectual funneling of the scientific enterprise to that which is seen as connected to and derivative from physical force exclusively, must yield to the recognition that the human being is demonstrably capable of exerting force on the world by taking account of all forces including the physical ones. We will get nowhere if we seriously and consistently take ourselves to be a simple resultant of physical forces.

Historically, science served the military by helping improve the technology of warfare, and mostly by increasing the available physical force of arms. Its role in such technology has characteristically been one of the main reasons for the support of science by governments, at least since the time of Napoleon; and it continues to be one of the main factors in the current support of science. A fashioning of the ideology of science around this function has taken place, expressed largely in that which I am calling positivism, taking physical force as the nucleus of all knowledge. One of the main consequences of this has been a great dampening of the advance of the social sciences through the systematic ignoring of human anthropogenesis as a major force in all events. We are left with a great understanding of ways of physical destruction by people, but precious little of the people who may exert the power of such destruction—and the people who could eliminate it.

References

Clausewitz, C. von. *On War* (M. Howard and P. Parat, trans.). Princeton: Princeton University Press, 1976.

Liddell Hart, B. H. *Strategy* (2nd Rev. Ed.). New York: Praeger, 1967.

Mao Tse-Tung. *Selected Military Writings.* Peking: Foreign Languages Press, 1968.

Sun Tzu. *The Art of War* (S. B. Griffith, trans.). New York: Oxford University Press, 1977.

9.4 Planning for Freedom

John P. Van Gigch

The Nature of Freedom

The problem of defining the concept of freedom has eluded definitive solution for a long time. Adler [1] tried to unify the many descriptors of freedom but decided

Reprinted by permission of John P. Van Gigch, "Planning for Freedom," *Management Science*, Vol. 22, No. 9, May 1976, 949–961. Coypright © 1976, The Institute of Management Sciences.

that several specifications rather than one were needed. He narrowed his choice to five concepts which were: "circumstantial freedom of self-realization," "acquired freedom of self-perfection," "natural freedom of self-determination," "political liberty" and "collective freedom." A second approach consists in enumerating "the system of liberties" which make up freedom, such as the liberty of speech, of association, of religious belief, of protection under the law, and so on. However, as Laski [8] points out, simple enumeration sidesteps the more difficult problem of determining the conditions under which these freedoms can or cannot be guaranteed and exercised.

Another approach which has been used in trying to deal with the concept of freedom is to distinguish between two kinds of concepts, that of "negative freedom" and of "positive freedom" [2], [12]. In that case, and as a result, two "camps" emerge, where adherents of negative freedom contend that "only the *presence* of something can render a person unfree," while those adhering to the idea of positive freedom hold that "the *absence* of something makes a person unfree" [12, p. 114]. However, this type of dichotomy has "encouraged the wrong sorts of questions" and is . . . "conducive to distortion of important views on freedom" [12, p. 114].

In talking about freedom, MacCallum adopts a triad or set of three variables which provides a starting point from which we can start to plan for freedom.

Freedom always involves: (a) agents or planners with *assumptions*, (b) system *conditions*, and (c) *opportunities* and/or *barriers*. We will elaborate on the possible dimensions of these variables and thus enlarge on the thesis that freedom can be planned. Different combinations in the triad will explain the existence of different varieties of freedom and explain how each variety can be anticipated when the "assumptions-conditions-opportunities" triad is defined.

The Agents' or Planners' Assumptions

The agents involved in the problem of freedom are the planners or designers of the system. These planners hold assumptions which play an important part in shaping the kind of freedom which prevails in the system. These assumptions shape the "Weltanschauung" or way in which the planner views the system, his "image of the world." Mason [14] has shown that

(a) a plan (or behavior pattern) is the result of a planner's interpretation of a set of data,
(b) this interpretation depends on the planner's "value system" or assumptions about the states of the world, and
(c) predictions about the configuration of the plan can be made, given the data set and the planner's assumptions.

When dealing with freedom, the planner's assumptions are related to their *concept of man* from which the *conditions* which prevail for freedom directly derive. Planners can either hold an optimistic or a pessimistic view of man and as a consequence will either rely on the "inner man" or on external checks to control man's behavior. These opposite views can be illustrated by comparing the value system which existed in two periods of ancient Greece [16]. During the ages of Pericles and Socrates (approximately fifth century B.C.) the planners have an optimistic "world view" of man. They consider him basically moral, rational, and interested in improving his personality. On the other hand, during the ages of Plato and Aristotle (approximately fourth century B.C.) a pessimistic view of man prevails; he is regarded as basically selfish, prey to his lowest tendencies where reason cannot be trusted and where man must be controlled with external checks. These two diametrically opposed concepts of man lead to opposed concepts of freedom. In the optimistic world, equality, material rights, participation, faith in the individual personality, unselfishness and self-determination are bound to prevail. By contrast, in the pessimistic world, there is natural inequality and limited participation of the individual whose nature, weaknesses and selfish tendencies must be controlled.

Conditions Prevailing in the Planning System

The second dimension in the designing triad of freedom corresponds to the *conditions* which exist in the system. These conditions can be characterized along the following eleven attributes or criteria:

(1) *Rationality*, which describes the role of reason and debate in the planning system.
(2) *Equality*, which describes how privileges and expertise are distributed among members.
(3) *Experts and Elites*, whose influence is the direct result of whether equality or inequality prevails in the system.
(4) *Participation*, which establishes the extent to which individual members can meaningfully contribute to the system's welfare.
(5) *Change*, which states the attitudes toward the preservation of institutions which are embedded in the planners' value systems.
(6) *Control*, which belongs to all the people, to elites or to certain factions depending on the degree to which participation and equality are regarded as a basis of the system's allocative mechanism.
(7) *Responsiveness*, which shows how the system is influenced by the needs and demands of its members.
(8) *Conflict*, which describes the manner in which disputes are settled and how divergent opinions are taken into account.
(9) *Technology*, which describes the "state of the art," i.e. the particular form of man's systems, tools, instruments, methodologies, advancements and capabilities through which his life at work and off work are organized.

(10) *The System's Morality*, which explains where the "ultimate good" and the interests of the individual citizen lie relative to those of the entire state. The nature of the "ultimate good" depends on the value placed on the welfare of "private man," the interest of the state, or the power of special groups.
(11) *The System's Optimum*, which is the maximum value of the system's objective function. In order to reach this optimum the system may rely on a completely decentralized "adjustment process" where all systems make individual decisions which contribute to the welfare of the total system subject to the overall systems constraints. The concept of "adjustment process" is borrowed from economics where centralization and decentralization are described in terms of an allocative mechanism by which the welfare of the central agency and of the subagencies are optimized relative to each other.[1] In these planning models, the optimum is reached either by centralizing decision-making among appointed elites or experts or by taking into account the power of factions which dominate the scene. A description of the system's optimum includes a determination of where the control of the means (technology) and of the ends (goals) is located in the system.

These conditions are compared in four different contemporary planning systems as shown in Table 1. The four planning systems are:

(1) The liberal model of democracy,
(2) The conservative model of democracy,

---

[1] The concept of decentralization is not contradictory to strong federal institutions which are deemed to manage public funds at the total system level.

(3) The broker rule model of democracy, and,

(4) The Marxian socialist-communist model.

It is pertinent to give here a brief definition of these four models in order to establish their scope. The descriptions of the first three are borrowed mostly from Livingston and Thompson [10]. The description of the fourth comes from a variety of sources (e.g. [4], [7], [11], [15]).

These models are not intended as full explanations of the political philosophies which they represent. They are only provided as examples to illustrate the differences which exist in their respective assumptions-conditions-opportunities triads. Real world economic and political systems are hybrid versions of those described below and possess properties of one or the other planning model. There are no unique liberal or conservative or broker rule models, but rather a number of them. Further "the meaning of liberalism or conservatism keeps changing over the years and centuries."[2] Even the meaning of communism and socialism differs from country to country and only represents in part the theoretical Marxist outline.

(1) The Liberal Model of Democracy

In its broadest terms, the liberal model of democracy emphasizes the role of the majorities but guarantees the inalienable rights of the minorities. It seeks the public interest with control of the government by the people. It has faith in the rational outcome of debate with equal participation of all citizens. It holds an optimistic notion of the nature of mankind according to which "public man" always strives to place the people's interest above his own.

[2] From one of the referee's statements. The author gratefully acknowledges the improvements which the referees' suggestions made to the original version of the paper.

(2) The Conservative Model of Democracy

Contrary to the idealistic and optimistic view held in the previous model, man is regarded as a rather weak being, and given to behave less rationally and more selfishly than could be expected. The political life of the community cannot rely solely on the contribution of the masses. Rather, the state must rely on an aristocracy, i.e., an institution of the "best men" who are chosen indirectly if possible. Hierarchy and aristocracy reflect the natural inequality of men. The governing elite is not assumed to be immune to the antisocial tendencies of other men. Therefore, restraints against natural vices and opportunism are provided. The system is deemed democratic because it does not rule out the participation of all, provided that the proper safeguards are taken and that checks and balances are built-in.

(3) The Broker Rule Model of Democracy

The broker rule model is said to be "a defense and justification of modern political processes" as found in American capitalism. The broker rule model is a "pluralistic model" which recognizes the participation of all partisan groups in the shaping of a compromise or a consensus, according to which the affairs of the system will be guided. Minorities and interest groups participate in the constant bargaining among "shifting coalitions" out of which evolve solutions which satisfy a majority of the groups. The politician acts as a broker among factions.

(4) The Marxian Socialist-Communist Model

Marxian theory holds that after the breakup of the capitalist system, the proletarian state will be established. This would be

TABLE 1 Attributes Which Characterize the Conditions Prevailing in Four Planning Systems

	Liberal Model	Conservative Model	Broker Rule Model	Socialist-Communist Model
RATIONALITY	Reason is held in esteem. It can be used as an instrument to obtain the "ultimate good" and to promote consensus. All reasonable arguments are allowed because the best plan evolves from "informed debate."	Passions can overpower reason. Reason cannot be trusted to control the passions of mankind. The solution of difficult public issues cannot be obtained in the heat of public debate, but rather by relying on the experts and the informed "elites."	Power can control reason. Complex issues are resolved by negotiation among interested factions. Confrontation can lead to power struggles. Reason can only be used as an instrument of persuasion among opposing parties.	Belief is held in the power of science and in man's ability to transform the society in which he lives. The solutions of problems must be scientific in order to replace the autonomy of decision-makers. Search for economic rationality leads to directives and to mandatory plans. Political and economic laws regulate the development and progress of society.
EQUALITY	All men are born equal. Wisdom is not the privilege of a few. All individuals are equally capable of contributing to the determination of the public welfare. Expertise can be held by the majorities as well as the minorities and is the result of the tolerant discussion of all alternatives by all concerned.	Not all men are born equal. Natural inequality justifies an intellectual hierarchy among men. The direction of the system is assigned to a "brain trust." Tyranny of this elite is avoided by a system of checks and balances. Limits must be placed on "unlimited power."	Equality or inequality stems from the uneven distribution of power. Power originates from social, economic or political status. Knowledge can also constitute a source of power.	All men have equal standing in society in relation to conditions of work and the distribution of goods resulting from it. According to the communist principle: "From each according to his ability: to each according to his needs." It is anticipated that classes and class antagonism will eventually disappear.

EXPERTS AND ELITES	Everyone can aspire to knowledge and hence to expertise. Elites and experts are not held in particular esteem unless they share their alleged superiority with others. The citizens *are* the planners.	Wisdom is the privilege of a body of experts. Elitism fosters the recognition of a body of experts or professionals with superior knowledge or influence which has more say on public issues than the rest of the community.	Elitism is a function of the relative power demonstrated by the factions.	Reliance on centralized control of the economic enterprise creates the necessity for a body of technocrats, to forecast, administer and supervise the fulfillment of plans. In its present form, a self-selected power elite holds and dominates political power. However, the promise is held that, in later stages of evolution, the state itself will "wither away" as an apparatus of compulsion and subordination.
PARTICIPATION	The participation of citizens is needed. Self-determination and a sense of achievement dictate the individual citizen's involvement in the debate of public issues. Knowledge and education are held in esteem. A more informed and better educated individual can more meaningfully participate in public debate.	As a result of natural inequities created by wealth, position and education not all members of the community can or are entitled to participate in final decisions. Citizens can participate through traditional institutions and body of experts. An indirect system of representatives ensures that all opinions are taken into account by planners and decision-makers.	Individuals with common interest must group to participate. Citizens participate through memberships in groups or factions of common interests.	All men must take active part in controlling public affairs. The people's efforts will lead to "breaking the bonds of necessity and achieving freedom" [3, p. 50]. They participate voluntarily because they believe in man's capacity for changing his environment. The collective will guided by the government arm ensures the success of policy and programmes [3, p. 49].

TABLE 1 *(continued)*

	Liberal Model	Conservative Model	Broker Rule Model	Socialist-Communist Model
CHANGE	Tradition and present forms of social institutions are not held sacred and are subject to evolution. Relativism in values is accepted.	Allegiance to traditional institutions ensures the preservation of order. The status quo must be protected in the name of stability. Slow change is allowed as long as respect for established institutions and commitment to tradition are observed. "Incrementalism" embodies slow movement in the direction of improvement.	Bargaining and negotiation hold the key to change. Previously held positions are used as starting points from which to initiate bargaining. To avoid conflict among factions, deciding for the average is sometimes expedient. The role of the broker is to hedge and avoid the dominance of any one faction. Leadership is diffused to avoid takeover or domination by a particular group.	Hegelian dialectic creates change from the conflict of thesis and antithesis from which a synthesis of ideas will emerge. Marxian dialectic uses an economic interpretation of history to explain social changes by attributing all events to the economic conditions of society [11, p. 73]. The "mode of production" sets the form and content of all other social institutions [11, pp. 73–75].
CONTROL	Control of the planning system rightfully belongs in the hands of the citizens. The people control the governing processes.	Control of the planning process belongs to the governing elite of experts who rightfully make decisions. Citizens have indirect control through representation and voting.	The control of decision-making rests with economic or political groups who hold power due to their number or their strategic position in the system.	Control rests with the administrative and political elite that holds the decision-making power at all levels of the system.
RESPONSIVENESS	The planning system is responsive to individual inputs. Through participation in the debate of	Individual inputs are heard when directed to appropriate experts, through specified chan-	The system is most responsive to factions controlling the decision-making power.	The system is not responsive to the individual, in the sense described in the other

public issues, the citizens feel that the system is responsive and sensitive to their demands and needs.	nels. A system of checks and balances insures that no partisan group imposes its views upon others.		planning models of the western world. It does not allow individuals sovereignty or pluralism in most aspects of life.
CONFLICT It is hoped that reasoned debate in the community's assembly assuages the minority and allows the majority to rule.	Once chosen, the elite and the experts decide where the truth lies. Therefore conflict can be resolved through hierarchical influence.	Conflict is resolved by middle of the road positions and by compromise.	Basically there is no conflict between the interests of society and those of the individual. The coercive power of the state only exists during early stages of transition from socialism to full communism in order to reconcile class antagonism and to assert the people's rights.
TECHNOLOGY The exercise of democracy can be enhanced if, through technology, increased literacy and knowledge, the lower social classes can improve their material well-being and increase control over their destiny. Technology can also bring disutilities or erosion of democracy through the enlargement of the gap between the managers and the managed [13].	Technology is institutionalized in order to reap the benefits of knowledge. Whether this leads to an enhancement or an erosion of freedom and democracy depends on the way in which the planners and technocrats define the social goals of the system and on the participation they allow to the mass of the population in setting them.	Knowledge and technical rationality can spell power. However, only the managers are "the influential." They act as brokers between the manager, the intellectual elite and the planners themselves to exclude virtually all others from the goal setting process [13].	Moral ideas are determined by the particular class position of the dominating social group. Therefore, the "mode of production," i.e. the economic structure of a given society, sets the form and content of all social institutions as well as their ethical notions. Morality stems directly from man's material needs and from his interest in making nature serve his purposes and those of society better [17, p. 250].

TABLE 1 *(continued)*

	Liberal Model	Conservative Model	Broker Rule Model	Socialist-Communist Model
THE SYSTEM'S MORALITY	The planning system seeks the welfare of its constituents and strives for the "ultimate good" which is decided among all the community members. The "ultimate good" is a "common belief" wrought in rational debate. The interests of the community come before the interests of any one individual. However, the natural rights of each man are protected and guaranteed against violation. "Public man" places the public service above his own and therefore serves "private man." Whereas reason is held as the instrument of truth, the decisions reached by man can be fallible and values are relative to time and place. The "ultimate good" is allowed to vary.	The ethics of the system are decided by the aristocracy or elite of goal-setters who control the distribution of justice and public welfare. The ultimate good is decided by the chosen few on the recommendations of experts. The morality of the system is grounded on the preservation of the "status quo," a value in itself. Institutions are grounded in traditions which have passed the test of time. Values are based on certain absolute truths which are accepted on faith, and cannot therefore be either relative to time and place or the subject of debate.	The concepts of the "ultimate good" and of the "public interest" are replaced by the shifting goals resulting from compromise and bargaining. The "common belief" is not the result of rational debate but rather reflects the power realities of the situation. There are no absolute ethics for the system. Standards are the result of rationalizations of interests and desires among the participant groups. The broker decides what is moral and suitable after weighing the power of the factions instead of their arguments. The "ultimate good" is an average compromise struck to satisfy those who dominate the decision-making process.	Moral truths are not absolute but relative to a particular economic form of society. Ethical considerations are not imposed upon man but derive logically from conditions of life in the society in which he lives. What is moral is what succeeds in advancing the material and cultural well-being of society. Therefore, "communist man" is willing to work without compulsion, places public welfare above personal interests, endeavors to improve and develop his individual capabilities in order to bring about the ultimate ideal [7, p. 250].

THE SYSTEM'S OPTIMUM

Optimization can be visualized as a decentralized model of organizations where the decentralized subsystems strive toward the system's optimum by way of a never ending "adjustment process." The decentralized decision-makers decide what the optimum or "ultimate good" will be and control the means and technology to achieve it. The system's optimum is never quite reached. Its focus changes as the system strives to reach it.

Optimization resembles the centralized model of organizations where control of the process is lodged in the centralized headquarters to which the decentralized locations are allowed to send the solutions proposals. These proposals are reviewed and modified until they meet and satisfy the headquarters' objectives and resource constraints. The decision-makers in the centralized headquarters decide on the means and the ends (Technology and Goals) of how the system's optimum or "ultimate good" will be reached.

The "ultimate good" or optimum is wrought in the heat of power struggles among factions. Control of the means and ends to achieve the optimum wavers from faction to faction depending on the balance of power. Each subsystem tries to optimize its own system. Due to the interplay of factions, the subsystems do not necessarily strive toward an overall system's optimum for which they do not have any particular regard. Progress toward consensus (if it exists) is the result of power plays instead of reasoned debate.

The rational organization of the productive forces through quantitative planning methods leads to increased efficiency of the economic mechanism. Optimal Planning Theory which deals with the application of mathematical allocative models is used to calculate physical as well as value indices by which the interests of national economic development can be "harmonized" with the maximization of local optimality criteria in each enterprise [5, p. 15].

"socialism" in the sense that the means of production will no longer be the private property of individuals but belong to the whole of society [11, p. 144]. Once the proletarian state is in operation, transition to full communism is anticipated which promises "free development of each" as the condition "for the free development of all" [9, p. 145], [17, p. 248]. The new society is without class, the workers (i.e., all of society) possess the entire fruits of production. The material base allows higher forms of pleasure, leisure, culture and freedom from economic worries. [11, p. 148].

The Opportunities and the Barriers

The third element of the triad by which freedom can be defined concerns the *opportunities* which enhance its exercise and the restraints or *barriers* which hinder it. These opportunities and barriers flow directly from the two other elements of the designing triad, i.e., the planners' or agents' assumptions and the conditions existing in each system. We proceed to describe these opportunities and barriers as they operate in each of the four planning systems chosen for study.

1. The Liberal Model of Democracy

1.1. Opportunities Which Enhance the Exercise of Freedom (a) Due to equality and participation, all citizens are planners and take part in the debate of public issues. (See Table 1.)
(b) Faith in the individual leads to self-determination. Increased education and knowledge leads to enhancement of the personality (through "self-realization" and "self-perfection") and a more meaningful contribution to the community.

(c) Through participation and involvement, the individual controls his own fate. Chances for coercion, compulsion or alienation are reduced.
(d) The system is responsive to inequities and criticism, thus promoting orderly change.
(e) The dissemination of knowledge gives socio-political power to lower social classes which contest the control of the managerial and technological elite. [13]

1.2. Barriers Which Hinder the Exercise of Freedom (a) Political freedom and self-determination are endangered when the system grows in size and complexity and becomes more anonymous and impersonal.
(b) Estrangement from the system results when it cannot match expectations with results.
(c) The growing "gap in political culture" between the managers and the managed causes "the erosion of the democratic ethos." [13]

2. The Conservative Model of Democracy

2.1. Opportunities Which Enhance the Exercise of Freedom (a) Commitment to and respect for established institutions foster the enjoyment of traditional freedom guaranteed by law.
(b) Allegiance to traditional symbols and customs ensures community of purpose.
(c) Limits on unlimited freedom guarantee opportunities of exercising all freedoms.
(d) As in the liberal model, increased technical rationality improves leverage and participation in the determination of the values and ends of the planning system. [13]

2.2. Barriers Which Hinder the Exercise of Freedom (a) Limits must be placed over man's actions to control human nature and his "factious tendencies."

(b) Participation in community affairs and decision-making is limited to experts and elites.

(c) Indirect participation and representation reduce the system's responsiveness to grievances and criticism.

(d) Technical organization increases negative effects and the hierarchical gap among classes. [13]

3. The Broker Rule Model of Democracy

3.1. Opportunities Which Enhance the Exercise of Freedom (a) The group becomes an important vehicle to resolve conflicts and vent criticism.

(b) Freedom boundaries are defined by the limits imposed by the collective society.

(c) Broker rule is an alternative to the tyranny of a few. Compromise is better than coercion.

(d) Under broker rule, standards reflect the collective morality of the majority in power.

3.2. Barriers Which Hinder the Exercise of Freedom (a) "Plurality of norms" has a levelling effect whereby norms never soar above the average.

(b) Power and force of partisan groups reign above reason.

4. The Marxian Socialist-Communist Model

This planning model is presented here to show that planning for freedom is related to the assumptions held by the planners and to the conditions obtaining in the system. The shape given to freedom depends directly on those two elements of the designing triad. Consequently, it is futile to argue that there is more or less freedom in one system than in another.

The "form" which freedom takes is different from system to system and one cannot judge the opportunities and barriers existing in one system when one holds assumptions applicable to another. As will be illustrated below, as far as the planners of the Marxian socialist-communist model are concerned, *there is* freedom in their system. The opportunities and barriers for its enjoyment are of a different kind than those existing in the democratic models explained earlier. They result directly from the values and conditions prevailing in the planning system.

4.1. Opportunities Which Enhance the Exercise of Freedom (a) *Elimination of wage slavery and exploitation*. The wage worker in a noncommunist society is a slave because he is not properly compensated for his labor. In a communist planning system, the exploitation of man by man becomes impossible, the means of production belong to the whole of society and democracy is transferred from the "rulers" to the "ruled" [11, pp. 113, 144].

(b) Overcoming and controlling the forces of nature by understanding necessity leads to freedom from anxiety over the individual's means of subsistence and over the material requirements of life [6, p. 266].

(c) Personal freedom will exist in a classless society whose participants take over control of productive forces which dictate the conditions of existence [17, p. 270].

4.2. Barriers Which Hinder the Exercise of Freedom (a) *Mode of Production*. The whole Marxian theory is based on the belief that the wage worker is not a free agent in modern society. He is bound to his employer to whom he sells his labor power. As a consequence of the accumulation of surplus value in the hands of the owners, the workers are pushed into a state of subservience. The existing "mode of production" creates a "possessing class" which oppresses the proletariat, prevents it from enjoying democracy and maintains barriers against freedom.

(b) *Intervention of the State.* During the early stages of social reform, the presence of the state and the dictatorship of the proletariat must be established to eliminate vestiges of inequality and class struggles. In later stages of the system's development, the state becomes unnecessary as an apparatus of repression, compulsion, and subordination. "Only then . . . it becomes possible to speak of freedom" when observation of the rules of social life occurs logically either through voluntary cooperative agreement or through "the individuals' communized psychologies" [11, p. 147].

(c) *Elimination of Barriers.* In the Soviet system, the existing party regime dominates government and controls individual destiny. It is reasoned that, as transition from socialism to full communism takes place, true pluralism without restrictions or barriers will eventually be available to all [11, p. 525].

Conclusions

Thus, we have tried to illustrate that there is no inherent dilemma between planning and freedom. More planning does not necessarily lead to less freedom. Rather, different kinds of planning spell different kinds of freedom(s). The planning paradigm consists of an "assumptions-conditions-opportunities" triad by which the types of freedom prevailing in a system are determined. Due to the disparity among the elements of the triad from system to system, it is difficult to make intersystem comparisons of the amounts of freedom which obtain. Further, one cannot tell whether the nature of freedom in one planning model is more desirable or advantageous than that in another. There is no way of adding the advantages provided by the opportunities to exercise freedom and subtracting the disadvantages due to the barriers which act to hinder it. It is futile to mount attacks on the form and quantity of freedom prevailing in one system, when viewed from the perspective based on the assumptions and conditions existing in another system. The debate or dilemma about which system provides more freedom remains unresolved. Rather, the issue revolves around the compatibility of one's views and values with the assumptions and conditions by which freedom is determined. Whether we cheer or deplore when a new opportunity for, or a new barrier against, freedom arises, depends on whether our own assumptions and beliefs are in consonance with the conditions existing in the planning system. Each system can justify its own "brand" of freedom by claiming compatibility between its constituents' values and the conditions of the system.

References

1. Adler, M. "Freedom as Natural, Acquired, and Circumstantial," in *Freedom: Its History, Nature and Varieties*, edited by Dewey, R. E. and Gould, J. A. The Macmillan Co., New York, 1970, pp. 68–75.

2. Berlin, I. "Two Concepts of Liberty," in *Freedom: Its History, Nature and Varieties, op. cit.*, pp. 84–93.

3. Bernard, Phillippe J. *Planning in the Soviet Union.* Pergamon Press, Oxford, 1966.

4. Drachkovitch, Milorad, M., ed. *Marxist Ideology in the Contemporary World, Its Appeals and Paradoxes.* F. A. Praeger, New York, 1966.

5. Ellman, Michael. *Planning Problems in the USSR—The Contribution of Mathematical Economics to Their Solution.* University of Cambridge, Cambridge, 1973.

6. Engels, F. *Anti-Dühring (Herr Eugen Dühring's Revolution in Science).* International Publishers, New York, 1939,

p. 125, as quoted in: *Reader in Marxist Philosophy*, edited by Selsam, H., and Martel, H. International Publishers, New York, 1963.

7. Halm, G. N. *Economic Systems: A Comparative Analysis*. Holt, Rinehart and Winston, New York, 1968.

8. Laski, H. J. "The Changing Content of Freedom in History," in *Freedom: Its History, Nature and Varieties, op. cit.*, pp. 48–55.

9. Lenin, V. I. *Handbook of Marxism*, E. Burns, comp. Random House, 1935, New York, as quoted in Loucks, W. N., and Whitney, W. G. *Comparative Economic Systems*. Harper and Row, New York, 1969.

10. Livingston, J. C., and Thompson, R. G. *The Consent of the Governed*. The Macmillan Co., New York, 2nd ed., 1966.

11. Loucks, W. N., and Whitney, W. G. *Comparative Economic Systems*. Harper and Row, New York, 1969.

12. MacCallum, Gerald C., Jr. "Negative and Positive Freedom," in *Contemporary Political Theory*, edited by de Crespigny, A., and Wertheimer, A. Aldine-Atherton, New York, 1970, pp. 107–126.

13. McDermott, J.: "Technology: The Opiate of the Intellectuals." *The New York Review of Books*, July 31, 1969, pp. 25–35.

14. Mason, R. O. "A Dialectical Approach to Strategic Planning." *Management Science*, Vol. 15, No. 8 (1969), pp. B-403–B-414.

15. Mayo, H. B. *Democracy and Marxism*. Oxford University Press, New York, 1955.

16. Pohlenz, M. *Freedom in Greek Life and Thought: The History of an Ideal*. The Humanities Press, New York, 1966.

17. Selsam, H., and Martel, H. (eds.). *Reader in Marxist Philosophy*. International Publishers, New York, 1963.

IV
Values and Goals

10
Finding Direction in Planned Change

Whatever else planning may mean, it signifies an anticipation of some future state of affairs and the confirmation of a vision of that future in the present in order to motivate, guide, and direct present action. A planner's present situation always includes a time perspective forward— a future different from the present, yet populated with more or less clearly delineated agents and counteragents, objects to be avoided, objects to be embraced, means to empower avoidance or embracing, and some context of interrelated factors and forces, human and nonhuman, benign, hostile, or neutral. Man as planner must climb out of his involvement in present transactions to look beyond the horizon of the present and to bring back a vision of the future to modify the tempo, quality, and direction of his present transactions.

It is the fact of change in the internal and external conditions of human life that makes planning important and necessary to time-bound men and women, choosing and acting of necessity within the medium of history. And it is the fact of change that makes planning difficult for time-bound men and women. If the future were to be like the present, there would be no need to give thought to preparing for it. Yet, since the future will be different from the present, men do not know how far to trust their present anticipations of it in preparing to meet and cope with it. All human planning is planning for change and requires judgments about the proper

409

balance between investment of energy and resources in the pursuit or avoidance of consequences we can now anticipate and the massing of free and uncommitted energy and resources for coping with unanticipated consequences.

Kenneth Boulding has illuminated the predicament of men in attempting to plan the future of the social systems in and through which they live in his distinction between "evolutionary systems" and "mechanical systems."

> One thing we can say about man's future with a great deal of confidence is that it will be more or less surprising. This phenomenon of surprise is not something which arises merely out of man's ignorance, though ignorance can contribute to what might be called unnecessary surprises. There is, however, something fundamental in the nature of our evolutionary system which makes exact foreknowledge about it impossible, and as social systems are in a large measure evolutionary in character, they participate in the property of containing ineradicable surprises.[1]

Mechanical systems have no surprise in them since time as a significant variable has been eliminated from them in the sense that they have no past or future and the present is a purely arbitrary point. The traditional lure among scientific students and planners of human affairs toward interpreting social systems as mechanical systems may rest on some inherent preference for a world of no surprise among scientific men. Yet system breaks which result in more or less sudden changes in the defining characteristics of the system itself seem to characterize the temporal careers of all human systems. And human planners must plan with the possibilities of system breaks somewhere within their field of consciousness.

We have spoken so far of the predicament of human planning in general. Yet planning always occurs within some time-bounded historical situation. What characteristics of the present historical situation have given new point and poignancy to men's efforts to find confident direction in planning for the future?

A radical increase in the rate of change in the conditions of life has thrown the problem of direction finding and planning into new perspective. Concentration of energy and resources in basic and applied research has resulted in a continuing revolution in the means and conditions of work, play, education, and family and community living. Men have found the established institutions and wisdoms from the past less and less dependable as guides to the effective and humane management of new knowledges and technologies in the conduct of life. Men in a slowly changing culture could validly assume that the ecological contours of their

---

[1] Kenneth E. Boulding, "Expecting the Unexpected: The Uncertain Future of Knowledge and Technology," Edgar L. Morphet and Charles O. Ryan (eds.), *Prospective Changes in Society by 1980* (Denver, Colo.: July 1966).

future life would be substantially similar to those of their past. Changes to be planned for could be seen as confinable and manageable within the patterns of a viable tradition out of the past. Modern men have been betrayed by tradition direction. They face both the hopes and terrors of an unknown future more directly than past men did, bereft of security in the guidance of traditional forms and wisdoms.

Finding direction for the future by projecting the forms and values of a traditional culture upon that future has been further undermined by the omnipresent fact of intercultural contact, confrontation, and mixing within nations and between nations. The development of vast networks of interdependence, the spread of mass media of communication, reduced security in spatial and political boundaries between cultures, due to space-destroying means of transportation and other related factors, have brought about uneasy contact and confrontation between traditionally segregated nations, classes, races, and subcultures. As we seek new bases for an interdependent future across these cleavages of culture by projecting the traditions of any one cultural tradition, the futility of this way of defining the future for purposes of planning becomes more and more apparent to modern men. If there is to be a common future, it must be constructed and reconstructed by men in a way to lead beyond the present maze of disparate and conflicting traditions. The outlines of the task have become clearer than the means for achieving it.

A third feature of contemporary man's struggles to find viable directions into his future is a widespread decline of confidence in a presiding Providence which will automatically and without human attention bring the plural and conflicting plans and actions of individual men and groups of men into the service of commonly valuable purposes. Confidence in some pre-established ordering principle within history—a principle which men can depend upon to bring meaningful and moral order out of the confusion and chaos of diverse and conflicting individual and group decidings and strivings—has taken many forms in the history of human affairs. The principle has been conceived theistically and naturalistically, personally and impersonally, immanently and transcendentally, pessimistically and optimistically. And it has been given many names—the Will of God, Fate, the Nature of Stoics and Taoists, the "Unseen Hand" of Adam Smith and the free-market mechanism of the classical economists, the Idea of Progress in Western liberalism, the historical inevitability of socialism in Marxism. One may recognize the common function which these versions of a superhuman directing principle have played in the direction of human affairs and in setting limits to human responsibility in planning man's future, without denying the differences which adherence to one version or another has made in the organization and deployment of human energies and resources. The effect of this confidence has been to narrow the range of human responsibility for finding and giving direction to the course of human history. Decline of confidence means a widening of man's responsibility for designing and inventing his own future. If there is to be an ordering principle in human planning, a principle attentive to the conservation and augmentation of human values, men must find, or better construct and apply, the principle through their own collective intelligence and volition.

In this human condition, it is not surprising that a new "discipline" of "futuristics" has emerged recently. The aim of "futuristics" is to help men and women find and keep direction in their efforts to envision and build a viable future for man on earth. Elise Boulding, in "Learning to Image the Future," offers a constructive critique of contemporary "futuristics" and envisions a way of imaging the future which incorporates the transcendence that human hope requires, which is egalitarian rather than elitist, and which is transnational rather than nationalistic in its scope. She also projects the kind of educational processes which men and women will require in learning to image a future for man and models of which, she argues, have already emerged in the contemporary scene.

Margaret Mead works out of a similar value commitment in "The Future as the Basis for Establishing a Shared Culture." She is impressed by the fragmentation, "the agglomeration of partly dissociated, historically divergent and conceptually incongruent patterns" of culture and subculture which now block men and women in their search for a better future for mankind. Imaginatively, Miss Mead envisions a focus upon a future to be jointly built as the basis for uniting young and old, men and women, people of various nationalities and religions, scholarly and nonscholarly, in going beyond the fragmentation of culture which now divides them into the construction of a shared culture. The future, unlike the past, is always newborn. To involve all living persons in constructing the future is to release and facilitate change and growth all around. Mead's method of grappling with the future is prophetic, in the sense that she is concerned not primarily with predicting but rather with invoking and shaping the future in the service of an overarching value—"shared culture."

The changes which contemporary men and women are undergoing, and, insofar as they can summon the directed energy and wit, changes which they are helping to shape and control, extend not alone to human institutions but to the internal organization of human persons, themselves and others. What kind or kinds of persons will social evolution elicit and require in the future? Louis Zurcher sketches the shape of persons now emerging in "The Mutable Self: A Self-Concept for Social Change." Zurcher's mutable self is the personal counterpart of the temporary human systems which Bennis, Slater, and others have seen as characteristic of post-bureaucratic society. John Dewey once identified the ultimate devotion of persons who live wisely in and with continuing change and who assume responsibility for directing it as commitment to the process of self-remaking. If Zurcher is empirically correct, contemporary society is now tending to support the development of mutable selves with such a devotion.

10.1 Learning to Image the Future

Elise Boulding

The intimate relationship between the reconstruction of education and the reconstruction of society has come out frequently in the preceding chapters. The capacity of a society to generate creative images of the future, that will act back on the present and draw it toward the envisioned tomorrow, is simultaneously reflected in and fostered by its educational institutions. It is in these institutions that the battle between the past and the future is fought. On the one hand children are prepared for the maintenance of existing structures through training in the social and technical skills familiar to the adult generation. They may even be trained to meet long-past crises, just as nations train soldiers to fight old wars. At the same time they must be prepared to adapt to, and even to create, new institutions and new possibilities for humankind. While the rhetoric of education all lies in the direction of creating new futures, the actuality lies much more in the re-creation of the past.

The rise of futuristics as an intellectual discipline is forcing education to reexamine its rhetoric and its reality. As the professional futurist moves in, the educator is waking up and saying, "Hey, the future is my business too! This is what I work

Originally published as "Futurism as a Galvanizer of Education," in N. Shimahara (Ed.), *Educational Reconstruction* (Columbus, Ohio: Charles Merrill Pub. Co., 1972).

References in the deleted parts of this essay have been removed and the remaining references renumbered.

with!" It is good that he does so since this is his best protection against an excessively technocratic futurism, which simply treats the future as a problem to be solved. The technocrat-cum-planner tends to see the educational system as a powerful tool to assist him in shaping the future he is blueprinting. If education is to be more than a complex piece of software for implementing certain types of futures in a technological society, a more indepth understanding of the dynamics of imaging the future, and the role of education in it, is required. . . .

We are discussing here a complex set of three-way interactions between society, the imaged future, and society's learning communities. Each of the three acts on the other two. In order to understand this interaction we need to examine (1) the nature of the imaging process, (2) the politics of imaging the future in a period of redistribution of social power, (3) the reservoir of human knowledge on which we draw in the imaging process, and (4) the changing character of the learning communities.

Imaging the Future

While the idea of envisioning the future is as old as human society, and in fact marks humankind off from other animal species, the specific term "image of the future" has come into usage rather recently. The scholar who has dealt the most delicately and sensitively with the concept is Fred Polak, one of the first of the post–World War II European futurists. Writing in the bleak aftermath of Nazism when it looked as if the future was closing off for Europe, he probed searchingly into the history of the West to try to identify the ground of past visions, and their effects on the societies that held them. *Was* there a relationship between man's imaging capacity and the future itself? *Did* the envisioned future act back upon the groping present, and draw it surely towards itself? And if this was indeed the case, what were the features of the image itself that gave it such power over the present?

In Polak's book, *The Image of the Future*,[1] he traces the relationship between prevailing images of the future and the ensuing future of succeeding periods of Judaeo-Christian society, getting a running start in Mesopotamia. His hypothesis that the image of the future acts as a time bomb going off in the future itself is amply demonstrated in this book. This time-bomb characteristic of the image stems from its combination of two elements, the eschatological and the utopian.

The *eschatological, or transcendent, is the element which enables the visionary to breach the bonds of the cultural present and mentally encompass the possibility of a totally other type of society, not dependent on what human beings are capable of realizing.* While transcendence refers to the supernatural dimension, there is a theoretically unspecified interaction between the known and the conviction concerning the eventually attainable imagined other.

The *totally other* is, of course, in fact not conceivable by man, but this term (an exact translation of the Dutch) is used without modification because it emphasizes the notion of discontinuity as a key aspect of dynamic social change. Kenneth Boulding's discussion of "Expecting the Unexpected"[2] points up the dilemma underlying the concept of discontinuity.[3] It is clear, however, that a society with an eschatological outlook, one which conceives the possibility, even the desirability, of drastic social change, is very different from the society that seeks familiar tomorrows.

The second element in the ideal-type image of the future is the humanistic utopian, or immanent, element which designates men as the copartners with nature (or God) in the shaping of The Other in the Here-and-Now. Polak suggests that the Judaic image of the future was an ideal embodiment of these twin elements. The Judaic conception of the Covenant, a unique bonding between man and the supernatural,[4] held man responsible for creating the new Zion out of the dusty materials of the planet Earth. Paradise was to be nowhere but here. But man had instructions, and he had to listen carefully to get them right. If he didn't listen, the deal was off—the covenant broken. It was the character of the instructions that set a handful of nomads apart from their fellow tribes in Syriac-Palestine.

This delicately balanced conception of the relationship between immanence and transcendence, man and the supernatural,

---

[1] Fred L. Polak, *The Image of the Future*, Elise Boulding (tr.) (New York: Oceana, 1961).

[2] Kenneth E. Boulding, "Expecting the Unexpected: The Uncertain Future of Knowledge and Technology," in *Prospective Change in Society by 1980 Including Some Implications for Education*, reports prepared for the first Area Conference, Designing Education for the Future, Edgar L. Morphet and Charles O. Ryan (eds.) (Denver: 1966), pp. 199–215.

[3] See also Peter F. Drucker, *The Age of Discontinuity* (New York: Harper & Row, 1968).

[4] The supernatural, which is used in several different ways by Polak, may in general be thought of as a kind of governor on the total ecosystem of the earth, standing outside that system even while partaking of it.

has never lasted for long, though it has reappeared from time to time in the history of the West. The pendulum has swung back and forth. Either God was taking care of everything and man had but to go along with it (St. Augustine), or everything was up to man and he'd better get with it (Comte). Furthermore, societies have alternated between optimistic and pessimistic views of the nature of reality and man. Four modes of imaging the future emerge from various combinations of attitudes to the basic categories of Seinmüssen (that which must be) and Seinsollen (that which ought to be):

1. *Essence optimism combined with influence optimism:* the world is good and man can make it even better.
2. *Essence optimism combined with influence pessimism:* the world is good but it goes of itself and man cannot alter the course of events.
3. *Essence pessimism combined with influence optimism:* the world is bad but man can make it better.
4. *Essence pessimism combined with influence pessimism:* the world is bad and there isn't a damn thing man can do about it.

Influence optimism can be further divided into direct and indirect influence optimism, depending on whether man is perceived as running the show or acting in partnership with the supernatural.[5] Clearly, a society suffering from both essence and influence pessimism is not generating any dynamic images of the future, and the social paralysis engendered by the lack of positive images of the future will lead to the death of the society,

---

[5] Questions may be raised concerning the nature of relationships between man and the supernatural which are not dealt with in Polak's theory. This relationship is formally specified as nonhierarchical, but the specification is exceedingly fuzzy given the difference between the dimension "human" and the dimension "supernatural."

according to Polak. The most dynamic society is the one with both essence and influence optimism, and if the image has eschatological elements with a sense of the possibilities of breakthrough to a totally new order, this adds to the dynamism. These eschatological elements always present a danger to any society, however, in that there is a tendency to spiritualize the other reality and come to think of it as realizable only in heaven, or in an afterlife, and not in this world. This is what happened to Christianity. The ever-deferred paradise, conceived as imminent in Jesus' time, was finally thought to be not for this world at all.

Out of the turbulence of the Middle Ages, when conflicting modes of viewing the future were doing battle with each other both inside and outside the church, came the great surges of influence optimism that characterized the Renaissance. From that time on the utopian and eschatological streams diverged more and more as the church retreated in the face of increasing confidence in man's capacity to shape his own destiny, with the aid of science. In the end only the pentecostal and adventist sects kept intact the concept of "the peaceable kingdom" as coming on earth, and the rest of the Christian church settled for a spiritualized kingdom within man or located at a comfortable remove in outer space.

Two sets of discoveries released the pent-up energy of the Middle Ages for utopian construction of possible future societies: scientific discoveries that opened up the possibilities of using nature as a tool to shape the environment, and voyagers' discoveries of exotically other cultural patterns which revealed that human society was highly malleable. The sixteen, seventeen and eighteen hundreds produced a heady array of "futures." These ranged from classical-style Platonic utopias such as Bacon's *New Atlantis*, which drew on a prevision of future scientific and technological developments to outline a kind of universal communism, through romantic, satirical, and rollicking utopias which combined sharp critique of the times with glimpses of an upside-down right-side-up society—Rousseau, Rabelais, Defoe, Swift, Fenelon, Holberg[6]—and on to the socialist utopias of Owen, Saint-Simon, and Fourier.[7] This is the point at which social scientists got into the utopia-writing business, and Comte and Marx each constructed utopian future societies based on "natural law," though Marx vehemently attacked the concept of utopism itself.[8]

Utopian writing about the future interacted with social experimentation and the more popular imagination to create social innovations in every sphere from the economic (the trade union movement, profit sharing, social security, scientific management) through the political (parliamentary democracy, universal suffrage) to the social (universal education, child welfare practices, women's "emancipation," New Towns, social planning).[9] As Polak says, most features of social design in contemporary Western society were first

figments of a utopia-writer's imagination.

Somewhere in the 1800s, however, something began happening to the "other space" and the "other time" of utopian fantasy. It began in Germany, home of the universalistic utopians Lessing (1730) and Kant (1785), in such works as Fichte's *Geschlossene Handelsstaat* (1800), which designs a specific future for a specific country—Germany. From this time on nationalism and an orientation toward the immediate future began eroding the creative imaging powers of the utopist. The sense that man can breach time and create the totally other is gone.

It is Polak's contention that the capacity to image the future is a core capacity in any culture that is manifested in every aspect of that culture. Therefore the decline in the ability to envision totally other "realities," the compressing of the mental perceptions of time and space into the here and now, will be revealed not only in the literature of an era, but also in its art, architecture, poetry and music, in its science and philosophy, and in its religion. Polak in fact documents this decline in imaging capacity in science, philosophy, and religion in the twentieth century. The predominantly Orwellian tone of twentieth century science fiction is presented as the most damaging evidence of all concerning the diseased futurism of the present. Prometheus is re-bound, tied up in knots by his own science and technology and fear of the future he had thought to master. What went wrong?

The cultural lag in ability to generate new visions appropriate to the complex knowlege structure of a hyperindustrialized society has been examined at length in contemporary social science literature. The rate of change itself is usually seen as the culprit. Whether or not the human imagination can adapt itself to reconceptualizing reality as fast as reality changes in this century of exponential growth curves is a subject for debate. An element usually left out of the debate, however, is

[6] Rousseau, *Confessions*; Rabelais, *L'Abbaye de Theleme*; Defoe, "Essays of Projects"; Swift, *Gulliver's Travels*; Fenelon, *Les Adventures de Telemaque*; Holberg, *The Underground Journey of Nicholas Klim.*

[7] Owen, *Signs of the Times, or the Approach of the Millennium* and *Book of the New Moral World*; Saint-Simon, *De la Réorganisation de la Société Européene*; Fourier, *The Social Destiny of Man, Theory of the Four Movements*, and *The Passions of the Human Soul.*

[8] There is some danger of overemphasizing the role that contact with other people's "differentnesses" has in generating a sense of transcendence. Such contact may simply extend the range of an invading culture's manipulative abilities rather than stimulate the envisioning of totally new kinds of social structures. If there were a direct correspondence between contact with other cultures and transcendence generation, the West would not now stand accused of having done so much harm to the world.

[9] Frank E. Manuel (ed.), *Utopias and Utopian Thought* (Boston: Beacon, 1967).

the disappearance of the eschatological sense of a totally other order of reality. The divorce of utopia from eschatology which characterized the Enlightenment appeared as a liberation of human thought at the time; but Polak points out that the utopian and eschatological modes are symbiotic, and either without the other goes into decline. Once the eschatological otherness of utopian images of the future was weeded out, utopias themselves came to be conceived as more and more static images of a boring, end-state of man. The true utopia is not static, however, but historically relative.[10]

The historical evolution of utopias is a part of the battle between past and future mentioned earlier, and it is in the setting of the learning community that much of this battle takes place. In tracing the decline of the imaging capacity Polak faults the university severely (as many others have done). In criticizing the standardization of learning and of mass output of students at the expense of nurturing a creative minority who can dream dreams and re-create society, however, he is guilty by implication of looking back to older models of the *universitas* in a society where few were educated. We can't go back. We live on a small, densely populated planet, and we want education for everyone. How do we regenerate our utopianizing capacity?

Polak emphasizes that it is the *eschatological* component of our thinking that has declined in every sector of society, including the educational. In the high mass-consumption societies of the West, we sit like so many spoiled children, with all our splintered and lifeless utopias scattered around us like so many broken toys. It is

not future shock[11] that is hurting us. We know that there will be more and better toys next year. What is hurting is that it is the day after Christmas, and we have lost our sense of the transcendent. What we can make, break, and fix is all there is. It is this loss of the sense of transcendence that has weakened our imaging capacity. Is the loss reparable? Can the learning community do anything about it?

The Politics of Imaging

Talk about the sense of transcendent smacks of elitist thinking. We think of it as a concept belonging exclusively to the province of the philosopher and the theologian, dreaming away in cloister or ivory tower. This leads to the question, are we the image makers, anyway? And for whom are the images? These are crucial questions in the libertarian age. Historically, the image makers have always been the intellectual elite. Whether or not they included "something for the masses" in their images of the future, they did their image making *for* society, not with it. There have been two parallel traditions of dealing with the masses in imaging the future in the Christian West. One has made use of an equalitarian model of the social structure, the other of a stratified model. Plato's *Republic* serves as the prototype of the stratified model, and reappears in Dante's *De Monarchia*, Jean Bodin's *La République*, Bacon's *New Atlantis*, Campanella's *City of the Sun*, and—in a subtle way—in Skinner's *Walden II*.

An early version of the equalitarian model is found in the Old Testament books of the Prophets, where an image of simple tribal patterns of nomadic days is held up in contrast to the wicked city which draws lines between rich and poor. Equalitarian utopias are scarce before the

[10]Elise Boulding, "Futuristics and the Imaging Capacity of the West," in *Human Futuristics*. Magoroh Maruyama and James A. Dator (eds.) (Honolulu: University of Hawaii, Social Science Research Institute, 1971), pp. 29–53.

[11] Alvin Toffler, *Future Shock* (New York: Random House, 1970).

Middle Ages, however. If they were written, the church probably suppressed them. In the twelfth century Joachim de Fiore ignored the interests of the ecclesiastical hierarchy and wrote of the coming of a radical new age on earth in which all men should be holy and equal, and the church would fade away. Three centuries later Thomas More's *Utopia* appeared as the first secular equalitarian utopia and became the prototype for all the modern equalitarian utopias. Karl Marx translated the equalitarian ideal into the industrial setting.

While both equalitarian and stratified models have reappeared again and again in utopian images of the future, our accumulated historical experience seems to tell us that only a hierarchically structured multiclass society has viability over time. (Melvin Tumin, Kingsley Davis and Wilbert Moore laid out the pros and cons of this hypothesis in their famous debate in 1953.[12]) It is startling, therefore, to realize in surveying the actual experiments in alternative communities, often based on a literary utopia, that the models in which people invest their lives are predominantly the equalitarian models. The willingness to invest one's own life-energy in these historically "unworkable" equalitarian models has increased dramatically in the past two decades.

The politics of imaging is complex. Primitive Christian communism and sophisticated ecclesiastical hierarchy have alternated inputs into the secular social structures of the West for two thousand years now. The industrial and technological revolutions, which concentrated social power in new ways while destroying once

functional feudal distribution systems, generated a new set of social inequities and also a constant flow of ideas about ways to remove them. The socialist utopists—Owen, Saint-Simon, Fourier—all contributed to the lessening of the inequities, and to the development of educational and welfare reforms in the name of an equalitarian ideal. Still, these utopists were all intellectual elitists working on behalf of, not with, the masses.

Today, the real polarization in society (as has often been noted) is not between the radical and the reactionary, but between the radical and the liberal.

Futurists are on the whole in the liberal tradition, and are in the business of imaging futures for people they know very little about. (This is equally true of many radicals.) However, it is not fair to lump all futurists together under one label, since there are substantially different approaches and value systems represented among them.

Within social science, futurism has taken various forms, including social planning in specialized and general systems-type planning, the development of special techniques such as brainstorming for inventing new futures, and the development of a variety of a conceptual tools for predicting the future *à la* Kahn and Wiener, Helmer, etc. Straddling the social and engineering sciences are the evolutionary nucleators such as Mead, Platt, and Doxiades. The ecological futurists range from Ward and Boulding, who offer a spaceship earth vision of the future, through social geographers and ecologists to whole-earth romanticists and pre-Raphaelite Aquarians. Finally there are the revolutionary futurists, some political, some nonpolitical, some militant, some gentle, and all dedicated to a completely new society for man—and there are the science fiction writers.

Most social science futurists are utopians. This means that they are operating on the premise that everything depends

[12] Kingsley Davis and Wilbert E. Moore, "Some Principles of Stratification," *American Sociological Review, 10* (April, 1945), pp. 242–49; Melvin Tumin, "Some Principles of Stratification: A Critical Analysis," *American Sociological Review, 18* (August, 1953), pp. 387–97. The Tumin article contains comments by Kingsley Davis and Wilbert E. Moore.

on humankind's evolving capacities as social artisans. Since humankind hasn't done too well so far, this leads the utopist to an elitist position, putting his superior capacities at the disposal of the as yet inarticulate masses. The utopian tradition is by and large the elitist liberal tradition, which takes seriously the responsibility of modifying social structures and removing inequities on behalf of those who suffer from them.

The libertarian radical futurists are operating on different premises. In the tradition of the politicized peasant chiliasts who followed on the heels of Joachim de Fiore in the Middle Ages, they believe in the possibility of a radical break in history. The concept of conscientization of the masses involves the conviction that there is something radically Other in every human being which can be awakened, and which once awakened represents a new kind of force in history which will lead to a totally new kind of society. The libertarian radical therefore refuses to do a Band-Aid job on existing structures, and he refuses to do the thinking of the masses for them. (I am using the term "libertarian radical" here to distinguish him from the authoritarian radical, who in fact does impose his thinking on the masses, and is not a true radical at all but only an angry, impatient elitist liberal who wants to do his thing right away.)

It is this burning sense of what conscientization can do for the mass of humankind that enables the libertarian radical to have confidence in the imaging process of the masses, and to work in the direction of coparticipation in the creation of images of the future (as well as in the creation of actual futures). Mao Tse-Tung and Paulo Freire arrive at these convictions along different routes, but they both base their work as evolutionaries on this process of coparticipation in imaging. Freire calls it dialogic education; the teacher-student learns from the students-teachers and then reflects back to them what he has learned

from them, with the additional insights and clarity he can provide.[13] Freire recognizes that Mao Tse-Tung is talking about the same thing when he says "we must teach in the masses clearly what we have received from them confusedly."[14] Freire distinguishes this dialogic approach very sharply from the authoritarian approach of the pseudoradical, in which the revolutionary decides what is best for the masses and then tells them. The traditional conception of the public school and university hardly fits this dialogue-with-the-masses approach. The learning community concept, however, does.

This is not the place to go into a discussion of the whole question of the possibility of a nonhierarchical society. The possibility of the learning community providing a nonhierarchical network of relationships within the larger society and generating images of possible futures within that society that draw on the life experiences and dreams of a great diversity of previously inarticulate social groups is an exciting one. It depends, however, on an eschatological view of humankind and history which is uncomfortable for today's liberal.

The Cultural Reservoir of Image-Material

Coparticipation in the development of images of the future on the part of diverse groups within a national society enriches the reservoir of image material, but still leaves out a vast array of cultural experience in human history. It is at this point that we become the most conscious that the universitas is not a universitas at all, but only a very ethnocentric community of scholars turned inward to the West,

[13] Paulo Freire, *Pedagogy of the Oppressed* (New York: Herder, 1971).
[14] Freire, *Pedagogy of the Oppressed*, p. 82n.

making occasional libations to other cultural traditions. Futurists are the worst offenders of all in this regard.

Their global ethnocentrism is an unintended by-product of an honest effort to think about the planet as a whole. To describe the macroproblems of the planet within the frame of reference of a particular Western sequence of experience, however, is about as appropriate as for the Australian bushman to describe the problems of the planet in terms of his own experience of desert life. The Australian bushman has a very sophisticated technology of environmental utilization, given the resources he has available. He knows how to find food and water and how to deal with distance, time, space, and heat in very remarkable ways. His knowledge, however, is useful in a very limited range of settings. Our knowledge covers more settings, but our cognitive map of the planetary sociosphere is still very inadequate.

This is serious, because the resources available to us for social change are limited by the thought models used to describe and label them. The intellectual reality constructs of the scientific subculture of the West make quite a few resources unavailable to us, including large chunks of human experience codified in non-Western historical records, and the possibility of living in multidimensional time. On the whole we think of ourselves as being "locked in" to a high technology society with the only imagined exits involving an unthinkable return to the past. The feeling of being locked in is a result of the acceptance of a peculiarly Western unilinear theory of development that postulates such a tight interlocking of physical technology and social patterns (the urbanization-industrialization-based media network theory of development) that we are convinced we can only go where urban-based technology will take us.

The Data Banks of History

Here is where history as a social resource can help free us. Complex communications networks have evolved in the absence of urbanization, as the horseback empire of Ghengis Khan demonstrates; this empire undertook the first mapping of the kingdoms of Europe when the local princes could not even find their way to each other's castles.[15] Pluralism and decentralized control is possible even with large-scale administrative systems of empire, as the millet system of the Ottoman Empire demonstrated, allowing a variety of religions and political subsystems to exist within an over-all Moslem administrative structure. A passion for learning can exist without a large-scale planned educational technology, as the sudden flourishing of lay teachers of the three R's outside the cathedral schools of the medieval European church demonstrated, once people got the idea that knowing how to read was advantageous.[16] A passion for experimentation with the building of new societies can exist without governmental subsidy by monarchies or parliaments, as the countless adventurous bands of Hittites, Celts, Phoenicians, Greeks, and other Mediterranean people showed in the second millennium BC, in organizing do-it-yourself utopian expeditions all around the Mediterranean.[17]

A passion for experimenting with forms of household organizations and kin patterning is endemic in human civilization, and the storied variants in primitive tribes are only a tiny fraction of the arrangements that have been tried. The 200-person communes of the European middle ages make our young people's counterculture

[15] Michael Prawdin, *The Mongol Empire: Its Rise and Legacy* (New York: Free Press, 1940, 1967).

[16] Philippe Aries, *Centuries of Childhood* (New York: Knopf, 1962), 2 vols.

[17] C. D. Darlington, *Evolution of Man and Society* (New York: Simon & Schuster, 1969).

experiments seem tame.[18] Humankind has developed many patterns for dealing with varying population densities over the past 10,000 years; and 7,000 years of experience with urbanism is no small heritage to draw on. Almost any kind of family or communal experiment that is being tried today has been tried over and over again under varying conditions—nomadic, settled rural, settled urban, seasonal migration, utopian colonization.

In short, the innovative spirit was not born in the West, and is not dependent on modern technology. Furthermore, there is no one-to-one correspondence between environmental resources and culture, any more than between technological resources and culture. Tightly packed and environmentally deprived Japan and the Netherlands would never have made it if they had depended on physical resources. Their chief resource was social ingenuity. Assuming that we are all potentially as ingenious as the Japanese or the Dutch, we are free to borrow social technology from India, Japan, China and elsewhere—technologies that were developed in totally different contexts but which can be adapted. Our main problem is to inventory all the existing social technologies so we know what we have to draw on. This we have not done because we think that what we have is all there is. The BLTMT[19] is a millstone around the neck of the West. There is nothing inherently wrong in projecting Basic Long-Term Multiform Trends, as long as we include all the forms—but a reading of futurist literature only gives us the Western variants.

Why this emphasis on borrowing from other social technologies? Are we really so badly off in the urban West, apart from some impending mineral shortages that can be solved by a combination of consumer education and new scientific discoveries? Maldistribution of existing resources is after all a soluble problem. Development theory tells us that the increase in individual rationality and social competence that modern urbanization makes possible will lead to a society both more equalitarian and more affluent than the one we have now.

The Mythology of Competence

In spite of the comforting doctrines of development theory, we are ambivalent on this question of competence. We think we have it, yet we fear we don't. Our fear of being locked in by current technologies indicates our uncertainty about our competence. There is good reason for this uncertainty. On the one hand, although we have been able to develop very complex large-scale systems of administration of physical and social resources in Europe and North America, there seems to be some evidence in the United States at least that at this moment we are unable to do anything but elaborate on present patterns. We may not be able to deal with structurally generated inequities because we cannot address ourselves to structural change. A paper by Roland Warren analyzes the participation of community decision organizations in the Model Cities Program and concludes that all the rhetoric about a redistribution of decision-making power among the peoples to be served by the Model Cities Program led to nothing but a reinforcement of existing structures.[20] After three years of major and well funded effort, nothing had changed. There were a variety of reasons for this failure, but one

[18] Marc Bloch, *Feudal Society* (Chicago: University of Chicago, 1961).

[19] Kahn and Wiener were among the first to make use of this terminology. See Kahn and Wiener, *The Year 2000* (New York: Macmillan, 1967).

[20] Roland L. Warren, "The Sociology of Knowledge and the Problems of the Inner Cities," *Social Science Quarterly*.

important one was a complete inability on the part of the persons involved to question habitual structures and behaviors. By leaning on a mythology of competence, they could avoid examining alternatives. . . .

The Changing Character of Learning Communities

By using the term "learning communities" for educational institutions, I have already built my own image of the future for education into this chapter. There seems to be some convergence among both educators and futurists on the notion of increased flexibility of organization of learning facilities and of teaching-learning relationships in the future. Billy Rojas' Delphi Survey on Alternative Educational Futures[21] indicates a surprising consensus on the part of futurist-oriented educators concerning the disappearance by 1980 of traditional curricula, teaching methods, and attendance requirements in the public schools at least of the more progressive states.

It is further widely held that community people and paraprofessionals will outnumber teachers in the schools by this date. There is a similar consensus on the disappearance of conventional academic departments and degree requirements in the universities. By 1985, many educators believe that "college departments at most state universities will become task-oriented rather than academically centered as at present. A 'department of environment' might be established, for instance, to eliminate pollution in a four-county area. When the task is accomplished, the department would phase out, its members

regrouping in other departments."[22] Students will collect modular credits for short-term academic experience, and cash them in like trading stamps for a diploma when the necessary number have been acquired.[23]

In general, the changes envisioned represent a freeing up of existing structures, but no real change in the conception of the university. Even the relatively radical statement "25 percent of colleges and universities [will be] governed by postbureaucratic administrations of type described by Warren Bennis,"[24] still assumes a recognizable campus structure. It is hard to get away from the banking conception of education, to use Freire's terminology, in which students become the vaults and the teachers the depositors. Even postbureaucratic administrations cannot administer co-intentional communities. The development on a large scale of learning collectives pursuing cointentionality in education is not yet within our capacity to imagine. And yet it may come about sooner than we think.

The rate of experimentation with nonhierarchical communal enterprises in economic production, scientific research, and information network development, as well as in educational ventures, is very high. The character of these enterprises can sometimes be identified by the use of the label "collective" in the name, but more often they have to be visited in order to discover this. The style of these enterprises is informal, provisional, task-oriented, and

[21] Billy Rojas, "Delphi Survey—Alternative Educational Futures" (Pippa Passes, Ky.: Alice Lloyd College, Futuristics Curriculum Project, 1971).

[22] Rojas, "Delphi Survey."

[23] This is already a pattern, of course. Students who dropped out in the early sixties as freshmen and sophomores are now, ten years later, returning to the campuses to collect enough credits for a B.A. They are taking a strictly utilitarian attitude towards this enterprise, doing the "shit work" uncomplainingly because they want the accreditation to upgrade their job opportunities. Often these returnees have done rather well in salaried jobs in the past few years, but are bored with their work.

[24] Rojas, "Delphi Survey."

network-oriented. They form and reform according to perceived tasks and perceived colleagues in given enterprises, and are continually "in touch" though a network which is as ad hoc as the groups, and yet is building up in a recognizable communal infrastructure that is transnational in character.

These collectives are enormously diverse in style and activity focus, but they give us important clues about future patterns of living, learning, working, and playing. The ones I will mention here all have a common orientation to the production of new knowledge which will be useful in the creation of a new society. That is, they all seek to be agents of social change. That is not in itself so unusual. But in addition they all choose to incorporate into their own communal structures the features of the radically new society as they are beginning to understand it. This means that they usually include both intellectuals and nonintellectuals in their group, and also include people of all age groups from grandparents to teen-agers, with one important group being young parents with small babies. Their principle of functioning is that everyone in the community has inputs to make of equal importance with everyone else, but in order to ensure this each member must teach the others what he knows best how to do. Thus, internationally known intellectuals will be seen baking bread and running mimeograph machines, and teen-agers will be sent out to speak in settings where "people of reputation" are expected to sit on the platform. At its best this kind of equalitarianism helps each member of the community to reach his highest level of potential functioning, and in place of the traditional superstar model of creativity which measures that creativity in the number of publications, etc., produced, a new communal style of creativity emerges that needs different measures, but can be identified in the continuous acts of shaping new social patterns. . . .

One of the major theoreticians of the new transnational, nonhierarchical, nonorganization collectives is Anthony Judge, Associate Executive Secretary of the Union of International Organizations in Brussels. He is in a unique position to observe the dynamics of the emergence of new transnational networks, and has developed an interesting model for transnational nonhierarchical systems. He also has a theory of nonorganizations appropriate to the fluidity of the ever-forming and re-forming collectives: all groups should be ad hoc and stay "potential organizations," constructing information and communication systems through the careful development of mailing lists and by-passing the membership approach, constitution, and so on, entirely. This avoids cluttering the social scene with superannuated organizations determined to live forever. Not a bad approach for universities!

The value of this type of fluidity eludes many in the older generation of scholars, businessmen, and activists, who set great store by the institutional "base of operations" they may have spent years building. Such people feel that the short lifespan of many collectives demonstrates definitively their lack of social viability. The possibility that the stability and permanence may be here in the networks themselves, rather than in particular organizational bases, is not easily accepted by persons equally committed to social change but operating with a more institution-based model for bringing about change. The *Source Catalogue* and its contemporaries, the *Whole Earth Catalogue*, the *Big Rock Candy Mountain*, and various directories of social change movements, all illustrate the network principle of action.

The Introduction to the *Source Catalogue* encapsulates this whole approach:

> Sharing is at the heart of revolutionary activity, and the sharing of information is primary in the struggle to return control of America to its people. Information is a source of power to determine our own lives

and the culture of our communities. We need information about our movement, its resources, projects, skills, and dreams in order to build the support networks needed to liberate this country and ourselves. . . .

The Source Collective's beginnings were with the Educational Liberation Front (ELF) Bus—a project-information center and Movement media-bookmobile that traveled 20,000 miles visiting fifty campus communities in 1969 and 1970. After a year's experience, it was obvious that we had collected too much material for one bus to pass on. From this realization came *Source*, whose original idea of one catalogue quickly expanded to the idea of thirteen 100 to 200 page catalogs, each covering a different area of the Movement.[25]

The learning communities of tomorrow are already here. They are new creatures entirely, and will not simply replace our existing learning institutions. They will grow side by side with them, modifying the character of all other institutions and social groupings and breaking down many social barriers of age, status, and affluence to which we have been long accustomed. The importance of existing institutions of learning will be lessened in a society which has increasing numbers of ELF buses driving around the country plugging people into networks.

While the new learning communities won't replace schools and universities, they will modify them. Co-intentional learning will be rediscovered, and within our more formal institutions many co-intentional groups of faculty and students will be formed, working in a new way with old skills. What kind of imaging of the future can we expect from more communally orientated educational groups? At present, the futurist on the university campus sets a high value on his capacity to dream up radically different alternatives for society by special techniques for jogging people loose from their mental ruts.[26]

One significant limitation upon brainstorming is the point made by Barnett that "the expectation of change always envisages limits upon its operations. Change is expected only between certain minimal and maximal boundaries."[27] Barnett cites the example of the Samoans who set a high value on innovations in design, but the range of total variation is so narrow that the untrained Western eye has difficulty in detecting differences between one design and another, whether in textiles, songs, or dances. Whether the range is wide or narrow, the cultural limits are firmly set. In short, the proverbial man from Mars might not be very impressed with the alternative futures dreamed up by the wildest of blue sky imagineers. While this kind of limitation operates on all human fantasizing, it operates much more strongly in a technique-oriented setting such as brainstorming than it does for the lone fantasist.

Neither brainstorming nor a sophisticated projection of future trends, then, will break us out of our technological trap. The sense for the totally other, the capacity for transcendence that Polak has said is seriously weakened in our society, will not recover via that route.

It is precisely in the learning communities that the capacity for transcendence is being reborn. They are building "fear-free unhassled envelopes of free space deep within the heartlands of the dominant culture" through "learning based on love."[28] In a bureaucratic society that appears to be destroying children and adults alike, these intentional learning

---

[25] *Source Catalogue*, "Communications: An Organizing Tool" (Chicago: Swallow Press, 1971).

[26] Alex Osborn, *Applied Imagination*, 3rd ed. (New York: Scribner's, 1963); William J. J. Gordon, *Synectics* (New York: Collier, 1961).

[27] H. G. Barnett, *Innovation: The Basis of Cultural Change* (New York: McGraw-Hill, 1953).

[28] Salli Rasberry and Robert Greenway (eds.), *Rasberry Exercises: How to Start Your Own School . . . and Make a Book* (Box 357, Albion, Calif.: The Freestone Publishing Company, 1970), p. 26.

groups feel that they are rescue operations for the human race.

There is a specific reason why the capacity for otherness is fostered in these educational settings, and it relates to the general direction that educational theory and practice has taken in recent decades. Stages of cognitive development have come in for a great deal of attention. The body of research dealing with emotional development, and particularly the interplay between experiences of human warmth in the family and other settings and the development of cognitive skills,[29] has had much less attention. That which has had least attention of all is the challenge of orchestrating different modes of knowing in order to allow for an integration of the cognitive and affective aspects of life experience.[30] In particular the spiritual-intuitive mode of knowing that draws on a special capacity to listen for what Peter Berger calls "signals of transcendence" has been ignored.[31] Imagine children being encouraged to sit and listen for signals of transcendence in a public school classroom! It is the discovery of the fruits of training in that kind of listening which has delighted many young people in their exploration of Eastern religions. That coin of that kind of knowledge is easily debased, however, when not carefully related to the development of cognitive and affective capacities. Gandhi's education for *Satya*

graha combines training in these three modes of knowing in a unique way that deserves much more attention.[32] There are traditions in the Christian church that draw on a combination of these three modes too. The tendency of the church to become separated from the world, and particularly for the lovers of God within the church to separate themselves further in monastic movements has usually led to a wildly imbalanced development of the spiritual-intuitive at the expense of the other modes of apprehending reality. The Benedictines have succeeded better than others in avoiding this imbalance.

Intentional learning communities today are exploring the nature of that balance, and developing ways of learning that will foster it. They are making mistakes, but that is because they are trying to do something which we have systematically avoided doing in recent centuries; and it will take time to discover how to do it.

The only way to understand the excitement, joy, and willingness to commit one's life totally to intentional community while by-passing many of the comforts that technological society offers that characterizes the members of these intentional learning communities is to recognize that they are in fact tapping this missing dimension of transcendence in modern life. Where others despair, they see visions of an awakened society—and they feel themselves to be coparticipants in the awakening.

Technocratic futurism cannot be the galvanizer of education. All that this kind of futurism can provide is some skills to do better what educators are already trying to do. That which will galvanize education is the sense of The Other. The signals are there. Are we listening?

---

[29] Bonnie Barrett Stretch, "The Rise of the Free School," *Saturday Review* (June 20, 1970), pp. 76–77.

[30] W. Ron Jones with Julia Cheever and Jerry Ficklin, *Finding Community: A Guide to Community Research and Action* (Palo Alto, Calif.: James E. Freel, 1971); P. S. Holzman, "The Relation of Assimilation Tendencies in Visual, Auditory, and Kinaesthetic Time-Error to Cognitive Attitudes of Leveling and Sharpening," *Journal of Personality*, 22 (1954), pp. 375–94.

[31] Peter L. Berger, *A Rumour of Angels* (New York: Doubleday, 1969).

[32] Elise Boulding, "The Child as Shaper of the Future" (unpublished "think piece," January 1972).

10.2 The Future as the Basis for Establishing a Shared Culture

Margaret Mead

1. The Present Situation

The world today is struggling with many kinds of disjuncture. Some derive from the progressive fragmentation of what was once a whole—as higher education has broken down into a mass of separate specialties. Some have come about with the development of world views that parallel and often contradict older and displaced—but not replaced—ways of viewing the world. Others result from a juxtaposition of vastly different and extremely incongruent world views within the national and also the world-wide context provided by our contemporary press and television coverage. Within the framework of the United Nations we have balloting for representatives both from countries with many hundreds of years of high civilization and from countries just emerging from a primitive way of life. Still others are the effect of changing rates in the production of knowledge which bring about unexpected discrepancies between the young and the old. In a sense, these different kinds of disjuncture can also be seen as related to the very diverse ways in which the emergent, changing world is experienced by people of different ages—particularly young children—who are differently placed in the world, the nation, and the community.

Discussion of this tremendous fragmentation and of the agglomerations of partly dissociated, historically divergent, and conceptually incongruent patterns has

Margaret Mead, "The Future as the Basis for Establishing a Shared Culture," reprinted by permission of *Daedalus*, Journal of the American Academy of Arts and Sciences, Boston, Massachusetts. Winter 1965, *Science and Culture*.

been conducted, too often, in a narrow or a piecemeal fashion which takes into account only certain problems as they affect certain groups. The recent "two cultures" discussion is an example of such an approach, in which neither the arts nor the social sciences are included in what is essentially a lament about the state of communication within a small sector of the English-speaking world, whose members for various reasons of contemporary position or achievement think of themselves as an elite. In another context it is demanded that children's textbooks should portray "realistically" the conditions in which many American children live, because the conventional house pictured in advertisements and schoolbooks is unreal to the underprivileged children who live in cabins and coldwater flats and tenements. Even though the aim was to rectify the consequences of social and economic fragmentation at one level, a literal response to this demand would result in further fragmentation of our culture at another level. Wherever we turn, we find piecemeal statements, each of which can be regarded as a separate and partial definition of the basic problem of disjuncture, and piecemeal attempts at solution, each of which, because of the narrowness of the context in which it is made, produces new and still more complicated difficulties.

Yet these partial definitions and attempts at solution point in the same direction. We are becoming acutely aware that we need to build a culture within which there is better communication—a culture within which interrelated ideas and assumptions are sufficiently widely shared so that specialists can talk with specialists in other fields, specialists can talk with laymen, laymen can ask questions of specialists and the least educated can participate, at the level of political choice, in decisions made necessary by scientific or philosophical processes which are new, complex, and abstruse.

Models for intercommunication of this kind—poorly documented but made vividly real through the treatment given them by historians—already exist, in the past, within our own tradition. One model, of which various uses have been made, is the Greek city, where the most erudite man and the simplest man could enjoy the same performance of a tragedy. Another, in which there has been a recent upsurge of interest, is medieval Europe, where the thinker and the knight, the churchman, the craftsman, and the serf could read a view of the world from the mosaic on the wall, the painting above the altar, or the carving in the portico, and all of them, however far apart their stations in life, could communicate within one framework of meaning. But such models are not limited to the distant past. Even much more recently, in Victorian England, a poet's words could be read and enjoyed by people of many different backgrounds, when he wrote:

> Yet I doubt not thro' the ages one
>   increasing purpose runs,
> And the thoughts of men are widen'd with
>   the process of suns.[1]

Whether or not the integration of culture which we construct retrospectively for these golden ages existed in actuality is an important question scientifically. But thinking about models, the question of actuality is less important. For the daydream and the vision, whether it was constructed by a prophet looking toward a new time or by a scholar working retrospectively, can still serve as a model of the future. Men may never, in fact, have attained the integration which some

[1] Alfred Lord Tennyson, "Locksley Hall" (1842).

scholars believe characterized fifth-century Athens. Even so, their vision provides a challenging picture of what might be attained by modern men who have so many more possibilities for thinking about and for controlling the direction in which their culture will move.

However, all these models—as well as the simpler model of the pioneering American farmer, dressed in homespun, reared on the King James version of the Bible, and sustained by simple foods and simple virtues—share one peculiarity. In each case the means of integration is a corpus of materials from the past. The epic poems of Homer, the Confucian classics, the Jewish and the Christian Scriptures—each of these, in giving the scholar and the man in the street, the playwright and the politician access to an articulate statement of a world view, has been a source of integration. But the community of understanding of what was newly created—the poem, the play, the set of laws, the sculpture, the system of education, the style of landscape, the song—still depended on something which had been completed in the past. Today there is a continuing complaint that we have no such source of integration, and many of the measures which, it is suggested, would give a new kind of order to our thinking are designed to provide just such a body of materials. There is, for example, the proposal to teach college students the history of science as a way of giving all of them access to the scientific view of the world. Or there is the related proposal to teach all students evolution, particularly the existing body of knowledge about the evolution of man and culture, as a way of providing a kind of unity within which all specialists, no matter how specialized, would have a common set of referents.

But such suggestions place too much reliance on the past and necessarily depend on a long time span within which to build a common, shared view of the world. In the present crisis, the need to establish a shared body of assumptions is a very pressing one—too pressing to wait for the slow process of educating a small elite group in a few places in the world. The danger of nuclear disaster, which will remain with us even if all stockpiled bombs are destroyed, has created a hothouse atmosphere of crisis which forces a more rapid solution to our problems and at the same time wilts any solution which does not reflect this sense of urgency. For there is not only a genuine need for rapid solutions but also a growing restiveness among those who seek a solution. This restiveness in turn may well become a condition within which hasty, inadequate solutions are attempted—such as the substitution of slum pictures for ideal suburban middle class pictures in slum children's textbooks—within too narrow a context. Speed in working out new solutions is essential if new and disastrous fragmentations are not to occur—but we also need an appropriate framework.

Measures taken at the college level to establish mutual understanding between the natural scientist and the humanist, the social scientist and the administrator, men trained in the law and men trained in the behavioral sciences, have a double drawback. The cumulative effect of these measures would be too slow and, in addition, they would be inadequate in that their hope lies in establishing a corpus based on something which already exists—a theory of history, a history of science, or an account of evolution as it is now known. Given the changing state of knowledge in the modern world, any such historically based body of materials becomes in part out of date before it has been well organized and widely taught. Furthermore, it would be betrayed and diluted and corrupted by those who did the teaching, as they would inevitably have to draw on their own admittedly fragmented education to convey what was to be learned. One effect of this fragmentation can be seen in attempts to express forms of new knowledge in imagery which cannot contain it, because the imagery is shaped to an earlier view of the world. In a recent sermon, for example, the Bishop of Woolwich presented a picture of dazzling contemporaneity in disavowing the possibility of belief in the corporeal ascension of Christ; but, then, in proclaiming a new version of the Scriptures, he used the image of the sovereignty of Christ—an outmoded image in the terms in which he was speaking.

In the last hundred years men of science have fought uneasily with the problem of their own religious belief, and men of God have hardened their earlier visions into concrete images to confront a science they have not understood. Natural scientists have elaborated their hierarchical views of "true" science into an inability to understand the nature of the sciences of human behavior, welcoming studies of fragmented aspects of human behavior, or an inappropriate reduction in the number of variables. Human scientists have destroyed the delicacy and intricacy of their subject matter in coarse-grained attempts to imitate the experimental methods of Newtonian physics instead of developing new methods of including unanalyzable components in simulations or in developing new methods of validating the analysis of unique and complex historical events. As a result we lack the capacity to teach and the capacity to learn from a corpus based on the past. The success of any such venture would be comparably endangered by the past learning of the teachers and the past learning of the students, whose minds would already be formed by eighteen years of exposure to an internally inconsistent, contradictory, half-articulated, muddled view of the world.

But there is still another serious drawback to most current proposals for establishing mutual understanding. This is, in general, their lack of inclusiveness. Whether an approach to past knowledge is narrowly limited to the English-speaking world or includes the whole Euro-American tradition, whether it begins with the Greeks or extends backward in time to include the Paleolithic, any approach through the past can begin only with one sector of the world's culture. Inevitably, because of the historical separation of peoples and the diversity of the world's cultures throughout history, any one view of any one part of human tradition, based in the past, excludes other parts and, by emphasizing one aspect of human life, limits access to other aspects.

In the newly emerging nations we can see clearly the consequences of the efforts made by colonial educators to give to distant peoples a share in English or French or Dutch or Belgian or Spanish culture. Ironically, the more fully the colonial educators were willing to have some members at least of an African or an Asian society share in their traditions and their classics, the more keenly those who were so educated felt excluded from participation in the culture as a whole. For the classical European scholar, Africa existed mainly in very specialized historical contexts, and for centuries European students were concerned only with those parts of Africa or Asia which were ethnocentrically relevant to Greek or Roman civilization or the early Christian church. Throughout these centuries, peoples without a written tradition and peoples with a separate written tradition (the Chinese, for example, or the Javanese) lived a life to which no one in Europe was related. With the widening of the European world in the fifteenth and sixteenth centuries, Europeans treated the peoples whom they "discovered" essentially as peoples without a past, except as the European connoisseur came to appreciate their monuments and archeological ruins, or, later, as European students selectively used the histories of other peoples to illustrate their own conceptions of human history. Consequently, the greater degree of participation felt by the member of one

of these more recently contacted societies in a French or an English view of the development of civilization, the more he also felt that his own cultural history was excluded from the history of man.

It is true that some heroic attempts have been made to correct for this colonial bias. Looking at a synchronic table of events, a child anywhere in the world may sit and ponder what the Chinese or the ancient canoe-sailing Hawaiians were doing when William the Conqueror landed in England. But almost inevitably this carefully constructed synchrony—with parallel columns of events for different parts of the world—is undone, on the one hand, by the recognition that the New World and the Old, the Asian mainland and the Pacific islands were *not* part of a consciously connected whole in A.D. 1066, and, on the other hand, by the implications of the date and the dating form, which carry the stamp of one tradition and one religious group within that tradition. It is all but impossible to write about the human past—the movements of early man, the building of the earliest known cities, the spread of artifacts and art forms, the development of styles of prophecy or symbolism—without emphasizing how the spirit of man has flowered at different times in different places and, time and again, in splendid isolation. Even in this century, the efforts to integrate the histories of the world's great living traditions have led, in the end, to a renewed preoccupation with each of these as an entity with its own long history.

Today, however, if we are to construct the beginning of a shared culture, using every superior instrument at our command and with full consciousness both of the hazards and the possibilities, we can stipulate certain properties which this still nonexistent corpus must have.

It must be equally suitable for all peoples from whatever traditions their present ways of living spring, and it must not give undue advantage to those peoples anywhere in the world whose traditions have been carried by a longer or a more fully formulated literacy. While those who come from a culture with a Shakespeare or a Dante will themselves be the richer, communications should not be so laden with allusions to Shakespeare or Dante that those who lack such a heritage cannot participate. Nor should the wealth of perceptual verbal detail in distinguishing colors, characteristic of the Dusun of Borneo or the Hanunóo of the Philippines, be used to make less differentiated systems seem crude. The possession of a script for a generation, a century, or a millennium must be allowed for in ways that will make it possible for all peoples to start their intercommunication on a relatively equal basis. No single geographical location, no traditional view of the universe, no special set of figures of speech, by which one tradition but not another has been informed, can provide an adequate base. It must be such that everyone, everywhere can start afresh, as a young child does, with a mind ready to meet ideas uncompromised by partial learning. It must be cast in a form that does not depend on years of previous learning— the fragmented learning already acquired by the college student or the student in the high school, the *lycée*, or the *Gymnasium*. Instead, it must be cast in a form that is appropriate for small children—for children whose fathers are shepherds, rubber tappers in jungles, forgotten sharecroppers, sailors or fishermen, miners or members of the dispossessed urban proletariat, as well as for the children whose forebears have read one of the world's scripts for many generations.

If this body of materials on which a new, shared culture is to be based is to include all the peoples of the world, then the peoples of the world must also contribute to it in ways that are qualitatively similar. If it is to escape from the weight of discrepant centuries, the products of civilization included within it must

be chosen with the greatest care. The works of art must be universal in their appeal and examples of artistic endeavor whose processes are universally available—painting, drawing, carving, dancing, and singing in forms that are universally comprehensible. Only after a matrix of shared understanding has been developed will the way be prepared for the inclusion of specific, culturally separate traditions. But from the first it must have the character of a living tradition, so it will be free of the static qualities of older cultures, with texts that have become the test of truth and forms so rigid that experimentation has become impossible. And it must have the qualities of a natural language, polished and pruned and capable of expansion by the efforts of many kinds of different calibres, redundant and sufficiently flexible so it will meet the needs of teacher and pupil, parent and child, friend and friend, master and apprentice, lawyer and client, statesman and audience, scientist and humanist in their different modes of communication. It is through use in all the complexity of relationships like these that a natural language is built and given form and content by many kinds of human beings, becomes a medium of communication that can be learned by every child, however slight its natural ability. This projected corpus should not be confused with present day *popular culture*, produced commercially with contempt for its consumers. Instead, by involving the best minds, the most sensitive and gifted artists and poets and scientists, the new shared culture should have something of the quality of the periods of folk tradition out of which great art has repeatedly sprung.

A body of materials having these characteristics must bear the imprint of growth and use. Yet it is needed now, in this century, for children who are already born and for men who either will preserve the world for a new generation to grow up in or who, in failing to do so, will doom the newly interconnected peoples of the world to destruction by means of the very mechanisms which have made a world community a possibility. The most immediate problem, then, is that of producing, almost overnight, a corpus which expresses and makes possible new processes of growth.

We believe that the existing state of our knowledge about the processes of consciousness is such that it is necessary for us only to ask the right questions in order to direct our thinking toward answers. Today engineering and the technology of applied physical science have outstripped other applied sciences because in these fields searching questions have been asked urgently, sharply, and insistently. This paper is an attempt to ask questions, set up a series of specifications, and illustrate the order of answer for which we should be looking. There will be better ways of formulating these questions, all of which have to do with communication, and better ways of meeting the criteria which will make answers possible. In fact, it is my assumption that the creation of a body of materials which will serve our needs will depend on the contribution and the participation of all those who will also further its growth, that is, people in every walk of life, in every part of the globe, speaking every language and seeing the universe in the whole range of forms conceived by man.

2. The Future as a Setting

I would propose that we consider the future as the appropriate setting for our shared world-wide culture, for the future is least compromised by partial and discrepant views. And I would choose the new future over the far future, so as to avoid as completely as possible new confusions based on partial but avowed totalistic projections born of the ideologies of certainty, like Marxism and Leninism, or the recurrent scientific dogmatisms

about the possibilities of space travel, the state of the atmosphere, or the appearance of new mutations. But men's divergent dreams of eternity might be left undisturbed, providing they did not include some immediate apocalyptic moment for the destruction of the world.

Looking toward the future, we would start to build from the unknown. In many cases, of course, this would be knowledge very newly attained. What we would build on, then, would be the known attributes of the universe, our solar system, and the place of our earth within this system; the known processes of our present knowledge, from which we shall proceed to learn more; the known treasures of man's plastic and graphic genius as a basis for experience out of which future artists may paint and carve, musicians compose, and poets speak; the known state of instrumentation, including both the kinds of instrumentation which have already been developed (for example, communication satellites) and those which are ready to be developed; the known numbers of human beings, speaking a known number of languages, and living in lands with known amounts of fertile soil, fresh water, and irreplaceable natural resources; the known forms of organizing men into functioning groups; and the known state of modern weaponry, with its known capacity to destroy all life.

These various kinds of knowledge would be viewed as beginnings, instead of as ends—as young, growing forms of knowledge, instead of as finished products to be catalogued, diagrammed, and preserved in the pages of encyclopedias. All statements would take the form: "We know that there are at least X number of stars" (or people in Asia, or developed forms of transportation, or forms of political organization). Each such statement would be phrased as a starting point—a point from which to move onward. In this sense, the great artistic productions of all civilizations could be included, not as the splendid fruit of one or another civilization, but on new terms, as points of departure for the imagination.

The frenetic, foolhardly shipping of original works of art around the world in ships and planes, however fragile they may be, can be looked upon as a precursor of this kind of change—as tales of flying saucers preceded man's first actual ventures into space. It is as if we already dimly recognized that if we are to survive, we must share all we have, at whatever cost, so that men everywhere can move toward some as yet undefined taking-off point into the future.

But if we can achieve a new kind of consciousness of what we are aiming at, we do not need actually to move these priceless objects as if they were figures in a dream. We can, instead, take thought how, with our modern techniques, we can make the whole of an art style available, not merely single, symbolic examples, torn from their settings. Young painters and poets and musicians, dancers and architects can, today, be given access to all that is known about color and form, perspective and rhythm, technique and the development of style, the relationships of form and style and material, and the interrelationships of art forms as these have been developed in some place, at some time. We have all the necessary techniques to do this. We can photograph in color, train magnifying cameras on the inaccessible details of domes and towers, record a poet reciting his own poetry, film an artist as he paints, and use film and sound to transport people from any one part to any other part of the world to participate in the uncovering of an ancient site or the first viewing of a new dance form. We can, in fact, come out of the "manuscript stage" for all the arts, for process as well as product, and make the whole available simultaneously to a young generation so they can move ahead together and congruently into the future. Given access to the range of the world's art, young artists can see in a new light those special activities and art objects to which they themselves are immediately related, wherever they are.

Working always within the modest limits of one generation—the next twenty-five years—and without tempting the massive consequences of miscalculation, we can include the known aspects of the universe in which our continuing experimental ventures into space will be conducted and the principles, the tools, and the materials with which these ventures are beginning. Children all over the world can be given accurate, tangible models of what we now know about the solar system, models of the earth, showing how it is affected by the large scale patterning of weather, and models showing how life on earth may be affected by events in the solar system and beyond. Presented with a clear sense of the expanding limits of our knowledge, models such as these would prepare children everywhere to participate in discoveries we know must come and to anticipate new aspects of what is as yet unknown.

Within these same limits, we can bring together our existing knowledge of the world's multitudes—beginning with those who are living now and moving out toward those who will be living twenty-five years from now. The world is well mapped, and we know within a few millions, how many people there are, where they are, and who they are. We know—or have the means of knowing—a great deal about the world's peoples. We know about the world's food supplies and can relate our knowledge to the state of those who have been well nourished and those who have been poorly fed. We know about the world's health and can relate our knowledge to the state of those who have been exposed to ancient plagues and those who are exposed to "modern" ambiguous viruses. We can picture the ways of living of those who, as children, were reared in tents, in wattle and daub houses, in houses made of mud bricks, in tenements and apartment houses, in peasant houses that have survived unchanged through hundreds of years of occupancy and in the new small houses of modern suburbs, in the anonymity of urban housing, in isolated villages, and in the crowded shacks of refugee settlements. We can define the kinds of societies, all of them contemporary, in which human loyalties are restricted to a few hundred persons, all of them known to one another, and others in which essential loyalties are expanded to include thousands or millions or even hundreds of millions of persons, only a few of them known to one another face to face. In the past we could, at best, give children some idea of the world's multitudes through books, printed words and meager illustrations. Today we have the resources to give children everywhere living experience of the whole contemporary world. And every child, everywhere in the world, can start with that knowledge and grow into its complexity. In this way, plans for population control, flood control, control of man's inroads on nature, plans for protecting human health and for developing a world food supply, and plans for sharing a world communication system can all become plans in which citizens participate in informed decisions.

None of this knowledge will in any sense be ultimate. We do not know what form knowledge itself will take twenty-five years from now, but we do know what its sources must be in present knowledge and, ordering what we now know, we can create a ground plan for the future on which all the peoples of the earth can build.

Because it must be learned by very young children and by the children of very simple parents, this body of knowledge and experience must be expressed in clear and simple terms, using every graphic device available to us and relying more on models than on words, for in many languages appropriate words are lacking.

The newer and fresher the forms of presentation are, the greater will be the possibility of success, for, as in the new mathematics teaching, all teachers—those coming out of old traditions and having long experience with special conventions and those newly aware of the possibilities of formal teaching—will have to learn what they are to teach as something new. Furthermore, parents will be caught up in the process, in one sense as the pupils of their children, discovering that they can reorder their own knowledge and keep the pace, and in another sense as supplementary teachers, widening the scope of teaching and learning. Knowledge arranged for comprehensibility by a young child is knowledge accessible to all, and the task of arranging it will necessarily fall upon the clearest minds in every field of the humanities, the sciences, the arts, engineering, and politics.

There is, however, one very immediate question. How are we to meet the problem of shared contribution? How are we to ensure that this corpus is not in the end a simplified version of modern western—essentially Euro-American—scientific and philosophic thought and of art forms and processes, however widely selected, interpreted within the western tradition? Is there any endeavor which can draw on the capacities not only of those who are specially trained but also those with untapped resources—the uneducated in Euro-American countries and the adult and wise in old, exotic cultures and newly emerging ones?

A first answer can be found, I think, in activities in which every country can have a stake and persons of every age and level of sophistication can take part. One such activity would be the fashioning of a new set of communication devices—like the visual devices used by very simple peoples to construct messages or to guide travelers on their way, but now raised to the level of world-wide intelligibility.

In recent years there has been extensive

discussion of the need for a systematic development of what are now called glyphs, that is, graphic representations, each of which stands for an idea: male, female, water, poison, danger, stop, go, etc. Hundreds of glyphs are used in different parts of the world—as road signs, for example—but too often with ambiguous or contradictory meanings as one moves from one region to another. What is needed, internationally, is a set of glyphs which does not refer to any single phonological system or to any specific cultural system of images but will, instead, form a system of visual signs with universally recognized referents. But up to the present no sustained effort has been made to explore the minimum number that would be needed or to make a selection that would carry clear and unequivocal meaning for the peoples of the world, speaking all languages, living in all climates, and exposed to very different symbol systems. A project for the exploration of glyph forms and for experimentation with the adequacy of different forms has been authorized by the United Nations Committee for International Cooperation Year (1965—the twentieth anniversary of the founding of the United Nations). This is designed as an activity in which adults and children, artists and engineers, logicians and semanticists, linguists and historians—all those in fact, who have an interest in doing so—can take part. For the wider the range of persons and the larger the number of cultures included in this exploration, the richer and the more fully representative will be the harvest from which a selection of glyphs can be made for international use.

Since meaning is associated with each glyph as a unit and glyphs cannot be combined syntactically, they can be used by the speakers of any language. But considerable experimentation will be necessary to avoid ambiguity which may lead to confusion or the adoption of forms which are already culturally loaded. The variety of meanings which may already be associated with certain forms can be illustrated by the sign + (which, in different connections, can be the sign for addition or indicates a positive number, can stand for "north" or indicate a crossroad, and, very slightly modified, can indicate a deceased person in a genealogy, a specifically Christian derivation, or stand for the Christian sign of the cross) or the sign O (which, in different connections, may stand for circumference or for 360°, for the full moon, for an annual plant, for degrees of arc or temperature, for an individual, especially female, organism, and, very slightly modified, can stand for zero or, in our alphabet, the letter O).

Work on glyphs can lead to work on other forms of international communication. In an interconnected world we shall need a world language—a second language which could be learned by every people but which would in no sense replace their native tongue. Contemporary studies of natural languages have increased our understanding of the reasons why consciously constructed languages do not serve the very complex purposes of general communication. Most important is the fact that an artificial language, lacking the imprint of many different kinds of minds and differently organized capacities for response, lacks the redundancy necessary in a language all human beings can learn.

Without making any premature choice, we can state some of the criteria for such a secondary world language. It must be a natural language, chosen from among known living languages, but not from among those which are, today, politically controversial. Many nations would have to contribute to the final choice, but this choice would depend also on the outcome of systematic experiments with children's speech, machine simulation, experiments with mechanical translation, and so on. In addition, it would be essential to consider certain characteristics related to the current historical situation. Politically, it should be the language of a state too small to threaten other states. In order to allow for a rapid development of diverse written styles, it must be a language with a long tradition of use in written forms. To permit rapid learning, it must be a language whose phonetic system can be easily learned by speakers of other languages, and one which can be easily rendered into a phonetic script and translated without special difficulty into existing traditional scripts. It should come from the kind of population in which there is a wide diversity of roles and occupations and among whom a large number of teachers can be found, some of whom are already familiar with one or another of the great widespread languages of the world. Using modern methods of language teaching, the task of creating a world-wide body of readers and speakers could be accomplished within five years and the language itself would change in the process of this world-wide learning.

Once a secondary world language is chosen, the body of knowledge with which we shall start the next twenty-five years can be translated into it from preliminary statements in the great languages, taking the stamp of these languages as divergent subtleties of thought, present in one language and absent in another, are channeled in and new vocabulary is created to deal with new ideas.

One important effect of a secondary world language would be to protect the more localized languages from being swamped by those few which are rapidly spreading over the world. Plans have been advanced to make possible the learning and use of any one of the five or seven most widespread languages as a second language. Fully implemented, this would divide the world community into two classes of citizens—those for whom one of these languages was a mother tongue and those for whom it was a second language—and it would exacerbate already existing problems arising from differences in the quality of communication—rapid and idiomatic among native speakers and slower, more formal and less spontaneous among those who have learned English, French, or Russian later. In contrast, one shared second language, used on a world-wide scale, would tend to equalize the quality of world communication and, at the same time, would protect the local diversity of all other languages.

Another important aspect of a shared culture would be the articulate inclusion of the experience of those who travel to study, work, explore, or enjoy other countries. One of the most intractable elements in our present isolating cultures is the interlocking of a landscape—a landscape with mountains or a desert, jungle or tundra, rushing cataracts or slow flowing rivers, arched over by a sky in which the Dipper or the Southern Cross dominates—and a view of man. The beauty of face and movement of those who have never left their mountains or their island is partly the imprint on the human form of a complex relationship to the scale and the proportions, the seasonal rhythms and the natural style of one special part of the world. The experiences of those who have been bred to one physical environment cannot be patched together like the pieces of a patchwork quilt. But we can build on the acute and vivid experiences of those who, reared in a culture which has deeply incorporated its environment, respond intensely to some newly discovered environment—the response of the countryman to the city, the response of the city dweller to open country, the response of the immigrant to the sweep of an untouched landscape and of the traveler to a sudden vista into the past of a whole people. In the past, the visual impact of discovery was recorded retrospectively in painting and in literature. Today, films can record the more immediate response of the observer, looking with fresh eyes at the world of the nomadic

Bushman or the people beneath the mountain wall of New Guinea, at the palaces in Crete or the summer palace in Peking.

We can give children a sense of movement, actually experienced or experienced only in some leap of the imagination. In the next twenty-five years we shall certainly not explore deep space, but the experience of movement can link a generation in a common sense of anticipation. As a beginning, we can give children a sense of different actual relationships to the physical environments of the whole earth, made articulate through the recorded responses of those who have moved from one environment to another. Through art, music, and film, we can give children access to the ways others have experienced their own green valleys and other valleys, also green. We can develop in small children the capacity to wonder and to look through other eyes at the familiar fir trees rimming their horizon or the sea breaking on their island's shore.

In the past, these have been the experiences of those who could afford to travel and those who had access, through the arts, to the perceptions of a poet like Wordsworth in *The Prelude*, or a young scientist like Darwin on his Pacific voyage, or painters like Catlin or Gauguin. With today's technology, these need no longer be the special experiences of the privileged and the educated elite. The spur to action may be the desire for literacy in the emerging nations or a new concern for the culturally deprived in older industrialized countries. And quite different styles of motivation can give urgency to the effort to bring the experience of some to bear on the experience of all.

Looking to the future, the immediacy of motivation is itself part of the experience. It may be an assertive desire to throw off a colonial past or a remorseful attempt to atone for long neglect. It may be the ecumenical spirit in which the Pope can say: "No pilgrim, no matter how far, religiously and geographically, may be the country from which he comes, will be any longer a stranger to this Rome. . . ."[2] It may be the belief that it is possible to remake a society, as when Martin Luther King said:

> I have a dream today . . . I have a dream that one day every valley shall be exalted, every hill and mountain shall be made low. The rough places will be made plain, and the crooked places will be made straight. And the glory of the Lord shall be revealed, and all flesh shall see it together. This is our hope. This is the faith that I go back to the South with. With this faith we will be able to hew out of the mountain of despair a stone of hope.[3]

Or it may be the belief, expressed by U Thant, that men can work toward a world society:

> Let us look inward for a moment on this Human Rights Day, and recognize that no one, no individual, no nation, and indeed no ideology has a monopoly of rightness, freedom or dignity. And let us translate this recognition into action so as to sustain the fullness and freedom of simple human relations leading to ever widening areas of understanding and agreement. Let us, on this day, echo the wish Rabindranath Tagore stated in these memorable words, so that our world may be truly a world
>
> Where the mind is without fear and the head is held high;
> Where knowledge is free;
> Where the world has not been broken up into fragments by narrow domestic walls;
> Where words come out of the depth of truth;
> Where tireless striving stretches its arms toward perfection. . . .[4]

[2] *The New York Times*, May 18, 1964.

[3] From the speech by the Rev. Martin Luther King at the March on Washington, *New York Post Magazine*, September 1, 1963, p. 5.

[4] From the Human Rights Day Message by (then) Acting Secretary-General U Thant, December 8, 1961 (United Nations Press Release SG/1078 HRD/11 [December 6, 1961]).

There are also other ways in which experience can more consciously be brought to bear in developing a shared understanding. All traditions, developing slowly over centuries, are shaped by the biological nature of man—the differences in temperament and constitution among men and the processes of maturation, parenthood, and aging which are essential parts of our humanity. The conscious inclusion of the whole life process in our thinking can, in turn, alter the learning process, which in a changing world has become deeply disruptive as each elder generation has been left behind while the next has been taught an imperfect version of the new. One effect of this has been to alienate and undermine the faith of parents and grandparents as they have seen their children's minds moving away from them and as their own beliefs, unshared, have become inflexible and distorted.

The policy in most of today's world is to educate the next—the new—generation, setting aside the older generation in the mistaken hope that, as older men and women are passed over, their outmoded forms of knowledge will do no harm. Instead, we pay a double price in the alienation of the new generation from their earliest and deepest experiences as little children and in the world by an older generation who still exercise actual power—hoarding some resources and wasting others, building to an outmoded scale, voting against measures the necessity of which is not understood, supporting reactionary leaders, and driving an equally inflexible opposition toward violence. Yet this lamentable outcome is unnecessary, as the generation break itself is unnecessary.

In the past the transmission of the whole body of knowledge within a slowly changing society has provided for continuity. Today we need to create an educational style which will provide for continuity and openness even within rapid change. Essentially this means an educa-

tional style in which members of different generations are involved in the process of learning. One way of assuring this is through a kind of education in which new things are taught to mothers and young children together. The mothers, however schooled, usually are less affected by contemporary styles of education than the fathers. In some countries they have had no schooling; in others, girls are warned away from science and mathematics or even from looking at the stars. So they come to the task of rearing their small children fresher than those who have been trained to teach or to administer. Child rearing, in the past fifty years, has been presented as almost entirely a matter of molding the emotional life of the child, modulating the effects of demands for cleanliness and obedience to permit more spontaneity, and of preserving an environment in which there is good nutrition and low infection danger. At the same time, we have taken out of the hands of mothers the *education* even of young children. So we have no existing rationale in which mother, child, and teacher are related within the learning process. What we need now, in every part of the world, is a new kind of school for mothers and little children in which mothers learn to teach children what neither the mothers nor the children know.

At the same time, grandparents who, perforce, have learned a great deal about the world which has gone whirling past them and in which, however outmoded they are declared to be, they have had to maintain themselves, can be brought back into the teaching process. Where patience, experience, and wisdom are part of what must be incorporated, they have a special contribution to make. Mothers of young children, lacking a fixed relationship to the growing body of knowledge about the world, provide freshness of approach; but older people embody the experience that can be transformed into later learnings. The meticulous respect for materials, coming from long experience with hand work, the exacting attention to detail, coming from work with a whole object rather than some incomplete part, and the patient acceptance of the nature of a task have a continuing relevance to work, whatever it may be. So also, the disciplined experience of working with human beings can be transformed to fit the new situations which arise when democracy replaces hierarchy and the discipline of political parties that of the clan and the tribe.

We have been living through a period in which the old have been recklessly discarded and disallowed, and this very disallowance resonates—as a way of life which has been repressed rather than transformed—in the movements of unaccountably stubborn reaction from which no civilization in our present world is exempt. Grandparents and great-grandparents—even those who are driven from their land to die in concentration camps and those who voluntarily settle themselves in modern, comfortable Golden Age clubs—live on in the conceptions of the children whose parents' lives they shaped. Given an opportunity to participate meaningfully in new knowledge, new skills, and new styles of life, the elderly can embody the changing world in such a way that their grandchildren—and all children of the youngest generation—are given a mandate to be part of the new and yet maintain human ties with the past which, however phrased, is part of our humanity. The more rapid the rate of change and the newer the corpus of knowledge which the world may come to share, the more urgently necessary it is to include the old—to transform our conception of the whole process of aging so their wisdom and experience can be assets in our new relation to the future.

Then we may ask, are such plans as these sufficiently open ended? In seeking to make equally available to the peoples of the world newly organized ways of moving into the immediate future, in a universe in which our knowledge is rapidly expanding, there is always the danger that the idea of a shared body of knowledge may be transformed into some kind of universal blueprint. In allowing this to happen we would, of course, defeat our own purpose. The danger is acute enough so that we must build a continuing wariness and questioning into the planning itself; otherwise even the best plan may result in a closed instead of an open ended system.

This means that we must be open ended in our planning as well as in our plans, recognizing that this will involve certain kinds of conscious restriction as well as conscious questioning. For example, we must insist that a world language be kept as a second language, resolutely refusing to consider it as a first language, in order to protect and assure the diversity of thought which accompanies the use of different mother tongues. We should also guard against a too early learning of the world language, so that the language of infancy—which also becomes the language of love and poetry and religion—may be protected against acquiring a too common stamp. We must insist on the inclusion of peoples from all over the world in any specific piece of planning—as in the development of an international system of glyphs—as a way of assuring a growing and an unpredictable corpus. We must be willing to forego, in large-scale planning, some kinds of apparent efficiency. If we are willing, instead, to include numerous steps and to conceive of each step somewhat differently, we are more likely, in the end, to develop new interrelationships, unforeseeable at any early stage. A more conscious inclusion of women and of the grandparental generation in learning and teaching will carry with it the extraordinary differences in existing interrelations between the minds and in the understanding of the two sexes and different age groups.

We can also take advantage of what

has been learned through the use of cybernetic models, and equip this whole forward movement of culture which we are launching with a system of multiple self-corrective devices. For example, criteria could be established for reviewing the kinds of divergences that were occurring in vocabulary and conceptualizations as an idea fanned out around the world. Similarly, the rate and type of incorporation of special developments in particular parts of the world could be monitored, and cases of dilution or distortion examined and corrected. Overemphasis on one part of knowledge, on one sensory modality, on the shells men live in rather than the life they live there, on sanitation rather than beauty, on length of life rather than quality of life lived, could be listened for and watched for, and corrective measures taken speedily.

A special area of concern would be intercommunication among all those whose specializations tend to isolate them from one another, scientist from administrator, poet from statesman, citizen voter from the highly skilled specialist who must carry out his mandate using calculations which the voter cannot make, but within a system of values clearly enough stated so that both may share them. By attending to the origins of some new communication—whether a political, a technical, or an artistic innovation—the functioning of the communication process could be monitored. Special sensing organs could be established which would observe, record, and correct so that what otherwise might become a blundering, linear, and unmanageable avalanche could be shaped into a process delicately responsive to change in itself.

But always the surest guarantee of change and growth is the inclusion of living persons in every stage of an activity. Their lives, their experience, and their continuing response—even their resistances—infuse with life any plan which, if living participants are excluded, lies on the drawing board and loses its reality. Plans for the future can become old before they are lived, but the future itself is always newborn and, like any newborn thing, is open to every kind of living experience.

10.3 The Mutable Self: A Self-Concept for Social Change

Louis A. Zurcher, Jr.

The person first develops an A mode self-concept based on body image and physical sense, then a B mode social self with a

Selected from pages 184–219, Louis A. Zurcher, Jr., *The Mutable Self: A Self-Concept for Social Change* (Beverly Hills, Cal.: Sage Publications, 1977). Zurcher uses the A, B, C, and D self-reference categories developed by Manford Kuhn for scoring responses to his Twenty Statements Test(TST). In using this text, persons are asked to write twenty statements in response to the question "Who Am I?" The responses

complex role set, lodged in relatively stable social structures. Those roles and structures can be made temporarily or permanently, slightly or intensely, unstable by the impact of technical and societal change, by disruption to the value or reward

are then sorted into the A, B, C, or D categories. The meanings of these categories are developed in the context of Zurcher's discussion.

Footnotes in edited portions of this paper have been deleted and the remaining footnote renumbered.

supporting them, by personal rejection of them, by their becoming obsolete or dysfunctional, and by conflict among component parts of the social structures or role sets. The instability or unacceptability of the structures and roles generates a C mode self-concept in the individual. He or she experiences concern, anxiety or confusion about the concept of self. The anchorages for self-definition are not dependable or acceptable. The person feels a need to resolve the uncertainty, to move away from the C self-concept mode. Depending upon the intensity of the stress and anxieties, and the degrees of freedom within the situation, the person may resolve the C mode by withdrawing into an A mode; finding a new, relatively stable and satisfying B mode; perseverating in the C mode; transcending to a D mode. If the C condition is repetitive or sustained enough, as it would be in rapid social change, if the C mode has not become rigidly chronic, and if the other modes have been experienced by and are in the individual's repertoire, he or she may develop a self-concept which not only is full but capably accommodates change— the Mutable Self.

It would be useful to construct a more detailed though also hypothetical case of a person experiencing dislocation from a B mode self-concept, and explore the options he might elect for further self-definition. Let us assume that the person is a male adult and has until recently been relatively well established in and satisfied with a B mode self-concept.

An Expository Case

In 1965 James Tempus was twenty-seven years old, single, and residing in New York City. He was Anglo, healthy, and in most every way an average member of the American middle class. He liked his occupation—stockbroker—which he had recently entered, having been educationally prepared for that job by acquiring a Bachelor's degree in finance. James considered himself to be "on the move upward" in the socioeconomic hierarchy. The future looked bright. He was, as he described it, "settled in" his social world. At this time he had no thoughts of marriage, although he felt he probably would eventually have a family of his own.

When administered the Twenty Statements Test in 1965, James quickly and easily provided the following responses:

I am: — a stockbroker (B)
— a Rotarian (B)
— a Republican (B)
— a University of Pennsylvania alumnus (B)
— a bachelor (B)
— a baseball fan (B)
— a happy person (C)
— a Presbyterian (B)
— a son (B)
— a member of the Junior Chamber of Commerce (B)
— a former Marine Officer (B)
— a Shriner (B)
— a golfer (B)
— a poker player (B)
— a boys' club coach (B)
— a football fan (B)
— a member of the Country Club (B)
— a good friend and a tough enemy (C)
— a hard-working person (C)
— trying to get further ahead financially (C)

James' TST profile clearly is B mode. His self-concept, at least as measured by the TST, indicates an anchoring of self in established and relatively stable social structures. He does not question those structures to any great degree, nor does he question his linking of identity with them.

Five years later it is 1970, and James is thirty-two years old. The United States has entered into a serious recession, the stock market has plummeted, not many

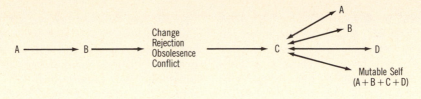

FIGURE 1

people are buying stocks. James' income has dropped considerably. As a less senior member of the brokerage company, James is very likely to be "furloughed" because of lack of market action. Several other people his own age and level of seniority have already been "let go" until things get better.

James' responses to the Twenty Statements Test now are dramatically different, and slowly and painfully given:

I am: — concerned about my job (C)
— worried about the future (C)
— wondering what the hell is happening to my life (C)
— nearly a pauper (C)
— thinking that the country is going to hell (C)
— tired of the hassle (C)
— disappointed (C)
— not going to give up (C)
— wishing things were different in the U.S.A. (C)
— probably going to quit the country club (C)
— going to buy a cheaper car (C)
— very angry about people's apathy in this country (C)
— going to kick a few hippies' asses (C)
— thinking about going back into the Marine Corps (C)
— losing my faith in people (C)
— too disgusted to finish this questionnaire (D)

James now clearly manifests the C mode self-concept. He reveals considerable concern about the stability, the dependability, of the important social structures around him. He expresses suffering because his self-concept, previously lodged in those social structures, is in effect being fractured by the disruption to the structures themselves. He is reflecting upon the conditions of his life, and upon ways of arranging a future in which personal and social stability might be reestablished. But he is not yet certain how he might best undertake that task, what he might do about his painful circumstances.

According to Figure 1, James has several choices. He can withdraw into an A mode, find a new B mode, remain for a longer time in the C mode, or move into a D mode. He also might, though it is not likely at this early point and without further sustained challenges to a series of B mode self-concepts, evolve the Mutable Self.

The Mutable Self usually does not develop quickly or easily. Its emergence in the individual generally follows many repetitions of B mode enactments and C mode reflections, along with A and D mode experiences. It can be a painful process—a travail. Mutable Self development can be accelerated in a society manifesting social change of such an order that it maintains, epidemically, conditions of psychological stress and self-concept disruption. The change can generate the crises which produce a personal and societal advancement.

Let it be assumed that James Tempus has evolved the Mutable Self after a long and tense period in the reflective C mode state. Let it also be assumed that he has experienced and has in his repertoire all four self-concept modes.

James' employers offer him the option of a "furlough" from his stockbroker job or a reduction in his base pay to 50 percent of its previous level. He chooses the half-time option. Certainly this arrangement does not provide him with the relative affluence to which he had become accustomed; the salary is enough, however, to cover his rent, food, and other basic expenses. He sells his car—"Who needs a car in New York, anyway?"—and resigns from the country club. He continues to play golf, but at the municipal course, and he has found a lower stakes poker group. He doesn't go to as many football games as he used to, and he has resigned from the junior chamber of commerce. He spends more time in his volunteer role as a boys' club coach. Thus James has continued some of the activities which contributed to his previous B mode self-concept. He enjoys them, but has come to view those social B mode enactments as more voluntary, less compulsive, less oriented toward the accomplishment of some specific material or status acquisition. He does not view his B mode enactments as part of the effort "to get further ahead financially."

James has taken up the sport of long-distance running. "I love the feel of running," he reflects. "I pick out different wooded areas, or riverside stretches, to run each day. The feel of my own body stretching and working is delightful. The breeze, the smell of the trees, the feel of the ground under my feet, all of it, is wonderful. I don't know how far I run, but I guess it must be several miles. I take about an hour each day, and alternate running and walking. I thought about keeping a record, but the hell with it. I do know I've lost weight, and have become trim. My doctor tells me my pulse rate and blood pressure have gone down considerably. I don't look pale anymore like I used to. Some of my business friends want me to join their jogging club, but I'd rather do it alone."

James has enacted an activity that would contribute physical A type components to his self-concept. He speaks of physical sensations, body image, and the exhilaration of experiencing his own sharpened sensory awareness. There is no compulsiveness in the pursuit of those A mode characteristics. When he is running, he is totally A mode. He does not define himself as a "runner," but experiences himself as a physical person. Yet his whole life is not tied up in running, in A mode experiences. He shifts with ease to the role of stockbroker, and defines himself as such, during that portion of each day when he must do so (and wants to do so) in order to provide himself with an income. And he enjoys the social B role of stockbroker now, just as he enjoys the physical A mode of running.

James has elected to become more involved in Zen Buddhism. He spends large portions of his weekends in the practice of *upaya* and engages daily in *Za-Zen* meditation. He reads more and more deeply into the philosophy of Zen, and listens with what he feels to be increasing understanding and appreciation of the lessons of Zen masters. At such times James clearly manifests an oceanic D mode self-concept and experiences himself as such. During his D mode times he detaches himself from social contact, turning himself outward into the broader experience of what he interprets to be the void, the suchness.

But the D mode self-concept does not dominate, steadily and continually, all of James' person. Just as he was able to turn from the situational enjoyment of the A mode running, he can turn from the situational enjoyment of the D mode meditation. From that D mode he can move to A mode, or B mode, enjoying himself equally well in those quite different experiences and self perceptions.

James still feels a bit "unsettled." He moves from A to B to D mode self-concept, situationally, easily, but every once in a while longs for the old certainty—when the social B mode dominated his self-concept across nearly all situations. Yet, he has developed a capacity to understand and accept that longing, that difficulty with uncertainty. James perceives the periods of uneasiness as part of being human, of being finite. Though he may not articulate it fully, he senses that the flexibility of moving (for the purposes of enjoyable experiences and personal development) among the A, B, and D self-concepts (and the situations which generate them) necessitates some degree of uncertainty, of gamble, of risk. The experience of the C mode self-concept situationally is part of the flexibility pattern—just as much a part as are the A, B, and D modes.

James also realizes that some people tend to emphasize, across situations, one self-concept mode more than the others. He himself now seems to emphasize the D mode slightly, though as a Mutable Self he possesses and expresses all four modes. But he is accepting of Mutable Selves who favor other modes. He even is tolerant of persons, not Mutable Selves, who are defensively caught in single modes. He no longer wants to "kick a few hippies' asses," nor is he "angry about people's apathy in this country" or continuing to lose his "faith in people." He is still concerned about citizen apathy, but not angry about it.

James retains the capacity to become engaged in civic action, when he sees that action to be related importantly to the maintenance of his and others' freedom to move voluntarily among the self-concept modes. James may enact the B mode role of social activist when such freedom is threatened, perhaps even joining a social movement; but the B mode enactment is purposive, does not manifest a means-end reversal, and is clearly viewed in the perspective of the wholeness of his person.

James proclaims that he feels good, "better than I have ever felt in my life."

His overall self-concept, the Mutable Self, is based squarely upon the experience of process, of change, of flow through the situations he encounters in everyday life. He has the flexibility to draw pleasurable experiences from a wide diversity of activities—physical, social, reflective, oceanic. In a sense, the shapes of his four selves (modes) are temporary, capable of changing, worthy of enactment but not sacrosanct, to be maintained in specific forms only so long as they contribute to a sense of fullness, to a sense of *living*. James has evolved a process perspective; he is oriented toward process experience. But the process has discrete chunks of direct contact with the structured social world. He treads the line, a delicate and sometimes painful line (the C mode), between I-Thou and I-It relations. James is operating in a "functionally marginal" position among social forms, picking and choosing from them, letting himself be A mode, B mode, C mode, or D mode, actively or passively, as his predilections dictate.

James does not hesitate to manifest self-disclosure, no matter which of the self-concept modes he may at the moment be enacting. His presentation of self is marked not by cynicism, not by defensiveness, but by openness—though he can erect a solid B mode facade if he judges it to be appropriate.

If given the Twenty Statements Test over a period of time, James would reveal himself to be in some settings A mode, in some B mode, in some C mode, and in some D mode. Thus, in order to get an assessment of the Mutable Self, the investigator needs to have a sample of self-concept evaluations from the person longitudinally, involving a diversity of social and experiential settings. Even then, a measure like the Twenty Statements Test would not be enough. The individual would have to be interviewed in depth in order to determine his or her attitude toward self, and to assess the diversity of self-concepts which he or she enacts in different social settings. The Mutable Self would be characterized by the kinds of flexibility, tolerance, openness, and diversity discussed so far. The interviews would reveal which of the modes in the Mutable Self configuration the person tended to emphasize (although the emphasis would not approach dominance).

The individual with a Mutable Self is the self-actualizer, the consciousness III (IV?) person, the creative self, the omega person, the Heraclitean self, the protean person, homo novis, the autonomous person, the fully functioning person, the productive person, the Mandala person. But those characterizations of "new self" tend explicitly or implicitly to suggest transcendence beyond the "throwness" or "suchness" of everyday life, beyond the finiteness, the bodily limitations, the social (B mode) and physical (A mode) exigencies of the here and now world. The person with the Mutable Self, though quite capable of transcendence (D mode), does not become detached from that reality.

The Mutable Self would be fully functional in societies which are theological/military, metaphysical/juridical, or science/industry; gemeinschaft or gesellschaft; mechanical or organic; fraught with cultural lag; class structured or classless; sensate, ideational, or idealistic; rational, traditional, or charismatic. The person may prefer one form of societal organization to another, that preference being guided by the degree to which the flexibility to experience, fully and freely, A/B/C/D self-concept modes is made available within the social structure.

Which raises the question: Has the person with the Mutable Self no commitments, no core of value-orientations, no teleological orientations other than to personal experience and growth? It has been noted that the Mutable Self is based upon what perhaps could be considered at the level of meta-needs; process experience; flexibility; tolerance; change; process

perspective; functional marginality. But is the Mutable Self chameleon-like—shallow—as whimsical as the most extreme and defensive C mode could be? Selfish? Almost psychopathic?[1] Indeed not. The orientation toward personal flexibility and tolerance for self-change *demands* acceptance of the personal flexibility and self-change of other human beings, and the diversity of expressiveness and alternative social forms which accompany those attributes. Such an orientation calls not only for a desire to enhance self-dignity, but to enhance the dignity of others in the context of self-extension. Furthermore, the flexibility that would provide the individual the opportunity to move among A, B, C, and D self-concepts necessitates that the person take responsibility for actions associated with that flexibility. Recall that the Mutable Self necessitates the realization and experience of all four self-concept modes. If any one of those realities is denied by the individual, the Mutable Self is not possible. The B mode component of the Mutable Self needs the consensual validation of other persons' B modes. The D mode contains within it the propensity for transcendence. For the Mutable Self, that transcendence must at least in part be oriented toward an understanding of the relations among human individuals and other pieces of existence in a broad philosophical or theological framework. The philosophical or theological framework brings with it the necessity of ethics, or rightness and wrongness, of distributive justice. This is the kind of evolutionary process that Kohlberg has called the universal ethic, Teilhard de Chardin saw as part of the omega person, and Alfred Adler characterized as being associated with the creative self. The reflective C mode may be the "gateway" to the Mutable Self, the introduction of process

[1] William McCord and John McCord, *The Psychopath: An Essay on the Criminal Mind* (New York: Van Nostrand, 1964).

orientation, but the oceanic D mode usually is the penultimate experience. Transcendence, if not compulsive or rigidly escapist, can provide the breadth of perspective and integrating principles which influence synthesis among, and accommodate dialectic between, the four self-concept modes.

The value for transcendence and the experience of transcendence necessitate an acceptance of transcendence in others. That acceptance generates the formulation of norms, even to the extent of binding laws, which protect the freedoms and flexibilities of other persons. The Mutable Self accepts those norms as being a part of the important realities of everyday life. If the norms become obsolete, perverted, or suffer a means-end reversal, individuals with Mutable Selves can be expected to ignore, countermand, or reformulate them.

The Mutable Self Diagrammed

The term "Mutable" in Mutable Self refers to the individual's capability for flexible, resourcefully directed, and autonomous change among A, B, C and D mode self-concepts. It further refers to the individual's ability to accommodate and, if necessary, control or modify those social situations and forms which support the four types of self-concept.

The Mutable Self constellation can be diagrammed as in Figure 2. A question still remains—and the diagram highlights it—concerning the driving force behind the Mutable Self. Is there some natural tendency toward balancing the A, B, C, and D mode self-concepts unique to and shared by human beings as a natural phenomenon? Where does that "natural" tendency come from? Physiological sources (rooted in the A mode)? Social forces, interactions, socialization processes (rooted in the B mode)? Conditions of stress, homeostatic pushes and pulls, necessity for consistency, need for certainty (rooted

in the C mode)? A spiritually based need for transcendence, a soul, an *intellectus agens*, an ultimate philosophical end (rooted in the D mode)? Different theorists have taken assorted positions on this issue; no one yet has provided *the* answer.

The position suggested here certainly is not radical, nor innovative—but it serves the purpose. Individuals develop Mutable Selves as part of the evolutionary process based initially on physical survival. People come to view themselves in ways that will facilitate the provision of sustenance, protection against physical vulnerabilities, and simple nurturing rewards. As expressed above, the earliest development of self-concept is A mode, based in physical needs, images, and identities.

Subsequently, the learning of social roles (B mode) becomes important as a way of dealing with the more sophisticated reward structures of society, and the more complicated demands society makes upon the individual for survival. Socially learned needs accumulate along the way—e.g., status, power, affiliation. The complexity of (and change in) the world in which people live generates inconsistency and contradiction in social roles (and the values, norms, and statuses upon which they are based). The individual must learn to deal with those inconsistencies (and the resulting C mode) to resolve them in one fashion or another in order to remain within the network of physical and social rewards.

In the socialization process individuals learn some values which point to transcendence, to "higher" goals (D mode). The attainment of those goals, or the manifestation of significant achievements leading to them, provide people with rewards meeting physical and social needs.

It is assumed that Allport was correct in concluding that though social and transcendent needs may be based in physical needs for survival, or may have been passively socialized into individuals,

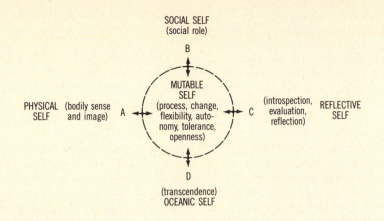

FIGURE 2

they can take on the characteristics of functional autonomy—develop a motivational base, a reward system, of their own. The A and B mode self-concepts have the potential to develop a motivational base of their own. So also the C mode, and the D mode. The Mutable Self, even if generated in and by conditions in which the previously more adaptive B mode constellations are breaking down, and where individuals are looking for solutions to troublesome C mode self-concepts, can develop a motivational base of its own. Process, change, flexibility, autonomy, tolerance, and openness may be rewarding for their own sake—and not only because they are associated with the mechanisms for survival in contemporary society, a society that is fraught with accelerated sociocultural change.

Thus, though the motivational basis for the evolution of the Mutable Self may be survival, the definition of survival becomes increasingly more complex, increasingly more sophisticated, and increasingly more encompassing of a mutual understanding of the dignity of other individuals' survival.

11

Some Value Dilemmas of the Change Agent

Value considerations have appeared in discussions of planned change and the change-agent role throughout this volume, even where the focus of the discussion has been upon historical, cognitive, or technological matters. In fact, the differentiation of planned change from other modes of human change is grounded in a cluster of value commitments on the part of the agent of planned change—a commitment to collaborative ways of working, a commitment to the basing of plans for change upon valid knowledge and information, and a commitment to reducing power differentials among men and groups of men as a distorting influence upon the determination of the tempo and direction of justifiable changes in human life. We have tried to be open about the value commitments of our enterprise throughout our discussion. What more needs to be said?

In the first place, the meaning of these overarching value commitments is frequently not clear in the complex and confused situations in which the change agent functions. Value considerations present themselves intertwined with cognitive and technical considerations, and it is often difficult to sort out the value component of decisions and judgments from other components when it needs most to be confronted in its own right. Confrontations of value differences and conflicts are often freighted with subjectivity and emotional heat as compared with confrontations of differences in cognitive and technical matters. And most of us are unsure of our ability to handle our subjectivity and emotional heat constructively. As a result, we tend to avoid value confrontations. This tendency is highly prevalent in behavioral-science types—and many change agents are behavioral scientists. For scientists have frequently been indoctrinated in a value-free ideal of science. In addition to the basically human difficulties in handling value confrontations constructively, behavioral scientists often suffer additional feelings of shame and guilt for being involved in value commitments at all, if these are, by definition, unscientific.

In addition, the conditions of society and culture, which were examined in the last chapter as placing processes of goal setting and direction finding in a radically new light, also load the value judgments and choices of change agents, where, behaviorally, values and value orientations function and perchance grow and develop, with new and wider responsibilities as indeed the choices of all men are now similarly loaded. We now know that we are no longer choosing wisely when we choose within the framework of assumed and unexamined traditions of belief and practice. We are literally legislating the future for ourselves and for others as we choose and act upon our choices. Since our value orientations are at least partial determinants of our choices, responsibility requires that we become clear about and responsible for our actual as well as our professed ideal values as they function or fail to function in the choices we make as change agents.

The purpose of this chapter is to illuminate some of the contexts in which value clarification and responsibility are required of change agents and, by extension, of behavioral scientists in their functioning as researchers as well as in their practitioner and policy-influencing functions. There is, thus, a wide spectrum of social interventions where the intention of the interveners is to influence the direction, tempo, and quality of social change. The intervention may be a micro-intervention as in processes of training and of organizational and community consultation. Or the intervention may be a macro-intervention as in processes of policy-determination with respect to such national issues as population control or such international issues as technical assistance and modernization. And there are various social interventions which fall between these two extremes.

In their book *The Ethics of Social Intervention*, Bermant, Kelman, and Warwick have dealt with a wide range of social interventions from psychotherapy with individuals, through behavior modification programs in institutions and projects in organization and community development, to national programs in population control. They have asked persons closely identified with various cases of social intervention to identify and clarify the ethical issues inherent in the case as they have experienced it. In addition, they have appended to the ethical analysis presented by "insiders" complementary ethical analyses of each case written by a neutral or critical "outsider." In a concluding chapter, Bermant and Warwick have prepared a summary which generalizes the ethical issues common to the entire range of interventions reported and analyzed in the book. The selection reprinted here is drawn from the summary chapter, in which the ethical issues in social intervention are categorized under three headings—"power," "freedom," and "accountability."

In a previously unpublished essay, Benne analyzes the "Moral Dilemmas of Managers." He clarifies the distinction between technical and ethical issues and describes the societal conditions which make the avoidance of ethical issues increasingly difficult for managers and other change agents. Benne clarifies the distinction between substantive advocacy and methodological (process) advocacy as possible stances for managers of human systems in the resolution of ethical dilemmas and recommends and elaborates the latter stance as most appropriate for managers in contemporary settings.

11.1 The Ethics of Social Intervention: Power, Freedom and Accountability

Gordon Bermant   Donald P. Warwick

The central ethical issue raised by this volume concerns the professional intervenor as an agent of power. Professional intervenors hold power deriving from their specialized knowledge, their privileged personal position, and connections with their clients. Often their clients are among the most influential in the society: corporate managers, government agencies, and international assistance organizations. Almost inevitably, the combination of a potent client and a skillful intervenor produces more leverage than is held by the population that is the target of the intervention. Regardless of anyone's intentions, ethical issues arise simply from the fact that a sizeable power differential exists

Selected from Chapter 18, Gordon Bermant, Herbert C. Kelman, and Donald Warwick (eds.), *The Ethics of Social Intervention* (Washington, D.C.: Hemisphere Publishing Corporation, 1978). Reprinted by permission of Hemisphere Publishing Corporation.
References within this article are maintained.

between the intervenors and those intervened upon. Additional problems arise when the exercise of power is veiled or obscured by the white coat of the physician, the open collar of the encounter group leader, or the bland smile of the presumably neutral mediator.

Clients of the professional intervenor are not always powerful. Sometimes they are a relatively weak interest group who approaches the intervenor as an avenue toward increased power or at least practical help. Other ethical issues arise in this context, particularly intentional or unintentional misrepresentations of the intervenor's skills and influence.

Thus *power*, both within and behind professional interventions, is the first theme that emerges from the eight species of intervention described in this book.

The second theme is *freedom*, particularly the freedom of citizens to choose the degree of their participation in programs of intervention. Traditionally, discussion has centered on the freedom to refuse to become a subject of intervention. The issue of informed consent, first explored in biological research and medicine, is now also of central importance in social experimentation. But there is another relevant facet of freedom here, namely, freedom of access to the mechanisms of social intervention and change. How should the power of professional intervenors be distributed within and between societies? What are the relations between the forms of intervention discussed in this book and more traditional forms of professional activity that fall within our definition of intervention, for example, legal advocacy? Should the availability of newer forms of professional intervention follow a marketplace model, a public service model, both, or neither?

The third theme of our discussion is *accountability*, which emerges out of concern for protecting freedom against abuses of power by professional intervenors. Practitioners of the newer forms of social intervention have not yet come to grips with the problems of determining the legitimate extent of their accountability as professionals. During the last several years physicians, attorneys, accountants, and engineers have been forced by a surge of professional malpractice litigation to reconsider their obligations. There is greater awareness that citizens can successfully press their complaints against incompetent or negligent professionals by filing suit. In part reactively, and in part through self-generated concern for the maintenance of high professional standards, various professional associations are reconsidering their codes of professional conduct. Practitioners of newer forms of social intervention can benefit from these experiences and perhaps avoid some mistakes already made by more established professions.

Power

Three separable but interacting power relationships arise in social interventions. They are the relationships between client and intervenor, the intervenor and the target of intervention, and the client and the target of intervention.

By "client," we mean the individual or institution who contracts and/or pays for the intervention. Sometimes the distinction between client and target disappears. For example an individual who chooses to obtain therapy from a mental health professional is the professional's client and target as well. The distinction between client and intervenor can also become blurred, for example, when a government agency conducts a social experiment using its own research staff instead of an outside contractor. But usually the role of the client is distinguishable from that of the intervenor.

Interventions aimed primarily at individual change show characteristic sets of power relationships. Thus, behavior therapy, encounter groups, and organization development exercises involve either of two sets of relationships. In one case, which is the more relevant to our concerns, the client is in a position of power relative to the target. In this variety of behavior therapy, the client is typically an arm or agent of the state, such as a judge who assigns therapy as a condition of probation. The therapist, also often an employee or agent of the state, shares a position of power with the client relative to the target.

To the extent that encounter groups are used as part of institutional therapies, they follow the pattern of behavior therapy. In organization development, senior management is usually the client, and subordinates are the targets of intervention. Hence the power relationships are the same as in the other two interventions.

The second set of power relationships arises when a client arranges to be the target of intervention. For example, an individual enters private therapy or an encounter group, or senior management hires an organization development specialist to work on its own problems and potential. The ethical problems facing the intervenor in this situation are simpler than in the former case, because the element of explicit or implicit coercion of the target's participation is absent. The major obligation for the intervenor is the fair representation of the risks, benefits, and costs associated with the intervenor's efforts. Because behavior therapists are more closely allied with the traditional model of health services delivery, the extent of their obligation is clearer than the responsibilities of the encounter group agent or organization development specialist. The problem appears to be particularly sticky for the encounter group agent, at least as Glidewell expresses it, because of the importance, for the encounter process, of leaving the goals and anticipated results of the process relatively undefined. Nevertheless, the purely power-based ethical issues in this setting are minor relative to those that arise when the interventions are institutionally mandated.

Power relations among client, target, and intervenor become particularly complex at the level of community interventions. In the situation described by Huey et al., there was an unusual financial arrangement in which the intervening agency paid for the intervention not only as a public service for the clients, but also in order to develop its skills in a new area of research and development. Several key problems in the case, as delineated by Guskin, arose from the intervenor's uncertainty about its own role in the intervention and the extent of its legitimate commitment to the client. While the first steps of the intervention were marked by strong initiatives, the intervenor soon found itself in a reactive posture and out of its technical and political depth. The channels of communication and decision within the

intervenor's organization were not always as open and quick as they should have been in such a delicate and volatile situation. As the project progressed, the scope of the intervenor's role and responsibilities underwent changes not fully understood by either intervenor or clients. Some problems might have been avoided if the client had been in a traditional fee-for-service arrangement with the intervenor. As it was, senior management of the intervening organization did not have the same obligation to the client as it would have had under a normal contractual arrangement. Initially, intervention was offered almost as a form of charity. However well intended, this power relation between intervenor and client weakened the client's position when the intervenor decided unilaterally to terminate involvement. The obvious lesson for the intervenor was the importance of establishing in advance, as clearly as possible, the limits on quality and quantity of services to be offered.

The Power of Definition

If a modern Machiavelli were to compose a handbook called *The Intervenor*, she or he might begin with the axiom that the intervenor's most important task is defining the problem to be solved in a way that minimizes impediments to solution. In particular, the intervenor should define the problem so as to forestall the need to justify the intervention. If one does not have to explain why intervention is necessary, one can move quickly to consider how to accomplish it.

Several chapters suggest that the most effective way to legitimate intervention is to portray it as promoting health or eliminating illness. "Health" and "illness" evoke such reflexive responses of acquiescence that the targets are likely to consider it precarious, if not sacrilegious, to challenge diagnoses made in those terms.

Conceptual ambiguities such as those described benefit intervenors and their clients at the expense of the targets of intervention. Stolz shows clearly how the "sick" label is used to the advantage of prison and hospital authorities and, more generally, the society. Laue and Cormick also underscore the politics of defining the disadvantaged as victims of social illness and, therefore, as in need of therapy by qualified professionals. However well-intentioned interventions based on this definition may be, they have the effect of keeping weaker groups in a passive, dependent role and of convincing them that they are unable to shape their own destinies.

If our latter-day Machiavelli were to give the targets of social intervention one bit of advice, it might be this:

> Get completely clear on what problem is to be solved and who has defined that problem. Insist that the intervenor do the same. Set forth the objectives to be achieved and the criteria by which they are to be be measured. And finally, let no mystique surrounding an institution or a profession replace or suppress discussion about the precise reasons for change.

Neutrality, Advocacy, and Forensic Social Science

Perhaps the most tangled knot of issues raised in earlier chapters concerns the possibility or desirability of intervenor neutrality and, conversely, the limits of legitimate advocacy. Laue and Cormick assail the notion of intervenor neutrality as inherently hypocritical and misleading. A posture of impartiality, they argue, serves only to strengthen the position of the disputant already in power. Other chapters demonstrate implicitly what Laue and Cormick make explicit: The most effective stance in the quest for power is the one that appears least political.

The significance of apparent neutrality for intervenor power surfaces most clearly in the choice of language used to label the intervenor and the intervention. There is tension, for example, between the descriptions of encounter groups given by Glidewell and by Back. Back, who is critical of the movement, speaks of the intervenor as the group's "leader." Glidewell, on the other hand, goes to some lengths to explain why he, and presumably other practitioners, prefer the more neutral term "agent." Back insists that there is more to this difference than a semantic quibble. What is at stake, he believes, is the intervenor's honesty with the targets of the intervention as well as the acceptance of professional responsibility. The advantage of a bland image is that it eases the pressures on the intervenor to explain the hidden agenda present in most encounter groups. The more one is identified as a leader, the greater the likelihood of challenges to that position, and the more visible the manipulations made by the person in question will be. While both Glidewell and Back would agree that the maintenance of a low-power profile is a key technique in the intervenor's repertoire, they disagree about the extent to which the intervenor should own up to being a personally responsible cause of group activity. By denying or concealing such responsibility, the intervenor becomes free to organize the intervention around his or her preferred notions of health, growth, or fulfillment. What Glidewell portrays as wholesome facilitation Back paints as irresponsible, covert manipulation.

The first is the proposition that social scientists sometimes hide their policy biases behind masks of impartiality. The chapters in this book and the history of the social sciences leave little doubt about the accuracy of this proposition. While social scientists all disavow rigged research and misrepresentation of auspices and intentions, they agree less about the ethics and wisdom of conscious partiality.

The second and more controversial

question is thus whether policy-related social science should be conducted in adversary form. Should the social scientist act more as a lawyer advocating the interests of a client, or as a scientist whose primary commitment is to the truth of a situation? If the choice is for the advocacy role, is it ethical to capitalize on the aura of objectivity that accrues to the social scientist willy-nilly because of the scientific stance of others in the field? When, for example, the social science advocate presents survey data on the effects of discrimination, should this be presented as objective information or as biased data designed to make a case for one side of a dispute? Can one have one's scientific cake while demolishing it with criticisms of its very existence?

In the debate over forensic or committed social science, much can be learned from the Anglo-American legal system. Litigation under this system is widely regarded as stylized combat, with lawyers behaving as adversaries whose adherence to prearranged rules of conduct is monitored by an impartial judge (Frankel, 1976). . . .

Public trust in the social scientist, as distinct from the adversary advocate, depends on the assumption that the social science professional will behave as a scientist. By some definitions, the term "forensic social science" would be a contradiction of terms, for it would imply professional behavior at variance with the commonly understood norms of science. These norms include three essential features.

First, the primary loyalty of the scientist qua scientist is to the faithful presentation of information obtained by generally accepted methods of data collection. The scientist may, of course, have a point of view about the issue under consideration, particularly when the research deals with policy questions. In this case, the opinion should be freely admitted, but not used to slant the collection and interpretation of data in favor of a predetermined policy option. It is precisely the point of good

scientific practice to provide data insulated from the scientist's preconceptions about what the right answer should be. The scientific method is, after all, a series of devices for producing a social consensus about reality (Ziman, 1968). Social science obviously falls short of the ideals established in the physical sciences for the establishment of consensus. But the principle remains that the role of the scientist demands adherence to the best methods available for obtaining reliable and relevant information. This allegiance should transcend loyalties to employers, favored causes, or preferred theories. Researchers who place the interests of their clients above their loyalty to sound methods will do as much mischief to social policy and public trust as the hypocritical scientists scored by Rivlin. Those who feel that the models and methods of natural science are inappropriate to intricate human beings and complex social realities should make their own positions clear and disavow not only the methods but the label of science. It is the height of hypocrisy to chastise social science for its imitation of natural science while simultaneously accepting benefits from the aura conferred by association with the latter.

Second, scientists, as distinct from adversary advocates, have a positive obligation to publish the results of their work. Again, the obligation follows from the nature of science, which is not only knowledge but *public knowledge* (Ziman, 1968). It simply will not do, as forensic social science would have it, for scientists to leave detailing the counter evidence to their opponents. One reason, as Warwick points out in his discussion of social experiments, is that the opponents may not have access to the necessary information. If the advocates of a particular policy about income are the only ones with access to evaluation data on a related social experiment, the possibility of fair advocacy for all sides breaks down. The scientist has a positive obligation to present conclusions based on all relevant evidence, and to open the data to others who could further this objective. To behave otherwise may be good advocacy, but it is bad science.

Third, scientists should resist attempts by clients or other interested parties to influence the scope and content of publication. There are legitimate exceptions to this principle, such as state secrets about nuclear energy or proprietary interests in data collected under a contract. Nevertheless there is no place in science for the equivalent of a general privilege of confidentiality, such as that seen between lawyer and client, about data. Nor should we be forced to assume that all data are presented to portray the client or the cause in the most favorable light possible. The great irony of an advocacy approach for social science is that it would be effective only so long as its audience did not know that it was in operation. If the public came to assume that social scientists, like defense lawyers, were being as selective as possible in their presentation of a case, public confidence in social science would crumble—and properly so.

In sum, social scientists and lawyers operate out of different traditions, with different public understandings about their roles, different protections for their clients, and different ethical codes. Any attempt to cast the social scientist in an adversary role without changing the institutional structure to accommodate that role seems foolhardy and ultimately destructive of the very notion of social science.

A Typology of Effects

Given the power flowing from the intervenor's image and expertise, what are the predominant political effects of social interventions?[1] Taken with the Introduc-

[1] The term "political" is used to cover any change in the distribution of power, influence, or authority in any of the units covered by the papers. These include the individual, the small

tion, the 16 chapters suggest a useful typology of effects that divide fairly well into categories of system maintenance and system change.

System Maintenance

Social intervention may help to maintain or strengthen a system in the following ways.

Moral Legitimation   The presence of highly visible, credentialed intervenors often reinforces the sense that the sponsoring body is upright, responsible, and entitled to its power and position. For example, organization psychologists or management consultants brought in for OD sessions lend the weight of their credentials and image to the firm that hires them. One has the sense that in settings ranging from prisons to population programs, social science professionals now play the role once performed by priests who conferred their benedictions on secular events. Kurt Back is more explicit about the religious overtones of the encounter group movement, but others, especially Stolz, Warwick, and Guskin, also point to the legitimating function of the intervenor.

Targeting   Intervenors play a key political role in defining the problem to be solved through intervention and the specific targets for action. This targeting or channeling function is especially significant when the intervenors accept without question the definitions of problems or deviance held by the populace or established by a society's legal code. Stolz provides a sound analysis of the moral difficulties raised when behavior modification specialists not only accept societal definitions of deviance but in effect wreak vengeance by applying their most painful techniques to those who are considered

group, the work organization, the community, the nation-state, and the international political system.

the greatest offenders. By embracing and acting on a society's or an organization's definitions of problems and of deviants, intervenors work to maintain the status quo.

Victimizing Carried to extremes, the process of targeting becomes victimizing. Social and political systems are often unified through the catharsis produced by scapegoating. As a way of achieving greater internal cohesion, nearly every society selects an enemy or demon on which it can project its guilt, frustrations, or discontents. In *The Crime of Punishment*, Karl Menninger (1968) argued, for example, that the American public needs both crime and punishment as a means of ritual purification. Whether in total societies or encounter groups, professional intervenors may play a significant political role by defining the enemy and by providing moral sanction and impetus for retribution. A clear example is seen in the field of population policy. Historically, the strongest support for the practice of sterilizing the mentally retarded came from specialists in eugenics. Their clinching argument, one that captured the attention of no less a figure than Oliver Wendell Holmes, was that the "feebleminded," knowing no restraint, would breed furiously and thus adulterate the society's gene pool. Subsequent research showed that the empirical assumptions of this argument were flawed, that its exponents were largely of upper-class origins, and that the entire exercise could well be considered a case of scapegoating. Who, after all, is likely to rally less support than the retarded, especially after they have been portrayed for several generations as not only incompetent but lascivious? Microcosmic versions of this phenomenon arise in encounter groups and in organization development exercises when some participants, particularly those who hold out against group norms, become subjects for special opprobrium. The point to be underscored is

that such scapegoating helps to maintain the system by channeling aggressions against the weak rather than against the powerful.

Retreatism Social interventions may further promote system maintenance by encouraging or aiding those who experience frustrations with the system to retreat into the self or into groups embracing emotional but not political expression. The clearest case is the encounter group movement, which, according to Back, has strong elements of sociopolitical withdrawal. Robert Merton, who first used the term "retreatism" in sociological analysis, also noted its political consequences:

> The competitive order is maintained but the frustrated and handicapped individual who cannot cope with this order drops out. Defeatism, quietism and resignation are manifested in escape mechanisms which ultimately lead him to "escape" from the requirements of the society (Merton, 1957, p. 153).

Adjustment Several of the chapters suggest ways in which interventions may encourage individuals and groups to adjust to a system by thinking, feeling, and acting within its prescribed limits. The most blatant example, cited by Stolz, is the application of behavior modification techniques to promote discipline and order in classrooms. Walton and Warwick also discuss the ethics of using organization development techniques to cool out opposition or otherwise to keep organizational tensions within manageable boundaries. At a broader level, Laue and Cormick are highly critical of intervenors who use their skills at crisis management to manipulate weak but intransigent parties into docile submission. Moreover, intervenors may in general promote adjustment by imparting or endorsing an ethic of feasibility. In this ethic, political, organizational, or other action is seen as acceptable only within the range of options approved by established authorities. The emphasis is on the possible and the practical, the down-to-earth and the nitty-gritty, rather than on schemes more disruptive to the underlying authority structures.

Intelligence Gathering Professional intervenors may further strengthen the hand of established authorities by gathering information on dissent or dissatisfaction. Increasing attention has recently been focused on the role of the professional as a double agent. Physicians, psychiatrists, psychologists, management consultants, OD practitioners, encounter group leaders, crisis intervenors, and others are often in a position to gather privileged information on the discontents and strategies of opponents to the system. Walton notes the ethical dilemmas faced by OD practitioners who are asked to provide appraisals of employees encountered in their work. These professionals are in a better position than line managers to detect or observe employee dissidence. Crisis intervenors and consultants operating in the interstices of conflicting interests face similar dilemmas.

Undermining Opposition The political advantage conferred by privileged information is that it gives managers and other authorities a better base for dealing with opposition. Professional intervenors may also wittingly or unwittingly work to undercut dissident forces. An unambiguous example arises when an encounter group leader or OD practitioner transposes what would otherwise be a labor-management issue into one of openness and trust in the here and now. Union leaders who may be perfectly able to protect their interests through conventional negotiating techniques may find themselves completely off-guard when confronted with a staged setting, an arcane language, and an elusive opponent. At a more subtle level, potential opposition may also be defused by group discussions relying on affective expression and group camaraderie to neutralize simmering conflicts over substantive issues like working conditions and pay rates. Union spokesmen have long been criticial of the human relations movement for its implicit but nonetheless powerful support of management through the promotion of worker satisfaction. Whether their criticisms have an ethical or merely a political basis is open to question, but at the very least they point up the internal political implications of management consulting and OD. Back, Walton, and Warwick are explicit about this set of issues for encounter groups and OD, as are Laue and Cormick for crisis management.

System Change

Whatever their boundary-maintaining effects, social interventions are, by definition, actions that produce or are designed to produce change. Many forms of deliberate intervention do not, of course, accomplish their stated objectives of change, but they may directly or indirectly bring about other significant modifications of individuals and social systems. The chapters in this book suggest four mechanisms by which systemic change can be effected.

Consciousness Raising One of the potentially profound effects of social intervention is the heightened consciousness that something is wrong with one's life and the associated conviction that the situation could be improved. The impetus given the feminist movement by women's "rap groups" in the late 1960s and early 1970s is an important recent example.

Beyond a generalized sense of a problem or a hope for positive change, the intervention may also help individuals to step back from the structures that surround them and understand, however dimly, the forces shaping their lives. Sartre (1956) described the process by which European workers came to awareness of the possibility of revolt against their suffering. According to Sartre, the key psychological ingredient was the *contemplation* of suffering as a state in itself. Without that explicit consciousness,

> Suffering cannot be in itself a *motive* for [the worker's] acts. Quite the contrary, it is after he has formed the project of changing the situation that it will appear intolerable to him. This means that he will have had to give himself room, to withdraw in relation to it, and will have to have effected a double nihilation: on the one hand, he must posit an ideal state of affairs as a pure *present* nothingness; on the other hand, he must posit the actual situation as nothingness in relation to this state of affairs. He will have to conceive of a happiness attached to his class as a pure possible— that is, presently as a certain nothingness— and on the other hand, he will return to the present situation in order to illuminate it in the light of this nothingness and in order to nihilate it in turn by declaring: *"I am not happy"* (p. 435).

Delegitimation Social interventions may also foster change by challenging the legitimacy of a given system or its rulers. Because legitimacy arises from shared beliefs that authority is rightfully exercised by certain individuals or groups, interventions can challenge legitimacy by persuasively challenging the foundations of those beliefs. In the field of population studies, Mahmood Mamdami (1972) performed this function in a controversial study titled *The Myth of Population Control*. The reason that the book generated such controversy was that Mamdami took exception to the commonly held assumption that smaller families were in the interest of poor villagers. His data from field research in India apparently show that there are many reasons, including compelling economic considerations, for villagers to have large families. Since 1972 this work has been regularly cited by critics of the international population control movement as evidence of the movement's misdirected efforts.

An intervention may also aim to weaken the power bases of established leaders. Sometimes the mere fact that a leader is challenged at all will undercut the perception that he or she is all-powerful and immune to criticism. Success in small-scale sorties may encourage larger assaults. Laue and Cormick imply that constant challenges are needed to keep entrenched powers off-guard. Williams, in turn, criticizes them for advocating a level of confrontation that may erode the underlying political consensus and respect for authority. Williams suggests, by implication, that too much delegitimation may ultimately work against justice by replacing the notion of agreed-upon fairness with the principle of push-and-shove. Finally, the conflicts and tensions produced by the intervention may place more strain on the system than it can accommodate. Laue and Cormick appear to endorse crises as a legitimate vehicle for promoting minority interests. But carried to an extreme, constant crises can completely debilitate a social or political system. Argentina, known among Latin American scholars as "the conflict society," provides a national example of the limits of political delegitimation.

Destabilization This term refers to deliberate efforts to kindle opposition, dissension, discord, and strife in a social or political system. Had we organized this volume before the overthrow of the Allende regime, we almost certainly would have added a set of papers on political interventions among nations, with special emphasis on Chile. We now have vivid documentation showing how the CIA, with the encouragement and assistance of multinational corporations, deliberately set out to foment dissension against the Allende regime in Chile. The methods used by CIA included covert payments to opposition groups, harassment through international organizations, and encouragement of criticism through diplomatic channels. Unfortunately, none of the papers in this volume deals even indirectly with the phenomenon of destabilization.

Enablement Interventions may further induce change by supplying opponents, minority groups, or other contending forces with the capacity, opportunity, means, or incentive to act. Laue and Cormick organize their paper around one form of enablement, the development of power for the powerless. Their discussion of empowerment is clear and cogent, but it does not exhaust the possibilities of enablement. Waymon notes how his intervention, which failed to meet its primary objective, seems to have led to an increased capacity on the part of the black corporation to deal with "City Hall" and the federal bureaucracy. As he puts it, "they are now the experts in housing and are widely sought as speakers, consultants, resource people, and so forth. They didn't get the housing units, but they did get added units of respect and status among themselves and among their peers and colleagues at all levels" (p. 325).

Interventions can also promote enablement by convincing people that they can be sources of social action. In some cases, this means contradicting the view that human actions are shaped by powerful external forces or insuperable biological drives. If people are convinced that their lives are shaped by forces beyond their control, they tend to act accordingly. Interventions can counter this tendency by teaching individuals and groups to see themselves as originators of action, capable of initiative, foresight, control, and above all, significant influence on others. Needless to say, this is not a matter simply of changing self-images, for objective power obviously counts, but increased efficacy has psychological as well as social and financial underpinnings. Glidewell, for example, makes explicit reference to increased competence and efficacy as the goals of encounter group participation.

Social interventions may promote system maintenance and system change in other ways, most notably through the actual contents of the intervention. Our list includes only the most common and general mechanisms.

Evaluation Criteria

Finally, questions of power arise in the choice of criteria for assessing the processes and outcomes of social interventions. Contending interests will affect, first of all, the performance criteria established for the evaluation. A growing literature in evaluation research (Gurel, 1975; Sjoberg, 1975; Weiss, 1975) documents the influence of political considerations on the choice of yardsticks for judging programmatic success. The chapter on the New Jersey–Pennsylvania Income Maintenance Experiment shows that the selection of evaluation standards is not a matter of political indifference. The experiment's designers made a political judgment in deciding to have the evaluation focus heavily on the work-leisure trade-off—whether people would stop working and enjoy leisure above a certain income floor. This decision reflected the interests of academic economists hoping to devise new tests for static equilibrium theory and of OEO officials seeking a novel but politically feasible income policy. As Warwick notes, the evaluation criteria might have been different had the program designers consulted the poor, employers, congressmen, and other interested parties.

The politics of evaluation also surfaces in the assessment of family planning programs. Although neither Lapham nor Tangri discusses the point, there is evidence that the primary data collected on these programs, and the ways in which they are interpreted, reflect pressures from donors, advocates, and other interest groups (Marino, 1971). Given that the same organizations that advocate and fund international family planning programs also are the major sources of support for evaluations, it is not surprising that there has been a bias in favor of results showing that the programs lead to decline in fertility rates. In a review of the literature, Hilton and Lumsdaine (1976) show the gaps between the data presented and the conclusions drawn about the impacts of family planning programs.

Considerations of power and vested interests are no less salient in the choice of ethical criteria for the evaluation of social interventions. In this book, the most striking case of politically resonant ethical judgment is Tangri's advocacy of women's interests in population programs. While other groups, particularly men, have some claims in this area, Tangri contends that they are distinctly secondary to the interests of women. She is also quite explicit about the premises for her ethical judgment:

> Any consideration of ethical issues in fertility control must recognize that we begin with a biological fact: only one of the sexes can have babies. The advantages and disadvantages, as well as risks and benefits associated with reproduction and its prevention do not accrue equally to both sexes. If they did—if there were no differences between the sexes in their reproductive functions—the same ethical considerations would apply to both sexes (p. 364).

Women's rights are primary, therefore, because women have a greater stake in reproduction and thus a greater moral claim to control over any social intervention having to do with reproduction. As a result,

> . . . the most important goal of population programs should be to give women control over their own bodies and reproduction, with fertility reduction a secondary goal; and . . . any program that will lead to reduction in fertility must also

encourage liberating social changes that will provide women with opportunities for alternative means of satisfaction and status (p. 364).

Because Tangri's paper is so frankly political in its endorsement of one set of group interests, it provides a useful foil for debate on the broader issue of whose needs and concerns should enter into judgments about the ethics of intervention. Several specific questions are raised by her arguments.

First, what are the moral grounds for asserting that one social group should have primary control or disproportionate influence over a given kind of intervention? Tangri rests her claim on a biological fact— only women can have babies. She does not spell out in any detail why this particular biological fact should confer special rights, nor does she indicate whether other biological facts, such as racial characteristics, size, and genetic deformities, call for similar entitlements. Do those born with Down's syndrome, for example, have the right to primary control over programs on mental retardation, since their stakes in such programs are larger than those of the nonretarded?

Second, even allowing the validity of the biological view, are there not parallel rights that might be accorded to men in population programs? Tangri focuses primarily on the risks and benefits of pregnancy, where women's interests are obviously stronger. But what standards should apply to population programs that are aimed at men, such as the massive vasectomy camps organized in India? Should women, because of their biology, determine the organization and implementation of these programs, which are directed exclusively at the reproductive apparatus of men? The argument developed by Tangri seems to suggest that where the stakes are greater for men than for women, men have stronger moral claims for control over policy.

Third, if a judgment is made that the interests of one group have ethical primacy, questions remain about how those interests should be defined, and by whom, within the entitled group. In the case of women and population programs there are many ambiguities. Does the ethical position outlined by Tangri represent the views of all women concerned with family planning programs? Quite clearly it does not. Even in the United States, the women's movement is divided, for example, on the question of abortion. When one moves to the international scene, the picture is even more complicated. In Latin America, women's groups that support some objectives of North American feminism object strongly to the tone and moral reasoning of the movement. Even stronger criticisms would be forthcoming if U.S. feminists, intending to speak for the women of the world, placed their own principles at the foundation of policies governing international family planning programs supported by U.S. funds. Third World critics, both men and women, would quickly denounce such influence as political and cultural imperialism.

Fourth, what ethical calculus should be applied to social interventions when more than one set of group interests is at stake? Perhaps to dramatize her argument, Tangri ducks the difficult moral and practical questions posed by trade-offs. Her treatment of family planning programs oversimplifies the ethical issues at stake by dealing mainly with male and female interests. Closer analysis of existing programs suggests that there are also other interests involved, including the donor agencies, social classes, ethnic groups, and competing programs with their clienteles. Using a broader evaluation framework than that presented in Tangri's paper, the policy analyst might come up with the following questions and dilemmas:

> When support for family planning programs comes from public funds (as it usually does), what priority should the promotion of women's interests hold vis-à-vis other possible areas of expenditure? For example, if family planning programs seem to be serving mainly urban, middle-class women, while malaria control programs benefit poor men and women in rural areas, how should decisions be made about the allocation of limited funds for health care? It would be difficult to sustain the argument that, whatever their income position, women's needs for fertility control should take precedence over the health or welfare needs of the entire population.

> An Asian country has two major ethnic groups—the Chinese, who are reasonably affluent, and the Malays, who are quite poor, especially in rural areas. Surveys show that the Chinese women are highly motivated to practice family planning and would welcome assistance with means. The Malay women, on the other hand, seem more concerned about having fewer of their babies die than about limiting births. Should the government spend its health/family planning money in helping the Chinese women control their fertility or in assisting the Malays to reduce infant mortality?

> The government of an African country discovers a segment of its population in which roughly equal numbers of both males and females show high rates of involuntary sterility. While the exact causes are not known, the government is confident that medical attention can relieve the condition for a significant number of those affected. Should the government-sponsored infertility clinics give greater or exclusive attention to women because of the devastating effect of infertility on their self-images, or to women and men in equal proportions as facilities permit?

These examples, and many others that could be constructed, show that ethical dilemmas posed by fertility control will not be resolved by any single-factor moral assessment. There is no reason to believe that other complex social interventions would respond any better to a unidimensional ethical scheme.

Freedom

The discussion thus far has suggested that the balance of power in social interventions is often stacked against the targets of change. Most of the chapters in this book recognize the disparity in power and express concern about its implications for human freedom. The commentaries on freedom revolve around three central issues: capacity, opportunity, and safeguards.

According to the definition proposed in the introductory chapter, freedom requires above all the capacity and the opportunity to choose. The same criteria apply to informed consent and voluntary participation in social intervention. If the individuals involved do not have the ability and information to perceive and weigh the consequences of their participation, or if they are coerced, constrained, or manipulated by environmental pressures to participate, then their freedom has been impaired. The difference between capacity and opportunity should not be overdrawn, for in many circumstances the ability to understand an intervention grows out of the opportunity for first-hand participation. Nevertheless, this distinction offers a convenient way of highlighting the issues of freedom posed in many interventions.

Capacity

A prime obstacle to freedom lies in people's inability to understand the nature and consequences of their particpation in interventions. Sometimes, as with retarded persons, the difficulty arises from mental disabilities. In other cases, the barrier is inadequate information about the intervention and its consequences. In still other cases, freedom is obstructed by a mixture of limited abilities and inadequate information.

A question raised but not adequately addressed in this book concerns the limits of disclosure. While most authors agree that informed consent as conventionally defined is ethically desirable in social interventions, they seem unsure about how far disclosure should be carried. For example, does the specialist on behavior modification have a moral obligation to reveal the precise techniques that will be used to reshape a person's behavior? Should the encounter group leader or agent set forth in clear terms not only the general nature of the experience but also the precise manipulations to be used? Is it desirable, for example, for the leader to explain why the furniture has been arranged in certain ways, why the group is to focus on the here and now, how the leader will operate to steer the group in particular directions, and so on? Should crisis intervenors lay all of their cards on the table, including full disclosure on the panoply of techniques at their disposal? Should administrators of family planning programs candidly admit that, despite the health rhetoric used by the clinic and the government, the true purpose of the program is a reduction in the birth rate? The chapters are, in general, silent on these questions, but they show little enthusiasm for full disclosure. Even Laue and Cormick, who go as far as any of the other authors in advocating openness, stop short of recommending complete revelation of techniques and intentions.

The most likely reason for this hesitation about total disclosure is that advance information about hidden agendas and backstage manipulations could easily undercut the intended effects of the intervention. Fully informed about how their agent operates, encounter group participants might focus too closely on the agent's actions or enter into the spirit of the game by trying to counteract the agent's influence through parallel tactics. Similar reactions might be seen in behavior modification, organization development, crisis interventions, and in any area of intervention where the intervenor relies on identifiable strategies and techniques. With housing, education, population, and income maintenance programs, on the other hand, the reactive effects of disclosure would probably be less striking. The reason is that this last set of programs relies less on covert manipulations and specific techniques than on skills and intentions that are closer to the surface. Even so, one could imagine some fallout from the income maintenance experiment if participants were told that the government wanted to see if they stopped working above a certain income level, or in family planning programs if clients were informed that the clinic had to meet certain targets of sterilizations in order to stay in operation the following year. Thus, the question of how much disclosure should be required in social interventions remains open in these chapters.

Opportunity

Individual freedom is also constrained by obstacles and pressures found in the environment. The most obvious pressure, which arises in several spheres of intervention, is outright coercion. The chapters indicate that individuals have been forced to receive behavior modification, to join encounter groups, to take part in organization development exercises, to be sterilized, and to submit to other interventions against their will. The difference between coercion and lesser degrees of pressure depends in large part on the severity of the sanctions applied against people who refuse to participate. Where the penalties for noncompliance are large, such as with the loss of a job or the threat of physical harm, the term "coercion" properly applies. There is strong opposition to coercion in this book. Glidewell, Back, Lapham, and Tangri are specifically opposed to the use of force in the interventions that they review. Stolz is clearly in favor of informed consent and opposed to the use of aversive

techniques as a form of retribution, but she leaves the door open to the coercive application of behavior modification techniques in certain limited circumstances.

In other cases, the constraint on freedom arises not from direct coercion but from group pressures or strong threats and inducements. In organization development, the management may clearly state that employees are free to participate or not, as they see fit. But this freedom may prove hollow if most members of a work group see fit to participate and the holdouts feel under pressure to close ranks. Both Walton and Warwick point out how the power imbalances commonly seen in OD exercises may deprive employees of genuine freedom of choice. The extent of group pressure may also affect freedom to depart from an ongoing intervention. In the case of encounter groups, Glidewell claims that one clear source of protection for participants is their right to leave at any time. He fails to note, however, that the potent forces of the here and now—forces he identifies as the prime source of influence in this intervention—may erect formidable psychological barriers to departure. Once the short-term group culture is created and individual positions are staked out, disaffected participants may think it an unconscionable loss of face to drop out at the height of their distress. Freedom may thus be compromised precisely because the encounter group has succeeded in convincing the participants to shed their normal identities and take up new roles in the constructed microculture. As Walton suggests in one of his examples, the same difficulty may arise in OD sessions. When one member elected to withdraw, the others set out in hot pursuit. These examples underscore the need to place freedom in the specific context of the intervention and the forces that it generates.

Finally and ironically, individual freedom may sometimes be seriously compromised by the offer of positive rewards and inducements. The most dramatic example in recent years, one mentioned by Lapham, is the use of financial and other material incentives to promote voluntary sterilization in India. In dozens of communities, family planning workers offered men and women money, food, clothing and other rewards for submitting to vasectomy or tubectomy. At first blush, the provision of such incentives might seem like the pure enhancement of freedom—the poor are helped and yet are not forced to accept anything that they do not want. But this is an overly rational assessment of the situation. At a deeper level, there is a serious ethical difficulty raised by the fact that these bonuses have the greatest appeal for those who have the fewest resources. To an Indian farmer earning 70 dollars per year, 20 dollars is a substantial amount of money. In a recent review of the ethics of population incentives, Veatch (1977) lays out the various moral problems raised by the use of incentives in population programs. Warwick's paper on social experiments also suggests that providing income supplements to the poor may carry liabilities as well as benefits for freedom. Once again the key question is whether the offer of incentives exploits the disadvantaged by playing on their economic need. A major difference between incentives for sterilization and income maintenance, however, is that in the former the rewards are used to induce individuals into actions that may lead to serious regret or harmful consequences, while with income maintenance the potential harms are relatively slight. Nevertheless, we must still ask if it is ethically justified to use material rewards to promote behavior change in social interventions. As a rule of thumb, we might suggest that the greater the difference in the attractiveness of the incentives across socioeconomic groups, and the greater the potential harms at stake in adopting the rewarded behaviors, the more serious the ethical issues posed by the inducements.

Safeguards

Given the many limitations of capacity and opportunity, what steps might be taken to safeguard human freedom in social interventions? The authors offer numerous suggestions, ranging from fairly conventional steps for the protection of human rights to far-reaching changes in the condition of participants. The suggestions differ especially in their underlying assumptions about the capacity to understand an intervention. Some, taking this ability for granted, focus mainly on improving the volume and quality of information needed for rational decisions. Others are less optimistic in their views about capacity and, at the extreme, feel that it is completely lacking. The following typology of proposed safeguards is organized around differences in assumed capacity to grasp the nature and consequences of social interventions.

Improved Information

Where it can be assumed that participants or target groups are in a position to understand the intervention and to protect their own interests if given adequate information, the challenge is to provide this information in the most intelligible manner possible. Glidewell insists that even a person undergoing psychotherapy is often in a position to decide about the costs and benefits of an encounter group experience. The key duty of the agent, therefore, is to supply the person with clear and complete descriptions of the likely costs and benefits of participation in the group and of the agent's professional qualifications. Glidewell also suggests that the agent request the potential participant to consider how useful the benefits of group participation will be. Glidewell thus assumes that most people need no development of their basic intellectual competence in order to be able to grasp the significance of an encounter group. What they lack is good information about the experience itself and about the background and experience of the leader/agent. Walton also presumes basic capacity in his recommendation that, as a protection for informed consent, OD services be more accurately labeled.

Participation

Several chapters cite joint participation and negotiation as effective means of aiding informed consent and otherwise protecting freedom. The assumption behind such proposals is that people have the basic capacity to protect their interests, but need more than information to do so. Specifically, they should have the chance to take part in decisions about whether there should be an intervention at all, when and where it should take place, and how it will be conducted. Walton emphasizes the importance of negotiations on the question of whether there should be an intervention. In addition to meeting an ethical desideratum, bringing the eventual targets of intervention into the early decision-making and planning stages alerts the intervenor and client to possible mistakes in the conception of the intervention. In particular, when the intervention is ill timed, strong objections during the planning stage can avoid the harms that would result if the original idea were implemented.

Stolz sees great merit in joint planning for behavior modification but notes the difficulties of carrying this out when the recipient is retarded, senile, incarcerated, or suffers other restraints on the freedom to participate. Glidewell regards negotiations about goals and limits as among the most significant protections for participant freedom in encounter groups. Huey and his associates also cite constant communication with community groups as a means of protecting the targets of change. An important and ironic flaw in the Seattle Urban Academy intervention was the lack of sufficient attention to communicating with groups in the establishment, partic-

ularly the school board. Warwick joins Rossi et al. in citing the lack of participation by policy makers and the heavy influence of academic economists as both ethical drawbacks and practical limitations on the New Jersey-Pennsylvania Income Maintenance Experiment. While the various chapters reveal many ambiguities about participation, such as who should participate in which decisions, with what knowledge, and to what limits, they generally endorse participation in threshold decisions and planning as an effective safeguard for freedom.

Empowerment

Laue and Cormick contend that, left to their own devices, the disadvantaged are often not in a position to participate as equals in negotiations about conflict resolution. The most ethical solution, therefore, is neither to rely on the survival of the fittest nor to turn the matter over to outside bodies, but to enlarge the ability of the weak to represent their own interests.

> The intervenor should promote the ability of the weaker parties to make their own best decisions through helping them obtain the necessary information and skills to implement power. The intervenor should assess the relative level of information, negotiating skills, and analytical ability of the parties and, if there is a considerable differential, help even the odds through training or other forms of advocacy (p. 221).

Accountability

Should social intervenors be held accountable for their professional action or inaction? If so, to whom, for what, and with what methods of enforcement? Perhaps predictably, our authors favor professional accountability as a principle, but none is specific about details. Adding to the usual hesitations about recommending restrictive standards may be the amorphousness of social intervention as a profession. With the exception of behavior therapy, which is rooted completely in psychology, none of the interventions is closely linked to a single academic discipline or an established profession. From encounter group leadership to family planning programs, from organizational development to the implementation of income maintenance experiments, virtually all the theories and skills of the behavioral and social sciences are brought to bear at some point. Some areas of intervention, such as organization development and crisis intervention, seem to be developing as hybrid specialties in their own right, while others, such as family planning programs, are acomplished by teams of individual specialists. Still other interventions, such as those exemplified by Waymon's work for the Corp, represent the application of nonspecialized savvy to particular problems. This diversity makes it difficult to set down detailed principles of accountability that will hold with equal validity across all spheres of social intervention. But we can explore some of the major issues of accountability and seek analogues from other professions, especially law.

Accountable to Whom?

Three interrelated meanings of accountability may be distinguished: personal, legal, and professional. First is the personal responsibility one takes for one's actions. There is a widespread presumption, recognized in such statements as the Nuremberg Code and the Universal Declaration of Human Rights, that individuals, no matter what their status or profession, are morally accountable for their behavior. Thus the social intervenor has no right to kill, maim, lie, cheat, steal, or otherwise violate accepted moral codes in carrying out an intervention. Just what those codes

should be and how obligatory they are for any individual are matters of endless debate, but the resulting ambiguities do not negate the concept of personal accountability. At the same time, some of the most severe moral dilemmas for the intervenor arise from conflicts between personal moral standards and the perceived requirements for effective interventions. To cite one example, the organizer of a compulsory sterilization program in India may feel simultaneously that such activities are a violation of human rights, yet are necessary to deal with the pressing social problem of population growth.

A second, very different, form of accountability, is legal liability. The essential notion behind malpractice litigation is that professionals are liable to their clients or patients for damages done and perhaps for additional penalties as well. We must distinguish, however, between the legal and the ethical aspects of liability. We may all agree that patients of physicians, clients of lawyers, and clients or targets of social intervenors have the right to take these professionals to court if they believe that (a) the professional has practiced negligently or unethically, (b) the patient, client, or target has been damaged thereby, and (c) alternative approaches for compensating the damaged party have not produced a satisfactory result. It is just as clear that the legal outcome of the suit is morally open: it may or may not reflect a just resolution of the dispute. Patients or their lawyers, for example, may misrepresent a physician's verbal statements to make a more compelling case to the jury. In general, the move to accountability through litigation may be taken as a failure of other, less drastic means of bringing a dispute to resolution. To date, the concept of legal liability for social intervenors has been more theoretical than actual, except in the areas of behavior therapy and encounter group leadership. But if the rise in malpractice suits against lawyers and physicians is any indication of what might be expected in these fields, the threat may soon become reality.

The earlier chapters point to several dilemmas concerning the locus of accountability in intervention. One is the question of relative accountability to the client and the target of the intervention. Stolz raises this issue very clearly for behavior therapy. Should the therapist be accountable mainly to the person receiving the therapy, the institution in which the person is confined, or the larger society? When there are conflicts of interest between the target and the client (the individual agency employing the therapist), how should they be resolved? Sarason and Sarason suggest that the therapist's obligation is to reconcile these interests by acting simultaneously as an advocate for the patient's welfare and as a promoter of institutional well-being. In theory this is an ideal resolution of the dilemma, but it will break down in the hard cases where the interests are in sharp conflict. From the standpoint of professional accountability, moreover, it leaves practitioners in a most vulnerable position, for they must harmonize conflicting interests with no accepted guidelines or principles for doing so. Given the current surge of malpactice suits, therapists are unlikely to be satisfied with broad injunctions to be effective dual agents. The problem of divided loyalties is also raised in other chapters, including the discussions of organization development, the Seattle Urban Academy program, the income maintenance experiment, and the population control programs. The chapters provide no conclusive answers, but they do suggest several working principles.

First, they underscore the need for intervenors to be clear about their accountability to their clients. Only too often, it seems, well-intentioned professionals enter a complex situation without a real understanding of whom they are working for and the potential conflicts of interest that might arise. Sometimes it is difficult to know in advance what directions the intervention will take once it is launched, and which actors and interest groups will present moral claims. But in many interventions even a modicum of forethought could alert intervenors to major pitfalls. Conscious of the hazards ahead, they could seek outside advice on responsible ways of resolving possible ethical dilemmas or take steps to reduce these dilemmas by astute negotiation of the terms of reference of their own interventions. Organization development practitioners, for example, might set down as a specific condition of their employment that management refrain from asking for appraisals of specific individuals or work units.

Second, several of the chapters make a strong case for open disclosure of the intervenor's prior commitments and loyalties to the client. If, for instance, a behavior therapist is primarily in the service of a prison and only secondarily concerned with the personal welfare of inmates, that therapist should make this fact clear to all concerned, including the inmates chosen for therapy. Similarly, as Laue and Cormick recommend, if a crisis intervenor is brought in to serve as an advocate for one of the parties to a dispute, this person should not pretend to be a mediator. In general, the question of who is to be served by professional intervenors seems fundamental and deserving of much more careful analysis than it has received in this volume.

A related question concerns the ethical obligations of the professional intervenor in dealing with the familiar dilemma of value neutrality versus commitment to superordinate moral standards. While, as noted earlier, most of the authors regard value neutrality as self-deceptive and misleading to others, they hedge their bets about positive commitment. At one extreme Stolz mentions behavior modification specialists who see themselves as "super technicians" with no obligation to question the values of those using their services. The problem of the intervenor as hired gun arises in every area of intervention. Walton asks if OD practitioners should question the values and practices of the organizations that hire them, including their definition of the problem to be solved by OD. His case studies suggest that the practitioners themselves are divided on this point. At the opposite extreme, Laue and Cormick take the position that there can be no neutrality, and that advocacy for the powerless is the order of the day. They do not indicate, however, whether crisis intervenors should wear their principles on their sleeves for all to see, or whether they should bill themselves as mediators but work, in essence, as closet advocates. The dilemma is acute, for intervenors who openly identify themselves as advocates for one side will obviously stand little chance of being hired as impartial mediators.

One of the more vexing problems raised in these chapters is the issue of accountability to society. Glidewell and Stolz, in particular, speak of society as an entity with rights and obligations in social intervention, but neither gives any precise indication of how its values and interests are to be articulated. Who speaks for society, and how does the intervenor deal with variations across classes, minority and ethnic groups, and other social divisions? And, when programs cross national lines, which society's standards should apply, and what status should be accorded such cross-cultural instruments as the Universal Declaration of Human Rights? In her chapter, Stolz makes two points that deserve emphasis. First, the mere fact that a society holds certain values, preferences, or prejudices does not make its norms a valid basis for ethical judgments about social interventions. For example, widespread moral disapproval of pedophilia does not provide automatic entitlement for behavior therapists to use aversive conditioning to change pedophiliacs. Second, given the nebulous definitions of society and its standards, it is all

too easy for intervenors to project their own biases onto this murky mass and then defend them as society's will. One unambiguous conclusion from this book is that interventions justified on the basis of society's interest should be subjected to careful scrutiny and strong moral challenge.

Accountable for What?

The second broad question of accountability centers on the precise contents of professional responsibility. The chapters suggest four areas in which abuses have been seen and professional standards may be needed.

Competence   Given the ill-defined and ''learn-as-you-go'' quality of many interventions, together with the unconventional blends of skills required to bring them to completion, is it meaningful to speak of minimal standards of competence for intervenors? Or, to turn the question around, are there some forms of professional incompetence that appear often enough to warrant concern? Several authors answer in the affirmative, pointing to two kinds of abuses. The first is a sheer lack of qualifications for undertaking the intervention. Guskin criticizes the Battelle consultants for having an inadequate background to advise Seattle's black community about educational changes. As a result, according to Guskin, the intervenors had to fall back on generalized process skills too diffuse for the task at hand. Similarly, Walton speaks of a competence-confidence gap in organization development, while Warwick criticizes OD practitioners who enter a new setting without adequate information about its context and unique features. Second, questions of competence arise in choosing particular models of intervention. Walton and Warwick question the ethics of force-fitting OD interventions to situations where they might not be appropriate, as when solutions derived from industrial organizations are uncritically applied to government agencies. Laue and Cormick are emphatic on this point:

> Intervenors trained in one conceptual approach . . . should not transfer their intervention models uncritically to a different system setting (a racial/community dispute involving multiple parties, for example). To do so is to increase the probability that issues will be diverted and that the outcomes will not meet the most basic needs of the disputants (pp. 221–222).

Truth Telling To judge from these chapters, one of the more common ethical abuses in social interventions is false advertising or raising unwarranted expectations about the intervenor's abilities. Back takes encounter groups to task for creating a kind of sociotherapeutic seduction. Glidewell also recognizes the issue of truth in advertising, but seems more sanguine than Back about handling it through open disclosure at the point of the participant's entry. Similar questions of truth telling arise in national family planning programs, particularly with communication campaigns promising the poor a better life if they limit their family to two children.

Honoring Guarantees of Confidentiality In many spheres of intervention, participants are told or assume that what they say and do will be held in confidence. Recipients of psychotherapy, participants in encounter groups and organization development, clients of family planning programs, and candidates for income maintenance may come to believe, rightly or wrongly, that their words, deeds, and misdeeds will not be held against them outside the intervention. The chapters point up several ethical difficulties with express or implied guarantees of confidentiality. The most obvious and the

easiest to resolve is the broken promise. As Walton's chapter makes clear, intervenors have violated promises of confidentiality by discussing the performance of OD participants with management. Such violations would seem to be a flagrant and unquestioned breach of personal and professional ethics. The ethical situation is more complicated when the intervenor, acting in good faith, promises confidentiality, but does not have the legal backing to honor the guarantee. Rossi and his associates show how this problem arose when a district attorney sought data on individual participants in the New Jersey–Pennsylvania Income Maintenance Experiment. While the sponsors of the experiment had every intention of honoring their promises, they found that their data enjoyed no legal protection or privilege and thus could be subpoenaed. Given these risks, the intervenor has two basic options: make the usual promises in the hope that the question of a subpoena will not arise; or tell the people involved that the intervenors will keep the information confidential, but that there is a slight chance that it could be subpoenaed by the government. As Warwick observes, the first choice suffers from inadequate disclosure of important information, while the second may so frighten respondents that they will not participate in the intervention. This dilemma is now being given serious consideration by the National Commission on the Protection of Human Subjects of Biomedical and Behavioral Research.

Higher-order Effects Though the authors of the lead chapters were asked to analyze the ethics of higher-order or unintended effects in social interventions, the response was limited. Even those who did comment on this question seem to have had a difficult time placing it in perspective. The most obvious reason is that higher-order and especially unintended effects are, almost by definition, elusive and outside the paradigms of conventional ethical assessment. Further, since these effects are likely to appear in areas two or three steps removed from the scene of direct action and may surface months or even years later, there are formidable problems in attributing causality. The chapters suggest nonetheless that the question remains ethically salient, if intellectually hazy. Glidewell argues, for example, that the intervenor has a manifest responsibility to assess the indirect outcomes of encounter groups. The task may be daunting, but there are options available, including controlled experiments and a more limited follow-up of selected participants. This type of long-term assessment would also go some distance in generating the kinds of information needed to deal with Back's criticisms of encounter groups.

Protection versus Paternalism: The Intervenor's Dilemma

The strongest undercurrent of ambivalence in these chapters courses around the issue of protecting those intervened upon against more powerful forces in the society, against the intervenors, and even against their own limitations and urges. In essence, the question boils down to the difference between responsible protection versus deleterious paternalism.

There seems to be little doubt that some groups of individuals, such as children, the retarded, and the institutionalized, do need protection against interventions designed by others. But what about normal adults, especially those who voluntarily seek out interventions such as encounter groups? Even here the authors reveal mixed feelings. Glidewell, for instance, generally leans toward treating adults, including those currently in psychotherapy, as rational decision makers who are able to act in their interest when given adequate information. Nevertheless, he holds that because agents have greater

knowledge than the participants about the pitfalls of encounter groups, they are obligated to set limits on the experience. Among the common protections are a ban on violence and drugs, limits on scapegoating, and a clear norm that individuals are free to join or stay apart from the group. Moreover, "one powerful limit on danger to individual welfare is the right to interrupt any activity in order to analyze its nature, its antecedents, and its consequences" (p. 90). Most of the other authors seem to agree with the principle implicit here: allow people to decide when they can exercise reasonably free choice, but institute protections when there is clear danger that inexperience would seriously impair judgment.

Laue and Cormick maintain that the most efficacious way of providing protection and avoiding paternalism is through empowerment. When the weak are strengthened to the point that they can challenge not only their opponents but also the intervenors, they are no longer in need of either external safeguards or professional tutelage. While at first sight, this seems an appealing solution to the problem of paternalism, closer examination suggests that it may simply displace the problem. It is, after all, the intervenors who decide who needs to be empowered, and how, and it is they who determine when the proper types and levels of empowerment have been attained. If the method operates as straightforwardly as Laue and Cormick imply, the intervenors only move to a position of higher-order paternalism. They seem to sit above the fray, pulling levers to draw some individuals and groups to a higher level of competence and leaving others where they are. Accountability is particularly difficult because none of the groups to be empowered is likely to ask why the intervenors have chosen them and not their opponents, or why they are being given some negotiating skills and not others. An impartial observer perched above both the intervenors and those with whom they work might further ask if those being empowered are being given the most effective skills and tools for challenging the position of the intervenors. Even with the best of intentions, and by Laue and Cormick's own persuasive logic, intervenors are interested in the intervention and, therefore, will be tempted to avoid forms of empowerment that may complicate their interventions. Thus, while there are many ethical merits to the strategy of empower-

ment, one would be naïve to treat it as a panacea for resolving complex questions of power. Taken as a whole, these chapters suggest that the dilemma of protection versus paternalism will remain alive as long as there are power differentials in social intervention. We further suggest that even the attempt to reduce these differentials will involve significant questions of professional power and accountability.

References

Frankel, M. E. The adversary judge. *Texas Law Review*, 1976, 54, 465–487.

Gurel, L. The human side of evaluating human services programs: Problems and prospects. In E. L. Struening & M. Guttentag (Eds.), *Handbook of evaluation research*, Vol. II. Beverly Hills, Calif.: Sage, 1975.

Mamdami, M. *The myth of population control: Family, caste and class in an Indian village.* New York: Monthly Review Press, 1972.

Marino, A. KAP surveys and the politics of family planning. *Concerned Demography*, 1971, 3, 36–75.

Menninger, K. *The crime of punishment.* New York: Viking, 1968.

Merton, R. *Social theory and social structure.* New York: Free Press, 1957.

Meyerhofer v. Empire Fire & Marine Insurance Co., 497 F.2d 1190 (2d Cir. 1974), *cert. denied*, 419 U.S. 998, Nov. 11, 1974.

Rivlin, A. M. Forensic social science. *Harvard Educational Review*, 1973, 43, 61–75.

Sartre, J. P. *Being and nothingness.* Trans.

H. E. Barnes. New York: Philosophical Library, 1956.

Sjoberg, G. Politics, ethics and evaluation research. In E. L. Struening & M. Guttentag (Eds.), *Handbook of evaluation research*, Vol. I. Beverly Hills, Calif.: Sage, 1975.

Veatch, R. M. Ethical principles in medical experimentation. In A. M. Rivlin & P. M. Timpane (Eds.), *Ethical and legal issues of social experimentation.* Washington, D.C.: Brookings Institution, 1975.

Veatch, R. M. Governmental incentives: Ethical issues at stake. *Studies in Family Planning*, 1977, 8, 100–108.

Warwick, D. P. Contraceptives in the third world. *Hastings Center Report*, 1975, 5, 9–12.

Weiss, C. H. Evaluation research in the political context. In E. L. Struening & M. Guttentag (Eds.), *Handbook of evaluation research*, Vol. I. Beverly Hills, Calif.: Sage, 1975.

Ziman, J. *Public knowledge: The social dimension of science.* Cambridge: Cambridge University Press, 1968.

11.2 Moral Dilemmas of Managers

Kenneth D. Benne

The work life of managers bristles with problems and choices that have a moral component as well as cognitive and technical aspects. This is as true of managers in organizations that produce and distribute services as it is of those that produce and distribute artifacts and other goods. Not infrequently, managers ignore or are unaware of the *moral* dilemmas which confront them and attribute their recurring and persistent quandaries to cognitive or technical deficiencies on their part or to factual conditions beyond their control. It is much more common for managers to seek help from consultants renowned for their cognitive or technical competence than for their ethical awareness or sagacity in moral matters. The training of managers is typically focused on relevant knowledge and technique and their effective uses, not on sensitivity and skill in clarifying and coping with ethical dilemmas.

Neglect of the Moral Dimension of Management Problems

There are a number of reasons for widespread unawareness, on the part of managers, of moral conflicts posed by their working lives and relationships. One reason lies in the nature of moral problems. What is being evaluated, judged, and perhaps reconstructed in *moral* deliberation is one's self in its future trends. Moral judgments, in contrast to cognitive and

This essay is a revision of a paper presented to a meeting of the Association of the Professional Directors (YMCA) in Toronto, Canada, in October 1980.

technical judgments, necessitate reevaluation of one's own value orientations or some aspect of them and the relationships and associations that sustain one as a moral person, not alone the handling of external and technical conditions and instrumentalities. One cannot exclude one's "subjectivity" from examination and judgment in resolving ethical quandaries as one can in the solving of technical problems, where "objectivity" is a prime value. And, where the manager is working in a pluralistic human environment, as one almost invariably must in a heterogeneous society like our own, he (or she) confronts value conflicts not only in himself (or herself) but between one's own cherished values and those of others. The resolution of moral problems always involves confrontation and attempted reconciliation of conflicting value orientations and interests. Often no consensual resolution is possible, as is ideally the case with technical problems. Confrontation of self and others in a state of moral ambiguity and conflict is painful, difficult and frustrating. It is comforting, though often false, to believe that our differences lie outside ourselves and the other selves with whom we work and that problems incorporating differences in value orientations can be solved by more adequate knowledge and technique, alone or primarily.

An examination of some of the ways in which managers, along with many other people, try to finesse or avoid the moral problems inherent in their role and work may be useful in broadening and sharpening managers' own ethical sensitivities. One way already suggested is to try to convert moral problems into technical problems.[1] In a technical problem, the difficulties to be overcome are externalized. The values and morally significant relationships of the problem solver are not part of the content which is being judged, tested, or reconstructed in the process of resolution. Nor are the conflicting values of others who are affected by the solution to be worked out part of the data to be considered in shaping a solution. A technical problem ideally requires an "objective" solution. "Subjective" aspects of the situation—my values or your conflicting values, my significant and personally sustaining relationships or your different ones—must be excluded from the processes of problem-solving in the interest of a sound technical solution. In a moral problem, my values and different significant relationships are part of the content of the difficulty to be overcome, part of what is weighed, tested and perhaps reconstructed in the deliberations and dialogue that lead to a viable solution. Those managers who seek *techniques* which will eliminate the pains and rigors of value conflicts in managing unresolved human situations are, in effect, though not necessarily in intent, seeking to depersonalize these situations and to short-circuit opportunities for moral learning and development in themselves and those around them. The spirit of "scientific management," though its vogue is long past, was in line with this effort to bypass the moral dilemmas of organizational leadership and to convert management to a "scientifically based technology." Actually, of course, "science" as a human enterprise is not value-free but has its own distinctive value orientation. And, in this sense, "scientific" management represented one value orientation among others, usually a conservative one, though the prestige of "science" may have, for a time, tended to silence questioning of it in both management and employee circles.

This observation leads to another way in which the value dimensions of organizational problems are frequently finessed. The method is to smuggle values in covertly, through the definition of problems in powerful and apparently value-neutral or consensual terms which are actually value-laden and, when analyzed, subject to various interpretations. Such terms, in addition to "science," are "health," "growth," "development," and "productivity." Value conflicts may be obscured if, for example, a problem can be defined in terms of finding the best way to augment organizational "health." Who can be sanely opposed to improved "health," leaving, for the moment, morticians and physicians out of account? The main point here is that smuggling pseudo-agreements about values into the definition of problem, by using apparently value-free goal language, does support the false assumption that management is only or primarily a technical matter which can circumvent moral dilemmas through expert manipulation of appropriate managerial skills and techniques.

Another way of avoiding ethical dilemmas in management is to attempt to substitute "law" for "ethics." This method involves getting higher authority to legislate or proclaim rules for handling various situations. Official codes of "ethics" may be used in this way. The manager relies on authoritative rules rather than on his or her own ethical judgments in combination with the ethical judgments of those with whom he or she works to validate his or her actions in controverted situations. It is no accident that in a heterogeneous society, in which various groups are becoming more and more articulate about their distinctive interests and con-

[1] For a fuller discussion of the distinctions between ethical and technical problems in group and organizational situations, see K. D. Benne, "Some Ethical Problems in Group and Organizational Consultation," in Bennis, Benne, Chin (eds.), *The Planning of Change*, 2d Edition (New York: Holt, Rinehart and Winston, 1969), pp. 595–604.

cerns, professionals are more and more involved in litigation which challenges the legitimacy of their decisions and actions. This includes professional managers, though of course other professionals—doctors, teachers, psychologists, and others—are involved in the same trend. Our common ethics and the authority that it once provided to practitioners who judged and acted within its framework has been fragmented. The only way that many see to resolve conflicting rights and interests is through an appeal to laws and processes of litigation. The public effect of this tendency to depend more and more on law to settle questions of conflicting values is ultimately to deprive law itself of moral authority and to reduce its influence to the power of the sanctions which it prescribes for those who break the law. The effect on professionals, including managers, is to reinforce their tendency to avoid ethical judgments and to conform to law, including established administrative policy, as a sufficient measure of right conduct.

Still another way to avoid recognizing, facing, and becoming responsible for the moral dilemmas presented by one's work environment is to narrow the range of morals to limited aspects of human life and conduct. Even though some students of morality have worked vigorously in recent years to widen the range of choices which have moral significance, to include collective or communal along with personal choices in the scope of ethics, most of us are still victims of our Puritan heritage in our thinking about morality, if not in our actual behavior. This inheritance tended to focus questions of morality on individual conduct and more particularly on sexual behavior and on the maintenance of property rights. Few of us when confronted with the term "moral turpitude" tend to think, for example, of managers whose careless disposal of chemical wastes undermines the health and life of large numbers of people as readily as we do of

a person who molests a child sexually or even of deviant sexual behavior between consenting adults.

There are actually two aspects to the problem just presented. One is the range of human conduct which requires moral consideration in life-decisions and which merits ethical scrutiny and scrupulosity. The other is the impersonality which attends the actions of large associations and corporations, public and private, and the difficulty of fixing moral responsibility for the human effects of their actions. To the first question, my own answer is that any action which has effects on the life and welfare of persons—persons other than the agent and the agent him/herself—requires moral scrutiny and evaluation. This scrutiny extends to the quality of the processes of choice which led to the actions. Another way of putting this is that the entire range of human goods presents relevant subject matter for ethical deliberation, not just those connected directly by custom, law, or policy to role-related rights, duties, and obligations. All persons, including managers, are ethically obligated to optimize the goods inherent in or consequent upon their choices and actions.

The second question presents both practical and theoretical difficulties. It is hard to fix personal responsibility for actions taken by a corporation. Somehow corporate responsibility needs to be brought into the range of ethical deliberation. Persons in an organization who knowingly allow morally indefensible actions to be taken by the corporation and do not try to block or reverse them share in the collective responsibility for the consequences. Corporations often defend themselves irrationally and irresponsibly against charges of wrongdoing in an effort to maintain a favorable public image, which much of their expenditure for advertising is designed to promote. People generally need to become educated to value more positively those organizations which admit demonstrable moral errors and voluntarily move to correct these than those which deny wrongdoing and communicate false images of their policies and of the consequences of these in action. Managers have a moral responsibility to further the process of re-educating the public concerning the evidences of corporate morality or immorality.

Societal Conditions Now Compelling Attention to Moral Dilemmas

Four societal conditions have contributed to growing awareness of the prevalent neglect and avoidance of essentially moral problems in the management of organizational and of societal affairs.

1. The first of these is the familiar fact of growing interdependence in our societal and economic life, both within the nation and across national boundaries as well. This fact need not be belabored. Management decisions taken in oil companies in Houston, Texas, have consequences for the health and survival of families in Massachusetts during cold winters and, at least until recently, for the economic and political life of people in Saudi Arabia. In turn, political and economic decisions taken in Saudi Arabia affect patterns of life of people throughout the U.S.A. in countless ways. Emphasis on the often neglected social-ethical responsibilities of managers in all sorts of organizations has only recently come to be a recognized part of managerial scholarship, research and education.

2. Even as social interdependence has grown within and between nations, groups of various sorts have articulated and asserted their distinctive interests and challenged the justice and moral adequacy of the dominant ethos which once provided a common moral underpinning for choices within nations, if not between them. The result has been accentuated intergroup conflicts along interracial, interreligious, interclass, interethnic, intergender, and intergenerational lines. Each group as it becomes conscious of its distinctiveness develops its own interpretation of justice and freedom, of rights and obligations. Where the consciousness takes a religious form, sacrally or ideologically, rights, duties, value orientations tend to take on an absolute cast. The difficulty of reconciling and compromising group value orientations becomes more and more difficult, even where social interdependence makes reconciliation more and more necessary for human survival.

3. Our common ethos was embodied in traditions, in unwritten and largely uncriticized assumptions, about right relationships among human beings both within and between organizations, between roles of employees and managers, between the majority and minorities, between the private and public sectors of our economy, etc. Our common traditions which provided a fairly workable foundation and reference point for validating solutions to ethical difficulties have been fragmented and shorn of their power to command universal assent. This has come not alone from the espousal and assertion of distinctive ways of life by various groups within our heterogeneous society. It has come also from radical changes in the conditions and ways of life which have followed upon the application of a growing science and a developing technology in every facet of our lives, not least in conditions of work and in the roles of organizational managers and employees.

Tradition-direction has broken down. Deliberate planning, policy-making, and changing have become the accepted way of conducting human affairs. If plans, policies, and changes are to embody livable values, acceptable to all affected by the plans, policies, and changes, they must be deliberately created and decided upon. Moral principles and ideals must be negotiated in order to provide an acceptable motivational basis for common effort among people who differ, often markedly, in their culturally inherited moral outlooks. Morale and workable organizational functioning require it. Managers must take the lead in forging and reforging a viable moral basis for common organizational efforts.

4. The need for a working ethic which is relevant to a changing technology and yet not subservient to it has come to be felt keenly as knowledge and related technology which make possible the radical manipulation of human attitudes and behavior have become realities. The management of organizations and political leadership have been quick to employ persons expert in "man-shaping" technologies, as Vance Packard termed them, to help them in engineering consent to policies and practices considered desirable by management and leadership.

It has been persons employed for this purpose, usually as consultants, who have become deeply concerned with the ethical use and abuse of the knowledge and technology at their command. It is the scruples of organizational consultants and trainers that have led to the best formulations now available concerning the ethical problems involved in intervening into the lives of other people to induce changes in their attitudes, value orientations, and behaviors.

As managers have come to accept and practice *consultative* management as the only form of management which can work under the societal conditions already outlined, it seems that an ethics of social intervention developed and tested by consultants for the guidance of their own efforts can be readily adapted by managers for their own use. This is the assumption on which the remainder of this essay is based.

Social Intervention: The Locus of Moral Dilemmas

The managerial role requires intervention into the lives and relationships of those whose work the manager supervises and directs. The manager is involved in setting and resetting goals for his/her unit of the organization in which he/she is employed. The manager is involved in attaining common action by other persons in pursuit of these goals. The manager is involved in setting standards of quality and productivity and in evaluating and the work of self and others in relation to these standards. The manager is involved in settling conflicts between persons and subgroups in his/her unit and in reconciling the work of his/her unit with the expectations and requirements of the larger organization and society of which his/her unit is a part.

All of these activities require social intervention by the manager into the lives of other persons and into the relationships between his/her self and other persons and between other persons. It is in these interventions that problems of moral choice are most frequently encountered. Problems of the use and abuse of power and authority, problems of influence and ways of influencing others—coercion and consent, command and collaboration, manipulation and facilitation, problems of responsibility and accountability—all of these have moral dimensions and aspects. The ethical problems are most acute and most apparent when interventions are designed to produce changes within the behavior and relationships of persons and organizational units. For it is in processes of changing that value considerations and conflicts with respect to the directions, quality and tempo of the changes to be effected are raised into consciousness, are articulated, and become unavoidable.

While ethical problems of intervention are most apparent in choices and actions designed to alter manager-staff or staff-

staff relationships, the moral significance of such choices is by no means limited to the quality of these internal relationships. In all such cases, the continuing moral integrity and morale of the manager are involved. This is an ethical matter. In a service organization, staff-client relations often present ethical difficulties. The effects of staff changes on staff-client relations are important ethical content in decisions about such changes. In most cases the effects of internal changes in a unit on the larger organization and its welfare are involved. These are part of the ethical content of problems and solutions. And, in many cases, internal changes have effects on the wider society in which this organization operates. These effects are part of the ethical content to be considered in shaping, directing and evaluating an intervention.

There are distinctions which are practically important, in some connections, between micro-interventions and macro-interventions. A macro-intervention in an organization might be illustrated by efforts to induce a major change in program direction and emphasis. A micro-intervention might be illustrated by a performance appraisal interview with an employee. For the present, this distinction is not of concern. Both kinds of intervention present occasions for ethical deliberation on the part of a morally sensitive manager.

One of the best current treatments of the ethical problems of social intervention identified four aspects of an intervention in which ethical questions are most likely to be confronted by a consultant or ethical analyst, and, by extension, a manager.[2] These are: choice of goals; definition of change targets; choice of means; and assessment of consequences. This analysis offers an important reminder that ethical problems are not confined to the beginning or end of an intervention but require attention throughout the course of a continuing and developing program of action.

Optimality and the Necessity of Bargaining

The search for or assertion of absolute and unchanging ethical rules and standards is a temptation for managers, as for other persons, in the presence of continually changing conditions, demands and expectations. In my opinion, it is a temptation to be resisted. The attempt to exempt some aspect of traditional morality from criticism by claiming absolute validity for it usually masks an effort to save some vested interest from rational criticism and possible revision. If there are perennially valid standards of moral conduct, they will find validation and revalidation in processes of continuing rational criticism at various times and places.

It is an often forgotten wisdom in ethical matters that ethical dilemmas present conflicting goods and rights, not conflicts between good and bad or right and wrong, for choice and decision. (The absolutist may try to convert a conflict among goods into a melodramatic struggle between the good guys and the bad guys. In melodramas, rationality is inapplicable—a struggle of competing powers is the prescribed form of action, each identifying the other as representing the powers of evil.) Where one good cannot be fully realized without thwarting or restricting the actualization of another good, the goods are in conflict—an ethical dilemma exists.

In the past, another effect of absolutistic moral orientations has been to prevent continuing moral inquiry and experimentation designed to produce a growing body of moral norms adequate to control for human benefit the powers put into human

[2] Bermant, Kelman, and Warwick, *The Ethics of Social Intervention* (New York: Hemisphere Publishing Corporation, 1978).

hands by a continually developing science and technology. The absolutist mentality is particularly dangerous in a time of accentuated intergroup conflicts. An absolutist outlook on the part of groups defending and promoting alternative moral orientations which are in conflict makes the creative synthesis of differences into a commonly acceptable view of right human conduct difficult or impossible to achieve and creates and maintains a debilitating state of continuing "holy" warfare, covert or overt, cold or hot.

The goal of deliberation about an ethical conflict is an "optimal" resolution of the conflict adequate to a time and place, not a determination of the ultimately right way of handling similar situations once and for all. "Optimality" is a word of great importance in my view of moral inquiry in a pluralistic world. It avoids the perils of perfectionism and absolutism on the one hand and the equally disheartening stance of moral indifference and despair on the other.

If this view is accepted, the attainment of an optimal resolution of value conflicts is a bargaining process. The responsible effort is to make the process one of "creative bargaining," as Max Otto named it, not one of unimaginative, timid, and mechanical compromise. This assumes a restored kinship between political and ethical deliberation, a kinship well understood by the classical Greeks but one which is often forgotten or denied in the modern world. Ethically sensitive managers should, I believe, develop processes of creative bargaining in dealing with value conflicts which at one and the same time redeem politics from sheer power manipulation and render ethical decisions which are socially relevant.

The Manager as Methodological Advocate

I fear that the socialization of most of us has led us to think of the moral hero or heroine as one who sticks to his or her ethical principles unswervingly without regard to counter arguments or the consequences of his/her perseverance for him/herself and for others. And the principles adopted by our putative moral hero or heroine are substantive goals or causes for which he or she stands. In the 1960s the substantive advocate of desirable changes was glorified and the "liberal" who evinced concern with the quality of the processes of deliberation and action through which changes were planned and worked out was vilified. I must confess that I was then and am still an unreconstructed liberal in my concern with the quality of the processes of choosing and changing through with decisions are made, executed, and evaluated.

Actually, there is a kind of advocacy sometimes evidenced and always required in morally conflicted situations other than the perseverant *substantive advocacy*, often identified with moral courage and strength. This other kind of advocacy may be called *methodological advocacy*. It is the kind of advocacy which I recommended to managers as a basis of strength in dealing with morally conflicted situations.[3] Managers, who accept the role of methodological advocate with respect to the settling of confused, controverted, morally conflicted situations, work on the assumption that there is a close interconnection between the moral quality of the means used by persons in resolving issues and the moral quality of the resolution attained. It is not true that managers have no substantive values with respect to the ends of human action. The assumption is rather that they, along with all other persons involved in a controverted situation, have such values.

[3] See K. D. Benne, "The Moral Orientation of Laboratory Methods of Changing and Learning" in Bennis, Benne, Chin, and Corey, *The Planning of Change*, 3d Edition (New York: Holt, Rinehart and Winston, 1976), pp. 496-505, for a fuller discussion of the distinction between substantive and methodological advocacy.

It is further assumed that persons involved now differ in their *ultimate* value orientations and in most cases will continue to do so. But managers should believe that differences in value orientation do not constitute a blemish upon or a threat to learningful common deliberation and action, if commitment to the use of methodologies which respect value differences and employ them to enrich and improve common action can be maintained by all parties in and through conflict situations.

The best safeguard to the continuation and enhancement of personal and subgroup differences within an interdependent yet heterogeneous society may well lie in the cultivation of common commitment to appropriate methodologies for dealing with ethical difficulties and issues. These must be methodologies which incorporate respect for differences, which build upon the extension of open expression of articulated differences by all parties in the arena of public deliberation, which require the imaginative weaving of moral differences into the fabric of common policies and decisions reached, and which conceive of conflict resolution as potentially a process of mutual and desirable learning, re-education, and change for all of those involved.

Recommended Norms for a Methodologically Oriented Ethic

I once formulated six norms which specify in outline the characteristics of an adequate process- or methodology-oriented ethic for our troubled times. At the time, I labeled them norms of a democratic ethic.[4] I still

[4] For a full discussion and defense of these norms, see K. D. Benne, "Democratic Ethics and Human Engineering," in Bennis, Benne, and Chin, *The Planning of Change*, 1st Edition (New York: Holt, Rinehart and Winston, 1961), pp. 141–148.

believe they define democracy as a moral process of conflict resolution in a pluralistic society. But I have since come to believe that their basis is broader than that of democracy as a political process. They are, I believe, consistent with the prophetic aspect of our Hebraic-Christian inheritance. And they partake of the open-ended values of science as a human enterprise and embody in a general way the values of the helping relationship as these have emerged from studies of therapeutic and educative processes. (It needs hardly be stated that I regard management as basically and ideally a facilitative and dialogic rather than a coercive and manipulative process.) I recommend these norms here, without defense and with a minimum of elaboration, for your consideration.

1. The process of resolving moral conflicts should be *collaborative*. This requires collaboration not alone between all those immediately involved in the conflict but with the "publics" affected by the resolution, at least by representation.

2. The process of resolving moral conflicts should be *educational and/or therapeutic* for all participants. A process of deliberation needs the best relevant information available about the conditions, effects, and costs of various proposed resolutions. Participants need to learn valid and unlearn invalid information. It is equally important that they must learn about their own values and empathically about the values of others, particularly those in conflict with them. Objective information and awareness of the values at stake must be blended in the creation of an optimal resolution.

3. The process of resolving moral conflicts should be *experimental*. The resolution reached should be adopted for try-out and not as a final revelation from Mt. Sinai. The resolution should include plans for periodic reevaluation of the decision in the light of experienced action upon it. Minority dissenters and "public" represen-

tatives should be included in the reevaluation process.

4. The process of resolving moral conflicts should be *task-oriented*, controlled by the requirements of the problems confronted and an evaluation of envisioned effects of the resolution in action from all contending perspectives, rather than oriented in the maintenance or extension of the prestige or power of those who advocate particular patterns of resolution.

5. The process of resolving moral conflicts should be *anti-individualistic*, yet include commitment to the establishment and maintenance of appropriate areas of privacy for individuals and subgroups and to the empowerment of persons and subgroups as creative units of influence in an interdependent organization and society.

As already emphasized, many of our most pressing moral problems are collective in character and require communal solutions. Traditional ethics has been oriented too exclusively to the control of individual conduct rather than to the guidance of group, organizational and societal behavior. Reemphasis is required. "Individualism" does not safeguard "individuality" in our time and place.

6. The process of resolving moral conflicts employed by persons, groups and organizations should itself be subject to continual review, evaluation and revision.

Conclusion

We live in a time when traditional moral community has been eroded and fragmented. Yet, without some measure of moral community, social processes degenerate into brutish power struggles, into Hobbes's war of all against all. Moral community can be restored only through deliberate and collaborative efforts by persons, groups, and organizations in all parts of our nation and world. Since human society is heterogeneous, optimal resolutions to moral dilemmas will be pluralistic in character. An experimental morality is required by a changing society. The most promising moral commitment in our time is to a process- and methodologically-oriented ethic. As John Dewey once remarked, "He who would think of ends seriously must think of means reverently." Managers should become examplars and advocates of such an ethic in their life and work.

Index